Exceptional Learners

FOURTEENTH EDITION

AN INTRODUCTION TO SPECIAL EDUCATION

DANIEL P. HALLAHAN
UNIVERSITY OF VIRGINIA

JAMES M. KAUFFMAN
UNIVERSITY OF VIRGINIA

PAIGE C. PULLEN
UNIVERSITY OF FLORIDA

 Pearson

330 Hudson Street, NY, NY 10013

Director and Portfolio Manager:
Kevin M. Davis
Content Producer: Janelle Rogers
Sr. Development Editor: Alicia Reilly
Media Producer: Lauren Carlson
Portfolio Management Assistant: Casey
Coriell
Executive Field Marketing Manager: Krista
Clark
Executive Product Marketing Manager:
Christopher Barry

Procurement Specialist: Carol Melville
Full Service Project Management: Cenveo®
Publisher Services
Cover Designer: Cenveo® Publisher Services
Cover Image: © Off Set–Shutterstock
Composition: Cenveo® Publisher Services
Printer/Binder: LSC Communications
Cover Printer: LSC Communications
Text Font: ITC Garamond Std. Regular

Credits and acknowledgments for materials borrowed from other sources and reproduced, with permission, in this textbook appear on the appropriate page within the text.

Every effort has been made to provide accurate and current Internet information in this book. However, the Internet and information posted on it are constantly changing, so it is inevitable that some of the Internet addresses listed in this textbook will change.

Cataloging-in-Publication Data is on file at the Library of Congress

8 2021

ISBN-10:   0-13-480693-x
ISBN-13: 978-0-13-480693-8

Daniel P. Hallahan, Ph.D., is Professor Emeritus of Education at the University of Virginia. At UVA, Hallahan served as a department chair (twice), director of doctoral studies, and elected representative (four three-year terms) to UVA's faculty senate. He held three endowed professorships, including the UVA Cavaliers' Distinguished Teaching Professorship. He received the UVA Outstanding Teaching Award and the Virginia State Council of Higher Education Outstanding Faculty Award. Hallahan was inaugural editor of *Exceptionality* and currently reviews for *Exceptional Children, Learning Disability Quarterly, The Journal of Special Education,* and *Exceptionality.* He is a past president of the Division for Learning Disabilities of the Council for Exceptional Children (CEC). In 2000 he received

the CEC Career Research Award. Hallahan's expertise covers a broad spectrum—learning disabilities, ADHD, autism, intellectual disabilities, blindness, deafness. Much of his early scholarship focused on cognitive strategy training for students with learning disabilities and ADHD. Most recently, he has focused on the need for more individualized, intensive special education instruction for students with disabilities. Hallahan is author of over 100 articles, over 40 chapters, and is coauthor or coeditor of 18 books, including *Handbook of Special Education* (2nd ed.) (with J. M. Kauffman & P. C. Pullen, Routledge, 2017) and *Special Education: What It Is and Why We Need It* (2nd ed.) (with J. M. Kauffman, P. C. Pullen, & J. Badar, Routledge, 2018). Some of his books have been translated into German, Spanish, Korean, and Arabic. Hallahan has taught thousands of pre-service and in-service teachers in the introductory course in special education, characteristics of students with learning disabilities, and characteristics of students with intellectual disabilities, as well as hundreds of Ph.D. students in research seminars.

James M. Kauffman, Ed.D., is Professor Emeritus of Education at the University of Virginia. He is a past president of the Council for Children with Behavioral Disorders (CCBD) and the recipient of several awards, including the 1994 Research Award of the Council for Exceptional Children, the 2006 award of the Society for Applied Behavior Analysis for Presentation of Behavior Analysis in the Mass Media, and the 2011 Distinguished Alumni Award from the University of Kansas School of Education. His primary research interests are emotional and behavioral disorders, learning disabilities, and the history of and policy in special education. He has published over 100 articles in refereed journals, authored or coauthored dozens of book chapters, and is author, coauthor, or coeditor of more than 20 books, including *Characteristics of Emotional and Behavioral Disorders of Children and Youth* (10th ed.) (with Timothy J. Landrum, Pearson, 2013), *Handbook of Special Education* (2nd ed.) (with J. M. Kauffman & P. C. Pullen, Routledge, 2017), and *Special Education: What It Is and Why We Need It* (2nd ed.) (with J. M. Kauffman, P. C. Pullen, & J. Badar, Routledge, 2018). In his career, Kauffman has taught thousands of pre-service and in-service teachers in courses on emotional and behavioral disorders and behavior management, as well as hundreds of Ph.D. students in doctoral seminars.

Paige Cullen Pullen, Ph.D., is the Literacy Initiatives Manager at the Lastinger Center for Learning and a Research Professor in the School of Special Education, School Psychology, and Early Childhood Studies at the University of Florida. Prior to her position at the University of Florida, Pullen held a joint appointment in University of Virginia's Department of Pediatrics and the Curry School of Education. Before earning her doctorate at the University of Florida in 2000, she had 12 years of K–12 teaching experience in general and special education. She has served as the Principal Investigator of federal and foundation-funded projects, has coauthored several books, including *Teaching Students with Learning Disabilities, and Students with Learning Disabilities* (with Cecil D. Mercer, Pearson, 2009; 2011), and has published numerous book chapters, peer-reviewed articles, and presented papers focused on evidence-based reading instruction for students with disabilities. Pullen is Executive Editor of *Exceptionality: A Special Education Journal* (Taylor & Francis). Pullen's research focuses on early language and literacy development and interventions to prevent reading disability for vulnerable populations (e.g., cultural differences, poverty, rural living environments), as well as the educational outcomes of children with developmental disabilities and those with chronic medical conditions. Pullen currently conducts reading research and professional development in Zambia and Botswana, Africa, as well as in the USA. She is the recipient of the prestigious UVA Seven Society's Excellence in Mentoring Award—2011 and the Curry School Foundation's Most Outstanding Professor Award. Pullen has taught thousands of pre-service and in-service teachers in the introductory course in special education and language and literacy intervention for students with disabilities.

PREFACE

Exceptional Learners: An Introduction to Special Education, Fourteenth Edition, is a general introduction to the characteristics of exceptional learners and their education. (*Exceptional* is the term that traditionally has been used to refer to people with disabilities as well as to those who are gifted.) This book emphasizes classroom practices as well as the psychological, sociological, and medical aspects of disabilities and giftedness.

We've written this text with two primary audiences in mind: those who are preparing to be special educators and those who are preparing to be general educators. Given the federal legislative mandates, as well as ethical concerns, for including students with disabilities in general education classrooms whenever possible, general educators must be prepared to understand exceptional learners. And they must be ready to work with special educators to provide appropriate educational programming for students with disabilities. This book is also appropriate for professionals in other fields who work with exceptional learners (e.g., speech-language pathologists, audiologists, physical therapists, occupational therapists, adapted physical educators, counselors, and school psychologists).

We believe we've written a text that reaches both the heart and the mind. Feedback we've received from students and instructors on previous editions strengthens our confidence that we've done so. Our conviction is that professionals working with exceptional learners need to develop not only a solid base of knowledge, but also a healthy attitude toward their work and the people whom they serve. Professionals must constantly challenge themselves to acquire a solid understanding of current theory, research, and practice in special education and to develop an ever more sensitive understanding of exceptional learners and their families.

WHAT'S NEW IN THIS EDITION?

As with all of our previous revisions, we've approached this one with an eye toward providing the reader with the latest, cutting-edge information on research and best practices in special education. The most obvious innovation is that this edition is available as FULLY DIGITAL, with over 200 interactive elements (primarily videos) hot-linked throughout the text. After careful consideration, we as well as the publisher, Pearson, are convinced that the electronic format offers multiple benefits for students, instructors, and us, the authors. For students it offers a much more affordable learning resource than the traditional text. For instructors it offers a way of engaging students and opening up myriad possibilities for class discussions and lectures. For us, the authors, it offers a way to bring to life teaching practices, to portray the human side of disabilities, to go into more depth on critical topics. Excuse the cliché, but "a picture is worth a thousand words" comes to mind.

New or Thoroughly Updated Content within Chapters

- *Chapters 6, 7, 8, 9:* Inclusion of new definitions of Specific Learning Disorder, Attention Deficit Hyperactivity Disorder (ADHD), Emotional and Behavioral Disorders, and Autism Spectrum Disorders (ASD), from the American Psychiatric Association's *Diagnostic and Statistical Manual of Mental Disorders, Fifth Edition* (DSM-5, 2013)
- *Chapter 1—Exceptionality and Special Education:* More emphasis on *abilities,* rather than *disabilities,* of students in special education

- *Chapter 2—Current Practices for Meeting the Needs of Exceptional Learners:* Updated and expanded coverage of special education in the context of the Common Core State Standards Initiative
- *Chapter 3—Multicultural and Bilingual Aspects of Special Education:* Updated percentages of students of various ethnic groups receiving special education
- *Chapter 4—Parents and Families:* Greater emphasis on the importance of *family resiliency* in the face of having a child with a disability
- *Chapter 5—Learners with Intellectual and Developmental Disabilities:* More succinct and clear-cut explanation of the critical role of *systematic instruction* for students with intellectual disabilities
- *Chapter 6—Learners with Learning Disabilities:* Expanded and more in-depth discussion of literacy instruction and learning disabilities; expanded discussion on identification of students with learning disabilities, including strengths and weaknesses in cognitive processing
- *Chapter 7—Learners with Attention Deficit Hyperactivity Disorder:* More emphasis on importance of executive functioning and behavioral inhibition
- *Chapter 8—Learners with Emotional or Behavioral Disorders:* A new Figure 8.1 depicting the process of early identification of emotional and behavioral disorders
- *Chapter 9—Learners with Autism Spectrum Disorders:* Importance of *neuronal underconnectivity* between the front and back of the brain in people with autism spectrum disorders
- *Chapter 10—Learners with Communication Disorders:* More streamlined coverage for definitions of speech and language disabilities
- *Chapter 11—Learners Who Are Deaf or Hard of Hearing:* Updated information on how sign language evolves naturally among people who are deaf, further demonstrating that sign language is a *bona fide language*
- *Chapter 12—Learners with Blindness or Low Vision:* The role humor can play in dispelling stereotypes about people who are blind
- *Chapter 13—Learners with Low-Incidence, Multiple, and Severe Disabilities:* Expanded coverage of traumatic brain injury, especially in the context of sports injuries
- *Chapter 14—Learners with Physical Disabilities and Other Health Impairments:* Research linking spina bifida and learning disabilities
- *Chapter 15—Learners with Special Gifts and Talents:* Difficulties of defining giftedness in a multicultural society

Special Features

UP CLOSE WITH   Features individuals who, in various ways, serve as inspirational role models for all people, whether with a disability or not. Some are accompanied by a video that brings to life the person's accomplishments.

PEER CONNECTIONS   We believe students reading this book will have a better understanding of exceptionality if they read about the lives of exceptional learners who are young adults. In *Peer Connections,* individuals with disabilities' personal stories help readers realize that their peers with disabilities are very much like themselves.

SUCCESS STORIES: SPECIAL EDUCATORS AT WORK   Special educators work in a variety of settings, ranging from general education classrooms to residential institutions. Although their main function involves teaching, these professionals also engage in a variety of activities, such as counseling, collaborating, and consulting. This feature, contained in several chapters, emphasizes the importance of education for students with special needs that is intensive, relentless, and specific, and includes questions for students that relate to CEC Standards.

MISCONCEPTIONS ABOUT EXCEPTIONAL LEARNERS: MYTHS AND FACTS BOXES
We start each chapter with a feature that juxtaposes several myths and facts about the

subject of the chapter. This popular feature, familiar to longtime users of previous editions, serves as an excellent advance organizer for the material to be covered.

MyLab for Education™

Learning Outcomes and Summaries of Content

Learning Outcomes begin each chapter to focus reader thinking about the topics to be covered in the upcoming pages, and these are directly associated with the chapter's section headings. Each chapter concludes with a Summary of the main ideas of the chapter, reinforcing the connection between learning outcomes and chapter content.

> ### ▶ LEARNING OUTCOMES

Learning Outcome 5.1: Understand why the term *intellectual disabilities* is used rather than *mental retardation*, how professionals define intellectual disabilities, and the prevalence of intellectual disabilities.

Learning Outcome 5.2: Learn the causes of intellectual disabilities.

Learning Outcome 5.3: Learn about assessments used to identify intellectual disabilities and some of the psychological and

behavioral characteristics of learners with intellectual disabilities.

Learning Outcome 5.4: Understand some of the educational considerations for people with intellectual disabilities and how professionals assess progress in academics and adaptive behavior.

Learning Outcome 5.5: Learn about issues that should be considered with respect to early intervention and transition to adulthood for learners with intellectual disabilities.

Video Examples

In all chapters, embedded videos provide illustrations of special education principles or concepts in action. These video examples show students, teachers, and families working in classrooms and providing their perspectives about real life situations. There are also several videos showing textbook authors Hallahan, Kauffman, and Pullen, as well as other experts in the field, discussing topics central to the field of special education, such as the Least Restrictive Environment, Inclusion, and current approaches to teaching students with special needs.

MyLab Education
Video Example 13.4
This video shows an example of the importance of interdisciplinary teamwork in implementing a successful educational program for a child with TBI.

Self-Checks

Throughout the chapters, you will find MyLab Education™ Self-Check quizzes. There are four to six of these quizzes in each chapter. These are meant to help readers assess how well they have mastered the concepts covered in the sections they have just read. Self-Checks are made up of self-grading multiple-choice items that provide immediate feedback on whether questions have been answered correctly or incorrectly, as well as rationales for both correct and incorrect answers.

Application Exercises

Most sections conclude with one or two application exercises that provide readers with opportunities to reflect upon chapter content and apply it to teaching and learning in real classrooms. Exercises usually include constructed-response questions. Readers receive immediate feedback on their responses to these questions in the form of model answers written by experts.

MyLab Education Self-Check 13.4

MyLab Education Application Exercise 13.4:
Small Group Instruction for Students with
Deaf-Blindness

Watch a video in which a teacher is working on a
language lesson with the students. Answer the
questions that follow.

Advanced Data and Performance Reporting Aligned to National Standards

Advanced data and performance reporting helps educators quickly identify gaps in student learning and gauge and address individual and classroom performance. Educators easily see the connection between coursework, concept mastery, and national teaching standards with highly visual views of performance reports. Data and assessments align directly to national teaching standards, including The Council for Exceptional Children (CEC), and support reporting for state and accreditation requirements.

Study Plan Specific to the Text

MyLab Education™ gives students the opportunity to test themselves on key concepts and skills, track their own progress through the course, and access personalized Study Plan activities.

The customized Study Plan is generated based on students' pretest results. Incorrect questions from the pretest indicate specific textbook learning outcomes with which the student is struggling. The customized Study Plan suggests specific enriching activities for particular learning outcomes, helping students focus. Personalized Study Plan activities may include e-book reading assignments, and review, practice, and enrichment activities.

After students complete the enrichment activities, they take a posttest to see the concepts they've mastered or areas where they still may need extra help.

MyLab Education™ then reports the Study Plan results to the instructor. Based on these reports, the instructor can adapt course material to suit the needs of individual students or for the entire class.

Assignments and Activities

Designed to enhance students' understanding of concepts covered in class, these assignable exercises show concepts in action (through videos, cases, and/or student and teacher artifacts). They help students deepen content knowledge and synthesize and apply concepts and strategies they have read about in the book. (Correct answers for these assignments are available to the instructor only.)

Building Teaching Skills and Dispositions

These unique learning units help students practice and strengthen the skills that are essential to effective teaching. After examining the steps involved in a core teaching process, students are given an opportunity to practice applying this skill via videos, student and teacher artifacts, and/or case studies of authentic classrooms. By providing multiple opportunities to practice a single teaching concept, each activity encourages a deeper understanding and application of concepts, as well as the use of critical thinking skills. After practice, students take a quiz that is transmitted to the instructor gradebook and performance reporting.

IRIS Center Resources

The IRIS Center at Vanderbilt University (http://iris.peabody.vanderbilt.edu), funded by the U.S. Department of Education's Office of Special Education Programs (OSEP), develops training enhancement materials for preservice and practicing teachers. The center works with experts from across the country to create challenge-based interactive modules, case study units, and podcasts that provide research-validated information about working with students in inclusive settings. In the MyLab Education™ course, we have integrated this content where appropriate.

Teacher Talk

This feature emphasizes the power of teaching through videos of master teachers, who tell their own compelling stories of why they teach. Each of these featured teachers has been awarded the Council of Chief State School Officers Teachers of the Year award, the oldest and most prestigious award for teachers.

Course Resources

The Course Resources section of MyLab Education™ is designed to help students put together an effective lesson plan, prepare for and begin a career, navigate the first year of teaching, and understand key educational standards, policies, and laws. It includes the following:

The **Lesson Plan Builder** is an effective and easy-to-use tool that students can use to create, update, and share quality lesson plans. The software also makes it easy to integrate state content standards into any lesson plan.

The **Certification and Licensure** section is designed to help students pass licensure exams by giving them access to state test requirements, overviews of what the tests cover, and sample test items.

The Certification and Licensure section includes the following:

State Certification Test Requirements: Here, students can click on a state and be taken to a list of state certification tests.

Students can click on the Licensure Exams they need to take in order to find

Basic information about each test

Descriptions of what is covered on each test

Sample test questions with explanations of correct answers

National Evaluation Series™ by Pearson: Here, students can see the tests in the National Evaluation Series (NES), learn what is covered on each exam, and access sample test items with descriptions and rationales of correct answers. Students can also purchase interactive online tutorials developed by Pearson Evaluation Systems and the Pearson Teacher Education and Development group.

ETS Online Praxis™ **Tutorials**: Here, students can purchase interactive online tutorials developed by ETS and by the Pearson Teacher Education and Development group. Tutorials are available for the Praxis I® exams and for select Praxis II® exams.

The **Licensure and Standards** section provides access to current state and national standards.

The **Preparing a Portfolio** section provides guidelines for creating a high-quality teaching portfolio.

Beginning Your **Career** offers tips, advice, and other valuable information on:

Resume Writing and Interviewing: Includes expert advice on how to write impressive resumes and prepare for job interviews.

Your First Year of Teaching: Provides practical tips to set up a first classroom, manage student behavior, and more easily organize for instruction and assessment.

Law and Public Policies: Details specific directives and requirements needed to understand under the Elementary and Secondary Education Act and the Individuals with Disabilities Education Act.

The **Multimedia Index** aggregates resources in MyLab™ by asset type (e.g., video or artifact) for easy location and retrieval.

Visit www.pearsonmylabmastering.com for a demonstration of this exciting new online teaching resource.

Support Materials for Instructors

The following resources are available for instructors to download on www.pearsonhighered .com/educators. Instructors enter the author or title of this book, select this particular edition of the book, and then click on the "Resources" tab to log in and download textbook supplements.

Instructor's Resource Manual (0-13-480683-2)

The Instructor's Resource Manual synchronizes all of the resources available with this textbook, providing a multitude of activities and ideas to help instructors teach their courses, whether traditional or online. Each chapter provides a teaching outline, learning activities, and handouts.

Test Bank (0-13-480691-3)

The Test Bank provides hundreds of test items, with answer keys, organized by chapter and ready for use in creating tests based on the textbook material.

PowerPoint™ Slides (0-13-480681-6)

The PowerPoint™ slides include suggested activities, key concept summaries, diagrams, and other graphic aids to enhance learning. They are designed to help students understand, organize, and remember core concepts and theories.

TestGen (0-13-480679-4)

TestGen is a powerful test generator that instructors install on a computer and use in conjunction with the TestGen test bank file for the text. Assessments, including equations, graphs, and scientific notation, may be created for both print or testing online.

TestGen is available exclusively from Pearson Education publishers. Instructors install TestGen on a personal computer (Windows or Macintosh) and create tests for classroom testing and for other specialized delivery options, such as over a local area network or on the web. A test bank, which is also called a Test Item File (TIF), typically contains a large set of test items, organized by chapter and ready for use in creating a test, based on the associated textbook material.

The tests can be downloaded in the following formats:
TestGen Testbank file—PC
TestGen Testbank file—MAC
TestGen Testbank—Blackboard 9 TIF
TestGen Testbank—Blackboard CE/Vista (WebCT) TIF
Angel Test Bank (zip)
D2L Test Bank (zip)
Moodle Test Bank
Sakai Test Bank (zip)

ACKNOWLEDGMENTS

We are grateful to those who provided valuable comments on the 13th edition: Lana Collet-Klingenberg, University of Washington–Whitewater; Young-Gyoung Kim, Clarion University of PA; Jean C. Faieta, Edinboro University of PA; Sara Hooks, Towson University.

We are once again thankful for the wonderful support and assistance we received from the folks at Pearson. Alicia Reilly, our Development Editor. No superlatives are strong enough to praise Alicia's work. We simply can't thank her enough for all she does for us. She is a jewel. Kevin Davis, Executive Editor, is a genius of the textbook publishing industry. He is a consummate professional—a perfect blend of cheerleader and taskmaster. We also are grateful for his and Ann Davis' extensive knowledge of fine restaurants.

Janelle Rogers, Content Producer for this edition, brought all the complex pieces of the project to completion flawlessly. Our copy editor, Kathy Smith, did a terrific job of keeping us stylistically and grammatically correct.

Some Final Thoughts

Given that this is the fourteenth edition, some readers might legitimately wonder whether authors Hallahan and Kauffman have kept abreast with current research. In a word: Yes. We assure you that they didn't approach this edition any differently than they did the first. In fact, if anything, they were energized by the freedom of expression that came with changing to digital format. Furthermore, the fresh perspective of Paige Pullen, the youngest co-author, ensures that 14th edition is **up to date and cutting-edge.**

For those loyal users of previous editions, we assure you that we weighed carefully each change or update. We hope you agree that our revisions reflect the myriad changes in the field of special education over the past few years as well as the information explosion brought about by ever more accessible computer databases and the Internet. We also hope you'll agree that we haven't failed in our continuing commitment to bring you the best that research has to offer for educating exceptional learners.

DPH
JMK
PCP

BRIEF CONTENTS

CONTENTS

chapter seven

Learners with Attention Deficit Hyperactivity Disorder 139

chapter eight

Learners with Emotional or Behavioral Disorders 166

chapter fifteen

Learners with Special Gifts and Talents 353

SPECIAL FEATURES

SUCCESS STORIES

chapter one

EXCEPTIONALITY AND SPECIAL EDUCATION

GettyMoodboard/Vetta/Getty Images

▶ LEARNING OUTCOMES

Learning Outcome 1.1: Become oriented to exceptionality and special education.

Learning Outcome 1.2: Understand the educational definition of exceptional learners.

Learning Outcome 1.3: Learn about the prevalence of exceptional learners in both high- and low-prevalence categories and how special education is defined.

Learning Outcome 1.4: Understand and appreciate the history and origins of special education, including legislation and litigation that have affected special education.

MISCONCEPTIONS ABOUT Exceptional Learners

MYTH Public schools may choose not to provide education for some students with disabilities.

FACT Federal legislation specifies that to receive federal funds, every school system must provide a free appropriate public education (FAPE) for every student, regardless of any disabling condition.

MYTH The causes of most disabilities are known, but little is known about how to help individuals overcome or compensate for their disabilities.

FACT In most cases, the causes of disabilities are not known, although progress is being made in pinpointing why many disabilities occur. More is known about the treatment of most disabilities than about their causes.

MYTH People with disabilities are just like everyone else.

FACT First, no two people are exactly alike. People with disabilities are unique individuals, just like everyone else. Often, most of their abilities are much like those of the average person who is not considered to have a disability. Nevertheless, a disability is a characteristic that is not shared by most people. It is important that disabilities be recognized for what they are, but individuals with disabilities must be seen as having many abilities—other characteristics that they share with the majority of people.

MYTH A disability is a handicap.

FACT A disability is an inability to do something, the lack of a specific capacity. A handicap, on the other hand, is a disadvantage that is imposed on an individual. A disability might or might not be a handicap, depending on the circumstances. For example, the inability to walk is not a handicap in learning to read, but it can be a handicap in getting into the stands at a ball game. Sometimes handicaps are needlessly imposed on people with disabilities. For example, a student who cannot write with a pen but can use a tablet or computer would be needlessly handicapped without such equipment.

GUIDING QUESTIONS

- How can we get oriented to exceptionality and special education?
- What is the educational definition of *exceptional learners*?
- What is the prevalence of exceptional learners?
- What is the definition of *special education*?

- What are the history and origins of special education?
- What legislation and litigation have affected special education?
- What is our perspective on the reasons for optimism regarding special education?

The study of exceptional learners is the study of both differences and similarities. The exceptional learner differs in some way from the average. In very simple terms, such a person might have problems or special talents in thinking, seeing, hearing, speaking, socializing, or moving. More often than not, she has a combination of special abilities or disabilities. Today, more than 6 million learners with these differences have been identified in public schools throughout the United States. About 1 of every 10 school-age students in the United States is considered exceptional. The fact that many so-called "normal" students have school-related problems makes the study of exceptionality essential.

The study of exceptional learners is also the study of similarities. Exceptional individuals are not different from the average in every way. In fact, most exceptional learners are average in more ways than they are not. And although not all individuals with Down syndrome are high functioning, the following feature demonstrates how many of these individuals aspire to and attain similar life goals as the typical adolescent or young adult (http://www.youtube.com/watch?v=VMoZhgN0V5o). Until recently, professionals—and laypeople as well—tended to focus on the differences between exceptional and nonexceptional learners, almost to the exclusion of the ways in which all individuals are alike. Today, we give more attention to what exceptional and nonexceptional learners have in common—to similarities in their characteristics, needs, and ways of learning. As a result, the study of exceptional learners has become more complex, and many so-called facts about children and youths with disabilities and those who have special gifts or talents have been challenged.

GETTING ORIENTED TO EXCEPTIONAL LEARNERS AND SPECIAL EDUCATION

MyLab Education
Video Example 1.1

Jennifer, who has a learning disability and a hand tremor, discusses stereotyping, hurtful words, and their emotional impact on a person with a disability.

Students of one of the hard sciences might boast about the difficulty of the subject matter because of the many facts they must remember and piece together. Students of special education face quite different problems. To be sure, they study facts, but the facts they must master are relatively few compared to the unanswered questions or ambiguities within their minds. Any study of human beings must take into account inherent ambiguities, inconsistencies, and unknowns. In the case of the individual who deviates from the norm, we must multiply all the mysteries of normal human behavior and development by those pertaining to the person's exceptionalities. Because no single theory of normal development is universally accepted, it is not at all surprising that relatively few definitive statements can be made about exceptional learners and that many controversies remain (Kauffman, 2008; Kauffman, Hallahan, & Pullen, 2017).

The Importance of Abilities

Many people with disabilities have abilities that go unrecognized because their disabilities become the focus of concern and distract attention from what the individual can do. We must study the disabilities of exceptional children and youths if we are to learn how to help them maximize their abilities in school. Some students with disabilities that are not obvious to the casual observer need special programs of education and related services to help them live full, happy, productive lives. However, we must not lose sight of the fact that the most important characteristics of exceptional learners are their abilities, not their disabilities.

Consider Nick Vujicic, a Serbian-Australian who was born with a rare disorder called **tetra-amelia**, which results in the absence of all four limbs. He has similar life goals—aspirations for meaningful relationships, gainful employment, and participation in athletics—but he is different in that he has no arms or legs. As educators, we need to focus on both similarities and differences. Moreover, we should be inspired by individuals such as Nick Vujicic to help individuals move beyond their disabilities to reach their maximum potential. We must not allow people's disabilities to keep us from recognizing their abilities or to become so much the focus of our concern that we overlook their capabilities.

Disability Versus Handicap

We recognize an important distinction between disability and handicap: A **disability** is an inability to do something, a diminished capacity to perform in a specific way (an impairment); a **handicap**, however, is a disadvantage imposed on an individual. Thus, a disability might or might not be a handicap, depending on the circumstances. Likewise, a handicap might or might not be caused by a disability. For example, blindness is a disability that can be anything but a handicap in the dark. In fact, in the dark, the person who has sight is the one who is handicapped. Needing to use a wheelchair might be a handicap in certain circumstances, but the disadvantage may be caused by architectural barriers or other people's reactions, not the inability to walk. Other people's insensitive responses can handicap those who differ from themselves (in color, size, appearance, language, and so on) by stereotyping them or not giving them opportunities to do the things they are able to do. When working and living with exceptional individuals who have disabilities, we must constantly strive to separate their disabilities from the handicaps. That is, our goal should be to confine the handicaps to those characteristics and circumstances that can't be changed and to make sure that we impose no further handicaps by our attitudes or our unwillingness to accommodate their disabilities.

Disability Versus Inability

Another important distinction is that between inability and disability. All disabilities are an inability to do something. However, not every inability to do something is a disability. That is, disability is a subset of inability: "A disability is an inability to do something that most people, with typical maturation, opportunity, or instruction, can do" (Kauffman & Hallahan, 2005, p. 30; see also Stichter, Conroy, & Kauffman, 2008). Consider age and ability. Most 6-month-old infants cannot walk or talk, but they are not thought of as having a disability because their inability is age appropriate. However, if that inability extends well past the time when most children learn to walk and talk, then we consider their inability a disability. Consider the role of instruction. An adult's inability to read is not a reading disability if she or he has not had reading instruction. Weigh the factor of typical adult human abilities. A typical adult male might not be able to lift 400 pounds, but this isn't considered a disability, because most men simply can't lift 400 pounds. Judging inability in the context of old age, the average 70-year-old can't run 10 miles, but most 70-year-olds can walk a considerable distance. Not being able to run 10 miles is not considered a disability for a 70-year-old, but being unable to walk *at all* is. The point is, simply, that disability is a significant difference from what we expect most people to be able to do, given their age, opportunities, and instruction.

Video Example from

MyLab Education
Video Example 1.2

Nick Vujicic is a Serbian-Australian who was born with a rare disorder called tetra-amelia, which results in the absence of all four limbs. Nick is more like than unlike people without disabilities. https://www.youtube.com/watch?v=SjbX6mDnMwM

MyLab Education Self-Check 1.1

MyLab Education Application Exercise 1.1:
Lauralee's Story: Am I More Alike than Different?

Watch the video clip of Lauralee. As you watch, think about
ways in which you and Lauralee are similar.

EDUCATIONAL DEFINITION OF *EXCEPTIONAL LEARNERS*

For purposes of education, exceptional learners are those who require special education and related services if they are to realize their full human potential (Kauffman & Hallahan, 2005). They require special education because they differ markedly from most students in one or more of the following ways: They may have intellectual disabilities, learning or attention disabilities, emotional or behavioral disorders, physical disabilities, disorders of communication, autism, traumatic brain injury, impaired hearing, impaired sight, or special gifts or talents. The chapters that follow define as exactly as possible what it means to have an exceptionality.

Two concepts are important to this educational definition of exceptional learners: (1) diversity of characteristics and (2) need for special education. The concept of diversity is inherent in the definition of exceptionality; the need for special education is inherent in an educational definition. Exceptional learners differ from most (typical or average) individuals in a particular way that is relevant to their education. Their particular educationally relevant difference demands instruction that differs from what most (typical or average) learners require (Kauffman & Hallahan, 2005; Kauffman & Konold, 2007; Stichter et al., 2008). Consider the case of Doug Landis, a successful artist who is gifted at drawing but is paralyzed from the neck down. Doug is an example of how the focus on persons with disabilities must be on what they can do rather than on how they are limited. (To learn more about this successful artist, see Up Close with Doug Landis).

- -

UP CLOSE with Doug Landis Doug Landis became quadriplegic (all four limbs are affected by paralysis) in high school as a result of a wrestling accident. After Doug's accident, his brother thought he was watching too much television and challenged him to start drawing by putting a pencil in his mouth. Using a pencil attached to a mouth stick, Doug has become a major artist whose detailed line drawings of wildlife are best known, but he is gifted at drawing many things. He has also made short animated films. Doug is an active member of the organization Mouth and Foot Painting Artists (http://www.mfpausa.com), which assists artists with disabilities to meet their financial needs. Doug Landis's exquisite drawings and paintings of wildlife (http://www.youtube.com/watch?v=55AFFtP2pSA) illustrate how the focus on persons with disabilities must be on what they can do rather than on how they are limited. You may see Doug's art on his website (http://www.mouthart.com). •

- -

Sometimes seemingly obvious disabilities are never identified, and the consequences for the person and her family, as well as for the larger society, are tragic (Kauffman & Brigham, 2009). Sometimes disabilities are identified but special education is not provided, and opportunities for the child's development are thus squandered. Although early identification and intervention hold the promise of preventing many disabilities from becoming worse, preventive action often is not taken (Kauffman, 2014; Kauffman & Brigham, 2009; Stichter et al., 2008). In fact, launched in 2004, the Centers for Disease Control and Prevention's (CDC's) "Learn the Signs. Act Early." campaign encourages the early identification of developmental disabilities, including autism. On its website, the CDC provides a library of videos to help parents and professionals track the development of young children (https://www.cdc.gov/ncbddd/actearly/milestones/milestones-in-action.html). The videos provide examples of developmental milestones for children birth to 5 years of age.

Special education does not always work as it should, but when it does, educators identify a student's disability early and provide effective special education. Pediatricians also are an important part of this process, particularly for young children, as they can refer patients for evaluation and early childhood special education services. In both early childhood special education and special education for school-age children, the child's parents are involved in the decision about how to address the student's needs, and the outcome of special education is the student's improved achievement and behavior.

Students with exceptionalities are an extraordinarily diverse group in comparison to the general population, and relatively few generalizations apply to all exceptional individuals. Their exceptionalities can involve sensory, physical, cognitive, emotional, or communication abilities or any combination of these. Furthermore, exceptionalities may vary greatly in cause, degree, and effect on educational progress, and the effects may vary greatly depending on the individual's age, gender, and life circumstances. Any individual presented as an example of an "exceptional learner" is likely to be representative of exceptional learners in some respects but unrepresentative in others.

The typical student who receives special education has no immediately obvious or visible disability. He (more than half of the students served by special education are males) is in elementary or middle school and has persistent problems in learning and behaving appropriately in school. His problems are primarily academic and social or behavioral, and may not be apparent to many teachers until they have worked with him for a period of weeks or months. His problems persist despite teachers' efforts to meet his needs in the regular school program in which most students succeed. He is most likely to be described as having a learning disability or to be designated by an even broader label indicating that his academic and social progress in school is unsatisfactory owing to a disability.

By federal law, schools should not identify these exceptional students as eligible for special education until careful assessment indicates that they are unable to make satisfactory progress in the regular school program without special services designed to meet their extraordinary needs. Federal special education laws and regulations include definitions of several conditions (categories such as learning disability, autism, and hearing impairment) that might create a need for special education. These laws and regulations require that schools provide special services to meet whatever special needs are created by a disabling condition that can't be met in the general educational program. The law doesn't require provision of special education simply because a student has a disability.

MyLab Education Self-Check 1.2

MyLab Education Application Exercise 1.2: Disability Categories: Prevalence Versus Percentages

Scan Chapters 5 through 14 in your text for an overview of *prevalence* figures for students with disabilities. Then, consider data provided by the U.S. Department of Education's National Center for Education Statistics to answer a few questions.

PREVALENCE OF EXCEPTIONAL LEARNERS

Prevalence refers to the percentage of a population or number of individuals having a particular exceptionality. Obviously, accurate estimates of prevalence depend on the ability to count the number of people in a given population who have a specific exceptionality.

The task of determining the number of students with exceptionalities might appear simple enough, yet the prevalence of most exceptionalities is uncertain and a matter of considerable controversy. Multiple factors make it difficult to state the number of exceptional individuals with great accuracy and confidence. These factors include vagueness in definitions, frequent changes in definitions, and the role of schools in determining exceptionality—matters that we discuss in later chapters (see also Kauffman, Hallahan, & Pullen, 2017).

Recent government figures indicate that over 6.7 million students (8.7%) between the ages of 6 and 21 years receive special education services in schools (U.S. Department of Education, 2016). It's important to keep in mind that the number of students served in special education is not necessarily equal to the number of students who actually have the disability. The latter is much more difficult to calculate than the former, because the federal government requires school districts to report the number of students with disabilities they are serving each year. Beginning in the mid-1970s, the number of students served by special education grew steadily, from about 3.75 million in 1976 to more than 6 million in the early 21st century. Most of the children and youths who are served by special education are between the ages of 6 and 17. Although preschoolers and youths ages 18 to 21 are being identified with increasing frequency as having disabilities, school-age children and youths in their early teens make up the bulk of the identified population.

The percentage of the special education population identified as having certain disabilities has changed considerably over several decades. For example, the number of students identified as having learning disabilities has more than doubled since the mid-1970s; these students now make up about half of the number of students receiving special education services. In contrast, the percentage of students whose primary disability is speech or language impairments declined substantially (but is growing again), and the percentage identified as having intellectual disabilities is now about half of what it was in 1976. No one has an entirely satisfactory explanation of these changes. However, they might in part reflect alterations in definitions and diagnostic criteria for certain disabilities and the social acceptability of the "learning disability" label. In subsequent chapters, we discuss the prevalence of specific categories of exceptionality.

High-Incidence and Low-Incidence Categories

Some disabilities occur with a relatively high frequency and are called *high-incidence disabilities* because they are among the most common. Learning disabilities, communication (speech and language) disorders, emotional disturbance, and mild intellectual disabilities are among those usually considered high incidence (Stichter et al., 2008). Other disabilities (such as blindness, deafness, severe intellectual disabilities, and traumatic brain injury) occur relatively rarely and are considered low-incidence disabilities.

Although the rates of occurrence of most of the high-incidence disabilities have remained relatively stable in the early 21st century, some of the low-incidence categories have increased dramatically. For example, the identification of **autism** or **autistic spectrum disorder** has increased dramatically since about 1995 (discussed further in Chapter 9; see also Stichter et al., 2008). In fact, some professionals speculate that it will eventually be considered a high-incidence disability. Other low-incidence categories showing a substantial increase in numbers include **traumatic brain injury (TBI)**, orthopedic impairments, and other health impairments. Increases in the first two are due to increases in spinal cord injury and in survival of severe physical trauma because of better medical care. As we point out in Chapter 7, the increase in OHI is due to an increase in ADHD, which is included in OHI.

Much of the increase in diagnosis of autism probably represents improved identification procedures along with identification of milder cases of autism, not an epidemic (National Research Council, 2001). Although some of the increase in TBI might represent better diagnosis, it might also reflect actual increases in brain injuries, as we will discuss in Chapter 13. Increases in orthopedic impairments might reflect the increasing survival rates of infants born with significant physical anomalies and of children involved in accidents. Reasons for the increase in ADHD are open for speculation. It may be partially the result of increased awareness.

MyLab Education Self-Check 1.3

DEFINITION OF SPECIAL EDUCATION

Special education means specially designed instruction that meets the unusual needs of an exceptional student and that requires special materials, teaching techniques, equipment and/or facilities. Students with visual impairments might require reading materials in large print or braille; students with hearing impairments might require hearing aids and/or instruction in sign language; those with physical disabilities might need special equipment; those with emotional or behavioral disorders might need smaller and more highly structured classes; and students with special gifts or talents might require access to working professionals. Related services—special transportation, psychological assessment, physical and occupational therapy, medical treatment, and counseling—might be necessary if special education is to be effective. The single most important goal of special education is finding and capitalizing on exceptional students' abilities.

The best general education cannot replace special education for those who need it; special education is more precisely controlled in pace or rate, intensity, relentlessness, structure, reinforcement, teacher–pupil ratio, curriculum, and monitoring or assessment (Pullen & Hallahan, 2015). We think it's a good idea to improve the education of all children, an objective of the federal education laws of the early 21st century; however, good or reformed general education does not and cannot replace special education for those students at the extremes of the range of disabilities (Kauffman & Konold, 2007; Pullen & Hallahan, 2015; Zigmond, 2007; Zigmond & Kloo, 2017 Zigmond, Kloo, & Volonino, 2009).

HISTORY AND ORIGINS OF SPECIAL EDUCATION

There have always been exceptional learners, but there haven't always been special educational services to address their needs (see Holmes, 2004; Metzler, 2006). During the closing years of the 18th century, following the American and French Revolutions, effective procedures were devised for teaching children with sensory impairments (i.e., those who were blind or deaf; Winzer, 1993). In 1829, Samuel Gridley Howe created the first residential school for students who were blind; the curriculum focused on both instruction in traditional reading, writing, and mathematics and the development of students' individual interests and abilities (Sapp & Hatlen, 2010). Early in the 19th century, the first systematic attempts were made to educate "idiotic" and "insane" children—those who today are said to have intellectual disabilities and emotional or behavioral disorders (or emotional disturbance; Kauffman & Landrum, 2006; Stichter et al., 2008).

In the prerevolutionary era, the best that society offered most children with disabilities was protection—asylum from a cruel world that had no place for them and in which they couldn't survive with dignity, if they could survive at all. But as the ideas of democracy, individual freedom, and egalitarianism swept across America and France, a change in attitude occurred. Political reformers and leaders in medicine and education began to champion the cause of children and adults with disabilities, urging that these "imperfect" or "incomplete" individuals be taught skills that would allow them to become independent, productive citizens. These humanitarian sentiments surpassed a desire to protect and defend people with disabilities. The early leaders sought to normalize exceptional people to the greatest extent possible and confer on them the human dignity they presumably lacked.

Contemporary educational methods for exceptional children can be traced directly to techniques pioneered during the early 1800s. Many (perhaps most) of today's vital, controversial issues have been concerns ever since the dawn of special education. Some contemporary writers believe that instruction in the history of special education is critically important in fostering understanding of today's issues because of the lessons we can learn from our past (e.g., Gerber, 2017; Kauffman & Landrum, 2006). In our discussion of major historical events and trends since 1800, we comment briefly on the history of people and ideas, the growth of the discipline, professional and parent organizations, and legislation.

People and Ideas

Many of the originators of special education were European physicians. They were primarily young, ambitious people who challenged the wisdom of the established authorities, including their own friends and mentors (Kanner, 1964; see also Kauffman & Landrum, 2006; Stichter et al., 2008).

Most historians trace the beginning of special education as we know it today to Jean-Marc-Gaspard Itard (1774–1838), a French physician who was an authority on diseases of the ear and education of students who are deaf. In the early 19th century, this young doctor began to educate a boy of about 12 years of age who had been found roaming naked and wild in the forests of France (he is sometimes referred to as the "wild child" or the "wild boy of Aveyron"). Itard's mentor, Philippe Pinel (1745–1826), a prominent French physician who was an early advocate of humane treatment of "insane" people, advised Itard that his efforts would be unsuccessful because the boy, Victor, was a "hopeless idiot." But Itard persevered. He did not eliminate Victor's disabilities, but he did dramatically improve the wild child's behavior through patient, systematic educative procedures (Itard, 1962). Several years ago, Mary Losure (2013) published a nonfiction book for children and adolescents that provides the history of the wild boy of Aveyron. Cases such as the wild boy of Aveyron bring into question the role of nature and nurture in human development (see the Focus on . . . The Nature–Nurture Controversy).

The ideas of the first special educators were truly revolutionary for their times. Following are some of the innovative ideas of Itard, Édouard Séguin, and their successors that form the foundation for present-day special education:

- *Individualized instruction,* in which the child's characteristics, rather than prescribed academic content, provide the basis for teaching techniques
- *A carefully sequenced series of educational tasks,* beginning with tasks the child can perform and gradually leading to more complex learning
- *Emphasis on stimulation and awakening of the child's senses,* to make the child more aware of and responsive to educational stimuli
- *Meticulous arrangement of the child's environment,* so that the structure of the environment and the child's experience of it lead naturally to learning
- *Immediate reward for correct performance,* providing reinforcement for desirable behavior
- *Tutoring in functional skills,* to make the child as self-sufficient and productive as possible in everyday life
- *Belief that every child should be educated to the greatest extent possible,* because every child can improve to some degree

So far, we've mentioned only European physicians who figured prominently in the rise of special education. Although much of the initial work occurred in Europe, many U.S. researchers contributed greatly during those early years. They kept informed of European developments as best they could, some of them traveling to Europe for the specific purpose of obtaining firsthand information about the education of children with disabilities.

Among the young U.S. thinkers who were concerned with the education of students with disabilities was Samuel Gridley Howe (1801–1876), an 1824 graduate of Harvard Medical School. Besides being a physician and an educator, Howe was a political and social reformer, a champion of humanitarian causes and emancipation. He was instrumental in founding the Perkins School for the Blind in Watertown, Massachusetts, and also taught students who were deaf and blind. His success in teaching Laura Bridgman, who was deaf and blind, greatly influenced the education of Helen Keller. In the 1840s, Howe was also a force behind the organization of an experimental school for children with intellectual disabilities (mental retardation) and was personally acquainted with Séguin.

When Thomas Hopkins Gallaudet (1787–1851), a minister, was a student at Andover Theological Seminary, he tried to teach a girl who was deaf. He visited Europe to

Video Example from

You Tube

MyLab Education
Video Example 1.3
Laurence Steinberg of Temple University explains the interaction of genetics and the environment and its role in human behavior; he highlights the need to break down the false dichotomy between genes and the environment.
http://www.youtube.com/watch?v=j-nnJpV1iuE

The Nature–Nurture Controversy

One of the oldest controversies involving the education of exceptional learners is the extent to which nature and nurture contribute to what a child becomes. What is attributable to biological factors such as genetics and other aspects of physical endowment, and what is attributable to environmental factors such as opportunity, encouragement, and teaching? The controversial idea was part of Itard's work in the early 19th century, and is still being debated by psychologists (e.g., Pinker, 2002) and popular writers (e.g., Gladwell, 2008) today.

For many years, theoreticians tended to view the nature–nurture issue from an either/or perspective: Either you believed that heredity held the key to determining intellectual development or you believed that the environment was the all-important factor. Today, however, most authorities believe that both heredity and the environment are critical determinants of intelligence. Some scientists have tried to discover how much of intelligence is determined by heredity and how much by the environment, but many view this quest as futile. They assert that heredity and environment do not combine in an additive fashion to produce intelligence. Instead, the interaction between genes and environment results in intelligence.

---

learn about educating the deaf and in 1817 established the first American residential school for students who were deaf (now known as the American School of the Deaf) in Hartford, Connecticut. Gallaudet University in Washington, D.C., the only liberal-arts college for students who are deaf, was named in his honor.

The early years of special education were vibrant with the pulse of new ideas. It isn't possible to read the words of Itard, Séguin, Howe, and their contemporaries without being captivated by the romance, idealism, and excitement of their exploits. The results they achieved were truly remarkable for their era. Today, special education remains a vibrant field in which innovations, excitement, idealism, and controversies are the norm. Teachers of exceptional children—and that includes all teachers—must understand how and why special education emerged as a discipline (see Gerber, 2017).

Normalization, Deinstitutionalization, and Inclusion

Among the major 20th-century ideas in special education is *normalization,* the philosophy that we should use "means which are as culturally normative as possible, in order to establish and/or maintain personal behaviors and characteristics which are as culturally normative as possible" (Wolfensberger, 1972, p. 28). With normalization, the barriers to the participation of people with disabilities in normal life are broken down. The concept of normalization was in itself important and led to related ideas, such as closing institutions and including exceptional learners in general education classrooms and schools.

Normalization continues to be a goal in special education and all other aspects of responding to disability. Breaking down barriers to participation of people with disabilities in activities with nonhandicapped individuals was one of the ideas leading to the **deinstitutionalization** movement of the late 20th century. At one time, it was common to place nearly all children and adults with intellectual disability (formerly mental retardation) and/or mental illness in residential institutions. In the 1960s and 1970s, systematic efforts were made to move people out of institutions and back into closer contact with the community. This led to more children with disabilities being raised by their families and resulted in the closure of many institutions regardless of the nature of the problems of the people involved. Today, smaller facilities within local neighborhoods are common. Transitional living homes (sometimes called halfway houses) exist for individuals with emotional difficulties, who no longer are thought to need the more isolated environment of a large institution. However, much still needs to be done to improve the quality of life for some people with disabilities who previously may have been in institutions. In fact, many people who formerly would have been in institutions are now homeless or in jail (see Earley, 2006; Goin, 2007; Nomani, 2007; Powers, 2017). Increasing numbers

MyLab Education
Video Example 1.4
Author Interview: A discussion of the term "full inclusion," and what that means for students being placed into special education services.

of individuals are homeless in the United States, and cognitive and mental health disabilities are significant risk factors for homelessness (Edens, Kasprow, Tsai, & Rosenheck, 2011; Mercier & Picard, 2011).

Perhaps the most controversial issue growing out of the idea of normalization is **inclusion**. Actually inclusion, or integration, has long been an issue with all exceptional students, including those with special gifts or talents. Although, historically, educators built educational programming for students with disabilities on the assumption that a variety of service delivery options need to be available (Crockett & Kauffman, 1999, 2001; Kauffman, Mock, Tankersley, & Landrum, 2008), inclusion of exceptional learners in ordinary classrooms with their nonexceptional peers has become the single most important issue for some advocates. The issue of inclusion became controversial among parents and others in the late 20th century and continues to be a topic of heated opinion and discussion.

At the unfolding of the 21st century, the inclusion controversy was sharpened, especially by the higher standards expected of all students. The direction the controversy will take is anyone's guess (see Bateman, 2017; Kauffman, Anastasiou, Badar, Travers, & Wiley, 2016; Kauffman & Hung, 2009; Kauffman & Landrum, 2018b; Zigmond & Kloo, 2017). We can't overemphasize the importance of intensive instruction in meeting the needs of exceptional learners. In our opinion, exceptional children should be placed where such instruction is most likely to be provided, even if that place is somewhere other than the general education classroom. It is critical that inclusion in the general education setting full time should not be at the expense of the specialized instruction that is required to help students with disabilities meet their academic potential.

Council for Exceptional Children and Development of the Profession

Special education didn't suddenly spring up as a new discipline or develop in isolation from other disciplines. The emergence of psychology and sociology and especially of the widespread use of cognitive tests in the early years of the 20th century had enormous implications for the growth of special education. Psychologists' study of learning and their prediction of school failure or success by means of tests helped to focus attention on children with special needs. Sociologists, social workers, and anthropologists drew attention to the ways in which exceptional children's families and communities responded to them and affected their learning and adjustment. Anecdotal accounts of intellectual disabilities or mental disorders can be found in the 19th-century literature, but they are not presented within the conceptual frameworks that we recognize today as psychology, sociology, and special education (Kauffman & Landrum, 2006). Even in the early 20th century, the concepts of disability seem crude by today's standards.

As the education profession itself matured and as compulsory school attendance laws became a reality, there was a growing realization among teachers and school administrators that a large number of students must be given something beyond the ordinary classroom experience. Elizabeth Farrell, a teacher in New York City in the early 20th century, was highly instrumental in the development of special education as a profession. She and the New York City superintendent of schools attempted to use information about child development, social work, mental testing, and instruction to address the needs of children and youths who were being either ill served in or excluded from general education classes and schools. Farrell was a great advocate for services for students with special needs. Her motives and those of the teachers and administrators who worked with her were to see that every student—including every exceptional child or youth—had an appropriate education and received the related health and social services necessary for optimum learning in school (Gerber, 2017). In 1922, Farrell and a group of other special educators from across the United States and Canada founded the Council for Exceptional Children (CEC), which is still the primary professional organization of special educators.

Contemporary special education is a professional field with roots in several academic disciplines—especially medicine, psychology, sociology, and social work—in addition to professional education. The discipline is sufficiently different from the mainstream of professional education to require special training programs but sufficiently like the mainstream to maintain a primary concern for schools and teaching.

Individuals, Parents, and Organizations

Individuals and ideas have played crucial roles in the history of special education, but it's accurate to say that much of the progress that has been made over the years has been achieved primarily by the collective efforts of parents and professionals. Professional groups were organized first, beginning in the 19th century. Effective national parent organizations have existed in the United States only since about 1950.

Many people have been influential in the development of special education or other opportunities for individuals with disabilities. Among them is the late President John F. Kennedy's sister Eunice Kennedy Shriver. Their sister Rosemary had an intellectual disability. Eunice Shriver originated the Special Olympics. Having sports competitions in which individuals with disabilities could compete no doubt enriched the lives of many. Even though the Special Olympics has generated criticism, it stands as an example of advocacy for caring and fair treatment of individuals with disabilities. Ms. Shriver (http://www.youtube.com/watch?v=0CukBoFytFY) undeniably changed the self-perception of many people with disabilities and also changed the general public's perceptions of individuals with disabilities for the better and improved the quality of life for many.

Although they offer membership to individuals who don't have exceptional children, parent organizations primarily comprise parents who do have such children and concentrate on issues that are of special concern to them. Parent organizations have typically served three essential functions: (1) provide an informal group for parents who understand one another's problems and needs and help one another deal with anxieties and frustrations, (2) provide information regarding services and potential resources, and (3) provide the structure for obtaining needed services for their children. Some of the organizations that came about primarily as the result of parents' efforts include the ARC (formerly the Association for Retarded Citizens), the National Association for Gifted Children, the Learning Disabilities Association of America, the Autism Society of America, and the Federation of Families for Children's Mental Health. (See the links to these organizations at the end of this chapter.)

Legislation and Litigation

Legislation (lawmaking) and litigation (defending one's rights under law) have played major roles in how students with disabilities are identified and educated. These roles have often been reciprocal, with one influencing the other and vice versa.

LEGISLATION Much of the progress in meeting the educational needs of children and youths with disabilities is attributable to laws requiring states and localities to include students with special needs in the public education system (Bateman, 2007, 2017; Bateman & Linden, 2006; Huefner, 2006). We focus here on significant legislation that represents a culmination of decades of legislative history. However, litigation (lawsuits or court decisions) has also played a major role in special education (see Yell, Crockett, Shriner, & Rozalski, 2017; Yell, Katsiyannis, & Bradley, 2017).

A landmark federal law was passed in 1975: the **Education for All Handicapped Children Act**, commonly known as PL 94-142* (Martin, 2013). In 1990, this law was amended to become the **Individuals with Disabilities Education Act (IDEA)**. In 1997, the law was amended again, but its name was not changed [see Bateman & Linden (2006) and Yell (2012) for details]. The law was reauthorized again in 2004, as the **Individuals with Disabilities Education Improvement Act (IDEIA)**. As a field, we still refer to the law simply as IDEA, as the basic requirements of the law have not changed. The federal law known as IDEA ensures that all children and youths with disabilities have the right to a free, appropriate public education.

---

*Legislation is often designated PL (for public law), followed by a hyphenated numeral; the first set of digits represents the number of the Congress that passed the bill, and the second set represents the number of that bill. Thus, PL 94-142 was the 142nd public law passed by the 94th Congress.

FOCUS ON

The Major Provisions of IDEA

Each state and locality must have a plan to ensure*:

Identification
Extensive efforts to screen and identify all children and youths with disabilities.

Free Appropriate Public Education (FAPE)
Every student with a disability has an appropriate public education at no cost to the parents or guardian.

Due Process
The student's and parents' rights to information and informed consent before the student is evaluated, labeled, or placed, and the right to an impartial due process hearing if they disagree with the school's decisions.

Parent/Guardian Surrogate Consultation
The student's parents (or guardian) are consulted about the student's evaluation and placement and the educational plan; if the parents (or guardian) are unknown or unavailable, a surrogate parent must be found to act for the student.

Least Restrictive Environment (LRE)
The student is educated in the least restrictive environment consistent with his or her educational needs and, insofar as possible, with students without disabilities.

Individualized Education Program (IEP)
A written individualized education program is prepared for each student with a disability, including levels of functioning, long-term goals, extent to which the student will *not* participate in the general education classroom and curriculum, services to be provided, plans for initiating and evaluating the services, and needed transition services (from school to work or continued education). Parents must be invited to the meeting and efforts made to enable them to attend.

Nondiscriminatory Evaluation
The student is evaluated in all areas of suspected disability and in a way that is not biased by his or her language or cultural characteristics or disabilities. Evaluation must be by a multidisciplinary team, and no single evaluation procedure may be used as the sole criterion for placement or planning.

Confidentiality
The results of evaluation and placement are kept confidential, though the student's parents (or guardian) may have access to the records.

Personnel Development, In-service
Training for teachers and other professional personnel, including in-service training for general education teachers, in meeting the needs of students with disabilities.

Detailed federal rules and regulations govern the implementation of each of these major provisions. The Code of Federal Regulations comprises the rules for implementation of the law.

Another landmark federal law, enacted in 1990, is the **Americans with Disabilities Act (ADA)**. ADA ensures the right of individuals with disabilities to nondiscriminatory treatment in other aspects of their lives; it provides protections of civil rights in the specific areas of employment, transportation, public accommodations, state and local government, and telecommunications. For information about the provisions for students under Section 504 of the ADA, you can go to www.ed.gov and in the "Search" box, type in "Americans with Disabilities Act Section 504."

IDEA and another federal law focusing on intervention in early childhood (PL 99-457) mandate a free appropriate public education for every child or youth between the ages of 3 and 21, regardless of the nature or severity of the disability. PL 99-457 also provides incentives for states to develop early intervention programs for infants with known disabilities and those who are considered to be at risk. Together, these laws require public school systems to identify all children and youths with disabilities and to provide the necessary special education and related services to these students.

The federal law we now know as IDEA was revolutionary because it was the first federal law mandating free appropriate public education for all children with disabilities. Its basic provisions are described in the Focus on . . . The Major Provisions of IDEA. "Celebrating 35 Years of IDEA" (http://www.youtube.com/watch?v=DUn6luZQaXE) provides a history of the legislation of the federal special education law.

Historically, legislation has been increasingly specific and mandatory. Beginning in the 1980s, however, a renewed emphasis on states' rights and local autonomy plus a political strategy of federal deregulation led to attempts to repeal some of the provisions of IDEA (then still known as PL 94-142) and loosen federal rules and regulations. Federal disinvestment in education and deregulation of special education programs remain popular ideas. It's not surprising that federal mandates for special education have come under fire. Dissatisfaction with federal mandates is due in part to the fact that the federal government contributes relatively little to the funding of special education. Although the demands of IDEA are detailed, state and local governments pay most of the cost of special education programs.

Some have characterized the legal history of special education as a "long, strange trip" (Yell, Rogers, & Rogers, 1998, p. 219). Special education law is highly controversial, and battles over IDEA are ongoing. The amendment and continuation of IDEA in 1997 and 2004 represented a sustained commitment to require schools, employers, and government agencies to recognize the abilities of people with disabilities, but the extent to which the 2004 revision of the law represents actual improvement is debatable (Turnbull, 2007; Vitello, 2007). IDEA and ADA require reasonable accommodations that will allow those who have disabilities to participate to the fullest extent possible in all the activities of daily living that individuals without disabilities take for granted. The requirements of ADA are intended to grant equal opportunities to people with disabilities in employment, transportation, public accommodations, state and local government, and telecommunications.

In the early 21st century, under the administration of President George W. Bush, the federal No Child Left Behind Act (NCLB) became a major factor in the focus of public schooling, including special education (see Huefner, 2006; Yell & Drasgow, 2005). NCLB was an attempt to improve the academic performance of all students, including those with disabilities. Under NCLB and its successor, the Elementary and Secondary Education Act (ESSA), most students with disabilities are to take standard tests of academic achievement and achieve at a level equal to students without disabilities. Moreover, NCLB included the requirement that all teachers be "highly qualified," a designation that left much to interpretation (Gelman, Pullen, & Kauffman, 2004). Some have noted that core requirements of NCLB were neither reasonable nor achievable, particularly with reference to special education (Kauffman, 2010; Kauffman & Konold, 2007; Rothstein, Jacobsen, & Wilder, 2006).

LITIGATION Laws often have little or no effect on the lives of individuals with disabilities until courts interpret exactly what the laws require in practice. Primarily through the actions of parent and professional organizations, exceptional children have been getting their day in court more frequently since IDEA and related federal and state laws were passed. Therefore, we must examine litigation to complete the picture of how the U.S. legal system may safeguard or undermine appropriate education for exceptional children.

Zelder (1953) noted that in the early days of public education, school attendance was seen as a privilege that could be awarded to or withheld from an individual child at the discretion of local school officials. During the late 19th and early 20th centuries, the courts typically found that disruptive children or those with mental retardation (intellectual disabilities) could be excluded from school for the sake of preserving order, protecting the teacher's time from excessive demands, and sparing children the discomfort of seeing others who are disabled. In the first half of the 20th century, the courts tended to

MyLab Education
Video Example 1.5
The Individualized Educational Program (IEP) is a critical element in IDEA. This video is an example of an IEP meeting. Note that the mother is included in the IEP meeting.

defend the majority of schoolchildren from a disabled minority. But now the old excuses for excluding students with disabilities from school are no longer valid.

Today, the courts must interpret laws that define school attendance as the right of every child, regardless of her disability. Litigation is now focused on ensuring that every child receives an education that is appropriate for her individual needs. As some legal scholars have pointed out, this doesn't mean that laws or litigation support full inclusion of all children with disabilities in general education (Bateman, 2017).

Litigation may involve legal suits primarily filed for either of two reasons: (1) because special education services aren't being provided for students whose parents believe their children deserve them or (2) because students are being assigned to special education when their parents believe that the assignment is unwarranted. Suits for special education have been brought primarily by parents whose children are unquestionably disabled and either are being denied any education at all or are being given very meager special services. The parents who file these suits believe that the advantages of their children's identification for special education services clearly outweigh the disadvantages. Suits against special education have been brought primarily by parents of students who have mild or questionable disabilities and who are already attending school. These parents believe that their children are being stigmatized and discriminated against rather than helped by special education. Thus, the courts today are asked to make decisions in which individual students' characteristics are weighed against specific educational programs.

Parents want their children with disabilities to have a free public education that meets their needs but doesn't stigmatize them unnecessarily and that permits them to be taught in the general education classroom as much as possible. The laws governing education recognize parents' and students' rights to such an education. In the courts today, the burden of proof is ultimately on local and state education specialists, who must show in every instance that the student's abilities and disabilities have been completely and accurately assessed and that appropriate educational procedures are being employed. Much of the special education litigation has involved controversy over the use of intelligence (IQ) and other standardized testing to determine students' eligibility for special education. Although the debate about IQ tests has been acrimonious, some scholars have found that IQ scores themselves haven't been the primary means of classifying children as eligible for special education (MacMillan & Forness, 1998).

One historic court case of the 1980s deserves particular consideration. In 1982, the U.S. Supreme Court made its first interpretation of PL 94-142 (now IDEA) in *Hudson v. Rowley*, a case involving Amy Rowley, a child who was deaf (*Board of Education of Hendrick Hudson v. Rowley*, 1982). The Court's decision was that appropriate education for a deaf child with a disability does not necessarily mean education that will produce the maximum possible achievement. Amy's parents had contended that she might be able to learn more in school if she were provided with a sign language interpreter. But the Court decided that because the school had designed an individualized program of special services for Amy and she was achieving at or above the level of her nondisabled classmates, the school system had met its obligation under the law to provide an appropriate education. In fact, Amy's education proved to be successful in that she went on to coordinate the American Sign Language Program at California State University East Bay, where she is currently an associate professor in Modern Languages and Literature.

School districts have used the precedent about the necessary level of benefits a student must be provided set in the *Rowley* case for decades; however, a new case may increase the level of benefit districts need to provide students with disabilities to meet FAPE. In the case of *Endrew F. v. Douglas County School District* (2017), the District used the *Rowley* language to argue that Endrew F. was receiving some benefit from the IEP, which met the letter of the law. The tenth district court interpreted *Rowley* to establish a rule that:

> a child's IEP is adequate as long as it is calculated to confer an " educational benefit [that is] merely . . . more than de minimis," 798 F. 3d 1329, 1338 (internal quotation marks omitted), and concluded that Endrew's IEP had been "reasonably calculated to

MyLab Education
Video Example 1.6
This video demonstrates how much a sign language interpreter can help a student with hearing impairment in the classroom. Note that during the interview, Joline, the interpreter, makes sure that the interviewer's questions are understood by the student.

enable [him] to make some progress," id., at 1342. The court accordingly held that Endrew had received a FAPE. (580 U.S. –No. 15–827. Argued January 11, 2017—Decided March 22, 2017, p. 2).

However, the U.S. Supreme Court decided in favor of Endrew F., stating in its opinion:

> When all is said and done, a student offered an educational program providing "merely more than de minimis" progress from year to year can hardly be said to have been offered an education at all. . . . The IDEA demands more. It requires an educational program reasonably calculated to enable a child to make progress appropriate in light of the child's circumstances. (580 U.S. --No. 15–827. Argued January 11, 2017—Decided March 22, 2017, p. 15).

Although the Court did not attempt to define "appropriate," it clearly set a new precedent for the level of benefit a child should receive from an IEP. The *Endrew F.* case, as well as other future cases, will undoubtedly help to clarify what the law means by "appropriate education" and "least restrictive environment." In Chapter 2, we go into more detail about the law and what it requires. We pay particular attention to writing individualized education programs (IEPs) and to the meaning of *least restrictive environment* (LRE).

REASONS FOR OPTIMISM

In this chapter, we've not presented a naively optimistic view of exceptionality and special education. The field faces many challenges. It's these very challenges, however, that make special education a dynamic field—a field not only worth studying but also of critical importance to millions of students with disabilities. We remain optimistic for these students' future because we know of so many teachers and other professionals who care, and because of the never ending scientific advances pertaining to disabilities.

Scientific Advances on Causal Factors of Disability

In the vast majority of cases, professionals are unable to identify the exact reason *why* a person is exceptional, but researchers are making progress in determining the causes of some disabilities. In Chapter 5, for example, we discuss the detection of causal factors in **Down syndrome**, a condition that results in the largest number of children classified as having moderate intellectual and developmental disabilities (mental retardation, which is now called either intellectual disability (ID) or intellectual and developmental disability (IDD)). Likewise, the incidence of **retinopathy of prematurity**, at one time a leading cause of blindness, has been greatly reduced since the discovery of its cause. The metabolic disorder **phenylketonuria (PKU)** was discovered decades ago, and now infants are routinely tested for PKU soon after birth, so that this type of intellectual disability can be prevented. More recently, the gene responsible for **cystic fibrosis**—an inherited condition characterized by chronic respiratory and digestive problems—has been identified. Advances in drug treatments appear to hold the potential for a cure for **muscular dystrophy**, another inherited disorder characterized by progressive degeneration of muscles (Zordan et al., 2013). In the future, the specific genes governing many other diseases and disorders will also likely be found. Scientific advances raise the possibility of medications or gene therapies to prevent or correct many disabling conditions. Physicians can now perform surgery to correct some identifiable defects on a fetus before birth (in utero), completely avoiding some conditions, such as **hydrocephalus** (an accumulation of fluid around the brain that can cause mental or physical disabilities if not corrected). And before long, research might lead to the ability to grow new organs from tissues taken from a person or from stem cells, perhaps allowing replacement of a poorly functioning lung, pancreas, or other internal organ and avoidance of the associated physical disabilities. Advances in reproductive technology also hold promise for preventing many disabilities (Kauffman & Hallahan, 2009).

Scientific Advances in Learning and Teaching

Besides these and other medical breakthroughs, research is enhancing understanding of the ways in which the individual's psychological, social, and educational environments are related to learning. For example, special educators, psychologists, and pediatricians are increasingly able to identify environmental conditions that increase the likelihood that a child will have learning or behavior problems (see Kauffman & Landrum, 2018b; Landrigan, Lambertini, & Birnbaum, 2012; Rauch & Lanphear, 2012).

Educational methodology has also made significant strides. In fact, compared to current knowledge about causes, the knowledge about how exceptional learners can be taught and managed effectively in the classroom is much more complete. Although special educators lament that not all the questions have been answered, considerably more is known today about how to educate exceptional learners than was the case years ago (see, for example, Kauffman, Hallahan, & Pullen, 2017).

One final point: We all must certainly learn to live with disabling exceptionalities, but we must never accept them. We prefer to think there is hope for the eventual eradication of many of the disabling forms of exceptionality. In addition, we believe that it is of paramount importance to realize that even individuals whose exceptionalities are extreme can be helped to lead fuller lives than they would without appropriate education.

My**Lab** Education Self-Check 1.4

My**Lab** Education Application Exercise 1.3: An Overview of the History of Special Education

For this exercise, you will need to refer to the section "History and Origin of Special Education" in your text.

▼ chapter one SUMMARY

How can we get oriented to exceptionality and special education?

- Exceptionality involves similarities and differences.

- Reasons for optimism include better treatment and education, medical breakthroughs, and prevention.

- Abilities as well as disabilities must be recognized.

- A disability is an inability to do something; a handicap is a limitation that is imposed on someone.

- Not all inabilities are disabilities; a disability is an inability to do something that most people, with typical maturation, opportunity, or instruction, can do.

What is the educational definition of *exceptional learners*?

- Exceptional learners are those who require special education services to reach their full potential.

- Many individuals with disabilities require special education services, but some do not.

What is the prevalence of exceptional learners?

- About 1 student in every 10 (about 10% of the student population) is identified as exceptional for special education purposes.

GettyMoodboard/ Vetta/Getty Images

- Some categories of disability are considered high incidence because they are found relatively frequently (e.g., learning disabilities, communication disorders, emotional or behavioral disorders).

- Some categories of disability are considered low incidence because they occur relatively rarely (e.g., blindness, deafness, deaf-blindness).

What is the definition of *special education*?

- *Special education* means specially designed instruction that meets the unusual needs of an exceptional student. It may include special materials, teaching techniques, or equipment and/or facilities.

- The trend is toward placement in environments closest to the general education classroom in format, especially for younger children.

What are the history and origins of special education?

- Special education became common in institutions and in major cities' public education systems in the 19th century.

- Physicians and psychologists played important roles in the early formation of special education.

- The Council for Exceptional Children (CEC) and many important parent and professional organizations were formed in the 20th century.

What legislation and litigation have affected special education?

- The primary federal law affecting special education is the Individuals with Disabilities Education Act (IDEA), enacted in the 1970s and reauthorized by the U.S. Congress in 2004.
- Also important is the Americans with Disabilities Act (ADA), which prohibits discrimination against persons with disabilities in employment and communications.
- In the 21st century, the No Child Left Behind Act (NCLB) also was important in the education of exceptional learners.

- Lawsuits (litigation) have added to interpretation of the meaning and application of the law.
- Some parents sue because they want their children with unquestionable disabilities to be identified for special education and provided services or because they want them placed in more specialized environments. Others sue because they feel their children have been incorrectly identified for special education or because they want to have them educated in less atypical situations.

What is our perspective on the progress of special education?

- Special education has made great progress, but making it better is a continuing struggle.

▼ INTERNET RESOURCES

Pertinent Organizations

- The major professional organization for practitioners, policymakers, and researchers in special education, with about 40,000 members is the Council for Exceptional Children (CEC) (http://www.cec.sped.org). CEC is made up of 17 divisions, each covering a different aspect of special education; for example, the Division for Learning Disabilities (http://teachingld.org), Division on Autism and Developmental Disabilities (http://daddcec.org), Council of Administrators of Special Education (http://www.casecec.org), and Division for Culturally and Linguistically Diverse Exceptional Learners http://community.cec.sped.org/ddel/home.
- CEC provides numerous member benefits: http://www.youtube.com/watch?v=QA4wwlyXT74&feature=c4-overview&playnext=1&list=TLZcuAELOx3Ss.

chapter two

CURRENT PRACTICES FOR MEETING THE NEEDS OF EXCEPTIONAL LEARNERS

Jim West/Alamy Stock Photo

▶ LEARNING OUTCOMES

Learning Outcome 2.1: Understand how students are evaluated and identified for special education services, including the use of Response to Intervention (RTI).

Learning Outcome 2.2: Understand the intent of special education law as it pertains to individualized education programs (IEPs), individualized family service plans (IFSPs), and transition plans for adolescents with disabilities.

Learning Outcome 2.3: Learn the various placement options and how they relate to least restrictive environment (LRE), inclusion of students with disabilities, and implementing inclusive teaching practices.

Learning Outcome 2.4: Understand the roles of general and special educators in providing exceptional learners an individualized education program.

Learning Outcome 2.5: Learn about integration of people with disabilities into society, including self-determination, universal design, and use of technology.

Learning Outcome 2.6: Become aware of the impact of standards-based reform on special education.

MISCONCEPTIONS ABOUT Learners with Disabilities

MYTH There is now a universally accepted model of response to intervention (RTI), which research has shown to be effective.

FACT Much variability exists in how RTI is implemented. This variation has contributed to the fact that there is little research on the effectiveness of RTI.

MYTH The concept of least restrictive environment (LRE) demands that all students with disabilities be educated in the general education classroom.

FACT LRE means that students are to be educated in the least separate setting given the student's individual learning, behavioral, and physical needs.

MYTH Research has established beyond a doubt that special classes are ineffective and that inclusion is effective.

FACT Research comparing special versus general education placement is inconclusive because most of these studies have been methodologically flawed. Researchers are now focusing on finding ways to make inclusion work more effectively.

MYTH Co-teaching (special education and general education teachers working together in the general education classroom) has a strong research base.

FACT Co-teaching can be successful, but it's a complicated model, and much research still needs to be done to determine how best to make it generally effective.

MYTH All professionals agree that technology should be used to its fullest to aid people with disabilities.

FACT Some believe that technology should be used cautiously because it can lead people with disabilities to become too dependent on it. Some professionals believe that people with disabilities can be tempted to rely on technology instead of developing their own abilities.

MYTH All students with disabilities must now be included in standardized testing associated with the Common Core State Standards (CCSS), just like students without disabilities.

FACT Most students with disabilities will be included in standardized tests used in CCSS, but some students will require adaptations of the testing procedure to accommodate their specific disabilities. Students with disabilities, however, can no longer be automatically excluded from participating in standardized assessment procedures.

GUIDING QUESTIONS

- How are students with exceptionalities evaluated and identified for special education services in school settings?

- How is the intent of special education law implemented in individualized education for students with disabilities?

- What are the various placement options for exceptional learners?

- What are some ways that teachers implement inclusionary practices?

- What are the current practices in collaboration between general and special educators?

- What are the roles of general and special educators in providing exceptional learners an individualized education program?

- What are the trends and issues in universal design?

- What are the current strategies in the use of technologies?

- What impact do standards-based reform and the Common Core State Standards (CCSS) have on special education?

- What are our concluding thoughts about providing services to exceptional learners?

Special education has a rich history of controversy and change. Controversy and change make teaching and studying disabilities challenging and exciting. The history of special education, described briefly in Chapter 1, is replete with unexpected twists and turns. Many developments in the past have had unanticipated consequences, and many of today's events and conditions will have consequences that we don't foresee.

Dramatic changes have occurred during the first two decades of the 21st century, and more changes will undoubtedly follow. One critically important issue in special education today is the identification of students for special education services, particularly in the area of specific learning disabilities. The long-term debate over methods of identification has resulted in response to intervention (RTI), an approach to identifying students with learning disabilities, which has captured the attention of researchers and practitioners alike. The movement toward multicultural special education—the subject of Chapter 3—has also been in the forefront of the special education field. In this chapter we explore the major trends in providing services to exceptional learners as well as the significant issues in responding to the needs of individuals with disabilities.

EVALUATION AND IDENTIFICATION OF EXCEPTIONAL LEARNERS

Although the landscape of special education has changed dramatically since the passage of PL 94-142: The Education for All Handicapped Children Act, one issue has remained constant. In 1975, the intent of the original law was the same as the intent today: to ensure that all children with disabilities receive a free appropriate public education (FAPE) (Yell, Crockett, Shriner & Rozalski, 2017). To provide students with disabilities the appropriate educational services in the setting that maximizes their potential (the least restrictive environment), schools must employ effective practices in identifying exceptional learners. A longstanding debate continues on how to best identify students who are exceptional learners. Regardless of the specific method of identification, the federal law requires that specific steps be followed in the process.

FOCUS ON

IDEA Requirements for Special Education Identification

Child Find. This is a requirement for states to identify and evaluate all children who may have a disability. It is each state's obligation to have a reasonable plan to locate children in the state even if they do not attend public schools (e.g., private schools, homeless, home-schooled). Once identified using "child find" strategies, the child is referred for special education evaluation.

Referral. School personnel, most likely the general education teacher, or a parent may make the referral or request for evaluation. The parents must give consent (verbal or written) before a child is evaluated.

Evaluation. Within 60 days of parental consent, the district must provide a full evaluation of the child in the areas of concern. Under IDEA, consent for evaluation does not mean consent for placement. The results of the evaluation help to determine the student's eligibility for special education and related services.

Eligibility Determination. To determine whether a student is eligible for services, a multidisciplinary team meets to determine (a) if the student has a disability, and (b) if as a result of the disability he or she needs special education or related services. If parents disagree with the decision, they may seek an outside evaluation.

Prereferral Interventions and Multidisciplinary Teams

The determination of eligibility for special education services has lifelong implications for students with disabilities. Consider the consequences for a student who is not provided appropriate, thoughtful interventions before a full evaluation is conducted. For an example, visit http://www.youtube.com/watch?v=KrapFXnZIDE.

Prereferral interventions developed by a **multidisciplinary team** may help prevent an inaccurate placement in special education. The purpose of prereferral interventions is to ensure that students receive evidence-based instruction before they are evaluated for special education. Typically, when a teacher observes that a child is struggling in school, a multidisciplinary team (e.g., the student's parents or guardian, a special education teacher, the student's general education teacher, counselor, administrators, school psychologist) is convened to identify alternative, evidence-based educational strategies for the student before making a referral for special education evaluation. The team reviews the information about the student and develops a plan for prereferral interventions that are implemented before a formal evaluation is conducted. If the student continues to struggle, he is referred for a full evaluation to determine eligibility for special education.

Although some variation of a prereferral process has been followed in schools for many years, since the passage of IDEA 2004, many states have followed a more systematic method of prereferral called response to intervention (RTI), particularly for identifying students with learning disabilities. Distinctions of RTI from earlier prereferral processes include universal screening, evidence-based interventions, multiple tiers of intervention that are increasingly more intense, frequent progress monitoring, and fidelity of implementation (Mellard & Johnson, 2008; Zirkel, 2011).

Response to Intervention

In the most recent reauthorization of the Individuals with Disabilities Education Act (IDEA), Congress included an additional option for determining eligibility for special education in the case of suspected learning disabilities that forces varying levels of support in general education before referral to special education. The regulations state: "in determining whether a child has a specific learning disability, states may rely on a process that determines whether the child responds to scientific, research-based intervention as a part of the evaluation." In practice, this concept has been termed **response to intervention (RTI).**

WHAT IS RTI? Response to intervention refers to a student's change (or lack of change) in academic performance or behavior as a result of instruction (Duhon, Messmer, Atkins, Greguson, & Olinger, 2009; Fuchs, Mock, Morgan, & Young, 2003; O'Connor, Sanchez, & Kim, 2017). In an RTI identification model, a student must first receive quality instruction in the general education classroom before being given a formal evaluation for special education services. Teachers gather data to determine whether the student is benefiting from that instruction. Only after educators determine that a student is nonresponsive to quality, research-based instruction by a general educator would a formal evaluation to special education occur.

RTI is usually associated with learning disabilities and academic learning. However, it has implications for students with any disability and is not confined to academic learning, but can be applied to social behavior as well (Cheney, Flower, & Templeton, 2008; Fairbanks, Sugai, Guardino, & Lathrop, 2007; Kauffman, 2014). Practitioners have applied various RTI approaches for students with disabilities, including emotional and behavioral disorders, intellectual disabilities, autism, and giftedness.

MULTITIERED MODEL FOR IDENTIFICATION The RTI approach is based on a multitiered model of prevention. No model is universally accepted; however, RTI typically provides for three progressively more intensive tiers of instruction for students who are experiencing difficulties (Fuchs, Fuchs, & Compton, 2012; Mercer, Mercer, & Pullen, 2011). Generally, Tier 1 includes universal screening to identify students who may be at risk of academic failure; implementation of quality, research-based instruction; and weekly monitoring of student progress (Fuchs, Fuchs, & Stecker, 2010; Silberglitt, Parker, & Muyskens, 2016). The teacher monitors the student's progress in the curriculum and in relation to peers and provides differentiated instruction. If the student's achievement improves, no other action is taken. If the student's performance doesn't improve, the student moves to Tier 2. In Tier 2, the student usually receives small-group instruction by a teacher or highly trained assistant three to four times per week with a research-validated program in the areas of difficulty (e.g., reading or writing). Tier 2 interventions should take place for approximately 6 to 8 weeks. If the student's performance doesn't improve at this level, a multidisciplinary team is convened to determine whether a student has a disability and therefore qualifies for Tier 3, which is special education. Tier 3 includes more intensive intervention provided by a special educator in an appropriate placement to be determined by the student's individualized education program (discussed later in this chapter). Figure 2.1 illustrates how instruction and possible placement in special education is facilitated in an RTI framework.

ASSESSMENT PRACTICES IN AN RTI MODEL The basic purposes of assessment in an RTI model are to identify students who may be at increased risk of school failure and to collect data to determine the effectiveness of instruction so that appropriate instructional decisions can be made (Mercer et al., 2011). The two most common forms of assessment in an RTI process are screening and progress monitoring.

Teachers or school psychologists use **screening instruments** to identify those students who may be at increased risk of school failure. Screening instruments are typically administered to an entire group of students and may be given to a large number of students in a short period of time. School personnel use results of the screening administrations to identify students for whom additional progress monitoring and Tier 2 instruction are required.

Progress monitoring assessments are frequent, quick-and-easy measures that teachers administer at regular intervals and that provide information on whether a student is learning as expected. The purpose of administering progress-monitoring instruments is to determine whether current instructional practices are appropriate for individual students and to identify instructional needs. One common form of progress monitoring is **curriculum-based measurement (CBM)**. CBM involves students' responses to their usual instructional materials; it entails direct and frequent samples of performance from the students' curriculum. CBM measures are commonly used as a way to determine students'

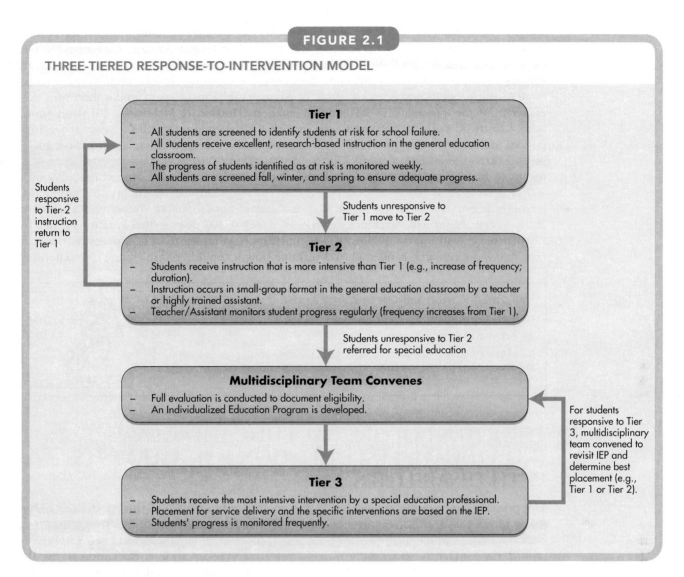

FIGURE 2.1

THREE-TIERED RESPONSE-TO-INTERVENTION MODEL

Tier 1
- All students are screened to identify students at risk for school failure.
- All students receive excellent, research-based instruction in the general education classroom.
- The progress of students identified as at risk is monitored weekly.
- All students are screened fall, winter, and spring to ensure adequate progress.

Students responsive to Tier-2 instruction return to Tier 1

Students unresponsive to Tier 1 move to Tier 2

Tier 2
- Students receive instruction that is more intensive than Tier 1 (e.g., increase of frequency; duration).
- Instruction occurs in small-group format in the general education classroom by a teacher or highly trained assistant.
- Teacher/Assistant monitors student progress regularly (frequency increases from Tier 1).

Students unresponsive to Tier 2 referred for special education

Multidisciplinary Team Convenes
- Full evaluation is conducted to document eligibility.
- An Individualized Education Program is developed.

For students responsive to Tier 3, multidisciplinary team convened to revisit IEP and determine best placement (e.g., Tier 1 or Tier 2).

Tier 3
- Students receive the most intensive intervention by a special education professional.
- Placement for service delivery and the specific interventions are based on the IEP.
- Students' progress is monitored frequently.

responsiveness to RTI; however, the ways in which teachers use these data differ (Burns, Silberglitt, Christ, Gibbons, & Coolong-Chaffin, 2016; Fuchs et al., 2007). We discuss CBM in more detail throughout the text as it relates to the assessment and instruction of students with various exceptionalities.

SUPPORT FOR RTI IDENTIFICATION MODELS Advocates of an RTI identification model claim that it will reduce the number of students referred to special education. The argument is that as a result of high-quality instruction provided at every level, RTI helps to determine whether a student truly has a disability or has just been subjected to poor or missing instruction (see Boardman & Vaughn, 2007). Another benefit of RTI is the implementation of **early intervening services**. In the 2004 IDEA reauthorization, along with the addition of RTI, the law provides for states to use up to 15% of special education funding for early intervening services. These funds may be used "to develop and implement coordinated, early intervening services, which may include interagency financing structures, for students in kindergarten through grade 12 (with a particular emphasis on students in kindergarten through grade three) who are not currently identified as needing special education or related services, but who need additional academic and behavioral support to succeed in a general education environment" (34 CFR 300.226(a)) (20 U.S.C. 1413(f)(1)).

HOW EFFECTIVE ARE RTI IDENTIFICATION MODELS? Unfortunately, little research evidence is available to determine whether RTI is effective. Only a few school districts in the country have used it on a wide scale and few large-scale systematic studies have been conducted (see Hughes & Dexter, 2011). Furthermore, the variability in RTI models makes it difficult to study its efficacy. A recent study of 31 state directors of special education provides evidence of the variability in RTI implementation (Hudson & McKenzie, 2016). In some school districts, students are remaining in Tier-2 interventions beyond a reasonable time period and are not being provided full evaluations in a timely manner. Nevertheless, IDEA gives schools the option of using RTI for identification of learning disabilities, as well as a means of improving instruction for all students. Recently, some have argued that although RTI is defensible as a way of improving early intervention and instruction for struggling learners, its use as a means of identifying disabilities is questionable (Boardman & Vaughn, 2007; Kavale, Kauffman, Bachmeier, & LeFever, 2008). We discuss these issues further in Chapter 6, on learning disabilities. RTI is much more complex than it appears on the surface, and more research is needed to determine how it should be implemented in schools.

MyLab Education Self-Check 2.1

MyLab Education Application Exercise 2.1:
Referral and Assessment

Refer to the section "Evaluation and Identification of Exceptional Learners" in your text and the "Perspectives and Resources" section in the IRIS Center Star Learning Module to respond to a few questions.

THE
IRIS
CENTER™

THE INTENT OF SPECIAL EDUCATION LAW: INDIVIDUALIZED EDUCATION FOR STUDENTS WITH DISABILITIES

The primary intent of the special education law passed in 1975 and the subsequent reauthorizations has been to require educators to focus on the needs of individual students with disabilities to ensure that they receive appropriate educational services. A multidisciplinary team that includes school or agency personnel as well as the parents and the individual, when appropriate, determines the services that an individual receives. The individualized education program (IEP) is the primary aspect of this focus; it spells out how a school plans to meet an exceptional student's needs. In addition to the IEP, the individualized family service plan (IFSP) for young children and the transition plan for adolescents are important aspects of providing appropriate individualized services to children and youth with disabilities. Reauthorizations of PL 94–142 have maintained the concepts of FAPE, LRE, and IEP, but have also moved toward students with disabilities having more opportunity to learn with their nondisabled peers.

Individualized Education Programs

The **individualized education program (IEP)** is the legal document that describes the educational services a student receives. IEPs vary greatly in format and detail from one child to another and from one school district to another. Table 2.1 provides a summary of the legal requirements of the IEP. Today, most schools, states, and districts have an online IEP management system. In addition, states typically have sample IEP documents that cover the federal and state guidelines. Check your state's department of education website for resources specific to your state.

Federal and state regulations don't specify exactly how much detail must be included in an IEP, only that it must be a written statement developed in a meeting of a representative of the local school district, the teacher, the parents or guardian, and (whenever appropriate) the child, and that it must include certain elements. The IEP that is written in most schools contains much information related to the technical requirements of IDEA in addition to the heart of the plan: its instructional components.

MyLab Education
Video Example 2.1
This video shows two teachers discussing the advantages of IDEA's focus on access to general education settings and curriculum.

TABLE 2.1 • **Legal requirements of the Individualized Education Program (IEP)**

According to the Individuals with Disabilities Education Act (IDEA) 2004, the required contents of an IEP include the following:

1. A statement of the child's present levels of academic achievement and functional performance. On many IEP forms, this is called the PLOP (present level of performance). In some cases the PLOP is now listed as the PLAAFP (present level of academic achievement and functional performance).
2. A statement of measurable annual goals, including academic and functional goals. The law states clearly that the goals should enable the child to access the general education curriculum.
3. A description of how the child's progress toward meeting the annual goals will be measured and when periodic reports on the progress the child is making toward meeting the annual goals will be provided.
4. A statement of the special education and related services and supplementary aids and services the child will receive. The services must be based on peer-reviewed research.
5. A statement of any individual appropriate accommodations that are necessary to measure the academic achievement and functional performance of the child on standardized achievement assessments. If the child is to take an alternate assessment instead of a particular regular state or districtwide assessment, a statement of why the child cannot participate in the regular assessment and why the particular alternate assessment selected is appropriate for the child.

The IEP also requires the following related-to-transition services for students at age 16:

1. Appropriate measurable postsecondary goals based on age-appropriate transition assessments related to training, education, employment, and independent living skills (if appropriate).
2. The transition services (including courses of study) needed to assist the child in reaching those goals.

The law also stipulates the make-up of the IEP team. The following individuals must be a part of the IEP team:

1. The parents of a child with a disability.
2. A minimum of one regular education teacher.
3. A minimum of one special education teacher or special education provider of the child.
4. A representative of the local educational agency. This individual should be qualified to provide, or supervise the provision of, specially designed instruction to meet the unique needs of children with disabilities, knowledgeable about the general education curriculum, and knowledgeable about the availability of resources.
5. An individual who can interpret the instructional implications of evaluation results.
6. Other individuals who have knowledge or special expertise regarding the child, including related services personnel as appropriate. The parents or the local education agency (LEA, i.e., school) may appoint these individuals as they see appropriate.
7. The child with a disability, whenever appropriate.

Source: Individuals with Disabilities Education Act, U.S. Department of Education.

Although the federal and state regulations do not specify how much detail should be included in the IEP, a recent court case, *Endrew F. v. Douglas County School District*, was heard before the U.S. Supreme Court (introduced in Chapter 1) that sheds light on the expectations of the IEP. The school district argued that a student need only make minimal progress toward IEP goals; however, in a rare but unanimous decision, the U.S. Supreme Court ruled in favor of Endrew F. and his family, stating that special education should offer more than minimum progress. Although it is unclear at this time how the court case will affect regulations and implementation of IDEA, this ruling is a "win" for students with disabilities.

When writing an IEP, the team should develop a document that is clear, useful, and legally defensible. The relationships among IEP components must be clear and explicit in order to maintain the focus of the individualized program—special, individually tailored instruction to meet unique needs. The process of writing an IEP and the document itself are perhaps the most important features of compliance with the spirit and letter of IDEA. Bateman and Linden (2006) summarize this compliance; when the IEP is prepared as intended by the law:

- The student's needs have been carefully assessed.
- A team of professionals and the parents have worked together to design a program of education to best meet the student's needs.
- Goals and objectives are stated clearly so that progress in reaching them can be evaluated.

Although compliance with the law is critical, what is of more importance is that the decisions that are made regarding the child's IEP determine his ultimate outcomes.

Video Example from

You Tube

MyLab Education
Video Example 2.2

IEP decisions determine ultimate outcomes. Consider this mom's perspective in the slideshow she prepared for her son's IEP meeting.
http://www.youtube.com/watch?v=8G-R5arIR7w

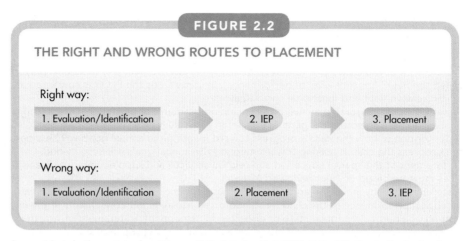

Source: Adapted with permission from Bateman, B. D., & Linden, M. A. (2006). *Better IEPs: How to develop legally correct and educationally useful programs* (4th ed.). Verona, WI: Attainment.

A major problem is that the IEP is often written at the wrong time and for the wrong reason (Bateman & Linden, 2006). As Figure 2.2 illustrates, the legal IEP is written after evaluation and identification of the student's disabilities and before a placement decision is made: Educators first determine what the student needs and then make a decision about placement in the least restrictive environment in which the needed services can be provided. Too often, we see the educationally wrong (and illegal) practice of basing the IEP on an available placement; that is, a student's IEP is written after available placements and services have been considered.

Another common error in writing the IEP is a reliance on state standards. A "standards-based" IEP is one that focuses on outcomes based on state standards rather than on individual student needs (Bateman, 2017). Clearly, state standards and access to the general education curriculum are important; however, a student's *individualized* education program should be based on outcomes appropriate for the child and not on dictated state standards. Drawing once again from the decision in the *Endrew F.* court case, Justice John G. Roberts wrote the following regarding access to general education curriculum and the IEP:

> A child's IEP need not aim for grade-level advancement if that is not a reasonable prospect. But that child's educational program must be appropriately ambitious in light of his circumstances, just as advancement from grade to grade is appropriately ambitious for most children in the regular classroom. The goals may differ, but every child should have the chance to meet challenging objectives (p. 3).

Individualized Family Service Plan

Federal laws now require that a variety of early intervention services be available to all infants and toddlers who are identified as having disabilities. Such services include special education instruction, physical therapy, speech and language therapy, and medical diagnostic services. As with school-age children with disabilities, a legal document, the **individualized family service plan (IFSP)**, describes the services that the child will receive. An IFSP is similar to an IEP for older children, but it broadens the focus to include the family as well as the child. In fact, federal regulations stipulate that the family must be involved in the development of the IFSP. Table 2.2 describes the legal requirements of an IFSP. As Noonan and McCormick (2006) note, an IFSP may be written for children up to 6 years of age, but usually an IFSP is written for infants and children up to 3 years of age, with the IEP being more common for children age 3 years and older.

Transition Plans for Adolescents with Disabilities

Most students complete high school and find jobs, enter a vocational training program, or go to college without experiencing major adjustment difficulties. We know that dropout and unemployment rates are far too high for all youths, especially in economically

TABLE 2.2 • Individuals with Disabilities Education Act (IDEA) requirements for the Individualized Family Service Plan (IFSP)

An IFSP must include:

1. A statement of the child's present level of development in these areas: physical (including vision, hearing, and health status), cognitive, communication, psychosocial, and adaptive behavior.
2. A statement of family strengths, resources, concerns, and priorities related to the child's development.
3. A statement of the major outcomes expected to be achieved for the child and family.
4. A statement of the frequency, intensity, and method of delivering the early intervention services necessary to produce desired outcomes for the child and family.
5. A statement of the natural environments where services will be provided or a statement explaining why services will not be provided in natural environments.
6. Projected dates for the initiation of services and anticipated duration of services.
7. The name of a service coordinator responsible for implementation of the IFSP and coordination with other agencies/professionals.
8. Steps to be implemented to ensure successful transition (a transition plan) to preschool services provided by the public schools.
9. Written consent from the parents or legal guardian.

depressed communities, but the outlook for students with disabilities is perhaps even worse. We must view published figures on dropout rates with caution because there are many different ways of defining the term and computing the statistics. Studies strongly suggest, however, that a higher percentage of students with disabilities, compared to students without disabilities, have difficulty in making the transition from adolescence to adulthood and from school to work. As a result, many individuals with disabilities do not achieve postsecondary degrees, are unemployed or underemployed, and have lower quality of life outcomes (Avellone & Taylor, 2017; Inge, 2017; Scanlon, 2017). Thus, transition to adulthood—which includes employment, postsecondary education, independent living, and community engagement—is an ongoing issue of great importance.

Federal laws, including IDEA, require attention to **transition plans** for older students, and these must be incorporated in students' IEPs. Transition services include a coordinated set of outcome-oriented activities that promote movement from school to postsecondary education, vocational training, integrated employment (including **supported employment**), continuing adult education, adult services, independent living, or community participation.

IDEA requires that each student's IEP contain a statement of needed transition services, when the student is 16 years of age and annually thereafter. (For students for whom it is appropriate or who are deemed at risk of failure, the transition statement must be included in the IEP at a younger age.) In addition, the IEP must include a statement of the linkages and/or responsibilities of each participating agency before the student leaves the school setting.

MyLab Education Self-Check 2.2

MyLab Education Application Exercise 2.2: IEP Components

For this exercise, you will use your text to review IEP components and compare those to an actual IEP that has been developed for a student.

PROVIDING SPECIAL EDUCATION: PLACEMENT ISSUES FOR EXCEPTIONAL LEARNERS

Several administrative plans are available for the education of exceptional learners, ranging from a few special provisions made by the student's general education teacher to 24-hour residential care in a special facility. Administrative plans for education vary according to the degree of physical integration—the extent to which exceptional and nondisabled students are taught in the same place by the same teachers.

Beginning with the least specialized environment, the general education teacher who is aware of the individual needs of students and is skilled at meeting them may be able to acquire appropriate materials, equipment, and/or instructional methods. This level might not require the direct services of specialists; the expertise of the general education teacher might meet the students' needs. Some students with disabilities can be accommodated without special education.

Alternatively, the general education teacher might need to *consult* with a special educator or other professional (e.g., the school psychologist) in addition to acquiring the special materials, equipment, or methods. The special educator might train or coach the general education teacher, refer the teacher to other resources, or demonstrate the use of materials, equipment, or methods. Alternatively, the general and special educators might *co-teach*, with each providing instruction and the special educator emphasizing instruction of the exceptional student(s).

A *resource teacher* provides services for students and teachers in a single school. The students served are enrolled in the general education classroom and work with the specially trained teacher for a length of time and at a frequency determined by the nature and severity of their particular problems. The resource teacher continually assesses the needs of the students and their teachers and usually works with students individually or in small groups in a special *resource room*, where special materials and equipment are available. Typically, the resource teacher also serves as a consultant to the classroom teacher, advising on how to instruct and manage the student in the classroom and perhaps demonstrating instructional techniques. The flexibility of the plan and the fact that the student remains with nondisabled peers most of the time have traditionally made this a particularly attractive and popular alternative.

One of the most visible—and, in recent years, controversial—service alternatives is the special *self-contained class*. Such a class typically enrolls 15 or fewer exceptional students with particular characteristics or needs. The teacher ordinarily has been trained as a special educator and provides all or most of the instruction, assisted by a paraeducator. The students assigned to such classes usually spend most or all of the school day separated from their nondisabled peers. Often, students with disabilities are included with nondisabled students during part of the day (perhaps for physical education, music, or some other activity in which they can participate well).

Special *day schools* provide an all-day special placement for exceptional learners who need this level of specialization or dedication to their needs. The day school usually is organized for a specific category of exceptional students and may contain special equipment necessary for their care and education. These students return to their homes during nonschool hours.

Hospital or *homebound instruction* is most often required by students who have physical disabilities, although it's sometimes an option for those with emotional or behavioral disorders or other disabilities when no alternative is readily available. Typically, the youngster is confined to the hospital or the home for a relatively short time, and the hospital or homebound teacher maintains contact with the general classroom teacher.

In a *residential school*, exceptional students receive 24-hour care away from home, often at a distance from their communities. This is the highest level of specialization or dedication on the continuum of alternative placements required by IDEA. These students might make periodic visits home or return each weekend, but during the week, they are residents of the institution, where they receive academic instruction in addition to management of their daily living environment.

Figure 2.3 illustrates the idea of variation in the separation of children from their general education classrooms and peers. It also illustrates the increasing specialization of environments. The degree to which education is "special" is a continuum. That is, education can be "sort of" special or very, very specialized.

FOCUS ON

Reality vs. What Might be Best for the Student

In practice, who educates exceptional students and where they receive their education depend on two factors: (1) in what ways and how much the student differs from typical students, and (2) what resources are available in the school and community. As we noted above, in the process of trying to find effective and economical ways of serving exceptional students, many school systems combine or modify these alternatives and the roles special educators and other professionals play in service delivery. School systems vary widely in the kinds of placements made for particular kinds of students.

It's important to point out that the second factor above (placement based on resources available) is based on reality, not law. In fact, according to federal law (IDEA), placement should be based on the needs of the student and not on what the schools can deliver. Although it's not a common occurrence, parents sometimes insist on a placement the school doesn't offer

(e.g., a separate class) or a private school specializing, for example, in learning disabilities, behavior disorders, or autism. If the school district doesn't agree, which is almost always the case, the parents can go to court; and if they win their case, the school must provide the appropriate placement and cover the costs.

Here are a couple of pertinent examples of placements for which parents sometimes sue:

- Some students have reading disabilities so severe that they need extensive and intensive instruction every day. Some schools don't provide that level of extensive and intensive instruction.
- Some students have such severe behavioral disabilities and/ or autistic behaviors (e.g., aggression, extreme withdrawal), that they need a greater degree of supervision than school districts can or want to provide.

Least Restrictive Environment

As we noted in Chapter 1, special education law requires placement of the student in the **least restrictive environment (LRE)**, which usually means that the student should be separated from nondisabled classmates and from home, family, and community as little as possible (see Yell, Crockett, Shriner, & Rozalski, 2017). That is, the student's life should be as normal as possible, and the intervention should be consistent with individual needs and not interfere with individual freedom any more than is absolutely necessary. For example, students should not be placed in special classes if they can be served adequately by resource teachers, and they should not be placed in a residential school if a special class will serve their needs just as well.

MyLab Education
Video Example 2.3
This video captures how one school defines and implements the least restrictive environment (LRE) at an IEP meeting.

FIGURE 2.3

CONTINUUM OF PLACEMENT OPTIONS SHOWING HYPOTHETICAL RELATIONSHIP BETWEEN DEGREE OF SEPARATENESS FROM GENERAL EDUCATION CLASSROOM PEERS AND DEGREE OF SPECIALNESS OF EDUCATION

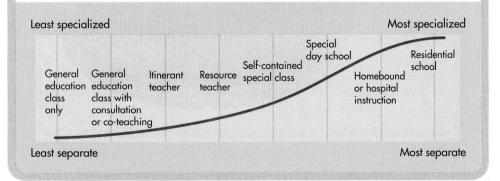

MyLab Education
Video Example 2.4
Authors Jim Kauffman and Paige Pullen discuss some of the misconceptions that surround the Least Restrictive Environment.

Although placement of exceptional students in the LRE is laudable, the definition of *least restrictive* is not as simple as it seems. Years ago, Cruickshank (1977), a pioneer in special education, pointed out that greater restriction of the physical environment does not necessarily mean greater restriction of psychological freedom or human potential (see also Bateman, 2007; Crockett & Kauffman, 1999, 2001). In fact, it is conceivable that some students could be more restricted in the long run in a general education class where they are rejected by others and fail to learn necessary skills than in a special class or day school where they learn happily and well (Gliona, Gonzales, & Jacobson, 2005; Kauffman, Bantz, & McCullough, 2002; Warnock, 2005).

It is important to keep our ultimate goals for the students in mind and to avoid letting the term *least restrictive* become a hollow slogan that results in shortchanging them in their education (Crockett & Kauffman, 1999, 2001; Huefner, 2006; Kauffman, 1995; Kauffman, McGee, & Brigham, 2004). Mercer and colleagues suggest that the *least restrictive environment* may be better termed the *most enabling environment* (Mercer et al., 2011). In the accompanying video, Drs. Kauffman and Pullen discuss what LRE really means.

Since the late 1980s, data have shown a steady trend toward placing more students with disabilities in general education classes and a corresponding trend toward placing fewer students with disabilities in resource rooms, separate classes, and separate facilities (U.S. Department of Education, 1995, 2005, 2009). Considerable variation exists in the placement of students with disabilities from state to state and among school systems within a given state. However, most exceptional students are now educated in general education classes. Nationwide, about 63% of exceptional children and youths are now served primarily in general education classes. Relatively few students with disabilities are placed outside of regular schools. Figure 2.4 shows the approximate percentage of students served in each type of placement as of 2014 (the most current data available as this text goes to press—release of federal data is always two or three years delayed) (U.S. Department of Education (2016).

Because children younger than 6 are usually only identified if they have relatively obvious or severe disabilities, they are less likely to receive education in general education classes and more often attend separate schools than do school-age children. Older

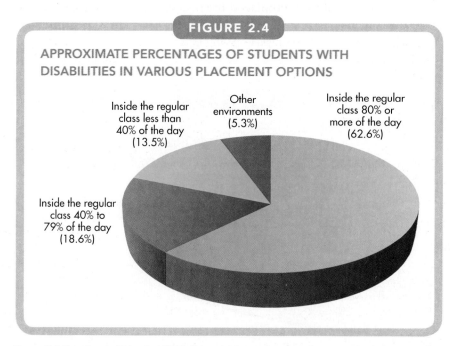

FIGURE 2.4

APPROXIMATE PERCENTAGES OF STUDENTS WITH DISABILITIES IN VARIOUS PLACEMENT OPTIONS

Inside the regular class less than 40% of the day (13.5%)

Other environments (5.3%)

Inside the regular class 80% or more of the day (62.6%)

Inside the regular class 40% to 79% of the day (18.6%)

Source: U.S. Department of Education. (2016). *Thirty-eighth annual report to Congress on implementation of the Individuals with Disabilities Education Act.* Washington, DC: Author.

teenagers and young adults more often attend special classes, separate schools, and other environments such as homebound instruction than do students in elementary and high schools because work-related educational programs for older teens with disabilities are frequently offered outside of the campuses of general education high schools.

Inclusion in Schools

Educators often use the term *inclusion* to describe teaching students with disabilities in the same environment as their age peers who don't have disabilities. Inclusion is now an issue in education worldwide (e.g., Anastasiou & Keller, 2017; Simpson & Kauffman, 2007; Warnock, 2005). Regardless of one's views, the controversy about the relationship between special and general education has made teachers more aware of the problems of deciding just which students should be taught specific curricula, which students should receive special attention or services, and where and by whom these services should be provided (Crockett & Kauffman, 1999, 2001; Kauffman & Hallahan, 1997, 2005b; Kauffman, Mock, Tankersley, & Landrum, 2008; Mock & Kauffman, 2005; Zigmond & Kloo, 2017).

Implementing Inclusive Teaching Practices

Whether or not one supports the concept of full inclusion, the fact is that most educators favor some degree of integration of students with disabilities with nondisabled students. Schools generally use four methods to help students with disabilities participate in the general education classroom:

1. Collaborative consultation
2. Co-teaching and other team arrangements
3. Curricula and instructional strategies
4. Accommodations and adaptations

The current trend is toward a variety of collaborative arrangements. All are intended to increase the cooperation between general and special education for the benefit of students with disabilities.

COLLABORATIVE CONSULTATION Once the IEP team has determined that a student in fact has a disability, the student may receive special education services within the general education classroom through **collaborative consultation**. In collaborative consultation, the special education teacher or psychologist acts as an expert who provides advice to the general education teacher. The special educator might suggest changes to instruction or additional supports, such as behavior plans or school–home notes.

CO-TEACHING Sometimes referred to as **cooperative** (or *collaborative*) **teaching**, co-teaching takes mutuality and reciprocity in collaborative consultation one step further (see Cook, McDuffie-Landrum, Oshita, & Cook, 2017; Scruggs, Mastropieri, & McDuffie, 2007; Walsh & Jones, 2004). **Co-teaching** between general and special educators means "two or more professionals delivering substantive instruction to a diverse, or blended, group of students in a single physical space" (Cook & Friend, 1998, p. 454).

Schools use many forms of co-teaching, but the most common appears to be for one teacher to instruct and the other to assist in some way (Scruggs et al., 2007). Sometimes, teachers find it very effective and workable. Other times, co-teaching can present incredible challenges to teachers and to students.

Unfortunately, research on how to ensure that co-teaching works is scarce. Zigmond (2007) argues that the popular co-teaching model of collaboration can't provide the kind of intensive instruction that students with learning disabilities and behavior disorders (and, presumably, many students with other disabilities as well) require if they are to make adequate progress. Moreover, she argues that special education teachers need special expertise in teaching specialized and individualized curricula. General education teachers are content specialists and should be trained by the "special education coach" to

MyLab Education
Video Example 2.5
Effective collaboration among general educators, special educators, and other professionals is a key ingredient in the successful participation of students with disabilities in general education classrooms.

address a wider range of instructional needs than they otherwise would have, but they can't take the place of special education teachers (Zigmond & Kloo, 2017).

Although there are no pat answers to the questions about how special and general education should work together to ensure that every student receives an appropriate education, it's clear that the relationship must be one of cooperation and collaboration. Despite their differing roles, general and special educators should not function on independent or mutually exclusive educational tracks. In Chapters 5 through 15, a special feature called "How Can I Help Students with … in the General Education Classroom" addresses specific issues of inclusion for each disability area.

CURRICULA AND INSTRUCTIONAL STRATEGIES In addition to teacher cooperation, specific curricula and instructional strategies can help students with disabilities succeed in the general education classroom. Cooperative learning is an instructional strategy that many proponents of inclusion believe is an effective way to integrate students with disabilities into groups of nondisabled peers. In cooperative learning, students work together in heterogeneous small groups to solve problems or practice responses.

Another research-based instructional strategy to enhance the integration of students with disabilities is peer-mediated instruction (Fuchs et al., 2001; Gardner et al., 2001; Maheady, Harper, & Mallette, 2001; see also Fulk & King, 2001, and the websites they list). Peer-mediated instruction may refer to peer tutoring, the use of peer confederates in managing behavior problems, or any other arrangement in which teachers deliberately recruit and train peers to help teach an academic or social skill to a classmate (Falk & Wehby, 2001).

When the whole class is involved, the strategy is referred to as classwide peer tutoring (CWPT); all students in the general education classroom routinely engage in peer tutoring for particular subject matter, such as reading or math (Greenwood, Arrega-Mayer, Utley, Gavin, & Terry, 2001; Kourea, Cartledge, & Musti-Rao, 2007). CWPT doesn't mean that the teacher provides no instruction. On the contrary, teachers must provide instruction in how to do peer tutoring and in the content of the tutoring sessions. Peers tutor each other to provide drill and practice of skills they already have.

Partial participation, another instructional strategy, entails having students with disabilities participate, on a reduced basis, in virtually all activities experienced by all students in the general education classroom. It questions the assumption that including students with severe intellectual or physical limitations is a waste of time because they cannot benefit from the activities in the same way as nondisabled students. Whether partial participation actually achieves these goals to the benefit of students is an open question.

INSTRUCTIONAL ACCOMMODATIONS AND ADAPTATIONS Instruction may be modified for learners with disabilities. Modifications usually take the form of amended materials or assignments and differ from changes in curricula or instructional strategies. Accommodations include changes in instruction that don't significantly change the content or conceptual difficulty level of the curriculum. Alternatively, adaptations generally involve more significant modifications of instruction than accommodations (Miller, 2002).

Tiered assignments (Tomlinson, 2001) are an example of adaptations, wherein teachers provide choices of varying difficulty for assignments on a single topic. For example, when studying a novel, some students might write paragraphs that identify and describe the characters; others might write paragraphs or papers that analyze the traits of each character, using examples.

MyLab Education
Video Example 2.6
Watch as Dr. Tom Smith explains what is meant by providing accommodations for students. This video also captures school personnel as they struggle to determine the proper role of extended time as an accommodation for special education students in the general education classroom.

MyLab Education
Video Example 2.7
In this video, Dr. Delores Gaunty-Porter discusses the role of teachers in determining methods for assessing students with disabilities, providing appropriate modifications and/or accommodations.

MyLab Education Self-Check 2.3
MyLab Education Application Exercise 2.3: The Continuum of Placement Options
Explain what you think the likely placement for Marty and Mwajabu would be.

TEACHERS' ROLES IN PROVIDING SPECIAL EDUCATION

We have noted that most students in public schools who have been identified as exceptional are placed in general education classrooms for at least part of the school day. Furthermore, there is good reason to believe that a large number of public school students who have not been identified as having disabilities or giftedness share many of the characteristics of those who are exceptional. Thus, while all teachers must be prepared to deal with exceptional students, it's unreasonable to expect all teachers to teach all exceptional students (Imray & Colley, 2017; Kauffman & Hallahan, 2005a; Mock & Kauffman, 2002; Zigmond, 2007; Zigmond & Kloo, 2017).

The roles of general and special education teachers are not always clear in a given case. Sometimes, uncertainty about the division of responsibility can be extremely stressful; teachers may feel uneasy because it's not clear whose job it is to make special adaptations for a pupil or just what they are expected to do in cooperating with other teachers.

Relationship Between General and Special Education

During the 1980s, radical reformers began recommending that special education be eliminated as a separate, identifiable part of education—calling for a single, unified educational system in which all students are viewed as unique, special, and entitled to the same quality of education. Although many of the suggested reforms have great appeal and some could produce benefits for exceptional students, the basis for integration of special and general education and the ultimate consequences this might bring have been questioned (e.g., Bateman, 2007; Crockett & Kauffman, 1999, 2001; Fuchs & Fuchs, 1994; Hockenbury, Kauffman, & Hallahan, 1999–2000; Imray & Colley, 2017; Kauffman, 1995, 1999–2000; Kauffman & Hallahan, 2005b; Martin, 1995; Mock & Kauffman, 2002, 2005; Warnock, 2005; Zigmond, 2007; Zigmond & Kloo, 2017).

MyLab Education
Video Example 2.8
Drs. Pullen and Kauffman discuss the challenges of meeting the needs of all children in the general education classroom.

These questions have no ready answers. Regardless of where one draws the line separating students who are considered to be at risk from students with disabilities, the line is arbitrary and leads to doubts about some students. In other words, no entirely clear distinction exists between *at risk* and *disability* because educational achievement and social competence can vary from a little to a lot, and no sudden, dramatic break exists in students' level of attainment (Boardman & Vaughn, 2007; Kauffman & Hallahan, 2005a; Kauffman & Konold, 2007).

Expectations for All Educators

One limitation of all teachers is that they can't accomplish the miracles portrayed in the popular media, even if they are very good at what they do (Moore, 2007). Real teachers can't be as perky, self-sacrificing, idealistic, and influential as those shown in films, and most teachers can't achieve the same results as those who win awards for exceptional performance. Competent teachers can make a significant difference in the lives of the children with whom they work, but the expectations set up by media portrayals—and too often by government or the general public—are unrealistic. Teachers, like those employed in other lines of work, must do the best they can with the resources at their disposal. Striving for excellence is admirable, but recognizing one's real-world limitations, keeping one's duties and accomplishments in perspective, and being happy with the best one can do, even if it's less than perfection, is as important for teachers as it is for students.

Regardless of whether teachers are specifically trained in special education, they may be expected to participate in educating exceptional students in any one of the following ways:

1. *Make maximum effort to accommodate individual students' needs:* Teaching in public schools requires dealing with diverse students in every class. All teachers must participate in the RTI process, making an effort to meet the needs of individuals

who might differ in some way from the average or typical student. RTI requires the implementation of evidence-based instruction that increases in intensity as necessary. Flexibility, adaptation, accommodation, and special attention are expected of every teacher. Special education should be considered necessary only when a teacher's best efforts to meet a student's individual needs aren't successful.

2. *Evaluate academic abilities and disabilities:* Although a psychologist or other special school personnel might administer formal standardized tests in academic areas to a student, adequate evaluation requires the teacher's assessment of the student's performance in the classroom. Teachers must be able to report specifically and precisely how students can and cannot perform in all academic areas for which they are responsible as part of the RTI process.

3. *Refer for evaluation:* By law, all public school systems must make extensive efforts to screen and identify all children and youths of school age who have disabilities. A student shouldn't be referred for special education unless teachers have made extensive and unsuccessful efforts to accommodate the student's needs in general education classes. Before referral, school personnel must document the strategies that have been used to teach and manage the student in general education. Referral is justified only if these strategies have failed. This is typically facilitated through the RTI process.

4. *Participate in eligibility conferences:* Before a student is provided special education, an interdisciplinary team must determine the student's eligibility. Therefore, teachers must be ready to work with other teachers and with professionals from other disciplines (e.g., psychology, medicine, or social work) in determining a student's eligibility for special education.

5. *Participate in writing individualized education programs:* Every student identified with a disability and receiving special education must have a written IEP. Teachers must be ready to participate in a meeting (possibly including the student and/or parents as well as other professionals) to develop the program.

6. *Communicate with parents or guardians:* Educators must consult parents (sometimes surrogate parents) or guardians during the evaluation of the child's eligibility for special education, formulation of the IEP, and reassessment of any special program that may be designed. Teachers must contribute to the school's communication with parents about the child's problems, placement, and progress.

7. *Participate in due process hearings and negotiations:* Parents, guardians, or students with disabilities themselves who are dissatisfied with the school's response to educational needs may request a due process hearing or negotiations regarding appropriate services. Teachers might be called on to offer observations, opinions, or suggestions in such hearings or negotiations.

8. *Collaborate with other professionals in identifying and making maximum use of exceptional students' abilities:* General and special education teachers are expected to share responsibility for educating students with special needs. In addition, teachers might need to collaborate with other professionals, depending on the given student's exceptionality (e.g., psychologists, counselors, physicians, physical therapists).

A high level of professional competence and ethical judgment is required to conform to these expectations. Teaching demands a thorough knowledge of child development and expertise in instruction. Furthermore, teachers are sometimes faced with serious professional and ethical dilemmas in trying to serve the needs of students and their parents, on the one hand, and in attempting to conform to legal or administrative pressures, on the other (Crockett & Kauffman, 1999; Kauffman & Hallahan, 2009). For example, when a teacher observes indications that a student might have a disability, should the teacher refer the student for evaluation and possible placement in special education, knowing that her school offers only inadequate or inappropriate services? Should a teacher who believes strongly that teenage students with mild intellectual disabilities need sex education refrain from giving students any information because sex education isn't part of the prescribed curriculum and is frowned on by the school board?

Expectations for Special Educators

In addition to being competent enough to meet the expectations for all teachers, special education teachers must attain further expertise in the following areas of skill and knowledge:

1. *Instructing students with learning problems, using evidence-based practices.* The majority of students with disabilities have more difficulty learning academic skills than do those without disabilities. This is true for all categories of disabling conditions because sensory impairments, physical disabilities, and intellectual or emotional disabilities all tend to make academic learning more difficult. Often, the difficulty is slight; sometimes it is extreme. Special education teachers must have more than patience and hope, though they do need these qualities; they must also have the technical skill to present academic tasks so that students with disabilities will understand and respond appropriately. Exceptional instruction is the key to improving special education (Kauffman & Hallahan, 2005a; Kauffman & Landrum, 2007). Table 2.3 lists eight dimensions of instruction that make special education special, although these dimensions are not unique to special education. That is, they are not dimensions of instruction that *only* special educators know about or use. They are modifications or alterations of instructional processes that all teachers use in some way. What makes special education special is not the instruction alone but instruction that is altered to meet the needs of exceptional learners.

2. *Managing serious behavior problems:* Many students with disabilities have behavior problems in addition to their other exceptionalities. Some, in fact, require special education primarily because of their inappropriate or disruptive behavior. Special education teachers must be able to deal effectively with more than the usual troublesome behavior of students. Besides having understanding and empathy, special education teachers must master techniques to draw out particularly withdrawn students, control those who are hyperaggressive and persistently disruptive, and teach critical social skills. Positive, proactive behavior intervention plans are essential for all students who receive special education and exhibit serious behavior problems,

TABLE 2.3 • **Dimensions of special education that can make it truly special**

DIMENSION OF INSTRUCTION	DEFINITION	ALTERATION OF INSTRUCTION
1. Pace (Rate)	Speed of lesson; speed of introducing new concepts	Made slower or faster to meet student characteristics
2. Intensity	Demandingness; difficulty; complexity	Size of steps in learning, number of trials, frequency of reviews adjusted to fit learner
3. Relentlessness or Persistence	Insistence; tenacity; stick-to-it-iveness	Repeated attempts, using different methods as required
4. Structure	Explicitness, predictability, teacher direction, tolerance, immediacy of consequences	Adjusted (tightened or loosened) to fit individual student
5. Reinforcement	Reward for desired behavior	Increased, made more frequent, immediate, and explicit or tangible as necessary
6. Pupil/Teacher Ratio (Class Size)	Number of students per teacher	Smaller, more individual
7. Curriculum	Content of instruction, purpose of activity	Determined by individual need
8. Monitoring (Assessment)	Keeping track of progress	Daily or near daily checking (testing) of achievement of specific tasks and goals

regardless of their diagnostic label or classification (Kauffman, Pullen, Mostert, & Trent, 2011; Landrum & Kauffman, 2006).

3. *Evaluating technological advances:* Technology is increasingly applied to the problems of teaching exceptional students and improving their daily lives. Special education teachers must be able to evaluate the advantages and disadvantages of using technology for teaching the exceptional children and youths with whom they work.

4. *Knowing special education law:* For good or ill, special education today involves many details of law. The rights of students with disabilities are spelled out in considerable detail in federal and state legislation. These laws, as well as the rules and regulations that accompany them, are constantly being interpreted by new court decisions. Special education teachers don't need to be lawyers, but they do need to be aware of legal requirements and prohibitions if they are to be adequate advocates for students with disabilities (Bateman, 2007; Huefner, 2006; Yell, 2006).

The knowledge and skills that every special education teacher is expected to master have been detailed by the primary professional organization of special educators, the Council for Exceptional Children (1998). These are general expectations and areas of competence that are required of every special educator; however, special educators have a responsibility to offer not just good instruction but instruction that is highly individualized, intensive, relentless, urgent, and goal directed (Hallahan, 2007; Kauffman & Hallahan, 2005a; Kauffman, Hallahan, Pullen, & Badar, 2018; Kauffman & Landrum, 2007; Pullen & Hallahan, 2015; Zigmond, 2003, 2007). To this end, the special feature "Responsive Instruction: Meeting the Needs of Students," in Chapters 3 to 15, provides information about research-based practices to help make instruction intensive, relentless, and goal directed.

MyLab Education Self-Check 2.4

MyLab Education Application Exercise 2.4: Teachers' Roles in an RTI Framework

Watch a video vignette about Response to Intervention and the roles of the general educator and special educator in meeting the needs of students with disabilities. Then answer the questions that follow.

Universal Design and Universal Design for Learning

Based on the architectural principles of **universal design**, **universal design for learning (UDL)** serves the general purpose of making learning accessible to more students in inclusionary programs. The idea is that with modifications of *representation* (materials), *expression* (methods of communication), and *engagement* (how students respond to curriculum), teachers can include a much wider range of students in typical classroom instruction (CAST, 2011; Spooner, Baker, Harris, Ahlgrim-Delzell, & Browder, 2007).

MAKING THINGS USABLE BY MORE PEOPLE   Access to the Internet by people with disabilities has significant implications for design. Section 508 of the Rehabilitation Act requires that federal agencies ensure equal access by those with and without disabilities to new information technology as well as information and services. Furthermore, IDEA urges educators to consider the use of assistive technology in servicing students with disabilities, to allow a greater diversity of students to be accommodated in typical classrooms (Spooner et al., 2007).

Making things usable by more people goes beyond the Internet. For example, teachers can design materials that increase accessibility for more students by creating them in ways that can be adjusted by the user (e.g., making the print larger, providing captions on videos, or creating PDF files that are in accessible formats). Accessible formatted PDF files can be used with a Brailler for individuals who are blind. Another example of making materials accessible is using a teaching microscope that projects the image on a large display, rather than having students with low vision use a standard microscope. In applying universal design to materials access, a teacher should ask herself, "*How can I make this content accessible to all of my students?*"

MyLab Education
Video Example 2.9
A teaching microscope makes science lab work accessible to students with visual impairments.

DOES UNIVERSAL DESIGN ELIMINATE THE NEED FOR CUSTOM DESIGN? One continuing issue is when to assume that the limits of universal design have been reached and go ahead with production. Inventors and designers may do their best to be "smart from the start" (Pisha & Coyne, 2001), but it is not possible to be certain that no potential user's needs have been overlooked. At some point, someone decides to put a gadget or technology into production under the assumption that the design is as universal as it can be made at that time.

Modifications of instruction used in UDL can make lessons appropriate for a wider range of students than has typically been the case. Thus, teachers must not overlook the possibility that they could be designing lesson plans that are appropriate for a greater variety of students. However, IDEA mandates individualized instruction. One curriculum is not likely to meet the letter or the intent of the law in terms of specialized instruction for students with disabilities. Perhaps the term *universal*, like the term *all*, should not be taken too literally, or it becomes self-defeating. Very likely, the need to "customize" for individuals will always exist. Even in instruction, some special education researchers note that students with disabilities need individualized instruction that is not most appropriate for students without disabilities (e.g., Zigmond, 2007).

Technological advances of all types can have implications for people with disabilities. Devices such as the Livescribe™ Echo® Smartpen allows the user to take notes, synchronized with audio, which can then be transferred to a computer or iPad.® Another new technology is Sonocent note-taking software (see https://www.sonocent .com/en-us/audio-notetaker). In addition to capturing audio, Sonocent allows the student to annotate during the recording and highlight important topics. In addition, the software breaks the recording into phrases and displays them on the screen. This powerful tool can help students with disabilities engage more fully in classroom activities.

Use of New Technologies

As technology becomes ever more sophisticated, the issue of independence will become ever more important. One general guideline might be that if the technology allows people with disabilities to do something they couldn't do without it, then the technology is in their best interest. However, if it allows them to do something new or better but at the same time imposes new limitations, then one might need to rethink the technology's benefits.

Technological advances of all types can have implications for people with disabilities. Advances in three technologies stand out as particularly important: (1) medical treatment, (2) human reproduction, and (3) communication. Some of these advances, particularly those in medical treatment and human reproduction, are highly controversial. The controversy is typically about whether something that *can* be done *should* be done, and it may involve two or three of the technologies we discuss. For example, should **cochlear implantations**, artificial inner ears (discussed further in Chapter 11), be used whenever possible to allow deaf children to hear? This issue involves both medical treatment and communication, and it could involve human reproduction as well. Should disabilities be corrected surgically before birth (in utero), if that is possible? Should the findings of fetal stem cell research be applied to cure or correct physical disabilities if possible? What characteristics of their children should parents be allowed to choose? These are some of the controversial ethical issues that we discuss in later chapters.

THE UPSIDE AND THE DOWNSIDE OF TECHNOLOGY As the pace of technology quickens, so do applications of these technologies to the daily lives of people with disabilities. In many ways, technologies expand the abilities of people with or without disabilities to access information, communicate, travel, and accomplish many other everyday tasks. Technological applications can also allow some people with disabilities to function like those without disabilities.

Some downsides are dependence on technology and the problem of reliability. People tend to rely on whatever technology they use rather than learn how to do things in alternative ways; as a result, they have no idea how to do things the "old-fashioned" way when a gadget malfunctions.

SHOULD WE DO SOMETHING BECAUSE WE CAN? An issue that is likely to become more controversial is whether we *should* do all the things that we *can* with new technologies. The moral and ethical dilemmas created by the availability of means to eliminate limitations such as being unable to hear, see, walk, or communicate—whether they are considered disabilities or not—will increase in years to come. Particularly troubling will be the issue of whether we *should* allow parents to create "designer babies" to any extent that we *can*. For example, should we allow parents to create children with (there are instances of couples who are deaf, for example, wishing to have a child who is also deaf) or without what most people consider disabilities? The ability to select embryos (or create them) with or without certain characteristics (e.g., deafness, dwarfism, diabetes, tendency toward schizophrenia or depression), in addition to presenting ethical dilemmas, raises difficult issues about the definition and meaning of disability (Kauffman & Hallahan, 2009).

MyLab Education Self-Check 2.5

MyLab Education Application Exercise 2.5: Assistive Technology in Action: Meet Elle
Watch a video about assistive technology and answer the questions that follow.

SPECIAL EDUCATION IN THE CONTEXT OF THE COMMON CORE STATE STANDARDS INITIATIVE

Since the late 20th century, state and federal policymakers have been concerned about what they perceive as a general decline in students' educational achievement and, as a result, have emphasized "standards-based" reforms. These reforms involve setting standards of learning that are measured by standardized tests. The reformers believed that teachers' expectations have been too low and that all students should be held to higher standards (see Finn, Rotherham, & Hokanson, 2001; Hoover & Patton, 2004; Pugach & Warger, 2001; Thurlow, 2000; Thurlow, Nelson, Teelucksingh, & Draper, 2001). The curriculum for students with disabilities has sometimes differed from the curriculum in general education. Failure to teach students with disabilities the same things that are taught in general education has been interpreted to mean that the expectations for these students are lower, resulting in their low achievement and failure to make a successful transition to adult life.

In the early stages of this standards-based reform movement, states began to develop standards of their own and create benchmark tests usually dependent on grade levels. For example, a state might have a certain level of proficiency expected of fourth-grade students, or they might have a high-stakes test students must to pass in order to obtain a high school diploma.

A strong movement, the **Common Core State Standards Initiative (2012)**, called for all states to accept a common set of standards. The National Governors Association (NGA) and the Council of Chief State School Officers (CCSSO) led the development of the Common Core State Standards, and in 2010 published a document delineating the standards (National Governors Association Center for Best Practices, Council of Chief State School Officers, 2010).

The **Common Core State Standards (CCSS)** cover English language arts and math for K–12. That is, the standards cover the competencies that students are expected to have at each grade in these areas. At this point, all but a handful of states have signed on to the Common Core Standards Initiative. Also, over a dozen states have formed the **Smarter Balanced Assessment Consortium (SBAC)** (www.smarterbalanced.org), which has created online assessments for English and math for grades 3–8 and high school aligned to the Common Core State Standards.

With respect to students with disabilities, the Common Core State Standards Initiative has put forth a statement, "Application to Students with Disabilities." Essentially, the

Initiative promotes the idea that students with disabilities should be held accountable regarding the general education curriculum. However, it notes that these students might need to have instructional supports, engaging students by presenting material in multiple ways and allowing for multiple modes of expression and accommodations, such as changing materials and procedures that do not alter the content of the general education curriculum. The CCSS mentions that students with severe cognitive deficits will need substantial supports and accommodations in order to access certain standards.

Concerns about the CCSS have been raised by several practitioners, researchers, and policymakers in the special education community. Although the Initiative has involved special educators in the development of the standards and the assessments (Thurlow, 2012), some are fearful that the standards will not be in the best interests of many students with disabilities. The standards-based reform movement and the CCSS have brought with them a heavy emphasis on access to the general education curriculum for students with disabilities. However, some special educators have questioned whether too much emphasis on the general education curriculum is at the expense of students learning skills such as study skills, daily living skills, and intensive reading instruction (Hoover & Patton, 2004; Pierangelo & Giuliani, 2006; Quenemoen & Thurlow & 2017; Zigmond, 2007). Also, what should be given up in music, art, poetry, physical education, and other areas to ensure progress on standardized tests in core curriculum areas of reading and math?

For many special educators, "the devil is in the details." Numerous questions arise: Should all standards apply to all students, regardless of disability? Under what circumstances are alternative standards appropriate? Under what circumstances should special accommodations be made in assessing progress toward a standard? Answering questions like these requires professional judgment in the individual case, and such judgment is required by law (see Bateman, 2007, 2017; Huefner, 2006; Johns, 2003; Kauffman & Hallahan, 2005a; Yell, 2006). Moreover, expecting all students with disabilities to score the same, on average, as students without disabilities is expecting the impossible (Kauffman, 2004; Kauffman & Konold, 2007; Kauffman & Wiley, 2004).

Assessment Issues in the Age of Accountability

The intent of the IDEA is to improve the instruction and outcomes of students with disabilities. Consequently, students with disabilities, with some exceptions, are included in the assessments of educational progress demanded of all students. Although assessment has always been an important factor in special education, it has taken the spotlight in the era of standards-based reform. NCLB required that the average scores of various subgroups of students be reported and that all groups, including students with disabilities, show progress. The Every Student Succeeds Act (ESSA), signed into law by President Obama in 2015, which replaced NCLB, also requires that students with disabilities participate in these assessments. The assessments in which students with disabilities are expected to participate in order for these comparisons to be made are considered outcome measures.

OUTCOME MEASURES Outcome measures differ from the screening and progress monitoring measures described earlier in the context of RTI. Educators use screening and progress measures to identify students who may be at risk for disability and to provide ongoing data to assist in program planning; they typically administer these measures in group settings. Outcome measures compare a student's performance with that of other students, or compare a state's or district's performance with that of other states or districts.

TESTING ACCOMMODATIONS Some students with disabilities who are included in standardized measures of achievement are entitled to receive testing accommodations. Testing accommodations are procedures that ensure equitable assessment access for students with disabilities (Thurlow, 2010). Although testing accommodation may involve altering the administration procedure or format of a test, the construct that is being measured does not change (Lazarus, Thurlow, Lail, & Christensen, 2009).

Accommodations for evaluation procedures might involve altering the setting, the presentation format, or the response format. The nature of the accommodation is based on the specific need of the student. Setting or scheduling accommodations alter the situation or time of the assessment, such as small-group administration and extended time. Presentation accommodations alter the way the assessment is presented to the student, such as having problems and directions read aloud. Response accommodations alter the way in which the student answers questions on the assessment, such as oral or typed responses.

Can We Solve the Dilemma of Standards and Disability?

Some consider it cruel to both students and teachers to require all students with disabilities, and those for whom the tests are inappropriate for other reasons, to take state exams (Kauffman, 2002, 2004; Kauffman & Konold, 2007; Kauffman & Wiley, 2004). However, testing to determine outcomes is necessary if we want to know whether programs for students with disabilities are "working" (Kauffman & Konold, 2007). Standardized tests have a legitimate place in assessing outcomes, and demonizing the tests themselves is not helpful. However, it's important to understand that "testing is useful only if you make the right comparisons for the right reasons" (Kauffman, 2002, p. 240). When it comes to special education, it's wrong to compare outcomes for students with disabilities to outcomes for students without disabilities. The right comparisons are contrasting students with disabilities who receive special education (or any given treatment) to those who don't receive it, or comparing students with disabilities before and after they receive special education (Kauffman, 2004; Kauffman & Hallahan, 2005a).

MyLab Education Self-Check 2.6

MyLab Education Application Exercise 2.6: Testing Accommodations for Students with Disabilities

Each state has its own policies related to accommodations. Read an information brief from the National Center on Educational Outcomes, noting the policies for your state, then answer the accompanying questions.

CONCLUDING THOUGHTS REGARDING SPECIAL EDUCATION

It is understandable to feel overwhelmed by the controversial nature of special education; a number of unanswered questions face our field. It seems that just as we find what we think are the right answers to a certain set of questions about how to educate students with disabilities, more challenging questions emerge.

It would be easy to view this inability to reach definitive conclusions as indicative of a field in chaos. We disagree. This constant state of questioning is a sign of health and vigor, an indication that special education is based on scientific understanding, not on philosophy or mere speculation. Far from seeking and providing final answers, science thrives on the unknown and on controversy. True, there are rules for inquiry: Science is all about examining the most reliable information (see Kauffman & Sasso, 2006a, 2006b; Mostert, Kavale, & Kauffman, 2008; Sasso, 2001, 2007).

The controversial nature of special education makes it exciting and challenging. We would be worried (and we believe people with disabilities and their families would be worried, too) if professionals in special education were suddenly in complete agreement on all important issues in the field. We should constantly strive to find better ways to provide education and related services for people with disabilities based on the best evidence we can obtain (Lloyd & Hallahan, 2007). In this endeavor, differences of opinion are inevitable.

▼ chapter two SUMMARY

Jim West/Alamy Stock Photo

How are students with exceptionalities evaluated and identified for special education services in school settings?

- Prereferral teams have a long history in the special education identification process.

- *Response to intervention* refers to students' response to scientific, research-based instruction.

- Although response to intervention has been suggested as a means of identifying students with learning disabilities, some question its usefulness as an identification tool.

How is the intent of special education law implemented in individualized education for students with disabilities?

- The primary concern of the law (IDEA) is that every child with a disability be given a free appropriate public education (FAPE).

- The IEP is an attempt to make certain an individualized program has been written for each child with a disability and that:
  - The student's needs have been carefully assessed.
  - A team of professionals and the parents have worked together to design a program of education to best meet the student's needs.
  - Goals and objectives are stated clearly so that progress in reaching them can be evaluated.

- The IEPs of students with disabilities must, by law, incorporate transition plans at a minimum by age 16.

- Early intervention is mandated by law; a cornerstone of early intervention is the individualized family service plan (IFSP).

What are the various placement options for exceptional learners?

- Special education may range from a few special provisions made by the student's general education teacher to 24-hour residential care in a special facility.

- Different placement options include the following, including combinations:
  - General education placement with the teacher making accommodations
  - General education with consultation with a special education teacher or co-teaching
  - Itinerant services from a specialist
  - Resource room services
  - Special self-contained class
  - Special day school
  - Hospital or homebound instruction
  - Residential school

- Federal law (IDEA) calls for placement in the least restrictive environment (LRE) that is compatible with the student's needs.

What are some ways that teachers implement inclusionary practices?

- Collaborative consultation
- Co-teaching and other team arrangements
- Curricula and instructional strategies
- Accommodations and adaptations

What are the current practices in collaboration between general and special educators?

- *Collaboration* with general education means that special educators and general educators work together in arrangements such as prereferral teams, consultation, and co-teaching.

- Some educators question the effectiveness of popular forms of collaboration such as co-teaching and recommend that special education teachers be involved either in training general education teachers to accommodate a wider range of students or in actually teaching students with disabilities.

What are the roles of general and special educators in providing exceptional learners an individualized education program?

- All educators are expected to:
  - Make maximum effort to accommodate individual students' needs.
  - Refer students who need evaluation.
  - Participate in eligibility conferences.
  - Participate in writing individualized education programs.
  - Communicate with parents and guardians.
  - Participate in due process hearings and negotiations.
  - Collaborate with other professionals in identifying and making maximum use of exceptional students' abilities.

- Special educators are expected to:
  - Instruct students with learning problems, using evidence-based practices.
  - Manage serious behavior problems.
  - Evaluate technological advances.
  - Know special education law.

What are the trends and issues in universal design?

- *Universal design* refers to the principle that a device or program should be workable for as many potential users as possible.

- Although devices and programs may be designed for a wide variety of users, few can be made usable by literally all, and custom designs will probably always be necessary for some users.

What are the current strategies in the use of technologies?

- The major technologies that are controversial for people with disabilities involve medical advances, human reproduction, and communication.

- There is controversy about whether we *should* do something just because we *can*.

What impact do standards-based reform and the Common Core State Standards (CCSS) have on special education?

- Students with disabilities are expected to participate in the CCSS.

- Proponents of participation suggest that special education has not been held accountable for students' progress.

- The CCSS states that students with disabilities should be held accountable regarding the general education curriculum, but some will need instructional supports and accommodations.

- Some educators argue that some students with disabilities should not be expected to live up to the same standards as their nondisabled peers and that too much emphasis on the general education curriculum is at the expense of students learning skills such as study skills, daily living skills, and intensive reading instruction.

What are our concluding thoughts about current practices in special education?

- We believe controversy indicates that the field of special education is alive and well.

- We should constantly strive to make special education better.

▼ INTERNET RESOURCES

Pertinent Organizations

- The United States Office of Special Education and Rehabilitative Services (http://www2.ed.gov/about/offices/list/osers/index.html) provides many links to resources and programs for exceptional children and their teachers.

- The major professional organization for practitioners, policymakers, and researchers in special education, with about 40,000 members, is the Council for Exceptional Children (CEC) (http://www.cec.sped.org). CEC is made up of 17 divisions, each covering a different aspect of special education; for example, the Division for Learning Disabilities (http://teachingld.org), Division on Autism and Developmental Disabilities (http://daddcec.org), Council of Administrators of Special Education (http://www.casecec.org), Division for Culturally and Linguistically Diverse Exceptional Learners (http://www.ddelcec.org).

- CEC provides numerous member benefits: http://www.youtube.com/watch?v=QA4wwlyXT74&feature=c4-overview&playnext=1&list=TLZcuAELOx3Ss.

- National Association of Special Education Teachers (http://www.naset.org) focuses on providing resources for special education teachers.

chapter three

MULTICULTURAL AND BILINGUAL ASPECTS OF SPECIAL EDUCATION

▶ LEARNING OUTCOMES

Learning Outcome 3.1: Understand the major issues in multicultural education and bilingual education and their implications for special education.

Learning Outcome 3.2: Understand the major issues pertaining to disproportionate representation of ethnic minority students in special education.

Learning Outcome 3.3: Understand the major issues in assessment as it pertains to culturally diverse populations.

Learning Outcome 3.4: Understand the major issues of instruction for culturally diverse populations.

MISCONCEPTIONS ABOUT Multicultural and Bilingual Aspects of Special Education

MYTH Multicultural education addresses the concerns of ethnic minorities who want their children to learn more about their history and the intellectual, social, and artistic contributions of their ancestors.

FACT This is a partial truth. In fact, multicultural education seeks to help the children of all ethnic groups appreciate their own and others' cultural heritages—plus our common American culture that sustains multiculturalism.

MYTH Implementing multicultural education is a relatively simple matter of including information about all cultures in the curriculum and teaching respect for them.

FACT Educators and others are struggling with how to construct a satisfactory multicultural curriculum and create multicultural instructional methods. Nearly every aspect of the task is controversial: which cultures to include, how much attention to give to each, and what and how to teach about them.

MYTH Multiculturalism includes only the special features and contributions of clearly defined ethnic groups.

FACT Ethnicity is typically the focal point of discussions of multiculturalism, but ethnicity is sometimes a point of controversy if it is defined too broadly (for example, by lumping all Asians, all Africans, or all Europeans together). Besides ethnic groups, other groups and individuals—such as people identified by gender, sexual orientation, religion, and disability—need consideration in a multicultural curriculum.

MYTH Disproportionate representation of ethnic minorities in special education is no longer a problem.

FACT Some ethnic minorities are still underrepresented or overrepresented in certain special education categories. For example, African American students, especially males, are overrepresented in programs for students with emotional disturbance and underrepresented in programs for gifted and talented students.

MYTH It's not possible to assess minority students because assessments are biased.

FACT Some assessments, especially those that are standardized, are culturally biased. But testing accommodations can reduce this bias, and response to intervention (RTI) is a promising method for culturally unbiased identification.

MYTH If students speak English, their teachers do not need to be concerned about bilingual education.

FACT Conversational English is not the same as the more formal and sometimes technical language used in academic curriculum and classroom instruction. Educators must make sure that students understand the language that is used in teaching, not just informal conversation.

GUIDING QUESTIONS

- What are some of the major issues concerning multiculturalism?

- How does multiculturalism play out in the United States?

- What are some of the important concepts about cultural diversity for education?

- What are some of the important issues concerning multicultural and bilingual special education?

- What are some of the important aspects of assessment in multicultural and bilingual special education?

- What are some of the major instructional issues concerning multicultural and bilingual special education?

Many nations and regions are splintered into factions, clans, tribes, and gangs. In some cases, this splintering has been accompanied by extreme cruelty of individuals or groups toward others. Differences—especially those of national origin, religion, ethnic origin, color, custom, sexual orientation, gender identity, social class, and disability—are too often the basis for viciousness. Prejudice remains a central problem of humankind. In this first quarter of the 21st century, slavery is still practiced in some nations of the world. Terrorists kill, maim, and threaten, and acts of war do the same. Not so long ago, systematic efforts were made in a supposedly highly "civilized" society to exterminate people with disabilities, and we would be wise to learn the lessons history can teach us about our personal and collective capacity for brutality. We refer here to the Eugenics Movement of the first few decades of the 20th century, in which sterilization of people with intellectual disabilities was relatively common. The most infamous case was that of Carrie Buck, who had been raped and whose sterilization purportedly to prevent her from bearing a child with disabilities was upheld by the U.S. Supreme Court in *Buck v. Bell*. (For more information see: https://en.wikipedia.org/wiki/Carrie_Buck).

In contrast to such deplorable discrimination, a mark of a truly civilized society is its acceptance and celebration of diversity. Few of us would actually want to live in a world without diversity. It's common to dwell on the problems associated with cultural differences. However, a world void of diversity would be dull and uneventful. Multiculturalism is an intricate component of the human experience and a significant force in the advancement of societies. Cultural diversity has sparked periods of advancement and change throughout history. The adventures of Marco Polo in China brought about changes in Italian culture and eventually the entire European continent. Similarly, when African slaves in America encountered European music, they blended it with their African music to create spirituals, and out of the spirituals grew other musical genres such as gospel, blues, jazz, and rock and roll. History provides countless examples of cultures learning from each other, as well as, unfortunately, countless examples of people of one culture devaluing individuals from another.

All cultures and ethnic groups of the world can take pride in much of their heritage, but all also bear a burden of indignity because at some time they have engaged in the ruthless treatment or literal enslavement of others. Sometimes this treatment has extended to minority members of their own larger group whose differences have been viewed as undesirable or intolerable.

In virtually every nation, society, religion, ethnic group, tribe, or clan, discrimination exists against those who are different. It's therefore critically important that we learn to accept the principle that those who differ from us are equals as human beings. Furthermore, all educators need to understand the purpose of **multicultural education**, which is for educational institutions and curricula to provide equal educational opportunities to students regardless of their gender, social class, ethnicity, race, disability, or other cultural identity. It also seeks to socialize students to a multicultural norm: acceptance of and respect for those whose culture differs from one's own and knowledge of our shared history. Schools play a central role in multicultural education.

Multiculturalism also involves the specter of collective versus individual pride and guilt in behavior. Is the entire group of people that comprise a culture justified in taking pride in the fact that one of their group has accomplished something notable? Is an entire group of people—perhaps a nation—guilty for the acts of some of its members? Clearly, the assignment of collective guilt is a convenient, time-honored way of perpetuating discrimination, ethnic cleansing, genocide, and other acts of violence. Collective pride can blind people to the faults of members of a group and create a false sense of worthiness.

THE UNITED STATES AND MULTICULTURALISM

MyLab Education
Video Example 3.1

In this video, Dr. Madeline Milian answers the question of how teachers can inject multiculturalism into their general curriculum.

Effective multicultural education promotes pride in students' own cultures and understanding and appreciation of different cultures among all students; it also ensures equal educational opportunities for all students, regardless of cultural background. America is an increasingly diverse country. Our desire should be to build a diverse society in which the personal freedom and pride of all cultural groups and respect for others' cultural heritage are the norm––a society in which fear, hate, and abuse are eliminated and in which guilt or accomplishment is not determined by association. Working toward this ideal demands a multicultural perspective, one from which we can simultaneously accomplish two tasks. First, we must renew our efforts to achieve social justice and take specific steps to understand and appreciate one another's cultures. Second, in doing so, we must pledge our first loyalty to common cultural values that make diversity a strength rather than a fatal flaw. We seek a commitment to our common humanity and to democratic ideals that bind people together for the common good and give all of them freedom for the rightful honoring of their heritage.

Since the civil rights movement of the 1960s, educators have become increasingly aware of the extent to which differences among cultural and ethnic groups affect children's schooling. Gradually, educators and others are coming to understand that the cultural diversity of the United States and the world demands multicultural education. Progress in constructing multicultural education has been slow, however, in part because of the way in which all cultural groups tend to view themselves as the standard against which others should be judged.

Education that takes full advantage of the cultural diversity in our schools and the larger world requires much critical analysis and planning. It can be very difficult for all cultural or ethnic groups to find common satisfaction in any specific curriculum, even if they are all seeking what they consider the multicultural ideal. Moreover, some argue that the more important goal is finding the common American culture and ensuring that our children have a common cultural literacy (Ravitch, 2003).

Even the metaphors that we use for dealing with cultural diversity and cultural unity are points of controversy. The United States has often been called a "cultural melting pot," but some now reject the notion of total melding or amalgamation; they reject the metaphor of an alloy in which metals are dissolved in each other and fused into a new substance. Instead, they use the metaphor of a "cultural salad bowl." Those who reject the alloy or melting pot metaphor want each identifiable group to be recognized as separate, distinct, and legitimate in its own right. To them, a salad is a better description because each ingredient (lettuce, tomatoes, onions, pine nuts, etc.) has its own distinct flavor; but when you mix the ingredients together, the salad takes on a taste of its own.

The solution is not as simple as becoming sensitized to differences. Too often, Eurocentrism is met with Europhobia, Afrocentrism with Afrophobia, homocentrism with homophobia, sensitivity to difference with hypersensitivity about being different. Nor is the solution to become "blind" to difference. Perhaps the solution includes both engendering sensitivity to differences and building confidence that one's own differences won't be threatened by others. The solution might also require helping students learn how to view themselves and others from different perspectives.

Interestingly, as of the writing of this text, the United States' policies on immigration are being hotly contested. At this point, President Trump's administration is attempting to limit the number of immigrants, especially those from Mexico and Latin America as well as several countries with majority Muslim populations. However, some Congress members and Governors are opposed to severe restrictions. And thus far, the Courts have stopped the travel ban. It is possible that eventually the U.S. Supreme Court will rule on its legality (Gerstein, 2017).

Multicultural education is challenging, but we are optimistic about it because it's an opportunity to face our nation's shared problems squarely and to extract the best human qualities from each cultural heritage. It provides the opportunity to develop an appreciation of our individual and shared cultural treasures and to engender acceptance, if not love, of all differences that are not destructive of the human spirit. The best antidote for cultural insularity is inclusiveness. Adherence to truly American values of multiculturalism overcomes insularity.

Multiculturalism is now a specialized field of study and research in education, and its full exploration is far beyond the scope of this chapter. Of particular concern to special educators is how exceptionalities are related to cultural diversity and the way in which special education fits within the broader general education context in a multicultural society. Cultural diversity presents particular challenges for special educators in three areas: assessment of abilities and disabilities, instruction, and socialization. Before discussing each of these challenges, we summarize some of the major concepts about education and cultural diversity that set the context for multicultural and bilingual special education.

MyLab Education
Video Example 3.2
In this video, Dr. Irma Olmedo provides advice on how to address biases that can exist in the classroom.

MyLab Education
Video Example 3.3
And in this video, Dr. Madeline Milian offers three things teachers should keep in mind when teaching English Language Learners (ELLs).

> My**Lab** Education **Self-Check 3.1**

EDUCATION AND CULTURAL DIVERSITY

The term *culture* has many definitions, although most include the following elements:

1. Values and typical behavior
2. Languages or dialects
3. Nonverbal communication
4. Awareness of one's cultural identity
5. Worldviews or general perspectives

These elements can together make up a national or shared culture. Within the larger culture are many **subcultures** that share the common characteristics of the larger culture. Subcultures needn't be small, and may, in fact, be the majority group in a given region, state, organization, or other group. European Americans are a subculture in the United States of America, although they have to date been the majority of Americans. But, of course, European Americans can be described as subcultures when designated by their region or nation of origin, as well as by other categories.

Subcultures include all of the various subcategories of people that one might name, including distinctions made on the basis of political party, ethnic identity, gender, sexual orientation, age, and disability. Subcultures may have unique values, behavior, languages or dialect, nonverbal communication, awareness, identity, and views. Some subcultures are voluntary (e.g., religion, political party), and some are involuntary (e.g., skin color,

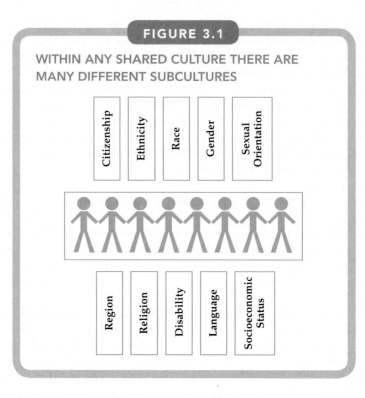

FIGURE 3.1

WITHIN ANY SHARED CULTURE THERE ARE MANY DIFFERENT SUBCULTURES

gender). Figure 3.1 illustrates that an individual might identify with the larger, general culture and also belong to many different subcultures. The variety of subcultures to which a person belongs affects his or her behavior. The larger, general culture in the United States consists of certain overarching values, symbols, and ideas, such as justice, equality, and human dignity. Within the United States, subcultures might share these common values but differ in many other ways.

The number of subcultures represented in U.S. schools has increased in recent decades because of the variety of immigrants from other countries. The number has also increased, however, because of greater recognition of and sensitivity to subcultures, such as those represented by disability, age, religion, and so on. Sexual orientation, in particular, which once was a topic that was either purposely or inadvertently ignored, has become germane to the discussion of subcultures. Many students, including many with educational exceptionalities, experience serious difficulties with what some have called the "invisible" culture of gay and lesbian youth.

Students who are "straight" might struggle with their own prejudices against homosexuals, which are all too often fostered by both their peers and adults and sometimes given justification by identification with a religious or political subculture. Gay and lesbian students are often harassed and abused verbally and physically in school and may suffer from serious depression or other psychological disorders as a result; even the appearance or assumption of being gay can lead to abuse (see Associated Press, 2004; Bell, 2004). Gay students need to be able to be themselves without fear of harassment or discrimination. Consider also that a student might be both gay or lesbian and gifted, physically disabled, intellectually disabled, or have another educational exceptionality.

Students from some subcultures in U.S. society do extremely well in school, but others don't. The factors accounting for the school performance of subcultures are complex, and social scientists are still searching for the attitudes, beliefs, traditions, and opportunities that foster the success of specific cultural groups. Although considerable evidence indicates that various ethnic minority communities have a positive influence on students' achievement and school behavior, we offer a couple of cautions. First, we need to guard against stereotypes—assumptions that one's cultural identity is sufficient to explain academic achievement or economic success. Second, the fact that some minority communities may have a strong influence on school success doesn't relieve schools of the obligation to provide a multicultural education. All students need to feel that they and their cultural heritage are included in the mainstream of American culture and schooling.

The general purposes of multicultural education are to promote pride in the positive aspects of one's own cultural heritage, encourage understanding of cultures that differ from one's own, foster positive attitudes toward cultural diversity, and ensure equal educational opportunities for all students. These purposes cannot be accomplished unless students develop an understanding and appreciation of their own cultural heritage, as well as an awareness and acceptance of cultures different from their own.

On the surface, teaching about cultures and engendering an acceptance and appreciation of cultural diversity appear to be simple. However, two questions immediately complicate things: (1) Which cultures shall we include? and (2) What and how shall we teach about them? The first question demands that we consider all the cultures that might be represented in the school and the difficulties inherent in including them all. In some urban school districts with large numbers of immigrant children, there may be more than 20 different languages spoken in students' homes within that district. Answering the second question is also problematic because it's often difficult to know what to teach and how. Some cultural groups find the traditions, ceremonies, values, holidays, and various characteristics of other cultures unacceptable or even offensive. That is, when it comes to what and how to teach about other cultures, the stage may be set for conflict. Treating all cultures with equal attention and respect can present substantial challenges.

Given the multiplicity of subcultures, each wanting—if not demanding—its precise and fair inclusion in the curriculum, it isn't surprising that educators sometimes feel caught in a spiral of factionalism and feuding. Additional questions about cultural values inevitably must be addressed: Which cultural values and characteristics should we embrace? Which, if any, should we shun? Would we, if we could, fully sustain some cultures, alter some significantly, and eliminate others? Consider, for example, cultures in which women are treated poorly and cultures that tolerate slavery. To what extent does every culture have a right to perpetuate itself? How should we respond to some members of the Deaf culture, for example, who reject the prevention of deafness or procedures and devices that enable children who are deaf to hear, preferring deafness to hearing and wishing to sustain the Deaf culture deliberately (see Kauffman & Hallahan, 2005; Mundy, 2002)?

Depending on how we define culture, the values of our own cultural heritage, and our role in multicultural education, we might find ourselves embroiled in serious cultural conflicts. No wonder that some describe the late 20th and early 21st centuries as an era of "culture wars." To deal effectively with the multicultural challenge, we must focus on the challenges that are most pertinent to special education.

MyLab Education Self-Check 3.2

MULTICULTURAL AND BILINGUAL SPECIAL EDUCATION

The subcultures that are of particular importance for special education are ethnic groups and exceptionality groups. Banks and Banks (2013) note that an *ethnic group* has a common historic origin and a shared identity, heritage, and tradition. It has value orientations, behavioral patterns, and often political and economic interests that differ from those of other groups in the larger society. An ethnic group may be a majority or a minority of people in a given country or region. We define an **exceptionality group** as a group sharing a set of specific abilities or disabilities that are especially valued or that require special accommodation within a given subculture. Thus, a person may be identified as exceptional in one ethnic group (or other subculture defined by gender, social class, religion, etc.) but not in another.

Ethnicity and Exceptionality

Multicultural *special education* must focus on *two primary objectives that exceed the general purposes of multicultural education*:

1. Ensure that ethnicity is not mistaken for exceptionality/disability.
2. Increase understanding of the subculture of exceptionality/disability and its relationship to other cultures.

ETHNICITY VERSUS EXCEPTIONALITY Ethnicity and exceptionality are distinctly different concepts. However, ethnicity can be mistaken for exceptionality when one's own ethnic group is viewed as setting the standard for all others. For example, patterns of eye contact, physical contact, use of language, and ways of responding to people in positions of authority vary greatly among ethnic groups. Members of each ethnic group must realize that what they perceive as deviant or unacceptable in their own group might be normal and adaptive in another ethnic group. That is, we must not mistakenly conclude that students have a disability or are gifted just because they are different.

It's undeniable that students from three ethnic minority groups are disproportionately identified for special education: American Indian or Alaska Native, Native Hawaiian or Other Pacific Islander, and African American (Oswald, Coutinho, Best, & Singh, 1999). Probably because of the regrettable history of slavery in the United States, as well as the greater numbers of African Americans among minorities, most of the attention regarding disproportionality has focused on African Americans. For example, looking at Table 3.1,

TABLE 3.1 • **Risk ratio for students 6 to 21 years of age within racial/ethnic groups by disability category**

DISABILITY	AMERICAN INDIAN OR ALASKA NATIVE	ASIAN	BLACK OR AFRICAN AMERICAN	HISPANIC/ LATINO	NATIVE HAWAIIAN OR OTHER PACIFIC ISLANDER	WHITE	TWO OR MORE RACES
All disabilities	1.68	0.47	1.41	1.01	1.59	0.90	0.87
Autism	0.94	1.11	0.99	0.79	1.32	1.16	0.97
Deaf-blindness	2.31	0.81	0.76	1.04	3.40	1.10	0.79
Developmental delay	4.09	0.41	1.68	0.69	2.35	0.91	1.24
Emotional disturbance	1.68	0.18	2.08	0.61	1.30	0.96	1.19
Hearing impairments	1.35	1.17	1.03	1.35	2.71	0.76	0.77
Intellectual disabilities	1.58	0.50	2.22	0.94	1.64	0.70	0.71
Multiple disabilities	1.90	0.63	1.36	0.73	1.94	1.11	0.72
Orthopedic impairments	1.01	0.88	0.86	1.21	1.50	0.97	0.76
Other health impairments	1.39	0.28	1.38	0.63	1.38	1.28	0.97
Specific learning disabilities	1.96	0.31	1.51	1.31	1.88	0.73	0.76
Speech or language impairments	1.40	0.69	1.02	1.08	1.09	0.99	0.90
Traumatic brain injury	1.70	0.51	1.09	0.71	1.59	1.29	0.90
Visual impairments	1.51	0.92	1.12	0.97	1.78	0.98	0.80

NOTE: Risk ratio compares the proportion of a particular racial/ethnic group served under *IDEA* to the proportion served among the other racial/ethnic groups combined. For example, if racial/ethnic group X has a risk ratio of 2 for receipt of special education services, then the proportion of students from that group receiving services is twice as great as that for all the other racial/ethnic groups combined. (USDOE, 2016) 38th Annual Report to Congress

FOCUS ON

What Causes Disproportionate Representation of African American Students in Special Education?

For decades, the overrepresentation of African Americans in special education has typically been blamed on (a) bias in tests used and/or (b) prejudice in teachers toward Black students (see Dunn, 1968, and Skiba, Poloni-Staudinger, Simmons, Feggins-Azziz, & Chung, 2005). After all, we know that some of the tests used to identify students with disabilities are culturally biased. And we know that some professionals lack an understanding of other cultures.

However, at the same time that these biases may exist, we also know that Black children are more likely to attend schools that are underfunded and understaffed. And we know that poverty puts children at risk for having disabilities and that some ethnic minorities (e.g., African Americans, Latinos/Hispanics, Native Americans) have higher rates of poverty. So, what is the reason that puts minority students at risk for being identified as disabled and placed in special education? Is it biased professionals and tests, or factors related to poverty?

As it turns out, it appears that both teacher and test bias *and* poverty are at play in causing the overrepresentation of African American students in special education. As we noted above, the prevailing view was that bias alone made minority students vulnerable to inappropriate placement in special education. However, relatively recently a team of researchers has vigorously challenged that point of view.

Paul Morgan and colleagues have analyzed the best available national data and concluded that poverty, not discrimination, is the major reason minority students are more likely to be identified for special education (Morgan et al., 2015). The statistics Morgan et al. have used are complex, but in essence, their analyses account for child, family, and school factors associated with minority populations that are likely causes of disabilities, such as

1. having a very low birth weight,
2. experiencing fewer interactions with health professionals who would recognize abnormal child development,
3. lacking in nutrition,
4. being raised in poverty,
5. lacking exposure to high levels of language interactions with adults,
6. having parents who are reluctant to have their child "stigmatized" with a special education label, and
7. attending poorly funded schools that are prone to avoid identifying students for special education because of the stress it puts on poorly trained staff.

When the prevalence of identification for special education is analyzed, taking into account the above child, family, and school factors, Morgan et al. conclude that, although they are disproportionately represented in special education, African American students are actually *underidentified* with respect to how many should be identified for special education.

As conscientious practitioners, policymakers, and researchers, we must assume that the problem of disproportionality in special education can be improved, if not solved. Important civil rights are at stake. On the one hand, children with disabilities have a right to appropriate education regardless of their ethnicity, even if their ethnic group is statistically overrepresented in special education. On the other hand, children also have a right to freedom from discrimination and segregation. The disproportional placement of ethnic minority students in special education strongly suggests that in some cases, students are misidentified and wrongly placed (and stigmatized and segregated) in special education, whereas in other cases, ethnic minority students' disabilities are ignored (and the students are therefore denied appropriate education) (Kauffman & Landrum, 2009).

---

we see that Black students are 1.41 times more likely to be identified for special education compared to the general population. In other words, almost half-again as many Black students compared to all students are in special education.

African American students are most at risk for identification as having a high-incidence disability, which are arguably the most reliant on clinical judgment for identification. For example, they are 2.08, 2.22, and 1.51 times more likely than the general population to be identified as emotionally disturbed, intellectually disabled, or learning disabled, respectively. The cause of this is controversial, to say the least. See Focus on "What Causes Disproportionate Representation . . . .?"

ASSESSMENT ISSUES IN MULTICULTURAL AND BILINGUAL SPECIAL EDUCATION

Assessment is a process of collecting information about individuals or groups for the purpose of making decisions. In education, assessment ordinarily refers to testing, interviewing, and observing students. Assessment serves various purposes, including

MyLab Education
Video Example 3.4

In this video, Dr. Paige Pullen discusses the challenges of ensuring that bilingual children's scores on tests are true measures of a student's ability and not due to language or cultural differences.

MyLab Education
Video Example 3.5

And in this video, Dr. Madeline Milian also discusses the challenges of determining whether an English language learner has a learning disability.

screening (quick measurement to determine who may need further assessment and possible intervention), diagnosis (measurement to identify specific problems), identification for special education services, progress monitoring (frequent measurement to help guide instruction), and evaluating outcomes (measurement to determine the effectiveness of educational programming). Clearly, assessment often results in important decisions about people's lives; therefore, great concern for accuracy, justice, and fairness in educational assessments is widespread in the United States.

Unfortunately, the accuracy of many educational assessments, especially those involving special education, is open to question (McDonnell, McLaughlin, & Morison, 1997; Utley & Obiakor, 2001a). Particularly when ethnic subcultures are involved, traditional assessment practices have frequently violated the U.S. ideals of fairness and equal opportunity regardless of ethnic origin, gender, or disability. That is, the assessment practices of educators and psychologists have frequently come under attack as being biased, resulting in misrepresentation of the abilities and disabilities of ethnic minorities and exceptional students, which may then result in classification and overrepresentation in special education rather than improved educational programming (Artiles, Rueda, Salazar, & Higareda, 2005; MacSwan & Rolstad, 2006).

Educators should be aware of the potential cultural biases in assessment procedures as they evaluate their students' progress toward annual goals and short-term objectives. As we discussed in Chapter 2, assessment practices have increased in the age of standards-based accountability. More students with disabilities are being included in state- and district-wide achievement tests. However, informal assessments of students' progress have also increased.

Fortunately, methods to monitor students' response to interventions have become more common as a result of legislation (e.g., IDEA, NCLB, ESSA). The increase in informal measures to assess student progress is particularly beneficial to students from diverse populations; progress monitoring assessments are typically less biased than traditional standardized tests. For example, **curriculum-based measurement (CBM)**, which entails direct and frequent samples of performance from the curriculum in which students are being instructed, is more useful for teachers than traditional testing and decreases the likelihood of cultural bias.

Standardized tests are often implemented to document students' achievement of annual goals, as well as for issues of accountability. These tests may be biased because many of the test items draw on specific experiences that students from different subcultures may not have had. For example, tests may be biased in favor of the likely experiences of European American, middle-class students or may be couched in language that is unfamiliar to members of a certain subculture (Singh, Baker, Winton, & Lewis, 2000). Testing accommodations are provided to students with disabilities and students with limited English proficiency for the purpose of assessing student knowledge on an equal basis with students without disabilities and for whom English is a first language. Accommodations should not give an advantage to students but should provide students an equal opportunity to demonstrate knowledge and skills.

Testing accommodations for English language learners should reduce the language barriers that may interfere with assessment results (Albus, Thurlow, Liu, & Bielinski, 2005). The most common accommodations include administration modifications (e.g., extended time and small-group and individual administration) and the use of a bilingual dictionary. Other accommodations include translation of tests to the student's native language and bilingual versions of tests, but these are not as common (Abedi, Hofstetter, & Lord, 2004). Unfortunately, empirical evidence isn't available on the efficacy of these accommodations. A study on the efficacy of using an English dictionary during testing did not demonstrate an advantage for students using this accommodation (Albus et al., 2005).

Response to Intervention in Multicultural and Bilingual Special Education

The problems in assessing students are numerous and complex, and no simple solutions exist (Thurlow, Nelson, Teelucksingh, & Draper, 2001; Utley & Obiakor, 2001a). Many of the problems are centered on traditional standardized testing approaches to assessment that have serious limitations: (1) They don't take cultural diversity into account, (2) they focus on deficits in the individual alone, and (3) they don't provide information useful in teaching.

Schools are using response to intervention (RTI), which we introduced in Chapter 2, more widely to identify students with disabilities. RTI practices may have distinct advantages for students who are culturally and linguistically diverse; however, the research that supports its use as an effective method of identification is based on monolingual students. Furthermore, the effective interventions on which RTI is based, particularly for identifying students with reading disability, have been validated only with monolingual, English-speaking students (Linan-Thompson, Vaughn, Prater, & Cirino, 2006).

Although educators have concerns about the current evidence base for using RTI with culturally and linguistically diverse learners, there are sensible reasons for thinking it is appropriate. Because RTI models are supposed to rely on quality instruction before identification, they may prevent students from falling behind and thus being identified for special education (Klingner & Edwards, 2006). In addition, RTI relies more heavily on curriculum-based measurement and less on standardized tests, which may contain cultural bias. Like other areas of assessment and instruction, more research is needed to determine whether RTI methods are appropriate for use with English language learners and other minority populations.

Issues in the Identification of Special Gifts and Talents

Finally, we note that fair and accurate assessment is an issue in identifying special gifts and talents as well as disabilities. Too often, the extraordinary abilities of students of color or other ethnic difference and students with disabilities are overlooked because of bias or ignorance on the part of those responsible for assessment. Alternative methods for identifying students for gifted and talented programs are being investigated. In one study (Pierce et al., 2007), an alternative identification procedure resulted in an increased representation of Hispanic and English language learners in a gifted program. In Chapter 1, we emphasized the importance of identifying the abilities as well as the disabilities of students. To that, we add the importance of being aware of culturally relevant gifts and talents and recognizing and valuing the abilities of minority students.

INSTRUCTION IN MULTICULTURAL AND BILINGUAL SPECIAL EDUCATION

A major objective of multicultural education is ensuring that all students are instructed in ways that don't penalize them because of their cultural differences and that, in fact, capitalize on their cultural heritage (see Council for Exceptional Children, 2000). The methods that are used to achieve this objective are among the most controversial topics in education today. All advocates of multicultural education are concerned with the problem of finding instructional methods that help to equalize educational opportunity and achievement for all cultural groups—that is, methods that break down the inequities and discrimination that have been part of the U.S. public education system and that IDEA seeks to eliminate. Yet considerable debate continues over the question of what instructional methods are most effective in achieving this goal.

If students' differences are ignored, then students will probably receive instruction not suited to their needs. They will likely fail to learn many skills, which will in turn deny them power and opportunity in the larger culture. For example, if we ignore non-English-speaking students' language and cultural heritage and prohibit them from using their native language, they may have great difficulty in school.

However, the solution to this problem is not necessarily recognition of students' differences, because instruction that is geared to individual students' subculture might teach only skills that are valued by the subculture. Because the larger or more general culture doesn't value these skills, the students' difference will be perpetuated. For example, if non-English-speaking students are taught in their native language and are not required to learn English, then their progress in the English-speaking society will be slowed.

In considering instruction in multicultural and bilingual special education, we discuss two general areas: (1) effective teaching for all, and (2) improving instruction for language minority students.

MyLab Education Self-Check 3.3

MyLab Education Application Exercise 3.1:
Making Assessment Culturally Relevant

A teacher talks about what she has learned from teaching students who are culturally or linguistically different (CLD). Another teacher demonstrates the use of program monitoring with computer software

---

Effective Teaching for All

INSTRUCTIONAL ISSUES Clearly, the problem of instruction in multicultural education isn't easily resolved. Most authorities now agree, however, that accepting and fostering cultural diversity must not be used as an excuse for not teaching students the skills they need to survive and prosper in the larger context of American culture.

Many educators call for instructional practices that are culturally sensitive or culturally responsive, meaning attuned to the particular cultural characteristics of learners (e.g., McIntyre, 2007; Shealey & Callins, 2007; Villegas & Lucas, 2007). The assumption underlying many assertions about culturally sensitive or culturally responsive instruction is that students with different cultural backgrounds need to be taught differently, that certain aspects of cultural heritage determine to a significant extent how students learn best. We might also hypothesize that certain methods of instruction are equally effective for all students in a culturally diverse group (see Council for Exceptional Children, 2000; Kauffman, Conroy, Gardner, & Oswald, 2008; Tyler, Yzquierdo, Lopez-Reyna, & Flippin, 2004). That is, some instructional approaches (e.g., direct instruction, cooperative learning, **classwide peer tutoring (CWPT)**, and cross-age grouping) allow teachers to provide culturally sensitive instruction to all members of a diverse group at once.

Sensitivity to individuals, regardless of their culture, and effective instruction are essential elements of multicultural education worthy of the name. If one assumes that culturally responsive teaching means helping students of color to learn to the greatest extent possible, then the above-mentioned scientifically valid methods might be the answer. Rather than seeking effective methods *specific* to *specific* ethnic groups, perhaps educators should focus on ensuring that minorities *have access to effective instruction validated with students regardless of ethnicity.*

In other words, in addition to creating an atmosphere of acceptance of cultural differences, teachers should be using instructional practices that have proven effective for students from a variety of backgrounds. Generally, researchers have found that effective instruction for students who are struggling or who have been identified for special education rests on the concept of *individualization* (Pullen & Hallahan, 2015). And this individualization is achieved through ensuring that each student has instruction that is explicit, systematic, intensive, and frequent; that provides an appropriate level of pacing, corrective feedback, and reinforcement; and that is often delivered in small groups.

Finally, a viable multicultural curriculum can't be created and simply handed out to teachers (Banks & Banks, 2013). Teachers must be committed to the endeavor because their values, perspectives, and teaching styles will affect what is taught and how. The effective implementation of a multicultural curriculum requires teaching strategies that are involvement oriented, interactive, personalized, and cooperative.

DISCIPLINARY ISSUES One of the most difficult tasks of teaching is socializing students through classroom discipline—that is, through the management of classroom behavior. Managing classroom behavior presents a serious challenge for nearly all teachers and a particularly difficult challenge for most special education teachers (see Evertson & Weinstein,

FOCUS ON

Teaching Tolerance and Appreciation of Differences

Effective teaching practices demonstrate sensitivity to each individual student's cultural heritage, sense of self, view of the world, and acquired knowledge and skills. Teaching about various cultures, individual differences, and the construction of knowledge should permeate and transform the curriculum (Banks & Banks, 2013). Teaching tolerance and appreciation of individual differences is a critical part of a curriculum sensitive to cultural differences.

By *tolerance*, we don't mean merely toleration of others who are seen as undesirable. Our definition entails appreciating and valuing—the opposite of rejection, denigration, or toleration of a necessary evil. As the publication, *Teaching Tolerance* (http://www.tolerance.org), views tolerance, it means working for equity and fair treatment, seeing those who are different in culture as equal. Tolerance and appreciation of difference is not, of course, limited to ethnic, regional, sexual orientation, or language differences but includes differences of all types, including disabilities.

Noted historian Ronald Takaki (1994), interviewed for an article in *Teaching Tolerance*, recalls that his grandparents were Japanese immigrant plantation laborers in Hawaii. Nobel laure-ate and author Elie Wiesel (2004), writing in the Sunday maga-zine *Parade*, recalls his rescue from a concentration camp. Both suggest that the American promise of equality and fairness can become a reality only if we free ourselves from a legacy of racism and prejudice. We can do so by acknowledging the reality of our past and learning more about ourselves and our heritage.

Although in some ways being tolerant toward others who are different seems so commonsensical and straightforward (http://www.youtube.com/watch?v=AdmjelOTUns), something that should hardly need to be taught, history and current-day events tell us that prejudice and bigotry are all too common in humankind. Overcoming prejudice and teaching students to appreciate those who are different from themselves is not easy. Moreover, this is not an area in which research can provide defin-itive guidelines. Yet proposed methods for how teachers can help students learn both self-esteem and tolerance of difference are promising (Banks & Banks, 2013; Utley & Obiakor, 2001c). For example, some schools focus on incorporating diversity by design or organizing anti-bias clubs that encourage understand-ing and tolerance of others (e.g., Bennett, 2000; Collins, 2000; Kissinger, 2017; McAfee, 2000).

2006; Kauffman, Mostert, Trent, & Pullen, 2011). Two considerations are critical: the relation-ship between the teacher's approach to classroom discipline and the parents' child-rearing practices, and the teacher's sensitivity to cultural differences in responses to discipline.

Teachers might have an approach to classroom discipline that they consider effec-tive and humane but that differs from some cultures' accepted child-rearing practices. Educators, like everyone else, are often ethnocentric, believing that their views are right and those of others are wrong based on cultural values. In a given case, they might be right, in that their view is more humane or effective, but they might also be insensitive to the values of students and their families. Teachers must be sensitive to individuals and families; in the case of discipline involving students of culturally diverse backgrounds, the teacher might face delicate decisions about what is best for the child. When do one's own beliefs about the treatment of children demand that a culturally condoned disci-plinary practice be confronted as inappropriate or, perhaps, even as abuse or neglect? Answering this question is not easy. Teachers' sensitivity should not allow them to ignore what reliable research tells us about human behavior (Kauffman et al., 2008).

In addition to determining the kind of instruction minority students who are disa-bled should receive, teachers need to address the important consideration of what can be done to educate *all students* about an understanding and appreciation for *differences of all kinds*. See Focus On "Teaching Tolerance and Appreciation of Differences."

Improving Instruction for Language-Minority Students

Students for whom English is a second language face the simultaneous demands of learning a new language and mastering traditional subject matter. Those who also have disabilities encounter a third demand of coping with the additional hurdles imposed by their exceptionalities. Bilingual special education is therefore particularly controversial, presenting difficult dilemmas and paradoxes. Moreover, some federal and state policies demand that students who aren't fluent in English must score, on average, the same as

MyLab Education
Video Example 3.6

In this video, teachers of bilingual students emphasize the need to use explicit instruction, which includes having students repeat the words being learned.

those who are fluent in English; this has created extraordinary controversy about language learning.

One approach to teaching language-minority students is to emphasize use of their native languages. In this approach, teachers initially provide all academic instruction in each student's native language and teach English as a separate subject. Later, when the students demonstrate adequate fluency in English, they make the transition to instruction in English in all academic subjects.

Another approach is to offer content-area instruction in English from the beginning of the student's schooling but at a level that is "sheltered," or constantly modified to make sure the student understands it. The goal of this approach is to help the student learn English while learning academic subjects as well.

In the first approach—native-language emphasis—students are taught for most of the day in their native languages and later make a transition to English. In the second, **sheltered-English approach**, students receive instruction in English for most of the school day from the beginning of their schooling. The question as to which approach is better for students with disabilities has not been answered, although it's clear that changing from one approach to the other when students change schools creates particular difficulties (Gersten & Baker, 2000). No matter which approach is used, teachers need to be explicit and systematic in their instruction and attentive to the bilingual child's need for practice and repetition in their second language.

Another issue for language-minority instruction is whether an emphasis on the natural uses of language or, alternatively, on skills such as vocabulary and pronunciation is most effective. However, this controversy might be based on a false dichotomy. What students need is an effective balance between skill building and language that is meaningful and relevant to their lives and interests (Gersten & Baker, 2000). Moreover, instruction of language-minority students must be consistent with effective teaching.

MyLab Education
Video Example 3.7

It is notable that CWPT concentrates on academic skills as well as social skills. In this video, Dr. Madeline Milean stresses that English language learners face challenges in two areas: academics and socialization.

CLASSWIDE PEER TUTORING **Classwide Peer Tutoring (Cwpt)** (http://www.youtube.com/watch?v=yf7PbFli9s8) is a research-validated teaching strategy that may be particularly useful in helping elementary school children who are not proficient to learn English more efficiently (Fulk & King, 2001; Greenwood, Arrega-Mayer, Utley, Gavin, & Terry, 2001). Because, by definition, CWPT necessitates that students *work together*, it offers opportunities for teachers to pair students to maximize appropriate interethnic interaction.

Evidence also suggests that peer tutoring is effective for improving important reading skills (i.e., DIBELS Nonsense Word Fluency and Phonemic Segmentation Fluency; Good & Kaminski, 2002) of Hispanic students (Calhoon, Al Otaiba, Cihak, King, & Avalos, 2007; Calhoon, Al Otaiba, Greenberg, King, & Avalos, 2006) and social interactions (Xu, Gelfer, Sileo, Filler, & Perkins, 2008).

MyLab Education
Video Example 3.8

It is important to learn about students' cultures in order to best meet their needs. In this video, the teacher explains what she does prior to lessons to ensure the success of students who are dual language learners.

IMPLEMENTING EFFECTIVE READING INSTRUCTION Of all academic skills, reading is critically important. It's a skill that is necessary for school and life success, and reading instruction should be based on the best scientific evidence possible (Reyna, 2004). However, students who are English language learners often have difficulty learning to read (McCardle, McCarthy, & Leos, 2005; Pollard-Durodola, Mathes, Vaughn, Cardenas-Hagan, & Linan-Thompson, 2006; Vaughn, Mathes, Linan-Thompson, & Francis, 2005). Fortunately, federal funding has provided extensive research on teaching reading skills to English language learners (McCardle & Leung, 2006). Researchers have been examining whether methods that are effective with monolingual students at risk for reading disability are also effective for non-English speakers. One important finding of this research program is that comprehensive interventions (i.e., including explicit instruction in phonemic awareness, alphabetic principle, fluency, vocabulary, comprehension) produced significant improvements for these students (Linan-Thompson et al., 2006; Vaughn, Cirino, et al., 2006; Vaughn, Linan-Thompson, et al., 2006; Vaughn, Mathes, et al., 2006). Less comprehensive interventions did not produce significant results (Denton, Anthony, Parker, & Hasbrouck, 2004).

For young children in particular, research increasingly points to the importance of an environment in which children have the opportunity to listen to reading, examine books, engage in activities such as saying nursery rhymes, writing, and seeing and talking about printed materials (Hammill, 2004; Peck & Scarpati, 2004). This means encouraging such literacy-related activities in the home, which cannot occur unless the teacher is competent in addressing cultural differences among families.

Reading Rockets, a project of PBS's WETA and funded by the federal government, focuses on providing resources for teaching reading. Going to http://www.readingrockets .org/ and entering "English Language Learners" in the search box takes you to multiple resources focused on English language learners and reading instruction.

SOME FINAL THOUGHTS ON MULTICULTURAL SPECIAL EDUCATION

Teaching in a multicultural society demands attention to the multitude of identities that students may have. It also demands awareness that any of these identities may carry the consequence of social rejection, isolation, and alienation. Many children with disabilities are lonely and need to develop friendships (Pavri, 2001). Our task as educators is to promote understanding of cultural differences and acceptance of individuals whose identities differ from one's own. Building pride in one's cultural identity is a particular concern in teaching exceptional students. As we have noted elsewhere, many people in the Deaf community prefer to be called *the Deaf*, which runs contrary to the current use of terms such as *hearing impaired*. Deaf people and blind people have begun to express pride in their identities and cultures and, at the same time, foster multicultural experiences involving other languages and customs (Gallucci, 2000). In fact, for increasing numbers of people with disabilities, labels are to be embraced, not hidden.

People from many segments of society—such as parents of children with disabilities, senior citizens, religious groups, and recovering alcoholics—find that congregating for mutual support and understanding enhances their feelings of self-worth. Educators need to consider the possible value of having students with disabilities congregate for specific purposes.

By trying to avoid labels and insisting that students with disabilities always be placed with those who do not have disabilities, perhaps we risk giving the message that those who have disabilities are less desirable or even are not fit to associate with as peers (Kauffman & Hallahan, 2005). Bateman (1994) suggests that "something is terribly and not very subtly insulting about saying a bright learning disabled student ought not attend a special school with other students who have learning disabilities because he needs to be with non-disabled students" (p. 516). In striving for true multicultural awareness, we might learn that it's more productive in the long run to embrace identities associated with exceptionalities, while working to increase tolerance and understanding of differences, than it is to avoid labels or refrain from congregating students with specific characteristics.

Finally, we note that education should not merely socialize students to fit into the existing social order. The goals of multicultural education include teaching students to work for social change, which entails helping students who are members of oppressed minorities become advocates for themselves and other members of their subcultures (Banks & Banks, 2013; Utley & Obiakor, 2001b).

MyLab Education Self-Check 3.4

MyLab Education Application Exercise 3.2:
Use of Native Languages and Culturally Relevant Materials
Listen to the podcast interview with Dr. Leonard Baca, watch the video about teaching diverse learners. Then respond to the questions that follow.

▼ chapter three SUMMARY

What are some of the major issues concerning multiculturalism?

- People of every identity take justifiable pride in aspects of their heritage.

- Some people of virtually all, if not all, identities have conducted themselves in ways that could possibly bring shame to their group.

- Collective guilt and collective pride are problems for every group.

How does multiculturalism play out in the United States?

- The United States is a very diverse society that seeks justice for all.

- Ideally, American culture is one that celebrates diversity within a framework of clearly defined common values.

What are some of the important concepts about cultural diversity for education?

- American society comprises many subcultures (cultures that are a part, not all, of the larger society), each of which is characterized by:
  - Values and typical behavior
  - Language or dialects
  - Nonverbal communication
  - Awareness of one's cultural identity
  - Worldviews or general perspectives

- Special education must foster achievement in the context of cultural diversity.

What are some of the important issues concerning multicultural and bilingual special education?

- Differentiating between ethnicity and exceptionality

- Dealing with disproportional representation of students from differing ethnicities

- Identification and classification procedures that result in accurate placement and services for students

What are some of the important aspects of assessment in multicultural and bilingual special education?

- Assessment that honors the student's cultural heritage and does not penalize the student

- Instruction that uses the students' cultural strengths and that involves teaching tolerance and appreciation of culture, working with families, improving language instruction for language-minority students, improving literacy instruction for language-minority students, and adopting effective teaching practices

What are some of the major instructional issues in multicultural and bilingual special education?

- Culturally sensitive teaching has been misinterpreted as determining specific teaching strategies for specific ethnic groups versus ensuring that all ethnic groups have access to evidence-based teaching strategies effective for all.

- Teaching tolerance is more than instruction on toleration of others who are different. It entails appreciating and valuing those who are different. Some schools have reported success in instituting anti-bias clubs or adopting a commercially available anti-bias curriculum.

Monkeybusinessimages/iStock/Getty images

▼ INTERNET RESOURCES

Pertinent Organizations

- The National Alliance of Black School Educators (www.nabse.org) provides resources for educators who are black.

- The National Association for the Education of African American Children with Learning Disabilities (http://www.aacld.org) serves persons with learning disabilities and their families.

- Fiesta Educativa (www.fiestaeducativa.org) provides information for Spanish-speaking families that have a child with a disability.

- The National Hispanic Education Coalition.

- The Mexican American Legal Defense Fund (www.maldef.org) focuses on numerous issues related to Hispanics/Latinos, including education. On its website, one can access information about the National Hispanic Education Coalition, an umbrella organization for 25 other organizations devoted to improving education opportunities for Hispanic/Latino students.

- The World Institute on Disability (www.wid.org).

- By typing "Hispanic/Latino" into the search box on the World Institute on Disability website (www.wid.org), the reader can access information on a variety of topics pertinent to students who are English language learners.

chapter four
PARENTS AND FAMILIES

Jaren Jai Wicklund/Shutterstock

LEARNING OUTCOMES

Learning Outcome 4.1: Learn how professionals' views of parents and families have evolved.

Learning Outcome 4.2: Learn about the effects of having a child with a disability on the family.

Learning Outcome 4.3: Understand Family Systems Theory, families' involvement in social supports, interventions, behavioral supports, collaboration with school professionals, and parent advocacy.

MISCONCEPTIONS ABOUT Parents and Families of Persons with Disabilities

MYTH Professionals need to focus their intervention efforts only on the parents, especially the mother, of children with disabilities.

FACT Professionals now believe that the family (including extended family) as well as friends should be included in intervention programming for children with disabilities.

MYTH Parents are to blame for many of the problems of their children with disabilities.

FACT Parents can influence their children's behavior, but so, too, can children affect how their parents behave. Research shows that some children with disabilities are born with difficult temperaments, which can affect parental behavior.

MYTH Parents must experience a series of reactions—shock and disruption, denial, sadness, anxiety and fear, and anger—before adapting to the birth of a child with a disability.

FACT Parents don't go through emotional reactions in lockstep fashion. They may experience some, or all, of these emotions but not necessarily in any particular order.

MYTH Many parents of infants with disabilities go from physician to physician, "shopping" for an optimistic diagnosis.

FACT Just the opposite is often true. Parents frequently suspect that something is wrong with their baby but are told by professionals not to worry—that the child will outgrow the problem. Then they seek another opinion.

MYTH The father is unimportant in the development of the child with a disability.

FACT Although they are frequently ignored by researchers and generally do experience less stress than mothers, fathers can play a critical role in the dynamics of the family.

MYTH Parents of children with disabilities are destined for a life of stress and misery.

FACT Some parents experience high degrees of disruption and stress, but over time many come to learn to cope. And some actually gain unanticipated positive benefits from having a child with a disability.

MYTH Siblings are usually unaffected by the addition of a child with a disability to the family.

FACT Siblings often experience the same emotional reactions as parents do, and their lack of maturity can make coping with these emotions more difficult.

MYTH The primary role of the early intervention professional should be to provide expertise for the family.

FACT Many authorities now agree that professionals should help parents become more involved in making decisions for the family.

MYTH The typical family in the United States has two parents, is middle class, and has only the father working outside the home.

FACT Demographics are changing rapidly. In many more families, both parents now work outside the home, and the numbers of single-parent families and families living in poverty have increased.

MYTH Parents who elect not to be actively involved in their child's education and treatment are neglectful.

FACT Although it's desirable for parents to be involved, it is sometimes very difficult for them to do so because of their commitments to other family functions (e.g., work and child care).

MYTH Professionals are always in the best position to help families of people with disabilities.

FACT Informal sources of support, such as extended family and friends, are often more effective than formal sources of support, such as professionals and agencies, in helping families adapt to a family member with a disability.

MYTH Teachers should respect the privacy of parents and communicate with them only when absolutely necessary—for example, when their child has exhibited serious behavior problems.

FACT Teachers should initiate some kind of contact with parents as soon as possible, so that if a problem such as a serious behavior infraction does occur, some rapport with the parents will already have been established.

GUIDING QUESTIONS

- How have professionals' views of parents changed?
- What are the effects of a child with a disability on the family?
- What are the best ways for families to be involved in treatment and education?

The birth of a child with a disability can have a profound effect on the family. But the exact nature of the effect is not always certain. Reactions of family members to the individual with a disability can run the gamut from absolute rejection to complete acceptance, from intense anger to intense love, from total neglect to overprotection. But most important, a child with disabilities does not always threaten the family's well-being. In fact, some parents and siblings testify that having a family member with a disability has strengthened the family bonds.

In this chapter, we explore the dynamics of families with children with disabilities and discuss parental involvement in treatment and education. First, however, we present a historical perspective of the role of parents and families of children who are disabled.

PROFESSIONALS' CHANGING VIEWS OF PARENTS AND FAMILIES

Today, knowledgeable professionals who work with exceptional learners are aware of the significance of the family; importantly, most recognize that *families* and not just parents are crucial for successful outcomes for persons with disabilities. A good way to put it is that "special education is inevitably a family affair" (Singer, 2017 p. 771). And when we talk about family, we should consider it in its broadest sense—siblings, relatives, in-laws, and close friends who may play a role identical to or similar to those of family members.

Although educators now recognize the crucial importance of considering the concerns of parents and families in treatment and educational programs for individuals who are disabled, this wasn't always the case. Professionals' views of the role of parents have changed dramatically. In the not too distant past, some professionals labeled parents as the primary cause of the child's problems or blamed parents when practitioners' interventions were ineffective. For at least three reasons, educators now know that automatically holding parents responsible for their children's problems is inappropriate.

First, research has shown that the direction of causation between child and adult behavior is a two-way street (Bell & Harper, 1977; Bellefontaine, Hastings, Parker, & Forman, 2006; Mangelsdorf & Schoppe-Sullivan, 2007). Sometimes the parent changes the behavior of the child or infant. However, sometimes the reverse is true. Research over several years has confirmed that parents' behavior toward their children can be affected by the behaviors of the children (ranging in age from infancy through adolescence) who have a wide variety of disabilities (Brooks-Gunn & Lewis, 1984; Mahoney & Robenalt, 1986; Orsmond, Seltzer, Greenberg, & Krauss, 2006; Slonims & McConachie, 2006; Smith, Greenberg, Seltzer, & Hong, 2008). For example, some infants who are disabled are relatively unresponsive to stimulation from caregivers, making it more difficult to interact with these children. With an understanding of the reciprocal nature of parent–child interaction, we're more likely to sympathize with a mother's frustration in trying to cuddle an infant with severe developmental disabilities or a father's anger in attempting to deal with his teenager who has an emotional or behavioral disorder.

Second, researchers have found that many parents of children with a disability are very adept at adjusting their interactions with their children to maximize positive development (Guralnick, Neville, Hammond, & Connor, 2008; L. E. Smith et al., 2008). Maternal and paternal instincts often help foster positive outcomes for children with disabilities. Although many researchers used to think that parents needed training to achieve a positive effect on their children, the prevailing philosophy now dictates that whenever possible, professionals should seek the special insights that parents can offer.

MyLab Education
Video Example 4.1

Kelly, Lauralee's mother, discusses parenting a daughter with Down syndrome. Kelly's relationship with her daughter provides an example of why it is critical to involve parents in providing services to individuals with disabilities. You will see more of Kelly and her daughter, Lauralee, throughout later chapters.

Third, authorities are less likely to view the purpose of early intervention as training parents to assume the role of quasi-therapist or quasi-teacher (Berry & Hardman, 1998). Instead, many professionals now believe that the goal of early intervention should be to develop and preserve the natural parent–child relationship as much as possible. In sum, a healthy parent–child relationship is inherently beneficial.

Recognizing the importance of the family, Congress has passed several federal laws stipulating that schools make a concerted effort to involve parents and families in the education of their children with disabilities. Current law mandates that schools attempt to include parents in crafting their children's individualized education programs (IEPs; see Chapter 1). In the case of infants and toddlers from birth through age 2 years, schools must involve parents in developing **individualized family service plans (IFSPs)**. The focus of the IFSP is family centered; it not only addresses the needs of the individual child who has a disability, but also focuses on the child's family by specifying which services the family needs to enhance the child's development.

In essence, families and teachers have a symbiotic relationship. Each group can benefit enormously from the other group (O'Shea & O'Shea, 2001). For example, they can each inform the other about what interests the child has so that the child can begin to form goals. They can each reinforce the same behaviors or skills that the child needs.

Unfortunately, in practice, parents do not always feel valued in their child's IEP meeting (Mueller, 2017). They often report that professionals use jargon and don't take time to seek or to listen to their opinions. And the disconnect between parents and professionals is even more pronounced for families from ethnic minorities. Cultural differences related to such things as parenting expectations, communication styles, and familiarity with the special education system can lead to misunderstandings and feelings of alienation.

MyLab Education Self-Check 4.1

The Effects of a Child with a Disability on the Family

The birth of any child has a significant effect on the dynamics of the family. The parents and other children must undergo a variety of changes to adapt to the presence of a new member. The effects on the family of the birth of a child with a disability can be even more profound. In fact, some have likened the impact for some families to that of post-traumatic syndrome disorder (PTSD) (Grasso, 2014).

For families who have a child with a disability, the everyday routines that most families take for granted are frequently disrupted (Keogh, Garnier, Bernheimer, & Gallimore, 2000; Stoneman & Gavidia-Payne, 2006). For example, the child with a disability might require alterations in housing (e.g., the family might decide to move closer to therapists), household maintenance schedules (e.g., chores might not be done as quickly because of lack of time), and even parents' career goals might change. For example, one survey of families with children with disabilities found that over half reported that one or more family members altered their work hours, worked fewer hours, changed jobs, or quit working altogether because of having a child with a disability (Anderson, Larson, Lakin, & Kwak, 2002).

It's important to note that the child with a disability can have an impact on both parents and siblings, and in different ways.

MyLab Education
Video Example 4.2

Unless you are a parent of a child with a disability, it is very difficult to understand and appreciate the challenges of raising a child with a disability.

Parents' Reactions

A STAGE THEORY APPROACH Traditionally, researchers and clinicians have suggested that parents go through a series of stages after learning they have a child with a disability. Some of these stages parallel the proposed sequence of responses that accompany a person's reactions to the death of a loved one. Based on interviews of parents of infants with serious physical disabilities, a representative set of stages includes shock and disruption, denial, sadness, anxiety and fear, anger, and finally adaptation (Drotar, Baskiewicz, Irvin, Kennell, & Klaus, 1975).

Several authorities have questioned the wisdom of this stage approach in understanding parental reactions. One argument against a strict stage model comes from the fact that many parents report that they don't engage in denial. In fact, they're often the first to suspect a problem. It's largely a myth that parents of children who are disabled go from physician to physician, "shopping" for a more favorable diagnosis. In fact, all too frequently, they have to convince the doctor that there is something wrong with their child.

Although parents might not go through these reactions in a rigid fashion, some do experience some or all of these emotions at one time or another. Commonly reported reactions are grief, loss, and especially guilt.

THE ROLE OF GUILT The parents of a child with a disability frequently wrestle with the feeling that they are in some way responsible for their child's condition. Even though absolutely no basis for such thoughts exists in the vast majority of cases, guilt is one of the most commonly reported feelings of parents of exceptional children. The high prevalence of guilt is probably due to the fact that the primary cause of so many disabilities is unknown. Accordingly, surveys indicate that many parents are either unsure of the basis for their child's disability or hold faulty beliefs about the cause (Zuckerman, Lindly, & Sinche, 2016). Uncertainty about the cause of the child's disability creates an atmosphere conducive to speculation by the parents that they are to blame.

DEALING WITH THE PUBLIC In addition to ambivalence about the cause of the child's disability, parents can feel vulnerable to criticism from others about how they deal with their child's problems. Parents of children with disabilities sometimes sense, correctly or not, that others are scrutinizing their decisions about such things as their child's treatment, educational placement, and discipline techniques (http://www.youtube.com/watch?v=mtdkw2Uq_Kg).

The public can sometimes be cruel in their reactions to people with disabilities. People with disabilities—especially disabilities that are readily observable—are inevitably faced with inappropriate reactions from those around them. Understandably, parents often assume the burden of responding to inappropriate or even cruel reactions from

MyLab Education
Video Example 4.3

Parents often experience a sense of grief, loss, and guilt when their child is diagnosed with a disability. However, some parents also feel empowered by a diagnosis that helps them to access the best services for their child.
http://www.youtube.com/watch?v=slJ5HnxzMX4

the public. A fear many parents have is that when they are not around, their children will undergo mistreatment and ridicule, with no one to defend them.

DEALING WITH THE CHILD'S FEELINGS In addition to dealing with the public's reactions to their child's disability, parents face the delicate task of talking with their child about his disability. This can be a difficult responsibility because parents need to address the topic without making the disability seem more important than it actually is. In other words, parents don't want to alarm the child or make the child more concerned about the disability than is necessary. At the same time, they should avoid sugarcoating the problems the child faces.

Also, the child with a disability usually has questions about it: How did I get it? Will it go away? Will it get worse? Will I be able to live independently as an adult? If possible, parents should wait for the child to ask specific questions to which they can respond, rather than lecture about generalities. However, it is a good idea for parents to talk honestly with the child at as early an age as possible, especially before the teenage years, when so many parents and children have problems communicating.

DEALING WITH EXTENDED FAMILY MEMBERS' FEELINGS Often overlooked is the impact that the child with a disability will have on extended family members (e.g., parents, grandparents, brothers, sisters). And their reactions are important because extended family members can often play a critical role in providing comfort and support to the immediate family.

Parents' Adjustment

Abundant evidence shows that parents of children with disabilities undergo more than the average amount of stress (Singer, Maul, Wang, & Ethridge, 2017). The stress is usually not the result of major catastrophic events but rather the accumulation of daily responsibilities related to child care. A single event, such as a family member coming down with a serious illness, can precipitate a family crisis, but its effects are even more devastating if the family was already under stress because of a multitude of daily hassles.

PARENTAL REACTION TO STRESS Contrary to what one might think, stress isn't always linked to the severity of the child's disability. For example, parents of children with more severe disabilities might have greater child-care burdens, but parents of children with milder disabilities might be more likely to experience additional stress related to what is usually felt by parents of children without disabilities (e.g., stress pertaining to school achievement, dating, driving a car). Stress, however, does appear to be more prevalent in parents of children who exhibit poor social skills and behavior problems (Bailey, Raspa, Humphreys, & Sam, 2011), especially if the problems involve socially offensive and disruptive behaviors (Hastings, Daley, Burns, & Beck, 2006; Orsmond et al., 2006).

The factors that appear to be most predictive of how parents will cope with the stress are their prior psychological makeup and marital happiness, and the quality and degree of informal support they receive from others. Although there are exceptions, it's fair to say that parents who were well adjusted and happily married before the birth of the child have a better chance of coping than do those who were having psychological or marital problems.

Social support that parents receive from each other, extended family members, friends, and others can be critical in helping parents cope with the stress of raising a child with a disability (Cantwell, Muldoon, & Gallagher, 2015; Plant & Sanders, 2007). The support can be physical, such as offering child care, or it can be psychological. Just having someone to talk to about problems can be helpful.

CHANGING VIEWS OF PARENTAL ADJUSTMENT At one time, most professionals assumed that parents of children with disabilities were destined for a life of stress and misery. Although professionals now know this assumption to be largely invalid, research does show that parents, especially mothers, of children with disabilities have an undeniably greater likelihood of depression. Across several studies, researchers have found that

FOCUS ON

Resiliency

Toward the end of the 20th century, a new area of psychological research on the effects of negative environmental factors emerged. Up until then, virtually all research on populations with physical, psychological, or economic vulnerabilities (e.g., illness, disabilities, poverty, wars) had focused on the *problems* these conditions caused and interventions to reduce their negative effect. The classic longitudinal study conducted by Emmy Werner and her colleagues changed the focus to people who were *not negatively affected* by such circumstances—those who were resilient in the face of extremely negative circumstances, such as poverty, alcoholism, and parental mental illness.

Werner followed a cohort of children from Kauai, Hawaii, who were born into high-risk families; she monitored them from infancy to the age of 40+, concentrating on those who overcame the odds by leading relatively successful lives (Werner, 2004). In general, they found that resilient adults had sociable temperaments as infants and toddlers and experienced positive support from at least one caring adult and/or organization while growing up.

At the beginning of the 21st century, a subset of researchers who focused on families of children with disabilities followed the same path as Werner's research on *individuals* and turned their attention to **resilient families**. There are many characteristics of family resilience (Ferguson, 2002; Scorgie & Sobsey,

2000; Singer et al., 2017; Skinner, Bailey, Correa, & Rodriguez, 1999), but some common findings are that the resilient family:

- learns from its negative experiences,
- looks for the positive influence of having a child with a disability (e.g., being more broadminded about differences in other people, being more concerned about social issues, taking a more philosophical/spiritual view of life),
- takes advantage of sources of support (e.g., extended family, friends, church members),
- balances the needs of the child with a disability with the needs of the rest of the family, including the parents,
- establishes routines, which help them structure their daily activities, and
- advocates for their child.

Interestingly, evidence suggests that Latino families are more likely than Anglo families to view having a child with a disability as a positive rather than a negative experience. One team of researchers (Blacher & Baker, 2007) attributes this to a philosophical attitude toward adversity as exemplified by the expression, "No hay mal que por bien no venga [there is nothing bad out of which good cannot come]" (Zuniga, 1992, p. 115). This attitude may also be due to the importance of the family in the Latino culture and the social supports that strong family ties can provide.

---

among mothers of children with developmental disabilities, 29% experienced depression, and others are at an increased risk of experiencing depression (Singer, 2006).

The figure of 29% certainly signals that mothers of children with disabilities are vulnerable to depression, but it's important to keep in mind that it also means that 71% did not become depressed. Furthermore, strong evidence indicates that this depression tends to diminish as the child grows older (Glidden & Jobe, 2006; Singer, 2006).

Although mothers of children with disabilities may be more prone to depression than fathers, the role of the father can be an important factor in helping reduce the degree of depression the mother experiences. Mothers of children with disabilities are less likely to exhibit depression if the father is actively involved in child-care activities (Laxman et al., 2015). And when fathers are more involved in child rearing and financial obligations of raising the child, positive effects are evident in infants as young as 6 months (Lewin et al., 2015).

Even though some families are able to gain resiliency, professionals should still have a heightened sensitivity to the possibility that parents of children with disabilities may experience varying levels of depression. Our intent is not to minimize the fact that the added stress a child with a disability often brings can have a devastating impact on the stability of the family. It's dangerous to assume, though, that the birth of a child with a disability automatically spells doom for the psychological well-being of the parents or for the stability of their marriage.

Siblings' Reactions

Although a relatively large body of literature pertains to parental reactions, much less information is available about siblings of people with disabilities. What is available, however, indicates that siblings can and frequently do experience the same emotions—fear, anger, guilt, and so forth—that parents do. Research indicates that siblings of children with disabilities are prone to exhibit anxiety about their brother or sister (Shivers & Dykens, 2017).

In some ways, siblings might initially have an even more difficult time than their parents in coping with some of these feelings, especially when they are younger. Being less mature, they might have trouble putting some of their negative thoughts into proper perspective. And they might be uncomfortable asking their parents the questions that bother them. These questions usually vary according to the type of disability and the age of the sibling. Young children might wonder what causes the disability, why their sibling takes so long to get ready for bed, or why their parents let the sibling behave so badly in public. Older children might wonder how to explain to their friends what's wrong with their sibling or what they should do when other children make fun of her or him. And even older children might be concerned about who will take care of their sibling when their parents die or whether they should seek genetic counseling (Gallagher, Powell, & Rhodes, 2006).

Siblings' Adjustment

Children, like parents, can adapt well or poorly to having family members with disabilities. Not much research exists on this topic. The little solid research evidence that does exist is in the area of intellectual disabilities and suggests that although siblings are at a slightly elevated risk, they are at lower risk than parents of experiencing depression and anxiety (Rossiter & Sharpe, 2001). As is the case with parents, however, some people report having benefited from having a sibling with a disability.

Why some siblings respond negatively whereas others do not isn't completely understood. Although not definitive, some evidence suggests that birth order, gender, and age differences between siblings have some bearing on adjustment. Although girls who are older than their sibling with a disability may experience more stress because their parents often rely on them to help with child care, research is mixed on whether they harbor more negative feelings than boys toward their siblings (Fiedler, Simpson, & Clark, 2007; Floyd, Purcell, Richardson, & Kupersmidt, 2009). At older ages, however, when siblings are adults, evidence shows that women experience more favorable attachments than men do to their sibling with a disability, and adults who are of the same gender as their sibling with a disability experience more favorable emotional responses (Orsmond & Seltzer, 2000).

Access to information is one key to adjustment for siblings of children with disabilities. As noted earlier, siblings have myriad questions pertaining to their sibling's disability. Straightforward answers to these questions can help them cope with their fears. Teachers, as well as parents, can provide answers to some of these questions. An excellent resource for providing information and support to siblings are *sibshops* (http://www.youtube.com/watch?v=JrRBAbd7n6Q), workshops (Meyer & Vadasy, 2008) specifically designed to help siblings of children with disabilities.

MyLab Education **Self-Check 4.2**

MyLab Education **Application Exercise 4.1: What Can Teachers Learn from Parents of Individuals with Disabilities?**

In this video, Kelly, Lauralee's mother, discusses parenting a daughter with Down syndrome. She discusses the concerns she has as a mother, challenges the family faced in Lauralee's early years, and what teachers can do to help.

A FAMILY-CENTERED APPROACH TO TREATMENT AND EDUCATION

As noted earlier, today, educators are more likely to recognize the positive influence parents can have on their exceptional children's development. This more positive attitude toward parents is reflected in educators' changed approach to involving parents in the treatment and education of their children.

At one time, most early intervention programs for families of children with disabilities operated according to the philosophy that the professionals had the expertise and the families needed that expertise to function. Most authorities today, however, advocate a **family-centered model** (Bailey, Raspa, Humphreys, & Sam, 2011; Mangelsdorf & Schoppe-Sullivan, 2007). Under a family-centered model, professionals encourage the families to make their own decisions with respect to services, while mobilizing resources and formal and informal supports for the family's goals. The family-centered approach is a model in which the professionals work *for* the family. Research indicates that a family-centered approach leads to positive outcomes for families (Bailey et al., 2011).

Family-centered models reflect a change from viewing parents as passive recipients of professional advice to recognizing them as equal partners in the development of treatment and educational programs for their children. The notion is that when professionals don't just provide direct services but also encourage the parents to help themselves and their children, the parents assume control over their own lives and avoid the dependency that is sometimes associated with typical professional–family relationships. Successful parent involvement focuses on the notion that parents' interaction with their children is critical (Sileo & Prater, 2012).

Achieving the right balance between offering assistance and allowing families to make independent decisions can be challenging. For example, interviews with parents have resulted in the following recommendations:

- Be direct—but don't tell us what to do.
- Tell the truth and be honest—but also be hopeful and encouraging.
- Be knowledgeable—but admit when you don't know the answer.
- Don't overwhelm—but don't hold back information. (Meadow-Orlans, Mertens, & Sass-Lehrer, 2003)

Family-centered models are consistent with another current trend in services for families with disabilities—wraparound service systems. **Wraparound service systems** involve using not only educational services, but also available community services (e.g., mental health, social welfare, juvenile justice, and so forth) to meet the individualized needs of children and their families (Fiedler et al., 2007). These various services are "wrapped around" the family so that service providers give attention to as many of the family's needs as possible.

Family Systems Theory

The emphasis on understanding the individual's behavior in the context of the family and understanding the family's behavior in the context of other social systems is the basic principle underlying **family systems theory** (Lambie, 2000). Researchers have developed several family systems theories, all of which assume that treatment and educational programs will be more likely to succeed if they take into account the relationships and interactions among family members. One model developed specifically with people with disabilities in mind includes four interrelated components: family characteristics, family interaction, family functions, and family life cycle (Turnbull, Turnbull, Erwin, & Soodak, 2006).

FAMILY CHARACTERISTICS **Family characteristics** include basic information about the family, such as the type and severity of the disability, the family's size, cultural background, socioeconomic status, coping styles, and special conditions (e.g., spousal abuse, maternal depression). Family characteristics help to determine how family members interact with both each other and those outside the family. These characteristics can include, for example, whether the child has learning disabilities or is deaf, is an only child or has five siblings, is of the upper middle class or lives in poverty, and so forth.

Recent trends in U.S. society make it even more important for educators to take into account family characteristics. In particular, teachers should be attentive to the expanding ethnic diversity in the United States, which has resulted in a wider mismatch between the ethnicities of teachers and students, especially students in special education. One of the difficulties facing many special education teachers, who are often white, is knowing how to involve families from a different culture.

Perhaps the most important thing to remember is that parents from diverse backgrounds do not have any one particular way of interacting with teachers or other professionals. For example, some researchers have found that family members from culturally and/or linguistically diverse backgrounds have a tendency to defer to professionals as the "experts," but other researchers have pointed out that these family members can sometimes mistrust school personnel (Parette & Petch-Hogan, 2000). In other words, professionals need to be alert to such possible differences and be ready to try to accommodate them. In the case of families being suspicious of schools, for example, teachers might try contacting people in the community (e.g., a minister, physician, retired teacher of the same ethnicity) who are trusted by the families to serve as bridges between the family and the school.

In addition to wider ethnic diversity, other changes in families include increases in the number of families in which both parents work outside the home, single-parent families, same-sex unions, and families living in poverty. Families particularly vulnerable to the stresses of raising a child with disabilities are those facing additional struggles arising from poverty or single-parent status. Although it possesses the world's largest economy, the United States' child poverty rate is the second highest out of 35 industrialized countries (UNICEF Office of Research, 2013). In the United States, 1 in 5 children live in poverty, with 1 in 3 Latino children and 1 in 2 Black children living in poverty. Furthermore, 36% of births are to unwed mothers (Shattuck & Krieder, 2013). Interestingly, the number of single-parent fathers is increasing dramatically, from only 14% of single parents being fathers in 1960 to 24% in 2011 (Livingston, 2013). Unfortunately, a higher prevalence of disabilities exists in single-parent families and families in poverty (Singer et al., 2017).

Another group whose numbers are on the rise and who face considerable challenges raising children with disabilities is military families. Separation resulting from deployment can put stress on the family. And the fact that the suicide rate and instances of post-traumatic stress disorder (PTSD) in soldiers returning from battle are alarmingly high increases the odds that military families experience stress.

The changing demographics of those in the military have contributed to these problems. An increasing number of low-income women are looking to the military for career opportunities; more than 80% of the military are married with children, and the military is the largest employer of single parents in the United States (Taylor et al., 2005). This stress not only has been difficult for the spouse of a soldier, but also has been especially difficult for the family when the mother is a soldier.

Coupled with these demographic changes—and to a certain extent influenced by them—families today live under a great deal of stress. For example, uncertainties regarding economic conditions over the past several years have increased stress on families. On the one hand, children need attention and reassurance more than ever; but on the other hand, because of pressures to earn a living, parents have fewer resources to draw on to provide comfort to their children.

These dramatic societal changes present formidable challenges in working with families of children with disabilities. As family configurations change, professionals need to alter their approaches. For example, approaches that are successful with two-parent families might not be suitable for single mothers. Also, professionals need to understand that today's parents are living under increasing stress and might find it correspondingly difficult to devote time and energy to working on behalf of their children.

FAMILY INTERACTION In the Turnbulls' model, **family interactions** reflect family cohesion and adaptability, important determinants of the "health" of a family (Turnbull et al., 2006). In general, families are healthier if they have moderate degrees of cohesion and adaptability.

Cohesion *Cohesion* refers to the degree to which an individual family member is free to act independently of other family members. An appropriate amount of family cohesion permits the individual to be her own person while at the same time drawing on other family members for support as needed. Families with low cohesion might not offer the child with a disability the necessary support, whereas the overly cohesive family might be overprotective. Research suggests that good cohesion has positive benefits for the child as well as other family members (Howell, Hauser-Cram, & Kersh, 2007; Magana, Schwartz, Rubert, & Szapocznik, 2006).

Otherwise healthy families often have difficulty finding the right balance of cohesion. They sometimes go overboard in wanting to help their children and, in so doing, limit their children's independence. Adolescence can be a particularly stressful time, when it's normal for teenagers to loosen their familial bonds. Adolescence is difficult for many families of children with disabilities; because of the disability, the family by necessity has often been more protective of the child. Cohesion can also be an issue for adults with disabilities. Current thinking dictates that people with disabilities should live in the community, but many will need support from their families to succeed. Living in the community demands a number of daily living skills—such as managing personal finances, keeping to a work schedule, and planning and preparing meals—that don't always come easily even to nondisabled young adults. Finding the right degree of independence from the family for young adults with disabilities can be a significant challenge.

Adaptability *Adaptability* refers to the degree to which families are able to change their modes of interaction when they encounter unusual or stressful situations. Some families are so chaotic that it's difficult to predict what any one member will do in a given situation. In such an unstable environment, the needs of the family member who is disabled might be overlooked or neglected. At the other end of the continuum are families characterized by extreme rigidity. Each family member has his or her prescribed family role. Such rigidity makes it difficult to adjust to the addition of a new family member, especially one with a disability. For example, the mother's involvement in transporting the child with a disability to therapy sessions might necessitate that the father be more involved in taking care of the other children.

Family Functions Family functions are the numerous routines in which families engage to meet their many and diverse needs—economic, daily care, social, medical, and educational.

An important point for teachers and other professionals to consider is that education is only one of several functions in which families are immersed. For some students, especially those with multiple disabilities, several professionals might be vying for the parents' time. It's natural, of course, for teachers to want to involve parents as much as possible. The bond between parents and professionals (e.g., teachers, speech therapists, physical therapists) can be critical to the child's development. At the same time, however, professionals need to respect the fact that their services are just one of the many functions to which families must attend.

Several authorities have reported that some families of students with disabilities prefer a passive, rather than an active, degree of involvement in their children's education (Turnbull & Turnbull, 2006). Families often have legitimate reasons for playing a more passive role. For example, in some cultures it's customary for parents to refrain from interfering with the roles of school personnel in educational matters. Furthermore, some parents might simply be so busy attending to other family functions that they are forced to delegate most of the educational decisions to teachers. Teachers should respect the parents' desire to play a relatively passive role in their child's education.

FAMILY LIFE CYCLE Several family theorists have noted that the impact of a child with a disability on the family changes over time (Berry & Hardman, 1998; O'Shea, O'Shea, Algozzine, & Hammitte, 2001) and have noted the value in looking at families of children with disabilities from a **family life cycle** perspective. Most family theorists consider four stages in the lives of families based on the ages of the children: early childhood, childhood, adolescence, and adulthood.

MyLab Education
Video Example 4.4
Kelly discusses her daughter, who has Down syndrome, and her budding romance with a young man named Crosby. Her continued story demonstrates a transition in life cycle changes.

Transitions between life cycle stages are often stressful for families, especially families with children who are disabled. We've already mentioned the difficulties facing families at the transition point when their child, as an adult, moves into more independent work and living settings. It's natural for parents to be especially concerned about what will happen to their child with a disability after they are too old to look after them or are deceased. A particularly difficult issue for some parents of children with disabilities who are entering adulthood is that of mental competence and guardianship. Parents who decide that their children are not competent to make rational choices without endangering themselves can go through legal channels to obtain guardianship of their children. **Guardianship** means that one person has the authority, granted by the courts, to make decisions for another person. Guardianship can range in degree from total to more limited or temporary authority to make decisions.

Another particularly troublesome transition can be from the relatively intimate confines of an infant or preschool program to the larger context of a kindergarten setting, which requires more independence on the part of the child. Furthermore, this transition can be equally troubling for parents as they learn to adjust to a new milieu of less familiarity and informality.

Transitions between stages are difficult because of the uncertainty that each new phase presents to the family. One of the reasons for the uncertainty pertains to replacements of the professionals who work with the child who is disabled. In particular, parents of a child with multiple disabilities, who requires services from multiple professionals, can experience ongoing anxiety about the switches in therapists and teachers that occur many times throughout the child's life, especially at transition points.

Social Support for Families

Families can derive tremendous benefit from social support provided by others (Cantwell et al., 2015; Gouin, da Estrela, Desmarais, & Barker, 2016; Lenhard et al., 2007). **Social support** refers to emotional, informational, or material aid that is provided to persons in need. In contrast to assistance that comes from professionals and agencies, social support is informal, coming from such sources as extended family, friends, church groups, neighbors, and social clubs.

ETHNICITY AND SOCIAL SUPPORT   Research shows evidence of familial and religious support in ethnic minority families (Harry, 2002; Magana et al., 2006). The values of some minority groups place heavy emphasis on caring for one's own family members, disabled or not. The family's church plays a major social support role for many minorities, again regardless of whether or not they are disabled.

PARENTAL SUPPORT GROUPS   One common type of social support, especially for parents of recently diagnosed children, is parental support groups that consist of parents of children with the same or similar disabilities. Such groups can be relatively unstructured, meeting infrequently with unspecified agendas, or they can be more structured. They serve as a means for parents to share their experiences, thus providing educational and emotional support. Parental support groups, however, are not of benefit to everyone. Some parents actually experience more stress from sharing problems and listening to the problems of others (Berry & Hardman, 1998).

PARENT CENTERS   The U.S. Department of Education has established more than 100 Parent Training and Information Centers and Community Parent Resource Centers; each state has at least one of these centers. The Technical Assistance Alliance for Parent Centers (http://www.taalliance.org/about/index.asp) assists and coordinates the work of these centers. The general purpose of the centers is to "provide training and information to parents of infants, toddlers, children, and youth with disabilities and to professionals who work with them. This assistance helps parents to participate more effectively with professionals in meeting their children's educational needs" (Technical Assistance Alliance for Parent Centers, 2009).

Behavioral Parent Training (BPT) and Coping Skills Interventions (CSI)

Some children with disabilities engage in behaviors that are particularly challenging for professionals and family members alike. Children with emotional or behavioral disorders and those with autism, for example, sometimes exhibit outbursts of aggressive or self-injurious behavior. As one team of researchers documented, such behaviors can have a profound impact on the family. At the end of one study, researchers exclaimed that they couldn't find the right words to describe adequately the emotional, physical, and social hardships families of children with significant behavior problems undergo (Fox, Vaughn, Wyatte, & Dunlap, 2002).

Such extreme behaviors often require more than just social support from friends and the community. Two successful approaches to managing parent stress are **Behavioral Parent Training (BPT)** and **coping skills interventions (CSI)** (Lindo, Kliemann, Combes, & Frank, 2016). The former focuses on the child's behavior and the latter focuses on the parent's behavior and thinking. BPT involves professionals helping parents to use behavioral principles to manage their child's problematic behavior. CSI involves helping parents use strategies to modify their reactions to their child's problematic behavior. In such cases, professionals may need to help families apply behavioral principles in interacting with their child. Researchers have found that programs emphasizing parents using behavioral principles to manage their child's difficult behavior have been successful (Skotarczak & Lee, 2015).

In implementing BPT or CSI, the focus can be on **family activity settings**, routines that families engage in, such as mealtimes, seasonal celebrations, visits to relatives, shopping, going on vacations, and eating in restaurants (Lucyshyn, Horner, Dunlap, Albin, & Ben, 2002; Singer, Goldberg-Hamblin, Peckham-Hardin, Barry, & Santarelli, 2002). Under the guidance of professionals, families typically begin by concentrating on just one or two settings before expanding to more. The key to reducing challenging behaviors in the home through BPT and CSI is close communication between parents, who know their children best, and professionals, who have the expertise to help parents apply behavioral principles effectively.

Communication Between Parents and Professionals

Virtually all family theorists and practitioners agree that no matter which particular approach one uses to work with parents, the key to the success of a program is how well parents and professionals work together. Even the most creative, well-conceived model will fail if professionals and parents cannot communicate effectively. Schools considered "parent-friendly" are most likely to foster productive communication (Sileo & Prater, 2012). Table 4.1 lists characteristics of parent-friendly schools.

Unfortunately, professional–parent communication doesn't come easily—which is not too surprising, considering the ingredients of the situation. On the one hand are the parents, who are trying to cope with the stresses of raising a child with a disability

MyLab Education
Video Example 4.5

Successful teachers keep in close communication with parents.

TABLE 4.1 • **Characteristics of Administrators and Practitioners at Parent-Friendly Schools**

- Administrators and practitioners at parent-friendly schools
  - schedule parent meetings at times convenient for parents
  - encourage and respond positively to parents who volunteer for school activities
  - invite parents to observe class activities (e.g., poetry readings, art project displays, student presentations, such as history or science units)
  - keep parents involved via such things as email, written notes, phone calls
  - appoint parents to advisory committees
  - encourage and respond positively to involvement of students' extended family and other sources of social support (e.g., friends of the family, clergy)
  - encourage and support parent advocacy for their child

MyLab Education
Video Example 4.6

Traveling notebooks, or home–school communications journals, as well as homework logs are excellent ways for teachers and parents to communicate.

in a complex and changing society. On the other hand are the professionals—teachers, speech therapists, physicians, psychologists, physical therapists, and so forth—who might be frustrated because they don't have all the answers to the child's problems.

A key to communicating with parents is to treat them with respect, accommodate their priorities, and be honest about their child (Sileo & Prater, 2012). The last aspect, if it entails negative feedback, requires diplomacy. Telling parents tactfully about their child's problem behavior (e.g., not following directions, talking back, provoking other students) is a skill not easily learned (Kauffman, Mostert, Trent, & Pullen, 2011).

It is critical that teachers receive information *from* parents as well as provide information *to* them. The parents have spent considerably more time with the child and have more invested in the child emotionally; they can be an invaluable source of information about the child's characteristics and interests. By keeping parents informed of activity in class, teachers can foster a relationship in which they can call on parents for support should the need arise.

Homework is one area in particular that's often a source of misunderstanding and conflict and that requires parental cooperation.

Most authorities agree that communication between the teacher and parents should start as soon as possible and that it should not be initiated only by negative student behavior. Parents, especially those who have children with behavior disorders, often complain that the only time they hear from school personnel is when their child has misbehaved. To establish a degree of rapport with parents, some teachers make a practice of sending an email or a brief form letter at the beginning of the school year, outlining the goals for the year. Others send periodic emails or newsletters or make occasional phone calls to parents. By establishing a line of communication with parents early in the year, the teacher is in a better position to initiate more intensive and focused discussions should the need arise. Three such methods of communication are parent–teacher conferences, home-note programs, and traveling notebooks.

PARENT–TEACHER CONFERENCES Parent–teacher conferences can be an effective way for teachers to share information with parents. Likewise, they're an opportunity for teachers to learn more about the students from the parents' perspective. In addition to regularly scheduled meetings open to all parents, teachers might want to hold individual conferences with the parents of particular students. Planning is key to conducting successful parent–teacher conferences. How the teacher initiates the meeting, for example, can be crucial. Among other things, teachers should welcome parents to the meeting, informally go over the goals of the meeting, begin by noting positive behaviors or strengths of the student, avoid jargon, and provide specific examples of the student's behaviors to be discussed (Mostert et al., 2011).

No matter the purpose of the meeting, research has shown that a key to communicating with parents is for professionals to talk about the child in such a way that it's obvious that they consider the child an individual, with unique strengths, weaknesses, and interests (Esquivel, Ryan, & Bonner, 2008). Nothing turns parents off more than getting the impression that their child is being defined by a diagnostic or special education category (e.g., learning disabled, behavior disordered).

FOCUS ON

Homework

A considerable amount of research has addressed how best to deal with homework assignments. Warger (2003–2004) reviewed much of this research and developed several pointers for teachers and administrators to consider.

Teachers should view homework as something that students should be able to do, as much as possible, on their own with no further instruction. It is frustrating for students, as well as

their parents, to be given assignments requiring the learning of new skills that haven't been part of work in the classroom.

Parents should provide as much structure as possible in the home to accommodate the child's doing his or her homework. The structure should pertain to the environment (e.g., quiet, well-lit, comfortable, distraction-free space) as well as family routine (e.g., allowing enough time for the child to work on his or her homework).

If the focus of the meeting is the student's poor work or misbehavior, the teacher will need to be as diplomatic as possible. Most authorities recommend that the teacher find something positive to say about the student while still providing an objective account of what the student is doing that is troubling. The teacher needs to achieve a delicate balance of providing an objective account of the student's transgressions or poor work while demonstrating advocacy for the student. If parents detect that the teacher is angry, this can make them apprehensive about the treatment the child might be receiving. Conveying only good news can also lose the parents' sense of trust. If the parents hear only good news, then they will be taken by surprise if a serious incident does occur.

MyLab Education
Video Example 4.7
Parent–teacher conferences with parents of children who are English language learners can be particularly challenging.

HOME-NOTE PROGRAMS Sometimes referred to as home-contingency programs, home-note programs are a way of communicating with parents and having them reinforce behavior that occurs at school (Jurbergs, Palcic, & Kelley, 2007; Kelley, 1990). By having parents dispense the reinforcement, the teacher takes advantage of the fact that parents usually have a greater number of reinforcers at their disposal than do teachers.

Teachers can choose from several types of home notes. (They can also elect to implement an electronic version of home notes via email or a website.) A typical home-note program consists of a simple form on which the teacher records "yes," "no," or "not applicable" to certain categories of behavior (e.g., social behavior, homework completed, homework accurate, in-class academic work completed, in-class academic work accurate). The form also may contain space for the teacher and the parents to write a few brief comments. The student takes the form home, has her parents sign it, and returns it the next day. The parents deliver reinforcement for the student's performance. The teacher often starts out sending a note home each day and gradually decreases the frequency until the notes are being sent once a week.

For home notes to work, it's important that both teachers and parents agree philosophically with a behavioral approach to managing student behavior. If either is opposed to using reinforcement as a means of shaping behavior, the home-note program is unlikely to succeed.

TRAVELING NOTEBOOKS **Traveling notebooks**, which go back and forth between school and home, are less formal than home notes and are particularly appropriate for students who see multiple professionals. The teacher and other professionals, such as speech and physical therapists, can write brief messages to the parents and vice versa. In addition, a traveling notebook allows the different professionals to keep track of what each is doing with the student.

Parent Advocacy

As we noted in Chapter 1, parent advocacy has played a critical role throughout the history of special education. Parents have been and continue to be influential in obtaining services for their children with disabilities.

The Individuals with Disabilities Education Act (IDEA) provides parents with a number of safeguards regarding their children. For example, they're entitled to a **due process hearing**, a noncourt proceeding held before an impartial hearing officer. Unfortunately, due process hearings don't always satisfy both sides, which can result in costly, drawn-out court proceedings. Each year, school districts across the United States spend well over $100 million resolving disputes between families of children with disabilities and school districts (Mueller, Singer, & Draper, 2008).

Although sometimes associated with the notion of confrontations between parents and professionals, ideally, parent advocacy can be a way to help prevent such disputes. Parents and professionals should work together in their efforts. Advocacy can foster needed or improved services for children while helping parents gain a sense of control over outcomes for their children. In advocating for their children, parents gain a sense of collective identity, which is key to changing both professional practices and professional and public beliefs (Turnbull, Shogren, & Turnbull, 2011).

Parents can focus their advocacy on helping their own children as well as other people with disabilities. The latter might involve volunteering for advisory posts with schools and agencies as well as political activism—for example, campaigning for school board members who are sympathetic to educational issues relevant to students with disabilities.

As important as advocacy is, not all parents have the personalities or the time to engage in such activities. Also, advocacy may be more or less suitable to some parents at various stages in their child's development. For example, some parents might be heavily involved in such efforts when their children are young but become exhausted over the years and reduce their involvement. On the other hand, some parents might not see the need for intervening on behalf of their children until they encounter problems later on—for example, in transition programming in the teenage years. The best advice for teachers is to encourage parents to be advocates for their children but respect parents' hesitancy to take on such responsibilities.

MyLab Education Self-Check 4.3

IN CONCLUSION

Today's knowledgeable educators recognize the tremendous impact a child with a disability can have on the dynamics of a family. They appreciate the negative as well as the positive influence such a child can exert. And they also realize that the family of a child with a disability can be a bountiful reservoir of support for the child as well as an invaluable source of information for the teacher. Although tremendous advances have been made, professionals are just beginning to tap families' potential for contributing to the development of their children with disabilities. Professionals are just beginning to enable families to provide supportive and enriching environments for their children. And professionals are just beginning to harness the expertise of families to provide the best possible programs for children.

▼ chapter four **SUMMARY**

How have professionals' views of parents changed?

- Professionals' views of parents are more positive than they once were for at least two reasons:
  - Not only can parent behavior influence child behavior, but the reverse can also occur.
  - The family can have a positive effect on the educational process.

- Congress has recognized the potentially positive influence by passing legislation mandating that families be involved in developing individualized education programs (IEPs) and individualized family service plans (IFSPs).

What are the effects of a child with a disability on the family?

- The addition of a child with a disability to a family can have significant effects on family dynamics and work patterns.

- Parental reactions to the birth of a child with a disability can involve a variety of reactions; guilt (even though unfounded) tends to be frequent.

- Parents must also deal with public reactions to their child as well as the child's feelings about having a disability.

- Substantial research shows that parents of children with disabilities undergo a great deal of stress.

  - How parents deal with the stress depends on their prior psychological makeup and marital happiness as well as the quality and quantity of social support they receive.

  - Current research indicates that many parents adjust well to having a child with a disability; some even benefit from the experience.

- Siblings of children with disabilities often experience some of the same emotions as the parents.

  - Siblings of the same gender and those who are close in age tend to have more conflicts, and at older ages, some evidence shows that women have a closer attachment to their sibling with a disability.

  - Having access to accurate information helps siblings to achieve a more positive adjustment.

What are the best ways for families to be involved in treatment and education?

- Most authorities advocate a family-centered model, whereby the families assume more decision making and professionals provide supports for families to achieve their goals.

- Most authorities also stress family systems theory. One such model (the Turnbulls') is composed of family characteristics, family interaction, family functions, and family life cycle (Turnbull et al., 2006).

- Social support—which involves emotional, informational, or material aid provided by nonprofessionals—is important for families.

  - Evidence suggests that some ethnic minority groups provide especially good social support.

  - Two common types of social support are parental support groups and Internet sites devoted to parents of children with disabilities.

- Behavioral Parent Training (BPT) and coping skills interventions (CSI) are important tools for parents who have children with challenging behaviors.

  - BPT consists of teaching parents to use behavioral principles to manage their child's problematic behavior.

  - CSI consists of teaching parents to modify and control their reactions to their child's problematic behavior.

- Communication between professionals and families is critical to involving families.

  - Parent–teacher conferences are an important means of communication, and preparation is a key to making them successful.

  - Home-note programs are a means for communication and a way for teachers to encourage parents to reinforce behavior that occurs at school.

  - Traveling notebooks are a way for one or more professionals to communicate with parents.

- Parent advocacy is an important way for families to become involved in the treatment and education of their children.

  - Advocacy need not be confrontational.

  - A common way to advocate is through active involvement in IEP meetings.

  - Teachers should encourage parent advocacy but respect parents who do not wish to be involved in this way.

▼ INTERNET RESOURCES

Parent and Professional Organizations

- The U.S. Department of Education's *My Child's Special Needs: Disabilities* website (http://www2.ed.gov/parents/needs/speced/edpicks.jhtml) offers several resources for parents of children with disabilities.

- The Washington State Fathers' Network (www.fathersnetwork.org) is devoted to information for fathers of children with disabilities and special health needs.

- Parents of children with severe disabilities often benefit from respite care (short-term, temporary care that allows parents to have some time to themselves). The National Respite Care Network (http://archrespite.org/home) features a respite care locator and other valuable services.

- Fiesta Educativa (www.fiestaeducativa.org) provides information for Spanish-speaking families that have a child with a disability.

- The National Center for Learning Disabilities website contains a variety of information for parents, including how to be advocates for their children. (http://www.ncld.org/parents-child-disabilities/ld-rights/how-parents-can-be-advocates-for-their-children).

- Founded in 1969, Parents Anonymous, Inc. (http://parentsanonymous.org), offers a number of resources for parents of children with or without disabilities.

- Wrightslaw (http://www.wrightslaw.com) specializes in legal advocacy for people with disabilities and their parents.

chapter five

LEARNERS WITH INTELLECTUAL AND DEVELOPMENTAL DISABILITIES

Angela Hampton/Bubbles Photolibrary/Alamy Stock Photo

▶ LEARNING OUTCOMES

Learning Outcome 5.1: Understand why the term *intellectual disabilities* is used rather than *mental retardation*, how professionals define intellectual disabilities, and the prevalence of intellectual disabilities.

Learning Outcome 5.2: Learn the causes of intellectual disabilities.

Learning Outcome 5.3: Learn about assessments used to identify intellectual disabilities and some of the psychological and

behavioral characteristics of learners with intellectual disabilities.

Learning Outcome 5.4: Understand some of the educational considerations for people with intellectual disabilities and how professionals assess progress in academics and adaptive behavior.

Learning Outcome 5.5: Learn about issues that should be considered with respect to early intervention and transition to adulthood for learners with intellectual disabilities.

MISCONCEPTIONS ABOUT Learners with Intellectual and Developmental Disabilities

MYTH Professionals agree about the definition of intellectual disabilities.

FACT Considerable disagreement exists among professionals about definition, classification, and terminology.

MYTH Once diagnosed as having intellectual disabilities, a person retains this classification for life.

FACT A person's level of intellectual functioning doesn't necessarily remain stable; this is particularly true for those individuals who have mild intellectual disabilities. With intensive educational programming, some persons can improve to the point that they are no longer classified as having intellectual disabilities.

MYTH Intellectual disability is defined by how a person scores on an IQ test.

FACT The most commonly used definition specifies that an individual must meet two criteria in order to be considered as having intellectual disabilities: (1) low intellectual functioning and (2) low adaptive skills.

MYTH In most cases, it's easy to identify the cause of intellectual disability.

FACT Although the mapping of the human genome has increased our knowledge about causes of intellectual disabilities, it's still difficult to pinpoint the cause of intellectual disabilities in many people, especially those with mild intellectual disabilities.

MYTH Psychosocial factors are the cause of the vast majority of cases of mild intellectual disabilities.

FACT Exact percentages aren't available, but researchers are finding more and more genetic syndromes that result in mild intellectual disabilities; hereditary factors are also involved in some cases.

MYTH The teaching of vocational skills to students with intellectual disabilities is best reserved for secondary school and beyond.

FACT Many authorities now believe it appropriate to introduce vocational content in elementary school to students with intellectual disabilities.

MYTH People with intellectual disabilities should not be expected to work in the competitive job market.

FACT More and more people who have intellectual disabilities hold jobs in competitive employment. Many are helped through supportive employment situations, in which a job coach helps them and their employer adapt to the workplace.

GUIDING QUESTIONS

- Why are most professionals now using the term *intellectual disabilities* instead of *mental retardation?*
- How do professionals define *intellectual disabilities?*
- What is the prevalence of intellectual disabilities?
- What causes intellectual disabilities?
- What methods of assessment are used to identify individuals with intellectual disabilities?
- What are some of the psychological and behavioral characteristics of learners with intellectual disabilities?

- What are some educational considerations for learners with intellectual disabilities?
- What issues should educators and other professionals consider with respect to early intervention for learners with intellectual disabilities?
- What are some important considerations with respect to transition to adulthood for learners with intellectual disabilities?

The education of students with intellectual disabilities has undergone remarkable changes in the past several years, in terms of both the quantity and the quality of services. Although teaching and parenting a child with intellectual disabilities still means meeting and overcoming many challenges, today, there are many more reasons for optimism. Teachers and other professionals are better prepared to use evidence-based treatments, and parents can look around and see examples of adults with intellectual disabilities who are holding jobs in competitive or semi-competitive work environments and living independently or semi-independently in the community.

Much of the success being achieved by people with intellectual disabilities is attributed to a change in philosophy that includes respecting their rights to be a part of decisions affecting their lives and emphasizing the use of natural supports. Later in the chapter, we discuss the important philosophical changes that have brought about the emphasis on self-determination and **natural supports**.

People with intellectual disabilities need more than well-intentioned philosophies to ensure that they reach their full potential with respect to independent employment and community living. They often need years of intensive instruction from special educators, working in tandem with other professionals, including general educators, to put the philosophies of self-determination and natural supports into effect.

Other changes have also had a profound effect on the field of intellectual disabilities in the past several years. Among the most significant is that this field has undergone a name change from *mental retardation* to *intellectual and developmental disabilities*.

WHAT'S IN A NAME? *MENTAL RETARDATION VERSUS INTELLECTUAL AND DEVELOPMENTAL DISABILITIES*

In January, 2007, the major professional organization for people with significant cognitive or intellectual disabilities—the American Association on Mental Retardation (AAMR)—changed its name to the American Association on Intellectual and Developmental Disabilities (AAIDD). To understand the reasons for this change, one needs to appreciate that throughout history people with subaverage intellectual abilities have been the subject of ridicule and scorn. Whatever name has been applied to these individuals by professionals has ended up being used pejoratively by the public. For example, it's probably surprising to many that as late as the early 1900s the terms *idiot*, *imbecile*, and *moron* were perfectly acceptable labels for those who, today, would be referred to as having severe, moderate, or mild intellectual disability or mental retardation, respectively. In fact, they were the "official" terms used by professionals and sanctioned by professional

FOCUS ON CONCEPTS ...

"Spread the Word to End the Word"

Conceived at the 2009 Special Olympics World Winter Games, the Spread the Word to End the Word campaign has been a catalyst for drawing attention to and for ending use of "retarded" or "retard" as an insult. The R-Word Website (r-word.org) provides testimonials, videos, and other resources, including a link whereby one can take a pledge not to use the r-word and to discourage others from using it. For example, they include examples of how you can respond when others, even friends and family members, use the r-word. As of November 9, 2017, over 710,998 people have taken the pledge.

The Spread the Word campaign has delivered its message in a number of ways, including public service announcements (http://www.youtube.com/watch?feature=player_embedded&v=oRUOL5Rm2XY).

---

organizations. Today, of course, very few would accuse someone of being overly politically correct if he viewed these terms as totally inappropriate and demeaning. A somewhat similar history has accompanied the term *mentally retarded*. Over the years it, too, especially its shortened form, *retard,* has come to be used as an insult.

The name change from AAMR to AAIDD did meet with some resistance, some of which continues to linger. Pointing to the historical use and abuse of terms such as *idiot,* some argue that trying to find a "slur-proof" term is fruitless. Others argue that, unlike *idiot,* the term *mentally retarded* has not become a slur except in its shortened form *retard*.

In 2010, federal legislation solidified the use of the term, *intellectual disability*. Public Law 111-256 mandated that *intellectual disability* replace *mental retardation* in many areas of the federal government. As of 2016, the term *mental retardation* was only being used in three states (Polloway, Bouck, Patton, & Lubin, 2017). You will note that we have titled the chapter, "Intellectual and Developmental Disabilities," but within the chapter, like many professionals, we've elected to go with the shortened term, *intellectual disabilities*.

Perhaps most important is that the term *intellectual disability* is actually more accurate than *mentally retarded* in describing the primary limitations of this group of individuals. One can also make the argument that *intellectual* is more accurate than *mental* because the latter is often used to refer to emotions, for example, *mental illness* (Glidden, 2006).

DEFINITION

The issue of defining intellectual disabilities or mental retardation has been contentious. For example, since the 1950s, the AAIDD has endorsed seven different definitions, with each successive clarification reflecting a more cautious approach to designating someone as mentally retarded or intellectually disabled. At least four reasons account for this more cautious attitude:

1. As we discuss later in the chapter, IQ tests are not infallible. Although they are the best measure we have of general intelligence and they are routinely used in the process of identifying people who have intellectual disabilities, a number of factors (e.g., examiner bias or lack of expertise or motivation of person being tested) can lead to their reduced reliability for individuals with low scores (Greenspan & Olley, 2015).
2. Professionals became concerned about the number of children from ethnic minority groups who were being diagnosed as having intellectual disabilities. For example, African American and Native American students are disproportionately identified by the public schools as having intellectual disabilities.
3. Some people believe that the diagnosis of intellectual disability results in a stigma that causes children to have poor self-concepts and to be viewed negatively by others.
4. Some professionals now believe that to a certain extent, intellectual disability is a socially constructed condition. For example, AAIDD conceives of intellectual disability not as a trait residing in the individual but as the product of the interaction between a person and her environment.

It's important to note that some of these points have not gone uncontested. For example, some authorities have argued that the AAIDD has gone too far in denying the existence of intellectual disability as an essential feature *within* a person (Baumeister, 2006). They acknowledge that all disabilities are socially constructed to a degree. For example, a deaf person's inability to hear would not be considered a disability if he were not living in a society in which virtually everyone communicated via spoken language. Likewise, a person with cognitive limitations would not be considered to have a disability except for the fact that intelligence is a critical factor for functioning in society. However, the fact is that not being able to hear what people are saying or to understand and solve problems puts a person at a distinct disadvantage in society at large.

Special educators are tasked with helping a person who has problems hearing or a person who has problems understanding to lead a productive and happy life. And in order to achieve these objectives, special educators address improving the inherent limitations such people have. At the same time, special educators (as well as society as a whole) should also be working to enhance society's awareness, understanding, and accommodation of persons with disabilities.

A number of researchers also have pushed back on the idea that ethnic minority students are overrepresented in special education. In fact, Paul Morgan and his colleagues have made the counterintuitive claim that minority students are *underrepresented* in special education (Morgan et al., 2015). It may be the case that schools are overreacting to criticisms of racial discrimination and, in questionable situations, are leaning toward non-identification.

It's beyond the scope of this textbook for us to go into this debate—the dispute involves relatively intricate statistical analyses. For the interested reader, we encourage you to read Morgan's research as well as those who challenge him (Skiba, Artiles, Lozleski, Losen, & Harry, 2015).

The AAIDD Definition

The current AAIDD definition reads as follows:

> [Intellectual disability] is a disability characterized by significant limitations both in intellectual functioning and in adaptive behavior as expressed in conceptual, social, and practical adaptive skills. This disability originates before age 18. (AAMR Ad Hoc Committee on Terminology and Classification, 2010, p. 1)

The AAIDD definition underscores two important points: Intellectual disability involves problems in adaptive behavior, not just intellectual functioning, and the intellectual functioning and adaptive behavior of a person with intellectual disabilities can be improved.

ADAPTIVE BEHAVIOR At one time, it was common practice to diagnose individuals as mentally retarded (intellectually disabled) solely on the basis of an IQ score. Today, we recognize that IQ tests are generally accurate but are not perfect. Furthermore, they are only one indication of ability to function. Professionals came to consider **adaptive behavior** in addition to IQ in defining intellectual disability because they began to recognize that some students might score poorly on IQ tests but still function well in their daily environment, e.g., be "streetwise"—able to travel via the subway system and resist involvement in gangs.

No single definition of adaptive behavior is universally accepted. One that many authorities see as theoretically sound is based on the notion that adaptive behavior consists of **social intelligence** and **practical intelligence** (Greenspan, 2006b). Social intelligence involves understanding and interpreting people and social interactions, such as being able to "read" when someone is angry, and not being gullible or easily tricked or manipulated. (We discuss gullibility in more detail later.) Practical intelligence involves the ability to solve everyday problems, such as preparing meals, using transportation systems, making change, using the Internet, and solving problems that are associated with particular job situations.

PEOPLE WITH INTELLECTUAL DISABILITIES CAN IMPROVE In the past, many authorities held little hope for significantly enhancing the functioning of people with intellectual disabilities; they essentially believed intellectual disability incurable. Today, however, the prevailing opinion is that the functioning of virtually all people with intellectual disabilities can be improved and that very few, especially those with very mild intellectual disabilities, can eventually improve to the point at which they are no longer classified as having an intellectual disability.

In agreement with the notion that intellectual disability is improvable, the developers of the current AAIDD definition hold that how well a person with intellectual disabilities functions is directly related to the amount of support he receives from the environment. The concept of supports is integral to the AAIDD's conceptualization of intellectual disabilities. The AAIDD defines **supports** as those strategies and resources that "a person requires to participate in activities associated with normative human functioning" (Thompson et al., 2009, p. 135). Supports can come in a variety of forms; for example, technological support (e.g., smart phones or tablets to provide a way of keeping in contact with others); social support (e.g., family, friends, and church members to offer assistance and friendship); organizational support (e.g., Best Buddies).

Classification of Intellectual Disabilities

Although AAIDD does not advocate such a classification scheme, most school systems classify students with intellectual disabilities according to the severity of their condition: **mild** (IQ of about 50 to 70), **moderate** (IQ of about 35 to 50), **severe** (IQ of about 20 to 35), and **profound** (IQ below about 20) **mental retardation** or **intellectual disabilities**, or a close approximation.

PREVALENCE

The average (mean) score on an IQ test is 100. Theoretically, we expect 2.27% of the population to fall 2 standard deviations (IQ = 70 on the Wechsler Intelligence Scale for Children, Fourth Edition, WISC-IV) or more below this average. This expectation is based on the assumption that intelligence, like so many other human traits, is distributed along a normal curve. Figure 5.1 shows the hypothetical normal curve of intelligence. This curve is split into eight areas by means of standard deviations. One standard deviation

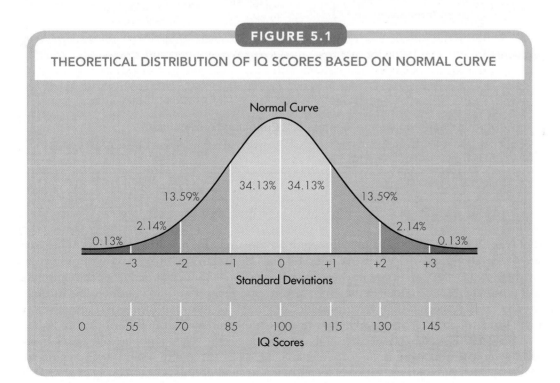

FIGURE 5.1

THEORETICAL DISTRIBUTION OF IQ SCORES BASED ON NORMAL CURVE

FOCUS ON

The Human Genome and ENCODE Projects: Ethical Issues Pertaining to Intellectual Disabilities

The U.S. Human Genome Project formally started in 1990 and ended in 2003. Among other things, the project has resulted in the identification of the 20,000 to 25,000 genes in human DNA and the sequences of three billion chemical base pairs that make up human DNA. The ENCODE (Encyclopedia Of DNA Elements) Project (http://www.youtube.com/watch?v=TwXX-gEz9o4w) began in 2003, with the goal of identifying all functional elements in the human genome sequence.

Practical benefits of the genome projects are that they help advance the ability to diagnose, treat, and eventually prevent genetic conditions, some of which cause intellectual disabilities. However, such potential breakthroughs have made some people uneasy. In addition to the usual questions related to such things as cloning and the creation of "designer babies," some have raised concerns specific to intellectual disabilities. For example, does the use of genetic information to prevent intellectual disabilities devalue the lives of those who have intellectual disabilities? In other words, does allowing people the option of preventing a disability send the message that people with that disability are less worthy of existence?

On the other hand, some argue that to renounce the use of genetic information to predict a disability in an unborn child can be ethically irresponsible, especially when the condition predicted is very likely to be severe. An example that's been used is that of Lesch-Nyan disease, which involves uncontrolled self-injurious behavior and requires almost constant restraint to prevent self-mutilation (Davis, 1997).

Of course, Lesch-Nyan is extremely rare, and most people with intellectual disabilities don't undergo such extreme suffering. However, these are the cases that make the issue of genetic testing so contentious.

---

equals 15 IQ points; 2.14% of the population scores between 55 and 70, and 0.13% scores below 55. Thus, it would seem that 2.27% should fall under 70. (See p. 89 for more on intelligence tests.)

However, the actual prevalence figures for students who are *identified* as having intellectual disabilities are much lower. In recent years, they have been well under 1%. Authorities surmise that this lower prevalence figure is due to one or a combination of three things: School officials (1) increased their use of adaptive behavior in addition to an IQ score to diagnose intellectual disabilities; (2) exhibited a preference to label students with IQs in the 70s as having learning disabilities because it's perceived as a less stigmatizing label (MacMillan, Gresham, Bocian, & Lambros, 1998); and/or (3) increased their propensity to identify children as having an autistic spectrum disorder (ASD) because of increased awareness of this condition. (We discuss this again in Chapter 9.)

MyLab Education **Self-Check 5.1**

MyLab Education **Application Exercise 5.1: Changing Terminology**
Respond to a question about the shift in terminology used to describe people once categorized as having mental retardation.

CAUSES

The past 20 years or so have witnessed an upsurge in research that has increased our understanding of causes of intellectual disabilities (http://www.youtube.com/watch?v=dyjFJ19DF9Y). Some of these discoveries have come as a result of the mapping of the human genetic code by the Human Genome Project and its continuation through the ENCODE Project, which have provided a wealth of information related to causes of many human illnesses. These advances have also engendered a number of thorny issues.

Not all causes of intellectual disabilities are genetically related, nor are all causes traceable to biological causes. A large percentage of cases (probably about 50%) remain for which we can't pinpoint the cause of a child's intellectual disabilities (Polloway et al., 2017).

FOCUS ON

Down Syndrome and Alzheimer's Disease

Researchers first noted a high prevalence of senility in persons with Down syndrome well over a century ago (Fraser & Mitchell, 1876, cited in Evenhuis, 1990). In the early 20th century, post-mortem studies of the brains of people with Down syndrome revealed neuropathological signs similar to those of people with Alzheimer's disease (Carr, 1994). It was not until the 1980s and 1990s, however, that scientists started to address this correlation seriously.

According to the postmortem studies, virtually all people with Down syndrome who reach the age of 35 have brain abnormalities very similar to those of persons with Alzheimer's disease (Alvarez, 2008; Hof et al., 1995). Although not inevitable, behavioral signs of dementia, or mental deterioration, occur in well over half of people with Down syndrome older than 60 years of age (Margallo-Lana et al., 2007). Unfortunately, maladaptive behaviors such as aggression, fearfulness, and sadness often increase as the dementia advances (Urv, Zigman, & Silverman, 2008).

Findings that link Down syndrome to Alzheimer's disease have made researchers optimistic about uncovering the genetic underpinnings of both conditions. For example, researchers have found that a particular protein may be the key to the rapid onset of Alzheimer's in people with Down syndrome (Wallace & Dalton, 2011). Interestingly, no evidence shows that Alzheimer's occurs more frequently in adults whose intellectual disabilities are due to other causes (Alvarez, 2008).

A common way of categorizing causes of intellectual disabilities is according to the time when the cause occurs: **prenatal** (before birth), **perinatal** (at the time of birth), and **postnatal** (after birth).

Prenatal Causes

We can group prenatal causes into (1) **chromosomal disorders**, (2) inborn errors of metabolism, (3) developmental disorders affecting brain formation, and (4) environmental influences.

CHROMOSOMAL DISORDERS As noted previously, scientists are making great strides in identifying genetic causes of intellectual disabilities. A few of the most common of these genetic syndromes are Down syndrome, Fragile X syndrome, Prader-Willi syndrome, and Williams syndrome.

Down Syndrome Many, but not all, genetic syndromes are transmitted hereditarily. However, by far the most common of these syndromes, **Down syndrome**, is usually *not* an inherited condition. Down syndrome involves an anomaly at the 21st pair of **chromosomes**. In the vast majority of cases of Down syndrome, the 21st set of chromosomes (the normal human cell contains 23 pairs of chromosomes) is a triplet rather than a pair; hence, the most common form of Down syndrome is also referred to as **trisomy 21**. Down syndrome is the most common form of intellectual disability that is present at birth (Polloway et al., 2017).

Down syndrome is associated with a range of distinctive physical characteristics, but it's important to keep in mind that they vary considerably in number and extent from one individual to another, making each person with Down syndrome unique, just as each individual without disabilities is unique. People with Down syndrome may have thick epicanthal folds in the corners of their eyes, making the eyes appear to slant upward slightly at the outside corners. Other common characteristics include small stature, decreased muscle tone (hypotonia), hyperflexibility of the joints, a small oral cavity that can result in a protruding tongue, short and broad hands with a single palmar crease, heart defects, and susceptibility to upper respiratory infections (R. L. Taylor, Richards, & Brady, 2005). Evidence also indicates a link between Down syndrome and Alzheimer's disease.

The degree of intellectual disability among people with Down syndrome varies widely (Stancliffe et al., 2012), but most individuals fall in the moderate range. In recent

MyLab Education
Video Example 5.1

Down syndrome is associated with a number of physical characteristics and health conditions in addition to intellectual disabilities.

years, more children with Down syndrome have achieved IQ scores in the mild intellectual disability range than previously, presumably because of intensive special education programming.

The likelihood of having a child with Down syndrome increases with the age of the mother (Weijerman et al., 2008). In addition to the age of the mother, researchers point to other variables as possible causes, such as the age of the father, exposure to radiation, and exposure to some viruses. Research on these factors is still preliminary, however.

Methods are available for screening for Down syndrome and some other birth defects. These methods include the following:

- **Maternal serum screening (MSS)**: A blood sample is taken from the mother and screened for the presence of certain elements that indicate the possibility of **spina bifida** (a condition in which the spinal column fails to close properly) or Down syndrome. If the results are positive, the physician can recommend a more accurate test, such as amniocentesis or chorionic villus sampling.
- **Amniocentesis**: The physician takes a sample of amniotic fluid from the sac around the fetus and analyzes the fetal cells for chromosomal abnormalities. In addition, the amniotic fluid can be tested for the presence of proteins that may have leaked out of the fetus's spinal column, indicating the presence of spina bifida.
- **Chorionic villus sampling (CVS)**: The physician takes a sample of villi (structures that later become the placenta) and tests them for chromosomal abnormalities. One advantage of CVS is that it can be done earlier than amniocentesis.
- **Nuchal translucency ultrasound**: This non-invasive procedure allows the physician to see the fluid from behind the fetus's neck; this can also be done earlier than amniocentesis. A greater than normal amount of fluid indicates the possibility of Down syndrome.

Fragile X Syndrome Fragile X syndrome is the most common known hereditary cause of intellectual disabilities. And it's the second most common syndrome, after Down syndrome, that causes intellectual disabilities (Polloway et al., 2017). In association with intellectual disabilities, Fragile X syndrome occurs in 1 in 4,000 males and 1 in 6,000 females (Meyer & Batshaw, 2002). In association with milder cognitive deficits, such as learning disabilities, the prevalence may be as high as 1 in 2,000 (Hagerman, 2001). It is associated with the X chromosome in the 23rd pair of chromosomes. In males, the 23rd pair consists of an X and a Y chromosome; in females, it consists of two X chromosomes. This disorder is called Fragile X syndrome because in affected individuals, the bottom of the X chromosome is pinched off in some of the blood cells. Fragile X occurs less often in females because they have an extra X chromosome, giving them better protection if one of their X chromosomes is damaged. People with Fragile X syndrome may have a number of physical features, such as a large head; large, flat ears; a long, narrow face; a prominent forehead; a broad nose; a prominent, square chin; large testicles; and large hands with nontapering fingers. Although this condition usually results in moderate rather than severe intellectual disabilities, the effects are highly variable; some people have less severe cognitive deficiencies and some, especially females, score in the normal range of intelligence (Dykens, Hodapp, & Finucane, 2000).

Prader-Willi Syndrome Prader-Willi syndrome is the result of a genetic abnormality, but very few cases are inherited. Prader-Willi syndrome has two distinct phases. Infants are lethargic and have difficulty eating. Starting at about 1 year of age, however, they become obsessed with food. In fact, Prader-Willi is the leading genetic cause of obesity. Although a vulnerability to obesity is usually their most serious medical problem, people with Prader-Willi are also at risk for a variety of other health problems, including short stature due to growth hormone deficiencies; heart defects; sleep disturbances, such as excessive daytime drowsiness and **sleep apnea** (cessation of breathing while sleeping); and **scoliosis** (curvature of the spine). The degree of intellectual disability varies, but the majority of individuals with Prader-Willi fall within the mild intellectual disability range, and some have IQs in the normal range (R. L. Taylor et al., 2005).

Williams Syndrome Williams syndrome is caused by the absence of material on the seventh pair of chromosomes. People with Williams syndrome have intellectual disabilities in the mild to moderate range (Mervis & Becerra, 2007). In addition, they often have heart defects, an unusual sensitivity to sounds, and "elfin" facial features. Williams syndrome typically occurs without any prior family history of the condition. In other words, it's not typically inherited; however, people who have Williams syndrome can pass it on to each of their children (Haldeman-Englert, 2008).

INBORN ERRORS OF METABOLISM **Inborn errors of metabolism** result from inherited deficiencies in enzymes used to metabolize basic substances in the body, such as amino acids, carbohydrates, vitamins, or trace elements (Medline Plus, 2007). One of the most common of these is **phenylketonuria (PKU)**. PKU involves the inability of the body to convert a common dietary substance—phenylalanine—to tyrosine; the consequent accumulation of phenylalanine results in abnormal brain development. All states routinely screen babies for PKU before they leave the hospital. Babies with PKU are immediately put on a special diet, which prevents the occurrence of intellectual disabilities. For example, milk, eggs, and the artificial sweetener aspartame are restricted because they contain significant amounts of phenylalanine. The need for a special diet often requires that parents and the rest of the family become involved in the treatment. At one time, physicians thought that the diet could be discontinued in middle childhood. However, authorities now recommend continuing the diet indefinitely, for two important reasons: Those who stop the diet are at risk for developing learning disabilities or other behavioral problems, and women with PKU who go off the diet are at very high risk of giving birth to children with PKU.

DEVELOPMENTAL DISORDERS OF BRAIN FORMATION A number of conditions can affect the structural development of the brain and cause intellectual disabilities. Some of these are hereditary and accompany genetic syndromes, and some are caused by other conditions such as infections. Two examples of structural development affecting the brain are microcephalus and hydrocephalus. In **microcephalus**, the head is abnormally small and conical in shape. The intellectual disability that results usually ranges from severe to profound. No specific treatment is available for microcephaly, and life expectancy is short (National Institute of Neurological Disorders and Stroke, 2008).

Hydrocephalus results from an accumulation of cerebrospinal fluid inside or outside the brain. The blockage of the circulation of the fluid results in a buildup of excessive pressure on the brain and enlargement of the skull. The degree of intellectual disability depends on how early the condition is diagnosed and treated. Two types of treatment are available: surgical placement of a shunt (tube) that drains the excess fluid away from the brain to the abdomen or insertion of a device that causes the fluid to bypass the obstructed area of the brain.

ENVIRONMENTAL INFLUENCES A variety of environmental factors can affect a woman who is pregnant and thereby affect the development of the fetus she is carrying. One example is maternal malnutrition. If the mother-to-be doesn't maintain a healthy diet, fetal brain development might be compromised.

A variety of substances, from obvious toxic agents, such as cocaine and heroin, to more subtle potential poisons, such as tobacco and alcohol, have harmful effects on a fetus. In particular, **fetal alcohol spectrum disorders (FASD)** include a range of disorders in children born to women who have consumed alcohol while pregnant. One of the most severe of those disorders is **fetal alcohol syndrome (FAS)**. Children with FAS are characterized by a variety of abnormal facial features and growth retardation, as well as intellectual disabilities. Although it's difficult to predict the effects of particular amounts of alcohol on the fetus, virtually all authorities (e.g., the Centers for Disease Control and the American Congress of Obstetricians and Gynecologists) are urging women who are pregnant or likely to become pregnant to refrain from drinking any alcohol.

The hazards of radiation to an unborn fetus have been recognized for some time. For example, physicians are cautious not to expose pregnant women to X-rays unless absolutely necessary, and the public has become concerned over the potential dangers of radiation from improperly designed or supervised nuclear power plants.

Infections in the mother-to-be can also affect the developing fetus and result in intellectual disabilities. A highly publicized relatively recent example is that of the outbreak of the **Zika virus** (spread by mosquito bites) in 2015 and 2016 in South America (especially Brazil) and Central America. When pregnant women are infected, they are at a very high risk of giving birth to babies with microcephaly and its resulting intellectual disability (McNeil, Romero, & Tavernise, 2016).

Rubella (German measles), in addition to being a potential cause of blindness, can also result in intellectual disabilities. Rubella is most dangerous during the first trimester (3 months) of pregnancy.

Perinatal Causes

A variety of problems occurring while giving birth can result in brain injury and intellectual disabilities. For example, if the child is not positioned properly in the uterus, brain injury can result during delivery. One problem that sometimes occurs because of difficulty during delivery is **anoxia** (complete deprivation of oxygen).

Low birthweight (LBW) can result in a variety of behavioral and medical problems, including intellectual disabilities (H. G. Taylor, Klein, Minich, & Hack, 2000). Because most babies with LBW are premature, the two terms—*LBW* and *premature*—are often used synonymously. LBW is usually defined as 5.5 pounds or lower, and it is associated with a number of factors: poor nutrition, teenage pregnancy, drug abuse, and excessive cigarette smoking. LBW is more common in mothers living in poverty. And surprisingly, worldwide, only Africa has a higher rate of premature births than North America (United States and Canada combined), with Asia and Latin America having a lower rate than the United States (Beck et al., 2010).

Infections such as **syphilis** and **herpes simplex** can be passed from mother to child during childbirth. These venereal diseases can potentially result in intellectual disabilities. (Herpes simplex, which shows as cold sores or fever blisters, is not usually classified as a venereal disease unless it affects the genitals.)

Postnatal Causes

We can group causes of intellectual disabilities occurring after birth into two very broad categories: those that are biological in nature and those that are psychosocial in nature.

BIOLOGICAL POSTNATAL CAUSES
Examples of biological postnatal causes are infections, malnutrition, and toxins. **Meningitis** and **encephalitis** are two examples of infections that can cause intellectual disabilities. Meningitis is an infection of the covering of the brain that may be caused by a variety of bacterial or viral agents. Encephalitis, an inflammation of the brain, results more often in intellectual disabilities and usually affects intelligence more severely. One of the toxins, or poisons, that's been linked to intellectual disabilities is lead. Although lead in paint is now prohibited, in impoverished areas where lead paint is common in housing, infants still become poisoned by eating lead-based paint chips. The effect of lead poisoning on children varies; high lead levels can result in death.

PSYCHOSOCIAL POSTNATAL CAUSES
Children who are raised in poor environmental circumstances are at risk for intellectual disabilities. It should be obvious that extreme cases of abuse, neglect, or understimulation can result in intellectual disabilities. However, most authorities believe that less severe environmental factors, such as inadequate exposure to stimulating adult–child interactions, poor teaching, and lack of reading materials, also can result in intellectual disabilities, especially mild intellectual disability. For example, in one large-scale study of 267,277 children, those who were born to teenage mothers who had fewer than 12 years of education were at increased risk for mild and moderate intellectual disabilities (Chapman, Scott, & Mason, 2002).

Although environmental causes of mild intellectual disabilities are undeniable, heredity can also play a role. For example, in a major study of heredity and mild intellectual disabilities, researchers looked at the degree of similarity in intellectual performance of monozygotic twins versus similarity in performance of dizygotic twins (Spinath, Harlaar,

Ronald, & Plomin, 2004). Monozygotic, or identical, twins come from the same egg and have the same genetic makeup. Dizygotic, or fraternal, twins come from separate eggs. In those who scored in the mild intellectual disability range, the degree of similarity was much higher in monozygotic twins than in dizygotic twins, thus indicating high heritability.

For many years, it's been assumed that psychosocial factors are the cause of the vast majority of cases of mild intellectual disabilities, whereas organic, or biological, factors are the cause of more severe intellectual disabilities. In recent years, however, authorities have begun to suspect that many cases of mild intellectual disabilities might be caused by specific genetic syndromes (Dykens et al., 2000; Hodapp & Dykens, 2007; Polloway, Smith, & Antoine, 2010). They point to the many cases of people with Prader-Willi syndrome and Williams syndrome, as well as females with Fragile X syndrome, who have mild intellectual disabilities, and they speculate that in the near future, new genetic syndromes will be discovered as causes of mild intellectual disabilities.

MyLab Education Self-Check 5.2
MyLab Education Application Exercise 5.2: Overview of Causes
This exercise asks you to create a graphic organizer to represent the causes of intellectual disabilities.

IDENTIFICATION

Assessment to determine whether a person has an intellectual disability addresses two major areas: intelligence and adaptive behavior.

Intelligence Tests

Many types of IQ tests are available. Because of the accuracy and predictive capabilities of IQ tests, school psychologists use individually administered tests rather than group tests when identifying students for special education. One of the most commonly used IQ tests for children is the WISC-V (Wechsler, 2003). The WISC-V consists of a Full-Scale IQ, as well as four composite scores: Verbal Comprehension, Perceptual Reasoning, Working Memory, and Processing Speed.

Although not all IQ tests call for this method of calculation, dividing mental age (the age level at which a person is functioning) by chronological age and multiplying by 100 provides a rough approximation of a person's IQ score. For example, a 10-year-old student who performs on an IQ test as well as the average 8-year-old (and thus has a mental age of 8 years) would have an IQ score of 80.

Compared to many psychological tests, IQ tests such as the WISC-V are among the most valid: The instrument measures what it is supposed to measure. A good indicator of the validity of an IQ test is the fact that it is generally considered the best single index of how well a student will do in school. It's wise to be wary, however, of placing too much faith in a single score from any IQ test. There are at least four reasons for caution:

1. An individual's IQ score can change from one testing to another, and although not common, sometimes the change can be dramatic (Whitaker, 2008).
2. All IQ tests are culturally biased to a certain extent. Largely because of differences in language and experience, people from minority groups are sometimes at a disadvantage in taking such tests.
3. The younger the child, the less validity the test has. Infant intelligence tests are particularly questionable.
4. IQ tests are not the absolute determinant when it comes to assessing a person's ability to function in society. A superior IQ score does not guarantee a successful and happy life, and a low IQ score does not doom a person to a miserable existence. Other variables are also important determinants of a person's coping skills in society. That is why, for example, professionals also assess adaptive behavior.

Adaptive Behavior

The basic format of instruments used to measure adaptive behavior requires that a parent, teacher, or other professional answer questions related to the person's ability to perform adaptive skills. We discuss some of these measures later in the section entitled, "Assessment of Adaptive Behavior."

PSYCHOLOGICAL AND BEHAVIORAL CHARACTERISTICS

Some of the major areas in which people with intellectual disabilities are likely to experience deficits are attention, memory, language, self-regulation, motivation, and social development. In considering psychological and behavioral characteristics, remember that a given individual with intellectual disabilities may not display all of these characteristics.

The importance of attention for learning is critical. A person must be able to attend to the task at hand before he can learn it. Often attending to the wrong things, persons with intellectual disabilities have difficulty allocating their attention properly.

People with intellectual disabilities have widespread memory difficulties, but they often have particular problems with working memory (Levorato, Roch, & Florit, 2011). **Working memory (WM)** involves the ability to keep information in mind while simultaneously doing another cognitive task. Trying to remember an address while listening to instructions on how to get there is an example of working memory.

Virtually all persons with intellectual disabilities have limitations in language comprehension and production. The exact types of problems depend largely on the cause of their intellectual disabilities (Abbeduto, Keller-Bell, Richmond, & Murphy, 2006).

Self-regulation is a broad term referring to the ability to regulate one's own behavior. People who have intellectual disabilities also have difficulties with metacognition, which is closely connected to the ability to self-regulate (Bebko & Luhaorg, 1998). **Metacognition** refers to a person's awareness of what strategies are needed to perform a task, the ability to plan how to use the strategies, and the evaluation of how well the strategies are working. Self-regulation is thus a component of metacognition. (We discuss metacognition again in Chapter 6.)

A key to understanding the behavior of persons with intellectual disabilities is to appreciate their problems with motivation (Switsky, 2006). Having usually experienced a long history of failure, they are likely to believe that they have little control over what happens to them. Therefore, they tend to look for external rather than internal sources of motivation.

People with intellectual disabilities are prime candidates for a variety of social problems. In addition to having difficulties making friends due to inappropriate behavior, they often lack awareness of how to respond in social situations (Snell et al., 2009). In fact, some researchers maintain that it is more accurate to consider social-emotional problems, such as mood disorders, obsessive-compulsive behaviors, and the like, as typical rather than rare (Woods, Freedman, & Derning, 2015).

UP CLOSE With The Late Robert Perske The only non-lawyer to be the recipient of the American Bar Association's Paul Hearne Award for Services to Persons with Disabilities, Robert Perske (1928—2016) (http://www.robertperske.com/Index.html) was a staunch advocate for people with disabilities for over 50 years. Perske attributed his dedication to society's most vulnerable citizens to his experiences as a 17-year-old soldier in the post–World War II, war-torn Philippine Islands. Perske's early career as the chaplain of the Kansas Neurological Institute, which served 250 children and young adults with intellectual disabilities, honed his sensitivities to people with intellectual disabilities. In his later years, Perske focused on exonerating people with intellectual disabilities who had provided false confessions to murder and/or rape.

FOCUS ON

Gullibility: From Puppets to the Supreme Court

One particular problem of responding in social situations that has received a great deal of research, especially in individuals with intellectual disabilities who have higher IQ scores, is gullibility. **Gullibility** can be defined as the "tendency to believe something, usually a highly questionable statement or claim, despite scanty evidence" (Greenspan, Loughlin, & Black, 2001, p. 102).

Stephen Greenspan, a prominent researcher in the field of intellectual disabilities, has made a strong case for social intelligence, gullibility in particular, as being the hallmark of intellectual disability, especially in those who have mild intellectual disabilities (Greenspan, 2004, 2006a, 2006b, 2009; Greenspan et al., 2001). Greenspan believes that gullibility likely results from a combination of cognitive and personality factors. The cognitive limitation is the inability to determine when something is a deceptive claim, and the personality factors relate to an overreliance on external motivational sources. Greenspan points to the character Pinocchio, from the classic 19th-century Italian children's novel of the same name, as the perfect example of someone who has mild intellectual disabilities by virtue of his gullibility. Made of wood, Pinocchio wants to be a "real" boy. He succumbs all too easily to temptation and being duped, with the outcome being his enduring a number of indignities. He eventually develops "social intelligence" and is able to return to his carpenter-maker, Gepetto, and turns into a flesh-and-bone boy.

The implications of gullibility beyond just marionettes from a children's fable are demonstrated by its role in how people with intellectual disabilities are dealt with by the legal system. Gullibility has figured into the wrongful conviction of numerous persons with intellectual disabilities. For example, false confessions are documented in at least 75 instances. Renowned advocate for persons with intellectual disabilities, Robert Perske, collected detailed information on dozens of these cases (Perske, 2008). (For more information on Perske, see *Up Close With Robert Perske*.) Just one example is of the case of Anthony Caravella, who was apparently harassed and beaten with a phone book by two policemen before confessing to the rape and murder of a woman in Miramar, Florida. There was no physical evidence tying Caravella to the crime, and he was found guilty primarily on police testimony. He said that he'd used a Pepsi bottle to hit her over the head—she had actually been stabbed and strangled. He referred to her as being a "girl"—she was actually 58 years old. Perske notes that a reporter, Maurice Possley from the *Chicago Tribune,* reported that Caravella said she was taller than he—she was eight inches shorter. He said he'd taken off her panties—they were partially on. Caravella served 26 years of a life sentence before being released based on DNA evidence.

The issue of gullibility of persons with intellectual disabilities has also been the topic of a landmark U.S. Supreme Court decision. After several years of debate in the courts, in 2002 the U.S. Supreme Court in *Atkins v. Virginia* ruled against the use of the death penalty for persons who have intellectual disabilities. Many of the arguments in favor of this decision focused on gullibility. Experts argued that, among other things, gullibility made such individuals vulnerable to being tricked into committing crimes without realizing their ramifications or to confessing to crimes that they had not actually committed (Patton & Keyes, 2006). The *Atkins* decision has also reinforced the claims of Greenspan and others that adaptive behavior, gullibility in particular, should figure more prominently in any future changes to the definition of intellectual disabilities (Greenspan & Switsky, 2006).

Linking Genetic Syndromes to Particular Behavioral Phenotypes

Until recently, most authorities paid little attention to the type of intellectual disability when considering behavioral characteristics. However, researchers have begun to find general patterns of behavioral characteristics, or **behavioral phenotypes**, associated with some of the genetic syndromes.

Researchers have identified the four genetic syndromes that we discussed in the section about the prenatal causes of intellectual disabilities—Down syndrome, Williams syndrome, Fragile X syndrome, and Prader-Willi syndrome—as having relatively distinctive behavioral phenotypes (Abbeduto, Murphy, et al., 2003, 2006, 2007; Dykens, 2001; Dykens et al., 2000; Fidler, Hepburn, Most, Philofsky, & Rogers, 2007; Hatton et al., 2003; Hodapp & Fidler, 1999; Mervis & Becerra, 2007; Moldavsky, Lev, & Lerman-Sagie, 2001; Roberts, Price, & Malkin, 2007). For example, people with Down syndrome often have significant impairments in language and grammar compared to visual-spatial skills; for individuals with Williams syndrome, the reverse is often true. In fact, the storytelling ability of the latter, including their ability to modulate the pitch and volume of their voices to interject emotional tone in their stories, together with their sociability and

TABLE 5.1 • **Links between genetic syndromes and behavioral phenotypes**

GENETIC SYNDROME	BEHAVIORAL PHENOTYPE	
	RELATIVE WEAKNESSES	RELATIVE STRENGTHS
Down syndrome	Receptive and expressive language, especially grammar Problems interpreting facial emotions Cognitive skills tend to worsen over time Early onset of Alzheimer's disease	Visual-spatial skills Visual short-term memory
Williams syndrome	Visual-spatial skills Math skills Fine-motor control Anxieties, fears, phobias Overly friendly Social relationships	Expressive language, vocabulary Verbal short-term memory Imitation of emotional responses Facial recognition and memory Musical interests and skills
Fragile X syndrome	Short-term memory Sequential processing Repetitive speech patterns Reading Social anxiety and withdrawal	Receptive and expressive vocabulary Long-term memory Adaptive behavior
Prader-Willi syndrome	Auditory processing Feeding problems in infancy Overeating, obesity in childhood and adulthood Sleep disturbances Obsessive-compulsive behaviors Math skills Working memory Social withdrawal	Relatively high IQ score (average about 70) Visual processing Facility with jigsaw puzzles

Based on data presented in: Abbeduto et al., 2003, 2007; Abbeduto, Murphy, et al., 2006; Bailey, Raspa, Holiday, Bishop, & Olmsted, 2009; Belser & Sudhalter, 2001; Dimitropoulos, Feurer, Butler, & Thompson, 2001; Dykens et al., 2000; Fidler et al., 2007; Fidler, Hodapp, & Dykens, 2002; Hatton et al., 2003; Hodapp & Dykens, 2007; John, Rowe, & Mervis, 2009; Kasari, Freeman, & Hughes, 2001; Mervis & Becerra, 2007; Mervis, Klein-Tasman, & Mastin, 2001; Moldavsky et al., 2001; Roberts et al., 2007.

elflike faces, have led to some speculation that the pixies, elves, or fairies depicted in folktales were people with Williams syndrome.

Table 5.1 lists some of the major behavioral characteristics associated with Down syndrome, Williams syndrome, Fragile X syndrome, and Prader-Willi syndrome. It's important to keep in mind that no one-to-one correspondence exists between the diagnosis and the characteristics. Not all individuals with each of these conditions will have all of the symptoms.

MyLab Education Self-Check 5.3

FOCUS ON

Williams Syndrome: An Inspiration for Pixie Legends?

English folklore is known for its depiction of "wee folk"—pixies, elves, fairies. The fact that people with Williams syndrome tend to possess facial characteristics similar to these figures —small stature, extreme sociability, and in fact, excessive friendliness (http://www.youtube.com/watch?v=gF4DiqEdN3w)—has sparked speculation among folklorists and biologists alike about whether the two were one and the same. Adding to this supposition is the fact that even though people with Williams syndrome usually have intellectual disabilities, sometimes they have a tendency to be lively storytellers and musically talented.

Historians and biologists have noted that folklore often serves the purpose of explaining real-life phenomena that are not very well understood. It is, therefore, not surprising that Williams syndrome has been linked to folktales of pixies and elves (Lenhoff, 1999). What's not clear is whether belief in elves and the like laid the foundation for society to consider people with Williams syndrome to be elves or vice versa. Given the extremely long history of many kinds of other-worldly beings, such as trolls, fairies, mermaids, and leprechauns, living in a variety of countries, such as Scandinavia, Germany, Ireland, Scotland, and England (see https://en.wikipedia.org/wiki/Thomas_Keightley), it's a good guess that it's the former.

EDUCATIONAL CONSIDERATIONS

In general, the focus of educational programs varies according to the degree of the student's intellectual disability or how much support the student requires. For example, the lesser the degree of intellectual disability, the more the teacher emphasizes academic skills; the greater the degree of intellectual disability, the more the teacher stresses functional skills, such as self-help, community living, and vocational skills. In practice, however, all students who have intellectual disabilities, no matter the severity level, need some instruction in academic, self-help, community living, and vocational skills. We focus on the elementary school level here; we discuss preschool and secondary programming in later sections.

A major issue facing special educators is how to ensure that students with intellectual disabilities have access to the general education curriculum, as dictated by the Individuals with Disabilities Education Act (IDEA; see Chapter 1), while also being taught functional skills. The more severe the level of intellectual disability, the more complex the issue of access. Authorities recommend a merger of functional and academic curricular standards. Blending academics and functional skills is embodied in **functional academics**, teaching academics in the context of daily living skills. Whereas children who do not have disabilities are taught academics (e.g., reading) to learn other academic content (e.g., history), the child with intellectual disabilities is often taught reading to learn to function independently. In functional reading, the child learns academics to do such things as read a newspaper or the telephone book, read labels on goods at the store, and fill out job applications.

Educational programming for students with intellectual disabilities often includes two features: systematic instruction and reinforcement.

Systematic Instruction

Research documents that **systematic instruction** is critical for students with intellectual disabilities (Drasgow, Wolery, Chezan, Halle, & Hajiaghamohseni, 2017). Systematic instruction involves the teacher:

1. selecting a well-defined target behavior (e.g., student will learn to read 8 consonant-vowel-consonant words, student will learn to sort socks, underwear, and t-shirts in a dresser);
2. implementing instruction consistently with respect to such things as sequencing and prompting/cueing;

MyLab Education
Video Example 5.2
This video shows a lesson focused on functional academics.

MyLab Education
Video Example 5.3
This video shows a teacher using systematic instruction along with reinforcement.

3. teaching foundational skills before teaching more advanced behaviors;
4. having a plan for how much to assist the student with verbal (e.g., "Put your socks in the bottom drawer.") or physical prompts/cues (pointing to the socks and the bottom drawer;) or modeling (e.g., the teacher puts the socks in the bottom drawer);
5. monitoring student performance and using that information to make changes to instruction as needed.

Reinforcement

Research has consistently shown that students who are positively reinforced for correct responses learn faster. Positive reinforcement ranges from verbal praise to tokens that can be traded for prizes or other rewards. For students with severe intellectual disabilities in particular, the more immediate the reinforcement, the more effective it is. The goal is to reach a point when the student doesn't have to rely on prompts and can be more independent.

Service Delivery Models

Placements for school-age students with intellectual disabilities range from general education classes to residential facilities. The degree of integration into general education tends to be determined by the level of severity; students who have less severe intellectual disabilities are the most integrated. Although schools have come a long way since passage of Public Law 94-142 (now IDEA), which prevented schools from turning away students with intellectual disabilities, there are many who believe that much of the momentum to educate students with intellectual disabilities in general education has begun to stall (Wehmeyer & Shogren, 2017).

The most recent report to Congress on the Implementation of IDEA (U.S. Department of Education, 2016) indicated that only 16.9% of students served under the category of intellectual disability spend 80% or more of their day in general education classrooms. Almost half (49.2%) of students with intellectual disability are educated in the general education classroom less than 40% of the day.

Even students with severe disabilities, however, are sometimes placed in general education classrooms, with schools providing extra support services (e.g., a special aide or special education teacher) in the class. Researchers have found classwide peer tutoring to be an effective technique for helping to integrate students with intellectual disabilities into general education classrooms (Delquadri et al., 1983; Greenwood, 1991). (See the accompanying Responsive Instruction feature.)

Although not all authorities agree on how much inclusion should be practiced, virtually all agree that placement in a self-contained class with no opportunity for interaction with students in general education classes is inappropriate. When students with intellectual disabilities are included in general education classes, it's important that special and general educators work together to plan for students to succeed. Without this planning the students are likely to be inattentive and socially isolated (Carter, Hughes, Guth, & Copeland, 2005; Kemp & Carter, 2006).

ASSESSMENT OF PROGRESS

Assessment of students with intellectual disabilities focuses on a variety of domains, including academic skills, adaptive behavior, and quality of life. The academic skills of students with intellectual disabilities may be assessed using methods that are common across disability categories, such as curriculum-based measurement (CBM). Some students with intellectual disabilities participate in standardized academic assessments. Many students with intellectual disabilities, however, require accommodations to participate in standardized assessments or receive an alternative assessment method if they cannot participate in traditional assessments with accommodations.

RESPONSIVE INSTRUCTION

Meeting the Needs of Students With Intellectual Disabilities

CLASSWIDE PEER TUTORING

What the Research Says

In an effort to meet the instructional needs of students with mild intellectual disabilities within inclusive settings, researchers have explored instructional methods that provide the necessary structure, individualization, and level of corrective feedback critical for success for this population. One such method is classwide peer tutoring (CWPT) (Delquadri, Greenwood, Stretton, & Hall, 1983). CWPT involves the use of peers to provide instruction and feedback in a reciprocal format. Paired students have the opportunity to serve as a tutor and as a tutee during each session. CWPT procedures were designed to address the need for higher levels of active academic engagement for all students, but particularly for students with the greatest academic deficits (Greenwood, 1991).

Research Study

A team of researchers conducted a study to examine the effectiveness of CWPT on the spelling performance of eight students (four students with mild intellectual disabilities and four students with no disabilities) participating in a general education class (Mortweet et al., 1999). The students with mild intellectual disabilities were included in general education classrooms for spelling, a social activity period, and lunch. The CWPT model was compared to traditional teacher-led instruction during the spelling period. The investigators used the following structure for the CWPT sessions:

1. Each student with mild intellectual disabilities was paired with a peer without disabilities.
2. Tutoring sessions occurred four times a week for 20 minutes per day.
3. Tutoring materials included the list of spelling words, point sheets, and practice sheets.
4. The teacher assigned each pair to one of two competing classroom teams. (Points earned by the pairs contributed to daily team point totals.) Partners and teams were reassigned on a weekly basis.
5. During each session, students served as the tutor for 10 minutes and as the tutee for the other 10 minutes.
6. Instruction consisted of the tutor reading the spelling word to the tutee. The tutee wrote the spelling word while saying each letter aloud. If the word was spelled correctly, the tutor awarded the tutee 2 points; if the word was spelled incorrectly, the tutor spelled the word correctly and the tutee wrote the word three times while naming each letter. The tutee could receive 1 point for correctly spelling the practice word. After 10 minutes, the roles were reversed.
7. The teacher assigned bonus points for pairs that were working cooperatively and following the instructional protocol.
8. When the 20-minute session was over, the teacher calculated team points on the basis of partner points. The winning team received privileges such as lining up first for recess.
9. Modifications made for the students with mild intellectual disabilities included shortened word lists, enlarged practice sheets, and tutee reading of words when the student with mild intellectual disabilities was the tutor and was unable to read the word.

Research Findings

When compared to the teacher-led condition, the CWPT resulted in improved academic performance for all students, increased amount of engaged academic time (approximately 5 to 10 minutes more per student per session), and positive acceptance from the teachers and students. Thus, CWPT provides teachers with a flexible instructional strategy to meet the varying needs of an inclusive classroom.

Applying the Research to Teaching

Given the effectiveness of CWPT, teachers can establish similar procedures in their classes. Tasks such as math facts, spelling, letter sounds, and word identification make great CWPT topics. Following the model established in the study, teachers can create their own tutoring materials. Key features of CWPT include partnering of a higher and a lower skilled student, explicit instruction in the tutoring activities (i.e., ample training before independent partner work), structured tasks for the tutor to guide the tutee in completing, reciprocal roles so the tutee has the opportunity to be a tutor, and use of points to reward desired behavior.

BY KRISTIN L. SAYESKI

Assessment of Adaptive Behavior

Assessments of adaptive behavior may be integrated with interventions so that services are provided in a data-based decision framework. One can use these assessments to provide outcome data on an individual's success following intervention. Typically, special educators or other professionals measure adaptive behavior indirectly, in that an "informant"

MyLab Education
Video Example 5.4

This video shows an example of Classwide Peer Tutoring being used with elementary-age students.

who is intimately familiar with the student provides information on a rating scale or in an interview (e.g., a parent, grandparent, teacher, or other primary caregiver). Several psychometrically sound instruments exist (Tasse et al., 2012). The Vineland Adaptive Behavior Scales—Third Edition (Vineland-3; Sparrow, Cicchetti, & Saulnier, 2016) is a popular measure of adaptive behavior for individuals from birth to 18 years. It includes several domains: communication, daily living skills, socialization, motor skills, and maladaptive behavior.

Assessment of Quality of Life

With the current emphasis on self-determination (which we discuss later in this chapter), more and more professionals are concerned with measuring the quality of life of persons with intellectual disabilities. However, measuring quality of life presents a challenge because a particular individual's perceived quality of life may differ from that of larger society (Brown & Brown, 2005; Cummins, 2005a). Consequently, outcome measures should include both objective and subjective measures that consider society's view of quality of life along with an individual's perceived level of satisfaction.

One measure commonly used to assess adolescents and adults with intellectual disabilities is the Quality of Life Questionnaire (QOL-Q; Schalock & Keith, 1993), which can be used with both English- and Spanish-speaking populations (Caballo, Crespo, Jenaro, Verdugo, & Martinez, 2005). It addresses five factors: satisfaction, well-being, social belonging, dignity, and empowerment/control (Schalock et al., 2002). A more objective scale is the BILD Life Experiences Checklist (Ager, 2003), which measures the extent to which an individual has ordinary life experiences. It comprises five areas including home, relationships, freedom, leisure, and opportunities for self-enhancement (Cummins, 2005b).

Testing Accommodations and Alternate Assessment

Testing accommodations are more likely to be used for students with milder intellectual disabilities, whereas alternate assessments are more likely to be used for students with more severe intellectual disabilities. Accommodations for students with intellectual disabilities on standardized tests can include modifications in scheduling, presentation format, and response format. Common scheduling accommodations include granting extended or unlimited time, or breaking the assessment into smaller, more manageable portions over several days. A typical presentation accommodation involves reading directions and problems to the student. Some students with intellectual disabilities may have physical difficulties and require response accommodations. For example, a student may dictate responses or use a tablet.

Alternate assessments are for students who can't be tested using traditional methods, even if accommodations are provided. Students with intellectual disabilities who participate in an alternate curriculum (e.g., life skills, vocational skills) instead of the general (more academic) curriculum may participate in alternate assessments. Alternate assessments should measure authentic skills, cover a variety of domains, and include multiple measures across time (Ysseldyke & Olsen, 1999). They can include direct observations of specific behaviors, checklists, rating scales, and curriculum-based measures. Several domains should be covered, for example, functional literacy, communication, leisure-recreation skills, domestic skills; and vocational skills (Spinelli, 2006).

MyLab Education Self-Check 5.4

MyLab Education Application Exercise 5.3: Who Is Star?

Watch a video featuring a little girl named Star, think about characteristics of students with intellectual disabilities, and then answer the questions that follow.

MyLab Education Application Exercise 5.4: Mini Case Study

Read a case study about Carrie, and respond to questions about the characteristics of students with intellectual disabilities.

SUCCESS STORIES: Nolan's Team of Parents and Professionals Helps Him Gain Access to the General Education Curriculum

Special Educator Sheryl Simmons: "Members of Nolan's team, including his parents, tailor materials to meet his needs in learning the general curriculum."

Nine-year-old Nolan Patrick Smith attends Sunflower Elementary School in Kansas.

These are the keys to his success:

- Intensive and strategic instruction
- Relentless collaboration among team members
- Specific goals and social supports

Nolan Smith, who has Down syndrome, is the second oldest of Kris Kohnke's and Sean Smith's four children. Within 3 weeks of his birth, Nolan started speech and language early intervention services. Intensive language and literacy instruction is still important to his success. Since he was an infant, Nolan has thrived on intensive, relentless, and specific special education.

- **Intensive and Strategic Instruction.** Nolan is now an outgoing 9-year-old boy with a broad range of cognitive abilities not easily summarized by a single score. He enjoys participating with children his age, but he struggles with reading, writing, and mathematics. Nolan reads at a first-grade level, and helping him move beyond sight words is a challenge. He's eager to decode text, and he has some strategies, but cognitive problems impede his progress. Handwriting is also challenging for Nolan, and he uses an adaptive keyboard for written assignments. "Nolan loves the computer," says Sean Smith. "Now the question is, how is he going to use it?"

  Nolan is easily distracted. Frequent prompts help keep him on task. "He can be silly, and the structure of the school day can be difficult for him," says Kris Kohnke. Nolan spends half the school day in third grade with 20 of his classmates. This year the focus of his inclusion is on academics (science and social studies) and social development. Nolan is learning that reading has a purpose, and he's eager to demonstrate what he knows. With the help of a paraprofessional, Nolan starts the morning with his classmates and goes to a quiet room for 60 minutes of intensive instruction in reading and mathematics with special educator Sheryl Simmons. He also gets strategic instruction in the resource room before joining his classmates for science, health, or social studies. "A visual approach works well for Nolan," says Mrs. Simmons, who adapts materials in visually stimulating formats to ensure he comprehends and can apply what he learns. According to his individualized education program (IEP), another successful strategy for Nolan is practicing answers to content-based questions

with an adult before sharing them with the class. This strategy reinforces his recall and reduces his tendency to stutter when he speaks.

- **Relentless Collaboration.** Much of Nolan's success depends on coordinated support from his parents, teachers, and therapists. "A real strength for Nolan is that he can understand concepts if we present them in multiple ways and in formats other than print," says Sean Smith. Nolan learned about rain forests through the efforts of relentless collaboration between home and school. His teachers modified a science study guide so Nolan's parents and his speech therapist could help him practice rain forest vocabulary. "By the time he took the pretest, he already knew the concepts of camouflage, endangered species, and global warming," says Sheryl Simmons. "He was so proud of his accomplishment."

  Collaboration with school personnel is a high priority. Nolan's parents meet every 3 weeks with Mrs. Simmons and Nolan's general education teacher to stay on top of communication and expectations for his progress. Nolan's annual goals are addressed but in the context of the third-grade classroom and curriculum. "With inclusion too many meetings happen 'on the fly,' and most IEP meetings are formal and nerve wracking," says Sean Smith. "By scheduling regular, informal meetings, we can talk more easily about Nolan and better target what he needs at school, and how we can support his learning at home."

- **Specific Goals and Social Supports.** Kris Kohnke and Sean Smith are strong advocates who want Nolan's goals to be practical and meaningful for him. This year's annual goals target sight-word vocabulary, reading fluency and comprehension, and building numeracy skills with money and time so Nolan can solve real-world math problems. Every other week he has a Lunch Bunch social skills group with the school counselor to strengthen his peer relationships. Nolan's goals for adapted physical education, and occupational and speech therapies help improve his physical coordination, self-care, and communication.

  Strengthening academic, functional, and social skills helps Nolan in his busy life outside of school. The four Smith children are active in their community, and Nolan is no exception. Lawrence Parks and Recreation's All-Star Sports and Special Olympics are a big part of his life, as are play-dates with teammate and best buddy, George. Nolan's parents

Continued

SUCCESS STORIES: Nolan's Team of Parents and Professionals Helps Him Gain Access to the General Education Curriculum

also make sure he participates in typical activities with his brother and sisters. "Sometimes it's hard on siblings when one child needs so much attention. Celebrations like the Down Syndrome Association's 'Buddy Walk' let Nolan's siblings see him in a positive way as part of a larger community," says Sean Smith. "This year 7000 people participated in Kansas City's celebration, and Nolan's sister said, 'look at all those other people with Down syndrome and their families and friends!'"

Reflecting on Your Own Professional Development: If you were Nolan's teacher . . .

- What are some areas about educating students with intellectual or developmental disabilities that you would need to know more about?
- What are some specific skills that would help you address his academic and behavioral challenges?
- What personal dispositions do you think are most important for you to develop in teaching students with limited cognitive abilities?

By Jean B. Crockett and Sean Smith

EARLY INTERVENTION

We can categorize preschool programs for children with intellectual disabilities as those intended to prevent intellectual disabilities or those designed to further the development of children who have already been identified as having intellectual disabilities. In general, the former address children who are at risk for mild intellectual disabilities, and the latter are for children with more severe intellectual disabilities.

Early Childhood Programs Designed for Prevention

Toward the end of the 20th century, the federal government began providing funds for several infant and preschool programs for at-risk children and their families, with the goal being to research their effects. Most such programs have focused on families in poverty. The Rand Corporation conducted a thorough analysis of 19 of these programs and concluded that most were highly effective for children and parents alike (Karoly, Kilburn, Cannon, 2005). Some of the programs were center-based, some home-based, and some were a combination of center- and home-based. They improved such things as academic achievement and employment while reducing poverty, special education placement, delinquency, and crime. And these outcomes yielded cost savings to society ranging from $1.80 to $17.07 for each dollar spent on the program.

Early Childhood Programs Designed to Further Development

Early childhood programs designed to enhance the development of children already identified with intellectual disabilities place a great deal of emphasis on language and conceptual development. Because these children often have multiple disabilities, other professionals—for example, speech therapists and physical therapists—are frequently involved in their education. Also, many of the better programs include opportunities for parent involvement.

Note in the accompanying Success Stories feature, for example, how much Nolan Smith's parents have collaborated with his teachers and therapists. Through practice with their children, parents can reinforce some of the skills that teachers work on. For example, parents of infants with physical disabilities, such as cerebral palsy, can learn from physical therapists the appropriate ways of handling their children to further their physical development. Similarly, parents can learn appropriate feeding techniques from speech therapists.

TRANSITION TO ADULTHOOD

In secondary school, the vast majority of students with intellectual disabilities take at least one vocational course and a life skills/social skills course. And when they do take general education courses, the majority receive a modified general education curriculum (Institute of Education Sciences, National Center for Special Education Research, 2009).

Although most authorities agree that the degree of emphasis on transition programming should be greater for older students, they also believe that such programming should begin in the elementary years. Three major areas to consider in planning for adulthood are life skills, employment skills, and self-determination skills. (See Figure 5.2.)

Life Skills

Life skills are one of those concepts that fit the colloquial expression, "I know it when I see it." Life skills are observable but hard to pin down with a precise definition. Most adults need these skills to live a fulfilling life by taking care of themselves and functioning in society. We have divided them into two categories: domestic skills and community skills.

Domestic and community skills have become more and more important with each passing year. It wasn't that long ago that professionals advised parents to place children with intellectual disabilities, even those with moderate intellectual disabilities, into

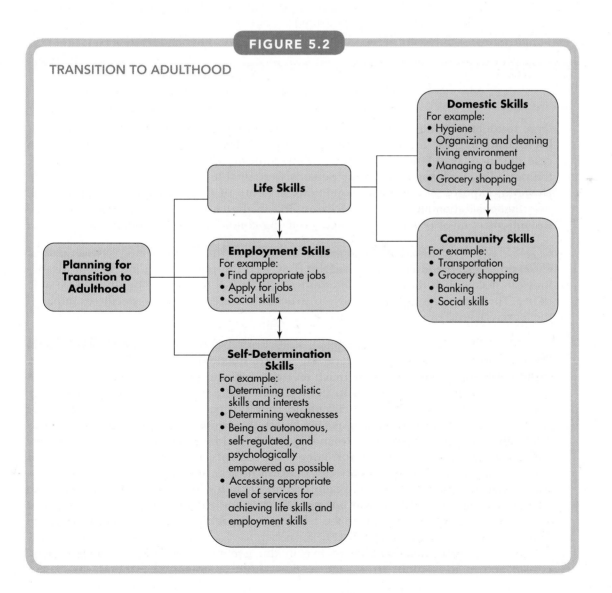

FIGURE 5.2

TRANSITION TO ADULTHOOD

Planning for Transition to Adulthood

Life Skills

Domestic Skills
For example:
- Hygiene
- Organizing and cleaning living environment
- Managing a budget
- Grocery shopping

Community Skills
For example:
- Transportation
- Grocery shopping
- Banking
- Social skills

Employment Skills
For example:
- Find appropriate jobs
- Apply for jobs
- Social skills

Self-Determination Skills
For example:
- Determining realistic skills and interests
- Determining weaknesses
- Being as autonomous, self-regulated, and psychologically empowered as possible
- Accessing appropriate level of services for achieving life skills and employment skills

The Changing Face of Living Options for People with Intellectual Disabilities

The early part of the 20th century in the United States witnessed an increase in the number of large residential institutions for people with intellectual disabilities. However, this growth was brought to a halt in the late 1960s. Not only was society beginning to be more accepting of individuals with intellectual disabilities, but there were several reports of overcrowding and sometimes abusive practices in these institutions. One of the most dramatic reports was *Christmas in Purgatory*, a pictorial essay on the squalid conditions of institutional life. Authored by Burton Blatt, a renowned advocate for persons with intellectual disabilities, and photographed by Fred Kaplan, this exposé was a major catalyst in turning the tide of public and professional opinion against large institutions (Blatt & Kaplan, 1966).

Although large residential facilities for people with intellectual disabilities still exist, as we noted earlier, they are fast disappearing. The trend is toward smaller **community residential facilities (CRFs)** (Lakin, Prouty, & Coucouvanis, 2006; Prouty, Coucouvanis, & Lakin, 2007). For example, since the 1970s, the number of residents with intellectual disabilities in CRFs has increased more than ten-fold, while those living in facilities of 16 or more has decreased more than three-fold. CRFs, or group homes, accommodate small groups (3 to 10 people) in houses under the direction of "house parents." Placement can be permanent, or it can serve as a temporary arrangement to prepare individuals for independent living. In either case, the purpose of the CRF is to teach independent living skills in a more normal setting than a large institution offers.

Some professionals question whether CRFs go far enough in offering opportunities for integration into the community. They recommend **supported living** (http://www.youtube.com/watch?v=9AWhEvWGrqY) in which persons with intellectual disabilities receive supports to live in more natural, noninstitutional settings, such as their own home, mobile home, condominium, or apartment. The idea is to enable them to choose to live in places that are available to typical residents in the community (Everson & Trowbridge, 2011). Some evidence shows that supported living arrangements lead to residents having more control over everyday choices (Ticha et al., 2012).

large residential institutions, and many of these children stayed there the rest of their lives. Living in these institutions meant that the residents' basic living needs were taken care of. There was little, if any, training in domestic or community skills because of the prevailing philosophy that such persons were unable to become more independent. However, exposés of inhumane conditions in some of these institutions triggered the **deinstitutionalization movement**, which resulted in the closing of many large residential institutions in favor of the more integrated living conditions we see today.

DOMESTIC SKILLS Domestic living skills involve such things as learning to wash dishes, cook, do laundry, and manage a budget. How well the person with intellectual disabilities can accomplish these tasks determines how independently he or she will be able to live. The accompanying Responsive Instruction feature provides a specific example of the "survival skill" of preparing meals.

COMMUNITY SKILLS Community living skills involve such things as using transportation, procuring health care, banking, going to restaurants, shopping for groceries, and so forth. These skills determine how much an individual can integrate into society. Special education teachers can do much to help prepare their students for community living (Everson & Trowbridge, 2011). For example, they can encourage them to volunteer for community service activities, such as Habitat for Humanity, soup kitchens, and the like. They can take field trips to local community residential facilities. And they can hold discussions of what their goals are for living arrangements, how to select a roommate, if they want one, and what skills they can perform now at home (e.g., help with laundry, washing dishes, house cleaning) to help prepare them for living more independently. In general, research has shown that attempts to train individuals for community survival skills can succeed, especially when the training occurs within the actual setting in which the individuals live (McDonnell, 2017).

In addition to skills needed to live in the general community, students can be encouraged to learn skills to engage in the school community (Dymond, 2017). For

RESPONSIVE INSTRUCTION

Meeting the Needs of Students with Intellectual Disabilities

USING TECHNOLOGY TO SUPPORT COOKING

What the Research Says

Independence is an important goal for many students with intellectual disabilities. Transition planning for students with intellectual disabilities typically includes strategies for promoting self-reliance through self-management and self-monitoring techniques (Sands & Wehmeyer, 2005). The process of food preparation, a valuable and economical aspect of independent living, has been studied by researchers for decades (Agran, Fodor-Davis, Moore, & Deer, 1989; Lancioni, O'Reilly, Seedhouse, Furniss, & Cunha, 2000; Martin, Rusch, James, Decker, & Trtol, 1982). The ability to prepare food creates the opportunity for both self-sufficiency and job employment. Researchers have used a variety of approaches, ranging from the use of static pictures to video modeling to video prompting to promote the development of independent cooking skills. Recent research has also looked to more portable, student-directed tools such as iPads, smart phones, or portable DVDs to promote multi-step skills such as cooking (Dymond, 2017). These technologies provide new avenues for support and independence.

Research Study

Mechling and colleagues (2008) had participants use portable DVD players as a support for completing cooking tasks. Three adults with moderate intellectual disabilities, ages 19 to 22, participated in the study. Each had the goal of preparing a simple meal as a part of his or her transition plan.

For the study, video segments of each step in the cooking process were created. Students could control the video by using the "Play," "Pause," and "Skip (Previous)" buttons on the portable DVD player. The modeling was provided from a subjective point of view (i.e., from the viewpoint of the student performing the task). To prepare the video, researchers conducted a step-by-step task analysis of the various cooking tasks (e.g., making grilled cheese, preparing a ham salad, cooking Hamburger Helper). The intervention included three phases: (1) teaching the students to use the DVD player—particularly, the play and repeat sequence process—to mastery, (2) cooking following the DVD self-prompting procedure, and (3) following the cooking steps without the DVD player. For each step in the video-prompting phase, students were evaluated as to whether they (a) successfully completed the step, (b) failed to complete the step, or (c) did not respond to the prompt. If a student failed to complete the step, three levels of prompting could occur. For the first prompt, a self-prompt, the student could replay the step using the skip/repeat function of the DVD player. For the second level of prompt, the instructor gave a verbal prompt. In the final level of prompt, the instructor completed the step.

Research Findings

All participants benefited from the intervention, as evidenced by an overall increase in the percentage of correctly completed steps. The steps that presented the greatest challenges were setting the digital timer, operating the stove dial, and waiting for the timer—all tasks involved in preparing the grilled cheese sandwich. Students did experience success in their ability to use the skip/repeat function of the DVD, but in many instances required instructor prompting to do so.

Applying the Research to Teaching

Teachers of students with intellectual disabilities can make use of the portable DVD player to support independent living tasks such as cooking. The dual advantages of relatively low-cost technology and student control through the play, pause, and repeat functions make portable DVD players a useful tool for teaching, which can transition with students as they move out of their educational settings. Teachers can create their own video models with prompts by following the steps established in the study by Mechling and colleagues (2008). After conducting a task analysis of skill, record simple video segments of each step. At the conclusion of each step, provide an auditory cue, "PAUSE," to prompt students to pause the video and conduct the step. Mechling and colleagues recommend identifying foods students like or activities students want to learn to increase student motivation and success with the tool.

BY KRISTIN L. SAYESKI

example, teaching students to become involved in attending school events and joining extracurricular clubs can help prepare them for developing skills needed for living in the broader, general community.

Employment

Overwhelming evidence shows that adults with intellectual disabilities have high rates of unemployment (Newman, Wagner, Cameto, & Knokey, 2009; Polloway et al., 2017). Although employment statistics for workers who have intellectual disabilities have been discouraging, most professionals working in this area are optimistic about the potential for providing training programs that will lead to meaningful employment for these adults. Research indicates that with appropriate training, individuals with intellectual disabilities can hold down jobs with a good deal of success, based on measures of attendance, employer satisfaction, and length of employment (McDonnell, Hardman, & McDonnell, 2003).

Schools often address preparing students with intellectual disabilities for employment by providing opportunities for them to gain experiences in the world of work. Some immediately place students in work settings, while others first introduce work experiences in the school setting and then gradually provide opportunities for working in real work settings (Drew & Hardman, 2007). For example, students might take field trips to various work sites, interview employees, or job-shadow an employee.

Once students with intellectual disabilities leave school, most of their employment options are subsumed under two very different kinds of arrangements: the sheltered workshop and supported competitive employment. Closely related to supported employment is customized employment.

SHELTERED WORKSHOPS A **sheltered workshop** is a structured environment in which a person receives training and works with other workers with disabilities on jobs requiring relatively low skills. This can be either a permanent placement or a transitional placement before a person obtains a job in the competitive job market. At one time, sheltered workshops were virtually the only type of employment available for persons with intellectual disabilities. Although sheltered workshops are still the most common work setting for individuals with disabilities (Winsor & Butterworth, 2008), more and more authorities are voicing dissatisfaction with these workshops. Among the criticisms are the following:

1. Workers make very low wages because sheltered workshops rarely turn a profit. Usually managed by personnel with limited business management expertise, they rely heavily on charitable contributions.
2. Sheltered workshops have no integration of workers who have disabilities with those who do not. This restricted setting makes it difficult to prepare workers who have intellectual disabilities for working side by side with workers without disabilities in the competitive workforce.
3. Sheltered workshops offer only limited job-training experiences. A good workshop should provide opportunities for trainees to learn a variety of new skills. All too often, however, the work is repetitive and doesn't make use of current industrial technology.

SUPPORTED COMPETITIVE EMPLOYMENT In contrast to sheltered employment, **competitive employment** provides jobs for at least the minimum wage in integrated work settings where most of the workers do not have disabilities. In **supported competitive employment** (http://www.youtube.com/watch?v=NRwo6AReqSA) the person with intellectual disabilities has a competitive employment position but receives ongoing assistance, often from a **job coach**. In addition to on-the-job training, the job coach might provide assistance in related areas, such as finding an appropriate job, interacting with employers and other employees, using transportation, and involvement with other agencies.

More research is needed; however, research now indicates that, when well-implemented, supported competitive employment leads to better employment outcomes (McDonnell et al., 2003). However, a couple of cautions are in order regarding supported competitive employment. First, research conducted thus far indicates that, similar to many reforms in special education, it is not yet being implemented widely enough to meet the demand. The funding and training required for proper implementation lags behind the research documenting its effectiveness. Second, although the ultimate goal for some adults with intellectual disabilities might be competitive employment, many will need supported employment for some period of time or even permanently.

In comparison to sheltered workshops, supported competitive employment is more in keeping with the philosophy of self-determination (discussed next). However, to achieve the goal of self-determination, clients should not become too dependent on their job coach. The role of the job coach therefore has changed in recent years. Many professionals now advocate that the job coach involve co-workers of persons with intellectual disabilities as trainers and/or mentors (Mank, Cioffi, & Yovanoff, 2003). After a period of time, the worker can be weaned from relying on the job coach and can learn to use more natural supports.

In addition to competitive employment, two other closely related employment models designed to foster self-determination are gaining in popularity: customized employment and self-employment.

CUSTOMIZED EMPLOYMENT Customized employment is similar to supported employment, but the latter has a stronger emphasis on individualizing and negotiating a job match (Inge & Moon, 2011). Customized employment involves four steps: (1) determining the interests and skills of the person with intellectual disabilities, (2) using that information to search for an appropriate job, (3) negotiating with the employer about how the person's skills are a match for what the employer needs, and (4) once hired, following up to ensure the individual has proper support and accommodations.

SELF-EMPLOYMENT As the term implies, self-employment refers to individuals who own their own business. In the case of persons with intellectual disabilities, this often means that a family member or close friend serves as a close "advisor" in helping them set up and maintain their enterprise. Good examples are businesses such as pet-sitting or housekeeping.

Self-Determination

A major goal of transition programming is to help persons with intellectual disabilities achieve as much self-determination as possible. Self-determination is the ability to act autonomously, be self-regulated, act in a psychologically empowered manner, and act in a self-realized manner (Wehmeyer & Mithaug, 2006). *Acting autonomously* means behaving according to your own preferences without dependency on others. Being *self-regulated* means evaluating and revising your own behavior. Being *psychologically empowered* means believing that you have control over events to the extent that you'll be able to influence desired outcomes. Being *self-realized* connotes knowing and accepting your own strengths and weaknesses and using that knowledge to attain goals.

Because people with intellectual disabilities have reduced cognitive ability, professionals and parents alike have traditionally considered them incapable of making their own decisions. In a sense, this paternalistic attitude often resulted in a self-fulfilling prophecy by not providing persons with intellectual disabilities an opportunity to take more control over their lives. Today, however, many professionals and parents champion the notion of promoting self-determination in persons who have intellectual disabilities.

One mistake that some of the more zealous proponents of self-determination make is to assume that self-determination will develop spontaneously in people who have intellectual disabilities. Given their history of learning deficits and vulnerability for developing **learned helplessness**, people with intellectual disabilities often find it difficult to become self-determined. Investigators have recently begun to develop methods of fostering self-determination (e.g., Devlin, 2011; Wehmeyer, Garner, Yeager, Lawrence, & Davis, 2006), but much more research is needed to determine the best ways to cultivate self-determination in students with intellectual disabilities.

An important consideration is that self-determination may be defined differently depending on the particular culture of the individual. Some cultures are more oriented toward valuing individuality and autonomy; others are less so. For example, some evidence indicates that Latina mothers of students with intellectual disabilities are less concerned with their children attaining independence as young adults because they value having them close to the family (Rueda, Monzo, Shapiro, Gomez, & Blacher, 2005).

One contentious issue related to self-determination regards the rights of persons with disabilities to have children and to be provided public social services to aid them in their parenting. Although becoming a parent may be out of the question for those who have severe disabilities, those with milder cognitive impairment can and do have children. Unfortunately, the research on parents who have intellectual disabilities is not definitive, but the available data suggest that these parents often face significant child-rearing challenges due to a combination of poverty and the lack of proper support systems (Tarleton & Ward, 2007). Research also suggests, however, that with appropriate support and systematic training, parents with intellectual disabilities can be successful parents (Kazdin, n.d.; Tymchuk, 2006; Wade, Llewellyn, & Matthews, 2008).

In keeping with the philosophy of self-determination programming, many professionals now recommend person-centered transition planning. **Person-centered planning** is similar to family-centered planning, which we discussed in Chapter 4, except that it focuses more on the individual than on the family. Person-centered planning is a consumer-driven model that encourages individuals to make their own decisions with respect to services while professionals mobilize resources and supports to help the individuals meet their goals.

Current employment figures and living arrangements for adults with intellectual disabilities might look bleak, but there is reason to be optimistic about the future. Outcomes for adults with intellectual disabilities are improving, albeit slowly, with respect to employment and living arrangements. With the development of innovative transition programs, many people with intellectual disabilities are achieving levels of independence in community living and employment that were never thought possible. Most of this success requires the collaboration of parents, students, and many professionals.

MyLab Education Self-Check 5.5

MyLab Education Application Exercise 5.5: Life Skills and Applied Academics

For this exercise, you will watch and respond to questions about two videos in which students participate in lessons that blend academics and functional or life skills.

MyLab Education Application Exercise 5.6: An Inclusive Protocol for Carlyn

For this exercise, click on the link to view the following video, and answer the questions about a little girl named Carlyn, in an early education setting.

MyLab Education Application Exercise 5.7: Vocational Training and Self-Determination

First, watch Evie Simmons-Reed take you on a tour of her high school's vocational training center. Next, watch Rachel, a 26-year-old woman with Down syndrome, at her job as a clerical assistant. Watch the videos, and then answer the questions that follow.

▼ chapter five SUMMARY

Why are many professionals now using the term *intellectual disabilities*?

- *Intellectual disabilities* is now used by many to refer to persons who, in the past, would have been designated as *mentally retarded*.
- The switch from *mental retardation* to *intellectual disabilities* is primarily due to the fact that the former, especially its shortened form, *"retard,"* has become a slur.

How do professionals define intellectual disabilities?

- The American Association on Intellectual and Developmental Disabilities (AAIDD) defines intellectual disability as "a disability characterized by significant limitations both in intellectual functioning and in adaptive behavior as expressed in conceptual, social, and practical adaptive skills. This disability originates before age 18."

Angela Hampton/ Bubbles Photolibrary/ Alamy Stock Photo

- The definition reflects two principles: (1) Intellectual disability involves problems in adaptive behavior, not just intellectual functioning, and (2) persons with intellectual disability can improve.

- Most schools and several professional organizations use the following classifications: mild (IQ score of about 50 to 70), moderate (IQ score of about 35 to 50), severe (IQ score of about 20 to 35), and profound (IQ score below about 20).

What is the prevalence of intellectual disabilities?

- From a purely statistical–theoretical perspective and relying only on scores on IQ tests, 2.27% of the population would be classified as having intellectual disabilities; however, fewer than 1% of the school-age population is identified as having intellectual disabilities.

- The reason for the lower prevalence in the schools is probably due to (1) schools using low adaptive behavior as well as low IQ scores as criteria and (2) a preference by some to identify students as having learning disabilities rather than intellectual disabilities because they perceive a learning disability to be less stigmatizing.

What causes intellectual disabilities?

- Prenatal causes include (1) chromosomal disorders, (2) inborn errors of metabolism, (3) developmental disorders affecting brain formation, and (4) environmental influences.

  - Chromosomal disorders include Down syndrome, Fragile X syndrome, Prader-Willi syndrome, and Williams syndrome. Down syndrome and Williams syndrome typically result from chromosomal abnormalities; Fragile X syndrome and Prader-Willi syndrome are inherited.

  - Phenylketonuria (PKU) is an example of a cause of intellectual disabilities due to an inborn error of metabolism.

  - Microcephalus and hydrocephalus are examples of disorders of brain formation.

  - Prenatal environmental influences include maternal malnutrition, fetal alcohol syndrome, and rubella (German measles).

  - Prenatal screening for Down syndrome and other conditions is available.

- Perinatal causes include anoxia (lack of oxygen), low birth weight, and infections such as syphilis and herpes simplex.

- Postnatal causes include those that are biologically or psychologically based.

  - Biological causes include traumatic brain injury and infections such as meningitis and encephalitis.

  - Psychosocial causes (e.g., inadequate exposure to stimulating adult–child interactions) can also cause mild intellectual disabilities.

  - Although environmental causes of mild intellectual disabilities are undeniable, heredity can also play a role. Most authorities now believe that heredity and environment interact to determine intelligence.

- Recent research suggests that many cases of mild intellectual disabilities are caused by specific genetic syndromes.

What methods of assessment are used to identify individuals with intellectual disabilities?

- Individual IQ tests are used to assess intelligence. The following cautions are important: (1) An individual's IQ score can change; (2) all IQ tests are culturally biased to some extent; (3) the younger the child, the less valid are the results; and (4) the ability to live a successful and fulfilling life does not depend solely on an IQ score.

- Adaptive behavior measures usually involve a parent, teacher, or other professional answering questions related to the person's independence and daily living skills and maladaptive behavior.

What are some of the psychological and behavioral characteristics of learners with intellectual disabilities?

- Major areas of problems for people with intellectual disabilities are attention, memory (especially working memory), language, self-regulation, motivation, and social development.

  - Some professionals have described the tendency toward gullibility as an aspect of social development that is particularly prevalent in persons with intellectual disabilities, especially those with mild intellectual disabilities.

- Researchers are beginning to link genetic syndromes to particular behavioral patterns, or phenotypes.

  - Down syndrome is linked to relatively low expressive language, relatively high visual-spatial skills.

  - Williams syndrome is linked to relatively low visual-spatial skills, relatively high expressive language skills.

  - Fragile X syndrome is linked to relatively low short-term memory, relatively high adaptive behavior.

  - Prader-Willi syndrome is linked to relatively low auditory processing and compulsive eating, and relatively high visual processing.

What are some educational considerations for learners with intellectual disabilities?

- The lesser the degree of intellectual disability, the more the teacher emphasizes academic skills; and the greater the degree of intellectual disability, the more emphasis there is on self-help, community living, and vocational skills.

- Authorities recommend a merger of functional and academic curricular standards, which can be accomplished by teaching functional academics.

- Effective teaching of students with intellectual disabilities involves *systematic instruction*: instructional prompts, consequences for performance, and strategies for the transfer of stimulus control.

- Although special classes for these students tend to be the norm, more and more students with intellectual disabilities are being placed in more integrated settings.

How do professionals assess the progress of students with intellectual disabilities?

- Curriculum-based measurement can be used to monitor *academic progress.*

- Interviews, observations, and self-reports, some of which are standardized, can be helpful in assessing *adaptive behavior.*

- Standardized questionnaires are available to assess *quality of life.*

- Accommodations for students with intellectual disabilities include modifications in
  - Scheduling (e.g., extended time)
  - Presentation format (e.g., reading directions to the student)
  - Response format (e.g., allowing the student to dictate responses)

- Alternate assessments for those who can't be tested using traditional methods, even with accommodations, may include direct observation of specific behaviors, checklists, and curriculum-based measures of functional literacy and leisure-recreation, domestic, and vocational skills.

What should educators consider with respect to early intervention for learners with intellectual disabilities?

- Preschool programs differ in their goals according to whether they are aimed at preventing intellectual disabilities or furthering the development of children who have already been identified as having them.

- In general, prevention programs are aimed at children who are at risk of developing mild intellectual disabilities, whereas programs for children who have been identified as having intellectual disabilities focus on children with more severe intellectual disabilities.

- Research supports the clear link between such interventions and success later in life.

What are some important considerations with respect to transition to adulthood for learners with intellectual disabilities?

- Promoting self-determination has become a major guiding principle in educating persons with intellectual disabilities.

- Transition programming involves two related areas: community adjustment and employment.

  - Community survival skills include managing money, using public transportation, and maintaining living environments. Large residential institutions are fast disappearing in favor of smaller community residential facilities (CRFs). Some people favor supported living, whereby people with intellectual disabilities live in their own apartment or home, over CRFs.

  - Two very different types of employment models are the sheltered workshop and supported competitive employment. Sheltered workshops offer structured training with other workers with disabilities on jobs requiring relatively low skills. Supported competitive employment involves receiving at least minimum wage in settings where most of the workers do not have disabilities, accompanied by ongoing assistance from a job coach. Two other models—customized employment and self-employment—share supported employment's goal of fostering self-determination.

▼ INTERNET RESOURCES

Professional Organizations

- Founded in 1876, the American Association on Intellectual and Developmental Disabilities (AAIDD) (http://www.aaidd.org/) is one of the oldest professional organizations in the world focused on intellectual disabilities.

- An organization that went to even greater lengths than AAIDD to change its name and avoid the term *mental retardation* is the Arc, formerly known as the Association for Retarded Citizens. The Arc (www.thearc.org) is primarily a parent organization and is a strong advocate for those with intellectual disabilities.

- The National Association for Down Syndrome (NADS) (www.nads.org) was founded in 1961 by a group of parents. Its Website provides information on resources as well as links to other sites devoted to Down syndrome.

- The Williams Syndrome Association (https://williams-syndrome.org/) is devoted to providing information to affected families.

- The National Organization on Fetal Alcohol Syndrome (http://www.nofas.org/) provides a variety of information for professionals and parents.

- The March of Dimes (http://www.marchofdimes.com/baby/premature_lowbirthweight.html) has information pertaining to low birthweight and its prevention.

- The National Fragile X Foundation (https://fragilex.org/) is devoted to providing information to affected families.

- The Prader-Willi Association (USA) (www.pwsausa.org/) is devoted to providing information to affected families.

chapter six

LEARNERS WITH LEARNING DISABILITIES

4X5 Collection/superstock

MISCONCEPTIONS ABOUT Learners with Learning Disabilities

MYTH IQ–achievement discrepancy is a straightforward, error-free way of determining whether a student has a learning disability.

FACT Numerous conceptual problems arise when using an IQ–achievement discrepancy.

MYTH Response to intervention (RTI) has been documented to be an error-free way of determining whether a student has a learning disability.

FACT Little research exists on RTI, especially when implemented on a large scale; therefore, many questions remain regarding how best to implement it.

MYTH All students with learning disabilities are brain damaged.

FACT Many authorities now refer to students with learning disabilities as having central nervous system (CNS) dysfunction, which suggests a malfunctioning of the brain rather than actual tissue damage.

MYTH The fact that so many definitions of learning disabilities have been proposed is an indicator that the field is in chaos.

FACT Although at least 11 definitions have been proposed at one time or another, professionals have settled on two: the federal definition and the definition from the National Joint Committee on Learning Disabilities. These two definitions differ in some ways, but they also have a lot in common.

MYTH The rapid increase in the prevalence of learning disabilities is due solely to sloppy diagnostic practices.

FACT Although poor diagnostic practices may account for some of the increase, there are plausible social/cultural reasons for it as well. In addition, evidence indicates that school personnel may "bend" the rules to identify students as having learning disabilities instead of the more stigmatizing identification of having intellectual disabilities.

MYTH We know very little about what causes learning disabilities.

FACT Although no simple clinical test exists for determining the cause of learning disabilities in individual cases, current research strongly suggests causes related to neurological dysfunction possibly resulting from genetic factors, toxins, or medical factors.

MYTH Math disabilities are relatively rare.

FACT Math disabilities may be just as prevalent (or close to it) as reading disabilities.

MYTH We needn't be concerned about the social-emotional well-being of students with learning disabilities because their problems are in academics.

FACT Many students with learning disabilities also develop problems in the social-emotional area.

MYTH Most children with learning disabilities outgrow them as adults.

FACT Learning disabilities tend to endure into adulthood. Most individuals with learning disabilities who are successful must learn to cope with their problems and make extraordinary efforts to gain control of their lives.

MYTH For persons with learning disabilities, IQ and achievement are the best predictors of success in adulthood.

FACT   The best predictors of success for adults with learning disabilities are perseverance, goal setting, realistic acceptance of weaknesses and ability to build on strengths, exposure to intensive and long-term educational intervention, and especially the ability to take control of their lives.

GUIDING QUESTIONS

- How do professionals define learning disabilities?
- How do professionals identify students with learning disabilities?
- What is the prevalence of learning disabilities?
- What causes learning disabilities?
- What are some of the psychological and behavioral characteristics of learners with learning disabilities?
- What are some educational considerations for learners with learning disabilities?

- How do professionals assess the academic progress of students with learning disabilities?
- What are some important considerations with respect to early intervention for learners with learning disabilities?
- What are some important considerations with respect to transition to adulthood for learners with learning disabilities?

Researchers, teachers, parents, policymakers, and even individuals with learning disabilities struggle to articulate the true essence of a learning disability (LD). The lack of ability of theoreticians and practitioners to define learning disabilities makes their existence no less real for the individuals who have them than if we were able to come to consensus on their definition and identification process. Millions of individuals with learning disabilities face academic and social problems and feel a sense of rejection and failure. At times, individuals without an understanding of learning disabilities have even perpetuated students' feelings of worthlessness. However, for individuals with learning disabilities there is opportunity for academic, social, and economic success.

The struggle to elucidate the nature of learning disabilities has often led to professional turmoil over the best ways to educate students with these disabilities. As the field has matured, however, greater consensus has developed about key issues, such as how to define and identify learning disabilities, what causes learning disabilities, and the best educational treatment approaches. Despite reaching a consensus, there is by no means unanimity on some of these issues. For example, healthy disagreements still exist with respect to the related issues of definition and identification. In fact, the American Psychiatric Association (APA) published the newest definition for "specific learning disorder" in the *Diagnostic and Statistical Manual of Mental Disorders, Fifth Edition* (DSM-V). In the following sections, we follow the history of the definitions and identification of individuals with LD.

DEFINITION

At a parents' meeting in the early 1960s, Samuel Kirk (1963) proposed the term *learning disabilities* as a compromise because of the confusing variety of labels that were being used to describe a child with relatively normal intelligence who was having learning problems. Such a child was likely to be referred to as *minimally brain injured*, a *slow learner, dyslexic*, or *perceptually disabled*.

Many parents as well as teachers found the label "minimal brain injury" problematic. **Minimal brain injury** refers to individuals who show behavioral but not neurological signs of brain injury. They exhibit behaviors (e.g., distractibility, hyperactivity, and perceptual disturbances) similar to those of people with real brain injury, but their neurological examinations are indistinguishable from those of individuals who do not have disabilities. Historically, the diagnosis of minimal brain injury was sometimes dubious because it was based on questionable behavioral evidence rather than on more solid neurological data. Moreover, minimal brain injury was not an educationally meaningful term, because such a diagnosis offered little real help in planning and implementing treatment. The term *slow learner* described the child's performance in some areas but not in others; and intelligence testing indicated that the ability to learn existed. *Dyslexic*, too, fell short as a definitive term because it described only reading disabilities, and many of these children also had problems in other academic areas, such as math. To describe a child as having *perceptual disabilities* just confused the issue further, for perceptual problems might be only part of a puzzling inability to learn. So the parents' group finally agreed on the educationally oriented term *learning disabilities*. Accordingly, they founded the Association for Children with Learning Disabilities, now known as the Learning Disabilities Association of America. A few years later, following the lead of the parents, professionals and the federal government officially recognized the term.

The interest in learning disabilities evolved as a result of a growing awareness that a large number of children were not receiving needed educational services. Because they tested within the normal range of intelligence, these children didn't qualify for placement in classes for children with intellectual disabilities. And although many of them exhibited inappropriate behavior disturbances, some of them did not. Placement in classes for students with emotional disturbance therefore was thought to be inappropriate. Parents of children who weren't achieving at their expected potential—children with learning disabilities—wanted their children's academic achievement problems corrected.

Several different definitions of learning disabilities have enjoyed some degree of acceptance since the field's inception in the early 1970s. Created by individual professionals and committees of professionals and lawmakers, each definition provides a slightly different slant. The two most influential definitions have been the federal definition and the definition of the National Joint Committee on Learning Disabilities (NJCLD). The definition of learning disorders in the *Diagnostic and Statistical Manual of the American Psychiatric Association* has played less of a role in the identification of children with LD in schools, although physicians use this definition frequently.

The Federal Definition

The majority of states use a definition based on the federal government's definition. This definition, first signed into law in 1975, was (with a few minor wording changes) adopted again in 1997 by the federal government and reauthorized in 2004. As we discuss in the next section, changes have occurred in identification procedures. However, the 2004 reauthorization of the Individuals with Disabilities Education Act (IDEA) did not change the definition contained in the 1997 reauthorization:

> GENERAL—The term "specific learning disability" means a disorder in one or more of the basic psychological processes involved in understanding or in using language, spoken or written, which disorder may manifest itself in an imperfect ability to listen, think, speak, read, write, spell, or do mathematical calculations.
> DISORDERS INCLUDED—Such term includes such conditions as perceptual disabilities, brain injury, minimal brain dysfunction, dyslexia, and developmental aphasia.
> DISORDERS NOT INCLUDED—Such term does not include a learning problem that is primarily the result of visual, hearing, or motor disabilities, of mental retardation, of emotional disturbance, or of environmental, cultural, or economic disadvantage. (IDEA, Amendments of 1997, Sec. 602(26), p. 13)

The NJCLD Definition

The National Joint Committee on Learning Disabilities (NJCLD), composed of representatives of the major professional organizations involved with students with learning disabilities, developed an alternative definition. They deemed it necessary to present their own definition because of dissatisfaction with the following factors in the federal definition:

1. *Reference to psychological processes:* Many of the early pioneers in the learning disabilities field believed that the processing of visual and auditory information, or the making sense of this information (as distinct from visual and auditory acuity problems of those identified as blind or deaf), was the underlying cause of academic problems, such as reading disabilities. Furthermore, they believed that training students in visual- and auditory-processing skills in isolation from academic material would help them conquer their reading problems (Frostig & Horne, 1964; Kephart, 1971; Kirk & Kirk, 1971). Researchers ultimately determined that these perceptual and perceptual-motor exercises did not result in benefits for students' reading achievement (for reviews see Hallahan, 1975; Hallahan & Cruickshank, 1973). In reaction to the widespread adoption of unproven perceptual training programs, the NJCLD objected to the "basic psychological processes" phrase.
2. *Omission of the intrinsic nature of learning disabilities:* The federal definition makes no mention of causal factors, but the NJCLD considered learning disabilities to be due to central nervous system (CNS) dysfunction within the individual.
3. *Omission of adults:* The NJCLD responded to the growing awareness that learning disabilities are not just a disability of childhood. They are a lifelong condition.
4. *Omission of self-regulation and social interaction problems:* The NJCLD responded to the growing awareness that students with learning disabilities often experience difficulties in self-regulation and social interaction.
5. *Inclusion of terms difficult to define:* The NJCLD believed that the federal definition was confusing because of its inclusion of terms such as *perceptual handicaps, dyslexia,* and *minimal brain dysfunction,* which had been so difficult to define (Hammill, Leigh, McNutt, & Larsen, 1981).
6. *Confusion about the exclusion clause:* The federal definition excludes a learning problem that is primarily due to other disabling conditions, such as mental retardation (intellectual disabilities), but it's vague with respect to whether one could have both a learning disability and another disability. The NJCLD preferred to be explicit about the possibility that someone with another condition, such as intellectual disability, could also have a learning disability.
7. *Inclusion of spelling:* The NJCLD believed that there was no need to mention spelling because it was included in writing.

On the basis of these seven purported weaknesses of the federal definition, the NJCLD proposed the following definition:

> Learning disabilities is a general term that refers to a heterogeneous group of disorders manifested by significant difficulties in the acquisition and use of listening, speaking, reading, writing, reasoning, or mathematical abilities. These disorders are intrinsic to the individual, presumed to be due to central nervous system dysfunction, and may occur across the life span. Problems in self-regulatory behaviors, social perception and social interaction may exist with learning disabilities but do not by themselves constitute a learning disability.
>
> Although learning disabilities may occur concomitantly with other handicapping conditions (for example, sensory impairment, mental retardation, serious emotional disturbance) or with extrinsic influences (such as cultural differences, insufficient or inappropriate instruction), they are not the result of those conditions or influences. (National Joint Committee on Learning Disabilities, 1989, p. 1)

The APA Definition

The definition used in the medical field is that of the American Psychiatric Association (APA). The APA definition of "specific learning disorders" includes four criteria:

1. Persistent (occurring for at least 6 months) academic problems in at least one of 6 areas: (a) inaccurate or slow and effortful reading, (b) poor reading comprehension, (c) poor spelling, (d) poor written expression, (e) poor number sense, (f) poor mathematical reasoning
2. Substantial discrepancy between actual and expected academic skill(s) based on chronological age that results in significant interference with academic, occupational, or daily living skills
3. Learning difficulties that began in school-age years but which might not become evident until task demands increase (e.g., timed test, tight deadlines, long reports)
4. Learning difficulties are not due to other disabilities, e.g., intellectual disabilities, visual or hearing impairment, English language learner, poor instruction

IDENTIFICATION

Identification procedures for learning disabilities are currently in a state of transition. As we noted in Chapter 1 earlier, the federal government reauthorized the IDEA in 2004. With this reauthorization, the way in which students may be found eligible for special education services because of having learning disabilities has changed dramatically. In this chapter, we discuss achievement–ability discrepancy, which was the traditional approach to identifying learning disabilities. Then we discuss response to intervention (RTI), which is the federally preferred way of identifying learning disabilities contained in the reauthorization. We say "federally preferred" because, even though the law allows for either one of these methods to be used, the wording of the law, as well as the research priorities of the federal government, definitely favor the use of RTI. For example, the law insists that states *must not require* the use of a severe discrepancy between intellectual ability and achievement; and it specifically requires that states *must permit* the use of RTI.

Achievement–Ability Discrepancy

Shortly after presenting its definition in 1977, the federal government published regulations on how to identify students with learning disabilities. The key element in these regulations was that to be identified as having a learning disability, the student needed to exhibit a "severe discrepancy between achievement and intellectual ability." In other words, a child who was achieving well below his potential would be identified as having a learning disability.

The federal government left it up to individual states to decide precisely how they determined whether a student had a severe discrepancy. Most states relied on an **IQ–achievement discrepancy**, which is a comparison between scores on standardized intelligence and achievement tests. Many states adopted different statistical formulas for identifying IQ–achievement discrepancies. However, some of the formulas are statistically flawed and lead to inaccurate judgments, and those that are statistically adequate are difficult and expensive to implement. Furthermore, they give a false sense of precision. That is, they tempt school personnel to reduce to a single score the complex and important decision of identifying a learning disability.

In addition to the problem of using formulas, some authorities have objected to using an IQ–achievement discrepancy on other conceptual grounds. For example, some authorities have pointed out that IQ scores of students with learning disabilities are subject to underestimation because performance on IQ tests is dependent on reading ability, to some extent. In other words, students with poor reading skills have difficulty expanding their vocabularies and learning about the world. As a result, they get lower-than-average scores on IQ tests, which lessen the discrepancy between IQ and achievement. Also, some educators have pointed out that the idea of discrepancy is practically useless in the earliest elementary grades. In the first or second grade, a child isn't expected to have achieved very much in reading or math, so it's difficult to find a discrepancy. Because of this delay in identification, the IQ–achievement discrepancy approach has been called a "wait-to-fail" model.

MyLab Education
Video Example 6.1
This video explains in detail how an IQ–achievement approach can lead to a delay in the identification of a student's learning disabilities.
https://www.youtube.com/watch?v=hgj2sqXtr6U

Response to Intervention or Response to Treatment

On the basis of the previously mentioned criticisms of IQ–achievement discrepancy, researchers proposed an alternative means of identifying students as having learning disabilities: a **response-to-intervention (RTI) or response-to-treatment approach.** As we noted in Chapter 2, no universally accepted RTI model exists. But, typically, it involves three tiers of progressively more intensive instruction, with monitoring of progress in each of the tiers. (See Figure 2.1.) Tier 1 involves instruction (which is supposed to be evidence based) that typically occurs in the general education classroom by the general education teacher. Those students who don't respond favorably move to Tier 2, in which they receive small-group instruction several times a week. Those not responding favorably to the small-group instruction are referred for evaluation for special education (Tier 3).

As we noted in Chapter 1, the jury is still out on the effectiveness of RTI in identifying students with disabilities, including learning disabilities (Fuchs, Fuchs, McMaster, Yen, & Svenson, 2004; Fuchs, Mock, Morgan, & Young, 2003; L. S. Fuchs, 2003; O'Connor, Sanchez, & Kim, 2017; Pullen & Hallahan, 2015; Pullen, Lane, Ashworth, & Lovelace, 2017; Vaughn & Fuchs, 2003). Some cautions raised include the following:

MyLab Education
Video Example 6.2
A discussion of the nuances of Response to Intervention (RTI) versus the I.Q.–Achievement Discrepancy Model.

- Little research evidence exists regarding the effectiveness of RTI in identifying students with learning disabilities, especially when implemented on a large scale.
- Most of what we do know about RTI is focused just on reading.
- Currently, many general education teachers are failing to use evidence-based instruction in Tier 1.
- Currently, considerable variability occurs in Tier 2 with respect to such things as type of instruction, duration of instruction, and who the instructor is (e.g., general education teacher, special education teacher, school psychologist, paraprofessional).
- Some students don't experience significant difficulties in reading until the third, fourth, or fifth grade, when skills required for reading become more complex; thus, the students go undiagnosed because most RTI models are implemented only in the early elementary grades.
- Some students referred to Tier 2 who do well enough to return to Tier 1 experience reading problems again and are referred back to Tier 2. This recycling between Tiers 1 and 2 may result in delaying them from what they really need, which is Tier 3.

MyLab Education
Video Example 6.3
Author Daniel Hallahan discusses the variation in the identification of students with learning disabilities across the United States.

Despite these cautions, most school administrators see RTI as promising a more reliable way of identifying students with learning disabilities. Virtually all states have implemented or are developing models of RTI for use by local school divisions (Berkeley, Bender, Peaster, & Saunders, 2009). And because the federal government has made funding of research on RTI a high priority over the next several years, there is hope that some of the concerns noted above can be ameliorated.

PREVALENCE

According to U.S. government figures, just under 5% of children between the ages of 6 and 17 years have been identified by the public schools as having learning disabilities. Learning disability is by far the largest category of special education. About half of all students identified by the public schools as needing special education have learning disabilities.

Increase and Decrease in Prevalence

From 1976–77, when the federal government first started keeping prevalence figures, to about 2000, the size of the learning disabilities category more than doubled. Many authorities maintain that the rapid expansion of the learning disabilities category reflects poor diagnostic practices. They believe that children are being overidentified, that teachers are too quick to label students with the slightest learning problem as having "learning disabilities" rather than entertain the possibility that their own teaching practices might be at fault. As we noted earlier, that's one of the reasons why the field has moved away from using the IQ–achievement discrepancy and toward RTI as a way of identifying students with learning disabilities. Others, however, argue that some of the increase might be due to social and cultural changes that have raised children's vulnerability to develop learning disabilities (Hallahan, 1992). For example, the number of children living in poverty has increased since the 1970s (Wright, Chau, & Aratani, 2010), and poverty is associated with higher rates of social and learning problems. Furthermore, even families who aren't in poverty are under more stress than ever before (Cohen & Janicki-Deverts, 2012), which takes its toll on both the time children have for concentrating on their schoolwork and their parents' ability to offer social support.

Still others maintain that a causal relationship exists between the decrease in the numbers of students who are being identified as having intellectual disabilities (mental retardation) and the increase in the numbers of students who are being identified with learning disabilities. Evidence suggests that when faced with a student who could qualify as having an intellectual disability, school personnel often bend the rules to apply the label of "learning disability" rather than the more stigmatizing label of "intellectual disability" (MacMillan, Gresham, & Bocian, 1998; MacMillan & Siperstein, 2002).

Even though the prevalence of students identified as having learning disabilities has doubled since the 1970s, it's significant that after peaking at 5.66% in the late 1990s, the rate has been gradually, but steadily, decreasing to its current level of just under 5%. This turnabout may be due to a conscious effort to be more conservative in identifying learning disabilities because so much concern has been raised about its seemingly endless growth. How much this decrease might be due to the emergence of RTI as a replacement of IQ–achievement discrepancy as an identification tool is not yet known.

MyLab Education
Video Example 6.4
Jennifer, who has a learning disability and a hand tremor, explains her disability, accommodations and learning strategies through high school and college.

Gender Differences

Boys outnumber girls by about 3 to 1 in the LD category (Cortiella, 2009). Some researchers have suggested that the greater prevalence of learning disabilities among males is due to their greater biological vulnerability. The infant mortality rate for males is higher than that for females, and males are at greater risk than females for a variety of biological abnormalities. Other researchers have contended, however, that the higher prevalence of learning disabilities among males might be due to referral bias. They suggest that boys are more likely to be referred for special education when they do have academic problems because of other behaviors that bother teachers, such as hyperactivity. Research on this issue is mixed (Clarizio & Phillips, 1986; Cortiella & Horowitz, 2014; Leinhardt, Seewald, & Zigmond, 1982; Shaywitz, Shaywitz, Fletcher, & Escobar, 1990). At this point, it's probably safest to conclude that

> some bias does exist but that the biological vulnerability of males also plays a role. For example, the federal government's figures indicate that all disabilities are more prevalent in males, including conditions that are difficult to imagine resulting from referral or assessment bias, such as hearing impairment (53% are males), orthopedic impairment (54% are males), and visual impairment (56% are males). (Hallahan, Lloyd, Kauffman, Weiss, & Martinez, 2005, p. 35)

MyLab Education Self-Check 6.1

CAUSES

For years, many professionals suspected that neurological factors were a major cause of learning disabilities. When the field of learning disabilities was emerging, professionals noted that many of the children displayed behavioral characteristics (e.g., distractibility, hyperactivity, language problems, perceptual disturbances) similar to those exhibited by people who were known to have brain damage, such as those who had suffered a stroke or a head wound (for review, see Hallahan & Mercer, 2002).

In the case of most children with learning disabilities, however, little neurological evidence exists of actual *damage* to brain tissues. Therefore, today, the term *dysfunction* has replaced *injury* or *damage*. A child with learning disabilities is now often referred to as having CNS dysfunction rather than brain injury. Dysfunction does not necessarily mean tissue damage; instead, it signifies a malfunctioning of the brain or CNS.

Researchers have documented neurological dysfunction as a probable cause of learning disabilities using neuroimaging techniques such as **magnetic resonance imaging (MRI)**, **functional magnetic resonance imaging (fMRI)**, **functional magnetic resonance spectroscopy (fMRS)**, and **positron-emission tomography (PET) scans**, as well as measuring the brain's electrical activity with **event-related potentials (ERPs**, also referred to as evoked potentials).

- An MRI sends magnetic radio waves through the head and creates cross-sectional images of the brain.
- fMRI and fMRS are adaptations of the MRI. Unlike an MRI, they are used to detect changes in brain activity while a person is engaged in a task, such as reading.
- A PET scan, like an fMRI or fMRS, is used while the person is performing a task. The subject is injected with a substance containing a low amount of radiation, which collects in active neurons. Using a scanner to detect the radioactive substance, researchers can tell which parts of the brain are actively engaged during various tasks.
- ERPs measure the brain's response to perceptual and cognitive processing. They result from the administration of an **electroencephalograph (EEG)**.

Using these neuroimaging techniques, researchers have accumulated evidence for structural and functional differences between the brains of people with and without learning disabilities, especially reading disabilities. *Structural differences* refer to such things as the size of the various areas of the brain. For example, researchers have found that the volume of certain areas of the brain is related to reading skills (Saygin et al., 2013). *Functional* refers to activity in the brain. Findings from these neuroimaging studies have been relatively consistent in identifying structural and/or functional differences in the **left temporal lobe** and areas around it in persons with dyslexia. (See Gabrieli, 2009 and Peterson & Pennington, 2015, for a review of this research.)

Using ERPs, researchers have determined that newborns' responses to speech stimuli are correlated with their language scores in preschool (Guttorm et al., 2005) and also predict whether they will have a reading disability at 8 years of age (Molfese, 2000). Evidence also suggests that ERP measures might someday be reliable enough to be used, along with educational and psychological tests, to identify children at risk for later development of reading disabilities (Hoeft et al., 2007).

Taken as a whole, these studies are not definitive evidence of a neurological basis for *all* students who are identified as having learning disabilities. However, the results have turned many people who were formerly skeptical into believers that CNS dysfunction could be the cause of many, if not most, cases of learning disabilities.

Even in cases in which one can be fairly certain that the person with learning disabilities has neurological dysfunction, the question still remains: How did the person come to have the neurological dysfunction? Possible reasons fall into three general categories: genetic factors, toxins, and medical factors.

Genetic Factors

Over the years, evidence has accumulated that learning disabilities can be inherited. The two most common types of studies that researchers use to examine the genetic basis of learning disabilities are familiality studies and heritability studies.

Familiality studies examine the degree to which a certain condition, such as a learning disability, occurs in a single family (i.e., the tendency for it to "run in a family"). Researchers have found that about 35% to 45% of first-degree relatives (the immediate birth family—parents and siblings) of individuals with reading disabilities also have reading disabilities (Hallgren, 1950; Olson, Wise, Conners, Rack, & Fulker, 1989; Pennington, 1990; Schulte-Korne et al., 2006), and the risk for having reading disabilities goes up for children when both parents have reading disabilities (Raskind, 2001). The same degree of familiality has also been found in families of people with speech and language disorders (Beichtman, Hood, & Inglis, 1992; Lewis, 1992; Schulte-Korne et al., 2006) and spelling disabilities (Schulte-Korne, Deimel, Muller, Gutenbrunner, & Remschmidt, 1996; Schulte-Korne et al., 2006).

The tendency for learning disabilities to run in families may also be due to environmental factors. For example, it's possible that parents with learning disabilities will pass on their disabilities to their children through their child-rearing practices. A more convincing method of determining whether learning disabilities are inherited is **heritability studies** that compare the prevalence of learning disabilities in identical (monozygotic, from the same egg) versus fraternal (dizygotic, from two eggs) twins. Researchers have found that identical twins are more concordant than are fraternal twins for reading disabilities, speech and language disorders, and math disabilities (DeFries, Gillis, & Wadsworth, 1993; DeThorne et al., 2006; Lewis & Thompson, 1992; Reynolds et al., 1996; Shalev, 2004). In other words, if an identical twin and a fraternal twin each have a learning disability, the second identical twin is more likely to have a learning disability than the second fraternal twin.

With the rapid advances in molecular genetics, an expanding body of research is attempting to pinpoint the genes involved in learning disabilities. Virtually all geneticists agree that no single gene causes a learning disability (Raskind, Beate, Richards, Eckert, & Berninger, 2013; Rubenstein, Matsushita, Berninger, Raskind, & Wijsman, 2011). Researchers are making rapid progress in identifying which genes are associated with learning disabilities (Eicher et al., 2016). And, interestingly, evidence suggests that some of these genes are associated with more than one type of learning disability, e.g., reading, math, and/or spelling disabilities (Hayworth et al., 2009; Plomin & Kovas, 2005).

It's important to keep in mind that, as exciting as these genetics findings are, just as was the case for intellectual disabilities (discussed in Chapter 5), the environment also plays an important role in learning disabilities. This is especially true in the early stages of learning; for example, early reading skills (Petrill, Deater-Deckard, Thompson, DeThorne, & Schatschneider, 2006).

Toxins

Toxins are agents that can result in a host of problems, such as headaches, poor memory, and even intellectual disability. One of the most common toxins known to result in these problems is lead, which is particularly toxic to children and the fetus in pregnant women. Unsafe levels of lead can be present in the air, water, food, and objects or surfaces painted with lead-based paint. At one time, many paints were lead-based, and young children were susceptible to lead poisoning from ingesting lead from toys and walls in their home. Lead-based house paint has been banned since the late 1970s. However, it still remains a problem in some older houses where lead-based paint has chipped off the walls.

Today, lead is all too frequently found in drinking water. Although U.S. public health officials had been warning for some time about unsafe levels of lead in water supplies, there has been a heightened awareness of the problem since 2014 when toxic levels of lead were discovered in Flint, Michigan. Researchers have accumulated strong evidence linking high lead levels in water to lower performance on IQ and achievement tests (Evens et al., 2015; Lanphear, Dietrich, Auinger, & Cox, 2000; Zhang et al., 2013). Air pollution, too, has considerable research support as a cause of learning impairments (Clark-Reyna, Grineski, & Collins, 2016). Similar to lead, children, whose brains are still developing, are especially vulnerable to toxins in the air.

Medical Factors

Several medical conditions can cause learning disabilities. Many of these can also result in intellectual disabilities, depending on the severity of the condition. For example, premature birth places children at risk for neurological dysfunction and learning disabilities (Aarnoudse-Moens, Weisglas-Kuperus, van Goudoever, & Oosterlaan, 2009), and pediatric AIDS can result in neurological damage resulting in learning disabilities.

MyLab Education Self-Check 6.2

PSYCHOLOGICAL AND BEHAVIORAL CHARACTERISTICS

Before discussing some of the most common characteristics of people with learning disabilities, we point out two important features of this population: People with learning disabilities exhibit a great deal of both interindividual and intraindividual variation.

Interindividual Variation

In any group of students with learning disabilities, some will have problems in reading, some will have problems in math, some will have problems in spelling, some will be inattentive, and so on. One term for such interindividual variation is *heterogeneity*. Although heterogeneity is a trademark of children from all the categories of special education, the old adage "No two are exactly alike" is particularly appropriate for students with learning disabilities. This heterogeneity makes it a challenge for teachers to plan educational programs for the diverse group of children they find in their classrooms.

Intraindividual Variation

In addition to differences among one another, children with learning disabilities also tend to exhibit variability within their own profiles of abilities. For example, a child might be 2 or 3 years above grade level in reading but 2 or 3 years behind grade level in math. Such uneven profiles account for references to *specific* learning disabilities in the literature on learning disabilities.

We now turn to a discussion of some of the most common characteristics of persons with learning disabilities.

Academic Achievement Problems

READING Reading poses the greatest difficulty for most students with learning disabilities; and reading affects every other academic subject in school. Students with reading disabilities or **dyslexia** are likely to experience problems in several of the major areas of reading: phonological awareness (more specifically, phonemic awareness), decoding, reading fluency, vocabulary, and reading comprehension (Mercer, Mercer, & Pullen, 2011). Most students with reading disabilities have difficulty at the early stages of reading (i.e., phonemic awareness and decoding), which in turn affects their ability to read with fluency and comprehension.

Reading is a complex process and requires the integration of many subskills. **Phonological awareness** is an understanding that the speech flow can be broken down into smaller units of sound such as words, syllables, onsets-rimes, and phonemes. **Phonemic awareness** is an understanding that specific words can be broken down into individual sounds. For example, the word *sat* has three **phonemes** or sounds: /s/ /ă/ /t/. Phonemic awareness is of critical importance; research substantiates a causal relationship between a lack of phonemic awareness skills and the inability to decode. **Decoding** is the ability to convert the printed words to spoken words and is highly dependent on phonemic awareness. First the student must be able to break a word into its individual sounds and then blend them together to say the whole word (i.e., **phonological recoding**). Students who are able to decode automatically will typically develop reading fluency. Students who have difficulty decoding invariably have problems with fluency. Reading fluency refers to the ability to read effortlessly and smoothly. **Reading fluency** comprises three skills—reading words: accurately, at an appropriate pace, and with prosody. **Prosody** entails making your oral reading sound like spoken language, using appropriate intonation and expression (Hudson, Lane, & Pullen, 2005).

SUCCESS STORIES: Hard Work at Home and School Helps Randy Read on Grade Level

Special Educator Celia Gottesman: "Unless you work harder, faster, and more intensively, they won't catch up."

Ten-year-old Randy Daniels is reading on grade level as he starts fifth grade at Lake Forest Elementary School in Florida. These are the keys to his success:

- Intensive instruction in reading and math
- Relentless progress monitoring
- Specific incentives and parental support

Randy Daniels ended third grade reading at a second-grade level, a full year behind many of his classmates. This year he has caught up, and he is proud of it. "I did it! I did it! I did it!" he said when he heard the good news. "Randy moved 2 years ahead in reading in 1 year with two intensive summer school experiences, and that's a tremendous achievement," says special educator Dr. Celia Gottesman. Hard work at home and at school helped Randy achieve success through intensive, relentless, and specific special education.

- **Intensive Instruction in Reading and Math.** Randy Daniels loves football and he likes to do his best, but last year he struggled to keep up in his regular class. In summer school Randy received intensive instruction for 90 minutes every day in a resource classroom with Celia Gottesman and Waltraud Schmid. Known to their students as Dr. G. and Mrs. Schmid, these special educators strengthened Randy's academic skills using a combination of formative assessment, direct instruction, and cognitive strategy training. "We also provided lots of positive reinforcement and personal attention," says Celia. The effective team of Gottesman and Schmid gets results, and this year their high-poverty school met its goals for adequate yearly progress (AYP). Celia Gottesman teaches reading and math to exceptional learners at Lake Forest Elementary. Waltraud Schmid also taught special education at the school before she retired. As a school volunteer, she now helps Celia plan and deliver systematic instruction 5 days a week. For Celia, teaching students with learning disabilities means accelerating progress as quickly as possible. "We assess frequently to see where students are, what academic and social skills they need, and how fast we can push them—and I'm a pusher," she says. She speaks candidly as the mother of three college graduates who have learning disabilities: "Unless you work harder, faster, and more intensively, they won't catch up."

    To improve Randy's reading fluency and comprehension, Celia modified the pace of instruction, and taught him in small groups with other students who struggled with similar concepts and vocabulary. She also taught evidence-based learning strategies to help him anchor academic content. In addition, Randy received supplemental one-on-one instruction daily from Waltraud Schmid, who inventoried his skill levels and charted his progress. "Mrs. Schmid was a pharmacist in

her first career," says Celia, "and you can be sure she knows the importance of collecting data."

- **Relentless Progress Monitoring.** Celia Gottesman bases instruction on multiple assessments. "We start the year with so much diagnostic information," she says. "We use many sources of data to plan our teaching and to monitor progress including scores on state tests, reading inventories, and curriculum-based measurement." In Randy's case, Mrs. Schmid used classroom materials to test his reading fluency and math facts. She graphed the number of words he read per minute and charted the number of correct and incorrect math facts daily across a 6-week period. This careful progress monitoring helped Celia guide Randy's instruction. "We have a mastery level in mind for each child based on their beginning scores. We isolate the skill we want to teach, we use validated methods to teach that skill, and then we measure the student's response to our instruction," says Celia. "We expected a 75-point increase for Randy on state achievement tests, but he made over 100 points in reading and over 200 points in math."

- **Specific Incentives and Parental Support.** According to his teachers, much of the credit for Randy's success goes to his mother, Leann Lee, who makes sure that he practices reading at home. "I don't want my son to become a statistic because he's a black male," says Mrs. Lee. "I want him to learn that he can succeed if he works hard." Mrs. Lee scheduled free tutoring after school and asked for Reading Mastery workbooks so she could help Randy. "I said to Dr. G, 'I need you to teach me how to teach Randy, so I can teach him at home.'" Leann Lee started an incentive program to raise his reading scores, and Randy is expected to read at least 30 minutes each day. His reward is playing in a local Pop Warner football league and his stepfather, Raymond Lee, is now the team coach. Randy has two younger sisters, and his parents both work full time. Their efforts to help him succeed have not been easy, but they have been worthwhile. "He's a busy little boy," says Leann. "Rewards motivate him, and what he's accomplished is awesome."

Reflecting On Your Own Professional Development

If you were Randy's teacher . . .

- What are some areas about educating students with learning disabilities that you would need to know more about?

- What are some specific skills that would help you address his learning disabilities?

- What personal dispositions do you think are most important for you to develop in teaching students with learning disabilities to succeed in mastering new skills?

By Jean B. Crockett

Reading fluency is highly associated with reading comprehension—those who read fluently typically, but not always, understand what they read. Problems with reading fluency are a major reason why students have difficulties with reading comprehension (Good, Simmons, & Kame'enui, 2001). **Reading comprehension** refers to the ability to gain meaning from print—the ultimate goal of reading.

All of the above-mentioned skills—phonological awareness, phonemic awareness, decoding, phonological recoding and reading fluency, as well as the **vocabulary base** they help build-interact with each other to make reading comprehension possible. At the Reading Rockets website (funded by the federal government, www.readingrockets. org), Dr. Reid Lyon, an expert on reading disabilities and the former Chief of the Child Development and Behavior Branch of the National Institutes of Health, explains how complex the reading process is and why individuals with learning disabilities struggle to gain reading skills (http://youtube.com/watch?v=VZmNpSYjMi4).

The good news is that, with intensive, explicit, and systematic instruction in a comprehensive reading program that includes attention to the above interplay of skills, most students with learning disabilities will learn how to read. For example, Randy Daniels, a student with a learning disability who received this specialized instruction in special education made great strides in reading. To learn more about Randy's program, read the accompanying Success Stories feature that describes his teachers' accomplishments and Randy's achievements. For more information on reading strategies for students with learning disabilities, visit the Reading Rockets website (www.readingrockets.org) as well as the websites of the major professional organizations listed at the end of this chapter (e.g., DLD and CLD).

MyLab Education
Video Example 6.5
In this video, the teacher expresses her appreciation for the effectiveness of explicit instruction.

WRITTEN LANGUAGE People with learning disabilities often have problems in one or more of the following areas: handwriting, spelling, and composition (Mercer et al., 2011). A specific learning disability in writing is called *dysgraphia*. Although even the best students can have less-than-perfect handwriting, the kinds of problems that some students with learning disabilities exhibit are much more severe. These children are sometimes very slow writers, and their written products are sometimes illegible.

Spelling can be a significant problem because of the difficulty (noted in the previous section) in understanding the correspondence between sounds and letters. In addition to the more mechanical areas of handwriting and spelling, students with learning disabilities frequently have difficulties in the more creative aspects of composition (Graham & Harris, 2011). For example, compared to peers who do not have disabilities, students with learning disabilities use less complex sentence structures; include fewer types of words; write paragraphs that are less well organized; include fewer ideas in their written products; and write stories that have fewer important components, such as introducing main characters, setting scenes, and describing a conflict to be resolved (Hallahan et al., 2005).

SPOKEN LANGUAGE Many students with learning disabilities have problems with the mechanical and social uses of language. Mechanically, they have trouble with **syntax** (grammar), **semantics** (word meanings), and, as we have already noted, **phonology** (the ability to break words into their component sounds and blend individual sounds together to make words).

The social uses of language are commonly referred to as **pragmatics**. Students with learning disabilities are often unskilled in the production and reception of discourse. In short, they're not very good conversationalists. They cannot engage in the mutual give-and-take that conversations between individuals require. For instance, the conversations of individuals with learning disabilities are frequently marked by long silences because they don't employ the relatively subtle strategies that their peers who do not have disabilities use to keep conversations going. They're not skilled at responding to others' statements or questions and tend to answer their own questions before their companions have a chance to respond. They tend to express task-irrelevant comments and make those with whom they talk uncomfortable. In one study cited often, for example, children with and without learning disabilities took turns playing the role of host in a simulated television talk show (Bryan, Donahue, Pearl, & Sturm, 1981). In contrast to children without disabilities, children with learning disabilities playing the host role allowed their guests without disabilities to dominate the conversation. Also, their guests exhibited more signs of discomfort during the interview than did the guests of hosts without disabilities.

MATH   Although disorders of reading, writing, and language have traditionally received more emphasis than problems with mathematics, the latter are now gaining a great deal of attention. A specific learning disability in mathematics is called **dyscalculia**. Authorities now recognize that math disabilities may be just as prevalent as or at least a close second to reading disabilities (Kunsch, Jitendra, & Sood, 2007; Swanson & Jerman, 2006). The types of problems these students have include difficulties with computation of math facts as well as word problems (Fuchs et al., 2011); trouble with the latter is often due to the inefficient application of problem-solving strategies. Researchers have found that processing deficits in working memory and retrieval from long-term memory are implicated in mathematics disability (Geary, Hoard, Nugent, & Bailey, 2011).

Perceptual, Perceptual-Motor, and General Coordination Problems

Studies indicate that some children with learning disabilities exhibit visual and/or auditory perceptual disabilities (for reviews, see Hallahan, 1975; Willows, 1998). A child with visual perceptual problems might have trouble solving puzzles or seeing and remembering visual shapes; for example, she might have a tendency to reverse letters (e.g., mistake *b* for *d*). A child with auditory perceptual problems might have difficulty discriminating between two words that sound nearly alike (e.g., *fit* and *fib*) or following orally presented directions.

Teachers and parents have also noted that some students with learning disabilities have difficulty with physical activities involving motor skills. They describe some of these children as having "two left feet" or "ten thumbs." The problems may involve both fine motor (small motor muscle) and gross motor (large motor muscle) skills. Fine motor skills often involve coordination of the visual and motor systems.

Disorders of Attention and Hyperactivity

Students with attention problems display characteristics such as distractibility, impulsivity, and hyperactivity. Teachers and parents of these children often characterize them as being unable to stick with one task for very long, failing to listen to others, talking nonstop, blurting out the first things on their minds, and being generally disorganized in planning their activities in and out of school. These problems are often severe enough to be diagnosed as **attention deficit hyperactivity disorder (ADHD)** (Mattison & Mayes, 2012). (We discuss ADHD more fully in Chapter 7.) Although estimates vary, researchers have generally found that almost half of students with ADHD also have a learning disability (Pastor & Reuben, 2008).

Memory Problems

Parents and teachers are well aware that students with learning disabilities have problems remembering such things as assignments and appointments. In fact, these adults often exclaim in exasperation that they can't understand how a child who is so smart can forget things so easily.

Students with learning disabilities have at least two types of memory problems: (1) **working memory (WM)** and (2) **retrieval of information from long-term memory (RLTM)** (Pong & Fuchs, 2017; Swanson, Kehler, & Jerman, 2010; Swanson, Zheng, & Jerman, 2009). Working memory involves the ability to hold information in memory for a short period of time in order to use it to solve a problem—for example, in a long division math problem, storing the numbers temporarily while working with them to solve the problem.

In addition to deficits in working memory, students with learning disabilities often have difficulty accurately and automatically retrieving information from long-term memory. For example, a student with a learning disability may know her math facts, but be unable to remember them with automaticity that allows for the use of this information in problem solving. A similar example is the inability of a student with dyslexia (reading disability) to access the sounds of the letters rapidly. Furthermore, research has suggested that performance anxiety moderates the effects of long-term memory retrieval among college students with mathematics learning disabilities (Prevatt, Welles, Li, & Proctor, 2010). That is, the deficits in long-term memory retrieval are further affected by students' anxiety related to the task in the area of their disability.

Researchers have found that one of the major reasons that children with learning disabilities perform poorly on memory tasks is that, unlike their peers without disabilities, they don't use strategies. For example, when presented with a list of words to memorize, most children will rehearse the names to themselves. They'll also make use of categories by rehearsing words in groups that go together. Students with learning disabilities are unlikely to use these strategies spontaneously. However, they can be taught memory strategies, such as rehearsal, which research indicates can enhance their academic performance.

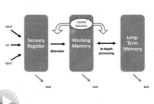

MyLab Education
Video Example 6.6
This 16-minute video provides an animated explanation of a three-component model of the human memory system.

Executive Function Problems

Executive functioning (EF) is an umbrella term covering cognitive processes that are necessary to control and regulate one's behavior—**self-regulation**. As we will discuss in Chapter 7 on ADHD, EF has been likened to the role of the conductor of an orchestra, the director of a movie, or the job of an air-traffic controller. There are both behavioral tests and questionnaires that measure EF. An example of a behavioral measure is the Tower of London Test (TLT) (Culbertson & Zillmer, 2017). The TLT, a 12-minute computerized test, requires moving three pegs (red, yellow, or blue), constrained by several difficult rules. To do well, planning, monitoring, and correcting one's moves are required.

LTM = organized network

MyLab Education
Video Example 6.7
This 5-minute video provides an animated explanation and illustration of long-term memory's constructive and organized nature.

Several different questionnaires have been developed to assess a person's executive functioning (Duckworth & Kern, 2011; Teglasi et al., 2015). Examples of items students typically evaluate themselves on in questionnaires are statements like: I have trouble planning ahead; I interrupt when others are talking; I make up my mind too quickly; I have problems changing course if things aren't going well; My work-space is cluttered.

Metacognition Problems

Metacognition refers to a student's ability to think about his own thinking and is critical to learning, memory, and academic achievement (Sperling, Richmond, Ramsay, & Klapp, 2012). Therefore, it's not surprising that individuals with learning disabilities often have problems with metacognition (Chevalier, Parrila, Ritchie, & Deacon, 2017). An important role of metacognition in learning is the ability to determine when you understand what is being taught or what you are reading and when you are struggling. Individuals with good metacognitive skills know when they are struggling and use "fix-up" strategies, whereas individuals with poor metacognitive skills may not even realize that they lack understanding. Think about your reading of this college textbook. There may be times that you need to reread a section because you didn't understand a concept, or you were distracted while you were reading. The ability to repair your comprehension by rereading demonstrates your skill in strategy selection and use.

How does the lack of metacognitive skills affect students with learning disabilities? We talk about this in three steps: the ability to (1) recognize task requirements, (2) select and implement appropriate strategies, and (3) monitor and adjust performance.

Regarding the first component—the ability to recognize task requirements—students with learning disabilities frequently have problems judging how difficult tasks can be. For example, they might approach the reading of highly technical information with the same level of intensity as when reading for pleasure.

An example of problems with the second component—the ability to select and implement appropriate strategies—occurs when students with learning disabilities are asked questions such as "How can you remember to take your homework to school in the morning?" They don't come up with as many strategies (e.g., writing a note to your-self, placing the homework by the front door) as students without disabilities do.

An example of the third component of metacognition—the ability to monitor or adjust performance—is comprehension monitoring. **Comprehension monitoring** refers to the abilities used while one reads and attempts to comprehend textual material. Many students with reading disabilities have problems, for example, in being able to sense when they are not understanding what they are reading. Good readers can sense this and make necessary adjustments, such as slowing down and/or rereading difficult passages. Students with reading problems are also likely to have problems in picking out the main ideas of paragraphs.

Social-Emotional Problems

Although not all, perhaps not even a majority, of children with learning disabilities have significant social-emotional problems, they do run a greater risk than do their peers without disabilities of having these types of problems. For example, they are at a greater risk for depression, social rejection, suicidal thoughts, and loneliness (Al-Yagon, 2007; Bryan, Burstein, & Ergul, 2004; Daniel et al., 2006; Maag & Reid, 2006; Mammarella et al., 2016; Margalit, 2006). For those who experience behavioral problems, the effects can be long-lasting and devastating. The scars from years of rejection can be painful and not easily healed in adulthood (McGrady, Lerner, & Boscardin, 2001).

One plausible reason for the social problems of some students with learning disabilities is that these students have deficits in social cognition. That is, they misread social cues and may misinterpret the feelings and emotions of others. Most children, for example, can tell when their behavior is bothering others. Students with learning disabilities sometimes act as if they are oblivious to the effect their behavior is having on their peers. They also have difficulty taking the perspective of others, of putting themselves in someone else's shoes.

Researchers have noted that problems with social interaction tend to be more evident in children who also have problems in math, visual-spatial tasks, tactual tasks, and self-regulation and organization (Rourke, 1995; Worling, Humphries, & Tannock, 1999). Some researchers have found that such children are similar to those with autism spectrum disorder (see Chapter 9) in their difficulties in "reading" the emotions of others (Semrud-Clikeman, Walkowiak, Wilkinson, & Minne, 2010). Individuals who exhibit this constellation of behaviors are referred to as having **nonverbal learning disabilities.** However, the term is somewhat of a misnomer because these people often exhibit subtle problems in using language, especially in social situations. Researchers have speculated that nonverbal learning disabilities are caused by malfunctioning of the right half of the brain because of known linkages of math, visual-spatial, and tactual skills to the right cerebral hemisphere. Evidence also indicates that individuals with nonverbal learning disabilities are at risk for depression, presumably because of the social rejection and isolation they may experience. In extreme cases, they have an increased risk of suicide (Bender, Rosenkrans, & Crane, 1999).

Motivational Problems

Another source of problems for many people with learning disabilities is their motivation, or feelings about their abilities to deal with many of life's challenges and problems. People with learning disabilities may appear content to let events happen without attempting to control or influence them. Psychologists refer to this as an external, rather than an internal, **locus of control.** In other words, these individuals believe that their lives are controlled by external factors such as luck or fate rather than by internal factors such as determination or ability (Hallahan et al., 2005). People with this outlook sometimes display **learned helplessness:** a tendency to give up and expect the worst because they think that no matter how hard they try, they will fail.

What makes these motivational problems so difficult for teachers, parents, and individuals with learning disabilities to deal with is the interrelationship between learning and motivational problems (Morgan & Fuchs, 2007). A vicious cycle develops: The student learns to expect failure in any new situation on the basis of past experience. This expectancy of failure, or learned helplessness, might then cause the student to give up too easily when faced with a difficult or complicated task. As a result, not only does the student fail to learn new skills but also he has another bad experience, which reinforces feelings of helplessness and even worthlessness—and so the cycle goes.

Inactive Learner with Strategy Deficits

Many of the psychological and behavioral characteristics we've described can be summed up by saying that the student with learning disabilities is an *inactive learner*, lacking in strategies for attacking academic problems (Hallahan et al., 2005). Specifically, research describes the student with learning disabilities as someone who doesn't believe in her own abilities (learned helplessness), has an inadequate grasp of what strategies are available for problem solving (poor metacognitive skills), and has problems producing appropriate learning strategies spontaneously.

The practical implication of this constellation of characteristics is that students with learning disabilities can have difficulties working independently. They're not likely to be "self-starters." Assignments or activities requiring them to work on their own may cause problems unless the teacher carefully provides an appropriate amount of support. As we discussed in Chapter 4, homework is a major problem for many students with disabilities; this is especially true for those with learning disabilities (Bryan & Sullivan-Burstein, 1998; Epstein, Munk, Bursuck, Polloway, & Jayanthi, 1998). Students' difficulties range from failing to bring home their homework to being distracted while doing homework, to forgetting to turn in their homework.

> **MyLab** Education Self-Check 6.3

EDUCATIONAL CONSIDERATIONS

In this section, we consider (1) cognitive training, approaches designed to use *strategies* to address learning and academic problems; (2) metacognitive training, approaches designed to help learners understand and know how to use cognitive strategies; (3) instructional approaches designed to address academics (reading, written language, math, and the content areas of science and social studies); and (4) two general approaches to instruction: direct instruction and peer tutoring.

Cognitive Training

Cognitive training involves three components: (1) changing thought processes, (2) providing strategies for learning, and (3) teaching self-initiative. Whereas behavior modification focuses on modifying observable behaviors, cognitive training is concerned with modifying unobservable thought processes, prompting observable changes in behavior. Cognitive training has proven successful in helping improve a variety of academic problems for many students with learning disabilities (Hallahan et al., 2005). It's particularly appropriate for students with learning disabilities because of its focus on problems of metacognition and motivation.

A variety of specific techniques fall under the heading of cognitive training. We briefly discuss four: self-instruction, self-monitoring, scaffolded instruction, and reciprocal teaching.

SELF-INSTRUCTION The purpose of **self-instruction** is to make students aware of the various stages of problem-solving tasks while they are performing them and to bring behavior under verbal control.

One study using self-instruction as an integral feature of instruction involved fifth- and sixth-grade students with learning disabilities solving math word problems (Case, Harris, & Graham, 1992). The five-step strategy that the students learned to use involved saying the problem aloud, looking for important words and circling them, drawing pictures to help explain what was happening, writing the math sentence, and writing the answer. Furthermore, students were prompted to use the following self-instructions:

1. *Problem definition:* "What do I have to do?"
2. *Planning:* "How can I solve this problem?"
3. *Strategy use:* "The five-step strategy will help me look for important words."
4. *Self-evaluation:* "How am I doing?"
5. *Self-reinforcement:* "Good job. I got it right."

SELF-MONITORING When **self-monitoring**, students keep track of their own behavior, often through use of two components: self-evaluation and self-recording (Hallahan, Kneedler, & Lloyd, 1983). Students evaluate their own behavior and then record whether the behavior occurred. Students can be taught to self-monitor a variety of academic behaviors. For example, after working on several math problems, students can check their answers and then record on a graph the number of correct answers. After several days, the student and teacher have an observable record of the student's progress.

SCAFFOLDED INSTRUCTION In **scaffolded instruction**, teachers provide assistance to students when they are first learning tasks, and then gradually reduce assistance so that eventually students do the tasks independently. For example, in one study, the teacher modeled a three-step strategy for writing, saying the steps aloud:

1. *Think*, who will read this, and why am I writing it?
2. *Plan* what to say using TREE (note Topic sentence, note Reasons, Examine reasons, note Ending).
3. *Write* and *Say More*. (Sexton, Harris, & Graham, 1998, p. 300)

While modeling the strategy, the teacher discussed various aspects of it with the students, and the students gradually memorized the strategy and implemented it on their own.

RECIPROCAL TEACHING Like scaffolded instruction, **reciprocal teaching** involves an interactive dialogue between the teacher and students in which the teacher–student relationship is similar to that of an expert (teacher) and an apprentice (student). The teacher gradually relinquishes her role as the sole instructor and allows the students to assume the role of co-instructor for brief periods. The teacher models and encourages the students to use strategies.

Metacognitive Training

Closely linked to cognitive training, metacognitive training addresses problems with planning ahead, selecting good learning strategies, and adjusting strategies based on performance. For example, a metacognitive training package focused on students defining goals and planning and monitoring their progress has been used to improve spelling and reading performance (Schiff, Ben-Shushan, & Ben-Artzi, 2017).

Instructional Approaches for Academics

By definition, students with learning disabilities experience academic problems in one or more areas, such as reading, writing, math, and content areas such as science and social studies. Although we discuss each separately, some rules of thumb are evident across these areas. As we noted in Chapter 1, special education instruction is precisely controlled in pace or rate, intensity, relentlessness, structure, reinforcement, teacher–pupil ratio, curriculum, and monitoring or assessment (Kauffman & Hallahan, 2005; Pullen & Hallahan, 2015).

INSTRUCTIONAL APPROACHES FOR READING In 2000, the National Reading Panel synthesized research on how children acquire reading and best practices for reading instruction (National Institute of Child Health and Human Development, 2000). This report identified five essential components of effective reading instruction: phonological awareness training, phonics instruction, fluency instruction, vocabulary instruction, and comprehension instruction. In addition, the most successful reading instruction is explicit and systematic.

As we noted earlier in this chapter, phonological awareness involves knowing that speech consists of small units of sound, such as words, syllables, and phonemes. Phonemic awareness, a component of phonological awareness, involves knowing that words are made up of sounds, or phonemes. Strong research evidence indicates that teaching students with reading disabilities to manipulate phonemes in words is highly effective in helping them acquire reading skills.

Phonics instruction involves learning the alphabetic system; that is, the pairing of letters and words with their sounds. Effective phonics instruction is explicit and systematic, and includes plentiful opportunities for practice (Mercer et al., 2011).

Reading fluency refers to the ability to read effortlessly and smoothly. Successful interventions for problems with reading fluency typically involve having the student read aloud. An especially effective technique is **repeated readings**, whereby students repeatedly (several times a week) read the same short passages aloud until they are reading at an appropriate pace with few or no errors.

A variety of methods are available for increasing students' listening and reading vocabulary. Some successful techniques for teaching vocabulary are mnemonic instruction, learning strategies using morphemic analysis, direct instruction, and multimedia instruction (Kuder, 2017). Because much of a person's vocabulary is learned indirectly, providing ample opportunities for reading a wide range of materials is important. With respect to directly teaching vocabulary, the most effective methods include "reviewing new or unknown words in a text prior to reading, extending instruction on specific words over time and across different contexts" (Mercer et al., 2011, p. 269).

Numerous strategies can help students comprehend what they are reading. Some involve the types of cognitive training strategies that we've already discussed; some involve content-enhancement strategies that we discuss later when describing approaches for content area instruction.

MyLab Education
Video Example 6.8
This video shows a science teacher teaching students to use mnemonics. Note how he is explicit in his directions.

INSTRUCTIONAL APPROACHES FOR WRITING The ability to read and write are closely linked. Students who exhibit reading disabilities also often have problems with writing. Researchers have determined that effective writing instruction for students with learning disabilities involves teaching students explicit and systematic strategies for planning, revising, and editing compositions (Graham & Harris, 2011).

Self-regulated strategy development (SRSD) (Graham & Harris, 2003; Harris, Graham, & Mason, 2003) is a research-based model that has been highly effective (Sreckovic, Common, Knowles, & Lane, 2014).). SRSD approaches writing as a problem-solving task that involves planning, knowledge, and skills. Within SRSD are several strategies focused on different aspects of writing. A good example is the story-writing strategy, *POW + WWW, What = 2, H = 2*. POW = **P**ick my idea; **O**rganize my notes; **W**rite and say more. WWW = **W**ho is the main character? **W**hen does the story take place? **W**here does the story take place? What = **W**hat does the main character do? and **W**hat happens then? H = **H**ow does the story end? and **H**ow does the main character feel?

MyLab Education
Video Example 6.9
In this video, the teacher provides explicit instruction on the value of using contextual clues for reading comprehension.

INSTRUCTIONAL APPROACHES FOR MATH Researchers have determined that certain principles characterize effective math instruction for students with learning disabilities. Probably the most important one is that the instruction needs to be explicit (Fuchs et al., 2011; Gersten et al., 2009). Constructivist, discovery-oriented approaches to math may succeed with students who don't experience learning problems, but students with learning disabilities need more structure and teacher direction. Some other principles are that the teacher should sequence the instruction to minimize errors, but when errors occur, they should be immediately rectified. The instruction should include cumulative review of concepts and operations, and the students' progress should be closely monitored.

INSTRUCTIONAL APPROACHES FOR SCIENCE AND SOCIAL STUDIES Students with learning disabilities often have problems with content areas such as science and social studies, especially when the primary means of delivering the content is through textbooks. Unfortunately, the current climate of standards-based learning and high-stakes testing has resulted in heavy emphasis on textbook-based science and social studies instruction—and textbook-based instruction does not align well with the weaknesses of students with learning disabilities in prior knowledge, reading, vocabulary, and memory. At the same time, however, the need for structure experienced by students with learning disabilities makes the use of activities-oriented instruction problematic. When activities-based instruction is carefully structured and sequenced, however, with emphasis on cumulative review and monitoring of student progress, it can be effective for students with learning disabilities (Scruggs, Mastropieri, Brigham, & Milman, 2017).

When textbooks are used, researchers have found that enhancing the content of science and social studies materials is very effective for students with learning disabilities (Gajria, Jitendra, Sood, & Sacks, 2007). **Content enhancement** can take many forms. It's a way of making materials more salient or prominent. Two particularly effective ways of enhancing content are graphic organizers and mnemonics. **Graphic organizers** "are visual devices that employ lines, circles, and boxes to organize information: hierarchic, cause/effect, compare/contrast, and cyclic or linear sequences" (Ellis & Howard, 2007, p. 1). **Mnemonics** involve using pictures and/or words to help remember information. For a description of mnemonics and how it can be used in the classroom, see the accompanying Responsive Instruction feature, "Mnemonics."

Direct Instruction

Direct Instruction (DI) focuses on the details of the instructional process. Commercial DI programs are available for several academic areas (e.g., reading, math, science, social studies). Advocates of DI stress a systematic analysis of the concept to be taught, rather than analysis of the characteristics of the student. A critical component of DI is task analysis. **Task analysis** involves breaking down academic problems into their component parts so that teachers can teach the parts separately and then teach the students to put the parts together in order to demonstrate the larger skill.

Originally pioneered by Sigfried Engelmann and the late Wesley C. Becker, DI programs consist of precisely sequenced, scripted, fast-paced lessons taught to small groups of 4 to 10 students, with a heavy emphasis on drill and practice. See the Responsive Instruction feature, "Direct Instruction," on page 129 for more information about DI in the classroom.

Direct Instruction programs are among the best-researched commercial programs available for students with learning disabilities. Use of these programs not only results in immediate academic gains, but also may bring long-term academic gains (Ellis & Fouts, 1997; Tarver, 1999).

MyLab Education
Video Example 6.10
Watch this video for a demonstration of a teacher using Direct Instruction.

Peer Tutoring

Teachers have successfully used several types of peer tutoring arrangements with students with learning disabilities. Two examples are **classwide peer tutoring (CWPT)** and **peer-assisted learning strategies (PALS)**. In Chapter 5, we discussed the use of CWPT for students with intellectual disabilities. Researchers have also extensively documented CWPT as effective for students with learning disabilities or those at risk for learning disabilities (Kourea, Cartledge, & Musti-Rao, 2007; Maheady, Harper, & Mallette, 2003). CWPT consists of "students who are taught by peers who are *trained* and *supervised* by classroom teachers" (Maheady et al., 2003, p. 1). "Trained" and "supervised" are emphasized because it's imperative that the teachers carefully structure the tutoring experience. In other words, the instruction isn't just turned over to the students.

RESPONSIVE INSTRUCTION

Meeting the Needs of Students with Learning Disabilities

MNEMONICS

Franklin Pierce (purse)
14 (forking)

FIGURE A   Mnemonic representation of Franklin Pierce, 14th president of the United States

Source: Adapted from Mastropieri, M. A., Scruggs, T. E., & Whedon, C. (1997). Using mnemonic strategies to teach information about U.S. Presidents: A classroom-based investigation. Learning Disability Quarterly, 20, 13–21. Copyright 1994 by Thomas E. Scruggs and Margo A. Mastropieri.

What Are Mnemonics?

The term *mnemonic* comes from the name of the Greek goddess of memory, Mnemosyne, whose name was derived from *mnemon*, meaning "mindful." Today, a mnemonic refers to any memory-enhancing strategy. Almost everyone has used a mnemonic at one time or another. To remember the order of the planets, many students learn the phrase "My Very Educated Mother Just Served Us Nachos." Music students trying to remember scales learn "Every Good Boy Deserves Fudge." Rhymes are another form of mnemonic—"*I* before *E*, except after *C*, or when pronounced as *A* as in *neighbor* and *weigh*." Mnemonics come in a variety of forms, but what defines a mnemonic is its ability to aid in the retention of certain information.

What the Research Says

Researchers have studied mnemonics and students with learning disabilities in both laboratory settings (i.e., one-to-one with trained experimenters rather than classroom

teachers) and classroom settings. Findings from these studies (Lubin & Polloway, 2016; Mastropieri & Scruggs, 1998; Scruggs et al., 2017) reveal the following gains made by students who are taught using mnemonics:

- Mnemonic keyword method resulted in increased recall of information.
- Small groups of students with learning disabilities could be taught using a variety of mnemonic strategies over a period of days without diminishing the effectiveness of the specific mnemonics.
- Mnemonic pictures aided in the comprehension and recall of information presented in science and history texts.
- Students with learning disabilities could be taught to create their own mnemonics and apply them successfully.
- Students with learning and behavior disorders benefited from teacher-created mnemonics and were able to retain the information longer than students who were not provided mnemonics.
- Mnemonics appeared to result in increased motivation, efficacy, and willingness to learn.

Implementing Mnemonics in the Classroom

Two effective mnemonic techniques are the keyword and peg-word methods (Lasley, Matczynski, & Rowley, 2002). (See Figure A.) When using a keyword approach, students are taught how to transform an unfamiliar word into a familiar word. For example, the word *accolade* could be associated with the keyword *Kool-Aid*. To associate *Kool-Aid* with the definition of *accolade*, students can think of someone making a toast to a guest of honor with a cup of Kool-Aid. Thus, the definition "giving praise" will be closely associated with *accolade* (Levin, 1993).

To use the peg-word strategy, students learn to correlate numbers with familiar rhyming words. The teacher creates a picture that incorporates the peg word along with the content associations. Teachers use this strategy when students need to remember the order of information or when a number is associated with the fact. For example, a student who is trying to remember that Monroe was the fifth president could combine the keyword for Monroe and the peg word *hive* for five. The image of bees carrying money to a hive would be the mnemonic (Mastropieri & Scruggs, 1998).

BY KRISTIN L. SAYESKI

PALS is based on research-proven, best practices in, for example, phonological awareness, decoding, and comprehension strategies (Fuchs & Fuchs, 2005; Fuchs, Fuchs, & Burish, 2000). PALS involves the pairing of a higher performing student with a lower performing student, with the pairs then participating in highly structured tutoring sessions. The students take turns being the "coach" (tutor) and the "reader" (tutee). More information is available on the PALS website at Vanderbilt University.

Service Delivery Models

For many years, the most common form of educational placement for students with learning disabilities was the special education resource room. In the mid-1990s, however, in keeping with the trend toward inclusion, the general education classroom surpassed the resource room as the most popular placement. In addition, the number of placements in separate classrooms has gradually diminished. Currently, about 70% of students with learning disabilities spend 80% or more of the school day in the general education classroom (U.S. Department of Education, 2016).

As we discussed in Chapter 2, more and more schools are moving toward some kind of cooperative teaching arrangement, in which general and special education teachers work together in the general education classroom. Some advocates believe that this model is particularly appropriate for students with learning disabilities because it allows them to stay in the general education classroom for all or almost all of their instruction. However, the research base for cooperative teaching is still in its infancy (Cook, McDuffie, Oshita, & Cook, 2017; Murawski & Swanson, 2001). See the How Can I Help feature on page 130 for a description of a co-teaching situation in an eighth-grade algebra class.

Because students with learning disabilities make up the largest category of special education students and because their academic and behavioral problems are not as severe as those of students with intellectual disabilities or behavior disorders, they are often candidates for full inclusion. However, all the major professional and parent organizations have developed position papers against placing all students with learning disabilities in full-inclusion settings. Research on the effectiveness of inclusion for students with learning disabilities also argues against using full inclusion for *all* students with learning disabilities (Zigmond & Kloo, 2017). Evidence indicates that the legal mandate of IDEA requiring the availability of a full continuum of placements is sound policy for students with learning disabilities.

ASSESSMENT OF PROGRESS

The notion of using assessment information to help plan educational strategies has gained much of its popularity from professionals working in the area of learning disabilities. For example, **curriculum-based measurement (CBM)** was developed largely by Deno and his colleagues (Deno, 1985; Fuchs, Deno, & Mirkin, 1984) of the University of Minnesota Institute for Research on Learning Disabilities (IRLD). In addition to CBM, teachers may administer other forms of informal assessments to monitor students' progress and make instructional decisions. This section provides a brief overview of CBM and other informal measures to monitor progress in the areas of mathematics, reading, and written expression.

MyLab Education
Video Example 6.11
This video shows a teacher using curriculum-based measurement.

Curriculum-Based Measurement

Teachers of students with learning disabilities are using CBM increasingly as a means to monitor academic progress and to document students' responsiveness to instruction.

CBM involves direct and frequent samples of performance on items from the curriculum in which students are being instructed. Each curriculum-based measure has multiple forms of equivalent difficulty that are administered at regular intervals to determine whether a student is making progress toward a specified goal (McMaster & Espin, 2007). Teachers implement the measures as short probes that require only minutes to administer.

RESPONSIVE INSTRUCTION

Meeting the Needs of Students with Learning Disabilities

DIRECT INSTRUCTION

EXERCISE 3

Say the Sounds

Note: Do not write the words on the board. This is an oral exercise.

1. Listen: fffeˉeˉeˉ. (Hold up a finger for each sound.)

2. Say the sounds in (pause) fffeˉeˉeˉ. Get ready. (Hold up a finger for each sound.) fffeˉeˉeˉ. (Repeat until the students say the sounds without stopping.)

3. Say it fast. (Signal.) Fee.

4. What word? (Signal.) Fee. Yes, fee.

5. (Repeat steps 2–4 for if, fish, sam, at, me, rim, she, we, ship, fat, miff.)

FIGURE A   A sample DI lesson

What Is Direct Instruction?

Direct instruction (DI) is a highly structured, teacher-directed method of instruction. The main features of DI programs are as follows:

- Field-tested, scripted lesson plans
- Curriculum based upon the theory of mastery learning (i.e., students do not move on until they have mastered the concept)
- Rapid pace of instruction highly dependent upon frequent teacher questioning and student response
- Achievement grouping
- Frequent assessments

Siegfried Engelmann developed DI in the 1960s on the basis of studies of beginning reading. Since the development of his early DI programs such as DISTAR Reading I (Engelmann & Bruner, 1969), DI programs have been developed in the areas of reading, language arts, mathematics, science, and social studies. One of the defining features of DI programs is that virtually every aspect of instruction undergoes careful evaluation before it is approved for inclusion in the program. Researchers evaluate everything from group size to teacher directions to method of student response, to achieve optimal effectiveness. As a result, DI programs have received the highest ranking for program effectiveness in an independent analysis of instructional programs (Ellis, 2001).

What the Research Says

To obtain an idea of the overall effectiveness of a program, researchers conduct what is called a meta-analysis. To conduct a meta-analysis, researchers identify all studies that have been conducted on a specific technique or program and statistically determine how effective the technique is as a whole. Since the inception of DI, several of these comprehensive evaluations have been conducted in regard to DI curriculum. A thorough meta-analysis made over 173 comparisons between DI and other programs. Results showed that (1) 64% of the comparisons resulted in statistically significant differences in favor of the groups using DI, (2) 35% of the comparisons showed no differences among programs, and (3) 1% showed differences in favor of programs other than DI (Adams & Engelmann, 1996). In short, the overall effectiveness of DI programs is among the highest in the field of education.

Implementing the Curriculum

To implement DI, teachers need to receive training in the program. Because of the highly structured nature of DI materials, many educators and administrators incorrectly assume that DI is "teacher-proof"; that is, anyone could be effective using the materials. Nothing could be further from the truth. Using the materials with ease, understanding the rationale for each component and therefore being able to communicate that to students, and pacing the instruction to meet the unique needs of a group of students all require teaching skills that cannot come from a script. After initial training, coaches or facilitators provide ongoing support for teachers who use DI programs to ensure that teachers are maximizing the effectiveness of the curriculum.

What Does DI Look Like?

The sample exercise in Figure A is an excerpt from Corrective Reading, an accelerated reading program for students in grades 3.5 through 12 who have not mastered the basics of decoding and comprehension.

In this decoding lesson, students work on phonemic awareness, letter–symbol identification, and sounding out words. The use of choral response increases opportunities for student engagement, and individual questioning ensures individual mastery.

Direct Instruction is a carefully evaluated instructional approach requiring specific training for teachers.

BY KRISTIN L. SAYESKI

HOW CAN I HELP?

Working with Students with Learning Disabilities in the General Education Classroom

"How can she help me if she doesn't know algebra like I do?"

How can co-teaching with a special educator to meet the needs of students with learning disabilities work if the special educator is not as much of a content area specialist as the general educator? Though you might think that would mean an end to equal collaboration in, say, a biology or advanced literature course, teachers of students with learning disabilities have knowledge about learning that can help make them an active part of any co-teaching team.

What Does It Mean to Be a Teacher of Students with Learning Disabilities?

Most programs for teachers of students with learning disabilities focus on the learning process and effective strategies for learning across the content areas. According to the Council for Exceptional Children (2003), teachers of students with learning disabilities should be ready and able to address a variety of academic learning problems, such as reading, math, spelling, and so forth. They should be able to help students apply these skills in the general education content areas, such as science, social studies, and so forth. Also, they should be able to teach these skills in several different settings, such as individually or in small or large groups.

Successful Strategies for Co-Teaching

Joan Hamilton is a former special educator who co-taught with general educators at the middle and high school levels. She describes a situation in which she was not the content specialist but was able to provide explicit strategy instruction to all students because of a successful co-teaching arrangement.

I was originally certified to teach social studies from 8th to 12th grades. When I began working in those classrooms, I realized that there were several students who really struggled to read the textbook I was using, and I became interested in learning disabilities.

After earning a Masters in Special Education, one of my first positions required co-teaching in an 8th-grade pre-algebra classroom. I knew the material, but wasn't as confident that I knew the best way to teach it. My co-teacher and I ended up with a class of 18 students, 11 of whom were identified with disabilities (nine with learning disabilities) and the rest had done poorly in their previous math courses. The textbook prescribed a rigid plan for the classroom: review homework, teach the next lesson, do some practice problems. The pacing guide provided by the district (and part of my co-teacher's evaluation criteria) did not leave many opportunities for creativity in instruction. Though we were both on the same 8th-grade team, we could use very little of the team meeting time to plan together. So, after many philosophical discussions, we plunged into the course. After a few weeks, we found a rhythm that seemed to work with the students.

First, my co-teacher taught the lesson as I took notes on the overhead for the students. I would often create a circle on the overhead with the example problem in the middle. As we worked the problem in the middle of the circle, I would use words to describe the step on the outside of the circle (see Rooney, 1998). This helped me understand how my co-teacher would teach the concept. And it provided the students with an annotated example problem.

Next, we both moved around the room to help students as they completed practice problems.

The next day, I did the homework review. This gave me the opportunity to return to the graphic organizers for review and to re-teach the steps of the problem as necessary (as my co-teacher had taught it earlier). It also allowed my co-teacher to circulate and to help individual students.

This co-teaching plan is probably a combination of the structures described in articles and books about co-teaching. It provided us with what we felt was the best support for our students, given the conditions of the classroom and curriculum. We had a few students fail the course because they just didn't even attempt to do much of the work. The majority, however, made it through the material and on to algebra with a basic understanding of the concepts and of how to structure their notes and ask questions.

BY MARGARET P. WEISS

In reading, for example, CBM typically focuses on oral reading fluency, which is determined by calculating the number of correct words per minute (CWPM) read on a grade-level passage. To monitor progress toward a specified goal, the teacher first gathers data to determine the student's current CWPM. The teacher then uses this information to calculate a **baseline data point**. Using data of **expected growth norms** (see, for example, Hosp, Hosp, & Howell, 2007), the teacher establishes a goal for the student and creates an **aim line** on a graph to depict where the student should be performing at a given point in time. The teacher assesses the student's reading on a CBM probe two or more times each week and graphs the data to determine if the student is on target to reach the specified goal.

Figure 6.1 illustrates a CBM graph for Billy, a fourth grader with a learning disability. Billy's teacher had gathered the baseline data point and determined that he read 56 CWPM. She then created an aim line for 18 weeks of instruction (one semester). Based on expected growth norms (Fuchs, L. S., Fuchs, D., Hamlett, Walz, & Germann, 1993; Hosp et al., 2007) and the baseline data point for CWPM, his teacher determined that Billy should be reading 79 CWPM by the end of the semester. After the first 5 weeks of instruction, Billy was on track to reach his goal by the end of the semester. However, during weeks 6 through 8, his CWPM began to decline, such that it looked like he wouldn't be able to reach his goal. At this point, the teacher adjusted the instruction by adding 15 minutes per day of peer tutoring, two times a week. From that point on, Billy improved and actually exceeded his goal, reading 82 CWPM by the end of the semester.

Although oral reading fluency probes are the most common form of CBM, teachers use additional methods to monitor student progress in other areas of reading (e.g., phonemic awareness, decoding, and comprehension), mathematics, spelling, and writing. In mathematics, researchers have developed CBMs that span topics in early mathematics through secondary skills. As early as prekindergarten, students may participate in CBM to demonstrate their knowledge of mathematics through various tasks (e.g., circling numbers to demonstrate numeral identification; Foegen, Jiban, & Deno, 2007). For school-age students, most CBMs focus on basic operations; however, CBM may be used for computation as well as conceptual knowledge. For more information on curriculum-based measurement and progress monitoring, search for the National Center on Student Progress Monitoring.

FIGURE 6.1

A PROGRESS-MONITORING CHART USING CURRICULUM-BASED MEASUREMENT ON ORAL READING FLUENCY FOR BILLY, A FOURTH GRADER WITH A LEARNING DISABILITY

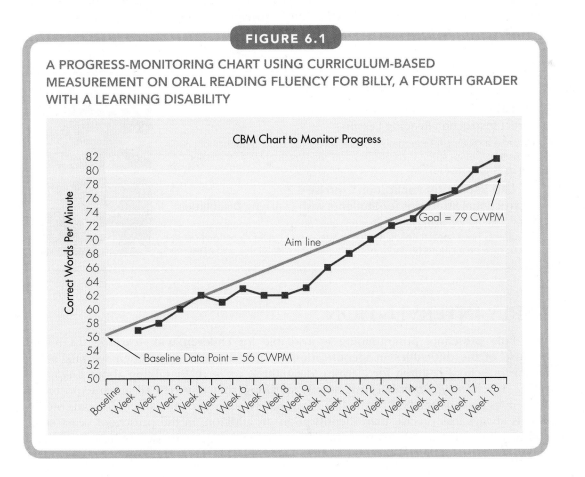

Informal Assessment

In addition to CBM, teachers may also use other informal measures to monitor student progress and plan for instruction. In the area of reading, for example, teachers can use an **informal reading inventory (IRI)**, a series of reading passages or word lists graded in order of difficulty. The teacher has the student read from the series, beginning with a list or passage that is likely to be easy for the student. The student continues to read increasingly more difficult lists or passages while the teacher monitors the student's performance. After compiling the results of the IRI, the teacher can use them to estimate the appropriate difficulty level of reading material for the student.

Mathematics dynamic assessment (MDA) is another example of an informal assessment that can inform instruction. Using MDA, the teacher integrates research-based assessment techniques including (1) examining mathematical understanding at concrete, semiconcrete, and abstract levels; (2) assessing mathematical interests and experiences; (3) examining error patterns; and (4) using flexible interviews (Allsopp, Kyger, & Lovin, 2008). This informal, yet comprehensive assessment process allows teachers to design effective instruction to meet the unique needs of students with learning disabilities.

Testing Accommodations

Accommodations for students with learning disabilities are similar to those for students with intellectual disabilities, as presented in Chapter 5. Many students with learning disabilities receive accommodations on standardized tests that alter scheduling, presentation format, and response format. The most common accommodations for students with learning disabilities are extended time and small-group setting administration.

Although testing accommodations are common for students with learning disabilities, particularly extended time, research is not clear on their effectiveness. For example, it's not clear whether accommodations provide an opportunity for students to demonstrate their knowledge without unfair advantage, or whether the accommodations actually boost their performance. Likewise, more research is needed to determine how to best match testing accommodations for specific students.

MyLab Education Self-Check 6.4

MyLab Education Application Exercise 6.1:
Direct Instruction Reading Lesson

Observe a reading lesson that follows a very structured sequence of steps to promote student vocabulary and reading fluency, and answer the questions that follow.

MyLab Education Application Exercise 6.2:
Instructional Strategies for Students with Learning Disabilities

In Mr. Wimberly's sixth-grade inclusion classroom of 27 students, 5 students have special needs. Watch a video and answer questions about how he includes his students with learning disabilities and ADHD.

EARLY INTERVENTION

Very little preschool programming is available for children with learning disabilities because of the difficulties in identification at such a young age. When we talk about testing preschool children for learning disabilities, we're really talking about *prediction* rather than *identification* because, strictly speaking, they haven't had much exposure to academics such as reading or math. Unfortunately, all other things being equal, prediction is always less precise than identification. In addition, in the preschool years some children do experience developmental delays. Some children who do not have disabilities show slow developmental progress at this young age, but soon catch up with their peers.

TABLE 6.1 • **Important developmental milestones**

- Delay in comprehension and/or expression of spoken language
  - Limited receptive vocabulary
  - Reduced expressive vocabulary ("late talkers")
  - Difficulty understanding simple (e.g., one-step) directions
  - Monotone or other unusual prosodic features of speech
  - Reduced intelligibility
  - Infrequent or inappropriate spontaneous communication (vocal, verbal, or nonverbal)
  - Immature syntax

- Delay in emergent literacy skills
  - Slow speed in naming objects and colors
  - Limited phonological awareness (e.g., rhyming, syllable blending)
  - Minimal interest in print
  - Limited print awareness (e.g., book handling, recognizing environmental print)

- Delay in perceptual-motor skills
  - Problems in gross or fine motor coordination (e.g., hopping, dressing, cutting, stringing beads)
  - Difficulty in coloring, copying, and drawing

Source: Adapted with permission from National Joint Committee on Learning Disabilities. (2006). *Learning disabilities and young children: Identification and intervention.* Retrieved from http://www.ldonline.org/about/partners/njcld

Even though it's wise to be cautious in identifying preschool children as having learning disabilities, researchers have determined that several risk factors are relatively good predictors of later learning disabilities. Table 6.1 provides a list of developmental milestones parents and teachers should monitor in the preschool years.

TRANSITION TO ADULTHOOD

At one time, professionals thought that children would outgrow their learning disabilities by the time they reached adulthood. We now know that this is far from the truth. While the long-term prognosis for individuals with learning disabilities is generally more positive than the prognosis for children with some other disabilities (e.g., behavior disorders), the potential for difficulty exists. Although the majority of students with learning disabilities don't drop out of school, their dropout rate of 25% is two to three times that of their peers without disabilities (Cortiella, 2009; Rojewski & Gregg, 2017). Also, many adults with learning disabilities have persistent problems in learning, socializing, holding jobs, and living independently (Scanlon, Patton, & Raskind, 2017). Even those individuals who are relatively successful in their transition to adulthood often must devote considerable energy to coping with daily living situations.

Factors Related to Successful Transition

How any particular adult with learning disabilities will fare depends on a variety of factors and is difficult to predict. Several researchers have addressed the topic of what contributes to successful adjustment of adults with learning disabilities (Bear, Kortering, & Braziel, 2006; Lindstrom & Benz, 2011; Rojewski & Gregg, 2017). Although IQ and achievement scores would seem to be the best predictors of success, according to successful adults with learning disabilities, the things that set them apart from those who are not as successful are the following:

- An extraordinary degree of perseverance
- The ability to set goals for oneself
- A realistic acceptance of weaknesses coupled with an attitude of building on strengths

- Access to a strong network of social support from friends and family
- Exposure to intensive and long-term educational intervention
- High-quality on-the-job or postsecondary vocational training
- A supportive work environment
- Being able to take control of their lives

The last attribute, in particular, is a consistent theme among the successful. They have not let their disability rule them; rather, they have taken the initiative to control their own destiny. As one adult remarked, on looking back at his days in secondary school:

> Having an LD is much akin to being blind or losing the use of an appendage; it affects all aspects of your life. In dealing with this, you have two choices. One, you can acknowledge the parasitic relationship the LD has with you and consciously strive to excel despite its presence.
> . . . The other path let(s) the LD slowly dominate you and become(s) the scapegoat for all your failings. Can't find a good job? Must be the LD. Relationships always fail? It's the LD. If you follow this destructive path, you spend the remainder of your life being controlled by your LD. (Queen, 2001, p. 15)

Eric Breeden (see accompanying Peer Connections) is a good example of an individual who did not allow a learning disability to interfere with his long-term goals.

Secondary Programming

Approaches to educating students with learning disabilities at the secondary level differ, depending on whether the goal is to prepare students for college or work. Students whose goal is to enter the workforce after high school are taught basic academic skills in math, language arts, and reading. They're also taught functional skills, such as on-the-job behavior, filling out job applications, and balancing a checkbook. It's often combined with work–study—supervised work experiences during the school day. Ideally, the student can explore a variety of jobs that might be of interest. Engaging in paid work experiences during high school is also beneficial for successful employment upon graduation (Rojewski & Gregg, 2011).

Students intending to pursue college work receive continued support in their academic subjects. Compared to elementary school, in high school the role of the special education teacher typically shifts even more to one of consultation with the general education teachers in the content areas (e.g., math, history, science). The general education teacher teaches the content, and the special education teacher recommends modifications to the format of the content and teaches the student strategies for learning. For example, the learning strategies model developed at the University of Kansas Center for Research on Learning focuses on teaching students to overcome their metacognitive deficits by using learning strategies (Deshler & Hock, 2007). The Kansas group has developed a variety of strategies that students can use to help them organize information and learn it more efficiently.

Regardless of whether the focus is on transition to work or to college, a key element to successful transition programming is empowering students to make informed choices and to take responsibility for their futures (Cobb & Alwell, 2009). One way of achieving this is to ensure that students take part in their transition planning. In addition to a **transition plan** (see Chapter 2), federal law now requires that schools develop a **summary of performance (SOP)** for individual students with a disability as they exit secondary school, whether by graduating or exceeding the age of eligibility. SOPs are designed to provide a summary of relevant information, such as assessment reports; accommodations that have been provided; and recommendations for future accommodations, assistive technology, and support services for use in employment, training, or postsecondary schooling. SOPs also have a section for the student to provide input. Because SOPs only began implementation in 2007–08, little research on their effectiveness exists.

PEER CONNECTIONS Eric Breeden

ERIC BREEDEN was born in Charlottesville, Virginia. At the time of this interview, he was a high school senior. Eric was diagnosed with a learning disability in fifth grade. His mother initially had concerns about disruptive behavior that his teachers were noticing in the classroom. Once Eric was diagnosed, changes were made in the classroom, and this behavior disappeared. Since fifth grade, Eric has had optional services that include sitting in the front of the classroom and having notes taken for him, more time for tests, and a resource class and teacher. Eric has found some of these adaptations more beneficial than others and has gone on to have a successful high school career. Eric is an avid athlete and is looking forward to going to college, where he hopes to play football and pursue a degree in criminal justice.

What do you do for fun? I hang out with friends and play football.

What is your favorite way to relax? I like to hang out at the house and listen to music.

What is something that you excel at? Sports! I do football, wrestling, and track.

What is your pet peeve? Losing and failing, giving up. In sports and in school.

Can you recall one teacher in particular who has been a positive influence in your life? Yes, I guess my preschool teacher. She made me love school. She was a fun teacher, and I still remember her today.

Is there anyone else (celebrity, family member) whom you regard as a role model? Why are they a role model for you? The football player, Ray Lewis, who plays for the Ravens. I admire him because he's one of the best in the NFL, but he doesn't talk about it. He's not cocky and doesn't brag, even though he's a great player.

What is the most difficult thing for you about having a disability? When I was diagnosed with a learning disability, in fifth grade, I started having a resource class and teacher. This was helpful in some ways because the teacher helped me stay organized and on top of my work. But it was hard once I got to high school, because I couldn't really take any extra elective classes like my peers. Because of the resource class, I couldn't fit an arts class or a foreign language into my schedule. This was difficult, but in tenth grade I decided that I wanted to try school without having a resource class. It worked out well, and now I still receive guidance from a resource teacher but I rarely notice my learning disability because I'm not singled out as much. I feel that I can do all of my work without a lot of trouble.

Do you see your disability as affecting your ability to achieve what you want in your life? No, I think that I will still be able to graduate high school. When I had my resource class I wasn't going to be able to graduate with an advance diploma because I couldn't take a foreign language. But when they let me stop resource class, I took Spanish, and now I will graduate with an advance diploma. I also plan to go to college, and even hopefully play football in college.

Has your disability affected your social relationships? No, not at all.

Are there any advantages to having a disability that others might be surprised to know? Not really. I mean I have the option to have notes written for me in my classes, and I also can have different test formats, like written copies. But I don't find that I use a lot of these services right now.

How do you think others perceive you? I think as funny and outgoing . . . and an athlete.

What is one thing that you would like others to know about you? I want to play football in college. Right now I play linebacker, stage key, and receiver, but I really hope to play in college, too.

Where do you see yourself 10 years from now? Having a job, hopefully in criminal justice, and having a family. Also, probably living in New York, Florida, or California.

Please fill in the blank: I couldn't live without _____. Sports!

Postsecondary Programming

Postsecondary programs include vocational and technical programs as well as community colleges and 4-year colleges and universities. More and more individuals with learning disabilities are enrolling in colleges and universities, and more and more universities are establishing special programs and services for these students.

In selecting a college, students and their families should explore what kinds of student support services are offered. Section 504 of the Vocational Rehabilitation Act of 1973 (Public Law 93–112) requires that colleges make reasonable accommodations for students with disabilities so that they will not be discriminated against because of their disabilities. Some typical accommodations are extended time on exams, allowing students to take exams in a distraction-free room, providing tape recordings of lectures and books, and assigning volunteer note takers for lectures.

MyLab Education
Video Example 6.12
In this video, Jennifer discusses the skills she developed to advocate for herself, as well as to determine which accommodations and support are helpful and which are not.

Even though students with disabilities are entitled to accommodations, they need to be much more proactive in order to receive these services than they were in the K–12 education system. Therefore, a potentially useful skill for college students with learning disabilities is *self-advocacy*: the ability to understand one's disability, be aware of one's legal rights, and communicate one's rights and needs to professors and administrators (Madaus & Banerjee, 2011). Although ideally, self-advocacy skills should be taught to students with learning disabilities in secondary school, many students come to college in need of guidance in how to advocate for themselves in a confident but nonconfrontational manner.

Much remains to be learned about programming effectively for students with learning disabilities in order for them to experience a rich, fulfilling adulthood. However, substantial strides are being made in the right direction. Between 1997 and 2007, the high school dropout rate was down 40%, and those graduating with a regular high school diploma was up 20% (Cortiella, 2009). And the numbers entering college are increasing.

MyLab Education Self-Check 6.5

▼ chapter six SUMMARY

How do professionals define learning disabilities?

- The most common definition is that of the federal government, which has been in effect since 1975 (with a few minor wording changes in 1997).

- The National Joint Committee on Learning Disabilities (NJCLD) presented a definition that differs from that of the federal government with respect to (1) no reference to psychological processes, (2) inclusion of intrinsic nature of learning disabilities, (3) inclusion of adults, (4) inclusion of self-regulation and social interaction problems, (5) omission of terms difficult to define, (6) purportedly less confusion regarding the exclusion clause, and (7) omission of spelling.

- In 2013, the American Psychiatric Association published a new definition for learning disabilities that eliminates the IQ–achievement discrepancy criteria for identification and uses a broad categorization of learning disabilities that does not specify the particular area of weakness.

How do professionals identify students with learning disabilities?

- Since the late 1970s, the major method of identifying learning disabilities had been to look for an IQ–achievement discrepancy.

- More recently, professionals have proposed use of a response-to-intervention (RTI) approach.

  - RTI is based on a multitiered (typically three tiers) model of prevention.

  - A variety of RTI models have been proposed and implemented.

  - Many questions still remain regarding large-scale implementation of RTI.

What is the prevalence of learning disabilities?

- Just under 5% of school-age students are identified as having learning disabilities, making learning disabilities the largest category of special education by far.

- The prevalence of learning disabilities has more than doubled since the late 1970s, but it has begun to decline somewhat since the late 1990s.

  - Some believe the increase reflects poor diagnostic practices.

  - Some believe that some of the increase may be due to social and cultural changes as well as reluctance to label students as having "intellectual disabilities."

- Boys with learning disabilities outnumber girls about 3 to 1.

  - Some believe that this is due to gender bias in referrals.

  - Some believe that this is partly due to boys being more vulnerable biologically.

What causes learning disabilities?

- With the advance of neuroimaging techniques, most authorities now believe that central nervous system (CNS) dysfunction underlies learning disabilities.

- Strong evidence indicates that many cases of learning disabilities are inherited.

- Toxins (e.g., fetal alcohol syndrome) and medical factors (premature birth) can also result in learning disabilities.

What are some of the psychological and behavioral characteristics of learners with learning disabilities?

- Persons with learning disabilities exhibit interindividual and intraindividual variability.

- Academic deficits are the hallmark of learning disabilities.

  - Reading disabilities are the most common form of academic disability and can be manifested in decoding, fluency, and comprehension problems.

    - Phonological awareness, the understanding that speech consists of units of sound (words, syllables, phonemes), underlies the ability to decode.

    - Phonemic awareness—understanding that words are made up of sounds or phonemes—is particularly important for learning to decode.

  - Writing disabilities, including handwriting, spelling, and composition, are common in students with learning disabilities.

  - Spoken language disabilities include problems with syntax (grammar), semantics (word meanings), phonology, and pragmatics (social uses of language).

  - Math disabilities include problems with computation and word problems.

- Some students with learning disabilities experience problems with perceptual, perceptual-motor, and general coordination.

- Many students with learning disabilities have problems with attention, and almost half of those with attention deficit hyperactivity disorder (ADHD) also have learning disabilities.

- Memory problems include problems with working memory (WM) and retrieval from long term memory (RLTM).

- Metacognitive problems include deficits in recognizing task requirements, selecting and using appropriate strategies, and monitoring and adjusting performance.

- Social-emotional problems include peer rejection, poor self-concept, and poor social cognition.

  - Problems with social interaction are more prevalent in students with problems with math, visual-spatial and tactual tasks, and self-regulation; such students are sometimes referred to as having nonverbal learning disabilities.

  - Motivational problems can include having an external locus of control and learned helplessness.

  - Some authorities believe that a composite of many of the preceding characteristics indicates that many students with learning disabilities are passive rather than active learners.

What are some educational considerations for learners with learning disabilities?

- Cognitive training focuses on (1) changing thought processes, (2) providing strategies for learning, and (3) teaching self-initiative.

  - *Self-instruction* involves having students say aloud what it is they are to do.

  - *Self-monitoring* involves having students self-evaluate and self-record while they are doing academic work.

  - *Scaffolded instruction* involves providing students with teacher support while they perform academic work.

  - *Reciprocal teaching* involves the teacher modeling correct performance and then having the student assume the role of co-teacher.

- Effective instructional approaches for reading are explicit and systematic and focus on phonological awareness, phonics, fluency, vocabulary, and comprehension.

- Effective writing instruction is explicit and systematic; an example is the self-regulated strategy development (SRSD) model.

- Effective math instruction is explicit, systematic, and sequenced to minimize errors, but with errors immediately rectified.

- Carefully structured and sequenced science and social studies instruction is effective, and content enhancement (e.g., graphic organizers, mnemonics) is a technique that helps make textbook-based instruction more effective.

- Direct Instruction (DI) focuses even more directly on academics than does cognitive training; a critical component of DI is task analysis, as well as the following:

  - Field-tested scripted lessons

  - Curricula based on mastery learning

  - Rapid instructional pace

  - Achievement grouping

  - Frequent assessments

- Using a peer tutoring strategy, students with learning disabilities are tutored by classmates without disabilities who are supervised and trained by the teacher.

- With respect to service delivery models, available research evidence indicates that a full continuum of placements is sound policy for students with learning disabilities.

How do professionals assess the academic progress of students with learning disabilities?

- Curriculum-based measurement (CBM) (brief samplings of academic performance) can be used to assess progress.

  - In reading, CBM typically focuses on correct words read per minute (CWPM).

  - CBM involves comparing the student's performance relative to a baseline point and an aim line based on expected growth norms.

- Informal reading inventories can be used to assess progress.

- Accommodations on standardized tests can include changes in scheduling and presentation and response formats.

What are some important considerations with respect to early intervention for learners with learning disabilities?

- Little preschool programming exists for children with learning disabilities because it's so hard to predict at that age which children will later develop academic problems.

- Even though prediction is not perfect, several developmental milestones are related to comprehension or expression of spoken language, emergent literacy skills, and perceptual skills that indicate risk for having learning disabilities.

What are some important considerations with respect to transition to adulthood for learners with learning disabilities?

- Factors related to successful transition include the following:
  - Extraordinary perseverance
  - Goal setting
  - Acceptance of weaknesses, combined with building on strengths
  - Strong network of social support
  - Intensive and long-term educational intervention
  - High-quality on-the-job or postsecondary vocational training
  - Supportive work environment
  - Taking control of one's life

- Secondary programming varies according to whether the goal is to prepare for work or college after graduation.
  - Those preparing for work receive training in basic academic skills, functional skills, and supervised work experiences.
  - Those preparing for college receive further academic training with support services from a special educator.
    - A key element to secondary programming is enabling students to make informed choices and to take responsibility for their futures.
    - In addition to a transition plan, the summary of performance (SOP) can be a potentially effective tool for transition to work or postsecondary education. The SOP includes information such as assessment reports, accommodations, recommendations for assistive technology, and support services.

- Postsecondary programs include vocational and technical programs as well as community colleges and 4-year colleges and universities.

- More and more students with learning disabilities are attending college. .

▼ INTERNET RESOURCES

Pertinent Organizations

- The Learning Disabilities Association of America remains the major parent organization for learning disabilities. Its website contains a variety of information on learning disabilities for parents and professionals: http://www.ldanatl.org

- The website for the National Center for Learning Disabilities contains several resources, such as position papers: http://www.ncld.org

- The Division for Learning Disabilities of the Council for Exceptional Children maintains a website devoted to research-based teaching practices: http://www.TeachingLD.org,

- Another professional organization providing information on learning disabilities is the Council for Learning Disabilities: http://www.cldinternational.org

- A helpful resource on both LD and ADHD is http://www.ldonline.com

- Decoding Dyslexia is a grass roots parent organization that focuses on ensuring that teachers are trained to provide evidence-based reading instruction (http://www.decoding-dyslexia.net/home.html)

chapter seven

LEARNERS WITH ATTENTION DEFICIT HYPERACTIVITY DISORDER

PeopleImages/Digitalvision/Getty Images

LEARNING OUTCOMES

Learning Outcome 7.1: Learn the history of, the clinical definition of, and the prevalence of attention deficit hyperactivity disorder.

Learning Outcome 7.2: Understand how attention deficit hyperactivity disorder is identified and the causes of attention deficit hyperactivity disorder.

Learning Outcome 7.3: Learn about the psychological and behavioral characteristics of learners with attention deficit hyperactivity disorder.

Learning Outcome 7.4: Understand educational and medication considerations for people with attention deficit hyperactivity disorder and how professionals assess progress to help plan educational strategies.

Learning Outcome 7.5: Learn about issues that should be considered with respect to early intervention and transition to adulthood for individuals with attention deficit hyperactivity disorder.

MISCONCEPTIONS ABOUT Learners with Attention Deficit Hyperactivity Disorder

MYTH All children with ADHD are hyperactive.

FACT Psychiatric classification of ADHD attempts to account for the fact that some persons display only inattention, or only hyperactivity/impulsivity, or both.

MYTH The primary symptom of ADHD is inattention.

FACT Recent conceptualizations of ADHD place problems with executive functioning and behavioral inhibition as the primary behavioral problems of ADHD.

MYTH ADHD is a fad, a trendy diagnosis of recent times in the United States with little research to support its existence.

FACT Literature indicates that physicians recognized the existence of attention problems and hyperactivity in the 18th, mid-19th, and early 20th centuries. Serious scientific study of attention problems began in the early and mid-20th century. A firmly established research base now supports its existence. And the prevalence of ADHD in several other countries is at least as high as it is in the United States.

MYTH ADHD is primarily the result of minimal brain injury.

FACT In most cases of ADHD, no evidence of actual damage to the brain exists. Most authorities believe that ADHD is the result of neurological dysfunction, which is often linked to hereditary factors.

MYTH African American children are more frequently identified as having ADHD than White children.

FACT National surveys indicate that the rate of identification of African American children and White children is the same. However, Latino/Hispanic children are less likely to be identified as having ADHD than African American and White children.

MYTH The social problems of students with ADHD are due to their not knowing how to interact socially.

FACT Most people with ADHD know how to interact, but their problems with behavioral inhibition make it difficult for them to implement socially appropriate behaviors.

MYTH Using psychostimulants, such as Ritalin, can easily turn children into abusers of other substances, such as cocaine and marijuana.

FACT No evidence shows that using psychostimulants for ADHD leads directly to drug abuse. In fact, evidence shows that those who are prescribed Ritalin as children are less likely to turn to illicit drugs as teenagers. However, care should be taken to make sure that children or others do not misuse the psychostimulants prescribed for them.

MYTH Because students with ADHD react strongly to stimulation, their learning environments should be highly unstructured in order to take advantage of their natural learning styles.

FACT Most authorities recommend a highly structured classroom for students with ADHD, especially in the early stages of instruction.

- What are the historical origins of attention deficit hyperactivity disorder (ADHD)?

- What is the current definition of ADHD?

- What is the prevalence of ADHD?

- What methods of assessment do professionals use to identify individuals with ADHD?

- What causes ADHD?

- What are some of the psychological and behavioral characteristics of learners with ADHD?

- What are some educational considerations for learners with ADHD?

- What are some medication considerations for learners with ADHD?

- How do professionals assess the academic, attention, and behavioral progress of students with ADHD?

- What are some important considerations with respect to early intervention for learners with ADHD?

- What are some important considerations with respect to transition to adulthood for learners with ADHD?

Fidgety Phil, the character in the poem (https://www.youtube.com/watch?v=LqmGK_NwGH4&list=RDLqmGK_NwGH4) by the German physician Heinrich Hoffmann (1865) is generally considered one of the first allusions in Western literature to what today is referred to as attention deficit hyperactivity disorder (ADHD) (Barkley, 2006c). Phil's lack of impulse control bears an uncanny similarity to today's conceptualization of ADHD as less a matter of inattention than a matter of regulating one's behavior. We discuss this conceptualization more fully later, but it's also important to point out here that Phil's excessive motor activity, or hyperactivity, may be characteristic of many children with ADHD but not all. Interestingly, Hoffmann also wrote another poem, "The Story of Johnny Head-in-Air," (http://www.youtube.com/watch?v=K_Qae-OE3f10) about a child who closely resembles children with ADHD who do not have problems with hyperactivity.

In addition to Hoffman's "poetic case studies," three early and scientifically oriented references to attention disorders are of interest; two pre-date Hoffmann, and one follows by about 40 years.

BRIEF HISTORY

The fact that there's a substantial history to the recognition of attention deficits is important. Today, ADHD is often the subject of criticism, being referred to as a phantom or bogus condition—sort of a fashionable, trendy diagnosis for people who are basically lazy and unmotivated. Although undoubtedly a few people hide behind an inappropriate diagnosis of ADHD, evidence indicates that the condition is extremely real for those who have it. And, as we point out in the next section, ADHD is not a recently "discovered," trendy diagnosis. An example of how ADHD is considered trendy is the following parody of "The Twilight Saga": http://www.youtube.com/watch?v=kuphC8lVa4A.

Dr. Melchior Adam Weikard's Textbook, "Der Philosophische Arzt"

The individual who is currently credited as the first to address the issue of attention deficits in the scientific literature is Dr. Melchior Weikard, a highly respected German physician, who served in numerous prestigious government positions, such as the court physician to an Empress, and the physician to a Prince-Bishop and a Tsar (Barkley & Peters, 2012). In his textbook published in 1775 (Weikard, 1775), he devoted a chapter to "Lack of Attention," in which he described the inattentive person as having deficits in concentration, being distracted by "every humming fly, every shadow, every sound, the memory of old stories [drawing] him off task to other imaginations. . . . [hearing] only half of everything. . . . (Barkley & Peters, 2012, p. 5).

Sir Alexander Crichton's Treatise "On Attention and Its Diseases"

About 20 years later, the treatise by the Scottish-born physician, Sir Alexander Crichton (1798), garnered even more attention than Weikard's publication (Palmer & Finger, 2001). Many of Crichton's notions regarding attention deficits are consistent with today's ideas. He noted that the ability to attend was not automatic but required active effort. And he theorized that a person could be born with attention disorders or could acquire them through diseases affecting the brain.

Dr. George F. Still's Children with "Defective Moral Control"

Writing much later than Crichton but more than a century ago, Dr. George F. Still, a physician, provided an even more scientific account to the medical profession of what we now call ADHD. Still delivered three lectures to the Royal College of Physicians of London in 1902 in which he described cases of children who displayed spitefulness, cruelty, disobedience, impulsivity, and problems of attention and hyperactivity. He referred to them as having "defective moral control" (Still, 1902, p. 1008). In the language of his day, Still was essentially saying that these children lacked the ability to inhibit or refrain from engaging impulsively in inappropriate behavior. (See Figure 7.1.)

Although Still's words are more than a century old, they continue to have relevance; one of the most influential current psychological theories is based on the notion that an essential impairment in ADHD is a deficit involving behavioral inhibition (Barkley, 1997, 2000a, 2000b, 2006e). Still's cases were also similar to discussions of today's population of persons with ADHD in at least five ways:

1. Still speculated that many of these children had mild brain pathology.
2. Many of the children had normal intelligence.
3. The condition was more prevalent in males than females.
4. There was evidence that the condition had a hereditary basis.
5. Many of the children and their relatives also had other physical or psychological problems, such as depression and tics.

We return later to Barkley's theory and to these five points. Suffice it to say here that Still's children with "defective moral control" today would very likely be diagnosed as having ADHD by itself or ADHD with **conduct disorder**, which is characterized by a pattern of aggressive, disruptive behavior (see Chapter 8).

Kurt Goldstein's Brain-Injured Soldiers of World War I

Kurt Goldstein reported on the psychological effects of brain injury in soldiers who had suffered head wounds in combat in World War I. Among other things, he observed in his patients the psychological characteristics of disorganized behavior, hyperactivity, **perseveration**, and a "forced responsiveness to stimuli" (1936, 1939). Perseveration, the tendency to repeatedly engage in the same behaviors, is often cited by clinicians as a characteristic of persons with ADHD. And their forced responsiveness to stimuli is akin to distractibility.

The Strauss Syndrome

Goldstein's work laid the foundation for the investigations of Heinz Werner and Alfred Strauss in the 1930s and 1940s (e.g., Werner & Strauss, 1939, 1941). Having emigrated from Germany to the United States after Hitler's rise to power, Werner and Strauss teamed

FIGURE 7.1

A REPRODUCTION OF DR. GEORGE STILL'S OPENING REMARKS FOR HIS CLASSIC LECTURES ON CHILDREN WITH "DEFECTIVE MORAL CONTROL."

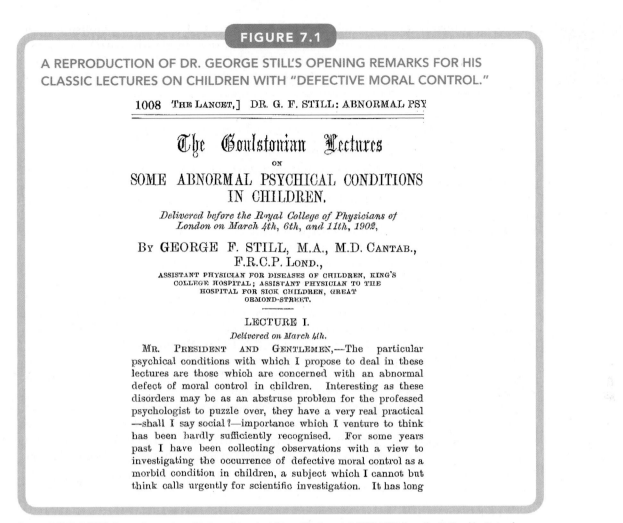

Source: Still, G. F. (1902). Some abnormal psychical conditions in children. *The Lancet, 1,* 1008–1012. From the National Institute of Mental Health.

up to try to replicate Goldstein's findings. They noted the same behaviors of distractibility and hyperactivity in some children with mental retardation (intellectual disabilities).

In addition to clinical observations, Werner and Strauss used an experimental task consisting of figure/background slides that were presented at very brief exposure times. The slides depicted figures (e.g., a hat) embedded in a background (e.g., wavy lines). Werner and Strauss found that, when asked what they saw, the children with supposed brain damage were more likely than those without brain damage to say that they had seen the background (e.g., "wavy lines") rather than the figure (e.g., "a hat") (Strauss & Werner, 1942; Werner & Strauss, 1939, 1941). After these studies, professionals came to refer to children who were apparently hyperactive and distractible as exhibiting the **Strauss syndrome**.

William Cruickshank's Work

William Cruickshank and colleagues, using Werner and Strauss's figure/background task, found that children with cerebral palsy were also more likely to respond to the background than to the figure (Cruickshank, Bice, & Wallen, 1957). This research extended the work of Werner and Strauss in two important ways. First, whereas Werner and Strauss had largely assumed that the children they studied were brain damaged, the children Cruickshank studied all had **cerebral palsy**, a condition that's relatively easy to diagnose. Cerebral palsy is characterized by brain damage that results in impairments in movement (see Chapter 14). Second, the children Cruickshank studied were largely of normal intelligence, thus demonstrating that children without intellectual disabilities

could display distractibility. Cruickshank was also one of the first to establish an educational program for children who today would meet the criteria for ADHD. At the time (the late 1950s), however, many of these children were referred to as "minimally brain injured." An important element of Cruickshank's program, which has stood the test of time, is to provide classroom structure and to minimize distractions.

Minimal Brain Injury and Hyperactive Child Syndrome

At about the same time as Cruickshank's extension of Werner and Strauss's work with children of normal intelligence, the results of a now classic study were published (Pasamanick, Lilienfeld, & Rogers, 1956). This study of the aftereffects of birth complications revived Still's (1902) notion that subtle brain pathology could result in behavior problems, such as hyperactivity and distractibility. Professionals began to apply the label of **minimal brain injury** to children of normal intelligence who were inattentive, impulsive, and/or hyperactive. Although popular in the 1950s and 1960s, the "minimal brain injury" label fell out of favor as professionals pointed out that it was difficult to document actual tissue damage to the brain (Birch, 1964).

"Minimal brain injury" was replaced in the 1960s by the label "hyperactive child syndrome" (Barkley, 2006c). **Hyperactive child syndrome** was preferred because it was descriptive of behavior and didn't rely on vague and unreliable diagnoses of subtle brain damage. This label's popularity extended into the 1970s. By the 1980s, however, it too had fallen out of favor as research began to point to inattention, not hyperactivity, as a major behavioral problem experienced by these children. In fact, some children exhibited attention problems without excessive movement.

This recognition of inattention as more important than hyperactivity is reflected in the current definition of ADHD and its immediate predecessors. However, as we discuss later, some authorities are now recommending that deficits in behavioral inhibition replace inattention as the primary deficit in ADHD. In any case, most authorities do not view hyperactivity as the primary deficit in ADHD.

DEFINITION

Most professionals rely on the American Psychiatric Association's (APA's) *Diagnostic and Statistical Manual of Mental Disorders*-5 (*DSM-5*) criteria to determine whether an individual has ADHD (American Psychiatric Association, 2013). The *DSM*-5 recognizes three subtypes of ADHD: (1) ADHD, Predominantly Inattentive Type; (2) ADHD, Predominantly Hyperactive-Impulsive Type; and (3) ADHD, Combined Type. Examples of criteria used to determine these subtypes include: (1) for inattention: trouble paying attention to details, difficulty sustaining attention, problems with organization, distractible; (2) for hyperactivity: fidgeting, leaving seat at inappropriate times, talking excessively; (3) for impulsivity: problems awaiting one's turn, interrupting others.

ADHD is widely recognized as one of the most frequent reasons, if not the most frequent reason, children with behavioral problems are referred to guidance clinics. The Centers for Disease Control and Prevention (CDCP) reports that between 7% and 9% of the school-age population has ADHD (CDCP, 2010). However, because the U.S. Department of Education does not recognize ADHD as a separate category of special education, it's difficult to estimate how many students with ADHD are served in special education. When the federal government began tracking the prevalence of students in all the major special education categories in the mid-1970s, ADHD was not included. This was due in part to two interrelated factors: (1) the research on this condition was still in its infancy, and (2) the advocacy base for children with ADHD was not yet well developed. In the early 1990s, advocacy groups lobbied for the inclusion of ADHD in these counts, but the U.S. Department of Education did not agree to add ADHD as a separate category. However, in 1991, it did determine that students with ADHD would be eligible for special education under the category "other health impaired" (OHI) "in instances where the ADD is a chronic or acute health problem that results in limited alertness, which adversely affects educational performance." Students with ADHD can also qualify for accommodations under another law: Section 504 of the Rehabilitation Act of 1973.

The growth of the OHI category since 1991 suggests that more and more students with ADHD are being identified as OHI. For example, since the mid-1990s the prevalence of students aged 6 to 17 years in the OHI category has quadrupled. However, the most recent published count of 1.07% for 2007–2008 (IDEA Data Tables, 2013) is still well below the prevalence estimates of 7% to 9% by the Centers for Disease Control and Prevention (CDCP, 2010). Many authorities think that fewer than half of students with ADHD who need special education services are receiving them.

ADHD occurs much more frequently in boys than in girls, with estimates of at least 2 to 1 (CDCP, 2010). Some have speculated that boys are identified more often than girls because boys tend to exhibit the highly noticeable hyperactive or impulsive type of ADHD, whereas girls are more likely to exhibit the inattentive type. Some gender bias in referral may exist, but our best research evidence suggests that it's not enough to account for the wide disparity in prevalence rates between boys and girls. Gender differences are likely due to constitutional, or biological, differences.

Some critics have asserted that ADHD is primarily a U.S. phenomenon, a result of our society's emphasis on achievement and conformity. However, statistics do not bear this out. Although it's difficult to compare prevalence rates cross-culturally because of differing diagnostic criteria, sampling techniques, and cultural expectations, the evidence strongly suggests that prevalence rates at least as high as those in the United States are found in several other countries. For example, a survey of the worldwide prevalence of ADHD that included Africa, the Middle East, Oceania, South America, Asia, North America, and Europe, indicated a worldwide prevalence of 3.4% to 5.29% (Polanczyk, Salum, Sugaya, & Rohde, 2015; Polanczyk, Silva de Lima, Horta, Biederman, & Rohde, 2007). Actually, some of the highest rates are for South America, Africa, China—6.26% (Wang et al., 2017) and Qatar—8.3% (Bradshaw & Kamal, 2017), not North America. Furthermore, research on the behavioral characteristics of persons identified as having ADHD in different countries indicates that they share the same core symptoms, which argues against ADHD being determined by cultural factors (Bauermeister, Canino, Polanczyk, & Rohde, 2010).

Some critics have also claimed that African American children, especially boys, are diagnosed disproportionately as having ADHD. However, research suggests that the rates of African American children identified as having ADHD are similar to those of White children (CDCP, 2010; Rowland et al., 2001). In fact, the CDCP (2010) found the only ethnic difference in rates is that Hispanic/Latino children are diagnosed with ADHD less frequently than other ethnicities.

MyLab Education Self-Check 7.1

MyLab Education Application Exercise 7.1: Types of ADHD

Read a case study about encouraging appropriate behaviors and answer the questions that follow.

MyLab Education Application Exercise 7.2: Interpreting Data

Consider data about students with ADHD who qualify for special education services and why the U.S. Department of Education determined they could be eligible under the category.

IDENTIFICATION

Findings like the preceding show that teachers and other professionals may not always be accurate in their ratings of attention and hyperactivity. Authorities therefore stress the importance of using several sources of information before arriving at a determination that an individual has ADHD. Most agree that there are four important components to assessing whether a student has ADHD: a medical examination, a clinical interview, teacher and parent rating scales, and behavioral observations. The medical examination is necessary to rule out medical conditions such as brain tumors, thyroid problems, or seizure disorders as the cause of the inattention and/or hyperactivity (Barkley & Edwards, 2006).

The clinical interview of the parent(s) and the child provides information about the child's physical and psychological characteristics, as well as family dynamics and interaction with peers. Although the interview is essential to the diagnosis of ADHD, clinicians need to recognize the subjective nature of the interview situation. Some children with ADHD can look surprisingly "normal" in their behavior when in the structured and novel setting of a doctor's office.

In an attempt to bring some quantification to the identification process, researchers have developed rating scales to be filled out by teachers, parents, and, in some cases, the child. Raters are asked such things as how often (never or rarely, sometimes, often, very often) the individual doesn't pay attention to details, is easily distracted, interrupts others, fidgets, and so forth. Whenever possible, the clinician should observe the student. This can be done in the classroom; clinicians who specialize in diagnosing and treating children with ADHD sometimes have specially designed observation rooms in which they can observe the child performing tasks that require sustained attention.

CAUSES

Probably because no simple diagnostic test, such as a blood test, is available for ADHD, much controversy has prevailed over what actually causes ADHD, as there have been numerous questionable causal theories put forth over the last century. (See the accompanying Focus on Concepts box, "Controversial Causal Theories of ADHD.") We now know, however, that strong evidence links neurological abnormalities to ADHD.

As we noted earlier, authorities in the early and middle parts of the 20th century attributed problems of inattention and hyperactivity to neurological problems resulting from brain damage. When researchers were unable to verify actual tissue damage in cases of ADHD, many professionals soured on the idea that ADHD was neurologically based. However, as we noted in our discussion of learning disabilities in Chapter 6, the development of neuroimaging techniques such as magnetic resonance imaging (MRI), positron emission tomography (PET) scans, and functional magnetic resonance imaging (fMRI) in the 1980s and 1990s allowed scientists for the first time to obtain more detailed and reliable measures of brain functioning. Using these techniques, researchers have made great strides in documenting the neurological basis of ADHD. As is the case with learning disabilities, research indicates that ADHD most likely results from neurological dysfunction rather than from actual brain damage. Evidence also points to heredity as playing a very strong role in causing the neurological dysfunction, with teratogenic and other medical factors also implicated to a lesser degree.

Areas of the Brain Affected: Frontal Lobes, Basal Ganglia, Cerebellum

Using neuroimaging techniques, several teams of researchers have found relatively consistent abnormalities in several areas of the brain in people with ADHD, most notably the frontal lobes, basal ganglia, and cerebellum (Frodl & Skokauskas, 2012; Hart, Radua, Nakao, Mataix-Cols, & Rubia, 2013).

PREFRONTAL, FRONTAL LOBES Located in the front of the brain, the **frontal lobes**—and especially the very front portion of the frontal lobes, the **prefrontal lobes**—are responsible for *executive functions*. Among other things, executive functions involve the ability to regulate one's own behavior. (We discuss executive functions more fully later.)

BASAL GANGLIA Buried deep within the brain, the **basal ganglia** are responsible for the coordination and control of motor behavior (Pinel, 2006).

CEREBELLUM The **cerebellum** is also responsible for the coordination and control of motor behavior. Although it's relatively small, constituting only about 10% of the mass of the brain, the fact that it contains more than half of all the brain's neurons attests to its complexity (Pinel, 2006).

Controversial Causal Theories of ADHD

Over the years, a number of myths have sprung up about what causes hyperactive behavior or ADHD. Most of these have little if any substantial scientific support. A good example is the purported influence of television and video games. Many people in the general public believe that by watching too much television or playing too many video games, children will acquire ADHD. One study did find that children who watch more television as preschoolers are rated as more inattentive at 7 years of age (Christakis, Zimmerman, DiGiuseppe, & McCarty, 2004). However, this isn't proof that watching television causes ADHD or even provokes higher rates of inattention. Attention problems, themselves, might cause children to want to watch more television. Or parents might find that one way to control their child's hyperactive behavior, at least for a short period of time, is to put them in front of a computer. Or parents who let their children watch more television may contribute in some other ways to their children's inattentive behavior. Perhaps they provide less supervision generally.

Another example of a controversial causal theory involves diet. In particular, sugar and food additives and artificial flavorings have been targeted as potential causes of ADHD. Parents and teachers have often complained that young children become more hyperactive when they ingest sugar in the form of soft drinks, cakes, and candies. However, careful research has demonstrated that this is *by and large* not the case (Millichap & Yee, 2012; Wolraich, Wilson, & White, 1995). One needs to consider that sugar often accompanies situations, such as parties, which are often stimulating and unstructured. This probably contributes to the popular notion that sweets cause hyperactivity.

Other environmental agents that some believe cause ADHD are artificial food colorings and additives. The original proponent of this theory was Benjamin Feingold, a pediatric allergist (Feingold, 1975) who proposed a strict diet devoid of these additives. Although substantial research has shown that this diet is not beneficial for *all* children with ADHD, there are studies providing suggestive data that there may be very small subgroups who have food allergies to such things as food colorings and additives (Bateman et al., 2004; Millichap & Yee, 2012).

At this point, the research evidence on these controversial theories (TV, video games, sugar, food additives/colorings) indicates that:

1. It's highly unlikely that too much TV or video games causes ADHD.
2. It's possible that sugar can trigger hyperactivity in a small subgroup of children with ADHD.
3. There is suggestive evidence that food additives and colorings might promote ADHD in a *very small subgroup* of children. If parents decide to try a diet that restricts these items with their child, they should keep a daily, perhaps even hourly, record of their child's behavior when on and off the diet.
4. Evidence does not support automatically placing all children with ADHD on restricted diets. (To do so results in a major disruption to family routine.)
5. Given that refined sugar is associated with several negative health conditions, e.g., obesity, diabetes, and tooth decay, parents might consider restricting it for general health reasons if not for ADHD.

Neurotransmitters Involved: Dopamine and Noradrenaline

Much exciting research is being conducted on neurotransmitter abnormalities that might cause ADHD. **Neurotransmitters** are chemicals that help in the sending of messages between neurons in the brain. Researchers have found that abnormal levels of two neurotransmitters—**dopamine** and **noradrenaline**—are involved in ADHD (Barkley, 2006b; Tripp & Wickens, 2009; Volkow et al., 2007).

Hereditary Factors

Most authorities agree that, in many cases, ADHD has a hereditary basis. Research indicates that no single ADHD-gene exists. Rather, multiple genes (at least 20) are involved. And many of these genes are linked to how neurotransmitters move from neuron to neuron (Floet, Scheiner, & Grossman, 2010; Li, Sham, Owen, & He, 2006; Sanchez-Mora et al., 2013). Evidence for the genetic transmission of ADHD comes from at least three sources: family studies, twin studies, and molecular genetic studies.

FAMILY STUDIES Generally, studies indicate that if a child has ADHD, the chance of his or her sibling or parent having ADHD is 4 to 8 times more likely than is the case for non-ADHD children and their immediate relatives (Willcutt et al., 2010). Furthermore, parents of children with attention deficit/hyperactivity disorder have 2.85 times the odds of parents of children without attention deficit/hyperactivity disorder of having a mental disorder, such as anxiety disorder (Cheung & Theule, 2016).

TWIN STUDIES Several researchers have compared the prevalence of ADHD in identical (monozygotic, from the same egg) versus fraternal (dizygotic, from two eggs) twins, when one of the members of the pair has ADHD. These studies consistently show that identical twins are almost 2 times more likely to both have ADHD than are fraternal twins (Willcutt et al., 2010)

MOLECULAR GENETIC STUDIES With the mapping of the human genome have come advances in **molecular genetics**, the study of the molecules (DNA, RNA, and protein) that regulate genetic information. Molecular genetic research on ADHD is in its early stages, but the research is consistent with the idea that several genes contribute to ADHD (Vorstman & Ophoff, 2013; Zheng, Lichtenstein, Asherson, & Larsson, 2013).

Toxins and Medical Factors

In Chapters 5 and 6, we discussed **toxins**—agents that can cause malformations in the developing fetus of a pregnant woman—as the cause of some cases of intellectual disabilities or learning disabilities. Although the evidence for toxins is not as strong as that for heredity, some of these same substances have been shown to be related to ADHD. For example, research indicates that some children with ADHD have higher levels of lead in their blood, suggesting a greater exposure than non-ADHD children to this known toxin (Nigg, Nikolas, Knottnerus, Cavanagh, & Friderici, 2010).

Other medical conditions may also place children at risk for having ADHD. Again, the evidence is not as strong as it is for heredity, but complications at birth and low birthweight are associated with ADHD (Levy, Barr, & Sunohara, 1998; Milberger, Biederman, Faraone, Guite, & Tsuang, 1997). Smoking during pregnancy is associated with having babies of low birthweight. Evidence also suggests that smoking by mothers-to-be puts their children who are already genetically predisposed (based on their dopamine-related genes) at an even greater risk of being diagnosed with ADHD (Neuman et al., 2007).

My**Lab** Education **Self-Check 7.2**

My**Lab** Education **Application Exercise 7.3: Eric**
Watch a video about identifying Eric's ADHD and describe the challenges he faces.

PSYCHOLOGICAL AND BEHAVIORAL CHARACTERISTICS

ADHD is characterized by a multiplicity of cognitive and behavioral deficits (Sjowall, Roth, Lindqvist, & Thorell, 2012). The effects of ADHD on psychological and behavioral functioning can be pervasive, with a major impact on quality of life (Danckaerts et al., 2010). For example, students with ADHD run a higher risk of incurring accidental injuries than their peers who do not have disabilities (Kang, Lin, & Chung, 2012; Shilon, Pollak, Aran, Shaked, & Gross-Tsur, 2011), which is logical given that so many have problems with inattention and impulsivity. And people with ADHD have a higher frequency of sleep disturbances (Hvolby, 2015; Silvestri et al., 2009).

The National Institute of Mental Health has identified several symptoms associated with the major behavioral characteristics identified by the DSM-5: inattention, hyperactivity, and impulsivity. See Table 7.1 for examples.

TABLE 7.1 • **Examples of symptoms associated with inattention, hyperactivity, impulsivity**

- Children who have symptoms of **inattention** may:
  - Be easily distracted, miss details, forget things, and frequently switch from one activity to another
  - Have difficulty focusing on one thing
  - Become bored with a task after only a few minutes, unless they are doing something enjoyable
  - Have difficulty focusing attention on organizing and completing a task or learning something new
  - Have trouble completing or turning in homework assignments, often losing things (e.g., pencils, toys, assignments) needed to complete tasks or activities
  - Not seem to listen when spoken to
  - Daydream, become easily confused, and move slowly
  - Have difficulty processing information as quickly and accurately as others
  - Struggle to follow instructions.

- Children who have symptoms of **hyperactivity** may:
  - Fidget and squirm in their seats
  - Talk nonstop
  - Dash around, touching or playing with anything and everything in sight
  - Have trouble sitting still during dinner, school, and story time
  - Be constantly in motion
  - Have difficulty doing quiet tasks or activities.

- Children who have symptoms of **impulsivity** may:
  - Be very impatient
  - Blurt out inappropriate comments, show their emotions without restraint, and act without regard for consequences
  - Have difficulty waiting for things they want or waiting their turns in games
  - Often interrupt conversations or others' activities.

Source: National Institute of Mental Health (2012). "Attention Deficit Hyperactivity Disorder." National Institutes of Health: NIH Publication No. 12-3572. P. 2. Retrieved from http://www.nimh.nih.gov/health/publications/attention-deficit-hyperactivity-disorder/index.shtml.

Deficits in Executive Functions and Behavioral Inhibition

The behavior symptoms listed in Table 7.1 provide a vivid picture of what the student with ADHD can look and sound like. Researchers have also examined what psychological processes underlie many of these symptoms. This research has pointed to two areas of difficulty, in particular, that appear to account for behavior symptomatic of ADHD: executive functions and behavioral inhibition.

EXECUTIVE FUNCTIONING **Executive functioning (EF)** is a term used to describe a number of processes involved in controlling and regulating behavior. It's been likened to the role of the conductor of an orchestra, the director of a movie, or the job of an air-traffic controller. Researchers and practitioners have provided several different definitions of EF, but most of them are highly similar, with nuanced differences. The definition generally contains the main skills that comprise EF: working memory (WM), inhibitory control or behavioral inhibition, and mental flexibility. (We discussed WM in Chapter 6, as the ability to hold information in memory for a short period of time so that it's available for further use. Mental flexibility refers to the ability to adjust one's behavior in order to adapt to changes in others' behavior or in the environment. We discuss behavioral inhibition below.)

Overwhelming evidence shows that ADHD results in EF deficits (Barkley, 1997; Goldstein & Kennemer, 2009; Weyandt, 2009b). The fact that a wealth of evidence indicates that EF is controlled by the prefrontal and frontal lobes of the brain fits nicely with the neuroimaging studies pointing to abnormality in these areas of the brain in persons with ADHD.

With diminished self-regulation or executive control abilities, students with ADHD find it exceedingly difficult to stay focused on tasks that require effort or concentration but that are not inherently exciting (e.g., many school-related activities). Substantial evidence shows that students with ADHD, indeed, have lower academic achievement than those without disabilities (Dittman, 2016; Frazier, Youngstrom, Glutting, & Watkins, 2007; Graham, Fishman, Reid, & Hebert, 2016).

BEHAVIORAL INHIBITION Closely related to executive functioning, **behavioral inhibition** involves the ability to delay a response; interrupt an ongoing response, if the response is deemed inappropriate because of sudden changes in the demands of the task; or protect a response from distracting or competing stimuli (Lawrence et al., 2002). The term *impulsivity* is frequently used to describe problems with behavioral inhibition. Problems in behavioral inhibition can be reflected in the inability to wait one's turn, to refrain from interrupting conversations, to resist potential distractions while working, or to delay immediate gratification to work for larger, long-term rewards (Tripp & Alsop, 2001).

An abundance of research points to problems with behavioral inhibition in people with ADHD (Barkley, 1997, 2000a, 2006e; Schachar, Mota, Logan, Tannock, & Klim, 2000; Semrud-Clikeman et al., 2000; Willcutt, Pennington, et al., 2001). (In fact, some have claimed that lack of behavioral inhibition is perhaps *the* defining characteristic of ADHD, Barkley, 2006e.)

Deficits in behavioral inhibition can also result in individuals having problems controlling emotions and arousal levels. They often overreact to negative or positive experiences. On hearing good news, for example, children with ADHD might scream loudly, unable to keep their emotions to themselves. Likewise, they are often quick to show their temper when confronted with frustrating experiences.

In the classroom, difficulties with behavioral inhibition, or manifestations of impulsivity, can present themselves during task switching or transitions. See the accompanying Responsive Instruction box for a description of research on this topic and how to apply the results to the classroom.

Adaptive Behavior

The concept of **adaptive behavior skills** (e.g., self-help, community use, home use, and so forth) has traditionally been associated with the area of intellectual disabilities. The definition developed by the American Association on Intellectual and Developmental Disabilities, for example, stipulates that intellectual disabilities be defined as impairments in intelligence and adaptive behavior (see Chapter 5). In recent years, authorities in the ADHD field have discovered that many children and adults with ADHD also have difficulties in adaptive behavior (Barkley, 2006a; Whalen et al., 2006). A good example is that people with ADHD have more problems related to driving as adolescents and young adults: more accidents and traffic violations (Cox, Merkel, Kovatchev, & Seward, 2000; Fischer, Barkley, Smallish, & Fletcher, 2007; Woodward, Fergusson, & Horwood, 2000). It's logical to assume that poor behavioral inhibition would lead to driving problems, and evidence shows that these problems may also be related to poor anger control (Richards, Deffenbacher, Rosen, Barkley, & Rodricks, 2007).

Social Behavior Problems

Research suggests that students with ADHD are more disliked by their peers than are students with any other kind of disorder (Mikami, Jack, & Lerner, 2009). In social situations, it often doesn't take long for students with ADHD to be ostracized. Unfortunately, the negative social status experienced by students with ADHD is difficult to overcome and is usually long lasting. And adding to their socialization problems, many students with ADHD also have social difficulties with their parents, siblings, and teachers (Mikami et al., 2009).

The enduring nature of social rejection easily leads to social isolation. The result is that many children and adults with ADHD have few friends, even though they may desperately want to be liked. This can set up a vicious circle in which they attempt to win friends by latching onto any chance for interaction with others. But their frantic need for

RESPONSIVE INSTRUCTION

Meeting the Needs of Students with ADHD

TASK SWITCHING: PREPARING STUDENTS WITH ADHD FOR CHANGE

What the Research Says

Many researchers contend that the primary deficit of students with ADHD is deficient behavioral inhibition (e.g., Barkley, 1997, 2000a, 2006e; Willcutt, Pennington, et al., 2001). In other words, once students with ADHD begin a task, it is difficult for them to mentally switch to a new activity. Researchers hypothesize that the executive controls needed to "inhibit" the current activity and "start up" the next differ for students with ADHD compared to students who do not have ADHD.

Research Study

A group of researchers examined the task-switching ability of students with and without ADHD (Cepeda, Cepeda, & Kramer, 2000). Results from the study indicated that clear performance deficits existed for unmedicated students with ADHD in the first trial after a task switch, even when the tasks were considered compatible, such as both tasks involving numbers. All students with ADHD, unmedicated or medicated, had higher "switch costs"—increased response time—when the new task was incompatible with the old task (e.g., switching from a number-identification task to a word-identification task). This type of task required the inhibition of thinking

about numbers and the preparation for thinking about letters and sounds. The findings suggest that differences do exist between students with and without ADHD in their ability to efficiently and effectively task switch.

Applying the Research to Teaching

Studies such as the one presented here indicate the need to support students with ADHD as they transition from one activity to another. Cognitive support for such transitions can include the following:

- Allow for time between asking a student to do or say something and expecting the response (i.e., increasing wait time).
- Avoid overloading a student's working memory (Barkley, Murphy, & Kwasnik, 1996) by limiting the number of steps or sequence of procedures a student must keep in working memory or by providing a visual for students to refer to.
- Create routinized procedures for daily transitions.
- Prepare students for the type of response that will be required when answering a question.
- Divide instruction into consistent, predictable sequences throughout the day.

BY KRISTIN L. SAYESKI

FOCUS ON

The Classic "Marshmallow Study"

In the late 1960s and early 1970s, Stanford psychologist Walter Mischel conducted several studies focused on the ability of pre-schoolers to delay gratification (Mischel & Ebbesen, 1970; Mischel, Ebbesen, & Zeiss, 1972). The original research was tagged the "marshmallow study" because of the innovative way Mischel and his colleagues measured how much the children were able to delay gratification. Generally, the child was brought into a room furnished with just a chair and table. The researcher placed a marshmallow on the table in front of the child and told her or him that the s(he) could eat the marshmallow now, but if s(he) waited until the researcher returned, s(he) could have two marshmallows. The adult then left the room and didn't return for about 15 minutes. In the meantime, researchers could watch the child via a two-way mirror. (There are several videos on YouTube showing examples of the gyrations some children go through in their attempt to resist the temptation of the marshmallow, e.g., http://www.youtube.com/watch?list=RD02x3S0xS2hdi4&v=Yo4 WF3cSd9Q.)

The major take-away message from the early set of studies was that, with age, children develop the ability to delay gratification or inhibit their behavior. But the most remarkable findings

came years later when researchers conducted several follow-up studies of the children from the original studies. Here are some examples of their findings. The 4- to 6-year-old children from the original studies who had been the least able to delay gratification:

- In adolescence, continued to display problems with inhibition. Furthermore, their SAT scores were lower (Shoda, Mischel, & Peake, 1990).
- When in their late 20s, they displayed more anxiety about being socially rejected by their significant others (e.g., spouses, partners) (Ayduk et al., 2000).
- When in their 30s, they had higher percentages of (BMI), a measure of body fat, which suggests that they were less able to maintain a healthy diet (Schlam, Wilson, Shoda, Mischel, & Ayduk, 2012).
- When in their 40s, still had difficulties with impulse control (Casey et al., 2011).
- When in their 40s, neuroimaging (Casey et al., 2011) revealed they had abnormalities in the frontal cortex and the basal ganglia—the two areas we discussed earlier in the section focused on causes of ADHD.

friendship, coupled with their deficient impulse control, ends up leading them to bother or pester the very people they are trying to befriend.

Given the problems in behavioral inhibition, it's not surprising that so many children and adults with ADHD end up socially ostracized. Unable to regulate their behavior and emotions, they are viewed as rude by others. It isn't that they don't know how to behave appropriately so much as that they are unable to do so (Landau et al., 1998). In other words, if asked what the appropriate behavior in a given situation should be, they can often give the socially acceptable answer. But when faced with choices in the actual situation, their deficits in behavioral inhibition lead them to make choices impulsively and to overreact emotionally.

Interestingly, researchers have found that, when they do have friends, the friendships tend to be close. And this friendship can be strong even in individuals who have relatively severe ADHD symptoms (Glass, Flory, & Hankin, 2012).

Coexisting Conditions

ADHD often occurs simultaneously with other behavioral and/or learning problems, such as learning disabilities or emotional or behavioral disorders. In addition, persons with ADHD run a higher risk than the general population for substance abuse.

LEARNING DISABILITIES Studies using careful diagnostic criteria have found about half of children with ADHD also have learning disabilities. Some authorities maintain that the relationship is strongest for students who have ADHD, Predominantly Inattentive Type (Marshall, Hynd, Handwerk, & Hall, 1997; Willcutt, Chhabildas, & Pennington, 2001).

EMOTIONAL OR BEHAVIORAL DISORDERS Estimates of the overlap with ADHD vary widely, but it's safe to say that 25% to 50% of people with ADHD also exhibit some form of emotional or behavioral disorder (Forness & Kavale, 2002; Hallahan & Cottone, 1997). Some people with ADHD can exhibit aggressive, acting-out behaviors, whereas others can manifest the types of withdrawn behaviors that accompany anxiety or depression. In fact, anxiety is evident in between 15% to 35% of children with ADHD, and they are especially vulnerable to having multiple anxiety disorders compared with children without disabilities (Schatz & Rostain, 2007).

SUBSTANCE ABUSE Adolescents with ADHD are more likely to experiment prematurely with alcohol, tobacco, or illicit drugs. A large-scale, longitudinal study found that the percentage of young adults with ADHD with substance dependence or abuse was high: nicotine (31%), alcohol (13%), cannabis (9%), cocaine (2%) (Pingault et al., 2013). Attention problems are linked with nicotine dependence, and oppositional behavior is linked with cannabis and cocaine dependence.

Some reports in the popular media have claimed that the treatment of ADHD with psychostimulants such as Ritalin leads children to take up the use of illegal substances. However, very little research backs up this claim (Connor, 2006).

Exactly why ADHD co-occurs with so many other learning and behavioral disabilities is unclear. Researchers are just beginning to tease out which of several possibilities are the most likely reasons for the extensive overlap between ADHD and other disabilities. For example, does having ADHD put one at risk for developing another disability, such as learning disabilities or depression? Or do ADHD and the other disability occur independent of each other? Is there a genetic basis to the coexistence of so many of these conditions? Research over the next few years should begin to provide more definitive answers to these questions.

MyLab Education **Self-Check 7.3**

MyLab Education **Application Exercise 7.4: Jake**

Read a case study about Jake, a student with ADHD, and answer the questions that follow.

EDUCATIONAL CONSIDERATIONS

In this section, we consider two aspects of effective educational programming for students with ADHD:

- Classroom structure and teacher direction
- Functional behavioral assessment and contingency-based self-management

Classroom Structure and Teacher Direction

As noted earlier, William Cruickshank was one of the first to establish a systematic educational program for children who today would meet the criteria for ADHD. Two hallmarks of Cruickshank's program were reducing stimuli irrelevant to learning and enhancing materials important for learning, and creating a structured program with a strong emphasis on teacher direction.

Because Cruickshank assumed that children with attention problems were susceptible to distraction, he reduced irrelevant stimuli as much as possible. For example, students' work spaces consisted of three-sided cubicles to reduce distractions. On the other hand, teachers were encouraged to use attractive, brightly colored teaching materials. The structure came in the form of a systematic schedule of activities for each child for virtually each minute of each day (Cruickshank, Bentzen, Ratzeburg, & Tannhauser, 1961).

It's rare today to see teachers using all the components of Cruickshank's program, especially the cubicles. For those students who are highly distractible, however, some authorities recommend the use of accommodations such as cubicles to reduce extraneous stimulation.

The degree of classroom structure and teacher direction advocated by Cruickshank is also rarely seen today. First, this intensity of structure could be achieved only in a self-contained classroom; most students with ADHD today are in general education settings. Second, most authorities today believe that a structured program is important in the early stages of working with many students with ADHD but that these students gradually need to learn to be more independent in their learning. For example, the National Institute of Mental Health (2012) has recommended several tips for parents emphasizing structure and routine for students with ADHD, which mirror Cruickshank's recommendations for teachers. See Table 7.2.

Functional Behavioral Assessment and Contingency-Based Self-Management

Functional behavioral assessment (FBA) is an important tool for teachers to use with students with emotional or behavioral disorders (we discuss this more in Chapter 8), as well as for students with many other types of disabilities when they also have behavioral

TABLE 7.2 • **Tips to help kids stay organized and follow directions**

Schedule Keep the same routine every day, from wake-up time to bedtime; include time for homework, outdoor play, and indoor activities. Keep the schedule on the refrigerator or on a bulletin board in the kitchen. Write changes on the schedule as far in advance as possible.
Organize everyday items Have a place for everything, and keep everything in its place. This includes clothing, backpacks, and toys.
Use homework and notebook organizers Use organizers for school materials and supplies. Stress to your child the importance of writing down assignments and bringing home the necessary books.
Be clear and consistent Children with ADHD need consistent rules they can understand and follow.
Give praise or rewards when rules are followed Children with ADHD often receive and expect criticism. Look for good behavior and praise it.

Source: National Institute of Mental Health (2012). "Attention Deficit Hyperactivity Disorder." National Institutes of Health: NIH Publication No. 12-3572. P. 11. Retrieved from http://nimh.nih.gov/health/publications/attention-deficit-hyperactivity-disorder/index.shtml.

MyLab Education
Video Example 7.2

Author Dan Hallahan discusses his early research on self-monitoring of attention with Paige Pullen.

MyLab Education
Video Example 7.3

Students with ADHD can be taught to monitor, record, analyze, and reinforce their own behavior. As you watch this video, notice how the individual students record their own behaviors, and the system used to reward the whole group when pre-selected target students exhibit appropriate behavior.

MyLab Education
Video Example 7.4

The degree to which students with ADHD can be successful in a general education setting is often dependent on the overall school policies of structure, discipline, and explicit expectations and instructions regarding student behavior. In this video, the teacher describes a school climate conducive to inclusion of students with ADHD.

problems. Therefore, it's often extremely useful in educational programming for students with ADHD. FBA involves determining the consequences, antecedents, and setting events that maintain inappropriate behaviors (Horner & Carr, 1997). Examples of typical functions of inappropriate behavior of students with ADHD are to avoid work and to gain attention from peers or adults (DuPaul & Ervin, 1996). Extensive research evidence is persuasive that FBA can be highly effective for students with ADHD (Miller & Lee, 2013).

Contingency-based self-management approaches usually involve having people keep track of their own behavior and then receive consequences, often in the form of rewards, based on their behavior (Davies & Witte, 2000; DuPaul, Arbolino, & Booster, 2009; Hallahan, Lloyd, Kneedler, & Marshall, 1982; Hallahan, Lloyd, Kosiewicz, Kauffman, & Graves, 1979; Hallahan, Marshall, & Lloyd, 1981; Shapiro, DuPaul, & Bradley-Klug, 1998). For example, the teacher might have students use self-monitoring to record how many times they left their seats during a class period. For directions about how to use self-monitoring in the classroom, see the accompanying Responsive Instruction box.

A combination of FBA and contingency-based self-management techniques has proven successful in increasing appropriate behavior of elementary and secondary students with ADHD (DuPaul, Eckert, & McGoey, 1997; Ervin, DuPaul, Kern, & Friman, 1998; Shapiro et al., 1998). In one study, for instance (Ervin et al., 1998), a combination of FBA and contingency-based self-management increased the on-task behavior of two adolescents with ADHD. For one of the students, the FBA interviews with the teacher and observations in the classroom led the researchers and teachers to conclude that the adolescent boy's disruptive behavior was a function of gaining peer attention. They based this assumption on evidence that the antecedents to his inattentive behavior included peers' looking his way, calling out his name, and making gestures toward him and that the consequences of his inattention included the peers' laughing or returning comments to him.

The contingency-based self-management phase involved the student evaluating his on-task behavior on a 5-point scale (0 = unacceptable to 5 = excellent) at the end of each math class. The teacher also rated the student's behavior and awarded the student points based on how closely the ratings matched. During writing class, the teacher awarded negative or positive points to members of the class depending on whether or not they responded to attention-seeking behaviors from any member of the class. In both classes, the students could use the points for privileges.

THE ROLE OF REINFORCEMENT Authorities have pointed to the crucial role that contingency plays in contingency-based self-management: Reinforcement of some kind, such as social praise or points that can be traded for privileges, is especially important for self-management techniques to be effective. For example, an extensive review of research found that contingency-based self-management strategies were more effective than self-management strategies without contingencies in leading to positive behavioral changes in students with ADHD (DuPaul & Eckert, 1997).

The use of behavioral procedures such as reinforcement is somewhat controversial, and some are opposed to their use (Kohn, 1993). Many authorities, however, consider them almost indispensable in working with students with ADHD. For example, behavioral procedures are an integral part of a set of intervention principles advocated by one team of authorities (Pfiffner, Barkley, & DuPaul, 2006). They note that, in particular, reinforcements usually need to be more salient and delivered more quickly and frequently for students with ADHD than for their peers who do not have disabilities.

Service Delivery Models

Because the U.S. Department of Education doesn't recognize ADHD as a separate special education category, we don't have statistics on how many of these students are served in different classroom environments. It's safe to assume, however, that one can find students with ADHD across the entire continuum of placements. But because, as we noted earlier, there is reason to believe that fewer than half receive any special education services, it's logical to assume that the majority of students with ADHD spend most of

RESPONSIVE INSTRUCTION

Meeting the Needs of Students with ADHD

THE BENEFITS OF SELF-MONITORING AND GROUP CONTINGENCY

What the Research Says

Many students with ADHD lack the ability to self-monitor. Self-monitoring requires the ability to appraise a situation and consider alternative ways of responding as well as possible outcomes associated with the various forms of responding (Shapiro, DuPaul, & Bradley-Klug, 1998). This inability to think before acting creates problems for students with ADHD in the areas of paying attention in class, responding to social situations appropriately, and finishing assigned tasks. To address these issues, teachers can help students learn to use self-management procedures to monitor, record, analyze, and reinforce their own behavior (Davies & Witte, 2000). Many studies have repeatedly demonstrated the effectiveness of teaching students such strategies (Cobb, Sample, Alwell, & Johns, 2006; Harris, Friedlander, Saddler, Frizzelle, & Graham, 2005; Lloyd, Hallahan, Kauffman, & Keller, 1998; Reid & Lienemann, 2006; Reid, Trout, & Schartz, 2005).

Although teaching self-management to students with ADHD has been proven to be effective, many teachers prefer whole-class or group-contingency plans. Within a group-contingency model, the behavior of one student is tied to the outcome of the whole group. Group-contingency models promote interdependence, as group members must work together to meet a goal (Tankersley, 1995). Under a group contingency, teachers can use the same behavior management approach for all students and don't have to differentiate their treatment of the few students who need help with self-management. Thus, group contingencies can be very effective for general education teachers whose classrooms include students with ADHD.

Research Study

One study examined the effects of a management program with third graders on the behaviors of students with ADHD in a general education classroom (Davies & Witte, 2000). All students—those with ADHD as well as students without disabilities—were responsible for monitoring their own behavior, and the researchers established contingencies for group performance. Procedures for the group intervention follow:

1. If any student displayed the target behavior [inappropriate verbalizations], she or he moved one dot from his/her group's chart from the green section into the blue section. If the child did not move the dot after about ten seconds, then the teacher moved a dot into the red section of the chart.

2. The rewards a group received were related to how many dots the group had in the green section of their chart at the end of the intervention period. Each group needed to have at least one dot left in the green section at the end of the intervention period to receive the reinforcer. [Each group started with five dots.] (Davies & Witte, 2000, p. 141)

Research Findings

Results from the study demonstrated a decrease in talking out of turn for the four students with ADHD. In addition, no evidence showed possible negative side effects of peer pressure, such as threats or negative verbal comments (Davies & Witte, 2000).

Applying the Research to Teaching

Findings from this study demonstrate the effectiveness of using self-management within the context of a group contingency. Teachers can implement similar management strategies through (1) targeting specific undesirable behaviors to be eliminated or specific desirable behaviors to be reinforced, (2) creating a chart for students to use for self-management, (3) communicating the procedures for recording behaviors on the chart (e.g., "If you do X, mark your chart" or "When the beeper beeps, check to see if you are doing X, then mark your chart accordingly"), or (4) connecting the self-management procedures to a group contingency (e.g., "If all students get over X points during the lesson, all students will get a homework pass").

BY KRISTIN L. SAYESKI

their time in general education classrooms. The accompanying How Can I Help? feature describes different ways to use co-teaching to help meet the needs of these students, whether they receive special education services or not.

As with all students with disabilities, the best placement for students with ADHD should be determined on an individual basis. Although full inclusion in a general education classroom might be appropriate for some students with ADHD, for students with severe ADHD problems, one needs to keep in mind that the best research-based practices for students with ADHD—that is, classroom structure, teacher direction, functional behavioral assessment, and contingency-based self-management—can be a challenge to implement in the general education classroom.

HOW CAN I HELP?

Working with Students with ADHD in the General Education Classroom

"How can I get this student focused?!"

What Does It Mean to be a Teacher of Students with ADHD?
Currently, the Council for Exceptional Children doesn't have specific competencies for teachers of students with attention deficit hyperactivity disorder (ADHD). As you read in this chapter, ADHD isn't recognized as a separate special education category by the U.S. Department of Education. These students, however, often have additional disabling conditions and are served by teachers with expertise in those areas. That expertise may include:

1. Understanding educational implications of characteristics of various exceptionalities
2. Understanding the effects of various medications on individuals with exceptional learning needs
3. Using procedures to increase the individual's self-awareness, self-management, self-control, self-reliance, and self-esteem

Successful Strategies for Co-Teaching
Co-teaching classroom configurations come in many forms, and all give teachers "more hands" to meet the needs of students with ADHD. Vaughn, Schumm, and Arguelles (1997) describe five basic models of co-teaching that provide co-teachers with opportunities to use the instructional strategies described in this chapter.

One Teach, One Drift
In this model, one teacher is responsible for instruction, and the other teacher drifts, monitoring students. This model allows the drifting teacher to redirect students who may be off task, to observe and mark student-monitoring forms, to provide feedback on individual students' attention and participation, and to deliver reinforcers or consequences on a frequent basis.

Station Teaching
In station teaching, co-teachers split content into two parts and students into three groups. Each teacher teaches one of the two content pieces at a station to a small group of students, and the other group works independently. The student groups rotate between stations. Teachers can break content down into smaller tasks that maintain the attention of all students. Each teacher can work with a small group of students, making it easier to ensure that they are focused and learning. It is also easier to help students work together and to provide reinforcers and consequences more frequently. The difficulty lies in making sure that students with ADHD can work appropriately in the independent station.

Parallel Teaching
In parallel teaching, the two teachers split the class into two groups and teach the same content to a smaller group of students. This model provides the same opportunities as station teaching, along with the chance to modify the instructional delivery of the same content material to meet the needs of the student.

Alternative Teaching
The alternative teaching model includes content instruction by one teacher to a large group of students and remedial or supplementary instruction by the other teacher to a small group of students. The teacher of the small group can modify delivery of content, control the delivery of consequences and rewards, and closely monitor and observe students. In addition, the teacher of the small group can incorporate instruction in strategies such as self-monitoring.

Team Teaching
In team teaching, co-teachers alternate or "tag team" in delivering instruction to the entire class. In this model, both co-teachers can be on the lookout for misconceptions, confusion, inattention, and disruption. Teachers can then address these issues during the flow of instruction rather than afterward or on an individual basis. In addition, co-teachers can work together to present content and learning strategies in unison to better meet the needs of all students.

In All Models
Teachers working together can discuss and better evaluate whether rules and instructions are clear, brief, and delivered in appropriate formats for students with ADHD. Co-teachers can also work together to better anticipate "rough spots" for students with ADHD, particularly during transition times, changes in routines, or complex tasks. The varying models of co-teaching provide the flexibility for teachers to adjust instructional delivery to meet both the objectives of the teachers and the needs of the students with ADHD.

Cautionary Note
All too often, co-teachers fall into the habit of using one model to the exclusion of others. This is unfortunate in that it may mean that one teacher doesn't participate actively in instruction and/or planning. This nonparticipation can lead to a lack of interest on the teacher's part and a disregard for that teacher on the students' part. The models of co-teaching were developed to match the needs of instruction. Both teachers should participate in instruction in a way that matches their expertise.

BY MARGARET P. WEISS

MEDICATION CONSIDERATIONS

One of the most controversial topics in all of special education is the treatment of ADHD with medication. **Psychostimulants**, which stimulate or activate neurological functioning, are by far the most frequent type of medication prescribed for ADHD. However, promising research is emerging on a number of nonstimulants. **Strattera** is an example of a nonstimulant that is also sometimes prescribed for ADHD (Childress, 2016). The most common stimulant prescribed for ADHD is methylphenidate, or **Ritalin**. **Adderall** and **Vyvanse** are other stimulants that are sometimes prescribed. The fact that physicians would prescribe a psychostimulant for someone who exhibits hyperactivity is, at first blush, counterintuitive. In fact, for years professionals referred to the **paradoxical effect of Ritalin** because its effects appeared to be the opposite of those one would expect in the case of someone who does not have ADHD. Researchers have concluded, however, that Ritalin influences the release of the neurotransmitters dopamine and norepinephrine, thus enabling the brain's executive functions to operate more normally (Arnsten et al., 2009; Connor, 2006; Floet et al., 2010). Responsiveness to stimulants is highly individual, so the dosage level and number of doses per day vary from person to person.

Use of stimulants for ADHD has increased steadily over the last several decades. Interestingly, African American children or children from low socioeconomic status (SES) homes are less likely to be treated with stimulants than white children or children from higher SES homes (Graves & Serpell, 2013). The reason for this discrepancy is debatable. Perhaps it is due to a combination of lack of access to medical/psychological services, cultural aversion to using medication for behavioral problems, and distrust of the medical system by individuals from low SES backgrounds.

Opposition to Ritalin

Not all professionals, parents, and laypeople are in favor of using pyschostimulants for ADHD. In fact, Ritalin has been the subject of numerous assaults in the media. Critics have appeared on nationally broadcast television shows such as *Oprah, Geraldo,* and *20/20,* as well as on evening and morning news shows. The Church of Scientology's objection to Ritalin has received much publicity due to Hollywood actor and Scientologist, Tom Cruise's criticisms of it. Although some criticisms have been relatively mild, others have ranged from assertions that ADHD is a bogus diagnosis to claims that professionals are trying to control children with medication and make them overly docile.

The Research Evidence

Over the last 30 to 40 years, dozens of research teams around the world have studied the effects of several medications on ADHD. Most of this research has focused on the psychostimulant Ritalin.

EFFECTIVENESS Despite all the negative publicity in the media, most ADHD authorities are in favor of Ritalin's use. After hundreds of studies, the research is overwhelmingly positive on the effectiveness of Ritalin in helping students to have more normalized behavioral inhibition and executive functioning (Connor, 2006; Meszaros et al., 2009; MTA Cooperative Group, 1999; Spencer, Biederman, & Wilens, 2010). Moreover, Ritalin not only leads to better results on parent and teacher rating scales, but also leads to higher academic achievement (Scheffler et al., 2009) as well as improved classroom behavior such as better note taking, on-task behavior, higher quiz scores, homework completion, and better written-language work (Evans et al., 2001).

NONRESPONDERS AND SIDE EFFECTS Even though research has demonstrated the general effectiveness of Ritalin, it's important to point out that it's not effective for everyone. Somewhere around 30% of those who take Ritalin do not have a favorable response (Barbaresi et al., 2006). In addition, some side effects are possible, including insomnia, reduction in appetite, abdominal pain, headaches, and irritability. There has also been speculation on the possibility that in a very small number of cases, Ritalin causes tics or increases their intensity in those who already have tics (DuPaul, Barkley, & Connor, 1998). There have been many anecdotal reports of a "rebound effect," in which a child exhibits irritability as the Ritalin wears off. In most cases, these side effects are mild and can be controlled. For example, in the case of the two most common side effects—insomnia and reduction in appetite—care should be taken not to take the Ritalin too close to mealtime or bedtime. In the case of the rebound effect, some physicians recommend using a time-release form of Ritalin.

DRUG ABUSE A popular misconception is that by taking Ritalin, children with ADHD are more likely to become abusers of drugs such as marijuana or cocaine as adolescents or young adults. Little if any documented evidence suggests that this occurs (Connor, 2006). In fact, evidence suggests that individuals with ADHD who are prescribed Ritalin as children are less likely to turn to illicit drugs as teenagers (Katusic et al., 2005). Some have speculated that perhaps those who are not medicated with Ritalin turn to other drugs to try to find "peace of mind" or to "chill out."

Cautions Regarding Medication

Although the research is overwhelmingly positive on the effectiveness of medication for increasing appropriate behavior, a number of cautions remain:

- Medication should not be prescribed at the first sign of a behavior problem. Only after careful analysis of the student's behavior and environment should medication be considered. The use of psychostimulants for ADHD in the United States increased approximately eight-fold from the 1970s to the 1990s (Wilens & Biederman, 1992), and in the first 5 years of the 21st century, the rate approximately doubled (Castle, Aubert, Verbrugge, Khalid, & Epstein, 2007). Although much of this increase in recent years can be attributed to an upsurge in prescriptions for females and adults coincident with the increase in diagnosis in these populations, it still should alert us to turning too quickly to medication as *the* answer to ADHD.
- Although research has demonstrated the effectiveness of medication on behavioral inhibition and executive functions, the results for academic outcomes have not been as dramatic. Thus, teachers shouldn't assume that medication will take care of all the academic problems these students face.
- Parents, teachers, and physicians should monitor dosage levels closely so that the dose used is effective but not too strong. Proper dosage levels vary considerably.
- Teachers and parents shouldn't lead children to believe that the medication serves as a substitute for self-responsibility and self-initiative.
- Teachers and parents shouldn't view the medication as a panacea; they, too, must take responsibility and initiative in working with the child.
- Parents and teachers should keep in mind that psychostimulants are a controlled substance. There has been a dramatic increase in persons who do not have ADHD using stimulants as a way of gaining a "high," or for secondary and college students of improving academic performance, or for athletes of gaining physical performance. Interestingly, research results are mixed on whether stimulants actually improve performance in these domains (Lakhan & Kirchgessner, 2012).
- Unfortunately, there has also been a dramatic increase in stimulant abuse. For example, between 2003 and 2013, national admissions to substance abuse treatment services for methylphenidate as a percentage of admissions for all illicit substances increased 25% (Substance Abuse and Mental Health Services Administration, 2015).
- The final key to the effective use of medication is communication among parents, physicians, teachers, and the child.

ASSESSMENT OF PROGRESS

Assessment of students with ADHD includes procedures for evaluating social and emotional behaviors and academic skills. Many of the procedures described in Chapter 6 on learning disabilities are also appropriate for students with ADHD.

Assessment of Academic Skills

As we discussed earlier, students with ADHD often experience difficulties with academic tasks as a result of inattention, impulsivity, and/or poor executive functioning skills. In addition, they're commonly diagnosed with learning disabilities as a co-existing condition.

Curriculum-based measurement (CBM), described in Chapter 6, is an appropriate method for monitoring academic progress for students with ADHD. An advantage of CBM for students with ADHD is that the measures take very little time to administer and they are focused on a particular task. CBM should be implemented with students with ADHD to ensure that academic progress is adequate.

Assessment of Attention and Behavior

Two methods are commonly used to assess a student's attention to tasks and social/emotional behavior: rating scales and direct observation. An example of a rating scale that can be used to measure student outcomes or to monitor student progress is the Conners-3 (Conners, 2007). The Conners-3 includes measures of oppositional behavior, inattention, anxiety, and social problems.

Teachers should also directly observe students on a regular schedule to monitor attention, academic engaged time, and disruptive behavior. Behavioral recording systems provide a framework to conduct systematic observations. For example, **momentary time sampling** allows the teacher to conduct brief observations and collect data on a specific set of behaviors. In momentary time sampling, the observer determines the length of the observation and divides it into intervals (e.g., 15 minutes may be divided into 15 intervals of 1 minute each). At the beginning of each interval, the observer records whether the student is exhibiting the behavior of interest and then does not observe the student until the beginning of the next interval.

Figure 7.2 provides an example of a momentary time-sampling chart for a student, Susie, who is working to increase her time on task. The observation lasted for 15 minutes. Glancing at Susie at the beginning of each minute, the observer placed a check mark in the box if Susie was attending to the task at the time sampled, and an *X* if she was not attending. At the end of the observation period, the teacher calculated the number of intervals Susie was on task to determine a percentage of on-task behavior for the 15-minute period. Susie was on task for 10 of the 15 intervals, or 67% of the time. Susie's teacher may use the momentary time-sampling procedure at regular intervals to monitor Susie's attention to tasks and modify interventions as needed.

A unique measure of student outcomes is the Telephone Interview Probe (TIP) (Corkum, Andreou, Schachar, Tannock, & Cunningham, 2007). This instrument uses brief telephone interviews of parents and teachers to determine the effects of interventions

---

FIGURE 7.2

MOMENTARY TIME SAMPLING—AN INTERVAL RECORDING PROCEDURE TO CAPTURE A REPRESENTATIVE SAMPLE OF A TARGET BEHAVIOR OVER A SPECIFIED PERIOD OF TIME.

Student Name: *Susie*

Date: *3/10/2011*

Setting: *Small - group reading* lesson

Time of day: *9:30 a.m.—9:45 a.m.*

	1	2	3	4	5	6	7	8	9	10	11	12	13	14	15
Attending to Task	✓	X	✓	✓	X	X	✓	✓	X	✓	✓	✓	X	✓	✓

10 /15 intervals = *67%*

for students with ADHD. It's particularly useful for evaluating the effects of psychostimu-lant medications on an individual at a specific time of day or setting. Many common rat-ing scales are limited to broader time frames and don't provide the specificity required to make decisions in regard to treatment with medications. The TIP provides ratings of inattention, impulsiveness, hyperactivity, oppositional behavior, and problem situations for three time points during the day (i.e., morning, afternoon, evening).

MyLab Education Self-Check 7.4

MyLab Education Application Exercise 7.5: Brandon
Watch a video about Brandon, a boy with ADHD, and two techniques that his teacher has developed to help him stay on task in the classroom.

MyLab Education Application Exercise 7.6: Accommodations
Read a case study about accommodations and then answer the questions that follow.

EARLY INTERVENTION

Diagnosis of young children with ADHD is particularly difficult because many young children who don't have ADHD tend to exhibit a great deal of motor activity and a lack of impulse control. However, in recent years the number of preschoolers identified as having ADHD has increased; the prevalence rates of 2% to 6% for preschoolers now rival the rates of 7% to 9% for school-age students. And perhaps maybe even more significant, parents report that ADHD symptoms in their children first begin to appear between the ages of 2 and 4 years (Posner, Pressman, & Grennhill, 2009).

Poor behavioral inhibition and inattention in preschool are predictors of ADHD symptoms and early literacy skills, respectively, in early elementary school (Campbell & von Stauffenberg, 2009; Walcott, Scheemaker, & Bielski, 2009). Therefore, early interven-tion for preschoolers with ADHD is critically important.

Because excessive activity and impulsivity are relatively normal for young children, pre-schoolers with ADHD can be particularly difficult to manage. Those preschoolers who really do have ADHD are a great challenge to parents and teachers. The impor-tance of the educational principles of classroom structure, teacher direction, functional behavioral assessment, and contingency-based self-management discussed previously in this chapter are all the more important for preschoolers. Given that even young children who don't have ADHD lack fully developed self-management skills, most profession-als recommend an even stronger emphasis on the use of contingencies in the form of praise, points, and tangible rewards.

MyLab Education
Video Example 7.5
Diagnosing ADHD in preschoolers is a challenge because children at this age are often very active and impulsive. However, in the case of some children, their ADHD behavior is obvious. For example, watch this video.

TRANSITION TO ADULTHOOD

Not too long ago, most professionals assumed that ADHD diminished in adolescence and usually disappeared by adulthood. However, authorities now recognize that, although the number of symptoms, especially those connected to hyperactivity (Weyandt, 2009a), may decrease, ADHD persists into adulthood. Research suggests that (1) about 50% of those diagnosed as having ADHD in childhood still persist with major symptoms as adults (Hechtman et al., 2016) and (2) about 4 to 5% of adults have ADHD (Ebejer et al., 2012; Michielsen et al., 2012).

Evidence is strong that working memory remains a problem for many adults with ADHD (Aldserson, Kasper, Hudec, & Patros, 2013). Researchers have found that adults with ADHD are poor decision makers. For example, instead of waiting to make a more informed decision, which is likely to result in a better reward, they choose a short-term gain even though they know they would obtain a better reward by wait-ing (Mowinckel, Pedersen, Eilertsen, & Biele, 2014). Researchers using some clever data

MyLab Education
Video Example 7.6
Careful observation and testing can help determine whether a preschooler has ADHD or is simply displaying high energy typical for his or her age.

FOCUS ON

Mind-Wandering

We've all experienced it: We're driving on a monotonous stretch of highway and suddenly realize our mind is somewhere else other than driving (an old acquaintance, an upcoming event, and so forth). Or we're reading a book and suddenly realize that our mind has wandered and we have to start reading the last paragraph or two again.

In general, measuring mind-wandering can be done in at least three ways: (1) ask respondents to rate how often their mind wanders; (2) while individuals perform a task, such as reading, ask them to stop and record every time they notice their mind has wandered; (3) give individuals a personal recording device and set it to prompt them randomly to record what they are pay-

ing attention to at that moment. Researchers have documented that adults with ADHD are vulnerable to mind-wandering (Franklin et al., 2014). For example, they've equipped individuals with mobile devices that randomly signal wearers throughout the day to record whether their minds have wandered. And, indeed, those with ADHD are much more likely to report that they were off-task. Likewise, researchers have had individuals perform a task, such as reading narrative text in a lab setting and interrupting them randomly to ask them whether they were paying attention or not. As predicted, people who have ADHD are more likely to report being off-task on these measures than those without ADHD.

---

collection techniques have also determined that adults with ADHD are likely to exhibit **mind-wandering**. See Focus on Concepts: Mind-Wandering.

Diagnosis in Adulthood

With the greater recognition of ADHD by the scientific community as well as by the popular media, many people are being diagnosed with ADHD in adulthood. In general, the more severe the symptoms in childhood, the more likely that adults with ADHD will be high school dropouts and experience employment problems (Fredricksen et al., 2014). However, the diagnosis of ADHD in adults can sometimes be controversial. In recent years, however, professionals have begun to make progress in identifying and treating ADHD in adults. It is important that a thorough clinical exam be conducted before diagnosing an adult as ADHD, especially if he or she was not previously identified in childhood. Within the history, the clinician looks for symptoms similar to those that children with ADHD display, although as mentioned, adults may have fewer symptoms, especially those related to hyperactivity. In addition, the symptoms may take a somewhat different form because they occur in a different context; for example, related to the work rather than the classroom environment or related to one's role as a spouse or parent rather than as a child in the family environment. For example, adults with ADHD may become bored easily with relatively routine work or have problems organizing their work schedule. Or they may have problems "tuning in" to what their spouse or children are saying, or overcommit themselves to too many household projects, such that many of them remain undone.

Adult Outcomes

Overall, adults with ADHD *tend* to have a number of poorer outcomes with respect to educational attainment, psychiatric problems (e.g., depression and anxiety), marital difficulties, driving infractions, and addictive behaviors, such as substance abuse and gambling addiction (Barkley & Murphy, 2007; Biederman et al., 2010; Fredricksen et al., 2014; Mohr-Jensen, C., & Steinhausen, H.-C., 2016; Mowinckel, Pedersen, Eilertsen & Biele, 2015; Ramsay, 2010; Rucklidge, Brown, Crawford, & Kaplan, 2007; Weyandt & DuPaul, 2006). Many of these outcomes are closely linked to the poor decision making noted above, with immediate gratification being favored over patiently thinking through the consequences of one's choices.

It's important to point out that not all adults with ADHD experience unfavorable outcomes. Many adults with ADHD actually appear to leverage their ADHD symptoms (e.g., high energy, thinking "outside the box") to become highly successful. (Examples of individuals with ADHD, many self-identified, are: Justin Bieber, Richard Branson, Jim

SUCCESS STORIES: Developing Self-Advocacy Skills to Get Needed Accommodations: Key to Josh's Success in College

Josh Bishop: "It's not like the work is hard; it's just getting it done!"

High school sophomore Josh Bishop hopes to play football on a team in the National Collegiate Athletic Association's Division I, despite his struggles with organization and time management.

These could be the keys to his success:

- Intensive classroom structure and consistent expectations
- Relentless positive reinforcement and behavioral support
- Specific accommodations and self-advocacy

Josh Bishop doesn't find schoolwork hard to do, but he finds it hard to get done. Special educator Jane Warner coordinates services for college students with disabilities at the university where Josh Bishop hopes to play football. She guides many students like Josh and encourages incoming freshmen with ADHD to begin their self-advocacy early. Although Josh does not receive special education services, his mother, Joni Poff, encourages him to seek out structures and supports so that he can meet his future goals.

- **Intensive Classroom Structure and Consistent Expectations.** Josh is a successful athlete, but in the classroom, he faces challenges. "I never have been very organized. I got by in elementary school, but middle school was a real wake-up call. In sixth grade, I'd get all my homework done in class. In seventh grade, I had homework due for every class."

Josh keeps an assignment book but admits that he doesn't use it faithfully. "When I've missed a deadline, sometimes I don't turn the work in at all. I know I need to do homework and I keep saying I'm going to do it, and then I don't turn it in and I get a zero. I can get work done at school, but I just can't get it done at home." According to his mother, "Josh does better with shorter time segments in a more structured setting. At home, he has trouble following through with sustained work. His pediatrician told me to back off. Josh takes medication during the day, and it's harder for him to concentrate in the evening."

Josh mentioned his medication but did not refer to his difficulties with completing written work, organizational skills, or attentiveness as being out of the ordinary. He would rather not be treated differently from other students, but he says that only a few teachers have provided the classroom structure that he needs. His mother thinks that the most successful teachers for Josh have been those who were very organized and made their expectations very clear. "They weren't wishy-washy. They were sympathetic that some things were difficult for Josh. They understood that he wasn't being purposefully lazy or disrespectful, but they still held high expectations for him."

- **Relentless Positive Reinforcement and Behavioral Support.** Josh was diagnosed by his pediatrician with

ADHD when he was 7 years old. "Josh always had a high activity level," recalls his mother. "In kindergarten, he was put on a behavior contract with stickers as positive reinforcement, but his first-grade teacher didn't follow through with his behavior management." By second grade, medication was recommended. Josh's family moved to a small school district where the local high school he attends has only 650 students. Contact between home and school has been close. But as he has matured and the academic demands have increased, says his mother, "high school has been difficult for Josh. Recently, I asked him to take advantage of a tutor or some structured support to help reinforce his behavior, but he seems determined to do it alone."

- **Specific Accommodations and Self-Advocacy.** Doing it alone is not always the answer, says Jane Warner. Students with ADHD frequently need support when they move from high school to college. "Study skills and time management are troublesome for students with ADHD. Things can start to fall apart. Students might miss several classes and think they can never go back, so they just sit out and their grades go down, their self-esteem starts to slip, and they hit the wall." Warner encourages students to disclose their learning needs confidently and make the primary contact with the office for disability services on campus. Students with ADHD who have not received special services in high school are advised to get the documentation they need for colleges to provide them with appropriate accommodations. "We prefer comprehensive evaluations that have been done by a qualified professional within the previous 3 years," says Warner. "IEPs are part of the puzzle, but IEPs can't be used as the only documentation for postsecondary accommodations."

Warner points out that current evaluations provide a clear picture of strengths and weaknesses, especially if the evaluator explains what the results mean in lay terms and makes specific educational recommendations. "Sometime between now and high school graduation," she says, "getting a current clinical evaluation will be a very important strategy for developing his self-advocacy and for moving Josh closer to reaching his goals."

Reflecting On Your Own Professional Development

If you were Josh's teacher...

- What are some areas about educating students with ADHD about which you would need to know more?
- What are some specific skills that would help you to address his academic and behavioral challenges?
- What personal dispositions do you think are most important for you to develop in teaching students with challenging behaviors posed by ADHD?

By Jean B. Crockett

Carrey, Ryan Gosling, Paris Hilton, Solange Knowles, Howie Mandel, Michael Phelps, Michelle Rodriguez, Charles Schwab, Will Smith, Justin Timberlake.)

Although we can point to highly successful adults with ADHD, they are the minority. One prestigious team of researchers found that children who persist into adulthood with the same ADHD symptoms that they demonstrated in childhood are at risk for such things as being fired from or quitting jobs, relying on public assistance, and engaging in risky sexual behavior (Hechtman et al., 2016).

COLLEGE If they attend a post-secondary school, students with ADHD tend to have more problems adjusting academically and socially than do their peers without disabilities. This shouldn't be surprising given the behavioral and social skills needed for successfully meeting the academic requirements and social complexities of academic life. Time management, an aspect of executive functioning, is a particular skill found lacking in some students with ADHD (Weyandt & DuPaul, 2013). See, for example, how much Josh Bishop in the Success Stories feature (p. 162) focuses on learning better time management in order to prepare for college. Note, too, that he is learning self-advocacy, something that will serve him well when he attends college.

One highly recommended technique for adults with ADHD, which is especially useful for those in college, is coaching. **Coaching** involves identifying someone whom the person with ADHD can rely on for support (Hallowell & Ratey, 2006). The coach, who can be a therapist or a friend, is someone who can regularly spend a few minutes to help keep the person with ADHD focused on goals. The coach provides the structure needed to plan for upcoming events and activities and heaps on praise when tasks are accomplished.

EMPLOYMENT One of the keys to successful employment, especially for persons with ADHD, is to select a job or career that maximizes the individual's strengths and minimizes weaknesses. Success often depends on pursuing a job that fits a person's needs for structure versus independence. It's recommended that those who work best with structure look for jobs with organizations that have a clear mission and lines of authority, with an emphasis on oversight from supervisors who have an understanding of ADHD. Those who find formal structures too confining should look for work environments that are flexible, have variety, and allow one to be independent (Hallowell & Ratey, 2006).

MARRIAGE AND FAMILY Given some of the behavioral characteristics of ADHD, it's not surprising that husbands and wives of people with ADHD frequently complain that their spouse is a poor listener, preoccupied, forgetful, unreliable, messy, and so forth. A person's ADHD can have a negative impact on the entire family. Parents who have ADHD may find it difficult to manage the daily lives of their children. As one parent put it, "I couldn't remember to brush my teeth when I was a kid, and now I can't remember to tell my kid to brush his teeth" (Weiss, Hechtman, & Weiss, 2000, p. 1060).

Many authorities recommend that the first step to treatment is to have all family members become educated about the facts associated with ADHD. Because ADHD is a family issue, they also recommend that all members of the family should be partners in its treatment.

In Summary

Even though people with ADHD are at risk for poorer outcomes, it's important to point out that many adults with ADHD have highly successful careers and jobs, and many have happy marriages and families.

There's little doubt that ADHD can be a lifelong struggle. However, with the appropriate combination of medical, educational, and psychological counseling, satisfactory employment and family adjustment are within the reach of most people with ADHD. Now that most authorities recognize that ADHD often continues into adulthood, more and more research will be focused on treatment of ADHD in adults. With this research should come an even more positive outlook for adults with ADHD.

MyLab Education Self-Check 7.5

▼ chapter seven **SUMMARY**

PeopleImages/
DigitalVision/Getty
Image

What are the historical origins of attention deficit hyperactivity disorder (ADHD)?

- In the mid-19th century, Dr. Heinrich Hoffmann wrote nursery rhymes about "Fidgety Phillip" and "The Story of Johnny Head-in-Air."

- In his textbook published in 1775, Dr. Melchior Adam Weikard devoted a chapter to "Lack of Attention."

- In 1798, Sir Alexander Crichton wrote a treatise on attention disorders.

- In 1902, Dr. George F. Still reported on children whom he referred to as having "defective moral control."

- In the 1930s, Kurt Goldstein reported on soldiers who had head wounds in World War I.

- In the 1930s and 1940s, Heinz Werner and Alfred Strauss reported on children with mental retardation (intellectual disabilities) who were assumed to be brain injured, referred to as having the "Strauss syndrome."

- In the 1950s, William Cruickshank extended Werner and Strauss's work to children with normal intelligence.

- In the 1950s and 1960s, professionals used the term *minimal brain injury* to refer to children who were of normal intelligence but who were inattentive, impulsive, and/or hyperactive.

- In the 1960s and 1970s, the term *hyperactive child syndrome* was popular.

What is the current definition of ADHD?

- Most professionals rely on the American Psychiatric Association's *Diagnostic and Statistical Manual of Mental Disorders (DSM-5)* for the definition of ADHD. Currently, the manual subdivides individuals into (1) ADHD, Predominantly Inattentive Type; (2) ADHD, Predominantly Hyperactive-Impulsive Type; and (3) ADHD, Combined Type.

What is the prevalence of ADHD?

- The best estimates are that 7% to 9% of the school-age population has ADHD; however, only 1.07% of the school-age population receive special education services.

- Boys with ADHD outnumber girls, most likely owing to biological differences and perhaps some referral bias.

What methods of assessment do professionals use to identify individuals with ADHD?

- Professionals usually use four methods of assessment: (1) a medical examination, (2) a clinical interview, (3) teacher and parent rating scales, and (4) behavioral observations. The behavioral observations can be done in the classroom and/or in the clinician's office.

What causes ADHD?

- Neuroimaging studies have identified four areas of the brain that might be affected in people with ADHD: the prefrontal and frontal lobes, the basal ganglia, and the cerebellum.

  - The prefrontal and frontal lobes are responsible for executive functions, or the ability to regulate one's behavior.

  - The basal ganglia and cerebellum are involved in coordination and control of motor behavior.

- Research has identified an imbalance in each of two neurotransmitters: dopamine and noradrenaline.

- Family studies, twin studies, and molecular genetic studies indicate that heredity may also be a significant cause of ADHD.

- Exposure to toxins such as lead, as well as medical factors such as complications at birth and low birth weight, can also be a cause of ADHD.

What are some of the psychological and behavioral characteristics of learners with ADHD?

- Three of the most common behavioral characteristics are inattention, hyperactivity, and impulsivity.

- Two of the most common psychological characteristics are difficulties in executive functioning and behavioral inhibition.

- People with ADHD also often experience problems in adaptive behavior and in their relationships with peers.

- Several conditions often co-exist with ADHD: learning disabilities and emotional-behavioral problems, such as depression and anxiety; people with ADHD are also at risk for substance abuse problems.

What are some educational considerations for learners with ADHD?

- Good educational programming for students with ADHD involves a high degree of classroom structure and teacher-directed activities.

- Good educational programming for students with ADHD involves functional assessment and contingency-based self-management.

  - Functional behavioral assessment (FBA) involves determining the consequences, antecedents, and setting events that maintain inappropriate behaviors.

  - Such approaches might also include self-monitoring or self-management programs, with students recording their own behaviors.

What are some medication considerations for learners with ADHD?

- Psychostimulants, such as Ritalin, are prescribed most often; Strattera, a nonstimulant, is also often prescribed.

- Scientific studies generally support the effectiveness of medication, and most authorities on ADHD favor its use.

- Some cautions about medication are that some people are nonresponders, dosage levels should be monitored closely, some people experience side effects (although these usually are not serious), children should not be encouraged to see the medication as a replacement for self-initiated behavioral control, and medication should not be the first response to problem behavior.

How do professionals assess the academic, attention, and behavioral progress of students with ADHD?

- Curriculum-based measurement can be used to assess progress in academics and attention and behavior.
  - Momentary time sampling is particularly useful for assessing behavioral progress.
- Testing accommodations often include small-group or individual administration in a quiet location, extended time, and frequent breaks.

What are some important considerations with respect to early intervention for learners with ADHD?

- Diagnosing ADHD in early childhood is difficult, partly because very young children typically have short attention spans and are motorically active.

- Principles of classroom structure, teacher direction, functional behavioral assessment, and contingency-based self-management are important for preschoolers with ADHD.
- Because young children typically do not have strong self-management skills, contingencies in the form of praise, points, and tangible rewards are important.

What are some important considerations with respect to transition to adulthood for learners with ADHD?

- At least 50% of children with ADHD continue to have difficulties in adulthood.
- The difficulties they have can include executive functioning, working memory, and time management.
- A thorough clinical history is critical in diagnosing ADHD in adults.
- Although exceptions exist, adults with ADHD tend to have less positive outcomes than the general population in terms of employment, marriage and family, and general social well-being.
- Coaching is a therapeutic technique often recommended for adults with ADHD.

▼ INTERNET RESOURCES

Professional Organizations

- The oldest organization focused on children and adults with ADHD is Children and Adults with Attention-Deficit Hyperactivity Disorder: www.chadd.org.
- An organization focused on adults with ADHD is the Attention Deficit Disorder Association: www.add.org.

- Totally ADHD (http://totallyadd.com) is a website that takes a relatively light and humorous view of ADHD; however, it also offers straightforward advice and does a good job of ensuring that it's accurate and scientifically based.

chapter eight

LEARNERS WITH EMOTIONAL OR BEHAVIORAL DISORDERS

Gawrav/E+/Getty Images

► LEARNING OUTCOMES

Learning Outcome 8.1: Understand the terminology used with, the definition and classification of, and the prevalence of learners with emotional or behavioral disorders.

Learning Outcome 8.2: Understand how learners with emotional or behavioral disorders are identified and the causes of emotional or behavioral disorders.

Learning Outcome 8.3: Learn about the psychological and behavioral characteristics of learners with emotional or behavioral disorders.

Learning Outcome 8.4: Understand some of the educational considerations for people with emotional or behavioral disorders, and how professionals assess progress to help plan educational strategies.

Learning Outcome 8.5: Learn about issues that should be considered with respect to early intervention and transition to adulthood for individuals with emotional or behavioral disorders.

MISCONCEPTIONS ABOUT Learners with Emotional or Behavioral Disorders

MYTH Most children and youths with emotional or behavioral disorders go unnoticed.

FACT Although it is difficult to identify the types and causes of problems, most children and youths with emotional or behavioral disorders, whether aggressive or withdrawn, are quite easy to spot.

MYTH Students with emotional or behavioral disorders are usually very bright.

FACT Some, but relatively few students with emotional or behavioral disorders, test high in intelligence; in fact, most have below-average IQs.

MYTH Most students who are seen by their teachers as a "pain in the neck" are not disturbed; they are disturbing to others, but they are not disturbed.

FACT Most students who are disturbing to others are also disturbed. One of the signs of emotional health and good adjustment is behaving in ways that do not cause others concern, being neither unusually aggressive and disruptive nor overly reticent and socially withdrawn.

MYTH Students with emotional or behavioral disorders exhibit problematic behavior constantly.

FACT Most students with emotional or behavioral disorders exhibit typical behavior most of the time. Their emotional or behavioral disorders are episodic.

MYTH Most students with emotional or behavioral disorders receive special education and/or mental health services.

FACT The vast majority of students with emotional or behavioral disorders are not identified and served in a timely fashion by either mental health services or special education. Only a small percentage (perhaps 20%) are served by special education or mental health services.

MYTH Most students with emotional or behavioral disorders need a permissive environment, in which they feel accepted and can accept themselves for who they are.

FACT Research shows that a firmly structured and highly predictable environment is of greatest benefit for most students.

MYTH Juvenile delinquency and the aggressive behavior known as conduct disorder can be effectively deterred by harsh punishment if children and youths know that their misbehavior will be punished.

FACT Harsh punishment, including imprisonment, not only does not deter misbehavior, but also creates conditions under which many individuals become even more likely to exhibit unacceptable conduct.

GUIDING QUESTIONS

- What terminology is used to describe emotional or behavioral disorders?

- What is the definition of *emotional or behavioral disorder?*

- How are emotional or behavioral disorders classified?

- What is the prevalence of emotional or behavioral disorders?

- What are the causes of emotional or behavioral disorders?

- How are emotional or behavioral disorders identified?

- What are the major educational considerations regarding emotional or behavioral disorders?

- How do professionals assess the progress of students with emotional or behavioral disorders?

- What are important considerations in early intervention for learners with emotional or behavioral disorders?

- What are important considerations in transition to adulthood for learners with emotional or behavioral disorders?

Most children and youths with emotional or behavioral disorders (EBD) aren't very good at making friends. Their most obvious problem is failure to establish close and satisfying emotional ties with other people who can help them. The friends they do have are often deviant peers (Kauffman & Landrum, 2018).

Some students with EBD are withdrawn. Other children or adults might try to reach them, but these efforts are usually met with fear or disinterest. In many cases, quiet rejection continues until those trying to be their friends give up. Close emotional ties are built around reciprocal social responses. People lose interest in others who don't respond to social overtures. (For a definition of EBD and what to look for, go to http://www.pacer.org/.)

Many students with EBD are isolated from others because they strike out with hostility and aggression. They're abusive, destructive, unpredictable, irresponsible, bossy, quarrelsome, irritable, jealous, defiant—anything but pleasant. Naturally, most other children and most adults choose not to spend time with individuals like this unless they have to. Some people strike back at youngsters who show these characteristics. It's no wonder that children and youths with EBD seem to be embroiled in a continuous battle with everyone. Teachers and well-behaved peers naturally tend to withdraw from them or avoid them, which reduces their opportunities to learn both academic and social skills.

A common but serious misunderstanding is that children with EBD aren't really disturbed; rather, they are just a pain in the neck. Students can be both disturbed *and* disturbing, have an emotional or behavioral disorder *and* irritate the teacher. True, some irritating students don't have an emotional or behavioral disorder. However, most children with EBD are irritating to teachers, whereas most children are neither irritating nor have such a disorder. Moreover, students who are consistently irritating are at high risk of acquiring EBD, if they don't already have a disorder, or of encouraging such disorders in others, simply because the reactions of their teachers and peers are likely to be so negative and hostile.

Another widespread misunderstanding is that children and youths with EBD exhibit their problematic behavior all the time—24/7. Most people don't seem to understand the fact that such disorders tend to be episodic, highly variable, and sometimes situation-specific (e.g., only when demands are placed on these students to perform or only outside their home or family). People often don't understand the fact that their own observation may catch these students at a time when the disability is *not* being exhibited. Many people also don't seem to realize that parents who have psychological disabilities may be very poor or unreliable reporters of these students' behavior at home. And often, people don't understand that a very good parent can have a really problematic child. Understanding the on-again, off-again nature of these disorders is critical. Expecting a youngster with EBD to exhibit problem behavior all the time is somewhat like expecting someone with a seizure disorder to have seizures all the time. Emotional or behavioral disorders aren't exhibited as consistently as is intellectual disability or cerebral palsy.

Where does the problem start? Does it begin with behavior that frustrates, angers, or irritates other people? Or does it begin with a social environment so uncomfortable or inappropriate that the child can only withdraw or attack? These questions can't be answered fully on the basis of current research. The best thinking today is that the problem isn't always just in the child's behavior or just in the environment. The problem arises because the social interactions and transactions between the child and the social environment are inappropriate—both the behavior *and* responses to it are problematic. This is an ecological perspective—an interpretation of the problem as a negative aspect of the child *and* the environment in which the child lives. And there are two equally serious mistakes people can make: First, assuming the problem is only in the child who exhibits inappropriate behavior; and second, assuming the child's behavior is not the problem, only the context in which it occurs. Sometimes the problem may begin with misbehavior, and sometimes it may begin with mismanagement. However, by the time special educators are involved, the problem usually involves both misbehavior *and* mismanagement.

TERMINOLOGY

Many different terms have been used to designate children who have extreme social-interpersonal and/or intrapersonal problems, including *seriously emotionally disturbed* (SED, formerly used in federal documents), *emotionally handicapped, emotionally impaired, behaviorally impaired, socially/emotionally handicapped, emotionally conflicted, seriously behaviorally disabled,* and *emotionally and behaviorally disordered* (EBD, the term now most often used). These terms don't designate distinctly different types of disorders. The different labels appear to represent only personal preferences for terms and slightly different theoretical orientations.

Until 1997, *seriously emotionally disturbed* (SED) was the term used in federal special education laws and regulations. *Seriously* was dropped from the terminology in 1997. *Emotionally disturbed* (ED) is still the term used in the Individuals with Disabilities Education Act (IDEA). The term *behaviorally disordered* is consistent with the name of the Council for Children with Behavioral Disorders (CCBD, a division of the Council for Exceptional Children) and has the advantage of focusing attention on the clearly observable aspect of these children's problems: disordered behavior. Many authorities favor terminology indicating that these children may have emotional or behavioral problems or both (Cullinan, 2004, 2007; Garner, Kauffman, & Elliott, 2014; Kauffman & Brigham, 2009; Kauffman & Landrum, 2018; Walker & Gresham, 2014). In 1990, the National Mental Health and Special Education Coalition, representing over 30 professional and advocacy groups, proposed the term *emotional or behavioral disorder* to replace *emotional disturbance* in federal laws and regulations (Forness & Knitzer, 1992). Unfortunately, the proposed terminology and definition have not yet been adopted by the federal government or most states (Polloway, Kauffman, Charles, Smith, & Patton, 2017).

Another term you may encounter is *prosocial*. Prosocial behavior is the opposite of antisocial behavior. It refers to desirable ways of behaving—obedience, friendliness, problem solving, and the kind of behavior that makes you want to be around someone. It includes skillfulness in making and keeping nondeviant friends, school success, staying within the limits of the law, and doing the kinds of things that are considered helpful, adaptive, and normal.

DEFINITION

Defining EBD has always been problematic. Professional groups and experts have felt free to construct individual working definitions to fit their own professional purposes. No one has come up with a definition that all professionals understand and accept (Kauffman & Landrum, 2006, 2018; Mundschenk & Simpson, 2014; Polloway et al., 2017; Walker, Yell, & Murray, 2014).

Defining emotional and behavioral disorders is somewhat like defining a familiar experience—anger, loneliness, or happiness, for example. We all have an intuitive grasp of what these experiences are, but forming objective definitions of emotional or behavioral disorders is difficult. Mental health and normal behavior have been hard to define precisely. It's no wonder, then, that the definition of EBD presents a special challenge. Conceptual models—assumptions or theories about why people behave as they do and what we should do about it—may offer conflicting ideas about just what the problem is. Emotional or behavioral disorders tend to overlap a great deal with other disabilities, especially learning disabilities and intellectual disability. Finally, each professional group has its own reasons for serving individuals with emotional or behavioral disorders. For example, clinical psychologists, school psychologists, social workers, teachers, and juvenile justice authorities all have their particular concerns and language. Differences in the focuses of diverse professions tend to produce differences in definition as well.

Current Definitions

There is general agreement that emotional or behavioral disorder refers to the following:

- Behavior that goes to an *extreme*—not just slightly different from the usual
- A problem that is *chronic*—one that does not quickly disappear
- Behavior that is *unacceptable* because of social or cultural expectations

THE FEDERAL DEFINITION The federal rules and regulations governing the implementation of IDEA define the term *emotionally disturbed* as follows:

i. The term means a condition exhibiting one or more of the following characteristics over a long period of time and to a marked extent, which adversely affects educational performance:
   A. An inability to learn that cannot be explained by intellectual, sensory, or health factors;
   B. An inability to build or maintain satisfactory relationships with peers and teachers;
   C. Inappropriate types of behavior or feelings under normal circumstances;
   D. A general pervasive mood of unhappiness or depression; or
   E. A tendency to develop physical symptoms or fears associated with personal or school problems.
ii. The term includes children who are schizophrenic. The term does not include children who are socially maladjusted unless it is determined that they are emotionally disturbed. (45 C.F.R. 121a5[b][8][1978])

These inclusions and exclusions (in ii above) are unnecessary (Bower, 1982; Kauffman & Landrum, 2018). Bower's five criteria (A–E above) for emotional disturbance indicate that schizophrenic children must be included and that socially maladjusted children cannot be excluded. Furthermore, the clause "which adversely affects educational performance" makes interpretation of the definition impossible, unless the meaning of educational performance is clarified. Does educational performance refer only to academic achievement? If so, then children with the behavioral characteristics listed but who achieve on grade level can be excluded.

One of the most widely criticized and controversial aspects of the definition is its exclusion of children who are socially maladjusted but not emotionally disturbed. Some states and localities have started to interpret social maladjustment as **conduct** disorder—aggressive, disruptive, antisocial behavior. The American Psychological Association and the CCBD have condemned this practice, which has no scientific basis (Kauffman & Landrum, 2018; Landrum, 2017).

AN ALTERNATIVE TO THE FEDERAL DEFINITION The National Mental Health and Special Education Coalition proposed an alternative definition in 1990 (Forness & Knitzer, 1992). We do not present their alternative in total because it is more than 25 years old and has not been adopted in federal law. It uses the terminology emotional or behavioral disorder, mentions cultural norms, includes social, vocational, and personal skills in addition to academic achievement, and states that problems are not temporary and must be exhibited in more than one environment.

MyLab Education
Video Example 8.1
Mel discusses fighting stigma with openness and success.

Some of the major advantages of Forness and Knitzer's (1992) proposed definition over the federal definition are:

- It uses terminology that reflects current professional preferences and concern for minimizing stigma.
- It includes both disorders of emotions and disorders of behavior, and it recognizes that they may occur either separately or in combination.
- It is school-centered but acknowledges that disorders exhibited outside the school setting are also important.
- It does not include minor or transient problems or ordinary responses to stress.
- It is sensitive to ethnic and cultural differences.
- It acknowledges the importance of trial interventions, but it does not require slavish implementation of them in extreme cases.
- It recognizes that students can have multiple disabilities.
- It includes the full range of emotional and behavioral disorders that are of concern to mental health and special education professionals, and it does so without problematic exclusions.

CLASSIFICATION

Classification of EBD is sometimes thought to follow psychiatric designations, particularly the categories suggested by the current version of the American Psychiatric Association's *Diagnostic and Statistical Manual of Mental Disorders, Fifth Edition* (DSM-5). Controversy about the manual has followed the release of every edition. Much of the controversy about DSM-5 has centered on the fact that classification depends primarily, if not exclusively, on the way people behave or feel—their symptoms of what is presumably mental illness, rather than a specific malfunction of the brain. However, teachers must manage behavior and emotions in everyday interactions. For teachers the DSM is important, but is sometimes less helpful than classification based on behavior (Mattison, 2014).

Researchers have identified two broad, pervasive dimensions of disordered behavior: externalizing and internalizing. **Externalizing behavior** involves striking out against others (see Furlong, Morrison, & Jimerson, 2004). **Internalizing behavior** involves mental or emotional conflicts, such as depression and anxiety (see Gresham & Kern, 2004). Some researchers have found more specific disorders, but all of the more specific disorders can be located on these two primary dimensions.

Individuals may show behaviors characteristic of both dimensions; the dimensions are not mutually exclusive. A child or youth might exhibit several behaviors associated with internalizing problems (e.g., short attention span, poor concentration) and several of those associated with externalizing problems as well (e.g., fighting, disruptive behavior, annoying others). Actually, **comorbidity**—the co-occurrence of two or more conditions in the same individual—is common. Few individuals with an emotional or behavioral disorder exhibit only one type of maladaptive behavior.

Children may exhibit any kind of troublesome behavior with any degree of intensity or severity. That is, any kind of problem behavior may be exhibited to a greater or lesser extent; the range may be from normal to severely disordered. For example, an individual might have a severe conduct disorder; exhibit an externalizing problem defined by overt, aggressive, disruptive behavior; or engage in covert antisocial acts such as stealing, lying, and fire setting. Individuals with **schizophrenia** have a severe disorder of thinking, not a mild one. They might believe that they are controlled by alien forces or might have other delusions or hallucinations (http://www.youtube.com/watch?v=PVHNGZ0Omx0). Typically, their emotions are inappropriate for the actual circumstances, and they tend to withdraw into their own private worlds.

PREVALENCE

Credible studies in the United States and many other countries have consistently indicated that at least 6% to 10% of children and youths of school age exhibit serious and persistent emotional/behavioral problems, but less than 1% of schoolchildren in the United States are identified as having emotional disturbance for special education purposes (Freeman, Paparella, Kauffman, & Walker, 2012; Kauffman & Landrum, 2018; Landrum, 2017). The U.S. Surgeon General's report early in this century and the 2013 report of the Centers for Disease Control and Prevention, as well as other studies, have shown that only a very small percentage of children with serious emotional or behavioral disorders receive mental health services (e.g., Costello, Egger, & Angold, 2005; Costello, Foley, & Angold, 2006; Forness, Freeman, Paparella, Kauffman, & Walker, 2012). Costello et al. (2005) concluded that this problem of underidentification poses a very serious health risk.

Looking at the evidence we have, we may conclude that the gap between estimates of the prevalence and provision of services by mental health and special education professionals is both huge and threatening (Forness et al., 2012; Kauffman, Mock, & Simpson, 2007; Kauffman, Simpson, & Mock, 2009). The most common types of problems exhibited by students who are placed in special education for EBD are externalizing—aggressive, acting-out, disruptive behavior. Boys outnumber girls in displaying these behaviors by a ratio of 5 to 1, or more. Overall, boys tend to exhibit more aggression than girls do, although antisocial behavior in girls is an increasing concern (see Coutinho & Oswald, 2011; Furlong et al., 2004; O'Brennan, Furlong, O'Malley, & Jones, 2014; Schaffner, 2006).

Juvenile delinquency and the antisocial behavior known as conduct disorder present particular problems in estimating prevalence. Disabling conditions of various kinds are much more common among juvenile delinquents than among the general population (Nelson, Leone, & Rutherford, 2004; O'Mahony, 2014). Moreover, the social and economic costs of delinquency and antisocial behavior are enormous. Students who exhibit serious antisocial behavior are at high risk for school failure as well as other negative outcomes (Kauffman & Landrum, 2018; Walker, Ramsey, & Gresham, 2004).

MyLab Education Self-Check 8.1

CAUSES

Philosophers, researchers, and others have attributed the causes of emotional or behavioral disorders to four major factors:

1. Biological disorders and diseases
2. Pathological family relationships
3. Undesirable experiences in schools
4. Negative cultural or supernatural influences

From the days of ancient Greek philosopher Plato to the present era, people have speculated about all of these (Goldstein, 2014—see esp. pp. 109–112; Scull, 2015). We focus further discussion on causes for which there is empirical evidence.

Although in the majority of cases, no conclusive empirical evidence indicates that one of these factors is directly responsible, some factors might give a child a predisposition to exhibit problem behavior, and others might precipitate or trigger it. That is, some factors, such as genetics, influence behavior over a long time and increase the likelihood that circumstances will trigger maladaptive responses. Other factors (e.g., observing one parent beating the other) might have a more immediate effect and might trigger maladaptive responses in an individual who is already predisposed to problem behavior.

Another concept important in all theories is the idea that contributing factors heighten the risk of a disorder. It's extremely unusual to find a single cause leading directly to a disorder. Usually, several factors together contribute to the development of a problem. In almost all cases, the question of what specifically caused the disorder can't be answered because no one really knows. However, professionals often do know the factors that place children at risk—the circumstances or conditions that increase the chances that a child will develop the disorder (see Cook & Ruhaak, 2014; Kazdin, 2008; Sprague & Walker, 2000). The upper list of factors in Figure 8.1 are conditions that heighten risk and may lead eventually to EBD. The lower list of factors in Figure 8.1 are things that lower risk and tend to be associated with the development of prosocial behavior skills that are typically required for school success. Information included in Figure 8.1 comes from Sprague and Walker (2000); Stichter, Conroy, and Kauffman (2008); and other summaries of research (e.g., Garner et al., 2014; Mash & Barkley, 2014; Walker & Gresham, 2014). However, it is important to understand that factors or conditions can change, that a child may experience mixed risk-heightening and risk-lowering factors, and that these are things that may change over time. The life course of a child is not fixed by any one factor or combination of factors. Educators must do their best to add whatever positive, risk-lowering factors they can, such as effective instruction, consistent discipline, warm relationships with students, and problem-solving and social skills. The earlier educators can intervene to lower risk, the better (see Dunlap & Fox, 2014; Walker, Severson, et al., 2014).

FIGURE 8.1

FACTORS THAT HEIGHTEN OR LOWER RISK AT VARIOUS STAGES OF DEVELOPMENT AND MAY LEAD TO EBD OR PROSOCIAL BEHAVIOR

	Age/Level		
preschool →	primary →	elementary/middle →	adolescence/high/adult
1 may lead to →	2 may lead to →	3 may lead to →	4

Factors heightening risk that may lead to --→ EBD

poverty, abuse, neglect	defiance of adults/authorities	truancy	failure or dropping out of school
harsh, inconsistent discipline	aggression toward peers	social rejection	violence and/or delinquency
caretaker substance abuse	low problem-solving skills	trouble at school or with law	substance abuse
observation of violence	lack of school readiness	drug use (including alcohol)	gang membership
negativity about school	cold or harsh teachers		adult criminality
family criminality or disruption	ineffective instruction		dependency on welfare

↗   ↗   ↗   ↗

Teachers should help students experience as many risk-lowering factors as possible as early as possible (↗)

↗   ↗   ↗   ↗

Factors lowering risk and may foster --→ prosocial behavior

nurturing, supportive parent(s)/adult(s)	obedience to adults/authorities	regular school attendance	school success/graduation
observation of prosocial behavior	school readiness	social and academic success	involvement in structured activities
positive attitudes toward school/education	positive interactions with others	liked by peers and teachers	contributions to community
family stability	good at problem-solving	involvement in extracurricular	avoidance of substance abuse
consistent discipline	warm, supportive teachers		
	effective instruction		

Biological Factors

Behaviors and emotions may be influenced by genetic, neurological, or biochemical factors, or by combinations of these. Certainly, a relationship exists between body and behavior, and it would therefore seem reasonable to look for a biological causal factor of some kind for certain disorders (Cook & Ruhaak, 2014; Cooper, 2014; Forness, Walker, & Serna, 2014; Grigorenko, 2014). For example, prenatal exposure to alcohol can contribute to many types of disability, including EBD. But only rarely is it possible to demonstrate a relationship between a specific biological factor and EBD.

For most children with EBD, no real evidence shows that biological factors alone are at the root of their problems. For those with severe and profound disorders, however, evidence often suggests that biological factors contribute to their conditions. Moreover, increasing evidence shows that medications may be helpful in addressing the problems of many or most students with emotional or behavioral disorders if they receive state-of-the-art psychopharmacology and if proper precautions are used (Konopasek & Forness, 2004, 2014; Locher, Koechlin, Zion, Werner, Pine, Kirsch, Kessler, & Kossowsky, 2017).

All children are born with a biologically determined behavioral style, or temperament. Although children's inborn temperaments may be changed by the way they are reared, some people have long believed that children with so-called difficult temperaments are predisposed to develop EBD. There is no one-to-one relationship between temperament and disorders, however. A difficult child might be handled so well or a child with an easy temperament treated so poorly that the outcome will be quite different from what one would predict on the basis of initial behavioral style (Keogh, 2003). Other biological factors besides temperament (e.g., disease, malnutrition, and brain trauma) can predispose children to develop emotional or behavioral problems. Substance abuse also can contribute to emotional and behavioral problems. Except in rare instances, it isn't possible to determine that these factors are direct causes of problem behavior (see Kauffman & Landrum, 2018; Landrum, 2017).

Emotional and behavioral disorders are, in essence, social phenomena, whether they have biological causes or not. The causes of emotional and behavioral disorders are seldom exclusively biological or psychological. Once a biological disorder occurs, it nearly always creates psychosocial problems that then also contribute to the emotional or behavioral disorder. Medication may be of great benefit, but it is seldom the only intervention that is needed (Forness & Beard, 2007; Konopasek & Forness, 2004, 2014). The psychological and social aspects of the disorder must also be addressed.

Family Factors

Even in cases of severe EBD, it isn't possible to find consistent and valid research findings that allow blaming parents (Kauffman & Landrum, 2018; Landrum, 2017). Very good parents sometimes have children with very serious EBD, and incompetent, neglectful, or abusive parents sometimes have children with no significant emotional or behavioral disorders. The relationship between parenting and EBD isn't simple, but some parenting practices are definitely better than others (see Heubeck & Lauth, 2014; Kazdin, 2008; Reinke, Frey, Herman, & Thompson, 2014).

Educators must be aware that most parents of youngsters with EBD want their children to behave more appropriately and will do anything they can to help them. These parents need support—not blame or criticism—to help them deal with very difficult family circumstances. The Federation of Families for Children's Mental Health was organized in 1989 to provide such support and resources, and parents are organizing in many localities to help each other in finding additional assistance.

School Factors

Some children already have EBD when they begin school; others develop such disorders during their school years, perhaps in part because of damaging experiences in the classroom. Children who exhibit disorders when they enter school may become better or worse according to how they are managed in the classroom (Furlong, Morrison, & Fisher, 2005; Kauffman & Brigham, 2009; Kauffman & Landrum, 2018; Landrum, 2017; Walker & Gresham, 2014). School experiences are no doubt of great importance to children, but as with biological and family factors, we can't justify many statements about how such experiences contribute to the child's behavioral difficulties. A child's temperament and social competence can interact with the behaviors of classmates and teachers in contributing to emotional or behavioral problems.

A very real danger is that children who exhibit problem behavior will become trapped in a spiral of negative interactions, in which they become increasingly irritating to and irritated by teachers and peers. In considering how teachers might be contributing to disordered behavior, they must question themselves about their academic instruction, expectations, and approaches to behavior management. Teachers must not assume blame for disordered behavior to which they are not contributing, but it's equally important that teachers eliminate whatever contributions they might be making to their students' misconduct (see Kauffman & Brigham, 2009; Kauffman & Landrum, 2018; Kauffman, Pullen, Mostert, & Trent, 2011).

Cultural Factors

Children, their families, and schools are embedded in cultures that influence them (see Anastasiou, Gardner, & Michail, 2011; Learoyd-Smith & Daniels, 2014; Skiba, Middelberg, & McClain, 2014). Aside from family and school, many environmental conditions affect adults' expectations of children and children's expectations of themselves and their peers. Adults communicate values and behavioral standards to children through a variety of cultural conditions, demands, prohibitions, and models. Several specific cultural influences come to mind: the level of violence in the media (especially including television, motion pictures, the Internet, and video games), the use of terror as a means of coercion, the availability of recreational drugs and the level of drug abuse, changing standards for sexual conduct, religious demands and restrictions on behavior, and the threat of nuclear accidents, terrorism, or war. Peers are another important source of cultural influence, particularly after the child enters the upper elementary grades.

IDENTIFICATION

It's much easier to identify disordered behaviors than it is to define and classify their types and causes. Most students with EBD don't escape the notice of their teachers. Occasionally, such students don't bother anyone and thus are invisible, but it's usually easy for experienced teachers to tell when students need help. Often, teachers fail to assess the strengths of students with EBD. However, it's important to include assessment of students' emotional and behavioral competencies, not just their weaknesses or deficits (Jones, Dohrn, & Dunn, 2004; Lane, Menzies, Oakes, & Germer, 2014; Oliver, Cress, Savolainen, & Epstein, 2014).

The most common type of EBD is conduct disorder, an externalizing problem that attracts immediate attention, so identification is seldom a real problem. Students with internalizing problems might be less obvious, but they aren't difficult to recognize (see Walker, Small, Severson, Seeley, & Feil, 2014). Students with EBD are so readily identified by school personnel, in fact, that relatively few schools bother to use systematic screening procedures. Also, the availability of special services for those with EBD lags far behind the need; and there isn't much point in screening for problems when no services are available to treat them. Children with schizophrenia are seldom mistaken for those who are developing normally. Their unusual language, mannerisms, and ways of relating to others soon become matters of concern to parents, teachers, and even many casual observers. Children with schizophrenia are a very small percentage of those with EBD, and problems in their identification aren't usually encountered. However, they might first be identified as having another disorder, such as attention deficit hyperactivity disorder or depression, and later be diagnosed with schizophrenia.

Even so, don't conclude that educators never have any question about whether a student has EBD. The younger the child, the more difficult it is to judge whether the behavior signifies a serious problem. And some children's EBD goes undetected because teachers aren't sensitive to the children's problems or because these children don't stand out sharply from other children in the environment who might have even more serious problems. Furthermore, cultural bias can work either way, leading educators to wrongly identify some children or fail to identify others. Even sensitive and unbiased teachers sometimes make errors of judgment. Also, keep in mind that some students with EBD don't exhibit problems at school.

Formal screening and accurate early identification for the purpose of planning educational intervention are complicated by the problems of definition we have already discussed (see Lane et al., 2014). In general, however, teachers' informal judgments have served as a reasonably valid and reliable means of screening students for emotional or behavioral problems (as compared with judgments of psychologists and psychiatrists). When more formal procedures are used, teachers' ratings of behavior have turned out to be quite accurate (Walker, Ramsey, & Gresham, 2003–2004a).

MyLab Education Self-Check 8.2

PSYCHOLOGICAL AND BEHAVIORAL CHARACTERISTICS

Describing the characteristics of children and youths with EBD is an extraordinary challenge because disorders of emotions and behaviors are extremely varied. Individuals may vary markedly in intelligence, achievement, life circumstances, and emotional and behavioral characteristics (Garner et al., 2014; Kauffman & Brigham, 2009; Walker & Gresham, 2014).

Intelligence and Achievement

The idea that children and youths with EBD tend to be particularly bright is a myth. Research clearly shows that the average student with an EBD has an IQ in the dull–normal range (around 90) and that relatively few score above the bright–normal range. Compared to the normal distribution of intelligence, more children with EBD fall into the ranges of slow learner and mild intellectual disability. On the basis of a review of the research on the intelligence of students with EBD, Kauffman and Landrum (2018) hypothesized distributions of intelligence as shown in Figure 8.2.

There are pitfalls in assessing the intellectual characteristics of a group of children by examining the distribution of their IQs. Intelligence tests aren't perfect instruments for measuring what we mean by intelligence, and it can be argued that EBD might prevent children from scoring as high as they are capable of scoring. Still, the lower-than-normal IQs for these students do indicate lower ability to perform tasks that other students perform successfully, and the lower scores are consistent with impairment in other areas of functioning (e.g., academic achievement and social skills). IQ is a relatively good predictor of how far a student will progress academically and socially, even in cases of severe disorders.

Most students with EBD are also underachievers at school, as measured by standardized tests. Students with an EBD do not usually achieve at the level expected for their mental age; seldom are such students academically advanced. In fact, many students with severe disorders lack basic reading and arithmetic skills, and the few who seem to be competent in reading or math often cannot apply their skills to everyday problems (Lane & Menzies, 2010; Nelson, Benner, & Bohaty, 2014).

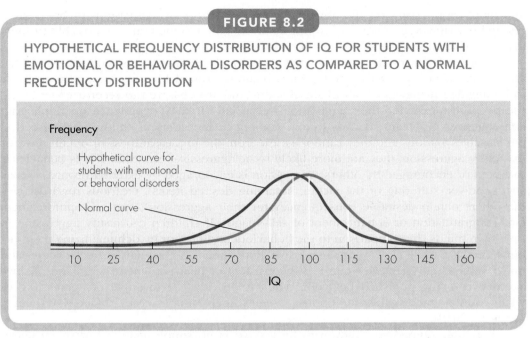

FIGURE 8.2

HYPOTHETICAL FREQUENCY DISTRIBUTION OF IQ FOR STUDENTS WITH EMOTIONAL OR BEHAVIORAL DISORDERS AS COMPARED TO A NORMAL FREQUENCY DISTRIBUTION

Source: Kauffman, James M.; Landrum, Timothy J., *Characteristics of Emotional and Behavioral Disorders of Children and Youth*, 9th Ed., ©2009. Reprinted and Electronically reproduced by permission of Pearson Education, Inc., New York, NY.

Social and Emotional Characteristics

Previously, we described two major dimensions of disordered behavior based on analyses of behavior ratings: externalizing and internalizing. The externalizing dimension is characterized by aggressive, acting-out behavior; the internalizing dimension is characterized by anxious, withdrawn behavior and depression. Our discussion here focuses on these two types.

A given student might, at different times, show both aggressive and withdrawn or depressed behaviors. Remember that most students with EBD have multiple problems. At the beginning of this chapter, we said that most students with EBD aren't well liked or they identify with deviant peers. Studies of the social status of students in regular elementary and secondary classrooms indicate that those who are identified as having EBD may be socially rejected. Early peer rejection and aggressive behavior place a child at high risk for later social and emotional problems. Many aggressive students who aren't rejected affiliate primarily with others who are aggressive.

The relationship between EBD and communication disorders is increasingly clear (Rogers-Adkinson & Griffith, 1999). Many children and youths with EBD have great difficulty in understanding and using language in social circumstances.

AGGRESSIVE, ACTING-OUT BEHAVIOR (EXTERNALIZING) As we noted earlier, conduct disorder is the most common problem exhibited by students with emotional or behavioral disorders. Hitting, fighting, teasing, yelling, refusing to comply with requests, crying, destructiveness, vandalism, extortion—these behaviors, if exhibited often, are very likely to earn a child or youth the label "disturbed." Normal children cry, scream, hit, fight, become negative, and do almost everything else children with EBD do, but not as impulsively and not as often. Youngsters of the type we are discussing here drive adults to distraction. These youths aren't popular with their peers either, unless they are socialized delinquents who don't offend their delinquent friends. They typically don't respond quickly and positively to well-meaning adults who care about them and try to be helpful.

Aggression has been analyzed from many viewpoints. The analyses having the strongest support in empirical research are those of social learning theorists and behavioral psychologists (Colvin, 2004; Leff, Waanders, Waasdorp, & Paskewich, 2014; Seeley, Severson, & Fixsen, 2014). Their studies take into account the child's experience

MyLab Education
Video Example 8.2

Negative reinforcement can be an effective way to increase a desired behavior.

MyLab Education
Video Example 8.3

It is easy to confuse different types of reinforcement. This video scenario explains positive reinforcement and how it differs from negative reinforcement.

MyLab Education
Video Example 8.4

Watch a video that explains the concept of shaping and its role in intermittent reinforcement.

and motivation, based on the anticipated consequences of aggression. In brief, these researchers view aggression as learned behavior and assume that it is possible to identify the conditions under which it will be learned.

Children learn many aggressive behaviors by observing parents, siblings, playmates, and people portrayed in the media. Individuals who model aggression are more likely to be imitated if they are high in social status and are observed to receive rewards and escape punishment for their aggression—especially if they experience no unpleasant consequences or obtain rewards by overcoming their victims. If children are placed in unpleasant situations and they cannot escape from the unpleasantness or obtain rewards except by aggression, they are more likely to be aggressive, especially if this behavior is tolerated or encouraged by others. Aggression is encouraged by external rewards (social status, power, suffering of the victim, obtaining desired items), vicarious rewards (seeing others obtain desirable consequences for their aggression), and self-reinforcement (self-congratulation or enhancement of self-image). If children can justify aggression in their own minds (by comparison to the behaviors of others or by dehumanizing their victims), they are more likely to be aggressive. Punishment can actually increase aggression under some circumstances: when it is inconsistent or delayed, when there is no positive alternative to the punished behavior, when it provides an example of aggression, or when counterattack against the punisher seems likely to be successful (see Kauffman & Landrum, 2018).

Teaching aggressive children to be less so is no simple matter, but social learning theory and behavioral research do provide some general guidelines. In general, research doesn't support the notion that it is wise to let children act out their aggression freely. The most helpful techniques include providing examples (models) of nonaggressive responses to aggression-provoking circumstances, helping the child rehearse or role-play nonaggressive behavior, providing reinforcement for nonaggressive behavior, preventing the child from obtaining positive consequences for aggression, and punishing aggression in ways that involve as little counteraggression as possible (e.g., using time-out or brief social isolation rather than spanking or yelling; Colvin, 2004; Kauffman et al., 2011; Walker et al., 2003–2004b, 2004). The accompanying Responsive Instruction box provides a description of a schoolwide strategy to reduce aggression and bullying.

The seriousness of children's aggressive, acting-out behavior shouldn't be underestimated. It was believed for decades that although these children cause a lot of trouble, they did not have disabilities as serious as children who are shy and anxious. Research has exploded this myth. When combined with school failure, aggressive, antisocial behavior in childhood generally predicts a gloomy future in terms of social adjustment and mental health, especially for boys. When we consider that conduct disorders and delinquency are highly correlated with school failure, the importance of meeting the needs of acting-out and underachieving children is obvious (Kauffman & Landrum, 2018; Walker et al., 2004).

IMMATURE, WITHDRAWN BEHAVIOR AND DEPRESSION (INTERNALIZING) In noting the seriousness of aggressive, acting-out behavior, we don't intend to downplay the disabling nature of immaturity and withdrawal or depression (for more on any type of disorder, including such things as anxiety disorders, go to http://psychcentral.com/ and search for the particular disorder or type of problem). Such disorders not only have serious consequences for individuals in their childhood years, but also carry a very poor prognosis for adult mental health. The child whose behavior fits a pattern of extreme immaturity and withdrawal or depression cannot develop the close and satisfying human relationships that characterize normal development. Such a child will find it difficult to meet the pressures and demands of everyday life (http://www.youtube.com/watch?v=fF5_kTwk8tQ). The school environment is the one in which anxious and withdrawn adolescents in particular experience the most distress (Masia, Klein, Storch, & Corda, 2001; Seeley et al., 2014).

RESPONSIVE INSTRUCTION

Meeting the Needs of Students with Emotional or Behavioral Disorders

STRATEGIES FOR REDUCING BULLYING

What the Research Says

In recent years, school bullying has become an increasing problem—particularly when interventions are not in place to reduce bullying. As many as 30% to 80% of students have been the victim of bullying while in school (Graham, 2010). Bullying can have a significant impact on the psychological and academic well-being of students. Not only does bullying occur in schools, but the ubiquity of technology has increased the occurrences of cyberbullying as well (Morgan, 2012).

Defining and identifying bullying may be difficult because there is not one set of behaviors that describe a bully. A report by Holt and Keys (2004) found that teachers often report lower bullying rates than students, indicating that teachers are not aware of the amount of bullying taking place in schools. Additionally, teachers typically label physical aggression as bullying but fail to include behaviors such as name-calling, verbal aggression, or intimidation as bullying. When these behaviors are overlooked, bullying can escalate, leading to hostile environments in schools.

Comprehensive Review of the Research

Jimenez-Barbero and his colleagues (2016) described a general review (meta-analysis) of the research on anti-bullying programs in schools. They found evidence that anti-bullying programs typically helped reduce frequency of victimization and violence in schools, although the strength of such effects was often too weak to be considered statistically significant. Some important variables, such as school climate, have not been studied sufficiently.

Other Research Findings

Unfortunately, other research has indicated that many bullying intervention programs are unsuccessful or have limited success (Morgan, 2012). Some programs, however, such as the *Olweus Bullying Prevention Program*, have documented success. The Olweus program is a schoolwide intervention program that may be used with any grade-level group—from kindergarten to high school. The program's goals are to reduce and prevent bullying problems among school children and to improve peer relations at school. Several research studies conducted in the United States have validated the use of this program across grade levels. Results indicated that bullying decreased as much as 45%. General outcomes included decreased reports of being bullied as well as decreased reports of bullying others.

Applying the Research to Teaching

The Olweus program includes specific guidelines for classroom teachers. These include: (a) establish rules and consequences related to bullying, (b) create a welcoming environment that fosters respect, (c) establish yourself as an authoritative figure in school safety, (d) positively reinforce appropriate behavior, (e) respond immediately to occurrences of bullying using consistent consequences, (f) actively listen to parent and student reports of bullying occurrences in the classroom, (g) notify parents if an incident occurs, and resolve the conflict in a timely manner, (h) refer victims to counseling as needed, (i) facilitate open classroom discussions regarding bullying, and (j) involve parents and provide them with information on bullying. Teachers, parents, and interventionists who are interested in using the Olweus Bullying Prevention Program can obtain information about materials, training, and support at http://www.olweus.org/.

BY KRISTIN L. SAYESKI

As in the case of aggressive, acting-out behavior, withdrawal and depression can be interpreted in many different ways. Proponents of the psychoanalytic approach are likely to see internal conflicts and unconscious motivations as the underlying causes. Behavioral psychologists tend to interpret such problems in terms of failures in social learning; this view is supported by more empirical research data than other views (Kauffman & Landrum, 2018; Walker & Gresham, 2014). A social learning analysis attributes withdrawal and immaturity to an inadequate environment. Causal factors may include over-restrictive parental discipline, punishment for appropriate social responses, reward for isolated behavior, lack of opportunity to learn and practice social skills, and models (examples) of inappropriate behavior. Immature or withdrawn children can be taught the skills they lack by arranging opportunities for them to learn and practice appropriate responses, showing models engaging in appropriate behavior, and providing rewards for improved behavior.

MyLab Education
Video Example 8.5
Jeanmarie, a teacher of students with EBD and adults with disabilities, discusses bullying prevention.

A particularly important aspect of immature, withdrawn behavior is depression. Only relatively recently have mental health workers and special educators begun to realize that depression is a widespread and serious problem among children and adolescents. Today, the consensus of psychologists is that the nature of depression in children and youths is quite similar in many respects to that of depression in adults. The indications of depression include disturbances of mood or feelings, inability to think or concentrate, lack of motivation, and decreased physical well-being. A depressed child or youth might act sad, lonely, and apathetic; exhibit low self-esteem, excessive guilt, and pervasive pessimism; avoid tasks and social experiences; and/or have physical complaints or problems in sleeping, eating, or eliminating. Sometimes depression is accompanied by such problems as bed-wetting (nocturnal **enuresis**), fecal soiling (**encopresis**), extreme fear of or refusal to go to school, failure in school, or talk of suicide or suicide attempts. Depression also frequently occurs in combination with conduct disorder.

Suicide is among the leading causes of death among young people ages 15 to 24. Depression, especially when severe and accompanied by a sense of hopelessness, is linked to suicide and suicide attempts. All adults who work with young people therefore must be able to recognize the signs of depression. Substance abuse is also a major problem among children and teenagers and may be related to depression (you may find more information about various mental disorders and suicide among children and teenagers at http://www.nami.org/).

Depression sometimes has a biological cause, and antidepressant medications have at times been successful in helping depressed children and youths to overcome their problems (Konopasek & Forness, 2004, 2014). However, antidepressant medications come with risks that must be carefully considered (Locher et al., 2017). In many cases no biological cause can be found. Depression can also be caused by environmental or psychological factors, such as the death of a loved one, separation of one's parents, school failure, rejection by one's peers, or a chaotic and punitive home environment.

Often, just having someone with whom to build a close relationship can be an important key in recovery from depression. Also, interventions based on social learning theory have often been successful in such cases (Gresham & Kern, 2004; Seeley et al., 2014; Swan, Cummings, Caporino, & Kendall, 2014). These interventions include instructing children and youths in social interaction skills and self-control techniques and teaching them to view themselves more positively.

Too often, the *emotional* aspects of EBD are overlooked, as well as what the experience of EBD is like from the student's perspective (Davies & Ryan, 2014; Place & Elliott, 2014). It is clear that along with behavior that is inappropriate, students with EBD suffer emotional trauma, including many emotionally wrenching experiences in school, and that they are often among the most marginalized students in schools.

MyLab Education Self-Check 8.3

MyLab Education Application Exercise 8.1:
Internalizing and Externalizing Behaviors
Read a case study about six students and answer the questions that follow.

EDUCATIONAL CONSIDERATIONS

Students with EBD typically have low grades and other unsatisfactory academic outcomes, have higher dropout rates and lower graduation rates than other student groups, and are often placed in highly restrictive settings. Whether such students are disproportionately over- or underrepresented, it is important that their cultural identity not determine that they receive special education services (Anastasiou, Kauffman, & Michail,

2016; Anastasiou, Morgan, Farkas, & Wiley, 2017). Their appropriate, successful education is among the most important and challenging tasks facing special education today (Landrum, Wiley, Tankersley, & Kauffman, 2014; Otten & Tuttle, 2010). Finding a remedy for the disproportionate representation of any group in programs for students with EBD is a critical issue. However, finding effective intervention strategies for diverse students is even more important if we are really to have successful multicultural education (Kauffman & Anastasiou, in press; Kauffman & Landrum, 2009; Kauffman, Conroy, Gardner, & Oswald, 2008; Kauffman et al., 2017).

Unfortunately, special educators have never reached a consensus about how to meet the challenge of educating students with EBD. Although a national agenda was written for improving services to students with emotional or behavioral disorders (Chesapeake Institute, 1994; see also Kauffman, 1997), it was so vaguely worded that it has been of little value in guiding the design of interventions (Kauffman & Landrum, 2006, 2018).

Educators have described several different conceptual models of education over the decades (Kauffman & Landrum, 2006). A combination of models now guides most educational programs (see Kauffman & Landrum, 2013, 2018, for a description and case illustrations of models). All credible conceptual models have two objectives: (1) controlling misbehavior and (2) teaching students the academic and social skills they need. The models don't focus on one objective to the exclusion of others, and they recognize the need for integrating all the educational, psychological, and social services these students require. More important than a particular conceptual model is the scientific approach, which demands adherence to an evidence base obtained by investigations following the scientific method (see Kauffman, 2011, 2014a, 2014b).

Balancing Behavioral Control with Academic and Social Learning

Some writers have suggested that the quality of educational programs for students with EBD is often dismal. They argue that the focus is often on external control of students' behavior, and say that academic instruction and social learning are too often secondary or almost entirely neglected. Teachers might not have knowledge and skills in teaching basic skills such as reading. Although the quality of instruction is undoubtedly low in too many programs, examples can be found of effective academic and social instruction for students at all levels (Gresham & Walker, 2014; Lane & Menzies, 2010).

Behavioral control strategies are an essential part of educational programs for students with externalizing problems (Colvin, 2004). Without effective means of controlling disruptive behavior, it's extremely unlikely that academic and social learning will occur. Excellent academic instruction will certainly reduce many behavior problems as well as teach important academic skills (Garner, 2014; Kauffman et al., 2011; Lane & Menzies, 2010; Nelson et al., 2014; Nicholson, 2014). Nevertheless, even the best instructional programs won't eliminate the disruptive behaviors of all students. Teachers of students with EBD must have effective control strategies, preferably involving students as much as possible in self-control. In addition, teachers must offer effective instruction in academic and social skills that will allow their students to live, learn, and work with others. Teachers must also allow students to make all the choices they can—manageable choices that are appropriate for the individual student (Kauffman et al., 2011).

MyLab Education
Video Example 8.6
Jeanmarie, a teacher of students with EBD and adults with disabilities, discusses how appropriate instruction, assessment, and learning targets impact classroom behavior.

Importance of Integrated Services

Children and youths with EBD tend to have multiple and complex needs. For most, life is coming apart in more ways than one. In addition to their problems in school, they typically have family problems and a variety of difficulties in the community (e.g., engaging in illegal activities, an absence of desirable relationships with peers and adults, substance abuse, difficulty finding and maintaining employment). Thus, children or youths with emotional or behavioral disorders might need, in addition to special education, a variety of family-oriented services, psychotherapy or counseling, community supervision, training related to employment, and so on. No single service agency can meet the needs of most of these children and youths, but it is clear that school plays an important role (Kauffman & Landrum, 2018). Integrating these needed services into a more coordinated and effective effort is now seen as essential.

Strategies That Work

Successful strategies at all levels, from early intervention through transition, balance concern for academic and social skills and provide integrated services. These strategies include the following elements:

MyLab Education
Video Example 8.7
Jeanmarie, a teacher of students with EBD and adults with disabilities, explains different ways to build positive relationships with parents, and how those strategies can help during difficult parent/ teacher conferences and interactions.

- *Systematic, data-based interventions:* Interventions are applied systematically and consistently and are based on reliable research.
- *Continuous assessment and progress monitoring:* Teachers conduct direct, daily assessment of performance, with planning based on this monitoring.
- *Practice of new skills:* Skills are not taught in isolation but are applied directly in everyday situations through modeling, rehearsal, and guided practice.
- *Treatment matched to problems:* Interventions are designed to meet the needs of individual students and their particular life circumstances and are not general formulas that ignore the nature, complexity, cultural context, and severity of the problem.
- *Multicomponent treatment:* Teachers and other professionals use as many different interventions as are necessary to meet the multiple needs of students (e.g., social skills training, academic remediation, medication, counseling or psychotherapy, and family treatment or parent training).
- *Programming for transfer and maintenance:* Interventions promote transfer of learning to new situations; quick fixes nearly always fail to produce generalized change.
- *Sustained intervention:* Many emotional or behavioral disorders are developmental disabilities and will not likely be cured but demand lifelong support.

Service Delivery

Only a relatively small percentage of children and youths with EBD are officially identified and receive any special education or mental health services (Forness et al., 2012). Consequently, the individuals who do receive special education tend to have very serious problems, although most have typically been *assumed* to have only mild disabilities. Perhaps students identified as having EBD (who may have intellectual disabilities or learning disabilities as well) tend to be placed in more restrictive settings than students in other high-incidence categories because their disabilities are more severe. Research verifies what teachers of students with emotional and behavioral disorders understand: "they teach students who are among the most dysfunctional youths in their community" (Mattison, 2004, p. 177; see also Mattison, 2014).

Undeniably, the problems of typical students with EBD are often more serious than many people have assumed. The term *severe* doesn't apply only to schizophrenia; a child can have a severe conduct disorder or severe depression, for example, and its disabling effects can be extremely serious and persistent.

TRENDS TOWARD INCLUSION Regardless of the nature or severity of the disorder, the trend in programs for students with EBD is toward integration into regular schools and classrooms whenever possible (Hornby & Evans, 2014). Even when students are placed in separate schools and classes, educators hope for reintegration into the mainstream. Integration of these students is typically difficult and requires intensive work on a case-by-case basis. Furthermore, some educators, researchers, and parents have made the case that students with emotional or behavioral disorders who are at high risk for ongoing problems need the structure and support of a special class; being in a separate class can be better than being included in general education (Brigham, Ahn, Stride, & McKenna, 2016; Kauffman, Bantz, & McCullough, 2002; Kauffman, Mock, Tankersley, & Landrum, 2008).

DIFFERENT NEEDS REQUIRE DIFFERENT PLACEMENTS Placement decisions for students with emotional or behavioral disorders are particularly problematic. Educators who serve students with the most severe emotional or behavioral disorders provide ample justification for specialized environments for these children and youths. That is, it's impossible to replicate in the context of general education in a neighborhood school the intensive, individualized, highly structured environments with very high adult–student ratios offered in special classes and facilities (see Brigham et al., 2016; Brigham & Kauffman, 1998; Kauffman & Badar, 2014, 2016; Kauffman & Brigham, 2009; Kauffman, Ward, & Badar, 2016; Zigmond & Kloo, 2017).

Hence, it's extremely important to maintain the full continuum of placement options for students with EBD as well as to make placement decisions on an individual basis after designing an appropriate program of education and related services. Students must not be placed outside general education classrooms and schools unless their needs require it. However, students' needs for appropriate education and safety take priority over placement in a less restrictive environment.

INSTRUCTIONAL CONSIDERATIONS Before being identified for special education, many students with EBD have been in general education where they could observe and learn from appropriate peer models. In reality, though, these students usually fail to imitate these models. They are unlikely to benefit merely from being with other students who have not been identified as having disabilities, because incidental social learning is insufficient to address their difficulties. For students with EBD to learn from peer models of appropriate behavior, most will require explicit, focused instruction about whom and what to imitate (Hallenbeck & Kauffman, 1995). In addition, they might need explicit and intensive instruction in social skills, including when, where, and how to exhibit specific types of behavior (Gresham & Elliott, 2014; McGrath, 2014; Walker et al., 2004).

The academic curriculum for most students with EBD parallels that for most students. The basic academic skills have a great deal of survival value for any individual in society who is capable of learning them; failure to teach a student to read, write, and perform basic arithmetic deprives that student of any reasonable chance for successful adjustment to the demands of everyday life. Students who don't acquire academic skills that allow them to compete with their peers are likely to be socially rejected (Garner, 2014; Kauffman & Landrum, 2018; Lane & Menzies, 2010; Nelson et al., 2014; Nicholson, 2014).

NEED FOR SOCIAL SKILLS Most students with emotional or behavioral disorders need specific instruction in social skills (Gresham & Elliott, 2014; McGrath, 2014). We emphasize two points: (1) Effective methods are needed to teach basic academic skills, and (2) social skills and affective experiences are as crucial as academic skills. How to manage one's feelings and behavior and how to get along with other people are essential features of the curriculum for many students with emotional or behavioral disorders. These children cannot be expected to learn such skills without instruction, because the ordinary processes of socialization obviously have failed.

Students with schizophrenia and other major psychiatric disorders vary widely in their behaviors and learning problems. Some might need hospitalization and intensive treatment; others might remain at home and attend regular public schools. Again, the trend today is away from placement in institutions or special schools and toward inclusion in regular public schools. In some cases, students with major psychiatric disorders who attend regular schools are enrolled in special classes.

NEEDS OF JUVENILE DELINQUENTS Educational arrangements for juvenile delinquents are hard to describe in general terms because *delinquency* is a legal term, not an educational distinction, and because programs for extremely troubled youths vary so much among states and localities. Special classes or schools are sometimes provided for youths who have histories of threatening, violent, or disruptive behavior. Some of these classes and schools are administered under special education law, but others aren't because the pupils assigned to them aren't considered emotionally disturbed. In jails, reform schools, and other detention facilities that house children and

MyLab Education
Video Example 8.8
Many students with emotional or behavioral disorders need explicit instruction in social skills. This video demonstrates explicit instruction on giving compliments.

Students with EBD in the General Education Classroom

"I don't want him in my classroom if he can't follow the rules!"

Statewide standards and policies of zero tolerance of certain acts have increased pressure on all teachers. Furthermore, many general educators don't receive sufficient training in classroom management. Many teachers are hesitant to collaborate with special educators to include students with EBD, even though many students who create discipline problems aren't identified as having a disability.

The expertise of any teacher of students with EBD includes understanding, assessing, and managing behavior to promote learning. The teacher needs the following skills:

1. Know a variety of prevention and intervention strategies for individuals who are at risk of emotional or behavioral disorders (for more on prevention, go to http://www.preventionaction.org/).
2. Use a variety of nonaversive techniques to control targeted behavior and maintain attention of individuals with emotional or behavioral disorders.
3. Establish a consistent classroom routine, and use skills in problem solving and conflict resolution.
4. Plan and implement individualized reinforcement systems and environmental modifications at levels equal to the intensity of the behavior.
5. Understand the advantages and limitations of instructional strategies and practices for teaching individuals with emotional or behavioral disorders.
6. Assess appropriate and problematic social behaviors of individuals.

Teachers particularly need competence in using positive behavioral interventions and supports (PBIS). More information about this can be found at www.pbis.org/.

Obviously, establishing clear rules and expectations for following those rules is the first step in managing behavior. However, some students require more support than others to meet those expectations.

BY MARGARET P. WEISS

MyLab Education
Video Example 8.9

Jeanmarie, a teacher of students with EBD and adults with disabilities, discusses the explicit instruction of routine and structure (classroom management).

MyLab Education
Video Example 8.10

Jeanmarie, a teacher of students with EBD and adults with disabilities, discusses explicit instruction of social problem-solving strategies.

adolescents, educational practices vary widely. Education of incarcerated children and youths with disabilities is governed by the same laws that apply to those who are not incarcerated, but the laws aren't always carefully implemented. Many incarcerated children don't receive assessment and education appropriate for their needs because of lack of resources, poor cooperation among agencies, and the attitude that delinquents and criminals are not entitled to the same educational opportunities as law-abiding citizens (Kauffman & Landrum, 2018; O'Mahoney, 2014; Sprague, Jolivette, & Nelson, 2014).

SPECIAL CHALLENGES FOR TEACHERS Given all this, it is clear that teachers of students with EBD need to be able to tolerate a great deal of unpleasantness and rejection without becoming counteraggressive or withdrawn. These students have been rejected by others; if kindness and concern were the only things they needed, they probably wouldn't be considered to have disabilities. Teachers cannot expect that caring and decency will always be returned and must be sure of their own values and confident of their teaching and living skills. They must be able and willing to make wise choices for students who choose to behave unwisely (Kauffman & Landrum, 2018; Kauffman et al., 2011; Kerr & Nelson, 2010). Training teachers to meet the academic and social needs of these students is extremely challenging (Blake & Behan, 2014).

Disciplinary Considerations

Classroom management and discipline are recognized as among the most difficult problems of teachers, both general and special education (Evertson & Weinstein, 2006; Kauffman et al., 2011). Students with EBD make behavior management even harder. Educators are now placing great emphasis on positive behavioral supports and behavior intervention plans for students with EBD. Increasingly, researchers recognize that problem behavior occurs less frequently in the classroom when the teacher is offering effective instruction, even though good instruction alone often isn't enough to resolve behavior problems.

Discipline is a controversial topic, especially for students with disabilities who exhibit behavior problems. Many teachers and school administrators are confused about what's legal. Special rules do apply in some cases to students who have been identified as having disabilities. In some instances, the typical school rules apply; in others, they don't. The issues are particularly controversial for students with EBD because, although their behavior might be severely problematic, the causes of their misbehavior are often difficult to determine.

Uncertainty or controversy usually surrounds a change in a student's placement or a suspension or expulsion due to very serious misbehavior such as bringing a weapon or illegal drugs to school. IDEA discipline provisions for students with disabilities are intended to maintain a safe school environment without violating the rights of students with disabilities to fair discipline, taking the effects of their disability into consideration (see Mayer & Cornell, 2010; Yell, Gatti, & Allday, 2014; Yell, Katsyiannis, & Bradley, 2017).

ZERO TOLERANCE One of the most dramatic and controversial measures involving discipline for serious offenses is known as **zero tolerance** (Skiba & Rausch, 2006). School administrators and teachers have been assumed to abuse their discretion in determining the punishment for certain serious offenses, such as bringing a weapon to school. Therefore, higher authorities (e.g., boards of education) in many cases removed discretion from the hands of teachers and lower administrators. The higher authorities prescribed a given punishment such as long-term suspension or expulsion for a particular offense, regardless of the circumstances surrounding the act. For example, an elementary school child who accidentally takes a paring knife to school in her lunch box might be expelled. A high school student who forgets to remove a roofing knife from his pocket and turns it in at the office because he knows he should not have it in school might be expelled. A student with intellectual disability who brings a toy gun to school, even though he does not understand that a gun is a weapon and even toy weapons are forbidden in school, might be expelled. The zero-tolerance rationale simply does not allow any exceptions for extenuating circumstances.

Teachers and school administrators are often unsure of just what freedom and constraints the law allows them in disciplining students with disabilities, even if they have a policy of zero tolerance. They must struggle to balance the rights of students with disabilities against the common good of maintaining a safe and orderly school environment.

Violence, disorder, and drugs in schools are serious problems that must be addressed (Mayer & Cornell, 2010). However, a fixed penalty for a given behavior without considering any circumstance or student characteristic presents particular problems for special education. All educators recognize the need for reasonable schoolwide discipline that brings a high degree of uniformity to consequences for particular acts. Nevertheless, special educators also argue for exceptions based on the relevance of the student's disability to the event in question, and note that zero tolerance has not made schools safer places.

MANIFESTATION DETERMINATION Special rules apply to managing some of the serious misbehavior of students who are identified as having disabilities. Again, in some cases, the typical school rules apply, but in others, they don't (see Yell et al., 2017, 2014). In any case, much of the special education advocacy regarding discipline is based on finding alternatives to suspension and expulsion for bringing weapons or drugs to school or for endangering others. Keeping students out of school is not an effective way of helping them learn how to behave acceptably.

Three concepts and related procedures provide the basis for much of the controversy surrounding the discipline of students with disabilities:

1. Determine whether the behavior is a manifestation of the student's disability.
2. Provide an alternative placement for the student's education for an interim period if temporary removal from the student's present placement is necessary.
3. Develop positive, proactive behavior intervention plans.

Deciding whether a student's misbehavior is a manifestation of disability is called a **manifestation determination (MD)**, based on the idea that it would be unfair to punish students for engaging in misbehavior that is part of their disability. However, if the misbehavior is not a manifestation of disability, then the usual punishment for students without disabilities should apply. For example, if a misbehavior is the result of a seizure or other neurological disorder or a manifestation of intellectual incapacity or emotional disturbance, then the student should not be punished for it.

The manifestation determination is a highly controversial issue, and some writers believe that it is more political than educational in purpose. Some people argue that the process actually undermines fairness since the rules or procedures for the MD are not entirely objective, the judgment about the causes of misbehavior will be subjective.

FUNCTIONAL BEHAVIORAL ASSESSMENT IDEA calls for **functional behavioral assessment (FBA)** if the student's behavior is persistently a problem, but the meaning of *functional assessment* isn't entirely clear in the context of the law. In behavioral science, the function of someone's behavior is the reason they do it. FBA assists educators in determining and altering the factors that account for a student's misconduct (see Martens & Lambert, 2014). Nevertheless, precisely what the law requires of special educators and other school personnel regarding FBA is often uncertain (Yell et al., 2017, 2014). Apparently, the intent of the law is to require teachers to assess student behavior in ways that lead to the selection of effective intervention strategies and to figure out how to support desirable behavior.

Supports for Desired Behavior

Perhaps the most critical part of the discipline provisions of IDEA is the requirement that schools must devise a positive **behavioral intervention plan (BIP)** for a student with disabilities who has behavior problems. The emphasis of this requirement is on creating proactive and positive interventions and avoiding punishment. When discipline is involved, the school must reevaluate the student's IEP and make efforts to address the misconduct that led to the problem, using positive (nonpunitive) means to the greatest extent possible.

An approach with support from research is **positive behavioral intervention and support (PBIS)** (Kauffman, Nelson, Simpson, & Mock, 2017). It integrates valued outcomes, the science of human behavior, validated procedures, and systems change to enhance quality of life and reduce problem behavior. Its primary goal is to improve the link between research-validated practices and the environments in which teaching and learning occur. This behaviorally based systems approach enhances the capacity of schools, families, and communities to design effective teaching and learning environments that improve lifestyle results (personal, health, social, family, work, recreation, etc.) for all children and youth. These environments apply contextually and culturally appropriate interventions to make problem behavior less effective, efficient, and relevant and to make desired behavior more functional. However, it does recognize the value of nonviolent negative consequences (punishment) in managing behavior.

INTERIM ALTERNATIVE EDUCATIONAL SETTING IDEA includes allowances for schools to use an **interim alternative educational setting (IAES)** in the discipline of a student with disabilities who cannot be managed satisfactorily in the general education classroom or school. For example, an IAES might be a separate special school serving students with behavior problems, a separate arrangement within the public school similar to in-school suspension, or a self-contained classroom. IAES is intended to encourage schools to use such alternatives rather than suspension or expulsion. The law doesn't define what an IAES must be, but only what it must provide: a continuation of education and modifications spelled out in the student's individualized education program (IEP). The IAES must also include specific programming to address and prevent the recurrence of the behavior that prompted the placement. Schools might use such settings for students with serious behavior problems as a way of preserving order and manageability of the typical classroom and school. However, regardless of the setting in which a student with emotional or behavioral disorders is placed, special educators should try to provide the most positive and functional behavioral support they can offer (Yell et al., 2017, 2014).

RESPONSIVE INSTRUCTION

Meeting the Needs of Students with Emotional or Behavioral Disorders

FUNCTIONAL BEHAVIORAL ASSESSMENTS

Functional behavioral assessments (FBAs) have become standard practice in the development of individualized education programs (IEPs), particularly the behavior intervention plan (BIP) component, for students with emotional or behavioral disabilities. Under IDEA, school districts are required to conduct an FBA and a BIP for any student with disabilities who receives disciplinary action that results in more than 10 days' suspension or a change in placement due to disciplinary issues. Unfortunately, the implementation of these assessments varies greatly, as does their effects. When implemented correctly, FBAs are effective. However, the burden is on school districts to ensure FBAs are implemented to the empirical standards established in the research.

The most common issues involving FBA/BIP development are:

- Failure to identify specific target behaviors
- Failure to verify the hypothesized function of the behavior
- Failure to connect the function of the behavior to the specific interventions identified in the BIP

Van Acker and colleagues (2005) created the following checklist for teams to self-evaluate their plans:

- Clearly identify the target behavior.
- Verify the hypothesized target behavior function.
- Develop a clear BIP indicating function of the behavior met through alternative, desirable behavior.
- Indicate positive behavioral supports.
- Modify physical or social context as a part of BIP.
- Plan for monitoring and evaluating BIP.

Watch this video (https://www.youtube.com/watch?v=9sIYgSZiZ28) and consider the teacher's remarks about carefully considering the student's point of view and the need to focus on offering support and attention to the needs of those involved.

BY KRISTIN L. SAYESKI

HOW SUCCESSFUL ARE MDS, FBAS, PBIS, AND IAES? The struggle to resolve discipline issues involving students with disabilities is ongoing. On the one hand, school administrators want the highest possible degree of uniformity of expectations (i.e., the same high expectations for all students). On the other hand, special educators and other advocates for students with disabilities see the absolute uniformity of disciplinary rules as failure to accommodate students' individual abilities and needs. The legal requirements regarding discipline, including suspension and expulsion, will continue to evolve as educators find more productive ways of dealing with serious misconduct. It is difficult to determine whether misbehavior is a function of a child's disability, and manifestation determinations will continue to be a matter of controversy for as long as the law requires them.

What are the components of a useful FBA? Can classroom teachers conduct such analyses without help from others? Some suggest that the FBA is considerably more complicated than many people think and that the law (IDEA) may have gotten considerably ahead of teachers' ability to do the necessary analyses. Although the idea is good, and a few educators may be able to perform a useful FBA, many functional analyses are poorly done (Fox & Gable, 2004). Can the manifestation of a disability always be found? What should we do if a disability's manifestation is unknown? In what settings can educators provide the necessary supports for positive behavior? With the proper behavioral supports, can all students with emotional or behavioral disorders succeed in the general education environment? These and other questions will no doubt perplex educators for many decades to come.

ASSESSMENT OF PROGRESS

The ongoing assessment program for students with EBD should include measures that address several domains of social-emotional behavior that influence academic learning, including interpersonal skills, study skills, motivation, and engagement (see Walker &

Gresham, 2014). Teachers typically use rating scales and direct observation to monitor students' progress in behavioral interventions. Many rating scales are available to assess students' social skills. Specific instruments are discussed in the literature (see, for example, chapters 7 through 13 in Walker & Gresham, 2014).

Numerous tests of academic achievement are also available. Unfortunately, the academic progress of students with EBD has often not been carefully monitored because of the greater concern for these students' social-emotional behavior. However, academic failure and troublesome behavior are often so interrelated that aiding students in becoming academically competent is critically important in helping them achieve better social and emotional adjustment. In fact, one of the signs that these students' social-emotional adjustment is improving is their acquiring academic skills (see Nelson et al., 2014; Nicholson, 2014).

MyLab Education **Self-Check 8.4**

MyLab Education **Application Exercise 8.2: Working with Students Who Have Behavioral Problems**

Watch and answer questions about a video showing Mr. Merkin's first grade classroom, and his handling of Tyra, a student with emotional and behavioral disorders.

EARLY INTERVENTION

Early identification and prevention are basic goals for any category of disability. For students with emotional or behavioral disorders, these goals present unique difficulties—yet also hold particular promise (Dunlap et al., 2006; Walker, Severson, et al., 2014; Walker & Sprague, 2007). The difficulties are related to the definition and measurement of EBD, especially in young children; the particular promise is that young children's social-emotional behavior is quite flexible, so preventive efforts seem to have a good chance of success (Kauffman, 2014c; Kauffman & Brigham, 2009).

Very young children are frequently difficult to assess or diagnose because they often respond with hyperactivity, aggressiveness, or defiance to whatever risk factor might be involved (Thomas & Guskin, 2001; see also Marshall, Brown, Conroy, & Knopf, 2017). Nevertheless, early identification and prevention of emotional or behavioral disorders—or what some have termed "challenging behavior"—is possible. First of all, young children and families who have access to mental health services and good medical care are less likely to have social, behavioral, or emotional problems (see Mattison, 2014; Vidair, Sauro, Blocher, Scudellari, & Hoagwood, 2014). Second, parents and teachers who are nurturing, positive and encouraging, and who develop healthy relationships with young children are less likely to see "challenging" behavior. Third, high-quality preschool education helps foster social competence and is associated with fewer behavior problems (see also Dunlap & Fox, 2014; Dunlap et al., 2006; Evans, Rybak, Strickland, & Owens, 2014; Marshall et al., 2017; Strain, Barton, & Bovey, 2014; Walker, Severson, et al., 2014).

The patterns of behavior that signal problems for the preschool child are those that bring them into frequent conflict with, or keep them aloof from, their parents or caretakers and their siblings or peers. Many children who are referred to clinics for disruptive behavior when they are 7 to 12 years of age showed clear signs of behavior problems by the time they were 3 or 4—or even younger. Infants or toddlers who exhibit a very "difficult temperament"—who are irritable; have irregular patterns of sleeping, eating, and eliminating; have highly intense responses to many stimuli and negative reactions toward new situations—are at risk for developing serious behavior problems unless their parents are particularly skillful at handling them. Children of preschool age are likely to elicit negative responses from adults and playmates if they are much more aggressive or much more withdrawn than most children their age. (Remember the critical importance of same-age comparisons. Toddlers frequently grab what they want, push other children down, and throw things and kick and scream when they don't get their way; toddlers normally don't have much finesse at social interaction and often hide from strangers.)

Because children's behavior is quite responsive to conditions in the social environment and can be shaped by adults, the potential for primary prevention—preventing serious behavior problems from occurring in the first place—would seem to be great. If parents and teachers could be taught effective child management skills, perhaps many or most cases could be prevented. Furthermore, one could imagine that if parents and teachers had such skills, children who already have EBD could be prevented from getting worse (secondary prevention). But the task of primary prevention is not that simple. For one thing, the tremendous amount of money and personnel that is needed for training in child management is not available. For another, even if the money and personnel could be found, professionals would not always agree on what patterns of behavior should be prevented or on how undesirable behavior could be prevented from developing (Kauffman, 1999, 2013, 2014c; Kauffman & Landrum, 2018).

If overly aggressive or withdrawn behavior is identified in a preschooler, what kind of intervention program is most desirable? Behavioral interventions are usually effective. A behavioral approach implies defining and measuring the child's behaviors and rearranging the environment (especially adults' and other children's responses to the child with the problem) to teach and support more appropriate conduct. In the case of aggressive children, social rewards for aggression should be prevented. For example, hitting another child or throwing a temper tantrum might result in brief social isolation or time-out instead of adult attention or getting one's own way (see Kauffman & Brigham, 2009; Kazdin, 2008; Walker, Severson, et al., 2014).

In summary, it is possible to identify at an early age those children who are at high risk for EBD. These children exhibit extreme aggression or social withdrawal and may be socially rejected or identify with deviant peers. They should be identified as early as possible, and their parents and teachers should learn how to teach them essential social skills and how to manage their problem behavior using positive, nonviolent procedures. If children with EBD are identified very early and intervention is sufficiently comprehensive, intense, and sustained, then there's a good chance that they can recover and exhibit developmentally normal patterns of behavior.

Nevertheless, research suggests that in practice early intervention typically doesn't occur (Dunlap et al., 2006; Forness et al., 2012; Kauffman, 2010, 2013, 2014c). The primary reasons given for the rarity of early, comprehensive, intense, and sustained intervention include worry about labeling and stigma, optimism regarding the child's development (i.e., the assumption that the child will "grow out of it"), lack of resources required to address the needs of any but the most severely problematic children, and ignorance about the early signs of emotional or behavioral problems.

TRANSITION TO ADULTHOOD

Programs designed for adolescents with EBD vary widely in aims and structure (Eber, Malloy, Rose, & Flamini, 2014; Unruh & Murray, 2014). Nelson and Kauffman (1977) described the following types, which remain, over four decades later, the basic options today:

- Regular public high school classes
- Consultant teachers who work with general education teachers to provide individualized academic work and behavior management
- Resource rooms and special self-contained classes to which students may be assigned for part or all of the school day
- Work-study programs in which vocational education and job experience are combined with academic study
- Special private or public schools that offer the regular high school curriculum in a different setting

- Alternative schools that offer highly individualized programs that are nontraditional in both setting and content
- Private or public residential schools

Incarcerated youths with EBD are an especially neglected group in special education (Sprague et al., 2014). The special educational needs of many (or most) of these teenagers who are in prison might be neglected because incarcerated youths are defined as socially maladjusted rather than emotionally disturbed. The current federal definition appears to allow denial of special education services to a large number of young people who exhibit extremely serious misbehaviors and have long histories of school failure.

It is difficult to design special education programs at the secondary level for students with EBD; this category of youths is so varied (see Cheney, Cumming, & Slemrod, 2014). Adolescents categorized for special education purposes as having EBD may have behavioral characteristics ranging from extreme withdrawal to aggressive delinquency, intelligence ranging from severe intellectual disability to highly gifted, and academic skills ranging from preschool to college level. It's hardly realistic to suggest that any single type of program or model will be appropriate for all such youths. In fact, youths with EBD, perhaps more than any other category of exceptionality, need a highly individualized, creative, and flexible education. Programs may range from teaching daily living skills in a sheltered environment to advanced placement in college, from general education placement to hospitalization, and from the traditional curriculum to unusual and specialized vocational training.

Transition from school to work and adult life is particularly difficult for adolescents with EBD. Many of them lack the basic academic skills necessary for successful employment. In addition, they often behave in ways that prevent them from being accepted, liked, and helped by classmates, employers, co-workers, and neighbors. It is not surprising that students with EBD are among the most likely to drop out of school and among the most difficult to train in transition programs (Wagner, 2014).

Many children and youths with EBD grow up to be adults who have real difficulties leading independent, productive lives. The outlook is especially grim for children and adolescents with conduct disorders. Contrary to popular opinion, the child or youth who is shy, anxious, or neurotic is not the most likely to have psychiatric problems as an adult. Rather, it is the conduct-disordered (hyperaggressive) child or youth whose adulthood is most likely to be characterized by socially intolerable behavior and lack of social competence (Walker et al., 2004). About half the children who are hyperaggressive will have problems that require legal intervention or psychiatric care when they are adults.

UP CLOSE with Kay Redfield Jamison: A Psychologist Who Knows What She's Talking About Kay Jamison is a clinical psychologist who has experienced what is known as bipolar disorder (formerly known as manic depression) since adolescence. Her childhood and early adolescence were characterized by wide swings of mood. Her autobiography, *An Unquiet Mind*, describes many of her experiences, including therapies and coping strategies. She has become a renowned authority on bipolar disorders. You may see an interview with her at http://www.youtube.com/watch?v=qF_AKQi7WJI, where you may find other videos involving her. For more information about her, you may visit her Facebook page or go to Wikipedia and search for Kay Redfield Jamison. •

Successful transition to adult life is often complicated by neglectful, abusive, or inadequate family relationships. A high percentage of adolescents with conduct disorder have family relationships of this nature. However, the emphasis on punishment and imprisonment, particularly of black males, appears to be counterproductive. The emphasis on punishment contributes to family deterioration and harsh conditions of life that perpetuate undesirable conduct.

Examples of relatively successful high school and transition programs are available, most of which utilize a behavioral approach. However, it is important to stress the term *relatively*. Educators have known for decades that many adolescents and young adults with severe conduct disorder appear to have a true developmental disability that requires intervention throughout their life span (see the early work of Wolf, Braukmann, & Ramp, 1987). By the time these antisocial youths reach high school, the aim of even the most effective program is to help them accommodate their disabilities (Walker et al., 2004). Rather than focusing on remediation of academic and social skills, these programs attempt to teach youths the skills they will need to survive and cope in school and community, to make a transition to work, and to develop vocations.

MyLab Education Self-Check 8.5

▼ chapter eight SUMMARY

Gawrav/E+/Getty Images

What terminology is used to describe emotional or behavioral disorders?

- The current term in federal laws is *emotionally disturbed*.

- The terminology of various states and localities is varied and sometimes confusing; it includes a variety of combinations of terms such as *emotional disturbance* and *behavioral disorder*. *Emotional or behavioral disorder* is the preferred term.

What is the definition of *emotional or behavioral disorder*?

- Any definition generally refers to behavior that goes to an extreme, a problem that is chronic, and behavior that is unacceptable because of social or cultural expectations.

- The current federal definition lists five characteristics, any one of which must be exhibited to a marked extent and over a period of time and adversely affect educational performance:

  - Inability to learn

  - Inability to establish satisfactory relationships

  - Inappropriate behavior

  - Pervasive unhappiness or depression

  - Physical symptoms, pains, or fears

- The major points of the definition of the National Mental Health and Special Education Coalition are that the behavior:

  - Is more than a temporary, expected response to stressful events in the environment.

  - Is consistently exhibited in two different settings, at least one of which is school.

  - Is unresponsive to direct intervention in general education, or the child's condition is such that general education interventions would be insufficient.

How are emotional or behavioral disorders classified?

- Psychiatric classifications are sometimes not as useful to teachers as behavioral descriptions.

- The most useful and reliable classifications are based on the primary dimensions of externalizing (acting against others) and internalizing (acting against self).

What is the prevalence of emotional or behavioral disorders?

- Most studies suggest that 5% to 10% of the child population have such disorders.

- Special education and mental health serve only a fraction of those needing help for serious disorders (i.e., less than 1% of the child population).

What are the causes of emotional or behavioral disorders?

- Causes are multiple and complex, and seldom can a single cause be identified.

- Major causal factors include biology, family, school, and culture.

How are emotional or behavioral disorders identified?

- Teacher judgment plays the most significant role.

- Most students are below average in tested intelligence and academic achievement.

- Students exhibit externalizing (aggressive toward others) or internalizing (immature, withdrawn, depressed) behavior or a combination of the two.

What are the major educational considerations regarding emotional or behavioral disorders?

- A balance between behavioral control and academic instruction is required.

- Integrated services are important.

- Strategies that work best include the following:

- Systematic, data-based interventions
- Continuous assessment and monitoring of progress
- Provision for practice of new skills
- Treatment matched to the problem
- Multicomponent treatment
- Programming for transfer and maintenance
- Commitment to sustained intervention
- Service delivery emphasizes inclusion when appropriate and the importance of a full continuum of alternative placements.
- Instruction should be highly structured and relevant to the student's life.
- Special disciplinary considerations include functional behavioral assessment (FBA) and positive behavioral intervention and support (PBIS).

How do professionals assess the progress of students with emotional or behavioral disorders?

- Professionals may use a variety of standardized scales and observations to assess behavior.
- Teacher judgment is an important aspect of assessment.

What are important considerations in early intervention for learners with emotional or behavioral disorders?

- Students with or at risk of EBD often are observed to be very different from their age mates.
- Early intervention is often suggested but seldom practiced.

What are important considerations in transition to adulthood for learners with emotional or behavioral disorders?

- For older students with EBD, programs must be highly individualized. No single plan will be appropriate in all cases.
- Transition is difficult but particularly important because the long-term and employment outcomes for most students are not good.

▼ INTERNET RESOURCES

Pertinent Organizations

- The Council for Children with Behavioral Disorders (a division of CEC, the Council for Exceptional Children) offers a variety of information about conferences, news, and publications at its website, http://www.ccbd.net/CCBD/Home/.
- The American Psychological Association offers information about many topics in psychology at its website, http://www.apa.org.
- The American Psychiatric Association offers important news and information about advocacy and psychiatric practice at its website, http://www.psych.org.
- The National Institute of Mental Health offers wide-ranging information on various topics in mental health at its website, http://www.nimh.nih.gov/index.shtml.

- The National Alliance on Mental Illness offers information, education, support, and advocacy at its website, http://www.nami.org.
- The Pacer Center offers a variety of information at its home website (http://www.pacer.org/), and you may find extensive information about EBD by searching for "emotional disturbance," "behavioral disorders," or "emotional or behavioral disorders."
- The National Federation of Families for Children's Mental Health (website http://www.ffcmh.org) offers a variety of information useful to families, children, and teachers.
- The Oregon Social Learning Center maintains a searchable website regarding children and families (http://www.oslc.org) that is particularly valuable to researchers, instructors, and students.

chapter nine

LEARNERS WITH AUTISM SPECTRUM DISORDERS

Photographee.eu/Shutterstock

► LEARNING OUTCOMES

Learning Outcome 9.1: Understand the most current definition of autism spectrum disorders (ASD) in an historical context and understand the prevalence of students with autism spectrum disorders.

Learning Outcome 9.2: Become familiar with the causes of autism spectrum disorders and how autism spectrum disorders are identified.

Learning Outcome 9.3: Learn about the psychological and behavioral characteristics of learners with autism spectrum disorders.

Learning Outcome 9.4: Understand some of the educational considerations for people with autism spectrum disorders, and how professionals assess progress to help plan educational strategies.

Learning Outcome 9.5: Learn about issues that should be considered with respect to early intervention and transition to adulthood for individuals with autism spectrum disorders.

MISCONCEPTIONS ABOUT Learners with Autism Spectrum Disorders

MYTH Autism is a single, well-defined category of disability.

FACT Autism comprises a wide spectrum of disorders and symptoms, ranging from very severe to relatively mild.

MYTH People with autism spectrum disorders have intellectual disabilities and can't be involved in higher education or professions.

FACT Autism spectrum disorders include people from the full range of intellectual capacity. Although a high percentage do have intellectual disabilities, many with milder forms, such as Asperger syndrome, are highly intelligent, earn graduate degrees, and are successful professionals.

MYTH All people with autism have impairments in some cognitive areas but are highly intelligent or geniuses in other areas.

FACT Only a very few people with autism have extraordinary skills. Called *autism savant syndrome,* these individuals are not geniuses in the traditional sense, but they possess very highly developed specific skills in such things as memorization, mathematics, art, or music in isolation from functional skills.

MYTH There is an autism epidemic that can't be explained.

FACT Undoubtedly, the number of diagnosed cases of has increased dramatically. Most authorities believe this is largely due to three things: a widening of the criteria used to diagnose autism, including the recognition of milder forms such as Asperger syndrome; a greater awareness of autism in the general public as well as in the medical, psychological, and educational professions; and the diagnosis of people as having autism who previously would have received a different diagnosis, e.g., as having intellectual disabilities (mental retardation). However, we can't rule out the possibility of toxins, such as air pollution, as contributing to the increase, if only a small way.

MYTH The measles, mumps, and rubella (MMR) vaccine causes autism.

FACT The Institute of Medicine of the National Academies commissioned a review of available evidence and concluded that the evidence favors rejection of a causal relationship between MMR vaccine and autism.

MYTH Bad parenting, especially cold, nonresponsive mothering ("refrigerator moms") can cause autism.

FACT No evidence indicates that bad parenting can cause autism. Furthermore, even if a parent is relatively unresponsive, this might be in reaction to the infant's low level of arousal or because of parental stress regarding the child's abnormal behavior.

GUIDING QUESTIONS

- What is the history behind autism spectrum disorders?

- How do professionals define autism spectrum disorders?

- What is the prevalence of autism spectrum disorders?

- What causes autism spectrum disorders?

- What methods are used to identify individuals with autism spectrum disorders?

- What are some of the psychological and behavioral characteristics of learners with autism spectrum disorders?

- What are some educational considerations for learners with autism spectrum disorders?

- How do professionals assess the progress of students with autism spectrum disorders?

- What are some important considerations with respect to early intervention for learners with autism spectrum disorders?

- What are some important considerations with respect to transition to adulthood for learners with autism spectrum disorders?

Autism spectrum disorders (ASD) involve myriad aberrant perceptual, cognitive, linguistic, and social behaviors. Although some consistent patterns of behavior accompany autism, a great deal of variation in symptoms also is exhibited by those who have autism. Not only do the symptoms vary, but the severity of the symptoms can be wide ranging. Some individuals with autism have deficits so severe that communicating with them requires enormous effort. Others, like Tim Page (2007), a Pulitzer Prize-winning former music critic for the *The Washington Post,* function in many respects at a very high level. For more information on Page, you can visit this site: http://en.wikipedia.org/wiki/Tim_Page_(music_critic).

HISTORICAL CONTEXT: KANNER'S AND ASPERGER'S PAPERS

The seminal work in the field of autism began with two scientific papers published one year apart (1943 and 1944) by physicians working independently: Leo Kanner (1943/1973) and Hans Asperger (1944/1991). Interestingly, both were born and raised in Vienna; however, Kanner came to the United States and wrote his historic paper in English. Asperger's work went largely ignored for many years, probably because it was published in German at the time of World War II.

Also interestingly, both Kanner and Asperger used the term *autistic* to refer to the children they were observing. Autism was a label that had been coined earlier in the 20th century (Bleuler, 1916/1951) and was used to refer to individuals who had an extremely narrow range of personal relationships and restricted interactions with their environment: "a withdrawal from the fabric of social life into the self. Hence the words 'autistic' and 'autism' from the Greek word *autos* meaning 'self'" (Frith, 2003, p. 5).

Kanner's Paper

Kanner (1943/1973) reported on the cases of 11 children from the Child Psychiatric Unit at Johns Hopkins University. Some of the major characteristics that distinguished these children were:

- An inability to relate to others in an ordinary manner
- An extreme autistic aloneness that seemingly isolated the child from the outside world
- An apparent resistance to being picked up or held by the parents
- Deficits in language including . . . echolalia. . . .
- Extreme fear reactions to loud noises
- Obsessive desire for repetition and maintenance of sameness
- Few spontaneous activities such as typical play behavior
- Bizarre and repetitive physical movement such as spinning or perpetual rocking (Scheuermann & Weber, 2002, p. 2)

A major conclusion that Kanner reached was that these children could be distinguished from children who had **schizophrenia** in at least three ways:

1. The children with schizophrenia tended to withdraw from the world, whereas the children with autism never seemed to have made any social connections to begin with.
2. The children with autism exhibited some unique language patterns, such as pronoun reversals (e.g., *I* for *it, he* for *she*) and **echolalia**, the repetition of words or phrases.
3. The children with autism did not appear to deteriorate in their functioning over time, as did some children with schizophrenia.

Asperger's Paper

Asperger (1944/1991) reported on four cases of children he observed in a summer camp who preferred to play alone and to not interact with other children. These children were similar to Kanner's cases with two notable exceptions. First, they had average intelligence, although they seemed to channel their intellectual pursuits into obsessive preoccupation in narrow areas, such as machinery or mathematical calculations. Second, their language was perceived as normal. (Later in this chapter, we'll discuss more recent research suggesting subtle language abnormalities.)

Asperger referred to his cases as having "autistic psychopathy." Nearly 40 years later, his work gained scientific notoriety when Lorna Wing (1981) published a paper that referred to Asperger's original paper and sparked interest in the topic. She was the one who suggested naming the syndrome after Asperger. And it was her paper that drew attention to the condition and was the catalyst for Asperger syndrome's becoming recognized as a condition meriting attention.

DEFINITION OF AUTISM SPECTRUM DISORDERS

Although autism has been a separate category under the Individuals With Disabilities Education Act (IDEA) since 1990, it and other similar disorders are now typically collected under a broader term: **autism spectrum disorders (ASD)**. The term *spectrum* emphasizes that the disabilities associated with ASD fall on a continuum from relatively mild to severe. The "gold standard" for diagnosing autism, the American Psychiatric Association's *Diagnostic and Statistical Manual of Mental Disorders-5 (DSM-5)* also uses the term autism spectrum disorders (ASD) (American Psychiatric Association, 2013).

Although the symptoms of ASD are wide ranging, the *DSM-5* divides them into two general domains: "social communication impairment" and "repetitive/restricted behaviors." It also states that the deficits begin in early childhood, even though they might not become evident until later, often when the child's poor communication skills become apparent.

The *DSM-5* no longer recognizes Asperger syndrome as a separate entity; instead, it emphasizes that ASD is an umbrella term. In practice, however, someone whose intellectual and verbal abilities are relatively high, but who still exhibits social communication deficits and repetitive/restricted behavior is often referred to as having Asperger syndrome. (We discuss this further in the later section on "Psychological and Behavioral Characteristics.")

PREVALENCE

In the past few years, the prevalence rate for autism spectrum disorder has increased dramatically. The first large-scale epidemiological survey of autism, conducted in the 1960s (Lotter, 1966), found a prevalence rate in the U.S. population of about 0.04% (1 out of 2,500). By 2000, the U.S. Centers for Disease Control and Prevention (CDCP) estimated the rate at 1 in 150; and as of the writing of this edition of the textbook, the most recent estimated rate has climbed to 1 in 68 (Centers for Disease Control and Prevention, 2016).

The public schools have kept pace with respect to the increasing prevalence of students identified as having ASD. The most current information from the U.S. Department of Education (IDEA Data Accountability Center, 2013) reported that from 2005 to 2011, the prevalence of students ages 6 to 21 who were identified as having ASD doubled, with the most recent rate being 0.59%.

A few important points should be noted about prevalence rates of autism:

1. First, the prevalence is 5 times higher for boys than for girls. As with other disabilities (e.g., learning disabilities, attention deficit hyperactivity disorder), reasons for this disparity vary from males being biologically more susceptible to neurological dysfunction to professionals having a biased tendency to refer and/or diagnose males when they exhibit behaviors outside the range of normalcy.

2. ASD occurs in all socioeconomic, ethnic, and racial groups. However, rates of autism are much lower in Latino populations, and when Latino children are diagnosed with autism it is likely to be at a later age than when white children are diagnosed. Paradoxically, Latina mothers of children who are eventually diagnosed with autism are more likely to be concerned about their child's development or behavior at an earlier age than are white mothers (Ratto, Reznick, & Turner-Brown, 2015). A possible explanation for this discrepancy between when Latina mothers first notice symptoms of autism and when their child is diagnosed is that they have less access to healthcare and/or are less adept at traversing the healthcare and school domains.

3. The prevalence rate is just as high, if not higher for countries in Europe and Asia.

4. The reasons for the growth in prevalence are disputable. However, researchers (Fombonne, 2001; Frith, 2003; National Research Council, 2001; Shattuck, 2006; Wing & Potter, 2002) have pointed to the following possibilities, individually or in combination:

   a. A widening of the criteria used to diagnose autism, including the recognition of individuals who are higher functioning;

   b. A greater awareness of autism in the general public as well as the medical, psychological, and educational professions;

   c. "Diagnostic substitution," the phenomenon of persons now being identified as having an autism spectrum disorder who previously would have been diagnosed as having intellectual disabilities (Coo et al., 2008) or as having developmental language disorders (Bishop, Whitehouse, Watt, & Line, 2008; Miller et al., 2013). For example, as we noted above, the prevalance of students identified by the public schools as having ASD doubled between 2005 and 2011; however, the prevalence of students identified as having intellectual disabilities fell by 22%. The schools are now identifying students with ASD and with intellectual disabilities at virtually the same rate.

5. Although the above four possible reasons for the increase are the ones backed up by scientific evidence, one can't rule out the possibility of some as yet undetected factor(s), such as toxins, contributing to the increase (CDCP, 2013; Hertz-Picciotto & Delwiche, 2009). For example, some preliminary evidence suggests a relationship between the amount of air pollution and the prevalence of autism (Volk, Lurmann, Penfold, Hertz-Picciotto, & McConnell, 2013).

FOCUS ON

Is There a Link Between Vaccinations and Autism?

In the late 1990s and early 2000s, a firestorm of controversy raged about whether the measles, mumps, rubella (MMR) vaccine can cause autism. Although the vast majority of the scientific community believes the debate should be extinguished for lack of evidence, there remain flickering beliefs within the public that the MMR vaccine should be avoided. How did this apparently specious theory come into existence? How can we explain its influence on the public at large? It's an interesting lesson in how science, the media, and public policy sometimes interact.

The Original Wakefield Paper

In 1998, Andrew Wakefield, along with 12 coauthors, published a paper in one of the most prestigious medical journals, *The Lancet*, on 12 cases of children who had been referred to a clinic in England for gastrointestinal problems and language deficits. Wakefield and colleagues reported two major findings pertinent to the issue of autism. First, they asserted that nine of the children were determined to be autistic. Second, parents or physicians of eight of the children attributed the onset of autistic symptoms to MMR vaccination; that is, the symptoms suddenly appeared a short time (48 hours to 2 weeks) after vaccination.

Public Reaction to the Wakefield Paper

Although Wakefield and colleagues stated that they did not *prove* that the MMR vaccine caused autism, such caveats were lost on some of the public. Once the possible connection between vaccines and autism was reported by the media, public fear spread quickly in Europe as well as North America.

Reemergence of Measles Outbreaks

After publication of the Wakefield article and its attendant publicity, a substantial decrease in the percentage of children receiving the MMR vaccination occurred in the United States. There's a strong probability that this decrease was the cause of reported measles outbreaks in England and the United States. For example, in the United States an outbreak occurred in 2008, and 90% of those infected hadn't been vaccinated (Centers for Disease Control and Prevention, 2008). And as recently as 2009, 1 out of 5 parents in the United States believed that vaccines could cause autism (Freed, Clark, Butchart, Singer, & Davis, 2010).

Several Authors Submit Retraction

Ten of the thirteen authors of the Wakefield paper also voiced concerns about the public reaction and offered a retraction (Murch et al., 2004). They pointed out that the major focus of the paper was on the intestinal abnormalities of the children

and that their data were "insufficient" to find a causal link between MMR vaccinations and autism. In light of the press coverage's potentially negative impact on public health, they considered it in the best interests of the public to retract their interpretations of the findings (Murch et al., 2004).

Commissioned Reports

In the United States, several federal agencies, including the prestigious Institute of Medicine of the National Academies, commissioned a review of the available evidence. They concluded that there was no evidence that vaccines cause autism (Institute of Medicine, 2004).

Because of the lingering controversy and the implications for public policy, the British General Medical Council (GMC) also initiated an investigation of the Wakefield research data. They found several irregularities in Wakefield's conduct (Flaherty, 2011). For example, they found that Wakefield had failed to disclose a potential conflict of interest—his name was on a patent for a new medicine designed to prevent measles, and he and one of his colleagues had not selected the participants for the study in an unbiased manner. Finally, the GMC Fitness to Practice Panel recommended revocation of Dr. Wakefield's medical license (General Medical Council, 2010).

Lancet Issues Retraction

On February 2, 2010, the *Lancet* published a retraction of the Wakefield et al. study, citing methodological flaws (Editors of *The Lancet*, 2010).

Some Parents Remain Unconvinced: Most of Scientific Community Remains Convinced

Despite overwhelming scientific epidemiological evidence to the contrary, many parents remain unconvinced that MMR vaccinations did not cause their children's autism. Some of this belief in vaccinations causing autism has been kept in the public eye by celebrities, such as the model/actress, Jenny McCarthy: http://www.youtube.com/watch?v=qGW4a96GqGc.

However, most scientists studying the matter hold that no evidence links the vaccine to autism spectrum disorders. They assert that the fact that a few children start showing signs of autism shortly after receiving the MMR vaccine is due to coincidence; the time the vaccination is administered coincides with the age when children start displaying signs of ASD that are *clearly observable* to laypeople and even some health care professionals. In addition, researchers have found that approximately one third of children who have ASD develop normally after birth until about 2 years of age, at which time their development regresses (Barger, Campbell, & McDonough 2013).

MyLab Education Self-Check 9.1

MyLab Education Application Exercise 9.1: ASD Controversy over Prevalence

After reading the section on prevalence in your text, consider the controversy over the rise of ASD in the United States

CAUSES

With the rapid increase in autism diagnoses has come an increase in research into the causes of the disorder. This research has dramatically altered our understanding of the condition. Early speculative causal theories have been replaced by a more scientifically based set of theories.

Early Causal Theories

Hans Asperger had conjectured that there was a biological and hereditary basis for autism (Hewetson, 2002). Kanner also speculated that the cause of autism was biological, but he noted that the parents of these children were not "warmhearted."

Even though Asperger and Kanner came down on the side of a biological basis for autism, the prevailing **psychoanalytic** ideas of the 1960s held sway for several years for professionals who were groping to find an answer to the origin of this puzzling condition. One psychiatrist in particular was extremely influential in promoting the idea that parents, especially mothers, were the cause of their children's autism. Perhaps influenced by Kanner's anecdotal reference to a handful of parents as not being warmhearted plus his later statement that "emotional refrigeration has been the common lot of autistic children" (Eisenberg & Kanner, 1956), Bruno Bettelheim (1967) conceived a theory that cold and unresponsive mothers caused autism. Most authorities attribute the term *refrigerator moms* (once used to refer to mothers of children with autism) to Bettelheim.

As we noted in Chapter 4, it wasn't too long ago that it was common to blame parents for the problems of their children, so Bettelheim's ideas were not viewed as radical. We now recognize that the direction of causation between child and adult behavior is a two-way street (Bell & Harper, 1977). It's reasonable to conclude that parents of a relatively unresponsive baby would over time come to display behaviors toward their infant that seemed cold and distant. Furthermore, we know that the families and parents of children with autism typically experience considerable stress because they are suddenly and unexpectedly confronted by the child's disability. Usually, their child does not look different from the typical child, and often he or she has gone through a short period of months or years of apparently normal development before the parents recognize that something is wrong. It's therefore understandable that parents would behave in ways that reflect stress and concern.

Today's Causal Theories

Scientists don't yet know precisely what's wrong with the brain in autism spectrum disorders, but they have established unequivocally that neurological—not interpersonal—factors are involved (National Institute of Health, 2013; National Research Council, 2001). Furthermore, they have strong evidence that genetics, neurological factors, and environmental contributions interact to result in autism in many cases (Stichter, Conroy, O'Donnell, & Reichow, 2017): Genetics can contribute to poor neuronal connections related to neurological anatomy and weakened synaptic strength that can result in vulnerability to environmental factors (e.g., toxic chemicals, maternal health issues, and early social deprivation) that results in symptoms of ASD.

However, given the range of symptoms and levels of severity of ASD, it's a reasonable guess that no single neurological or genetic cause exists.

NEUROLOGICAL BASIS OF AUTISM SPECTRUM DISORDERS Researchers using neuro-imaging techniques have documented that children and adults with ASD have neurological deficits in several areas of the brain. In fact, because so many areas are affected, many authorities now think that autism is better conceived as a disorder of neural *networks* rather than as being due to an abnormality in one particular part of the brain. More specifically, research suggests that the brain cells of individuals with autism exhibit deficient connectivity, referred to as **neuronal underconnectivity**, which disrupts the cells' ability to communicate with each other (Elison et al., 2013; Glessner et al., 2009; Just, Campbell, & McDonough, 2013; Just, Keller, Malave, Kana, & Varma, 2012; Wolff et al., 2012).

Researchers have found neuronal underconnectivity between the front and back of the brain in individuals with ASD. In particular, they point to deficiencies in communication between the **frontal lobes**, which are largely responsible for executive functioning and in the back of the brain, the **occipital lobes**, which are largely responsible for visual perceptual processing (Elison et al., 2013; Just, Campbell, & McDonough, 2013; Just et al., 2012; Wolff et al., 2012). Notably, researchers have found this underconnectivity in infants as young as 6 months of age.

See Up Close with Temple Grandin (and Her Brain) for further explanation of neuronal underconnectivity.

UP CLOSE with Temple Grandin (and Her Brain) Temple Grandin (http://www.grandin .com) (http://en.wikipedia.org/wiki/Temple_Grandin), perhaps the most well-known person with ASD, has arguably reached celebrity status. A best selling author, autism advocate, subject of several stories in the popular media, subject of an HBO documentary, included in *Time 100*'s list of the most influential people in the world in the "Heroes" category, Grandin is also renowned in the world of science. With a Ph.D. in animal science, Grandin is an authority on the design of more humane facilities for livestock, maintaining that her own extraordinary sensory abilities due to ASD help her to identify with how animals perceive their environment. •

As a high functioning person with ASD, Grandin has been able to articulate how her perceptions differ from those of others. Among other things, she emphasizes how much she "thinks" in pictures. By volunteering to have neuroimaging performed on her brain, she is helping scientists to better understand neuronal underconnectivity, as well as why she and many others with high functioning autism have well-developed visual and spatial processing abilities and poor social skills.

Another interesting line of neurological research involves the brain and head size of people with autism (Courchesne, Campbell, & Solso, 2011; Elder, Dawson, Toth, Fein, & Munson, 2008; Fukomoto et al., 2008; Piven, Arndt, Bailey, & Andreason, 1996). Studies indicate that the brains and heads of young children with autism tend to grow suddenly and excessively starting perhaps as early as the first year of life. This is then followed by a deceleration, such that they are about normal in size by adolescence. The significance of abnormally high rates of brain growth in the first 2 years is underscored by the fact that this is a time of critical importance to brain organization.

Theories vary, but some believe that the abnormal brain growth may be linked to elevated levels of growth hormones (Mills et al., 2007). Interestingly, another hormone-based theory of autism has drawn considerable attention among scientists as well as the popular media. Some researchers have claimed that those who, before birth, have high levels of **androgen** (a hormone that is responsible for controlling the development of male characteristics) in their mothers' amniotic fluid are more likely to exhibit autistic traits as children (Auyeung et al., 2009; Baron-Cohen, 2002, 2003; Baron-Cohen, Auyeung, Ashwin, & Knickmeyer, 2009). Based on these findings, some have come to refer to persons with autism as having an **extreme male brain (EMB)**. The theory remains plausible, but most of the scientific community continue to be skeptical about its validity (Barbeau, Mendrek, & Mottron, 2009; Falter, Plaisted, & Davis, 2008; Skuse, 2009). One of many criticisms is that the theory is based on a relationship between androgen and autistic traits in the general population, not between androgen and those who have actually been diagnosed with autism.

INTESTINE-MICROFLORA-BRAIN BASIS OF AUTISM SPECTRUM DISORDERS An emerging area of research into causal mechanisms of autism involves microflora, especially bacteria, living in the intestines. Several research studies have demonstrated that children with autism are more likely than children without autism to exhibit gastrointestinal distress, such as chronic diarrhea and constipation (Buie et al., 2010; Coury et al., 2012; Kohane et al., 2012). For example, in a survey sponsored by the Centers for Disease Control and Prevention, children with autism were 7 times more likely than children without autism to have experienced diarrhea/colitis in the last 12 months (Shieve et al., 2012). Furthermore, researchers have found a correlation between the severity of autism symptoms and the level of bacteria in the gut (Adams, Johansen, Powell, Quig, & Rubin, 2011).

Based on the evidence of a higher prevalence of gastrointestinal disorders in persons with autism, other teams of researchers have turned their attention to the biological makeup of the intestines of these individuals. Several research teams have found that the levels and types of bacteria differ in persons with autism, with some bacteria elevated and some depressed compared to individuals without autism (Kang et al., 2013; Parracho, Bingham, Gibson, & McCartney, 2005).

Other researchers have used mice as their subjects to test out the possibility of reducing autistic-like symptoms (Hsaio et al., 2013). By experimentally manipulating the intestinal bacteria in mice, they induced autistic-like symptoms, such as aloofness, anxiety, and repetitive physical movement. Taking it one step further, they "treated" the mice with a probiotic. Not only were there positive changes in their intestines, but the mice displayed fewer "autistic" symptoms—less anxiety, better social behavior, and less repetitive digging.

Although this research on the link between intestinal bacteria and autism is promising, it is important to keep in mind that it is still highly exploratory. How much, and whether, it leads to beneficial treatments for preventing or treating children with autism is unknown. However, it has already led to a better understanding of autism's biological features.

GENETIC BASIS OF AUTISM SPECTRUM DISORDERS Scientific evidence for autism having a hereditary component is very strong (Sutcliffe, 2008; Tick, Bolton, Happé, Rutter, & Rijsdijk, 2016). Studies have shown that when a child is diagnosed with autism, the chances are 15% that his younger sibling will be also be diagnosed with autism. This percentage is 25 to 75 times higher than in the population as a whole (Sutcliffe, 2008). When a monozygotic (identical, one egg) twin has autism, the chances are much greater that the other twin will also have autism than is the case with dizygotic (fraternal, two eggs) twins. Furthermore, even if they aren't diagnosed as having autism, family members of those with autism are more likely to exhibit autistic-like characteristics at a subclinical level, such as a lack of close friends, a preoccupation with narrow interests, and a preference for routines (Stone, McMahon, Yoder, & Walden, 2007; Volkmar & Pauls, 2003).

In addition to a direct hereditary cause of autism spectrum disorders, evidence now shows that sporadic genetic mutations are involved in some cases. Researchers have found that tiny gene mutations—spontaneous deletions and/or duplications of genetic material—that can result in autism are sometimes passed down to children from one or both parents (Autism Genome Project Consortium, 2007; Sebat et al., 2007).

Research has yet to identify all the exact genes involved. However, researchers are overwhelmingly consistent in stating that no single "autism gene" exists; multiple genes are involved, and the same genes are not implicated in all people with autism.

IDENTIFICATION

The diagnosis of autism is often made by a psychiatrist using criteria established by the American Psychiatric Association's *DSM-5* (2013), which focus on communication skills, social interactions, and repetitive and stereotyped patterns of behavior. In addition to observing the child in the examining room and taking a detailed history from parents, clinicians can use behavioral observation instruments and ask parents and/or teachers to fill out behavior checklists. Two instruments, both of which are standardized, are together generally considered the "gold standard" for diagnosing autism: the Autism Diagnostic Observation Schedule (ADOS) and the Autism Diagnostic Interview-Revised (ADI-R) (Le Couteur, Haden, Hammal, & McConachie, 2008; Stichter et al., 2017). Meant to be used together, the ADOS involves observing the child in several semi-structured play activities and the ADI-R is used to interview caregivers about the child's functioning in language/communication, reciprocal social interaction, and restricted, repetitive, and stereotyped behaviors.

Not that long ago, most authorities didn't think it possible to diagnose children with ASD until they were 2 or 3 years old. That opinion has changed. For example, the American Academy of Pediatrics recommends that pediatricians be on the alert for signs of autism at all well-child preventive care visits and that screening be done at 9-, 18-, 24-, and 30-month-old visits. As we noted earlier in our discussion of underconnectivity, researchers have discovered differences in the brains of infants as young as 6 months of age who then went on to develop autism. See Table 9.1 for a list of warning signs for ASD.

As noted in Table 9.1, an indicator for autism is loss or regression in babbling, speech, or social skills in a young child. Parents of some children with autism have often claimed that their child progressed normally for about the first 2 years and then abruptly began to regress in behavior. Research suggests that **autistic regression** occcurs in about 1 out of 3 cases of children with autism (Barger, Campbell, & McDonough, 2013). Researchers have begun to document that these parents' perceptions are, in fact, valid (Landa, Holman, Garrett-Mayer, 2007; Werner & Dawson, 2005). In one study, for example, researchers compared the home videotapes of first-year and second-year birthday parties and found that children whose parents said they had regressed had indeed shown signs of regression (Werner & Dawson, 2005). These findings also help explain why some parents have believed that vaccinations caused their children's autism (see the preceding Focus On . . . Is There a Link Between Vaccines and Autism?).

MyLab Education
Video Example 9.1
Obtaining a diagnosis of ASD is often a lengthy process. The mother in this video is typical in her description of her daughter's eventual diagnosis as ASD.

MyLab Education Self-Check 9.2

MyLab Education Application Exercise 9.2: Causes of Autism Spectrum Disorder
Read the section on Causes of ASD, and then consider the causal theories and how they have changed over the years.

TABLE 9.1 • **Warning Signs for ASD**

EARLY WARNING SIGNS
no babbling or pointing by age 1 no single words by 16 months or two-word phrases by age 2 no response to name loss of language or social skills poor eye contact excessive lining up of toys or objects no smiling or social responsiveness

LATER WARNING SIGNS
impaired ability to make friends with peers impaired ability to initiate or sustain a conversation with others absence or impairment of imaginative and social play stereotyped, repetitive, or unusual use of language restricted patterns of interest that are abnormal in intensity or focus preoccupation with certain objects or subjects inflexible adherence to specific routines or rituals

Source: National Institute of Health. (2013)

PSYCHOLOGICAL AND BEHAVIORAL CHARACTERISTICS

As noted earlier, the *DSM-5* considers ASD symptoms to fall under two general categories: social communication impairment and repetitive/restricted behaviors, so we've organized our discussion of the psychological and behavioral characteristics of ASD into these two categories. It's important to keep in mind the notion of ASD as being on a "spectrum," with a wide range of symptoms and levels of impairment. Also, as we noted earlier, the *DSM-5* doesn't recognize Asperger syndrome as a distinct category within ASD. However, because this change didn't occur until 2013, much of the research on ASD was done with individuals designated as having Asperger Syndrome. A general rule of thumb is that persons with ASD whose intellectual and verbal abilities are relatively high but who still have problems with social communication and/or repetitive/restricted behaviors are often referred to as having Asperger syndrome.

Impaired Social Communication

Many of the social interaction problems that individuals with autism exhibit involve deficits in social responsiveness. Parents of children with ASD often notice that their babies or toddlers don't respond normally to being picked up or cuddled. The young child with ASD might not show a differential response to parents, siblings, or their teachers compared to other strangers. They might not smile in social situations, or they might smile or laugh when nothing appears funny. Their eye gaze often differs significantly from that of others; they sometimes avoid eye contact with others or look out of the corners of their eyes. They might show little or no interest in other people but be preoccupied with objects. They might not learn to play normally. These characteristics persist and prevent the child from developing typical attachments to their parents or friendships with their peers.

COMMUNICATIVE INTENT Many children with ASD lack **communicative intent**, or the desire to communicate for social purposes. Some have severe language impairments and some can be **mute**; they use no, or almost no, language (Scheuermann & Webber, 2002). Those with severe impairments in language typically show abnormalities in intonation, rate, volume, and content of their oral language. Their speech sounds "robotic," or they might exhibit echolalia, parroting what they hear. They might reverse pronouns (e.g., confuse *you* and *I* or refer to themselves as *he* or *she* rather than *I* or *me*). Using language as a tool for social interaction is particularly difficult. If they do acquire language, they might have considerable difficulty using it in social interactions because they're unaware of the reactions of their listeners.

JOINT ATTENTION Deficits in social communication are often linked to impairment in the ability to engage in joint attention (Adamson, Bakeman, Deckner, & Romiski, 2009; Clifford & Dissanayake, 2008; Murray et al., 2008). **Joint attention** is the process by which an individual alerts another person to a stimulus via nonverbal means, such as gazing or pointing. For example, one person may gaze at another person, and then point to an object, and then return their gaze back to the other person. In this case, the pointing person is "initiating joint attention" by trying to get the other to look at the object. The person who looks to the referenced object is "responding to joint attention" (Joint Attention, n.d.). Researchers have found that the joint attention abilities of 3-year-olds with autism predicted their engagement in close and conflict-free friendships at 8 to 9 years of age (Freeman, Gulsrud, & Kasari, 2015).

PRAGMATICS People with Asperger syndrome may be able to express themselves using age-appropriate vocabulary and grammar, but they often exhibit numerous idiosyncratic language and language-related behaviors. They often have problems with **pragmatics**, the social uses of language (Colle, Baron-Cohen, Wheelwright, & van der Lely, 2008). For example, they might speak using an abnormal voice inflection, such as a monotone, talk too loudly or too quickly or slowly, not be adept at taking turns talking in a conversation, engage in monologues, or repeat the same thing over and over. In Chapter 6, we noted that people with learning disabilities can also experience problems with pragmatics; however, the deficits in pragmatic skills of individuals with Asperger syndrome are usually much more severe and pervasive.

A major reason that people with Asperger syndrome have so much difficulty in social interactions is that they aren't adept at reading social cues. In fact, at times, they can appear clueless about what constitutes appropriate social behavior. Because they can be highly verbal and intelligent, others may get the impression that they are willfully disregarding social etiquette. By "turning off" those around them, they become further ostracized from their peer group, making it difficult to make and keep friends and to interact with others.

Deficits in recognizing emotions, facial expressions, and vocal intonation may underlie the problems many people with ASD have in reading social cues. For example, people with ASD have more difficulty identifying the appropriate emotion when shown pictures of faces or recordings of voices displaying various emotions (e.g., sadness, happiness, fear, anger, surprise, and so forth) (Doi et al., 2013; Uljarevic & Hamilton, 2013).

Many of the social interaction difficulties of those with Asperger syndrome are due to their inability to think about situations in a nuanced way. They are often overly literal in how they "read" the behavior and language of others. And they often interpret situations using logic to the exclusion of emotion or sentiment. For example, they are prone to take things said to them literally. One person with Asperger syndrome noted that it took him until college to realize that when someone said, "I feel like a pizza," that it meant he felt like *eating* a pizza (Shore, 2003).

Another way of looking at the social problems for individuals with Asperger syndrome is captured by the notion of the hidden curriculum (Myles & Simpson, 2001, 2003). The **hidden curriculum** refers to the "dos and don'ts" of everyday living that most people learn incidentally or with very little instruction from others: behaviors or ways of acting that most of us take for granted.

All of these problems with social interaction are often misinterpreted as the person with Asperger syndrome's not wanting to engage socially with others. This may be true for some, but not for all people with autism. Numerous autobiographical accounts written by individuals with autism reveal that they often long to socialize with others (Causton-Theoharis, Ashby, & Cosier, 2009). They experience feelings of isolation. In addition, they often experience social anxiety about engaging socially with others (Kuusikko et al., 2008).

Repetitive/Restricted Behaviors

People with ASD are prone to abnormal sensory perceptions. Accordingly, they may display **stereotyped motor or verbal behaviors**: repetitive, ritualistic motor behaviors such as twirling, spinning objects, flapping the hands, and rocking, similar to those that are evident in some people who are blind (see Chapter 12). Another characteristic frequently seen in individuals with autism and related disorders is extreme fascination or preoccupation with objects and a very restricted range of interests. Children with autism might play ritualistically with an object for hours at a time or show excessive interest in objects of a particular type. They can become upset by any change in the environment (e.g., something out of place or something new in the home or classroom) or any change in routine; some individuals with autism seem intent on the preservation of sameness and have extreme difficulty with change or transition (Adreon & Stella, 2001; Myles & Simpson, 2001).

The abnormal sensory perceptions of people with ASD can sometimes be manifested by being hyperresponsive or hyporesponsive to particular stimuli in their environment (Ben-Sasson et al., 2009). For example, some people with ASD experience hypersensitivity to visual stimuli, such as being overly sensitive to fluorescent lights, and others can be overly sensitive to touch. Interestingly, some people with autism are totally the opposite of hyperresponsive. They are very *un*responsive to auditory, visual, or tactile stimuli. In fact, to the casual observer, some appear to be deaf or blind. Still others have a combination of hypersensitivity and hyposensitivity, for instance, being oblivious to loud noises such as a fire alarm but overreacting to someone whistling at a great distance. It's important to point out that the degree of sensory sensitivity and the number of stimuli to which one is sensitive are what make people with ASD different from the general population. In other words, research has shown that it is not unusual for some people who do *not* have ASD to exhibit some sensory sensitivity (Robertson & Simmons, 2013). For example, it may be perfectly normal for an individual to dislike having his or her hair cut because the clippings fall on the face, neck, shoulders, and so forth or to dislike strong smells in a candle/soap shop—these are two things asked on a questionnaire frequently used to diagnose autism (Baron-Cohen, Wheelright, Skinner, Martin, J. & Clubley, 2001).

Perhaps not surprisingly given their penchant for objects and repetition and their difficulties in interacting with people, children with ASD are likely to spend about twice as much time as their typically developing peers engaged in watching television and playing video games (Mazurek & Wenstrup, 2013). And their video game usage is more likely to become compulsive. On the other hand, also probably not surprising given their aversion to social interaction, children with ASD have a tendency to spend very little time using social media.

Some people with autism experience a neurological mixing of the senses, or synaesthesia. **Synaesthesia** occurs when the stimulation of one sensory or cognitive system results in the stimulation of another sensory or cognitive system. Daniel Tammet, who has autism savant syndrome (which we discuss below) and has set the European record for reciting Pi from memory, to 22,514 decimal places, experiences several forms of synaesthesia—for example, endowing such things as numbers, figures, and so forth with emotions, colors, textures and personalities. His biography, *Born on a Blue Day* (Tammet, 2006) refers to Wednesday, the day on which he was born, because he "sees" Wednesday as being blue. Other examples of his synaesthesia include seeing 1 as a flash of white light, 9 as blue or as loud voices arguing, 333 as beautiful, and 289 as ugly.

FOCUS ON

Autism Savant Syndrome

Some individuals with autism have such extraordinary skills that at first blush, one thinks they are geniuses. These individuals fall into the extremely rare classification of **autism savant syndrome**. Although their autistic symptoms can be severe, with serious developmental delays in overall social and intellectual functioning, they have remarkable skills or talents, which often involve preoccupation with the memorization of facts. A person with autism savant syndrome might have extraordinary capabilities in such things as playing music, drawing, or mathematical calculations. For example, when given a date that is far into the future, such as March 2, 2020, some autistic savants are immediately able to say that this will be a Monday. The same person, however, might not have the functional mathematical skills to be able to purchase items in a grocery store.

Interestingly, in 1887, Dr. J. Langdon Down reported on several cases of what would later become two key disability classifications—"Down syndrome," named for Dr. Down, and "idiot savants" (Down, 1887). At the time, *idiot* was an accepted medical term for persons who today are referred to as having intellectual disabilities, and Down used it to point out that such individuals were savants (from French, *savoir* = *to know*) in the face of having severe intellectual impairment. Toward the end of the 20th century, the designation "autistic savant" replaced

"idiot savant," because the earlier phrase had acquired the status of being pejorative (Treffert, 2013).

The following are some of the more well-known cases of autistic savant syndrome. As you'll see, some are apparently born with the condition, whereas others acquire it as the result of some kind of brain injury.

- Daniel Tammet's extraordinary math calculation skills: http://www.youtube.com/watch?v=ai9fq8k6_j8
- Matt Savage's spectacular jazz piano skills: http://www.youtube.com/watch?v=xfzRn9kmx_U
- Stephen Wiltshire's amazing visual memory and drawing skills: http://www.youtube.com/watch?v=jVqRT_kCOLI

Because the skills of individuals who are autistic savants are so extraordinary, they are often covered in the media. This fact—along with publicity that accompanies films such as *Rain Man* (Guber & Levinson, 1988), *Shine* (Scott & Hicks, 1996; a film loosely based on the life of pianist David Helfgott), and *Mozart and the Whale* (Naess & Bass, 2005)—has led to the misconception in the general public that most, if not all, people with autism have amazing talents. Although precise figures are not available, most estimates indicate that autism savant syndrome is rare among those with autism spectrum disorder.

Attempts to Construct a Unifying Theory of Autism Spectrum Disorders

Although a wide variety of psychological and behavioral characteristics have been attributed to individuals with autism spectrum disorders, some researchers have attempted to build theories that can account for many of the behaviors displayed. The three most prominent theories identify the major impairments as being accounted for by problems in (1) executive functioning, (2) weak central coherence, or (3) theory of mind (Frith, 2003; National Research Council, 2001; Volkmar & Pauls, 2003). Even though none of these three theories alone can explain all the myriad problems displayed, together they help us begin to build a composite picture of autism spectrum disorders.

EXECUTIVE FUNCTIONING   In Chapter 7, we noted that many people with ADHD exhibit difficulties in **executive functioning (EF)**. EF is usually even more impaired in people with autism spectrum disorders. Their ability to plan ahead in a thoughtful way is sabotaged by their problems with working memory (WM), inhibitory control or behavioral inhibition, and mental flexibility (Luna, Doll, Hegedus, Minshew, & Sweeney, 2007; Semrud-Clikeman, Fine, & Bledsoe, 2013; van Rijn et al., 2013; Wang et al., 2017). Furthermore, impaired EF has been found in preschoolers with autism spectrum disorders (Smithson et al., 2013).

CENTRAL COHERENCE   Some authorities have identified people with autism as having weak **central coherence** (Frith, 2003), the natural inclination for most people to bring order and meaning to information in their environment by perceiving it as a meaningful whole rather than as disparate parts. Individuals with autism, on the other hand, get caught up in details in classic "not being able to see the forest for the trees" fashion.

Interestingly, some people with autism don't seem to recognize that their way of processing information is disjointed, nor do they appear to have any desire or need to bring coherence to their fragmented perceptions:

> A patient exhibiting autistic symptoms from early childhood obsessively collected information about the addresses of juvenile courts. It is unknown how this extremely odd interest arose. However it came about, it would be less odd if it emerged from a general interest in courts, buildings, or town plans. In this case it would not be just a fragment, however well studied, but part of a bigger picture. But this was definitely not the case for this patient. When asked why he did not want to know about the addresses of nonjuvenile courts, he replied, "They bore me to tears." This was not a joke on his part. The remark showed a total lack of understanding that interests are expected to be justified as part of a coherent pattern of likes and dislikes, and not arbitrary. (Frith, 2003, pp. 157–158)

THEORY OF MIND   Theory of mind (ToM) is impaired in individuals with ASD (Schuwerk, Jarvers, Vuori, & Sodian, 2016); and the more severe the ToM impairment, the lower the cognitive abilities and severity of autism symptoms. **Theory of mind (ToM)** refers to a person's ability to take the perspective of other people. It's the ability to "read" the mind of other people with respect to characteristics such as their intentions, feelings, beliefs, and desires. The reading of social cues is another way of saying that a person can anticipate and understand what another is probably thinking. Most of us are able to infer the emotional state of those with whom we are conversing by interpreting cues, such as tone of voice and facial expressions. We're able to gauge how others are reacting to what we're saying using similar cues. And these are valuable skills to have when interacting socially with other people. Therefore, it's no surprise that ToM impairment in individuals with ASD can result in problems with social skills (Mazza et al., 2017).

People with autism spectrum disorders have varying degrees of difficulty inferring the thoughts of others (Kaland, Callesen, Moller-Nielson, Mortensen, & Smith, 2008). Some, in fact, don't seem to understand that their thoughts are different from those of others. See the accompanying Focus on feature for a study demonstrating the theory-of-mind problems exhibited by children with autism.

FOCUS ON

Theory of Mind: The Sally and Anne Experiment

In what has become regarded as a classic study of theory-of-mind problems, researchers investigated whether children with autism ages 6 to 16 years could recognize that others can have false beliefs that affect their judgment (Baron-Cohen, Leslie, & Frith, 1985). Using two dolls (Sally and Anne), an investigator played out a scenario to three groups of children (ASD, Down syndrome, no disabilities). The scenario was designed to determine how capable the children were in understanding what the thinking of another child would be.

Each child was tested individually, with the following steps:

1. The child is introduced to two dolls—Sally, who has a basket and Anne, who has a box.
2. Sally puts a marble into her basket and covers it up.
3. Sally leaves the room.
4. Anne takes the marble from Sally's basket and hides it her own box.
5. Sally comes back into the room.
6. The experimenter asks the child, "Where do you think Sally will look for the marble?"

If the child says that Sally will look in her own basket for the marble (not in Anne's box), the conclusion is that he or she is able to recognize Sally's perspective, which reflects having a "theory of mind" (Baron-Cohen, Leslie, & Frith, 1985).

The vast majority of the children without disabilities and even the children with Down syndrome answered correctly. However, only a few of the children with autism spectrum disorder gave the correct response. They were unable to understand that Sally had no way of knowing that the item had been switched—that to her way of thinking, the marble was where she had left it.

MyLab Education Self-Check 9.3

MyLab Education Application Exercise 9.3:
Characteristics of Autism Spectrum Disorder
The videos for this exercise illustrate some of the diverse characteristics associated with autism spectrum disorder.

EDUCATIONAL CONSIDERATIONS

As we have mentioned, the characteristics of autism spectrum disorders are quite varied. When these characteristics are severe, they typically carry a very guarded prognosis, even with early, intensive intervention. A significant percentage of children with severe symptoms are unlikely to recover completely, although they might make substantial progress (National Research Council, 2001). Those on the mild end of the spectrum, however, can make enough progress that they can lead happy, productive lives, being employed and living independently.

Educational Programming Principles for Students with Autism Spectrum Disorders

Most researchers agree that educational programming for students with autism spectrum disorders should include (1) direct instruction of skills, (2) instruction in natural settings, and (3) behavior management, when needed, using functional assessment and positive behavioral intervention and support.

DIRECT INSTRUCTION OF SKILLS Effective instruction for students with autism spectrum disorders usually requires a highly structured, directive approach that uses basic principles of behavioral psychology for analyzing tasks and how best to teach them. **Applied behavior analysis (ABA)** is a highly structured approach that focuses on teaching functional skills and continuous assessment of progress. Grounded in behavioral learning theory, ABA is a comprehensive approach that emphasizes positive reinforcement or rewarding of desired behaviors. In its original conceptualization, ABA also meant punishing undesired behaviors. Today, many professionals avoid or de-emphasize the use of punishment, and research suggests that this has not resulted in a decrease in effectiveness (Sallows & Graupner, 2005). ABA has a wealth of research evidence attesting to its effectiveness with several different populations including persons with autism (Bishop-Fitzpatrick, Minshew, & Eack, 2013; Grindle et al., 2012; Simpson et al., 2005).

INSTRUCTION IN NATURAL SETTINGS Educators of students with autism spectrum disorders are increasingly emphasizing applying behavioral psychology in natural settings and in natural interactions—the kinds of settings and interactions that children without disabilities enjoy. Researchers are constantly trying to make better instructional use of the natural interactions by which children normally learn language and other social skills.

BEHAVIOR MANAGEMENT Students with autism spectrum disorders, especially those with severe levels of autism, sometimes display highly inappropriate behaviors, such as biting, hitting, or screaming. As we mentioned in our discussion of intellectual

RESPONSIVE INSTRUCTION

Meeting the Needs of Students with Autism Spectrum Disorders

USING VIDEO MODELING AND VIDEO SELF-MODELING

What the Research Says

A growing number of studies have demonstrated the effectiveness of video modeling and video self-modeling for increasing the functional, vocational, social communication, and behavioral skills of students with autism (Hart & Whalon, 2012; Mason, Davis, Ayres, Davis, & Mason, 2016). During video modeling (VM) a competent peer or adult demonstrates a behavior or skill that the target student will later perform. Video self-modeling (VSM) involves the student watching a video of himself or herself competently completing a task. Research has shown that viewing video models is a powerful teaching technique (Burton, Anderson, Prater, & Dyches, 2012; Hart & Whalon, 2012). Video modeling, however, has been largely applied to non-academic tasks. With increasing numbers of students with autism being served in general education classrooms, researchers are now exploring the efficacy of VM and VSM for increasing academic skills.

Two Research Studies

Two recent studies examined the impact of video-based instruction on the academic skills development (mathematics and science) of students with autism and intellectual disabilities. Burton and colleagues (2012) worked with four adolescent boys (3 with autism and 1 with an intellectual disability) using VSM to complete mathematical story problems. For the study, students were first videotaped following a script that would demonstrate the problem-solving steps needed for this new skill. Then, during the intervention phase, students would watch the VSM on an iPad while completing the same problem on paper. Similarly, Hart and Whalon (2012) worked with one adolescent student with autism and an intellectual disability to increase his participation in a science class. For their study, Hart and Whalon created a VSM of the student responding correctly (unprompted) to the science teacher's questions. During the intervention, the student would watch the video on an iPad in class just prior to instruction starting. Then, the researchers would take data on the number of times the student responded during instruction.

Research Findings

In both studies, the researchers found that viewing a video self-model on an iPad was an effective instructional approach. Burton et al. found that across all four participants the use of VSM resulted in students successfully learning and applying the new problem-solving skills. Hart and Whalon's study demonstrated that watching the VSM increased the students' accurate, unprompted responding in class.

Applying the Research to Teaching

In both studies researchers used flip cameras and scripts to create simple video self-models. They then would edit the videos using video editing software, such as iMovie, before loading the video onto an iPad. Video editing allowed the researchers to cut out any prompting or cuing that occurred in order for the final model to be a smooth, accurate delivery of the skill. The large touch screen of the iPad allowed for easy access and viewing. Teachers can follow these same steps to develop VSM within their own classrooms.

disabilities, ADHD, and emotional or behavioral disorders (see Chapters 5, 7, and 8), authorities recommend that a combination of **functional behavioral assessment (FBA)** and **positive behavioral intervention and support (PBIS)** can help reduce or eliminate these behaviors. FBA involves determining the consequences, antecedents, and setting events that maintain such behaviors (Horner, Albin, Sprague, & Todd, 2000; Hurl, Wightman, Haynes, & Virues-Ortega, 2016). *Consequences* refer to the purpose the behavior serves for the person. *Antecedents* refer to things that trigger the behavior. *Setting events* take into account the contextual factors in which the behavior occurs. For example, students might be more likely to exhibit inappropriate behavior toward the end of the day when they are more tired.

PBIS involves finding ways to support positive behaviors of students rather than punishing negative behaviors. It focuses on the total environment of the student, including instruction.

Evidence-Based Specific Practices and Programs for Students with Autism Spectrum Disorders

In an extensive review of 456 studies, researchers (Wong et al., 2015) identified 27 specific practices or programs that qualified as *evidenced-based*, i.e., met rigorous methodological standards. We'll highlight a few of the most popular practices and programs.

EVIDENCE-BASED SPECIFIC PRACTICES Examples of evidence-based specific practices are video self-modeling and social narratives. For information on Video Self-Modeling, see the Responsive Instruction on Video Self-Modeling. Social narratives are brief stories (which can also contain drawings or pictures) describing social situations (e.g., going to the grocery store, playing during school recess, flying on an airplane) that present possible social interaction challenges while offering examples of appropriate responding. Teachers or therapists can individualize the stories according to particular social encounters with which the individual struggles.

EVIDENCE-BASED PROGRAMS Examples of programs that meet the requirements for being evidence-based are Picture Exchange Communication System (PECS), Treatment and Education of Autistic and Related Communication Handicapped Children (TEACCH), and Pivotal Response Training (PRT). Because the deficits exhibited by students with ASD range widely with respect to type and severity, no one program is appropriate for all. PECS focuses on language, TEACCH stresses structure, organization, and use of visual cues, and PRT targets pivotal, or key, skills that, once learned, can lead to progress in other skill areas.

For students with relatively severe language deficits, the Picture Exchange Communication System (PECS) involves the use of pictures to help students initiate and maintain functional communication. (See the accompanying Responsive Instruction feature on PECS.)

The TEACCH (Treatment and Education of Autistic and Related Communication Handicapped Children) approach places heavy emphasis on structure. The physical environment has boundaries for such things as group work, independent work, and play. Activities are structured, using scheduling, organization, and routine, so that children know what they will be doing throughout the day. A key element of the program is its emphasis on visual cues, such as labeling, color coding, pictures of tasks, and so forth. To see an example of how TEACCH works, see http://www.youtube.com/watch?v=ddGLJ2r4rcw.

An approach with considerable research behind it that uses a broader, more comprehensive intervention framework is that of pivotal response teaching (or training) (Bozkus-Genc & Yucesoy-Ozkan, 2016; Duifhuis, 2017; L. K. Koegel, Koegel, Harrower, & Carter, 1999; R. L. Koegel & Koegel, 2006). **Pivotal response teaching (PRT)** (https://education.ucsb.edu/autism/pivotal-response-treatment) is based on the assumption that some skills are critical, or pivotal, for function in other areas. Thus, by focusing intervention on these pivotal skills, the effects of the intervention can more easily spread to other

RESPONSIVE INSTRUCTION

Meeting the Needs of Students with Autism Spectrum Disorders

PICTURE EXCHANGE COMMUNICATION SYSTEM (PECS)

What the Research Says

A significant number of children with autism have difficulty acquiring speech. It's estimated that one third to one half of children with autism lack functional communication (National Research Council, 2001). For these children, teachers can use augmentative and alternative communication systems such as sign language, voice-output communication aids (VOCA), or symbols and pictures to supplement or support communication development.

The Picture Exchange Communication System (PECS) is one augmentative and alternative communication (AAC) system that educators have successfully used to support the communication needs of individuals with autism (Sulzer-Azaroff, Hoffman, Horton, Bondy, & Frost, 2009). Using PECS, individuals with no or limited speech can initiate requests and describe observations through the use of pictures. PECS can be used as an alternative communication system (i.e., the *primary* means of communication) or as an augmentative communication support (i.e., in conjunction with speech or the development of functional language).

Comprehensive Review of the Research

In 2009, Sulzer-Azaroff and colleagues conducted a comprehensive review of the research on PECS. The goal of the review was to synthesize the scientific evidence supporting PECS effectiveness. In their review, they identified 34 data-based, published research articles on PECS. To be included in the review, the research needed to follow the PECS protocol and provide data on the outcomes of the study. The studies varied in purpose (e.g., some studies looked at the use of PECS to facilitate functional communication, while others looked at the effect of PECS on turn taking, the development of spoken communication, changes in behavior, in comparison to other AAC systems such as sign language or VOCA); settings (e.g., special and regular schools, preschools, in

homes); instructors (e.g., teachers, parents, consultants, university personnel); and measures (e.g., correct response rates, spontaneous communication, length and complexity of communication). The majority of participants in all the studies, however, experienced improvement in communication as a result of the PECS intervention.

Research Findings

Given the variation in research studies examined, the specific effects of PECS varied across studies. General outcomes included improved communication between participants and adults such as caregivers, teachers, parents, and members of the community and the ability to initiate requests. Studies that compared PECS to other AAC options typically found that PECS worked as well as or better than other options in terms of enhancing communication (Sulzer-Azaroff et al., 2009). Individual studies also demonstrated increases in speaking, decreases in acting out or aggressive behaviors, and the generalization of communication to new or novel settings.

Applying the Research to Teaching

One commonality across all studies was adherence to the PECS protocol for implementation. PECS implementation consists of six phases: (a) Phase I: exchanging single pictures for desired activities or items, (b) Phase II: using the single pictures in new places or with different people, (c) Phase III: discriminating among pictures (i.e., selecting from two or more things), (d) Phase IV: constructing simple sentences such as pairing the "I want" picture with a desired item, (e) Phase V: learning to use PECS in response to the question, "What do you want?" and (f) Phase VI: using PECS to comment on the environment with simple sentence starters such as "I see," "I hear," and "I feel." The majority of studies included in the review of research achieved Phases III or IV with their participants.

BY KRISTIN L. SAYESKI

---

skill areas. PRT emphasizes using ABA's structured approach of continuous assessment and reliance on behavioral learning theory to teach pivotal skills. Some of these pivotal areas are *motivation, self-management, initiations,* and *responding to multiple cues*—all areas of difficulty for many persons with autism spectrum disorders. Motivation is obviously critical to many areas of learning. PRT fosters motivation by emphasizing natural rewards of the child's own choosing. Thus, the teacher uses materials for which the child shows a preference. Managing one's own behavior is a skill that leads to autonomy and independence from the control of others. Because many of these students are passive and disengaged from their environment, PRT focuses on teaching them to more actively initiate responses, such as asking simple questions as the situation dictates, for example, "What's that?" or "What happened?" Teaching the skill of responding to multiple cues

FOCUS ON

Animal Assisted Interventions (AAI): What's the Evidence?

Using animals to help treat children with autism spectrum disorders has mushroomed in popularity. At first blush, for the general public, the notion of children with ASD "connecting" with animals when they can't relate to people seems reasonable. At first blush for scientists, however, the notion of dolphins or horses as aid to reduce symptoms of ASD seems far-fetched.

Fortunately, researchers have begun to turn their attention to whether AAI has merit. A systematic review of AAI (O'Haire, 2013) suggests that AAI has achieved the status of "proof of concept," a term borrowed from the business world, indicat-ing that a new product has enough positive research support to bring it to market.

Equine therapy, in particular, has been found by several researchers to benefit persons with ASD (Anderson & Meints, 2016; Borgi et al., 2016; Gabriels et al., 2015; Lanning, Baier, Matyastik, Krenck, & Tubbs, 2014; Ward, Whalon, Rusnak, Wendell, & Paschall, 2013). The therapy has involved horseback riding, as well as grooming and stable chores.

For more on therapeutic riding, see this video, which aired on PBS: http://www.youtube.com/watch?v=-ax6UvG_7kg.

---

targets the student's tendency to focus on environmental stimuli in an overly selective manner, perhaps staring for long periods of time at just one or a few objects or focusing on only one aspect of an object. PRT encourages the training of multiple cues.

MyLab Education
Video Example 9.2
Both separate and more inclusive settings have their advantages and disadvantages. In this video, a mother explains why she likes the separate setting in which her daughter is currently placed.

Service Delivery Models

Currently, we don't have precise figures on how many students with ASD are in the various eeducational environments, e.g., general education classrooms, special education classrooms, and so forth. However, it's safe to say that with the increase in prevalence of ASD has come an increase in the percentage of these students in neighborhood schools and general education classrooms, especially at younger ages. In this model, general educators and special educators work together to meet the individual needs of students with autism. However, little research describes how this collaboration should look in the classroom.

One promising format might be the Autism Spectrum Disorder Inclusion Collaboration model (Simpson, deBoer-Ott, & Smith-Myles, 2003). Nevertheless, some of the effective instruction of children with autism spectrum disorders requires one-on-one teaching or teaching in very small groups, and sometimes this can't be done effectively in the general education classroom.

Even when such intensive instruction is offered in specialized settings, state-of-the-art teaching emphasizes the most natural possible human interactions. At the preschool level, teachers emphasize natural interactions in general education classrooms with peers who do not have disabilities. At the elementary level, educators are including more children with autism spectrum disorders in cooperative learning groups in general education classrooms with their peers who do not have disabilities.

ASSESSMENT OF PROGRESS

Two critical areas of assessment for students with autism spectrum disorders are progress in language development and social/adaptive behavior.

Monitoring Progress in Language Development

For many students with autism spectrum disorders, their language acquisition can significantly affect their long-term life outcomes. Ongoing progress monitoring of language development can help the teacher or therapist determine if an intervention is meeting the needs of the student. The National Institute on Deafness and Other

MyLab Education
Video Example 9.3
And in this video, a teacher describes how a student with ASD was successfully integrated into general education.

HOW CAN I HELP?

Students with ASD in the General Education Classroom

"I don't know anything about students with autism spectrum disorder. How can this work?"

Successful Strategies for Collaboration

Collaboration strategies for students with autism spectrum disorders are rather new, and few have been tested for effectiveness in the general education classroom. Nevertheless, researchers are working to create models that are effective and support both the general and special educators who are working "by the seat of their pants" at this point. One such model is the Autism Spectrum Disorder Inclusion Collaboration model (Simpson et al., 2003), which "emphasizes shared responsibility and shared decision making among general educators, special educators, and support personnel. The model also permits consideration of both learner behaviors and instructional factors" (p. 117). The model includes five main components: (1) environmental and curricular modifications, general education classroom support, and instructional methods; (2) attitudinal and social support; (3) coordinated team commitment; (4) recurrent evaluation of inclusion procedures; and (5) home–school collaboration. The model isn't prescriptive in its recommendations for how collaboration should look in the classroom, but it does list specific items that should be in place in each component in order for collaboration to work. These items include:

Environmental and Curricular Modifications

- Availability of appropriately trained support personnel
- In-service training
- Implementation of appropriate instructional methods
- Availability of paraeducators
- Adequate teacher planning time
- Reduced class size

Attitudinal and Social Support

- School administration has positive attitude toward inclusion
- Administrative support for those working to include students with autism spectrum disorders
- Dissemination of information about autism spectrum disorders
- Use of curricula and experiences to facilitate understanding and sensitivity toward students with autism spectrum disorders
- Social interaction training for students with autism spectrum disorders

Coordinated Team Commitment

- Clear definition of roles for service delivery personnel
- Effective communication
- Shared decision making

Recurrent Evaluation of Inclusion Practices

- Evaluating appropriate supplemental aides and services
- Evidence of benefit from participation and education
- Student demonstration of appropriate participation

Home–School Collaboration

- Meaningful participation
- Suitable administrative supports
- School's willingness to listen

BY MARGARET P. WEISS

MyLab Education
Video Example 9.4
In this video, two teachers discuss the value of interdisciplinary collaboration among several practitioners, e.g., special education teacher, speech and language therapist, occupational therapist, etc.

Communication Disorders convened a work group that determined that assessment of expressive language, particularly for young children with autism spectrum disorders, should include measures from multiple sources (Tager-Flusberg et al., 2009). These sources include natural language samples collected in various communicative contexts, parent report via questionnaire or interviews, and direct assessment through standardized measures. The content of language assessments should be comprehensive, including measures of phonology, vocabulary, syntax, and pragmatics.

Teachers can have parents fill out the MacArthur-Bates Communicative Development Inventories (Fenson, 2007; Fenson et al., 2006) to monitor progress in language development (Luyster, Lopez, & Lord, 2007; Luyster, Qiu, Lopez, & Lord, 2007). These inventories cover the age range from 8 to 37 months. Teachers may select the Clinical Evaluation of Language Fundamentals-5 (CELF 5; Wiig, Semel, & Secord, 2013) for older students. The CELF-5 measures receptive, expressive, grammatical, and semantic skills for individuals ages 5 to 21.

Monitoring Progress in Social/Adaptive Behavior

Comprehensive interventions for students with autism spectrum disorders invariably include a focus on social and adaptive behavior. Taking only 5 to 10 minutes to administer, the PDD Behavior Inventory™ Screening Version (PDDBI™-SV) (Cohen, 2011) is designed to monitor progress in social/adaptive behavior of students 18 monhs to 12½ years old.

The Social Responsiveness Scale (SRS) (Constantino & Gruber, 2005) is a parent/teacher scale that may be used to monitor progress in social/adaptive behavior (social awareness, social information processing, reciprocal social communication, social anxiety, and avoidance). The SRS evaluates the severity of social impairment of individuals with autism spectrum disorders between the ages of 4 and 18.

The Autism Social Skills Profile (ASSP) (Bellini & Hopf, 2007) is a standardized outcome measure that examines social skills of children and adolescents with autism spectrum disorder. The ASSP is completed by teachers or parents and includes three subscales: (1) Social Reciprocity, (2) Social Participation/Avoidance, and (3) Detrimental Social Behaviors.

The Childhood Autism Rating Scale 2nd Edition (Cars2) (Schopler, Bourgondien, Wellman, & Love, 2010) is frequently used for screening and diagnostic purposes and can also be used to evaluate the effectiveness of interventions (Cohen et al., 2003). CARS focuses on behaviors that deviate from those of typically developing children and is appropriate for children over 2 years old.

MyLab Education **Self-Check 9.4**

MyLab Education **Application Exercise 9.4: Behavioral Interventions for Learners with ASD**

Read a case study about Paula, a student with ASD; then answer the corresponding questions.

EARLY INTERVENTION

Most early intervention programming focuses on children with relatively severe degrees of autism spectrum disorders rather than those with milder issues because the former are more likely to be diagnosed earlier. For example, Asperger syndrome is rarely diagnosed in the preschool years.

To be most effective, education and related interventions for students with autism must be early, intensive, and highly structured and should involve families. Early, intensive intervention may produce remarkable gains in many young children with autism spectrum disorders, although no intervention yet can claim universal success in enabling these children to overcome their disabilities completely. Research reveals that the vast majority of children diagnosed as having ASD at an early age (about 2½ years old) do not improve when tested again at 5½ years of age (Venker, Ray-Subramanian, Bolt, & Weismer, 2013).

Research indicates that the following are essential features of effective preschool programs for children with autism spectrum disorders:

- Entry into intervention programs as soon as an autism spectrum diagnosis is seriously considered
- Active engagement in intensive instructional programming for a minimum of the equivalent of a full school day, 5 days (at least 25 hours) a week, with full-year programming varied according to the child's chronological age and developmental level
- Repeated, planned teaching opportunities generally organized around relatively brief periods of time for the youngest children (e.g., 15- to 20-minute intervals), including sufficient amounts of adult attention in one-to-one and very small group instruction to meet individualized goals
- Inclusion of a family component, including parent training
- Low student–teacher ratios (no more than two young children with autistic spectrum disorders per adult in the classroom)

- Mechanisms for ongoing program evaluation and assessments of individual children's progress, with results translated into adjustments in programming (National Research Council, 2001, p. 175)

Better understanding of the role of parents has led to having parents work together with others as "co-therapists" in many treatment programs. If early intervention is to be as intensive and pervasive as required, family involvement is essential. A program that is based on the features recommended by the NRC, including emphasis on the role of parents as interventionists, is the **early intensive behavioral intervention (EIBI)** program. Anchored in the applied behavior analysis (ABA) tradition, EIBI requires considerable time commitments from therapists and parents in implementing very structured training on discrete skills, starting when children are about 2 to 3 years old. Some professionals therefore have been cautious in recommending it. Several extensive research reviews, however, have found it to be effective in improving language and functional skills in many, although not all, young children with autism (Eldevik et al., 2009; Howlin, Magiati, & Charman, 2009; Matson, Tureck, Turygin, Beighley, & Rieske, 2012; Reichow & Wolery, 2009). And researchers have found that EIBI is more effective when implemented before 2 years of age (MacDonald, Parry-Cruwys, Dupere, & Ahearn, 2014).

TRANSITION TO ADULTHOOD

Autism spectrum disorder is a condition that invariably continues into adulthood. We will discuss transition to adulthood for students with autism spectrum disorders with more severe symptoms and students with less severe symptoms. In general, regardless of symptom severity, fewer than half of young adults with ASD are employed, which is even less than young adults with intellectual disabilities (Shattuck et al., 2012). Research, however, indicates that programming that includes internships in the last year of high school in work environments using applied behavior analysis can be highly effective (Wehman et al., 2013).

MyLab Education
Video Example 9.5
In this video, two students with ASD discuss their plans for transition from secondary school to living and working in the community.

Transition Programming for People with More Severe Autism Spectrum Disorders

Although the outcomes for adults with autism are better than they once were, they are still a long way from what we should hope they'd be. For example, the majority of adults with autism don't live independently (Hendricks & Wehman, 2009). In many ways, their outcomes are similar to those of individuals with intellectual disabilities, and their outcomes depend to a certain degree on their level of cognitive functioning (Cederlund, Hagber, Billstedt, Gillberg, & Gillberg, 2008). Transition programming for people with autism therefore follows virtually the same principles as those for people with intellectual disabilities (see Chapter 5). Transition planning should begin as early as the elementary years and become gradually more intensive in the middle school and secondary years. The current prevailing philosophy is **person-centered planning**, whereby the person with the disability is encouraged to make her own decisions as much as possible. More and more people with autism are being integrated into the community in small **community residential facilities** and in **supported living** settings, such as their own homes or apartments. The goal for work settings is for people with autism to be in **competitive employment** or **supported competitive employment**.

Transition Programming for People with Less Severe Autism Spectrum Disorders

Much of the planning for transition to adulthood for people with Asperger syndrome addresses issues of social interaction. Research suggests that social interaction issues, especially for those with Asperger syndrome, tend to increase as they reach adolescence and adulthood (Myles & Simpson, 2003). Unfortunately, this increase in difficulties in social interactions works against their achieving success in employment. Research also indicates that when people with Asperger syndrome do experience job difficulties, the cause is usually inappropriate social interactions rather than job performance (Gerhardt, 2003).

In transition programming for people with any kind of disability, it is always important that employers, college instructors, and those in similar positions have a solid understanding of the nature of the disability. In many cases, the person with Asperger syndrome may be misunderstood because he or she is intelligent but engages in eccentric behaviors.

More and more colleges and universities are developing programs for students with ASD, although many more are needed. Authorities recommend that in order to be successful, these programs should be individualized for each student. It is also critical that the people who provide services to these students are devoted workers because the work can be stressful and a substantial time commitment is required (Barnhill, 2016).

It is fair to ask just how much the social eccentricities of people with Asperger syndrome should be tolerated or how much these behaviors actually interfere with the culture of the workplace. Most people would agree that there is room for improvement in society's attitudes toward those who behave differently from the norm but do not bother or harm others. In many cases, it's probably reasonable to ask how much it matters that an individual employee does not fit in socially with the rest of the workforce if she gets the job done.

Many people with Asperger syndrome, in fact, are becoming advocates for themselves and others who have their condition. For example, see the website, Wrong Planet: http://www.wrongplanet.net.

MyLab Education Self-Check 9.5

MyLab Education Application Exercise 9.5
Transition Planning for Secondary Study
This exercise addresses ways in which schools can promote successful transition programming.

▼ chapter nine SUMMARY

What is the history behind autism spectrum disorders?

- In 1943, Leo Kanner reported on cases of children, whom he labeled as "autistic," who had major problems in communication and social interactions, as well as bizarre repetitive movements and an obsessive dislike of change.

- In 1944, Hans Asperger reported on cases of children, whom he referred to as having "autistic psychopathy," whom he thought had normal intelligence and language but who were socially isolated and had obsessive interests in extraordinarily narrow areas.

How do professionals define autism spectrum disorders?

- ASD is characterized by clinically significant deficits in social communication and by restricted, repetitive patterns of behavior, interests, and activities.

- People who have Asperger syndrome have higher cognitive and language skills than those with classic autism, but they have problems in other areas, especially social interaction.

What is the prevalence of autism spectrum disorders?

Photographee.eu/ Shutterstock

- Prevalence figures have risen dramatically in the past 30 to 40 years, with the U.S. Centers for Disease Control and Prevention (CDCP) now estimating that 1 out of 68 persons has ASD.

- Males outnumber females 5:1 in ASD.

- Most authorities maintain that the increase in autism is due to a widening of the criteria for ASD, a greater awareness of autism spectrum disorders, and diagnostic substitution (e.g., persons now identified as having an autism spectrum disorder previously might have been identified as having intellectual disabilities).

What causes autism spectrum disorders?

- Early causal theories were influenced by psychoanalytic thinking and blamed parents, often mothers, for causing autism by being too cold and unresponsive.

- Today's causal theories point to a neurological and genetic basis for autism.

- Neuronal underconnectivity between the frontal lobes and the occipital lobes of the brain is a likely cause of autism spectrum disorder.

- Evidence indicates that heredity as well as spontaneous genetic mutations are involved in causing autism.

- Evidence indicates that no single gene results in autism.

- The best scientific evidence indicates that the measles, mumps, rubella (MMR) vaccinations do not cause ASD.

What methods are used to identify individuals with autism spectrum disorders?

- For autism, the clinician uses criteria that focus on communication skills, social interactions, and repetitive and stereotyped patterns of behavior.

  - Some early signs of autism are a lack of the following: no babbling or pointing by age 1, no single words by 16 months or two-word phrases by age 2, no response to name, loss of language or social skills, poor eye contact, excessive lining up of toys or objects, no smiling or social responsiveness.

  - Clinicians often use two instruments that are considered the "gold standards" for diagnosing ASD: the Autism Diagnostic Observation Scale (ADOS) and the Autism Diagnostic Interview—Revised (ADI-R).

What are some of the psychological and behavioral characteristics of learners with autism spectrum disorders?

- People with ASD have deficits in social interaction, communication, and cognition; they also have repetitive and stereotyped patterns of behavior, and some have abnormal sensory perceptions.

  - Most lack communicative intent, the desire to communicate socially. Many infants and young children with autism display a lack of joint attention, the process of one person alerting another to a stimulus via nonverbal means, such as gazing or pointing.

  - They have cognitive deficits similar to those of people with intellectual disabilities; some have additional peculiarities, such as processing things visually and spatially rather than conceptually or linguistically.

  - Some, who are referred to as having autism savant syndrome, have extraordinary specialized skills.

  - Examples of abnormal sensory perceptions are being hyperresponsive, hyporesponsive, or having synaesthesia (a mixing of sensory information).

- Compared to people with more severe ASD, those with Asperger syndrome often display a milder degree of impairments or abnormalities in social interaction, communication, repetitive and stereotyped patterns of behavior, cognitive processing, and sensory perceptions.

  - People with Asperger syndrome often have difficulties with social interactions, understanding the hidden curriculum (the dos and don'ts of everyday living), and taking things too literally.

- Another communication challenge in Asperger syndrome is in pragmatics, the social uses of verbal and nonverbal communication skills.

- Three theories have been proposed to account for the many deficits in autism spectrum disorders. No single one explains all the deficits of all the disorders, but together they begin to build a composite picture.

  - Problems with executive functions, including working memory, self-regulation of emotions, and the ability to plan ahead.

  - Problems with central coherence involve paying too much attention to details or parts in cognitive processing, thereby leading to impairments in conceptualizing coherent wholes.

  - Problems with a theory of mind lead to impairments in taking another person's perspective, or being able to "read" what others might be thinking.

What are some educational considerations for learners with autism spectrum disorders?

- Educational programming for students with autism spectrum disorder includes direct instruction of skills, including applied behavior analysis (ABA); instruction in natural settings; and behavior management, when needed, using functional assessment and positive behavioral intervention and support (PBIS).

- Examples of approaches for students with autism spectrum disorder include the Picture Exchange Communication System (PECS), TEACCH, and pivotal response teaching (PRT).

How do professionals assess the progress of students with autism spectrum disorders?

- Progress in language development and social/adaptive behavior can be monitored using one or more scales designed for such purposes.

What are some important considerations with respect to early intervention for learners with autism spectrum disorders?

- The most effective early intervention programs are intensive, use principles of applied behavior analysis (ABA), are highly structured, and involve families. One such program that has been effective for some but not all children is the Early Intensive Behavioral Interventions (EIBI) program.

- Early intervention programs often use natural interactions to teach students in natural environments, including general education classrooms to the extent possible.

What are some important considerations with respect to transition to adulthood for learners with autism spectrum disorders?

- For those with more severe ASD, the emphasis is on person-centered planning, with living arrangements in community residential facilities or supported living settings and placement in competitive employment or supported competitive employment situations.

- For those with less severe ASD, such as Asperger syndrome, the focus is often on improving social interactions both in employment and in postsecondary settings.

▼ INTERNET RESOURCES

Professional, Parent, and Government Organizations

- Autism Speaks™ (www.autismspeaks.org) is the largest and most influential advocacy organization focused on persons with ASD.

- The Organization for Autism Research (http://www .researchautism.org) focuses on applied research for ASD.

- For a comprehensive overview of Autism Spectrum Disorders, see the National Institute of Neurological Disorders and Stroke Website: http://www.ninds.nih.gov/disorders/ autism/autism.htm.

- The National Institute of Mental Health maintains a website with information on several areas of disability, including ASD. For more information, go to www.nimh.nih.gov and click on the topic of ASD.

chapter ten
LEARNERS WITH COMMUNICATION DISORDERS

Monkey Business/Vetta/Getty Images

▶ LEARNING OUTCOMES

Learning Outcome 10.1: Understand the definition and prevalence of communication disorders.

Learning Outcome 10.2: Learn about the difference between communicative differences and disorders and learn the major disorders of speech and language.

Learning Outcome 10.3: Understand some of the educational considerations for people

with communication disorders, and how professionals assess progress to help plan educational strategies.

Learning Outcome 10.4: Learn about issues that should be considered with respect to early intervention and transition to adulthood for individuals with communication disorders.

MISCONCEPTIONS ABOUT Learners with Communication Disorders

MYTH Children with language disorders always have speech difficulties as well.

FACT It is possible for a child to have good speech yet not make any sense when he or she talks; however, most children with language disorders have speech disorders as well.

MYTH Individuals with communication disorders always have emotional or behavioral disorders or intellectual disabilities.

FACT Some children with communication disorders are normal in cognitive, social, and emotional development.

MYTH How children learn language is now well understood.

FACT Although recent research has revealed quite a lot about the sequence of language acquisition and has led to theories of language development, exactly how children learn language is still unknown.

MYTH Stuttering is primarily a disorder of people with extremely high IQs. Children who stutter become stuttering adults.

FACT Stuttering can affect individuals at all levels of intellectual ability. Some children who stutter continue stuttering as adults; most, however, stop stuttering before or during adolescence with help from a speech-language pathologist. Stuttering is primarily a childhood disorder, found much more often in boys than in girls.

MYTH Disorders of phonology (or articulation) are never very serious and are always easy to correct.

FACT Disorders of phonology can make speech unintelligible; it is sometimes very difficult to correct phonological or articulation problems, especially if the individual has cerebral palsy, intellectual disabilities, or emotional or behavioral disorders.

MYTH There is no relationship between intelligence and communication disorders.

FACT Communication disorders tend to occur more frequently among individuals of lower intellectual ability, although they may occur in individuals who are extremely intelligent.

MYTH There is not much overlap between language disorders and learning disabilities.

FACT Problems with verbal skills—listening, reading, writing, speaking—are often central features of learning disabilities. The definitions of language disorders and several other disabilities are overlapping.

MYTH Children who learn few language skills before entering kindergarten can easily pick up all the skills they need, if they have good peer models in typical classrooms.

FACT Early language learning is critical for later language development; a child whose language is delayed is unlikely to learn to use language effectively merely by observing peer models. More explicit intervention is typically required.

MYTH English language learners who have acquired proficient social language will also succeed in academic tasks.

FACT Basic interpersonal communication skills (BICS) do not ensure students' academic success. Students require proficiency in more advanced language skills, referred to as cognitive academic language proficiency (CALP), to succeed in academic areas.

GUIDING QUESTIONS

- How are communication disorders defined?
- What is the prevalence of communication disorders?
- What is the difference between communicative differences and disorders?
- What are the major disorders of language?
- What are the major disorders of speech?

- What are the main educational considerations for communication disorders?
- What are the major features of assessment of progress for students with communication disorders?
- What are the major aspects of early intervention for communication disorders?
- What do educators emphasize in transition for students with communication disorders?

Communication is such a natural part of our everyday lives that we seldom stop to think about it. In fact, communication occurs in everything we do. Social conversation with families, friends, and casual acquaintances is normally so effortless and pleasant that it is hard to imagine having difficulty with it. Hulit and Howard (2010) describe how speech is such a part of the human experience that we often take it for granted. Most of us only have feelings of uncertainty about the adequacy of our speech or language when we are in stressful or unusual social situations, such as talking to a large audience or being interviewed for a job. If we always had to be aware of and concerned about communicating, we would worry about every social interaction we had.

For some people, however, communication is not effortless and pleasant. Their communication may take great effort. For instance, some individuals have serious problems producing a sufficiently clear voice quality, described as a *voice disorder*, and other individuals are unable to comprehend the language that others produce, described as a *receptive language disorder*. Paste this URL into your browser to see individuals who are unable to produce fluent speech, or speech of an appropriate rhythm and rate; this is a *fluency disorder*, or stuttering (http://www.youtube.com/watch?v=2Jk3AtlfWKQ).

Not all communication disorders involve disorders of speech. Not all speech disorders are as handicapping in social interactions as stuttering, nor is stuttering the most common disorder of speech. About 5% of all children stutter for six months or more. About three-quarters discontinue stuttering by late childhood, leaving about 1% of the population with a long-term problem. Approximately an even percentage of girls and boys experience the onset of stuttering; however, about four times more boys than girls stutter long-term (Owens, Metz, & Farinella, 2015; The Stuttering Foundation, 2017).

Today, difficulties like those the children in the previous video experienced are viewed within the broad context of communication disorders because of the obstacles they present to social interaction, which is the major purpose of language. The children's stuttering resulted in an inability to convey thoughts and feelings and a fear of being unable to say certain words. In thinking about communication disorders, three elements of communication must be considered: the contexts in which communication occurs (e.g., in a group, in the classroom), the functions expressed by communication or the reasons one communicates (e.g., to request, to comment, to reason), and the actual execution of communication comprehension and expression.

DEFINITIONS

Speech and language are tools used for communication. **Communication** is the process of sharing information and involves many **communicative functions**, such as seeking social interaction, requesting objects, sharing ideas, and rejecting an object or interaction. It requires sending messages in understandable form (encoding) and receiving and understanding messages (decoding). It always involves a sender and a receiver of messages, but it does not always involve oral language. Communication can also be nonverbal; in fact, much of the meaningful interaction among humans is nonverbal. (Owens et al., 2015). Language (both verbal and nonverbal) and speech are important tools for human communication. A **communication disorder** impairs the ability to transmit or receive ideas, facts, feelings, and desires and may involve language or speech or both, including hearing, listening, reading, or writing.

MyLab Education
Video Example 10.1

In this video, the clinician is assessing a young child's receptive language using the Peabody Picture Vocabulary Test.

Language is the communication of ideas—sending and receiving them—through an arbitrary system of symbols used according to certain rules that determine meaning. Encoding or sending messages is referred to as **expressive language**. Decoding or understanding messages is referred to as **receptive language**. When people think of language, they typically think of oral language. **Speech**—the neuromuscular activity of forming and sequencing the sounds of oral language—is the most common symbol system used in communication between humans. Without the rule-governed symbol system that we call language, we would have only grunts and groans, not speech.

Some languages, however, are not based on speech. For example, American Sign Language (ASL) does not involve speech sounds; it is a manual language used by many people who cannot hear speech. **Augmentative and alternative communication (AAC)** (https://www.youtube.com/watch?v=r3m8_YmTDDM) for people with disabilities involving the physical movements of speech may consist of alternatives to the speech sounds of oral language (e.g., picture boards, ASL, gestures, and electronic devices that produce speech).

The American Speech–Language–Hearing Association (ASHA) provides definitions of disorders of communication, including speech disorders, language disorders, and variations in communication (differences or dialects and augmentative systems) that are not disorders. **Speech disorders** are impairments in the production and use of oral language. They include disabilities in making speech sounds, producing speech with a normal flow, and producing voice.

Language disorders include problems in comprehension and expression. Remember that language is governed by rules. The problems—rule violations—may involve the form (phonology, morphology, syntax), content (semantics), or use of language (pragmatics).

- **Phonology** refers to the rules governing speech sounds—the particular sounds and how they are sequenced.
- **Morphology** refers to the rules that govern alterations of the internal organization of words, such as adding suffixes and other grammatical inflections to make proper plurals—verb tenses, for example.
- **Syntax** refers to the rules of organizing sentences in a meaningful way, including, for example, guidelines about using subjects and predicates and placing modifiers correctly.
- **Semantics** refers to the rules about attaching meanings and concepts to words.
- **Pragmatics** refers to the rules about using language for social purposes.

Language disorders may involve any one or a combination of these five subsystems of language. Differences in speech or language that are shared by people in a given region, social group, or cultural/ethnic group should not be considered disorders. For example, African American English (Ebonics or Black English Vernacular), Appalachian English, and the Cajun dialect are varieties of English, not disorders of speech or language. These differences are governed by their own rules and reflect the cultural and linguistic diversity of North America. As long as speech and language are guided by consistent rules of a language community, they are not disorders, although they may differ from what we are accustomed to hearing and saying.

Similarly, the use of AAC systems does not imply that a person has a language disorder. Rather, such systems support people who have temporary or permanent inabilities to use speech satisfactorily for communication. Those who use AAC systems might or might not have language disorders in addition to their inability to use speech.

PREVALENCE

Establishing the prevalence of communication disorders is difficult because they are extremely varied, sometimes difficult to identify, and often occur as part of other disabilities (e.g., intellectual disabilities, brain injury, learning disability, or autism). About a million children—approximately one fifth of all children who are identified for special education—receive services primarily for language or speech disorders. Speech-language therapy is one of the most frequently provided related services for children with other primary disabilities (e.g., intellectual disabilities or learning disability).

About 8% to 9% of preschool children and about 5% of students in elementary and secondary grades have speech disorders; about 2% to 3% of preschoolers and about 1% of the school-age population have language disorders. Communication disorders of all kinds are predicted to increase during the coming decades, as medical advances preserve the lives of more children and youths with severe disabilities that affect communication. Therefore, schools need more **speech-language pathologists (SLPs)**, special and general education teachers need greater knowledge of communication disorders, and teachers need to be more involved in helping students learn to communicate effectively.

MyLab Education Self-Check 10.1

MyLab Education Application Exercise 10.1: Pragmatic Language

This exercise asks you to demonstrate your understanding of the different kinds of language disorders identified by the American Speech–Language–Hearing Association (ASHA).

COMMUNICATION VARIATIONS

The fact that certain students don't use the speech or language that is expected in school does not necessarily mean that they have a language disorder. The more important question is whether these students are effective communicators in their speech and language community (see Harris & Schroeder, 2013). Someone with a language difference that is also a disorder has difficulty communicating in every language environment, including the home language community.

Systematic language variations that are rule governed are considered **dialects** (Vinson, 2007). A dialect may lead to a misdiagnosis of a language disorder. The speech or language of black children, for example, could mistakenly be judged to indicate disorder when it is merely different from standard American English. Conversely, a speech or language deficit of a black child may be attributed to the dialect, resulting in underdiagnosis (Stockman, 2010). Although a language variation or dialect does not constitute a language disorder, an individual may both have a language disorder and exhibit a variation that is not a disorder. Such an individual will be unable to communicate effectively even with others who use the same language variation.

Encouraging the communication of children whose cultural heritage or language patterns are not those of the professional's subculture is of increasing concern to classroom teachers and speech-language clinicians (see Chapter 3). On the one hand, care must be taken not to mistake a cultural or ethnic difference for a disorder; on the other hand, disorders that exist in the context of a language difference must not be overlooked.

When assessing children's language, the professional must be aware of the limitations of normative tests and sources of potential bias.

A child might not have a language disorder, yet have a communicative difference that requires special teaching to promote academic achievement and social communication. Children of nondominant cultures must be taught the rules for effective communication in the dominant culture. However, professionals must also understand and accept the effectiveness of a child's home language in its cultural context. Failure to teach children the skills they need to communicate effectively according to the rules of the dominant culture will deny them many opportunities. In effect, children of minority language groups might need to learn to live in two worlds: one in which their home language is used and one in which school language is used.

Many students for whom language difference is an issue do not speak entirely different languages, but variations peculiar to certain groups of speakers—that is, dialects. In fact, most Americans speak with various dialects. It is interesting to think about the attitudes of Americans in relation to which dialect is correct. Go to this website to see a demonstration of opinions on dialect: https://www.youtube.com/watch?v=4kW3K3OclnE.

For example, one dialect that differs from standard American English (and is not a language disorder) is Appalachian English. Insert this address: https://www.youtube.com/watch?v=5PTML-P3Hl0 into your browser to see how folks in Appalachia speak a variation of English with features that are not shared by other English dialects. Teachers must understand—and help their students understand—that other dialects are not inferior or limited language systems. Furthermore, teachers must recognize cultural differences regardless of the communication device being used. Multicultural issues arise in all communication interactions, including those in which AAC is used (Goldstein & Iglesias, 2017).

Families differ greatly in the ways they talk to children and in the language they expect children to use. Although students might not have language disorders, their language variations could put them at a disadvantage in using language in an academic context. Consequently, some people have suggested that children who come to school without mastery of the English of their textbooks should be taught it directly and consistently (e.g., Raspberry, 2001). Other recommendations include but are not limited to the following:

- Show sensitivity to and knowledge of the student's cultural values.
- Ask for help from families and knowledgeable colleagues.
- Visit the student in his or her natural environment; interact with the student in classroom settings with his or her peers.
- Know and respect the features of the community's dialects.

A major concern today in both special and general education is teaching children who are learning English as a second language, who are non-English proficient, or who have limited English proficiency. Bilingual education is a field of concern and controversy because of the rapidly changing demographics in many American communities. Spanish-speaking children make up a rapidly growing percentage of the students in many school districts. Moreover, a large number of children from various nations have immigrated to the United States during the past decade. Many of these children have no proficiency or limited proficiency in English, and some have disabilities as well. Bilingual special education is still a developing field. As we discussed in Chapter 3, finding the best way to teach children to become proficient in English, particularly when they have disabilities as well as language differences, is a special challenge for the 21st century.

LANGUAGE DISORDERS

Communication disorders cannot be understood without knowledge of normal language development. So before we discuss the disorders of language and speech, we provide a brief description of normal language development. Language disorders are discussed first and more extensively than speech disorders, because the primary focus of speech-language pathologists and other specialists in communicative disorders has shifted from speech to language during the evolution of special education and related services (Owens et al., 2015).

The newborn makes few sounds other than cries. Within a few years, however, the human child can form the many complex sounds of speech, understand spoken and written language, and express meaning verbally. The major milestones in this ability to use language are fairly well known by child development specialists, although the underlying mechanisms that control the development of language are still not well understood. Which parts of the process of learning language are innate, and which parts are controlled by the environment? What is the relationship between cognitive development and language development? These and many other questions about the origins and uses of language cannot yet be answered definitively.

Children develop speech and language, reaching developmental milestones at certain ages (https://www.youtube.com/watch?v=uFC4UK5rk4E). Along with the linked video, several resources are available that describe the typical development of speech, language, and communication. These can be found on the Internet from organizations such as the American Speech Language Association, the Centers for Disease Control and Prevention, and the American Academy of Pediatrics. The child with a language disorder may eventually reach many or most of the milestones shown for normal development, but at a later age than typically developing children. It is important to note that children sometimes seem to "catch up" in language development, only to fall behind typical development again at a later age.

No one knows exactly how children learn language, but we do know that language development is related in a general way to physical maturation, cognitive development, and socialization. The details of the process—the particulars of what happens physiologically, cognitively, and socially in the learning of language—are still being debated. Nelson (1998) discusses six theories of language that have dominated the study of human communication at various times. The six theories and research based on them have established the following:

1. Language learning depends on brain development and proper brain functioning. Language disorders are sometimes a result of brain dysfunction, and ways to compensate for the dysfunction can sometimes be taught. The emphasis is on biological maturation.
2. Language learning is affected by the consequences of language behavior. Language disorders can be a result of inappropriate learning, and consequences can sometimes be arranged to correct disordered language. The emphasis is on behavioral psychology.
3. Language can be analyzed as inputs and outputs related to the way information is processed. Faulty processing may account for some language disorders, and more effective processing skills can sometimes be taught. The emphasis is on information processing.
4. Language is acquired by a biological process that dictates rules governing the form, content, and use of language. Language disorders are the result of a failure to acquire or employ rule-governed aspects of language, and these disorders may be overcome by helping an individual induce or learn these rules. The emphasis is on a linguistic or nativist perspective.
5. Language is one of many cognitive skills. Language disorders reflect basic problems in thinking and learning, and sometimes these disorders can be addressed effectively by teaching specific cognitive skills. The emphasis is on cognitive development.
6. Language arises from the need to communicate in social interactions. Language disorders are a breakdown in ability to relate effectively to one's environment, and the natural environment can sometimes be arranged to teach and support more effective interaction. The emphasis is on social interaction.

All these theories contain elements of scientific truth, but none can explain the development and disorders of language completely. Each of the six theories has advantages and disadvantages for assessing language disorders and devising effective interventions. Advances in neurological imaging technology may lead to better understanding of the biological bases of language (Foundas, 2001). However, pragmatic or social interaction theory is widely viewed as having the most direct implications for speech-language pathologists and teachers because it focuses most directly on how communication skills can be fostered through adult–child interaction (Owens, 2014).

Language involves listening and speaking, reading and writing, technical discourse, and social interaction. Language problems are therefore basic to many of the disabilities discussed in this book, especially hearing impairment, intellectual disabilities, traumatic brain injury, autistic spectrum disorder, and learning disability.

Classification of Language Disorders

Language disorders can be classified according to two primary dimensions: domain (subsystem or type) and etiology (cause). ASHA (www.asha.org) also provides definitions on its website and suggests a classification scheme involving five subsystems or types of language: phonological (sounds), morphological (word forms), syntactical (word order and sentence structure), semantic (word and sentence meanings), and pragmatic (social use of language). Difficulty with one of these dimensions of language is virtually certain to be accompanied by issues with one or more of the others. However, children with language disorders often have particular struggles with one dimension.

Another way of classifying language disorders is based on the presumed cause (etiology) or related conditions. Classification by etiology provides two subtypes: primary and secondary. A **primary language disorder** has no known cause. A **secondary language disorder** is caused by another condition, such as intellectual disabilities, hearing impairment, autism spectrum disorder, cerebral palsy, or traumatic brain injury.

A scientific approach to problems demands classification, but human beings and their language are very difficult to categorize. Therefore, all classification systems contain ambiguities, and none can account for all cases.

Ryan, the student described in the accompanying Success Stories feature, is a perfect example of this concept. He suffered a brain injury and, with the help of his family and involved professionals, he learned to communicate again. Ryan was fortunate enough to experience a full recovery, but his struggles with communication are fresh in his mind.

Primary Language Disorders

Specific language impairment (SLI) refers to a language disorder that has no identifiable cause; it is an unexpected and unexplained variation in the acquisition of language (Silliman & Scott, 2006). These disorders result in significant limitations in language and are not due to intellectual disabilities, the perceptual problems that characterize language learning disability, hearing problems, and so on (Owens, Metz, & Farinella, 2015). Often, SLI involves multiple aspects of language. Academic problems, particularly in the areas of reading and writing, are common for children with SLI (Choudhury & Benasich, 2003; Kohnert, Windsor, & Yim, 2006; Peterson, Pennington, Shriberg, & Boada, 2009; Tomblin, 2010).

Early expressive language delay (EELD) refers to a significant lag in expressive language (i.e., the child doesn't have a 50-word vocabulary or use 2-word utterances by age 2) that the child won't outgrow. About half the children whose language development is delayed at age 2 will gradually catch up developmentally with their age peers; however, the other half will not catch up and will continue to have language problems throughout their school years.

Language-based reading impairment involves a reading problem (i.e., dyslexia) based on a language disorder. This disorder cannot be identified until the child begins learning to read and has problems. Research of such abilities as phonological awareness, alphabet knowledge, and grammatical speech have helped in identifying children who are vulnerable to this kind of disorder (McNeil, Justice, Gillon, & Schuele, 2017; Vellutino, Fletcher, Snowling, & Scanlon, 2004). A significant percentage of children who manifest language impairments in kindergarten will have obvious reading problems by second

SUCCESS STORIES: Through Coordination of Medical and Educational Services, Ryan Moves from Rehabilitation to School Reentry Successfully

Ryan McGarr: "When I look back, I realize how slow I was as a result of the head injury."

College student Ryan McGarr was severely injured in a Thanksgiving Day car wreck during his junior year in high school. An innovative traumatic brain injury (TBI) project provided a bridge between his rehabilitation services and school reentry.

These are the keys to his success:

- Intensive coordination of services and supports
- Relentless instruction in academics and vocabulary development
- Specific goals for compensatory strategies and teacher training

Ryan McGarr remained in a coma for 3 days after his injury, and his residual difficulties in language and cognitive processing presented academic challenges. Special educator Nancy Maher-Maxwell directed a specialized TBI project for the Nassau County Board of Cooperative Educational Services in New York. When Ryan was injured, she coordinated his medical and educational services. She also trained his teachers to meet his individual needs as he reentered school after the accident. Ryan credits his success to intensive, relentless, and specific special education along with spontaneous neurological recovery and a strong desire to achieve.

- **Intensive Coordination of Services and Supports.**
  Kathy McGarr was grateful that someone at the hospital told her about the TBI project: "Just the trauma, and trying to take care of your other children—the whole family tends to fall apart. I didn't have the concentration or anything to deal with this." According to Maher-Maxwell, "Research suggests that kids who have this connection between rehabilitation and school reentry, along with ongoing staff support once they've returned, have greater success rates than those who don't."

  Ryan returned to school part time in April of his junior year. He went to an outpatient rehabilitation center for therapies in the morning and then to his local public high school in the afternoon for English, social studies, art, and resource room. He returned to school full time for his senior year, carrying a full program of academic courses with resource room support for 45 minutes daily.

- **Relentless Instruction in Academics and Vocabulary Development.** Nancy Maher-Maxwell remembers that when she met Ryan 6 weeks after the accident, he was determined to graduate with his class and wanted tutoring. "The psychologist at the hospital, who evaluated him 9 weeks after the accident, told me

Ryan would probably never finish school and that I was overwhelming him with academics," says Mrs. McGarr, "but it was what he wanted, and I had to let him try to do it." To start the process, Maher-Maxwell contacted Ryan's school district. His former English teacher agreed to be his home tutor. With Maher-Maxwell's help, her lessons were individualized, concentrating on vocabulary and word meanings. She used flash cards and together with Ryan made up funny sentences using mnemonics to help him remember information. Instead of giving him a chapter to read in history, she chunked material to be learned by breaking it up into smaller units.

- **Specific Goals for Compensatory Strategies and Teacher Training.** The TBI project coordinated Ryan's reentry into the regular educational environment by providing workshops as well as ongoing support for his teachers. Training emphasized Ryan's need to take in new information in a variety of ways. Teachers learned techniques to reinforce study skills, such as taking notes, outlining chapters, and organizing projects. "Often the typical high school teacher will lecture on the subject, expect the kids to take good notes, and evaluate them on a test. Because of the disruptions in the learning systems of students with TBI, there may be a slower rate in processing, so extended time is often necessary both in teaching and in testing," Maher-Maxwell says.

His mother recalls that it was hard to tell whether Ryan would regain his language abilities. "In speech therapy, he had a terrible time with categorization skills. His therapist asked him to name five green vegetables, and he couldn't do it! What was even more surprising was that he couldn't imagine that anyone could!"

TBI is an acquired injury that demands new adjustments. "If I hadn't spoken with Nancy," says Mrs. McGarr, "I wouldn't have known to put Ryan in a resource room, since he never needed special education before." Head injuries can also make the future harder to predict. "That early neuropsychological evaluation that said he could forget about his academic aspirations never took into account Ryan's determination and the compensatory strategies that special education could provide," says Maher-Maxwell.

Ryan still finds that he is more easily distracted than he used to be, and he continues to need extended time on some college exams. He remains confident about the future, saying, "I'll succeed in the world doing whatever I want to do. I have no doubts about that."

By Jean B. Crockett

grade (Catts, Adlof, Hogan, & Ellis Weismer, 2005; Catts, Fey, Zhang, & Tomblin, 2001; Sawyer, 2006). Although phonological awareness has garnered much of the attention for the past two decades, research also provides some evidence that pragmatic, syntactic, and semantic knowledge is predictive of later reading comprehension (Catts et al., 2001; DeThorne, Petrill, Schatschneider, & Cutting, 2010; Muter, Hulme, Snowling, & Stevenson, 2004; Silliman & Scott, 2006), again indicating significant risk for children with language impairment. Research also suggests that the magnitude of the reading impairment is greater when the language impairment is paired with a speech sound disorder (Peterson et al., 2009).

Secondary Language Disorders

The literature on language disorders often includes discussion of the particular communication impairments of individuals with other specific disabling conditions, such as intellectual disabilities or autism spectrum disorder (e.g., Owens, 2014). Difficulty in using language in social interactions and relationships is now seen as a basic problem in many disorders.

Emotional and behavioral disorders, for instance, may range from social reticence or withdrawal to severe acting out and aggression (McCabe & Marshall, 2006; Rogers-Adkinson & Griffith, 1999). Young children who have language disorders might have special difficulty in developing skills in social interaction because they do not interpret social circumstances correctly and have difficulty expressing themselves.

Language impairment may also limit individuals' social interaction with peers. For example, in a study of adolescents' use of cell phone technology, students with SLI texted their friends less frequently than their peers without SLI, resulting in fewer opportunities to develop social networks (Conti-Ramsden, Durkin, & Simkin, 2010).

SPEECH DISORDERS

Speech disorders are very heterogeneous—that is, many different types, degrees, and combinations exist. Speech disorders pose a wide variety of challenges to the communication abilities of school children.

We provide only brief descriptions of the major disorders affecting the speech of school-age children. Most speech disorders are treated primarily by a speech-language pathologist, not by a classroom teacher. However, both general and special education teachers are expected to work collaboratively with speech-language pathologists in assessment and intervention.

Phonological Disorders

Phonological disorders occur in children younger than 9 years of age. These disorders do not include the normally developing young child's inability to say words correctly. The cause of the disorder is often unknown, but for some reason children with phonological disorders do not understand the rules for producing the sounds of their language. Their speech sound production differs from age-appropriate, culturally based expectations. These children don't seem to understand how to differentiate and produce the phonemes or sounds of language to construct intelligible words. This disorder occurs in about 4 or 5 in 100 children, somewhat more often in boys than in girls.

Phonological disorders are difficult to distinguish conceptually from articulation disorders (Owens et al., 2015). Children with an articulation disorder simply have trouble producing sounds correctly. In contrast, children with a phonological disorder seem to have a poor inner representation of the sounds of language. They might not understand the contrasts between sounds or the distinctiveness of sound, which results in problems with how speech sounds are produced. For instance, children who do not have an internal representation of consonants at the end of words produce *hat* as *ha* and *dog* as *do*.

Phonology is critical to literacy. Learning to read requires an understanding of the alphabetic principle—that letters work systematically to represent sounds, and these sounds can be blended together to form words (Lane & Pullen, 2004). **Phonological awareness** is an understanding of the sound structure of language; it includes the abilities to blend sounds into words, to segment words into sounds, and to otherwise manipulate the sounds of spoken language. The following website shows how young children begin learning to recognize smaller units of sound within a word (https://www.youtube.com/watch?v=OOkCt-YtzEk). Without phonological awareness, a student cannot make sense of the alphabetic principle, which results in an inability to decode words. Some, but not all, children with phonological disorders lack phonological awareness. Some have serious problems with verbal working memory (remembering what was said or what they want to say) or word learning and word retrieval. Deficits in working memory and word retrieval are considered a phonological processing disorder. This disorder of the phonological system of language affects speech sound production and often affects literacy as well.

MyLab Education
Video Example 10.2

This video shows a speech language therapist assessing a child with Down syndrome's articulation skills and providing instruction.

Articulation Disorders

Articulation disorders involve errors in producing sounds. The problem is not an underlying phonological problem but a disorder in which the individual omits, substitutes, distorts, or adds speech sounds. Lisping, for example, involves a substitution or distortion of the /s/ sound (e.g., *thunthine* or *shunshine* for *sunshine*). Missing, substituted, added, or poorly produced word sounds can make a speaker difficult to understand or even unintelligible. Such errors in speech production may also carry heavy social penalties, subjecting the speaker to teasing or ridicule.

When are articulation errors considered a disorder? That depends on a clinician's subjective judgment, which will be influenced by the clinician's experience, the number and types of errors, the consistency of these errors, the age and developmental characteristics of the speaker, and the intelligibility of the person's speech (see Bernthal, Bankson, & Flipsen Jr., 2017). In the following video, a speech-language pathologist discusses the red flags that help you to recognize an articulation disorder (https://www.youtube.com/watch?v=nr92TSlBvA4).

Young children make frequent errors in speech sounds when they are learning to talk. Many children do not learn to produce all the speech sounds correctly until they are 8 or 9 years old. Furthermore, most children make frequent errors until after they enter school. Thus, the age of the child is a major consideration in judging the adequacy of articulation. Another major consideration is the characteristics of the child's language community, because children learn speech largely through imitation. For instance, a child who is reared in the Deep South might have speech that sounds peculiar to residents of Long Island, but this does not mean that the child has a speech disorder. Remember that there are differences that are not disorders.

Lack of ability to articulate speech sounds correctly can be caused by biological factors. For example, brain damage or damage to the nerves controlling the muscles that are used in speech may make it difficult or impossible to articulate sounds (Bernthal, Bankson, & Flipsen, Jr., 2017; Cannito, Yorkston, & Beukelman, 1998). Among children with other disabilities, especially intellectual disabilities and neurological disorders such as cerebral palsy, the prevalence of articulation disorders is higher than that in the general population. Abnormalities of the oral structures, such as a cleft palate, can make normal speech difficult or impossible. Relatively minor structural changes, such as loss of teeth, can produce temporary errors. Poor articulation may also result from a hearing loss.

Most schools screen all new pupils for speech and language problems, and in most cases, a child who still makes many articulation errors in the third or fourth grade will be referred for evaluation. Older children and adults sometimes seek help on their own when their speech draws negative attention. The decision to include or not include a child in speech-language therapy depends on several factors, including the child's age, developmental characteristics, and the pathologist's assessment of the likelihood that the child will self-correct the errors and of the social penalties, such as teasing and shyness, the child is experiencing. If the child misarticulates only a few sounds but does so consistently and suffers social embarrassment or rejection as a consequence, an intervention program is usually necessary.

Voice Disorders

People's voices are perceived as having pitch, loudness, and quality. Changes in pitch and loudness are part of the stress patterns of speech. Vocal quality is related not only to production of speech sounds, but also to the nonlinguistic aspects of speech. Voice disorders, though difficult to define precisely, are characteristics of pitch, loudness, and/ or quality that are abusive of the **larynx**; hamper communication; or are perceived as markedly different from what is customary for someone of a given age, sex, and cultural background (Robinson & Crowe, 2001).

Voice disorders can result from a variety of causes and can be grouped into three primary categories including functional disorders, organic disorders, and neurological disorders (Anderson & Shames, 2011). Disorders that are a result of damage to the larynx (i.e., trauma) are considered functional disorders. Physical conditions, including growths in the larynx (e.g., nodules, polyps, or cancerous tissue) that have affected the structure or function of the larynx, are considered organic disorders. Disorders that are a result of nervous system dysfunction are considered neurological disorders.

Misuse or abuse of the voice also can lead to a vocal quality that is temporarily abnormal. High school cheerleaders, for example, frequently develop temporary voice disorders due to the formation of nodules (calluses) on their vocal cords (Campbell, Reich, Klockars, & McHenry, 1988). The same kind of problem can be caused by a child's screaming. Teachers and others who constantly use a very loud voice, whether expressing passionate beliefs, talking over noisy conditions, or speaking in a room with poor acoustics, may also develop voice problems.

Disorders resulting from misuse or abuse of the voice can damage the tissues of the larynx. So can smoking or inhaling substances that irritate the vocal folds. Sometimes a person has psychological problems that lead to a complete loss of voice (**aphonia**) or to severe voice abnormalities.

Voice disorders having to do with **resonance**—vocal quality—may be caused by physical abnormalities of the oral cavity (such as **cleft palate**) or damage to the brain or nerves controlling the oral cavity. Infections of the tonsils, adenoids, or sinuses can also influence how the voice is resonated. Most people who have severe hearing loss typically have problems in achieving a normal or pleasingly resonant voice. Finally, sometimes a person simply has not learned to speak with an appropriately resonant voice. This problem has no biological or deep-seated psychological causes; rather, it appears that the individual has learned faulty habits of positioning the organs of speech.

Teachers need to observe children for common symptoms of voice disorders, such as hoarseness, aphonia, breathiness, odd pitch (voice too high or too low pitched), or an inappropriately loud or soft voice. A teacher who notes possible problems should ask a speech-language pathologist to conduct an evaluation. Teachers should also monitor their own voices for indications of vocal stress.

Fluency Disorders

Normal speech is characterized by some interruptions in speech flow. Especially when a child is learning to talk, we can expect normal **dysfluencies**. These are the hesitations, repetitions, and other interruptions of normal speech flow that are entirely normal parts of learning to use language. All of us occasionally get speech sounds in the wrong order (e.g., saying *revalent* for *relevant*), speak too quickly to be understood, pause at the wrong place in a sentence, use an inappropriate pattern of stress, or become dysfluent—that is, stumble and backtrack, repeating words or phrases, and fill in pauses with *uh* while trying to think of how to finish what we have to say. It is only when the speaker's efforts are so intense or the interruptions in the flow of speech are so frequent or pervasive that they prevent understanding or draw extraordinary attention that they are considered disorders. Besides, listeners have a greater tolerance for some types of dysfluencies than others. Most of us will more readily accept speech-flow disruptions that we perceive as necessary corrections of what the speaker has said or is planning to say than disruptions that appear to reflect the speaker's inability to proceed with the articulation of what he has decided to say (Robinson & Crowe, 2001).

The most frequent type of fluency disorder is stuttering. **Stuttering** is different from normal dysfluency in both the rate and the type of dysfluency. Children who stutter produce dysfluencies at a greater rate than children who do not stutter. The dysfluencies include part-word repetitions ("I wa-wa-want . . ."), sound prolongations ("It is at my hhhhhouse . . ."), and sound blocks ("My name is Mike . . ."). Stuttering can also consist of related secondary behaviors that are intended to avoid or escape the dysfluency, such as gestures, head nods, and eye blinks. It also includes negative feelings about communication on the part of those who stutter.

Stuttering is not a common disorder; about 1% of children and adults are considered stutterers. More boys than girls stutter. Many children quickly outgrow their childhood dysfluencies. These children generally use regular and effortless dysfluencies, appear to be unaware of their hesitancies, and have parents and teachers who are unconcerned about their speech patterns. Those who stutter for more than 1.5 to 2 years appear to be at risk for becoming chronic stutterers (Conture, 2001).

A child who appears to stutter should be evaluated by a speech-language pathologist. Early diagnosis is important to avoid the development of chronic stuttering. Unfortunately, many educators and physicians do not refer potential stutterers for in-depth assessment, because they are aware that dysfluencies are a normal part of speech-language development. Among experts, there is a lack of consensus on the optimal time and method for early identification and intervention (Onslow, Packman, & Payne, 2007). Persistent stuttering that goes untreated can result in a lifelong disorder that affects the ability to communicate, to develop positive feelings about oneself, and to pursue certain educational and employment opportunities that are not available to individuals with fluency disorders (Conture, 2001).

Motor-Speech Disorders

The muscles that make speech possible are under voluntary control. When damage occurs to the areas of the brain that control these muscles or to the nerves leading to the muscles, the ability to speak normally is disturbed. These disorders may involve controlling speech sounds (**dysarthria**) or planning and coordinating speech (**apraxia**). Both dysarthria and apraxia affect the production of speech, slow its rate, and reduce intelligibility (Owens, Evans, & Haas, 2000). Keep in mind, too, that dysarthria and apraxia are not mutually exclusive; that is, an individual can have both problems. Because these disorders are caused by a neurological problem, they are often called *neurogenic disorders of speech*.

By listening to the person's speech and inspecting her speech mechanism, the speech-language pathologist assesses the ability of the person with a motor-speech disorder or neurogenic speech disorder to control breathing, phonation, resonation, and articulatory movements. Medical, surgical, and rehabilitative specialists in the treatment of neurological disorders also must evaluate the person's problem and plan a management strategy. In cases in which the neurological impairment makes the person's speech unintelligible, an AAC system might be required.

MyLab Education
Video Example 10.3

In this video, Dr. Carol Dudding conducts a motor-speech assessment.

DYSARTHRIA Difficulties in speaking may occur because the individual cannot control precisely the muscles governing breathing, the larynx, the throat, the tongue, the jaw, and/or the lips. Depending on the nature of the injury to the brain, perceptual and cognitive functions may also be affected; the individual may have a language disorder in addition to a speech disorder.

Dysarthria is characterized by slow, labored, slurred, and imprecise speech. As a result of brain injury, the person's respiratory support for making speech sounds is affected, and his speech may be characterized by shallow breathing, hoarseness, and reduced loudness. The person might not be able to produce speech sounds precisely because of muscle weakness.

APRAXIA Apraxia is characterized by a disruption of motor planning and programming so that speech is slow, effortful, and inconsistent. A person with this disorder may recognize that she is making errors and try to correct them, but the attempts at correction make it even harder to understand what the person intends to say. Owens and co-workers (2000) provide the following example of the speech of someone with apraxia:

> O-o-on . . . on . . . on cavation, cavation, cacation . . . oh darn . . . vavation, of, you know, to Ca-ca-caciporenia . . . no, Lacifacnia, vafacnia to Lacifacnion . . . On vacation to Va-cafornia, no darn it . . . to Ca-caliborneo . . . not bornia . . . fornia, Bornfifornia . . . no, Balliforneo, Ballifornee, Balifornee, Californee, California. Phew, it was hard to say Cacaforneo. Oh darn. (p. 416)

Developmental apraxia is a disorder of motor planning that emerges as the child develops speech and language skills. Children with this disorder show significant delays in the ability to produce speech sounds and to organize sounds into words for effective communication. **Acquired apraxia** has similar symptoms, but it occurs because of a stroke or other type of brain damage after learning speech. Usually, the person with apraxia knows that she is making errors, wants to correct them, knows what she wants to communicate, but simply cannot do so. Consequently, apraxia is an unusually frustrating disorder for the speaker.

MyLab Education **Self-Check 10.2**

MyLab Education **Application Exercise 10.2:**
Speech and Language Disorders

Watch three videos to observe different speech and language disorders illustrated by Allyson, Diana, and Star. Then, answer the questions that follow.

EDUCATIONAL CONSIDERATIONS

Children with all types of disabilities are increasingly placed in general education classrooms. This means that all teachers must become aware of how they can address language problems in the classroom (Owens, 2014; Throneburg, Calvert, Sturm, Paramboukas, & Paul, 2000). Helping children overcome speech and language disorders is not the responsibility of any single professional. Rather, identification is the joint responsibility of the classroom teacher, the speech-language pathologist, and parents. The teacher can carry out specific suggestions for individual cases. By listening attentively and empathetically when children speak, providing appropriate models of speech and language for children to imitate, and encouraging children to use their communication skills appropriately, the classroom teacher can help not only to improve speech and language, but also to prevent some disorders from developing in the first place. A campaign in the UK, called HELLO, aims to increase awareness of how speech, language, and communication disorders affect a child in school and in life (https://www.youtube.com/watch?v=EZ02NkT9GMY).

Facilitating the Social Use of Language

In considering language development, the primary role of the classroom teacher is to facilitate the social use of language. The fact that a student has a language or speech disorder does not necessarily mean that the teacher or clinician must intensify efforts to teach the student about the form, structure, or content of language. Rather, language must be taught as a way of solving problems by making oneself understood and making sense of what other people say.

The classroom offers many possibilities for language learning. It should be a place in which almost continuous opportunities exist for students and teachers to employ language and obtain feedback in constructive relationships. Language is the basic medium through which most academic and social learning occurs in school. Nevertheless, the language of school, in both classrooms and textbooks, is often a problem for students and teachers. The accompanying Responsive Instruction feature provides a strategy for enhancing one aspect of social language, personal narratives, for students who use AAC.

School language is more formal than the language many children use at home and with playmates. It is structured conversation, in which listeners and speakers or readers and writers must learn to be clear and expressive, to convey and interpret essential information quickly and easily. Without skill in using the language of school, a child is certain to fail academically and virtually certain to be socially unsuccessful as well.

Teachers need the assistance of speech-language specialists in assessing their students' language disabilities and in devising interventions. Part of the assessment and intervention strategy must also include examining the language of the teacher. Problems in classroom discourse involve both how teachers talk to students and how students use language. Learning how to be clear, relevant, and informative and how to hold listeners' attention are problems not only for students with language disorders but also for their teachers. The Focus On . . . Talking with Students feature offers some general guidelines for how teachers should talk with students.

Question-Asking Strategies

One example of the role of the teacher's language in classroom discourse is asking questions. Teachers often ask students too many questions in areas of their identified weaknesses, thereby inadvertently curtailing the students' use of expressive language. For example, a teacher might ask a preschooler who does not know colors to identify colors repeatedly. Or a teacher may overuse yes/no questions (e.g., "Is this blue?" "Are you finished?"), which curtail the child's engagement in extended dialogues or provocative conversations. Unfortunately, teachers might not know how to modify their questions to teach concepts effectively, so their questions merely add to children's confusion.

Teachers can use alternative question-asking strategies to help students think through problems successfully. When students fail to answer higher-order questions because these are beyond their level of information or skill, the teacher should reformulate the problem at a simpler level. After students solve the intermediate steps, the teacher can return to the question that was initially too difficult.

Teachers sometimes do not clearly express their intent in questioning students or fail to explicitly delimit the topic of their questions. For example, a teacher might ask, "What are you going to tell me?" (not being clear about intention) or "How have you been feeling recently?" (asking a question that is too general or not sufficiently focused). Consequently, students become confused. Teachers must learn to clarify the problems under such circumstances. Teachers must also give unambiguous feedback to students' responses to their questions. Too often, teachers do not tell students explicitly that their answers are wrong, for fear of showing nonacceptance. Lack of accurate, explicit feedback, however, prevents students from learning the concepts involved in instruction. Our points here are these:

- The teacher's role is not merely to instruct students about language but also to teach them how to use it. More specifically, the teacher must help students learn how to use language in the context of the classroom.
- The teacher's own use of language is a key factor in helping students learn effectively, especially if students have language disorders.

Teachers need to keep in mind, too, that language disorders can change with a child's development. Just because a child has receptive or expressive language within

RESPONSIVE INSTRUCTION

Meeting the Needs of Students with Communication Disorders

ENHANCING THE PERSONAL NARRATIVES OF STUDENTS WHO USE AAC

What the Research Says

Many students who use augmentative and alternative communication (AAC) experience difficulty in creating personal narratives (Soto, Solomon-Rice, Caputo, 2009). Personal narratives, stories about ideas or events one has experienced or is thinking about, can play an important role in shaping how young children understand the world around them and connect with others (Nelson, 1993). Through personal narratives, children organize and remember events; attach significance to events; share event knowledge with others, thus creating a shared experience; and attach adult values that shape their understanding of events. Children who use AAC can be restricted in their telling of personal narratives due to limitations of the AAC device or support used and by their lack of experience in creating narratives (Soto et al., 2009).

Research Study

Soto and co-workers (2009) sought to examine the effects of teaching personal narrative construction to students who used AAC on the organization and complexity of their narratives. Three elementary-aged students participated in the study. Two of the participants had cerebral palsy and used multimodal communicators (Vantage II™). The other participant had severe verbal apraxia and used a variety of modalities for communication including vocalizations, the use of Signing Exact English (SEE) signs (Gustason & Zawolkow, 1993), a picture communication system, and an 84-location Vantage II™.

For the intervention, three different interventionists worked individually with students for approximately 1 hour twice a week over a 6-month period. Each intervention session consisted of two activities: (a) personal photo description and (b) emotional states description. During each activity, the interventionist showed the student a photo of either a personal event such as a birthday or vacation (for the personal photo activity) or a child displaying an emotional state such as happy, sad, or angry (for the emotional states activity). The interventionist asked the students if they remembered the event or could describe how the pictured child felt. The interventionist then used a variety of strategies to extend and validate the response. These included asking open-ended questions, fill-in-the-blank sentences, binary choices, modeling of strategic vocabulary including new words and wording formats, and visual story mapping. The interventionist wrote the narrative on a large piece of paper visible to the student and asked the student to edit the story as needed.

Research Findings

Soto and colleagues (2009) used a variety of tools to evaluate the narratives generated by the participants. Each narrative was coded in terms of dimensions of discourse (e.g., topic maintenance, event sequencing, explicitness, referencing, conjunctive cohesiveness, and fluency), linguistic complexity (e.g., number of different words and total number of words), number of clauses, number of syntactical features, and story complexity (e.g., identification of characters, emotional states of characters, setting, initiating event, and resolution).

All three participants improved in their overall organization, ability to add descriptive detail, use of linguistic complexity, number of clauses expressed, and ability to create narratives with greater story complexity.

Applying the Research to Teaching

Four features that have been shown to support personal narrative development are:

- Interactive engagement during narrative development that includes the use of open-ended questions, verbal prompts, binary choices, verbal scaffolds, and modeling.
- Use of a visual guide such as a story map and written record of the narrative.
- Strategies to connect emotional state to an event as research has shown that children tend to remember events associated with an emotional experience.
- Repeated opportunities to engage in personal narrative development.

Teachers can incorporate these features into instruction designed to teach and support the development of personal narratives in students with communication disorders.

FOCUS ON

Talking with Students

Suggestions for Talking with Students

- Choose a topic of interest to the student. Comment on the student's thinking, feelings, and experiences, as the student describes them by providing models of other words or phrases.

- After initiating the conversation, let the student take the lead. Show interest in and, if appropriate, excitement about what the student says.

- Try not to ask lots of questions, and when you do ask questions, ask open-ended ones for which explanations are appropriate.

- Use appropriate wait time with your questions; don't demand an immediate response, but give the student enough time to formulate an answer. Be comfortable with some open or empty spaces in the conversation; don't rush.

- Encourage question-asking in return, and give honest and open answers (except, of course, decline politely to answer inappropriate or highly personal questions).

- Keep your voice at an appropriate level, keep your pace moderate, and keep the conversation light and humorous unless the topic of conversation is serious and humor is inappropriate.

- Avoid being judgmental or making snide remarks about the student's language. If the student thinks you are judgmental or if you correct every error, he will stop talking to you. Demonstrate acceptance of the student's language.

- Do not interrupt the student when she is talking, and listen attentively to her ideas; show respect.

- Provide as many opportunities as you can for the student to use language in social situations, and respond appropriately to the student's attempts to use language to accomplish his goals.

---

the normal range at one age doesn't mean that it will be within the same range at a later age. Language intervention can change the nature and course of a child's language abilities, but even with therapy, a child might have persistent language problems.

Teaching Literacy: Reading and Written Expression

Developing literacy is a special problem for many students with speech and language disorders. As noted earlier in this chapter, students with language impairments often have reading deficits in both word-recognition skills and comprehension. It is less common for individuals who have pure speech disorders to have difficulties with reading, but those with language, or language and speech problems are indeed at significant risk for reading disability (Snowling & Hayiou-Thomas, 2006). In particular, students who have poor phonological awareness are typically unable to learn how to decode without intervention. **Decoding** refers to the ability to transfer the written words into speech. For those students with language impairments who learn how to decode, many will still have difficulty with reading comprehension. Thus, it is critical for the classroom teacher, speech-language pathologist, and special education teacher to work together to provide explicit and systematic intervention in reading for children with language impairments.

In addition to reading problems, students with language impairment also have difficulty with written expression. As students progress through the grades, written language takes on increasing importance. Students are expected to read increasingly complex and difficult material and understand its meaning. In addition, they are expected to express themselves more clearly in writing. The interactions teachers have with students about their writing—the questions they ask to help students understand how to write for their readers—are critical to overcoming disabilities in written language (MacArthur, Pilippakos, Graham, & Harris, 2012).

Finally, intervention in language disorders employs many of the same strategies used in intervention in learning disabilities. Metacognitive training, strategy training, and other approaches discussed in Chapter 6 are typically appropriate for use with students who have language disorders (see also Hallahan, Lloyd, Kauffman, Weiss, & Martinez, 2005; Mercer & Pullen, 2009).

ASSESSMENT OF PROGRESS

A primary purpose of language assessment is to inform instruction. An intervention plan based on assessment must consider the content, form, social context, and use of language. That is, it must consider the following:

- What the child talks about and should be taught to talk about
- How the child talks about things and how the child could be taught to speak of those things more intelligibly
- How the child functions in the context of the child's linguistic community
- How the child uses language and how the child's language use could be made to serve the purposes of communication and socialization more effectively

After developing the intervention plan, educators implement an ongoing assessment plan to monitor progress and identify outcome measures and to ensure that the student is meeting programmatic goals. Methods for monitoring the progress of students with language impairments may use a system of dynamic assessment that involves a cycle of teaching, followed by testing, and then reteaching as necessary (Ehren & Nelson, 2005). Teachers administer **dynamic assessments** during the learning process, and the speech-language pathologist (SLP) determines how the student performs with and without support (Anderson & Shames, 2011). This information guides intervention as the speech-language pathologist establishes what the student can do and where the student needs further intervention. Teachers can use dynamic assessments in the context of a response-to-intervention (RTI) program by speech-language pathologists (Ehren & Nelson, 2005).

Teachers can also use **curriculum-based language and communication assessment (CBLA)** to monitor students' progress. CBLA differs from curriculum-based measurement (CBM) discussed in Chapter 6 in that it measures a student's speech, language, and communication skills required to learn the school curriculum (Staskowski & Nelson, 2007). CBLA generally measures the communication skills required to participate in the school curriculum and the strategies the student employs to conduct curricular tasks. Based on the observations related to these two areas, the speech-language pathologist then determines what skills the student needs to acquire and how to modify the task to ensure success.

As in other areas of education, the current trend requires that service providers demonstrate the value of communication intervention in terms of student outcomes. Currently, speech-language pathologists may rely on the National Outcomes Measurement System (NOMS) to measure the outcomes of students in communication interventions. In an effort to assist speech-language pathologists in documenting treatment outcomes, the American Speech Language Hearing Association formed the National Center for Treatment Effectiveness in Communication in the early 1990s (Mullen & Schooling, 2010). A result of these efforts is the NOMS, an online database assessment system. The speech-language pathologist employs a series of scales that measure functional communication, and then evaluates these data, along with demographic and diagnostic data, to generate a report of outcomes based on the individual's intervention plan.

EARLY INTERVENTION

Early intervention is critically important for two primary reasons:

1. The older the child is when intervention is begun, the smaller the chance that he or she will acquire effective language skills (other things being equal).
2. Without having functional language, the child cannot become a truly social being (Warren & Abbaduto, 1992). Of all the skills in which a child may be lagging, language—communication—is the most important, as it is the foundation of academic and social learning.

Early Development and Early Intervention

The study of children's early development has shown that the first several years of life are a truly critical period for language learning. Educators have known for a long time that much of children's language, literacy, and social development depends on the nature and quantity of the language interactions they have with parents or other caregivers. In the homes of children who come to school ready to learn, the language interactions between parents and children have typically been frequent, focused on encouragement and affirmation of the children's behavior, emphasized the symbolic nature of language, provided gentle guidance in exploring things and relationships, and demonstrated the responsiveness of adults to children. By contrast, children who enter school at a disadvantage tend to have experienced much lower rates of language interaction; to have heard primarily negative, discouraging feedback on their behavior; and to have heard language that is harsh, literal, and emotionally detached.

In a now classic study, Hart and Risley (1995) compared the language experiences of children of professional parents, working-class parents, and parents on welfare. The contrasts in language experiences and the effects observed in children's academic achievement and behavior are stark, but the differences are unrelated to income or ethnicity. Rather, the differences are related to how and how much the parents talked to their children. As summed up by the authors:

> Our data showed that the magnitude of children's accomplishments depends less on the material and educational advantages available in the home and more on the amount of experience children accumulate with parenting that provides language diversity, affirmative feedback, symbolic emphasis, gentle guidance, and responsiveness. By the time children are 3 years old, even intensive intervention cannot make up for the differences in the amount of such experience children have received from their parents. If children could be given better parenting, intervention might be unnecessary. (p. 210)

Thus, it appears that the key to preventing many disabilities related to language development is to help parents improve how they relate to their children when they are infants and toddlers. Nevertheless, for many young children, intervention in the preschool and primary grades will be necessary. But such intervention must be guided by understanding of children's families, particularly the primary caretaker's (usually the mother's) views of language development (Hammer & Weiss, 2000). Preschoolers who require intervention for a speech or language disorder occasionally have multiple disabilities that are sometimes severe or profound.

Language is closely tied to cognitive development, so impairment of general intellectual ability is likely to have a negative influence on language development. Conversely, lack of language can hamper cognitive development. Because speech is dependent on neurological and motor development, any neurological or motor problem might impair a child's ability to speak. Normal social development in the preschool years also depends on the emergence of language, so a child with language impairment is at a disadvantage in social learning. The preschool child's language therefore is seldom the only target of intervention.

MyLab Education
Video Example 10.4

In this video, the teacher/therapist is using a child-centered approach.

Early Intervention in Delayed Language Development

Children with language disorders may follow the same sequence of development as most children but achieve each skill or milestone at a later-than-average age. Some children with language disorders reach final levels of development that are significantly below those of their peers who don't have disabilities. Still other children may be generally delayed in language development but show great discrepancies in the rate at which they acquire certain features of language.

Some children develop language late but will eventually develop age-appropriate speech and language (Vinson, 2007). Yet many children whose language development is delayed show a developmental lag that they won't outgrow (Owens, 2014). They are frequently diagnosed as having intellectual disabilities or another developmental disability. Sometimes these children come from environments where they have been deprived of many experiences, including the language stimulation from adults that is required for normal language development, or they have been severely abused or neglected. Regardless of the reasons for a child's delayed language, however, it's important to understand the nature of the delay and to intervene to give him or her the optimal chance of learning to use language effectively.

Some children 3 years of age or older show no signs that they understand language and do not use language spontaneously. They might make noises, but they use them to communicate in ways that may characterize the communication of infants and toddlers before they have learned speech. In other words, they may use **prelinguistic communication**. For example, they may use gestures or vocal noises to request objects or actions from others, to protest, to request a social routine (e.g., reading), or to greet someone.

When assessing and planning intervention for children with delayed language, it is important to consider what language and nonlanguage behaviors they imitate, what they comprehend, what communication skills they use spontaneously, and what part communication plays in their lives. It's also important, particularly with young children, to provide intervention in the contexts in which children use language for normal social interaction. For example, parents or teachers may use **milieu teaching**, a strategy to teach functional language skills in the natural environment. In this approach, teaching is built around the child's interests. When the child requests some action, object, or activity from the adult, the adult prompts the child's language and gives access to what is requested contingent on an attempt to communicate. Milieu teaching is a naturalistic approach, in that it encourages designing interventions that are similar to the ordinary conversational interactions of parents and children. Prelinguistic communication may be a good indication of a child's later ability to use language (Calandrella & Wilcox, 2000). The effectiveness of a milieu teaching approach may depend, at least to some extent, on mothers' responsiveness to their children's prelinguistic communication (Yoder & Warren, 2001).

MyLab Education
Video Example 10.5

In this video, the therapist interacts with a young child to obtain a speech sample. Consider what the therapist is able to learn about the child's language and how this knowledge will be helpful in planning intervention.

Involvement of Families

Researchers have become increasingly aware that language development has its beginning in the earliest mother–child interactions. Concern for the child's development of the ability to communicate can't be separated from concern for development in other areas. Therefore, speech-language pathologists are a vital part of the multidisciplinary team that evaluates an infant or young child with disabilities and develops an individualized family service plan (IFSP; see Chapters 2 and 4). Early intervention programs involve extending the role of the parent. This means a lot of simple play with accompanying verbalizations. It means talking to the child about objects and activities in the way most mothers talk to their babies. But it also means choosing objects, activities, words, and consequences for the child's vocalizations with great care to enhance the likelihood that the child will learn functional language (Fey, Catts, & Larrivee, 1995).

MyLab Education
Video Example 10.6

In this video, the teacher/ therapist is using a more teacher/therapist-directed approach.

Early childhood specialists now realize that prelinguistic intervention is critical for language development—that is, intervention should begin before the child's language emerges. The foundations for language are laid in the first few months of life through stimulating experiences with parents and other caretakers (Koury, 2007). In the early years of implementing IFSPs, educators emphasized assessing families' strengths and needs and training parents how to teach and manage their children. More recently, professionals have come to understand that assessing families in the belief that professionals know best is often misguided. Parents can indeed be helped by professionals to play an important role in their children's language development. But the emphasis today is on working with parents as knowledgeable and competent partners whose preferences and decisions are respected (Hammer & Weiss, 2000; see also discussion in Chapter 4).

Intervention in early childhood is likely to be based on assessment of the child's behavior related to the content, form, and especially the use of language in social interaction. For the child who has not yet learned language, assessment and intervention will focus on imitation, ritualized and make-believe play, play with objects, and functional use of objects. At the earliest stages in which the content and form of language are interactive, it is important to evaluate the extent to which the child looks at or picks up an object when it is referred to, does something with an object when directed by an adult, and uses sounds to request or refuse things and call attention to objects. When the child's use of language is considered, the earliest objectives involve the child's looking at the adult during interactions; taking turns in and trying to prolong pleasurable activities and games; following the gaze of an adult; directing the behavior of adults; and persisting in or modifying gestures, sounds, or words when an adult does not respond. In the preschool, teaching discourse (conversation skills) is a critical focus of language intervention. In particular, preschool teachers emphasize teaching children to use the discourse that is essential for success in school. Children must learn, for example, to report their experiences in detail and to explain why things happen, not just add to their vocabularies. They must learn not only word forms and meanings but also how to take turns in conversations and maintain the topic of a conversation or change it in an appropriate way. Preschool programs in which such language teaching is the focus may include teachers' daily individualized conversations with children, daily reading to individual children or small groups, and frequent classroom discussions.

Current trends are directed toward providing speech and language interventions in the typical environments of young children. This means that classroom teachers and speech-language pathologists must develop a close working relationship. The speech-language pathologist might work directly with children in the classroom and advise the teacher about the intervention that he can carry out as part of the regular classroom activities. Alternatively, the speech-language pathologist might work with the teacher directly to help her incorporate effective instructional practices for these students. The child's peers may also be involved in intervention strategies. Because language is essentially a social activity, its facilitation requires involvement of others in the child's social environment—peers as well as adults (Audet & Tankersley, 1999; Fey et al., 1995; Prizant, 1999).

Normally developing peers have been taught to assist in the language development of children with disabilities by doing the following during playtimes: establish eye contact; describe their own or others' play; and repeat, expand, or request clarification of what the child with disabilities says. Peer tutors can help in developing the speech and language of their classmates who may use different dialects (McGregor, 2000). Another intervention strategy involving peers is sociodramatic play. Children are taught in groups of three, including a child with disabilities, to act out social roles such as those people might take in various settings (e.g., a restaurant or shoe store). The training includes scripts that specify what each child is to do and say, which the children can modify in creative ways.

MyLab Education Self-Check 10.3

MyLab Education Application Exercise 10.3:
Educational Considerations

This exercise asks you to watch three short video clips about students with various communication disorders, and then apply some of the information you've learned in this chapter.

TRANSITION TO ADULTHOOD

In the past, adolescents and adults in speech and language intervention programs generally fell into three categories: (1) the self-referred, (2) those with other health problems, and (3) those with severe disabilities. Adolescents or adults might refer themselves to speech-language pathologists because their phonology, voice, or stuttering is causing them social embarrassment and/or interfering with occupational pursuits. These are generally people with long-standing problems who are highly motivated to change their speech and obtain relief from the social penalties their differences impose.

Adolescents and adults with other health problems might have experienced damage to speech or language capacities as a result of disease or injury, or they might have lost part of their speech mechanism through injury or surgical removal. Treatment of these individuals always demands an interdisciplinary effort. In some cases of progressive disease, severe neurological damage, or loss of tissues of the speech mechanism, the outlook for functional speech is not good. However, surgical procedures, medication, and prosthetic devices are making it possible for more people to speak normally. Loss of ability to use language is typically more disabling than loss of the ability to speak. Traumatic brain injury may leave the individual with a seriously diminished capacity for self-awareness, goal setting, planning, self-directing or initiating actions, inhibiting impulses, monitoring or evaluating one's own performance, or problem solving. Recovering these vital language-based skills is a critical aspect of transition of the adolescent or young adult from hospital to school and from school to independent living (Klein & Moses, 1999).

Individuals with severe disabilities might need the services of speech-language pathologists to help them achieve more intelligible speech. They might also need to be taught an alternative to oral language or given a system of augmented communication. One of the major problems in working with adolescents and adults who have severe disabilities is setting realistic goals for speech and language learning. Teaching simple, functional language—such as social greetings, naming objects, and making simple requests—may be realistic goals for some adolescents and adults.

A major concern of transition programming is ensuring that the training and support provided during the school years are carried over into adult life. To be successful, the transition must include speech-language services that are part of the natural environment. That is, the services must be community based and integrated into vocational, domestic, recreational, consumer, and mobility training activities. Speech-language interventions for adolescents and young adults with severe disabilities must emphasize functional communication—understanding and making oneself understood in the social circumstances that are most likely to be encountered in everyday life (Justice, 2006). Developing appropriate conversation skills (e.g., establishing eye contact, using greetings, taking turns, and identifying and staying on the topic), reading, writing, following instructions related to recreational activities, using public transportation, and performing a job are examples of the kinds of functional speech-language activities that may be emphasized.

Today, educators are placing much more emphasis on the language disorders of adolescents and young adults who do not fit into other typical categories of disabilities. Many of these individuals were formerly seen as having primarily academic and social problems that were not language related. But now it is understood that underlying many or most of the school and social difficulties of these adolescents and adults are basic disorders of language, which are a continuation of difficulties experienced earlier in their development.

Some adolescents and adults with language disorders are excellent candidates for strategy training, which teaches them how to select, store, retrieve, and process information (see Hallahan et al., 2005; see also Chapter 6). Others, however, don't have the required reading skills, symbolic abilities, or intelligence to benefit from the usual training in cognitive strategies. Whatever techniques are chosen for adolescents and older students, the teacher should be aware of the principles that apply to intervention with these individuals.

MyLab Education Self-Check 10.4

MyLab Education Application Exercise 10.4:
David's Transition from High School

Read a case about David, a high school junior preparing for transition to post-secondary education, and respond to the questions that follow.

▼ chapter ten SUMMARY

How are communication disorders defined?

- Communication involves sharing information between two individuals or among more than two individuals.
- Communicative functions include requesting, rejecting, commenting, arguing, and reasoning, among others.
- Communication disorders may involve language or speech or both, and they impair communicative functions.
- Language is sending and receiving ideas—expression and reception—through an arbitrary system of symbols used according to rules.
- Speech is the neuromuscular activity of forming and sequencing the sounds of oral language.

What is the prevalence of communication disorders?

- Reasonable estimates are that about 8% to 9% of preschool children and about 5% of students in elementary and secondary grades have speech disorders.
- Probably about 2% to 3% of preschoolers and about 1% of the school-age population have language disorders.

What is the difference between communicative differences and disorders?

- Differences include dialects, regional differences, language of ethnic minority groups, and nondominant languages.
- An individual with a difference that is not a disorder is an effective communicator in her language community, whereas someone with a disorder has impaired communication in all language environments.

What are the major disorders of language?

- There are many different theories of language development and the disorders of language.
- Language disorders may be primary (no known cause) or secondary (attributable to another condition or disability).
- Primary language disorders include specific language impairment (SLI), early expressive language delay (EELD), and language-based reading impairment.
- Secondary language disorders include those related to emotional or behavioral disorders or any other disability, such as intellectual disabilities or autism spectrum disorder.

What are the major disorders of speech?

- Speech disorders are a heterogeneous group of problems related to the production of oral language, including the following:
  - *Phonological disorders*—problems in understanding the sound system of language
  - *Articulation disorders*—problems in producing correct speech sounds
  - *Voice disorders*—problems in producing appropriate pitch, loudness, or quality of voice

- *Fluency disorders*—problems in maintaining speech flow
- *Motor-speech*—problems in speaking due to neuromotor damage, including the following:
  - *Dysarthria*—problems in controlling the production of speech sounds
  - *Apraxia*—problems in planning and coordinating speech

Monkey Business/Vetta/Getty Images

What are the main educational considerations for communication disorders?

- The classroom teacher needs to work with others in three main areas:
  - Facilitating the social uses of language
  - Question asking
  - Teaching literacy: Reading and written language

What are the major features of assessment of progress for students with communication disorders?

- A primary purpose of language assessment is to inform instruction.
- Assessment for intervention requires attention to the following:
  - What the child talks about and should be taught to talk about
  - How the child talks about things and how he could be taught to speak of those things more intelligibly
  - How the child functions in the context of his linguistic community
  - How the child uses language and how her use of it could be made to serve the purposes of communication and socialization more effectively
- Progress-monitoring assessments are dynamic and should follow a cycle of teaching, testing, and reteaching.
- Progress-monitoring assessments include curriculum-based language assessment (CBLA).
- Assessment of student outcomes should be implemented to confirm that learning has occurred.

What are the major aspects of early intervention for communication disorders?

- Early intervention is based on early language development.
- Early intervention usually involves working with individuals who have delayed language.
- Early intervention requires working with families.

What do educators emphasize in transition for students with communication disorders?

- Transition involves helping students use the language demanded for successful employment.

▼ INTERNET RESOURCES

Pertinent Organizations

- The website of the American Speech–Language–Hearing Association at http://www.asha.org is an important site to visit for extensive information about communication disorders.

- For more information about cleft lip, cleft palate, and other craniofacial deformities and effects on speech, see SMILES at http://www.cleft.org/.

- The Stuttering Foundation of America (http://www.stuttersfa.org/) and the National Center for Stuttering (http://www.stuttering.com/) offer more information about stuttering.

- Talk With Me Baby, sponsored by the Atlanta United Way and with support from the Barbara Bush Foundation, is an initiative to encourage parents to talk with their babies. It focuses on all hospital staff modeling verbal interaction with the newborn. http://www.talkwithmebaby.org/

chapter eleven

LEARNERS WHO ARE DEAF OR HARD OF HEARING

Sladic/Shutterstock

► LEARNING OUTCOMES

Learning Outcome 11.1: Understand the definition, classification, and prevalence of individuals who are deaf or hard of hearing.

Learning Outcome 11.2: Learn about the anatomical and physiological characteristics of the ear, the causes of hearing impairments, and how hearing impairments are identified.

Learning Outcome 11.3: Understand some psychological and behavioral characteristics of people with hearing impairments.

Learning Outcome 11.4: Learn about some educational considerations for people with hearing impairments and how professionals assess progress to help plan educational strategies.

Learning Outcome 11.5: Learn about issues that should be considered with respect to early intervention and transition to adulthood for individuals with hearing impairments.

MISCONCEPTIONS ABOUT Learners Who Are Deaf or Hard of Hearing

MYTH People who are deaf are unable to hear anything.

FACT Most people who are deaf have some residual hearing.

MYTH Deafness is not as severe a disability as blindness.

FACT Although it's impossible to predict the exact consequences of a disability on a person's functioning, in general, deafness poses more difficulties in adjustment than does blindness. This is largely due to the effects hearing loss can have on the ability to understand and speak oral language.

MYTH It's unhealthy for people who are deaf to socialize almost exclusively with others who are deaf.

FACT Many authorities now recognize that the phenomenon of a Deaf culture is natural and should be encouraged. In fact, some are worried that too much mainstreaming will diminish the influence of the Deaf culture.

MYTH In learning to understand what is being said to them, people with a hearing impairment concentrate on reading lips.

FACT *Lipreading* refers only to visual cues arising from movement of the lips. Some people who have a hearing impairment not only read lips but also take advantage of a number of other visual cues, such as facial expressions and movements of the jaw and tongue. They are engaging in what is referred to as *speechreading*.

MYTH Speechreading is relatively easy to learn and is used by the majority of people with a hearing impairment.

FACT Speechreading is extremely difficult to learn, and very few people who have a hearing impairment actually become proficient speechreaders.

MYTH American Sign Language (ASL) is a loosely structured group of gestures.

FACT ASL is a true language in its own right, with its own set of grammatical rules.

MYTH People within the Deaf community are in favor of mainstreaming students who are deaf into general education classes.

FACT Some within the Deaf community have voiced the opinion that general education classes are not appropriate for many students who are deaf. They point to the need for a critical mass of students who are deaf in order to have effective educational programs for these individuals. They see separate placements as a way of fostering the Deaf culture.

MYTH Families in which both the child and the parents are deaf are at a distinct disadvantage compared to families in which the parents are hearing.

FACT Research has demonstrated that children who are deaf who have parents who also are deaf fare better in a number of academic and social areas. Authorities point to the parents' ability to communicate with their children in ASL as a major reason for this advantage.

GUIDING QUESTIONS

- How do professionals define and classify individuals who are deaf or hard of hearing?
- What is the prevalence of hearing impairment?
- What are some basic anatomical and physiological characteristics of the ear?
- How is hearing impairment identified?
- What causes hearing impairments?
- What are some psychological and behavioral characteristics of learners with hearing impairments?

- What are some educational considerations for learners with hearing impairments?
- How do professionals assess the progress of students with hearing impairments?
- What are some important considerations with respect to early intervention for learners with hearing impairments?
- What are some important considerations with respect to transition to adulthood for learners with hearing impairments?

To be deaf, or even hard of hearing, often places a person in a difficult place somewhere between the world of the hearing and the world of the Deaf. A hearing impairment can put a person at risk for isolation—an isolation caused primarily by communication problems. As we see in this chapter, even if the hearing impairment isn't severe enough for a child to be classified as "deaf," but rather as "hard of hearing," the child with a hearing impairment is at a distinct disadvantage in virtually all aspects of English language development. The importance of the English language in U.S. society, particularly in school-related activities, is obvious. Many of the problems that people with hearing impairment have in school are due primarily to their difficulties in English. We explore this issue in some depth in this chapter.

A related controversy brought up by Martha Sheridan (2001) is the debate about whether the child who is deaf should be educated to communicate orally or through manual sign language. Sheridan is typical of the approximately 90% of those who are deaf, in that both her parents are hearing (Mitchell & Karchmer, 2004; National Institute on Deafness and Other Communication Disorders [NIDCD], 2017) and had chosen not to learn sign language. Also common, unfortunately, is the difficulty that Sheridan had learning to speechread, or to use visual information (including lip movements) from a number of sources, to understand what is being said.

Again, like others in the same situation, Sheridan eventually went on to immerse herself in the Deaf community. She found her identity as a Deaf person through her experiences at Gallaudet University, the primary postsecondary institution for students with hearing impairment:

> Gallaudet was a major gateway for me. It was the pot of gold at the end of my search for self, and it represented the beginning of the rest of my life. It was at Gallaudet that I discovered what it means to be deaf. . . . Here, and with sign language, my love for learning blossomed. (Sheridan, 2001, pp. 7–8)

But not all people who are deaf elect to join the Deaf community. Some become fluent enough in spoken English to function in mainstream society. Others are able to straddle both the world of the hearing and the Deaf. But regardless of the outcome, virtually all people who are deaf, as well as their parents, struggle with critical choices about oral versus manual modes of communication and cultural identity. With respect to the latter, in fact, many members of the Deaf community consider themselves part of a cultural minority rather than as having a disability.

All of these thorny issues make deafness one of the most challenging fields of study in all of special education. As you would surmise from our discussion of other special education areas, this challenge is evident in attempts to arrive at a definition of hearing impairment.

DEFINITION AND CLASSIFICATION

By far the most common way of classifying hearing impairment is the distinction between *deaf* and *hard of hearing*. Although it's common to think that being deaf means not being able to hear anything and that being hard of hearing means being able to hear a little bit, this is generally not true. Most people who are deaf have some residual hearing. Complicating things is the fact that professionals in different fields define the two categories differently. The extreme points of view are represented by those with a physiological orientation versus those with an educational orientation.

Those who maintain a strictly physiological viewpoint are interested primarily in the measurable degree of hearing impairment. Children who can't hear sounds at or above a certain intensity (loudness) level are classified as deaf; others with a hearing impairment are considered hard of hearing. Hearing sensitivity is measured in **decibels** (units of relative loudness of sounds). Zero decibels (0 dB) designates the point at which the average person with normal hearing can detect the faintest sound. Each succeeding number of decibels that a person cannot detect indicates a certain degree of hearing impairment. Those who maintain a physiological viewpoint generally consider people with hearing impairments of about 90 dB or greater to be deaf and people with impairments at lower decibel levels to be hard of hearing. For comparison purposes, 90 dB is the approximate loudness of a lawn mower (American Academy of Otolaryngology—Head and Neck Surgery, 2007).

People with an educational viewpoint are concerned with how much the hearing impairment is likely to affect the child's ability to speak and develop language. Because of the close causal link between hearing impairment and delay in language development, these professionals categorize primarily on the basis of spoken language abilities. *Hearing impairment* is a broad term that covers individuals with impairments ranging from mild to profound; it includes those who are deaf or hard of hearing. Following are commonly accepted, educationally oriented definitions for *deaf* and *hard of hearing*:

- A deaf person is one whose hearing disability precludes successful processing of linguistic information through audition, with or without a hearing aid.
- A person who is hard of hearing generally has residual hearing sufficient to enable successful processing of linguistic information through audition, with the assistance of a hearing aid. (Brill, MacNeil, & Newman, 1986, p. 67)

Educators are extremely concerned about the age of onset of hearing impairment. Again, the close relationship between hearing impairment and language delay is the key. The earlier the hearing impairment occurs in life, the more difficulty the child will have developing the language of the hearing society (e.g., English). For this reason, professionals frequently use the terms **congenitally deaf** (those who are born deaf) and **adventitiously deaf** (those who acquire deafness at some time after birth).

Two other frequently used terms are even more specific in pinpointing language acquisition as critical: **Prelingual deafness** refers to deafness that occurs at birth or early in life before speech and language develop. **Postlingual deafness** is deafness that occurs after the development of speech and language. Experts differ about the dividing point between prelingual and postlingual deafness. Some believe that it should be at about 18 months; others think it should be lower, at about 12 months or even 6 months (Meadow-Orlans, 1987).

Some professionals find it useful to classify according to hearing threshold levels, such as mild (26 to 40 dB), moderate (41 to 55 dB), moderate-severe (56 to 70 dB), severe (71 to 90 dB), and profound (91 dB and above) (Andrews, Leigh, & Weiner, 2004). These levels of loss of hearing sensitivity cut across the broad classifications of deaf and hard of hearing, which stress the degree to which speech and language are affected rather than being directly dependent on hearing sensitivity.

Deafness: Disability or Cultural Difference?

In considering issues of definition, it's important to point out the growing sentiment among people who are deaf that deafness should not even be considered a disability (Padden & Humphries, 2005). For the vast majority of society, it seems fairly obvious that deafness is a disability. However, it is far from obvious to many people who are deaf, who argue that instead of being considered as having a disability, people who are deaf should be viewed as a cultural minority with a language of their own: sign language (Ladd, 2003; Lane, 2002; Padden & Humphries, 1988).

As Harlan Lane puts it:

> What is the source of the belief that being a Deaf person entails an inherent biological limitation? Why is deaf associated with loss rather than difference or gain (different language, different culture, etc.)? I submit that it is because the society that has elaborated the concept of deaf is largely hearing and conceptualizes deaf as a loss of hearing. Indeed, the difference in hearing of a person born Deaf and one born hearing is called "hearing loss," although the Deaf person didn't lose anything. (Lane, 2002, p. 366)

Note that Lane (2002) at times uses the term *Deaf* with a capital *D* and at other times does not. Although some variance occurs, those who view deafness as a cultural difference rather than a disability use the lowerecase *deaf* to refer to the sensory aspect of deafness, i.e., measures of sensory acuteness, whereas the uppercase, *Deaf*, is used to refer to the community of people who are deaf—the Deaf culture.

Knowing that some within the Deaf community do not believe that deafness is a disability presents an interesting and challenging problem for educators and other professionals. Should their wishes be honored? Special educators, in particular, are trained to help remediate differences and to try to make people with such differences as "normal" as possible. Would it be professionally irresponsible not to find students who are deaf and who are eligible for special education services and then provide those services to them?

Later in the chapter, we discuss more thoroughly the nature and purpose of the Deaf culture. For now, it's enough to be aware of the challenges that have been raised to the very notion of considering deafness a disability.

MyLab Education
Video Example 11.1

Watch as Belisa tells her story of having a moderate to severe hearing impairment. You will hear more from Belisa as you read through this chapter.

Some authorities object to adhering too strictly to any of the various classification systems. Because these definitions deal with events difficult to measure, they're not precise. Therefore, it is best not to form any hard-and-fast opinions about an individual's ability to hear and speak solely on the basis of a classification of his hearing disability.

PREVALENCE

Estimates of the number of children with hearing impairment vary considerably, due to such factors as differences in definition, populations studied, and accuracy of testing. The U.S. Department of Education's statistics indicate that the public schools identify about 0.10% of the population from 6 to 21 years of age as deaf or hard of hearing (U.S. Department of Education, Office of Special Education and Rehabilitative Services, Office of Special Education Programs, 2016). Although the Department of Education doesn't report separate figures for the categories of deaf versus hard of hearing, strong evidence indicates that students who are hard of hearing are far more prevalent than those who are deaf (Mehra, Eavey, & Keamy, 2009). Furthermore, some authorities believe that many children who are hard of hearing and could benefit from special education are not being served.

Hearing impairment is more prevalent in ethnically diverse populations and in those who are living in poverty (Andrews, Shaw, & Lomas, 2011). Furthermore, another important statistic is that of those children who have hearing impairment, over 30% come from Spanish-speaking homes (Gallaudet Research Institute, 2011). In addition, relatively large numbers of other non-English-speaking immigrants are deaf. The relatively high numbers of students who are deaf and come from non-English-speaking families creates significant challenges for the schools. Deafness by itself makes spoken language acquisition in the native language very difficult, let alone deafness plus attempting to learn a second language.

ANATOMY AND PHYSIOLOGY OF THE EAR

The ear is one of the most complex organs of the body. The many elements that make up the hearing mechanism are divided into three major sections: the outer, middle, and inner ear. The outer ear is the least complex and least important for hearing; the inner ear is the most complex and most important for hearing. Figure 11.1 shows these major parts of the ear.

The Outer Ear

The outer ear consists of the auricle and the external auditory canal. The canal ends with the **tympanic membrane (eardrum)**, which is the boundary between the outer and middle ears. The **auricle** is the part of the ear that protrudes from the side of the head. The part that the outer ear plays in the transmission of sound is relatively minor. Sound is collected by the auricle and is funneled through the external auditory canal to the eardrum, which vibrates, sending the sound waves to the middle ear.

FIGURE 11.1

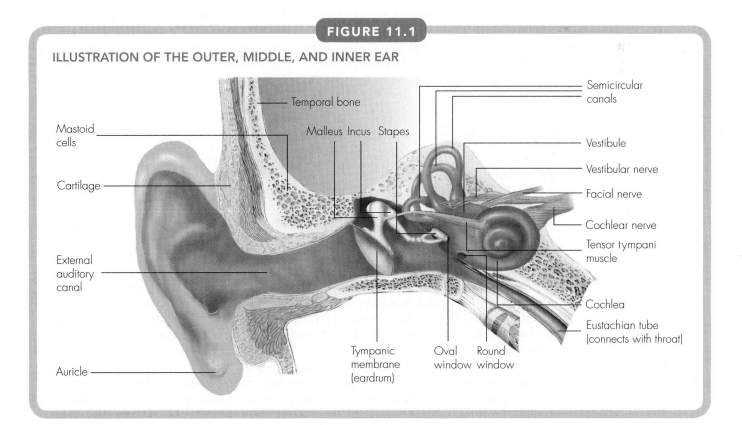

ILLUSTRATION OF THE OUTER, MIDDLE, AND INNER EAR

The Middle Ear

The middle ear comprises the eardrum and three very tiny bones (**ossicles**) called the **malleus** (hammer), **incus** (anvil), and **stapes** (stirrup), which are contained within an air-filled space. The chain of the malleus, incus, and stapes conducts the vibrations of the eardrum along to the **oval window**, which is the link between the middle and inner ears. The ossicles function to create an efficient transfer of energy from the air-filled cavity of the middle ear to the fluid-filled inner ear.

The Inner Ear

About the size of a pea, the inner ear is an intricate mechanism of thousands of moving parts. Because it looks like a maze of passageways and is highly complex, this part of the ear is often called a *labyrinth*. The inner ear is divided into two sections according to function: the vestibular mechanism and the cochlea. These sections, however, do not function totally independently of each other.

The **vestibular mechanism**, located in the upper portion of the inner ear, is responsible for the sense of balance. It's extremely sensitive to such things as acceleration, head movement, and head position. Information about movement is fed to the brain through the vestibular nerve.

By far the most important organ for hearing is the **cochlea**. Lying below the vestibular mechanism, this snail-shaped organ contains the parts necessary to convert the mechanical action of the middle ear into an electrical signal in the inner ear that is transmitted to the brain. In the normally functioning ear, sound causes the malleus, incus, and stapes of the middle ear to move. When the stapes moves, it pushes the oval window in and out, causing the fluid in the cochlea of the inner ear to flow. The movement of the fluid in turn causes a complex chain of events in the cochlea, ultimately resulting in excitation of the cochlear nerve. With stimulation of the cochlear nerve, an electrical impulse is sent to the brain, and sound is heard.

MyLab Education
Video Example 11.2
This video shows how the ear works. http://www.youtube.com/watch?v=MlKvReMGu5Q&feature=fvwrel.

IDENTIFICATION OF HEARING IMPAIRMENT

There are three general types of hearing tests: screening tests, pure-tone audiometry, and speech audiometry. Depending on the characteristics of the examinee and the use to which the results will be put, the audiologist may choose to give any number of tests from any one or a combination of these four categories.

Screening Tests

Screening tests are available for infants and for school-age children. As a result of an initiative by the federal government, about 95% of all newborns are screened for hearing (Lomas et al., 2017). Ideally, a 1-3-6 rule is followed; babies are screened at the hospital by 1 month, with those who show signs of hearing loss followed up by 3 months and entering a family intervention program by 6 months. Unfortunately, many who are identified at 1 month slip through the cracks and aren't followed up or for whatever reason are not identified until they enter school (Northern & Downs, 2014).

Some of the screening tests involve computer technology to measure **otoacoustic emissions**. The cochlea not only receives sounds but also emits low-intensity sound when stimulated by auditory stimuli. These sounds emitted by the cochlea are known as *otoacoustic emissions*, and they provide a measure of how well the cochlea is functioning.

Many schools have routine screening programs in the early elementary grades. These tests, especially those that are group rather than individually administered, are less accurate than tests done in an **audiologist**'s office. Children detected through screening as having possible problems are referred for more extensive evaluation.

Pure-Tone Audiometry

Pure-tone audiometry is designed to establish the individual's threshold for hearing at a variety of different frequencies. Frequency, measured in **hertz (Hz)** units, has to do with the number of vibrations per unit of time of a sound wave; the pitch is higher with more vibrations, lower with fewer. A person's threshold for hearing is simply the level at which she can first detect a sound; it refers to how intense a sound must be before the person detects it. As mentioned earlier, hearing sensitivity, or intensity, is measured in decibels.

Pure-tone audiometers present tones of varying intensities, or decibel levels, at varying frequencies, or pitch (hertz). Audiologists are usually concerned with measuring sensitivity to sounds ranging from 0 to about 110 dB. A person with average-normal hearing can barely hear sounds at a sound-pressure level of 0 dB. The zero-decibel level is frequently called *the zero hearing-threshold level,* or **audiometric zero**. Because the decibel scale is based on ratios, each increment of 10 dB is a tenfold increase in intensity. This means that 20 dB is 10 times more intense than 10 dB, and 30 dB is 100 times more intense than 10 dB. Whereas a leaf fluttering in the wind registers about 0 dB, normal conversation is about 60 dB, and, as we stated earlier, a power lawnmower is about 90 dB (American Academy of Otolaryngology—Head and Neck Surgery, 2007).

Hertz are usually measured from 125 Hz (low pitch) to 8,000 Hz (high pitch). Frequencies in speech range from 80 to 8,000 Hz, but most speech sounds have energy in the 500- to 2,000-Hz range.

Testing each ear separately, the audiologist presents a variety of tones within the range of 0 to about 110 dB and 125 to 8,000 Hz until she establishes the level of intensity (dB) at which the individual can detect the tone at a number of frequencies: 125 Hz, 250 Hz, 500 Hz, 1,000 Hz, 2,000 Hz, 4,000 Hz, and 8,000 Hz. For each frequency, the audiologist records a measure of degree of hearing impairment. A 50-dB hearing impairment at 500 Hz, for example, means the individual can detect the 500-Hz sound when it is given at an intensity level of 50 dB, whereas the average person would have heard it at 0 dB.

Speech Audiometry

Because the ability to understand speech is of prime importance, audiologists use **speech audiometry** to test a person's detection and understanding of speech. The **speech-reception threshold (SRT)** is the decibel level at which one can understand speech. One way to measure the SRT is to present the person with a list of two-syllable words, testing each ear separately. Audiologists often use the decibel level at which the person can understand half the words as an estimate of SRT level. One's ability to hear speech with background noise interference can also be tested. For a demonstration, go to www.hear-it.org and click on the "Online Hearing Test" box.

CAUSES

We discuss causes with respect to the type of hearing impairment (conductive, sensorineural, and mixed) as well as the location of the hearing impairment (outer, middle, or inner ear).

Conductive, Sensorineural, and Mixed Hearing Impairment

Professionals classify causes of hearing impairment on the basis of the location of the problem within the hearing mechanism. There are three major classifications: conductive, sensorineural, and mixed hearing impairments. A **conductive hearing impairment** refers to an interference with the transfer of sound along the conductive pathway of the middle or outer ear. A **sensorineural hearing impairment** involves problems in the inner ear. A **mixed hearing impairment** is a combination of the two. Audiologists attempt to determine the location of the dysfunction. The first clue may be the severity of the loss. A general rule is that hearing impairments greater than 60 or 70 dB usually involve some inner-ear problem. Audiologists use the results of pure-tone testing to help determine the location of a hearing impairment. They then convert the results to an audiogram—a graphic representation of the weakest (lowest-decibel) sound the individual can hear at each of several frequency levels. The profile of the audiogram helps to determine whether the loss is conductive, sensorineural, or mixed.

Hearing Impairment and the Outer Ear

Although problems of the outer ear are not as serious as those of the middle or inner ear, several conditions of the outer ear can cause a person to be hard of hearing. In some children, for example, the external auditory canal does not form, resulting in a condition known as *atresia*. Children may also develop **external otitis**, or "swimmer's ear," an infection of the skin of the external auditory canal. Tumors of the external auditory canal are another source of hearing impairment.

Hearing Impairment and the Middle Ear

Although abnormalities of the middle ear are generally more serious than problems of the outer ear, they, too, usually result in a classification as hard of hearing rather than deaf. Most middle-ear hearing impairments occur because the mechanical action of the ossicles is interfered with in some way. Unlike inner-ear problems, most middle-ear hearing impairments are correctable with medical or surgical treatment.

The most common problem of the middle ear is **otitis media**—an infection of the middle-ear space caused by viral or bacterial factors, among others. Otitis media is common in young children. At least 80% of children are diagnosed with otitis media at least once before they are 10 years old (Thrasher, 2009). It is linked to abnormal functioning of the eustachian tubes. If the eustachian tube malfunctions because of a respiratory viral infection, for example, it cannot do its job of ventilating, draining, and protecting the middle ear from infection. Otitis media can result in temporary conductive hearing impairment, and even these temporary losses can make the child vulnerable for having language delays (Feldman et al., 2003). If untreated, otitis media can lead to rupture of the tympanic membrane.

Hearing Impairment and the Inner Ear

The most severe hearing impairments are associated with the inner ear. In addition to problems with hearing sensitivity, a person with inner-ear hearing impairment can have additional problems, such as sound distortion, balance problems, and roaring or ringing in the ears.

Causes of inner-ear disorders can be hereditary or acquired. Genetic or hereditary factors are a leading cause of deafness in children. In fact, over 400 different varieties of hereditary deafness have been identified (Lomas et al., 2017). Scientists have identified mutation in the **connexin-26 gene** as the most common cause of congenital deafness.

Acquired hearing impairments of the inner ear include those due to bacterial infections (e.g., meningitis, the second most frequent cause of childhood deafness), prematurity, viral infections (e.g., mumps and measles), anoxia (deprivation of oxygen) at birth, prenatal infections of the mother (e.g., maternal rubella, congenital syphilis, and cytomegalovirus), Rh incompatibility (which can now usually be prevented with proper prenatal care of the mother), blows to the head, side effects of some antibiotics, and excessive noise levels.

Two of the preceding conditions deserve special emphasis because of their relatively high prevalence. **Congenital cytomegalovirus (CMV)**, a herpes virus, is the most frequent nongenetic cause of deafness in infants (Centers for Disease Control and Prevention, 2013). Over half of adults by age 40 are infected with CMV. Fortunately, very few of those infected develop the symptoms, which are usually severe. However, babies born to mothers with CMV are particularly vulnerable to its adverse effects, such as hearing impairment. CMV can result in a variety of other conditions, such as intellectual disabilities, visual impairment, and Attention Deficit Hyperactivity Disorder (ADHD) (Lomas et al., 2017).

Environamental factors can also cause hearing impairment. Chief among environmental causes are repeated exposure to loud music, gunshots, or machinery.

MyLab Education Self-Check 11.2

MyLab Education Application Exercise 11.2:
Ashley's Hearing Impairment

Watch two video clips about a 9-year-old girl named Ashley. She presents her own history of hearing loss, and then her mother talks about Ashley's hearing loss.

PSYCHOLOGICAL AND BEHAVIORAL CHARACTERISTICS

Consider this question: If you were forced to choose, which would you rather be—blind or deaf? On first impulse, most of us would choose deafness, probably because we rely on sight for mobility and because many of the beauties of nature are visual. But in terms of *functioning in an English language-oriented society*, the person who is deaf is at a much greater disadvantage than is someone who is blind.

Spoken Language and Speech Development

By far the most severely affected areas of development in the person with a hearing impairment are the comprehension and production of the English language. We stress *English* because it is the predominant language in the United States of those who can hear. In other words, people who have hearing impairment are generally deficient in the language used by most people of the hearing society in which they live. The distinction is important, because people who have hearing impairment can be expert in their own form of language: *sign language*.

Nevertheless, it's an undeniable fact that individuals with hearing impairment are at a distinct disadvantage in several critical areas. This is true in terms of language comprehension, language production, and speech. Speech intelligibility is linked to (1) degree of hearing impairment and (2) the age of onset of the hearing impairment. Even after intensive speech therapy, it's rare for children with prelingual profound deafness to develop intelligible speech (Marschark, 2002). Infants who can hear their own sounds and those of adults before becoming deaf have an advantage over those born deaf. Children who are deaf are handicapped in learning to associate the sensations they feel when they move their jaws, mouths, and tongues with the auditory sounds these movements produce. In addition, these children have difficulty hearing adult speech, which children without impairment can hear and imitate.

Table 11.1 provides general examples of the possible effects of various degrees of hearing impairment on English language development. This is only a general statement of these relationships, because many factors interact to influence language development in the child with hearing impairment.

Sign Language

Although children who are deaf face extraordinary challenges in learning a spoken language, with exposure they can easily learn **sign language**. However, historically, sign language has suffered from several misconceptions, including the belief that it is not a true language. The notion that sign language is simply a primitive, visual representation of oral language similar to mime was first challenged by the pioneering work of William Stokoe at Gallaudet University. A linguist, Stokoe submitted that, analogous to the phonemes of spoken English, each sign in ASL consists of three parts: handshape, location, and movement (Stokoe, 1960; Stokoe, Casterline, & Croneberg, 1976). For many years,

TABLE 11.1 • **Degrees of hearing impairment and impact on communication**

HEARING LEVEL	DESCRIPTOR	IMPACT ON COMMUNICATION
10–15 dB	Normal	No impact on communication.
16–25 dB	Slight	In quiet environments, has no difficulty recognizing speech, but in noisy environments, has difficulty understanding faint speech.
26–40 dB	Mild	In quiet conversational environments where the topic is known and vocabulary is limited, has no difficulty in communicating. Has difficulty hearing faint or distant speech, even if the environment is quiet. Has challenges in following classroom discussions.
41–55 dB	Moderate	Can hear conversational speech only at a close distance. Group activities, such as classroom discussions, present a communicative challenge.
56–70 dB	Moderate-Severe	Can hear only loud, clear conversational speech and has much difficulty in group situations. Often, the individual's speech is noticeably impaired though intelligible.
71–90 dB	Severe	Cannot hear conversational speech unless it is loud, and even then, cannot recognize many of the words. Can detect, though not always identify, environmental sounds. The individual's speech is not altogether intelligible.
91 dB +	Profound	May hear loud sounds, but cannot hear conversational speech at all. Vision is the primary modality for communication. The individual's own speech, if developed at all, is not easy to understand.

Source: Schirmer, Barbara R., *Psychological, Social, and Educational Dimensions of Deafness,* 1st Ed., ©2001. Reprinted and Electronically reproduced by permission of Pearson Education, Inc., New York, NY.

Stokoe's colleagues scoffed at him, but research in several areas has proved that he was correct in asserting that sign language is a true language.

GRAMMATICAL COMPLEXITY OF SIGN LANGUAGE Researchers have continued to refine Stokoe's (1960) work on sign language grammar, confirming its complexity. For example, like spoken language, sign language has grammatical structure at the sentence level (syntax) as well as at the word or sign level (Goldin-Meadow, 2003). Handshapes, location, and movement are combined to create a grammar every bit as complex as that of spoken language.

NONUNIVERSALITY OF SIGN LANGUAGE Contrary to popular opinion, no single, universal sign language exists. Just as geographical or cultural separations result in different spoken languages, they also result in different sign languages. For example, people who are deaf in France communicate in French Sign Language, and those in the United States use American Sign Language (ASL). A person who is deaf visiting a foreign country has difficulties communicating with others who are deaf, much as a hearing person does. This is because sign languages, like spoken languages, evolve over time through common usage. In other words, sign language was not invented by any one person or a committee of people. The 18th-century French clergyman Charles-Michel de l'Eppe is often referred to as the "father of sign language." On hearing this, some people assume that de l'Eppe invented sign language. However, he did promote the usage of French Sign Language, which already existed within the Deaf community. This is not to diminish his profound impact on advocating for using sign language in educating students with hearing impairments.

THE BLACK AMERICAN SIGN LANGUAGE (BASL) DIALECT Just as there are different sign languages associated with different countries, there are also different sign language dialects. These different dialects are usually due to differences in geographic locations within a country. The BASL dialect is an interesting example of this, in that the "geographic" discrepancy is based on segregation existing in schools hisorically. Just as black hearing students were segregated, so too were black deaf students (McCaskill et al., 2011).

FOCUS ON

The Impact of Cochlear Implants on Language

Since at least the mid- to late-20th century, scientists have sought to develop a way of electrically stimulating the cochlea in persons with deafness in order to bring them sound. After decades of research, scientists have developed what has come to be known as a cochlear implant. The Food and Drug Administration (FDA) approved the first cochlear implant for use in adults ages 18 and older in the 1980s. Starting in 2000, the FDA approved cochlear implantation for children 12 months or older. Worldwide, over 324,200 devices have been implanted. In the United States, at least 58,000 devices have been implanted in adults and 38,000 in children (National Institute of Deafness and Other Communication Disorders, 2016).

Cochlear implantation involves surgically inserting electronic elements under the skin behind the ear and in the inner ear. A small microphone worn behind the ear picks up sounds and sends them to a small computerized speech processor worn by the person. The speech processor sends coded signals to an external coil worn behind the ear, which sends them through the skin to the implanted internal coil. The internal coil then sends the signals to electrodes implanted in the inner ear, and these signals are sent on to the auditory nerve. (See Figure 11.2.)

Research indicates that, in general, implantation increases the ability to hear, thus resulting in better speech and language production (Geers & Hayes, 2011). However, implantation does not always lead to better literacy skills, such as reading, spelling, and writing. The prospects for increasing reading comprehension are increased when instruction focuses on explicit instruction in phonological skills (Lederberg, Miller, Easterbrooks, & Connor, 2014).

In the case of children, research shows that the earlier the transplant takes place, the better the child's ability to hear and speak (Geers, Moog, Biedenstein, Brenner, & Hayes, 2009; Sarant, Harris, & Bennet, 2015). However, results can still vary substantially from individual to individual, which makes the decision to pursue cochlear implantation potentially challenging, especially for parents of children who are deaf (Lomas et al., 2017).

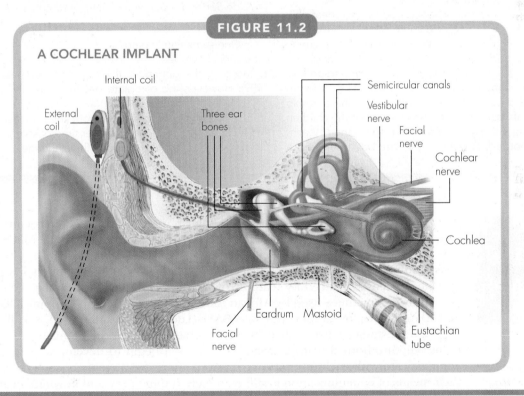

FIGURE 11.2

A COCHLEAR IMPLANT

Internal coil
External coil
Three ear bones
Semicircular canals
Vestibular nerve
Facial nerve
Cochlear nerve
Cochlea
Eardrum   Mastoid
Facial nerve
Eustachian tube

The establishment of schools and separate classes for black deaf students dates as far back as the mid-1850s. Because integration of black students into schools didn't "formally" occur until 1954, with the Supreme Court's ruling in *Brown v. Board of Education*, BASL had over 100 years to evolve among African American students who were deaf. In fact, just as integration of African American hearing students has been slow to take place, so has integration of African American deaf students. For example, the last black deaf school did not integrate until 1978 (McCaskill et al., 2011).

FOCUS ON CONCEPTS

The Birth and Evolution of Nicaraguan Sign Language

For years researchers have claimed that sign languages evolve naturally over time wherever there is a critical mass of persons who are deaf. The need to communicate is a driving force in the development of sign language. Although these scholars' conclusions were compelling, much of their work was based on retrospective analyses of sign languages that were already in existence. However, beginning in the 1970s, researchers were presented with a rare opportunity to study and document the evolution of sign language in Nicaragua:

> Before the 1970s, there was no deaf community in Nicaragua. Deaf people were largely isolated from each other, and used simple home sign systems and gesture 'mímicas' to communicate with their families and friends. The conditions necessary for a language to arise occurred in 1977, when a center for special education established a program initially attended by 50 young deaf children. The number of students at the school . . . grew to 100 by 1979, the year of the Sandinista revolution.
>
> In 1980, a vocational school for adolescent deaf children was opened. . . . By 1983 there were over 400 deaf students enrolled in the two schools. Initially, the language program emphasized spoken Spanish and lipreading, and the use of signs by teachers limited to **fingerspelling** (using simple signs to sign the alphabet). The program achieved little success, with most students failing to grasp the concept of Spanish words. However, while the children remained linguistically disconnected from their teachers, the schoolyard, the street, and the bus to and from

school provided fertile ground for them to communicate with each other, and by combining gestures and elements of their home-sign systems, a pidgin-like form, and then a creole-like language rapidly emerged. They were creating their own language. This "first-stage" pidgin . . . is still used by many of those who attended the school at this time.

> Staff at the school, unaware of the development of this new language, saw the children's gesturing as mime, and as a failure to acquire Spanish. Unable to understand what the children were saying to each other, they asked for outside help, and in June 1986, the Nicaraguan Ministry of Education contacted Judy Kegl, an American Sign Language linguist from Northeastern University. As Kegl and other researchers began to analyze the language, they noticed that the young children had taken the pidgin-like form of the older children to a higher level of complexity, with verb agreement and other conventions of grammar. This more complex sign language is now known as *Idioma de Señas de Nicaragua* (ISN). (*Nicaraguan Sign Language*, 2010)

One surprising finding has been that over time, the youngest signers have been the ones who have been most influential in changing the grammar of ISN (Kegl, Senghas, & Coppola, 1999). However, the complete development and perpetuation of ISN is dependent on a complex interplay between the generations (Senghas, 2003). The bottom line is that sign language, like spoken language, changes over time based on intergenerational interactions among users of the language.

MyLab Education
Video Example 11.3

Fingerspelling, in which words are spelled out using a **manual alphabet**, is also often used to supplement sign language or an oral approach. This video shows the manual alphabet.

Interestingly, just as certain spoken English dialects are sometimes considered inferior, so too have students using BASL been looked down upon (Lucas & McCaskill, 2007). The lower status of BASL parallels the way in which English spoken by African Americans is sometimes viewed by the hearing population. In fact, researchers have noted that BASL has been influenced by features of hearing African Americans" speech. For example, phrases sometimes used by African Americans, such as "Stop Tripping," "Girl, please," and "Dang," have found their way into BASL (Lucas, Bayley, McCaskill, & Hill, 2015).

Several studies have verified the evolutionary aspect of sign languages. For example, twins who are born deaf to hearing parents soon begin to develop a signing system to communicate with each other. However, even after several years of such communication, their means of communication is still extremely rudimentary and nowhere near as sophisticated as ASL. The Nicaraguan Sign Language Study, described in the accompanying Focus on Concepts feature, has also documented how sign languages change over time.

DEVELOPMENTAL MILESTONES OF SIGN LANGUAGE Considerable evidence indicates that children who are deaf reach the same language development milestones in sign that children who can hear reach in spoken language, and do so at about the same time (Emmorey, 2002; Goldin-Meadow, 2003). For example, they manually "babble" at about the same time as infants who can hear verbally babble. And infants who are deaf sign their first words and two-word phrases at about the same time that hearing infants verbalize their first words and two-word phrases.

NEUROLOGICAL FOUNDATIONS OF SIGN LANGUAGE Further evidence that sign language is a true language comes from studies showing that sign language has the same neurological underpinnings as does spoken language. In Chapter 6, we noted that areas within the left cerebral hemisphere of the brain are primarily responsible for language. However, we were referring to spoken language. Interestingly, using neuroimaging techniques, researchers have collected substantial evidence showing that the left hemisphere of the brain is also the primary site responsible for sign language acquisition and use (Campbell & MacSweeney, 2004; Emmorey, 2002; Waters et al., 2007). Also, stroke patients who are deaf are more likely to have deficits in signing if the stroke is to the left hemisphere than if the right hemisphere is damaged.

Intellectual Ability

For many years, professionals believed that the spoken language of individuals who are deaf was a sign that they also had intellectual deficiencies. As was noted earlier, however, we now know that although they might not have a spoken language such as English, if they use American Sign Language, these individuals are using a true language with its own rules of grammar.

Any intelligence testing of people who have hearing impairment must take their English language deficiency into account. Best practice dictates that professionals use multiple measures, with an emphasis on using non-verbal, performance tests, rather than verbal tests. Especially if the performance tests are administered in sign, they offer a much fairer assessment of the IQ of a person with a hearing impairment. In addition, standardized tests of ASL skills are available (Enns, Zimmer, Broszeit, C., & Rabu 2013; Morere & Allen, 2012; Simms, Baker, & Clark, 2013).

Academic Achievement

Unfortunately, most children who are deaf have large deficits in academic achievement. Reading ability, which relies heavily on English language skills and is probably the most important area of academic achievement, is most affected. For example, the average 15-year-old student with a hearing impairment has a deficit of at least 5 years in reading (Trezek, Wang, & Paul, 2010). Even in math, their best academic subject, students with hearing impairment trail their hearing peers by substantial margins.

Interestingly, the same areas of weakness—phonological and phonemic awareness—that are evident in many students with reading disabilities (see Chapter 6) are also characterstic of students with hearing impairment, many of whom have reading problems (Park, Lombardino, & Ritter, 2013). In fact, a comparison of the phonology skills of students with mild to moderate inner ear-based hearing loss are similar to those of students with reading disabilities (Park & Lombardino, 2012). The link between hearing impairment and phonological and phonemic difficulties is logical given that phonology, by definition, refers to the *sounds* of language.

Furthermore, researchers have found phonics-based intervention for students who are deaf or hard of hearing can result in a positive impact on language development (Gilliver, Cupples, Ching, Leigh, & Gunnourie, 2016; Wang, Spychala, Harris, & Oettig, 2013). In particular, they have found that the more explicit the instruction is, the more effective the impact is on language (Miller, Lederberg, & Easterbrooks, 2013). Using sign language to support phonics-based instruction has also been found to be effective in teaching writing and reading (Andrews, Hamilton, Misener-Dunn, & Clark, 2016).

Several studies have demonstrated that children who are deaf who have parents who are deaf have higher levels of achievement and better language skills than do those who have hearing parents. Researchers do not agree about the cause (Powers, 2003). However, many authorities speculate that the positive influence of sign language is the cause. Parents who are deaf might be able to communicate better with their children through the use of ASL, providing the children with needed support. In addition, children who have parents who are deaf are more likely to be proficient in ASL, and ASL can aid these children in learning written English and reading.

Social Adjustment

Students with hearing impairment are at risk for problems in interacting socially with their peers (Lauggen, Jacobsen, Rieffe, & Wichstrom, 2016). Social development and personality development in the hearing population depend heavily on communication, and the situation is no different for those who are deaf. People who can hear have little difficulty finding people with whom to communicate. People who are deaf, however, can face problems in finding others with whom they can converse. Studies have demonstrated that many students who are deaf are at risk for poor self-concepts (Mekonnen, Hannu, Elina, & Matti, 2016) and loneliness (Martin, Bat-Chava, Lalwani, & Waltzman, 2010; Wauters & Knoors, 2007). Two factors are important in considering the possible isolation of students who are deaf: inclusion and hearing status of the parents.

Researchers have shown that, without implementing strategic grouping, very little interaction typically occurs in inclusive settings between students who are deaf and those who are not (Kluwin, Stinson, & Colarossi, 2002). This is not always possible, however, because of the low prevalence of hearing impairment. Some interventions using cooperative learning have succeeded in increasing the interactions between students who are deaf and their peers who can hear (Kluwin et al., 2002).

Some authorities believe that the child who is deaf and has parents who can hear runs a greater risk of being unhappy than the child who has parents who also are deaf. Many parents who can hear, as well as parents who are hard of hearing, don't become proficient in ASL (Mitchell & Karchmer, 2005) and are unable to communicate with their children easily. Given that about 90% of children who are deaf have hearing parents (Mitchell & Karchmer, 2004), this problem in communication might be critical.

The need for social interaction is probably most influential in leading many people with hearing impairment to associate primarily with others with hearing impairment. If their parents are deaf, children who are deaf are usually exposed to other deaf families from an early age. Nonetheless, many people who are deaf end up, as adults, socializing predominantly with others who are deaf, even if they have hearing parents and even if, as children, they didn't come into contact with many other children who were deaf. This phenomenon of socializing with others who are deaf is attributable to the influence of the Deaf culture.

THE DEAF CULTURE In the past, most professionals viewed isolation from the hearing community on the part of many people who are deaf as a sign of social pathology. Now most professionals agree with the many people who are deaf who believe in the value of having their own Deaf culture. They view this culture as a natural condition emanating from the common bond of sign language.

The unifying influence of sign language is the first of six factors noted by Reagan (1990) as demarcating the Deaf community as a true culture:

1. *Linguistic differentiation* is at the heart of Deaf culture; many within the Deaf community view themselves as bilingual, with individuals possessing varying degrees of fluency in ASL and English (Ladd, 2003; Padden & Humphries, 2005). People who are deaf continually shift between ASL and English as well as between the Deaf culture and that of the hearing (Padden, 1996).
2. *Attitudinal deafness* refers to whether a person thinks of himself as deaf. It might not have anything to do with a person's hearing acuity. For example, a person with a relatively mild hearing impairment might think of herself as deaf more readily than does someone with a profound hearing impairment.
3. *Behavioral norms* within the Deaf community differ from those in hearing society. A few examples of these norms, according to Lane, Hoffmeister, and Bahan (1996), are that people who are deaf value informality and physical contact in their interactions with one another, often giving each other hugs when greeting and departing, and their leave-takings often take much longer than those of hearing society. Also, they are likely to be frank in their discussions, not hesitating to get directly to the point of what they want to communicate.

4. *Endogamous marriage* patterns are evident from surveys showing rates of in-group marriage as high as 90%. The Deaf community tends to frown on "mixed marriages" between people who are deaf and those who are hearing.

5. *Historical awareness* of significant people and events pertaining to people who are deaf permeates the Deaf community. They are often deferential to elders and value their wisdom and knowledge pertaining to Deaf traditions.

6. *Voluntary organizational networks* are abundant in the Deaf community. Some examples are the National Association of the Deaf, the World Games for the Deaf (Deaf Olympics), and the National Theatre of the Deaf.

CONCERN FOR THE EROSION OF DEAF CULTURE Many within the Deaf community and some professionals are concerned that the cultural status of children who are deaf is in peril (Lane et al., 1996; Padden & Humphries, 2005). They believe that the increase in inclusion is eroding the cultural values of the Deaf culture. In the past, much of Deaf culture was passed down from generation to generation through contacts made at residential schools, but if they attend local schools, today's children who are deaf may have little contact with other children who are deaf. Many authorities now recommend that schools involve members of the Deaf community in developing classes in Deaf history and culture for students who are deaf who attend local schools.

DEAF ACTIVISM: THE GALLAUDET EXPERIENCE Considering all groups with exceptionalities, those who are deaf have been one of the most, if not the most, outspoken about their rights. Even though some might think that the Deaf community is in peril of losing its identity, it's still very active in advocating a variety of social, educational, and medical policies. Two good examples of this activism are Gallaudet's Deaf President Now and Unity for Gallaudet Movements (see the accompanying Personal Perspectives) and the debate over cochlear implants.

DEAF ACTIVISM: THE COCHLEAR IMPLANT DEBATE Deaf activists have also been aggressive in attacking what they consider an oppressive medical and educational establishment. An example of just how much this segment of the Deaf community is at odds with many professionals is its opposition to the medical procedure of cochlear implantation.

Although the manufacturers of these devices, as well as many members of the medical community, view cochlear implants as miraculous, many within the Deaf community oppose them, viewing the process as physically and culturally invasive:

> I expect that most Americans would agree that our society should not seek the scientific tools or use them, if available, to change a child biologically so he or she will belong to the majority rather than the minority—even if we believe that this biological engineering might reduce the burdens the child will bear as a member of a minority. Even if we could take children destined to be members of the African American, or Hispanic American, or Native American, or Deaf American communities and convert them with bio-power into white, Caucasian, hearing males—even if we could, we should not. We should likewise refuse cochlear implants for young deaf children even if the devices were perfect. (Lane, 1992, p. 237)

The Deaf community has not had to confront the issue raised by Lane: whether to have the surgery even if it were to result in perfect hearing. Although perfect hearing through cochlear implants might not be just around the corner, enormous strides in technology have resulted in many more cases than ever before of greatly improved hearing for people with implants. These more positive results are making it more difficult for those who are deaf, or their parents, to decide whether to choose cochlear implantation. One problem is that in order to reap the benefits of improved hearing from the implant, many professionals recommend intensive oral instruction. As we discuss later, many within the Deaf community favor manual (ASL) over oral teaching methods. So they are concerned that persons with implants may not gain enough exposure to sign language. But the majority of children with implants still don't attain hearing and speaking skills within the range of hearing children. Again, this is a far cry from a cure, but for some, it's enough of an improvement to elect to undergo the surgery.

PERSONAL PERSPECTIVES

Gallaudet's Deaf President Now and Unity for Gallaudet Movements

Deaf President Now Movement

A prominent and historic example of Deaf activism occurred in the 1980s at Gallaudet University, a liberal arts college for the deaf and hard of hearing, when students and faculty protested the board of trustees' selection of a hearing president. Since its founding in 1864, Gallaudet had never had a deaf president. But when on March 6, 1988, the trustees announced the appointment of yet another hearing president, faculty and students took to the streets and halls in protest. Having successfully shut down the university, organizers of the Deaf President Now Movement issued four demands:

1. that a deaf president be named immediately;
2. that the chair of the board resign;
3. that the board, which consisted of 17 hearing and 4 deaf members, be reconfigured to include a majority of deaf members; and
4. that there be no reprisals.

After 8 days of protest, the board acceded to all four demands, the most significant of which was the naming of a long-time faculty member who was deaf—I. King Jordan—as president of the university.

Unity for Gallaudet Movement

Upon Jordan's retirement, the board announced on May 1, 2006, the appointment of the vice president of the university, Jane K. Fernandes, to be Jordan's successor. Students and faculty once again protested, holding rallies and blocking entrances to the school. The protests continued during the Fall semester, with more than 100 students arrested for blocking entrances.

Given that Fernandes is also deaf, accounts vary as to why such a negative reaction occurred (Christiansen, 2009; Takruri, 2006; Tapper & Sandell, 2006). Some cited what they considered a flawed, noninclusive selection process, but many pointed to concerns that Fernandes was not "deaf enough." They objected to her having stated that she wanted to be more inclusive by admitting more students with cochlear implants as well as those who had not grown up learning sign language. (Fernandes herself reportedly grew up using speech and speechreading and didn't learn sign language until she was in her 20s.)

In October 2006, Fernandes was removed as president by the board. In December, 2006, the board named Robert Davilla as an interim president. Deaf since the age of 8, Davilla had previously served in a number of high-level government and university positions. Also deaf, T. Alan Hurwitz became president in May, 2010. Hurwitz, whose background is engineering, came to the position after being president of the National Technical Institute for the Deaf. In 2016, Roberta Cordano became the first female deaf president of Gallaudet.

DEAF ACTIVISM: THE GENETIC ENGINEERING DEBATE Ironically, deaf activists can also put scientific discoveries to use to help sustain the Deaf culture, but not without facing thorny ethical concerns (Emery, Middleton, & Turner, 2010; Middleton, Emery, & Turner, 2010). Earlier, we noted the discovery of the mutation of the connexin-26 gene as the leading cause of deafness in children. Parents could use such information to increase their chances of having a baby who is deaf. (Contrary to what many in hearing society assume, when both parents are deaf, they usually would prefer to have a baby who is deaf.) For example, they could use **in vitro fertilization**, a procedure that is used to help infertile couples, whereby egg cells from the mother are fertilized in the laboratory and then placed in the mother's uterus. Parents who are deaf could choose to retain only fertilized eggs that have the connexin-26 mutation. Another option that actually has been used by deaf couples is artificial insemination by a donor who has a high probability of carrying genes leading to deafness (Mundy, 2002; Sanghavi, 2006).

MyLab Education **Self-Check 11.3**

MyLab Education **Application Exercise 11.3:**

The Impact of Hearing Loss: Mini Case Study

Read a mini case study about Fiona, a three-year-old with profound hearing loss, and answer the questions that follow.

SUCCESS STORIES: Bailea, a Kindergartener with a Cochlear Implant, Benefits from Early Intervention and Co-Teaching

Special Educator Heather Miles: "Set expectations high, and really work to meet them."

Five-year-old Bailea Kohler uses a cochlear implant in an inclusive kindergarten class.

These are the keys to her success:

- intensive early intervention and structured routines
- relentless focus on teamwork
- specific interventions in auditory-verbal learning

"I JUST LOVE BAILEA," says special educator Heather Miles. "She's strong willed and very curious about things." Bailea's father says she's an energetic and happy 5-year-old. "She always has bumps and bruises from trying to keep up with her older sister, Madison." Bailea was born deaf to hearing parents, Stacia and Mike Kohler. She has a cochlear implant, and she has benefited from intensive, relentless, and specific special education.

- **Intensive Early Intervention and Structured Routines.** At first, Bailea's doctors predicted her hearing would improve. "When she failed to hear doors slam or dogs bark, I reached out to everybody I could to find the best for her," says Stacia. When she was 12 months old, Bailea started intensive speech and language services 3 days a week at the Saginaw Hearing Center, in Saginaw, Michigan. An audiologist recommended a cochlear implant, but before surgery Bailea was required to wear hearing aids for 6 months. "It was a constant fight, and she tried to pull them out," recalls Stacia. "Bailea had surgery to implant the cochlear device when she was 19 months old. Her hearing specialist drove 3 hours to the University of Michigan in Ann Arbor, in an ice storm to visit Bailea in the hospital. The professionals who worked with us were like family."

  Structured routines have been important. "Bailea likes being in charge," says Heather, and she started kindergarten at age 5 with temper tantrums when she couldn't make her needs known. Classmates were positive models, but structured interactions and instruction helped her communicate. "We use a picture schedule to provide students with visual supports for learning. We also use tape to assign places for students to sit on the carpet during group time. Bailea's special place is near the front so she can scoot away if she needs to." Bailea's language skills are not strong, and her attention span is short in group settings. "Sometimes," says Heather, "the loudness of talking and laughter can get a bit much, and she needs to get away."

- **Relentless Focus on Teamwork.** Coordinated teamwork is critical to Bailea's success. Heather Miles has collaborated for 7 years with Bailea's kindergarten teacher, Mrs. English, who also has experience as a special educator. Their classroom is equipped with a portable FM speaker that amplifies sounds for any of the 19 students who might benefit. Heather spends 2 hours daily with Mrs. English, co-teaching reading and language arts in the morning, and writing in the afternoon. Sometimes Bailea joins Heather in a larger group for Direct Instruction (discussed in Chapter 6), and other times they work together in a separate classroom. Both teachers meet monthly with the speech and hearing specialists to ensure everyone is working toward the same goals. An audiologist sees Bailea weekly in the classroom and regularly attends team meetings. Says Heather, "She makes practical suggestions by telling us where the FM reception is best in the room, and she observes Bailea's behavior to monitor the volume and functioning of the cochlear implant." School personnel aren't responsible for adjusting implanted devices, so Bailea's parents let the medical team at the University of Michigan know about any problems that might be occurring with the implant in the classroom.

- **Specific Interventions for Auditory-Verbal Learning.** The Kohlers credit the team with helping Bailea develop the desire to hear. At home, 11-year-old sister Madison patiently helps Bailea to communicate. It hasn't been easy. The fragile cochlear device breaks easily—three times in recent months—but her new implant is smaller and less bulky than the original device. The new technology seems to make a positive difference in her ability to distinguish sounds, says Heather. "When I work with her individually, she can develop a thought, and together we stretch the words into a sentence. Now, she can write phonetically in a manner that most people can read." Bailea's language skills are delayed, so Heather monitors the rate with which she speaks and takes extra time to explain things in detail. "Bailea mimics what others are doing but she doesn't always grasp the concept. If directions call for using scissors to cut out three characters and put them in the story order, she would look at others cutting, but not really understand what she's supposed to do next." Heather uses a variety of assessments at least every 2 weeks to monitor Bailea's early literacy skills and to chart her progress. "We set expectations high," she says, "and really work to meet them."

EDUCATIONAL CONSIDERATIONS

Formidable problems face the educator who works with students who are deaf or hard of hearing. One major problem is of course communication. Dating back to the 16th century, debate has raged about how individuals who are deaf should converse

(Lane, 1984). This controversy is sometimes referred to as the **oralism–manualism debate**, to represent two very different points of view: Oralism favors teaching people who are deaf to speak, whereas manualism advocates the use of some kind of manual communication. Manualism was the preferred method until the middle of the 19th century, when oralism began to gain predominance. Currently, most professionals recommend both oral and manual methods in what is referred to as a **total communication** or **simultaneous communication** approach (Andrews et al., 2004). However, many within the Deaf community believe that even the total communication approach is inadequate, and they advocate for a **bicultural-bilingual approach**, which promotes ASL as a first language and supports instruction in the Deaf culture.

We first discuss the major techniques that make up the oral approach and the oral portion of the total communication approach; then we explore total communication, followed by a discussion of the bicultural-bilingual approach.

Oral Approaches: The Auditory-Verbal Approach and the Auditory-Oral Approach

THE AUDITORY-VERBAL APPROACH The **auditory-verbal approach** focuses exclusively on using audition to improve speech and language development (Andrews et al., 2004). It assumes that most children with hearing impairment have some residual hearing that they can use to their benefit. It relies heavily on amplification technology, such as hearing aids and cochlear implants, and stresses that this amplification technology should be instituted at as young an age as possible. This approach also places a heavy emphasis on speech training. Because children with hearing impairments have problems hearing their own speech or that of others and often hear speech in a distorted fashion, they must be explicitly instructed in how to produce speech sounds.

THE AUDITORY-ORAL APPROACH The **auditory-oral approach** is similar to the auditory-verbal approach, but it also stresses the use of visual cues, such as speechreading and cued speech. Sometimes inappropriately called *lipreading*, **speechreading** involves teaching children to use visual information to understand what is being said to them. *Speechreading* is a more accurate term than *lipreading* because the goal is to teach students to attend to a variety of stimuli in addition to specific movements of the lips. For example, proficient speechreaders read contextual stimuli so that they can anticipate certain types of messages in particular situations. They use facial expressions to help them interpret what is being said to them. Even the ability to discriminate the various speech sounds that flow from a person's mouth involves attending to visual cues from the tongue and jaw as well as the lips. For example, to learn to discriminate among vowels, the speechreader concentrates on cues related to the degree of jaw opening and lip shaping.

Cued speech is a way of augmenting speechreading. In cued speech, the individual uses handshapes to represent specific sounds while speaking. Eight handshapes are cues for certain consonants, and four serve as cues for vowels. Cued speech helps the speechreader differentiate between sounds that look alike on the lips. Although it has some devoted advocates, cued speech is not used widely in the United States.

CRITICISMS OF THE ORAL APPROACH Several authorities have been critical of using an exclusively oral approach with students who have hearing impairment (Lane et al., 1996; Padden & Humphries, 2005). In particular, they object to the deemphasis of sign language in this approach, especially for children who are deaf. These critics assert that it's unreasonable to assume that many children with severe or profound degrees of hearing impairment have enough hearing to be of use. Therefore, denying these children access to ASL is denying them access to a language to communicate.

Critics of the oral approach also point out that speechreading is extremely difficult and that good speechreaders are rare (Andrews et al., 2004). It's easy to overlook some of the factors that make speechreading difficult. For instance, speakers produce many sounds with little obvious movement of the mouth. Another issue is that the English

FOCUS ON

Bad Lip Reading (Or "Humorous Homophenes")

Started in 2011, the YouTube channel, BadLipReading, rocketed to popularity, with 6 million subscribers and over 800 million "views" as of March 19, 2017. Taking advantage of the plethora of homophenes in the English language—different sounds that are visually identical when spoken—the site contains several scenarios of politicians, athletes, celebrities, and so forth, who are made to look silly as they emit nonsensical statements. Visit the BLR channel for numerous examples. https://www.youtube.com/user/BadLipReading

---

language has many **homophenes**—different sounds that are visually identical when spoken. For example, a speechreader cannot distinguish among the pronunciations of *p*, *b*, and *m*. Speakers also vary in how they produce sounds. Finally, factors such as poor lighting, rapid speaking, and talking with one's head turned are further reasons why good speechreading is a rare skill (Menchel, 1988). See the Focus on Bad Lip Reading feature for an amusing use of homophenes.

Total Communication/Simultaneous Communication

As we noted previously, most schools have adopted the total communication approach, a combination of oral and manual methods. Total communication involves the simultaneous use of speech with one of the **signing English systems**. These signing systems are approaches that professionals have devised for teaching people who are deaf to communicate. **Fingerspelling**, the representation of letters of the English alphabet by finger positions, is also used occasionally to spell out certain words.

Dissatisfaction with total communication has been growing among some professionals and many within the Deaf community. The focus of the criticism has been on the use of signing English systems rather than ASL. Unlike ASL, signing English systems maintain the same word order as spoken English, thereby making it possible to speak and sign at the same time. Defenders of signing English systems state that the correspondence in word order between signing English systems and English helps students to learn English better. Advocates of ASL assert that the use of signing English systems is too slow and awkward to be of much benefit in learning English. They argue that word order is not the critical element in teaching a person to use and comprehend English.

Advocates of ASL believe that fluency in ASL provides students with a rich background of information that readies them for the learning of English. Furthermore, they argue that ASL is the natural language of people who are deaf and that it should be fostered because it is the most natural and efficient way for students who are deaf to learn about the world. Unlike ASL, signing English systems are not true languages. They have been invented by one or a few people in a short period of time, whereas true sign languages such as ASL have evolved over several generations of users. Many of the critics of the total communication approach advocate the bicultural-bilingual approach.

The Bicultural-Bilingual Approach

Although several variations of the bicultural-bilingual approach exist, most contain these three features (Schirmer, 2001):

1. ASL is considered the primary language, and English is considered the secondary language.
2. People who are deaf play an important role in the development of the program and its curriculum.
3. The curriculum includes instruction in Deaf culture.

MyLab Education
Video Example 11.4
In this video, second grade children without hearing impairment are learning to use sign language.

Bilingual education for students who are deaf can be structured so that ASL is learned first, followed by English, or the two can be taught simultaneously.

Research directly bearing on the efficacy of bicultural-bilingual programs is in its infancy. At this point, we know that such programs hold great promise and that ASL may contribute to the reading and writing skills of students who are deaf (Simms, Andrews, & Smith, 2005). However, research comparing ASL, signing English systems, and the various approaches has been insufficient to conclude that only one approach should be used. Rather, it is probably safest to conclude that

> No fail-safe, success-guaranteed method exists for educating deaf children, though periodically through the history of deaf education various methods have been proposed as the pedagogical solution. In the 1960s and 1970s, total communication was considered to be the answer. In the 1980s and 1990s, bilingual education was touted as the solution. With the increase in cochlear implants, greater numbers of children are being educated orally/aurally . . . and oral/aural approaches have seen renewed interest. Ultimately, the profession may recognize that only a range of approaches can meet the needs of a range of deaf children. (Schirmer, 2001, p. 203)

Technological Advances

A number of technological advances have made it easier for persons with hearing impairment to communicate with and/or have access to information from the hearing world. This technological explosion has primarily involved five areas: hearing aids, captioning, telephones, computer-assisted instruction, and the Internet. The accompanying Responsive Instruction feature describes one way of using assistive technology to enhance literacy skills of children who are deaf or hard of hearing.

MyLab Education
Video Example 11.5

Belisa explains the importance of technology as an accommodation for her hearing impairment. Note the challenges that she discusses with hearing aids in large classes.

HEARING AIDS There are three main types of hearing aids: those worn behind the ear, those worn in the ear, and those worn farther down in the canal of the ear. The behind-the-ear hearing aid is the most powerful and is therefore used by those with the most severe hearing impairment. It's also the one that children most often use because it can be used with FM systems that are available in some classrooms. With an FM system, the teacher wears a wireless lapel microphone, and the student wears an FM receiver (about the size of a cell phone). The student hears the amplified sound either through a hearing aid that comes attached to the FM receiver or by attaching a behind-the-ear hearing aid to the FM receiver. Whether a student will be able to benefit from a hearing aid by itself depends a great deal on the acoustic qualities of the classroom.

MyLab Education
Video Example 11.6

This video shows several types of hearing aids.

Although hearing aids are an integral part of educational programming, some children who are deaf can't benefit from them because of the severity and/or nature of the hearing impairment. Generally, hearing aids make sounds louder, not clearer, so if a person's hearing is distorted, a hearing aid will merely amplify the distorted sound.

It is critical for the student, parents, and teachers to work together to ensure the maximum effectiveness of any device. This means that the teacher should be familiar with its proper operation and maintenance.

TELEVISION, VIDEO, VIDEO GAMES, MOVIES AND YOUTUBE AND CAPTIONING At one time, viewers needed a special decoder to access captioned programs. Federal law now requires that TVs with screens over 13 inches must contain a chip to allow one to view captions without a decoder—and also stipulates that virtually all new programming must be captioned. However, advocates such as the National Association of the Deaf continue to press for more and better captioning. One need only watch a live news show on TV to see how inaccurate some of the captions can be.

Captioning of video games is becoming more common. Many DVDs and programs available from streaming services are captioned as well. The Rear Window captioning system displays captions on transparent acrylic panels that movie patrons can attach to the cup holders on their seats. The captions are actually displayed in reverse at the rear of the theater, and viewers see them reflected on their acrylic screen.

RESPONSIVE INSTRUCTION

Meeting the Needs of Students Who Are Deaf or Hard of Hearing

ASSISTIVE TECHNOLOGY

What the Research Says

Historically, assistive technologies for students who are deaf or hard of hearing have focused on addressing hearing needs or aiding in communication. These traditional technologies include amplification systems, cochlear implants, captioning services, and telecommunication devices for the deaf (TDDs/TTYs). Newer assistive technologies, however, can go beyond simply supporting communication to address the unique *learning* needs of students who are deaf or hard of hearing. Videophones, webcams, 3D avatars, interactive white boards (e.g., Smart-Boards™), student response systems, and reading and writing software programs are some of the new technologies that can facilitate and enhance learning outcomes.

One learning challenge for many students who are deaf or hard of hearing is in learning to read (Paul, 1998). Some researchers hypothesize that because the majority of deaf children have hearing parents, these children may lack early literacy experiences, which contributes to later difficulties in learning to read. Research on typically developing children has demonstrated the benefits of shared reading on later reading development (Snow, Burns, & Griffin, 1998). Newer assistive technologies can support parents and teachers in creating shared storybook reading experiences that provide opportunities for learning story grammar, internalizing concepts of print, and mastering complex syntax and vocabulary that are unique to the written language experience (Mueller & Hurtig, 2010).

Research Study

Mueller and Hurtig (2010) conducted a study to see if an electronic storybook with signing support enhanced the shared storybook reading experience. Four children under the age of 5 and their mothers participated in the study. For a period of 5 weeks, the mother–child dyads received five different e-books on a touch screen tablet PC to read together.

The books, created using the Iowa Signing E-book, included interactive features such as embedded questions, clickable text (e.g., each word was linked to a video clip of the sign for that word), and page navigation. Parents received e-training for each book that included suggestions on how to engage their child during reading and video models on how to sign the story. Each week the story format would alternate between presentation of the story with a video of a signing narrator and presentation without the signing narrator. During both formats, mothers were expected to supplement the reading of the story through signing.

Research Findings

Overall, participants spent more time engaged in shared storybook reading when the books included the signing narrator. Although this time was only an increase of a few minutes per book, it resulted in 30% to 60% more time engaged in reading. In addition, the mothers interested in learning to sign spent more time with the parent training e-books during the nonsigning narrative weeks. Finally, both mothers and children increased their signed vocabulary over the course of the study.

Applying the Research to Teaching

Shared storybook reading is an important component of early literacy experiences. Due to their lack of signing ability, many hearing teachers and parents are reluctant to engage in shared storybook reading with children who are deaf (Moeller & Luetke-Stahlman, 1990). E-books that include signing components can facilitate the shared reading experience by providing this necessary visual support for both students and their hearing facilitators. Teachers can extend the findings of this study and think about ways that new technologies, such as webcams and interactive whiteboards, can provide similar supports (i.e., a visual signing component) during the instruction and independent work of students who are deaf or hard of hearing.

BY KRISTIN L. SAYESKI

Google now offers a way for people to caption the videos they make. The videos can be imported directly to 3Play Media, a company that creates captions that are automatically sent to YouTube and added to the videos. Google also provides tools for YouTube video developers to use to create their own captions.

TELEPHONE ADAPTATIONS At one time, people with hearing impairments had problems using telephones, either because their hearing impairment was too great or because of acoustic feedback (noise caused by closeness of the telephone receiver to their hearing aids). However, ironically, text messaging with smart phones has now become a very useful way for those with hearing impairments to communicate. Also, another primary means for communication are **text telephones (TT)**, sometimes referred to as *TTYs* *(teletypes)* or *TDDs (telecommunication devices for the deaf)*. People can use a TT connected to a telephone to type a message to anyone else who has a TT. A special phone adaptation allows people without a TT to use the pushbuttons on their phone to "type" messages to people with a TT.

The federal government now requires each state to have a relay service that allows a person with a TT to communicate with anyone through an operator, who conveys the message to a person who does not have a TT. The TT user can carry on a conversation with the non-TT user, or the TT user can leave a message.

Another expanding technology is **video relay service (VRS)**. VRS enables people who are deaf to communicate with people who hear through a sign language interpreter serving as an intermediary. For example, the person who is deaf can communicate in sign over television or video camera over the Internet to the interpreter, who then speaks to the hearing caller and also signs the response back to the person who is deaf.

COMPUTER-ASSISTED INSTRUCTION The explosion of computer and related technology is expanding learning capabilities for people who are deaf and their families. For example, visual displays of speech patterns on a computer screen can help someone with hearing impairment to learn speech. Software programs and online videos showing people signing are also available for use in learning ASL.

Another example of computer-based technology is C-Print. With C-Print, a person who hears uses an abbreviation system that reduces keystrokes to transcribe on a computer what is being said by, for example, someone lecturing. Students who are deaf can read a real-time text display on their computers as well as receive a printout of the text at a later time.

VIRTUAL REALITY-HOLOGRAM-3-D-SIGNING AVATARS Researchers are also working on using gesture-recognition technology to help young children who are deaf practice ASL skills (Brashear et al., 2006; Lee, Henderson, & Brashear, 2005). The child sits in front of a monitor and wears special wireless gloves whose movement can be monitored by the computer to determine how accurately the child is signing.

Perhaps the most experimental research of all focused on technology for people who are deaf has been the development of avatars that use sign language. The future potential use for signing avatars is virtually limitless. Consider the possibility of avatars being used as sign language interpreters in college classeooms. Or consider the possibility of having this textbook transliterated or available in sign language similar to how Recordings for the Blind and Dyslexia make textbooks available for persons who are blind or who have reading disabilities.

THE INTERNET The Internet has opened up a variety of communication possibilities for people who are deaf. Besides e-mail, blogs, and instant messaging, which have been around for a while, the flow of social networking sites, such as Facebook, Twitter, and so forth, seems constant. All of these can serve as vehicles for the Deaf community to stay connected and for people with and without hearing impairments to communicate with each other.

Service Delivery Models

Students who are deaf or hard of hearing can be found in settings ranging from general education classrooms to residential institutions. Since the mid-1970s, more and more of these students have been attending local schools in self-contained classes, resource rooms, and general education classes. Currently, about 87% of students with hearing impairments between the ages of 6 and 21 attend classes in local schools, and 60% spend at least 80% of their time in the general education classroom (U.S. Department of Education, Office of Special Education and Rehabilitative Services, Office of Special Education Programs, 2016). Even though students with hearing impairment are now included to a very high degree in general education classrooms, they are still served in special schools or residential settings more than students in most other disability categories, with about 9% in the former and 4% in the latter type of placement.

HOW CAN I HELP?
Collaboration and Co-Teaching of Students Who Are Deaf or Hard of Hearing

"If he can't hear me, how can I teach him?"

Working with a teacher of students who are deaf or hard of hearing may mean learning a new language or learning to work with interpreters. This may cause anxiety and initial reluctance on the part of the general education teacher to try to collaborate. In all cases, the general educator who is being asked to collaborate has a right to a thorough understanding of the abilities of the student (not just the disabilities) and of the goals the special educator has set for the collaboration.

What Does It Mean to Be a Teacher of Students Who Are Deaf or Hard of Hearing?

The focus of training for teachers of the deaf or hard of hearing is not on content but on the assessment, characteristics, and management of hearing impairments. Again, these teachers have special skills that they can offer the general educator, such as:

1. An understanding of the communication features (e.g., visual cues, accommodations) that are necessary to enhance cognitive, emotional, and social development of students with hearing impairments.
2. An ability to modify incidental language experiences (e.g., communicating with other students and friends when working in groups) to fit the visual and other sensory needs of individuals who are deaf or hard of hearing.
3. A knowledge of strategies to facilitate cognitive and communicative development in individuals who are deaf or hard of hearing. (Council for Exceptional Children, 2003).

Tapping into these areas of expertise will certainly help in a collaborative situation, but it takes more than expertise in a teaching area to make a collaboration work, as evidenced by the following example.

Successful Strategies for Co-Teaching

Cindy Sadonis (a teacher of students who are deaf/hard of hearing) and Connie Underwood (a third-grade teacher) worked collaboratively to include Joe and Brittany. Joe used hearing aids but had language deficits, and Brittany had a profound hearing loss and used both sign and oral language.

Cindy: I teach nine students with hearing impairments in grades K through 5. The students receive a range of special education services. All students, however, are mainstreamed for library, music, PE, guidance, and special events.

Connie: I teach a general education third-grade class. There are 17 students. I had worked with students with hearing impairments in my general education classroom in the past, and although the experiences were positive in many ways, I felt that I was connecting with the students "at a distance."

Cindy: We were both apprehensive despite being friends, co-workers, and experienced teachers. I went into Connie's room, and she and her third-grade students came into my room.

Connie: I had three main fears. First, was I going to be able to communicate with Joe and Brittany without an interpreter? Yikes! My signing skills were labored, elementary, and painfully wrong at times. Second, how much more planning and time would this take? When I was lead teacher, Cindy interpreted and observed and was ready the following week with lessons on the same theme. I became a support in her room when she became the lead teacher. Third, I was concerned about student relationships. Without prompting, our students began signing as they tried to communicate, and by the latter part of the year it was amazing how much communication was going on at the lunch table, in PE, and even secretively (or so the kids thought) in the classroom.

There were times when Brittany and Joe still felt different and when my students found it much easier to engage in conversations with their friends without hearing losses.

Cindy: It's important to know that collaborative teaching to this degree is often difficult, largely due to schedule. Positive teacher attitudes are required if inclusion is to succeed. Challenges presented themselves along the way for us, too. Social interaction was always an area of need despite our best efforts. As teachers, we have highs and lows, too. Working through them has helped us continue to move in the right direction.

For more information on hearing impairments, visit the National Institute of Deafness and Other Communication Disorders at www.nidcd.nih.gov/health/kids/index.htm

BY MARGARET P. WEISS

Many people within the Deaf community have been critical of the degree of inclusion that is occurring (Aldersley, 2002; Lane et al., 1996; Padden & Humphries, 2005; Siegel, 2000). For example, several national organizations, including the National Association for the Deaf, have issued statements supporting the full continuum of placements, including residential schools. They argue that residential schools (and, to a lesser extent, day schools) have been a major influence in fostering the concept of a Deaf culture and the use of ASL. Inclusion, they believe, forces students who are deaf to lose their Deaf identity and places them in a hearing and speaking environment in which it is almost

MyLab Education
Video Example 11.7

This video shows an inclusive classroom in which the teacher uses both American Sign Language (ASL) and spoken English.

impossible for them to succeed. In particular, critics of inclusion argue that when a student who is deaf is placed in a setting with children who do not have a disability, she is usually the only student with a hearing impairment in the class. This lack of a "critical mass" of students who are deaf can lead to two interrelated problems: (1) a lack of peers with whom the student who is deaf can communicate and (2) a high degree of social isolation (Lomas, Andrews, & Shaw, 2017).

Even though inclusion can present problems for many students who are deaf, by no means is it a negative experience for all students. Research on the effects of integrating students who are deaf with hearing peers has consistently found that social and academic outcomes vary depending on the individual. For some, full integration is beneficial; for others, a separate setting is best. Researchers have found that effective inclusive programming for students who are deaf is related to support from the school administration and parents and opportunities for instruction in the general education classroom by special educators trained in deaf education (Schirmer, 2001). For an example of how this can work, read the accompanying How Can I Help? feature.

ASSESSMENT OF PROGRESS

Many students who are deaf or hard of hearing are educated in inclusive settings with their peers who do not have a disability. As we noted earlier, however, these students characteristically underachieve in academic areas. To ensure that they receive appropriate instruction, it's critical to assess their progress and outcomes in academic subject areas. Additionally, students who are deaf or hard of hearing are often included in state- and district-wide assessments. Teachers should understand appropriate accommodations and alternate assessments specific to this population of students (Cawthon, 2009).

Assessing Academic Skills

Assessment of academic skills for students who are deaf or hard of hearing includes measures to monitor student progress and evaluate student outcomes. Progress monitoring measures are similar to those used to assess students who hear. Research suggests that the technical adequacy of various methods of curriculum-based measurement (CBM) is appropriate for students who are deaf or hard of hearing (Allinder & Eccarius, 1999; Cheng & Rose, 2009). Based on this research, teachers can feel confident in administering CBM probes to monitor progress in reading fluency and comprehension as well as written expression and math.

The STAR Reading, Math, and Early Literacy Assessments (Renaissance Learning, 2006) are also useful for monitoring the academic progress of students who are deaf or hard of hearing. These measures are computerized assessment tools that provide immediate information on student skills to assist with instructional planning. The National Center on Student Progress Monitoring evaluated this measure and found that it met high standards of rigor in progress monitoring (U.S. Department of Education, National Center on Progress Monitoring, 2006).

Performance on measures documenting academic outcomes has significant implications for students; these assessments, however, may not be technically appropriate for students who are deaf or hard of hearing. Unfortunately, most standardized assessments are biased toward the majority culture (Mason, 2005). Educators must consider these biases carefully when making decisions as a result of students' outcomes. Despite these concerns, it's important to have methods to evaluate students' academic achievement.

Testing Accommodations

As students who are deaf or hard of hearing are being included in standardized assessments at higher rates, states are developing guidelines for the use of accommodations. Wide variability exists in how each state provides accomodations for students with hearing impairment (Lomas, Andrews, & Shaw, 2017). However, the most common presentation accommodations for these students are sign interpretation for directions and for test questions, extended time, and small-group or individual administration (Cawthon, 2010). Most states allow signing directions without restriction, but some states consider the accommodation for signing questions nonstandard (Lazarus, Thurlow, Lail, Eisenbraun, & Kato, 2006). A nonstandard accommodation often affects scoring and interpretation of the test. Students who are deaf or hard of hearing also receive response accommodations such as signing responses to an interpreter.

MyLab Education Self-Check 11.4

MyLab Education Application Exercise 11.4:
Inclusive Classroom Practices
Watch a video about inclusive practices that support students with hearing impairment. Then answer the questions that follow.

EARLY INTERVENTION

Education for infants and preschoolers with hearing impairments is of critical importance. Such programs not only can help facilitate the development of the children but also may be beneficial in reducing parents' stress levels (Lederberg & Golbach, 2002).

Because language development is such an issue for children who have hearing impairment and because early childhood is such an important time for the development of language, it's not surprising that many of the most controversial issues surrounding early intervention in the area of deafness focus on language. As indicated in our earlier discussion of oralism versus manualism, some people maintain that English language should be the focus of intervention efforts, and others hold that ASL should be used starting in infancy.

Children who are deaf and whose parents are deaf are likely to do better than children who are deaf with hearing parents. For example, in infancy, they develop ASL at a rate similar to the rate at which hearing infants of hearing parents develop English. But infants who are deaf who have hearing parents don't develop either English or ASL at as fast a rate. This may be because day-to-day interactions between mothers and infants are more facilitative and natural when both the infant and parents are deaf than when the infant is deaf and the parents are hearing.

In addition to facility with ASL, parents who are deaf also have the advantage of being better prepared to cope with their infant's deafness (Meadow-Orlans, 1990). Most parents who are hearing are unprepared for the birth of a child with hearing impairment, whereas parents who are deaf can draw on their own experiences in order to offer helpful support to their child who is deaf.

Hearing parents, especially if they want to teach their infants sign language, may need help in understanding the importance of the visual modality in communicating with their infants (Bornstein, Selmi, Haynes, Painter, & Marx, 1999). Hearing parents need to understand, for example, that the eye gaze of the infant who is deaf is extremely important because it's her way of expressing interest and motivation. The parents' eye gaze is also important because it can facilitate the child's communication and language development by helping direct the infant's attention (Clark et al., 2015).

Hearing parents of children who are deaf face a quandary over how to provide their children with appropriate sign language models. Both signed English and ASL, especially the latter, are difficult to learn to a high degree of fluency in a relatively short time. And like any language, ASL is harder to acquire as an adult and can rarely be learned to the same degree of fluency as that possessed by a native ASL signer.

The fact that about 90% of children who are deaf have parents who are hearing underscores the importance of intervention for many infants who are deaf. In fact, many

MyLab Education
Video Example 11.8

Belisa explains how important it is for teachers of young children to have high expectations for students with hearing impairment.

authorities believe that the need for early intervention is far greater for families with hearing parents of a child who is deaf than for families in which both the parents and the child are deaf (Andrews & Zmijewski, 1997).

Educators have established preschool intervention projects to teach the basics of sign language to the parents of children who are deaf as well as to the children themselves. Such projects are generally successful at teaching the rudiments of sign to parents and infants. Once the child is ready to progress beyond one- and two-word signed utterances, however, it's important that native signers be available as models. Authorities recommend a practice that is popular in Sweden: Adults who are deaf are part of early intervention efforts because they can serve as sign language models and can help hearing parents form positive expectations about their children's potential (Lane et al., 1996). Even though hearing parents might never be able to communicate fluently in sign language, it is important that they continue to sign with their child. Not only does signing allow parents a means of communicating with their child but it also demonstrates that they value the child's language and the Deaf culture.

TRANSITION TO ADULTHOOD

Unemployment and underemployment (being overqualified for a job) have been persistent problems for persons with a hearing impairment, especially women (Punch, Hyde, & Creed, 2004; Schirmer, 2001). The reasons for the difficulty experienced by individuals with hearing impairments in finding appropriate and satisfying employment have a lot to do with a poor understanding among the members of the population who do not have hearing impairments of what it means to have a hearing impairment and of possible accommodations in the workplace. Likewise, people with hearing impairments, themselves, often aren't prepared to ask for the right accommodations and have difficulties making good career choices (Punch, 2016).

MyLab Education
Video Example 11.9

Belisa, who has hearing impairment, explains how social interactions are difficult for her in the college setting.

Some evidence indicates, however, that this bleak picture is slowly beginning to change. The primary reason for this change has been the expansion of postsecondary programming for students with hearing impairment. A 15-year follow-up of graduates with hearing impairment from 2- and 4-year colleges found that a college education made a substantial difference in having a satisfying career and life (Schroedel & Geyer, 2000).

Postsecondary Education

Before the mid-1960s, the only institution established specifically for the postsecondary education of students with hearing impairment was Gallaudet College (now Gallaudet University). Except for this one institution, these students were left with no choice but to attend traditional colleges and universities. However, traditional postsecondary schools were generally not equipped to handle the special needs of students with hearing impairment. It's little wonder, then, that a study by Quigley, Jenne, and Phillips (1968) identified only 224 people with hearing impairment who were graduates of regular colleges and universities in the United States between 1910 and 1965.

Findings such as these led to the expansion of postsecondary programs. The federal government has funded a wide variety of postsecondary programs for students with hearing impairment. The two best-known ones are Gallaudet University and the National Technical Institute for the Deaf (NTID) at the Rochester Institute of Technology. The NTID program, emphasizing training in technical fields, complements the liberal arts orientation of Gallaudet University. At NTID, some students with hearing impairment also attend classes at the Rochester Institute of Technology with students who hear.

In addition to Gallaudet and NTID, well over 100 postsecondary programs are now available in the United States and Canada for students with hearing impairment. By law, Gallaudet and NTID are responsible for serving students from all 50 states and territories. Others serve students from several states, from one state only, or from specific districts only.

Although many people who are deaf who enroll in higher education choose to attend Gallaudet, NTID, or colleges with special programs, some go to traditional colleges and universities. These students usually take advantage of the expanding roles of university programs that have been established to facilitate the academic experiences of students with disabilities. One of the accommodations often recommended is to provide sign language interpreters in the classes students with hearing impairment attend.

SIGN LANGUAGE INTERPRETERS Even though most authorities would agree that having a sign language interpreter is one of the best accommodations, it's important to keep in mind that this is a far cry from leveling the academic playing field for students with hearing impairments. First, there is a national shortage of adequately trained interpreters (Schick, Williams, & Kupermintz, 2006). To appreciate the scope of the shortage, one can visit www.indeed.com, type in a city or a state and search for positions for "sign language interpreters." For example, as we write this, on November 16, 2017, by entering "sign language interpreter" and "Virginia" into the search boxes, 62 jobs are listed. To put this in context, entering "Spanish interpreter" or "Arabic interpreter" yields only 23 and 16 jobs, respectively.

Even when students with hearing impairment have access to highly trained interpreters, the amount of information they can take in falls well below that of their hearing peers. In other words, when hearing students and students who are deaf hear and see (through interpretation) the same lecture, the students who are deaf don't learn as much of the material (Marschark, Pelz et al., 2005; Marschark, Sapere, Convertino, & Seewagen, 2005; Marschark, Sapere, Convertino, Seewagen, & Maltzen, 2004).

The role of interpreters generates a debate over using ASL versus transliteration. **Transliteration,** which is similar to signed English, maintains the same word order as spoken English. ASL, by contrast, requires the interpreter to digest the meaning of what is said before conveying it through signs. Most college instructors have limited, if any, experience in working with sign language interpreters. Even so, it is critical that instructors and interpreters work closely together to provide the optimum learning experience for students who are deaf while not disrupting other students in the class (Seal, 2004).

Family Issues

With regard to raising a family, people who are deaf often face unique challenges. National statistics indicate that 95% of adults who are deaf choose deaf spouses, and 90% of the offspring of these marriages have normal hearing (Buchino, 1993). These hearing children often serve as interpreters for their parents. Being called on to interpret for one's parents can help to develop self-confidence around adult authority figures (e.g., doctors, lawyers, insurance agents), but it can also force one to face some unpleasant biases, as the following story from a hearing child of deaf parents demonstrates:

> Curled up in the seat, chin dug into my chest, I noticed there was a lull in the conversation. Dad was a confident driver, but Mom was smoking more than usual.
>
> "Something happened? That gas station?" Mom signed to me.
>
> "No, nothing," I lied.
>
> "Are you sure?"
>
> "Everything is fine." Dad and I had gone to pay and get directions. The man behind the counter had looked up, seen me signing and grunted, "Huh, I didn't think mutes were allowed to have driver's licenses." Long ago I'd gotten used to hearing those kind of comments. But I never could get used to the way it made me churn inside. (Walker, 1986, p. 9)

These children also sometimes resent that being called on to interpret for their parents has interfered with their social lives (Buchino, 1993).

There has been a long tradition of preparing students who are deaf for manual trades (Lane, 1992). But unskilled and semiskilled trades are fast disappearing from the workforce in favor of jobs requiring higher-level skills. As a result, adults who are deaf face even greater obstacles when they enter the job market.

Although the educational, work, and social opportunities for adults who are deaf are often limited, there are reasons to be optimistic about the future. With the continued expansion of transition programming, postsecondary education, and greater public awareness of the potential of people who are deaf, there is promise for a brighter outlook for adults who are deaf.

MyLab Education Self-Check 11.5

MyLab Education Application Exercise 11.5:
Hearing Parents/Deaf Child: Issues and Challenges

Watch an interview with the mother of Ashley, a child with hearing impairment, and answer the question that follows.

▼ chapter eleven SUMMARY

How do professionals define and classify individuals who are deaf or hard of hearing?

- Professionals with a *physiological* perspective use a decibel loss of 90 dB or greater as the cutoff for deafness.

- Those with an *educational* perspective classify individuals as deaf if they can't process linguistic information, with or without a hearing aid; they classify individuals as hard of hearing if they can process this information with the help of a hearing aid.

- *Congenital versus adventitious deafness* refers to being born deaf versus acquiring deafness after birth; *prelingual deafness* versus postlingual deafness refers to deafness occurring before versus after speech and language development.

- Sentiment is growing in the Deaf community that those who are deaf should be considered as a cultural/linguistic minority rather than disabled.

What is the prevalence of hearing impairment?

- About 0.10% of students from 6 to 21 years of age are identified as having hearing impairment; those classified as hard of hearing are more prevalent than those identified as deaf.

- More than half of students identified as having hearing impairment are minorities, and over 30% come from Spanish-speaking homes.

What are some basic anatomical and physiological characteristics of the ear?

- The outer ear consists of the auricle and external auditory canal.

- The middle ear consists of the eardrum and three tiny bones (ossicles): the malleus, incus, and stapes.

Sladic/Shutterstock

- The inner ear consists of the vestibular mechanism and the cochlea; the former monitors balance, and the latter is the most important for hearing because it is responsible for sending electrical impulses to the brain via the cochlear nerve.

How is hearing impairment identified?

- Screening tests for infants often measure otoacoustic emissions, low-intensity sound emitted from the cochlea when stimulated.

- Pure-tone audiometry assesses decibel (intensity) and hertz (frequency) levels.

- Speech audiometry assesses the ability to detect and understand speech.

What causes hearing impairments?

- Conductive hearing impairments involve the middle or outer ear, sensorineural hearing impairments involve the inner ear, and mixed hearing impairments involve both.

- The causes of impairments of the outer ear include infections of the external canal or tumors.

- Impairments of the middle ear are often due to malfunctioning of the ossicles; otitis media is a common cause of temporary middle-ear hearing problems.

- Impairments of the inner ear usually result in greater hearing impairment than do those of the middle or outer ear; impairments of the inner ear can be hereditary or acquired, but the former are much more common. Genetic or hereditary factors are the leading cause of deafness in children, with mutation of the connexin-26 gene now considered the most common cause of congenital deafness.

What are some psychological and behavioral characteristics of learners with hearing impairments?

- The most severely affected area is comprehension and production of English.
- Sign language is the primary language of most people in the Deaf community.
  - Each sign consists of three parts: handshape, location, and movement.
  - Sign language is a true language, as evidenced by the facts that sign language is as grammatically complex as spoken language, there is no universal sign language, children who are deaf reach the same language milestones and at the same times as do those who can hear, and the neurological underpinnings of sign language are the same as those for spoken language.
- Deafness doesn't affect intelligence.
- Most students who are deaf have extreme deficits in academics, especially reading.
  - Students who are deaf who have parents who are deaf do better academically.
  - A supportive home environment is associated with higher achievement.
- Students who are deaf might face limited opportunities for social interaction.
  - The inclusion movement can result in students who are deaf not having peers who are deaf with whom to communicate.
  - About 90% of children who are deaf have hearing parents, most of whom are not proficient in sign language.
  - Many authorities recognize the Deaf culture as a means of healthy social communication. There is concern that the Deaf culture might be eroding owing to inclusionary programming. Deaf activists have raised issues with respect to cochlear implants and genetic engineering.

What are some educational considerations for learners with hearing impairments?

- The oral approach consists of the following:
  - The auditory-verbal approach, which focuses on using audition to improve speech and language development.
  - The auditory-oral approach, which is like the auditory-verbal approach with the addition of using visual cues such as speechreading and cued speech.
- The manual approach stresses sign language.
- Most educational programs use a total communication (simultaneous communication) approach, a blend of oral and manual techniques, the latter being a type of signing English system in which the English word order is preserved.
- Some advocate for a bicultural-bilingual approach, which consists of three features: ASL is considered the primary language, people who are deaf are involved in the development of the program and curriculum, and the curriculum involves instruction in Deaf culture.
- Educational placement of students who are deaf includes the full continuum, but more inclusive settings are becoming more and more popular, with about 86% of students who are deaf attending classes in regular schools and 52% spending the vast majority of their time in general education classrooms. Many within the Deaf community are concerned that the inclusion movement results in the absence of a "critical mass" of students who are deaf, which can result in social isolation.
- Numerous technological advances are occurring in hearing aids; television, video, and movie captioning; text telephone technology; computer-assisted instruction; and the Internet.

How do professionals assess the progress of students with hearing impairments?

- Using sign language, professionals can implement CBM to monitor progress in academics, such as reading fluency, reading comprehension, writing, and math.
- The most common accommodations for standardized assessments include sign interpretation for directions and for test questions, extended time, and small-group or individual administration.

What are some important considerations with respect to early intervention for learners with hearing impairments?

- Families of children who are deaf with hearing parents might be in greater need of early intervention programming than families in which the parents are deaf.
- Because it is difficult for hearing parents to become fluent in sign language, native signers are a part of some intervention programs.

What are some important considerations with respect to transition to adulthood for learners with hearing impairments?

- In addition to Gallaudet University and the National Technical Institute for the Deaf, several postsecondary programs are now available for students with hearing impairment.
- A common accommodation in college is the use of sign language interpreters. Transliteration involves maintaining the same word order as English, whereas ASL does not.
- Ninety percent of the children of two parents who are deaf have normal hearing. These children often face challenges of negotiating between the Deaf community and hearing society.
- There has been a long tradition of preparing many students who are deaf for manual trades; however, these trades are disappearing.
- Expanded transition programming, postsecondary education, and public awareness promise a brighter outlook for adults who are deaf.

▼ INTERNET RESOURCES

Organizations Focused on People Who are Deaf and Hard of Hearing

- Founded in 1951, the World Federation of the Deaf (http://wfdeaf.org) is one of the oldest international organizations concerned with disabilities. The WFD focuses on international issues pertaining to those who are deaf or hard of hearing.

- The National Association of the Deaf (www.nad.org) concentrates on promoting and preserving the civil rights of persons who are deaf or hard of hearing.

- An excellent website is maintained by the National Institute on Deafness and Other Communication Disorders of the National Institutes of Health. On this site you can access a number of interesting demonstrations, including a video that explains how the ear works: www.nidcd.nih.gov

- Visit the National Theatre of the Deaf's website to look for upcoming performances in your area: www.NTD.org

- Two examples of publications devoted to issues of concern to the Deaf community are the magazines *Silent News* and *Deaf Life*. The former also has an online edition (www.silentnews.com/index.html). On the site, it presents itself as "a good glimpse into the Deaf community." Deaf Life's website has chat rooms for adults and some just for children: http://www.deaflife.com/

- The National Association of the Deaf had for years been opposed to cochlear implants. However, in the fall of 2000, it issued a policy statement that was much more neutral in tone; see http://www.nad.org/issues/technology/assistive-listening/cochlear-implants

- Signing Savvy is a website offering a "dictionary" of videos of ASL signs for spoken words: https://www.signingsavvy.com/

- About.Com has a listing of the most popular Facebook sites focused on people who are deaf: http://deafness.about.com/od/deafcommunity/tp/deafonfacebook.htm

- Children of Deaf Adults (CODA; www.coda-international.org) is an organization devoted to children of adults who are deaf. As stated on the website, "CODA is an organization established for the purpose of promoting family awareness and individual growth in hearing children of deaf parents. This purpose is accomplished through providing educational opportunities, promoting self-help, organizing advocacy efforts, and acting as a resource for the membership and various communities."

LEARNERS WITH BLINDNESS OR LOW VISION

▶ **LEARNING OUTCOMES**

Learning Outcome 12.1: Understand the definition, classification, and prevalence of individuals with blindness or low vision.

Learning Outcome 12.2: Learn about the anatomical and physiological characteristics of the eye, the causes of visual impairments, and how visual impairments are identified.

Learning Outcome 12.3: Understand some psychological and behavioral characteristics of people with blindness or low vision.

Learning Outcome 12.4: Learn about educational considerations for people with visual impairments and how professionals assess progress to help plan educational strategies.

Learning Outcome 12.5: Learn about issues that should be considered with respect to early intervention and transition to adulthood for individuals with blindness or low vision.

MISCONCEPTIONS ABOUT Learners with Blindness or Low Vision

MYTH People who are legally blind have no sight at all.

FACT Only a small percentage of people who are legally blind have absolutely no vision.

MYTH People who are blind have an extra sense that enables them to detect obstacles.

FACT People who are blind do not have an extra sense. Some can learn to develop echolocation skills by noting the change in echoes as they move toward objects. Likewise, better acuity in other senses does not arise on its own, but through intense concentration, they can develop fine discriminations in their remaining senses.

MYTH People who are blind have superior musical ability.

FACT People who are blind are not inherently gifted in music; however, many pursue musical careers as one way in which they can achieve success.

MYTH Stereotypic behaviors (e.g., body rocking, head swaying) are always maladaptive and should be totally eliminated.

FACT Although more research is needed, some authorities maintain that these behaviors, except when they are extreme, can help persons who are blind regulate their levels of arousal.

MYTH Braille is not very useful for the vast majority of people who are blind; it should only be tried as a last resort.

FACT Very few people who are blind have learned braille, primarily due to fear that using it is a sign of failure and to a historical professional bias against it. Authorities now acknowledge the utility of braille for people who are blind and for those with low vision whose conditions are likely to eventually lead to blindness.

MYTH If people with low vision use their eyes too much, their sight will deteriorate.

FACT Only rarely is this true. Wearing strong lenses, holding books close to the eyes, and using the eyes rarely harm vision.

MYTH Mobility instruction should be delayed until elementary or secondary school.

FACT Many authorities now recognize that even preschoolers can take advantage of mobility instruction, including the use of a cane.

MYTH The long cane is a simply constructed, easy-to-use device.

FACT Learning to use the long cane requires extensive, intensive instruction.

MYTH Guide dogs take people where they want to go.

FACT The guide dog does not "take" the person anywhere; usually, the person must first know where he or she is going. The dog can be a protection against unsafe areas or obstacles.

MYTH Technology will soon replace the need for braille and for mobility aids such as the long cane and guide dogs. In addition, a breakthrough for restoring complete sight through technology is just around the corner.

FACT As amazing as some of the technologies are in the field of vision impairment, it's doubtful that they will replace braille, the long cane, or guide dogs anytime soon. Research on artificial vision is exciting, but it too does not promise huge practical benefits for some time.

GUIDING QUESTIONS

- How do professionals define and classify learners with blindness and low vision?
- What is the prevalence of visual impairment?
- What are some basic anatomical and physiological characteristics of the eye?
- How is visual ability measured?
- What causes visual impairments?
- What are some of the psychological and behavioral characteristics of learners with visual impairments?
- What are some educational considerations for learners with visual impairments?

- How do professionals assess the progress of students with visual impairments in academic and functional skills and make testing accommodations for them?
- What are some important considerations with respect to early intervention for learners with visual impairments?
- What are some important considerations with respect to transition to adulthood for learners with visual impairments?

Of all the special education categories, we perhaps feel particularly uncomfortable interacting with persons with visual impairment. Visual impairments seem to evoke more awkwardness than most other disabilities. Why are we so uncomfortably aware of blindness? For one thing, blindness is visible. We often don't realize that a person has impaired hearing, for example, until we actually talk to him or her. The person with visual impairment, however, usually has a variety of symbols: a cane, physically abnormal eyes, thick or darkened glasses, a guide dog.

Perhaps we tend to be self-conscious around people who are blind because of the role that eyes play in social interaction. Poets, playwrights, and songwriters have long recognized how emotionally expressive the eyes can be for people who are sighted. Those of us who are sighted know how uncomfortable it can be to talk with someone who doesn't make eye contact with us. Think how often we've heard someone say or have ourselves said that we prefer to talk face to face on an important matter, rather than over the telephone.

In addition, although blindness is the least prevalent of all disabilities, at least in children, people dread it. It is reportedly the third most feared condition; only cancer and AIDS outrank it (Jernigan, 1992). Perhaps we fear loss of vision because the sense of sight is linked so closely with the traditional concept of beauty. We derive great pleasure from our sight. Our feelings about others are often based largely on physical appearances that are visually perceived. Additionally, our use of language reinforces a negative view of blindness (Kleege, 1999). For example, think of how often you've heard these expressions, in which *blind* is used with negative connotations: "blind alley," "blind spot," "blind to (fill in the term)."

With a bit of reflection, however, it becomes obvious that our anxieties about blindness are largely irrational. Most of our apprehension is because of our lack of experience interacting with individuals with visual impairment. It's not until we talk to people who are blind or read about their appreciation of sounds, smells, and touch that we begin to realize that sight is not the only sense that enables us to enjoy beauty or socialize with other people. Ironically, people who are blind themselves sometimes feel awkward about their blindness, not knowing exactly how to deal with it, especially when they aren't provided with appropriate social supports. Noted poet and author, Stephen Kuusisto, was blind from birth but was well

into his adult years before he stopped the charade of trying to "pass" as a sighted person. Once at peace with his blindness, he was able to turn his energies to more productive endeavors, such as being a successful author. A major theme of Kuusisto's work is that people who are blind vary in their response to being blind. Some actually gain an inner strength from adversity. For example, in his poem, "Elegy for Ray Charles and His Mother," Kuusisto describes how the mother of the legendary icon of soul music, Ray Charles, demanded that he do household chores, such as cutting firewood and carrying water, thereby making sure to instill in Charles a work ethic at least as strong as that for children who aren't blind.

However, a major impediment to being able to accept one's blindness is society's reactions to people who are blind. Like anyone with a disability, the person who is blind wants to be treated like everyone else. Most people who are blind do not seek pity or unnecessary help. In fact, they can be fiercely protective of their independence.

In this chapter, we hope to dispel several myths about blindness. We start by presenting a fact that most sighted people do not know: The majority of people who are blind can actually see.

DEFINITION AND CLASSIFICATION

The two most common ways of describing someone with visual impairment are the legal and educational definitions. Laypeople and medical professionals use the former; the latter is the one educators favor. The two major classifications are blindness and low vision.

Legal Definition

The legal definition involves assessment of visual acuity and field of vision. A person who is **legally blind** has visual acuity of 20/200 or less in the better eye even with correction (e.g., eyeglasses) or has a field of vision so narrow that its widest diameter subtends an angular distance no greater than 20 degrees. The fraction 20/200 means that the person sees at 20 feet what a person with normal vision sees at 200 feet. (Normal visual acuity is thus 20/20.) The inclusion of a narrowed field of vision in the legal definition means that a person may have 20/20 vision in the central field but severely restricted peripheral vision. Legal blindness qualifies a person for certain legal benefits, such as tax advantages and money for special materials.

In addition to this classification of blindness is a category referred to as **low vision** (sometimes referred to as *partially sighted*). According to the legal classification system, persons who have low vision have visual acuity falling between 20/70 and 20/200 in the better eye with correction.

Educational Definition

Many professionals, particularly educators, find the legal classification scheme inadequate. They have observed that visual acuity is not a very accurate predictor of how people will function or use whatever remaining sight they have. Although a small percentage of individuals who are legally blind have absolutely no vision, the majority can see to some degree.

Many who recognize the limitations of the legal definitions of blindness and low vision favor the educational definition, which stresses the method of reading instruction. For educational purposes, individuals who are blind are so severely impaired they must learn to read **braille**, a system of raised dots by which people who are blind read with their fingertips. It consists of quadrangular cells containing from one to six dots whose arrangement denotes different letters and symbols. Alternatively, they use aural methods (audiotapes and recordings). Those who have low vision can read print, even if they need adaptations such as magnifying devices or large-print books.

It's important to note that even though people with low vision can read print, many authorities believe that some of them can benefit from using braille. (We discuss this later in the chapter.) This is why we previously emphasized that those who are considered blind must use braille to read.

PREVALENCE

Blindness is primarily an adult disability. Most estimates indicate that blindness is approximately one-tenth as prevalent in school-age children as in adults. The federal government classifies only about 0.04% of the population ranging from 6 to 21 years of age as "visually impaired," which includes those who are blind or who have low vision. This is probably an underestimate because many blind children also have other disabilities, and school systems are instructed to report only the "primary" condition. So, for example, some students who are both blind and have intellectual disabilities might be designated as being in just one of the categories—"blind" or "having intellectual disability." The fact remains, however, that visual impairment is one of the least prevalent disabilities in children.

MyLab Education **Self-Check 12.1**

MyLab Education **Application Exercise 12.1:**
What Does Visual Impairment Mean?

Watch a video to see a range of students participating in a mixed grade classroom at a school for students with visual impairments, and then answer the questions that follow.

ANATOMY AND PHYSIOLOGY OF THE EYE

The anatomy of the visual system is extremely complex, so our discussion here focuses on only basic characteristics. Figure 12.1 shows the functioning of the eye. Basically, the physical object that you see becomes an electrical impulse that is sent through the optic nerve to the visual center of the brain, the occipital lobes. Before reaching the optic nerve, light rays reflecting off the object being seen pass through several structures within the eye. The light rays do the following:

1. Pass through the **cornea** (a transparent cover in front of the iris and pupil), which performs the major part of the bending (refraction) of the light rays so that the image will be focused
2. Pass through the **aqueous humor** (a watery substance between the cornea and lens of the eye)
3. Pass through the **pupil** (the contractile opening in the middle of the **iris**, the colored portion of the eye that contracts or expands, depending on the amount of light striking it)
4. Pass through the **lens**, which refines and changes the focus of the light rays before they pass through the **vitreous humor** (a transparent gelatinous substance that fills the eyeball between the retina and lens)
5. Come to a focus on the **retina** (the back portion of the eye, containing nerve fibers connected to the **optic nerve**, which carries the information back to the brain)

Here is a visual demonstration of how the eye works. (http://www.youtube.com/watch?v=LpjbOhtcD0A&feature=endscreen&NR=1)

IDENTIFICATION OF VISUAL IMPAIRMENT

Visual acuity is most often measured with the **Snellen chart**, which consists of rows of letters (for individuals who know the alphabet). For the very young and/or those who cannot read, the chart has rows of the letter *E* arranged in various positions, and the person's task is to indicate in what direction the "legs" of the *E*'s face.

FIGURE 12.1

THE BASIC ANATOMICAL FEATURES OF THE EYE AND THE VISUAL PROCESS

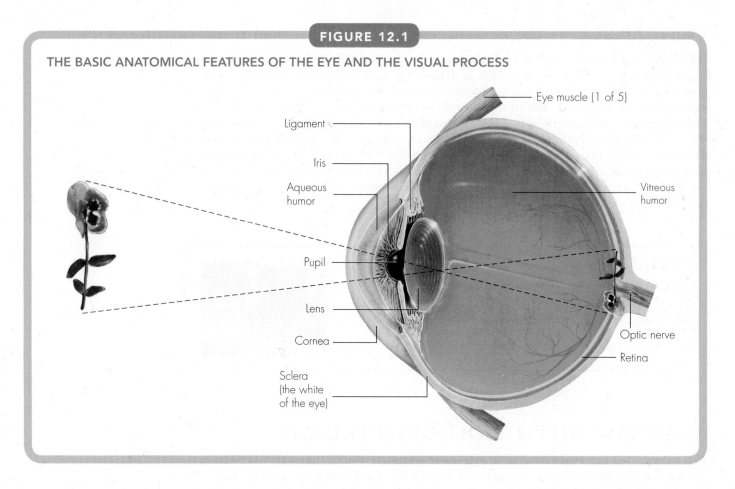

Although the Snellen chart is widely used and can be very helpful, it does have some limitations. First, it's a measure of visual acuity for distant objects, and a person's distance and near vision sometimes differ. Assessing near vision usually involves naming letters that range in size from smaller to larger on a card that is at a typical reading distance from the person's eyes.

Second, and more important, visual acuity doesn't always correspond with how a student actually uses his vision in natural settings, which have variable environmental conditions (e.g., fluorescent lighting, windows that admit sunshine, highly reflective tile floors). Vision teachers, therefore, usually do a functional vision assessment. A **functional vision assessment** involves observing the student interacting in different environments (e.g., classroom, outdoors, grocery stores), under different lighting conditions to see how well the student can identify objects and perform various tasks (Zebehazy & Lawson, 2017).

CAUSES OF VISUAL IMPAIRMENT

Causes Affecting Children and Adults

When considering both children and adults, the most common visual problems are the result of errors of refraction. **Refraction** refers to the bending of the light rays as they pass through the various structures of the eye. **Myopia** (nearsightedness), **hyperopia** (farsightedness), and **astigmatism** (blurred vision) are examples of refraction errors that affect central visual acuity. Although each can be serious enough to cause significant impairment (myopia and hyperopia are the most common impairments of low vision), wearing glasses or contact lenses usually can bring vision within normal limits.

FIGURE 12.2

VISUAL PROBLEMS: (A) MYOPIA, (B) HYPEROPIA

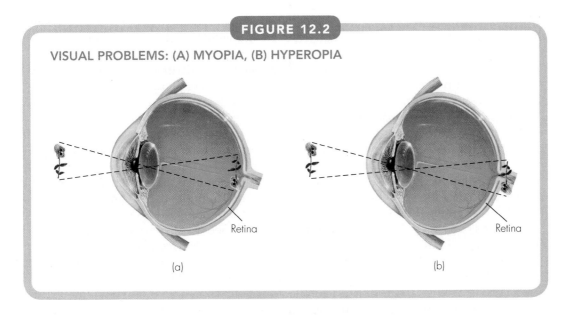

Retina

Retina

(a)   (b)

Myopia results when the eyeball is too long; hyperopia results when the eyeball is too short. As shown in Figure 12.2, for myopia, the light rays from the object are in focus in front of, rather than on, the retina (12.2a); and for hyperopia, the light rays from the object are in focus behind, rather than on, the retina (12.2b). Myopia affects vision for distant objects, but close vision may be unaffected. When the eyeball is too short, hyperopia (farsightedness) results. Hyperopia affects vision for close objects, but far vision may be unaffected. If the cornea or lens of the eye is irregular, the person is said to have astigmatism. In this case, the light rays from the object in the figure are blurred or distorted.

Among the more serious impairments are those caused by glaucoma, cataracts, and diabetes. These conditions occur primarily in adults, but each, particularly the latter two, can occur in children. **Glaucoma** is actually a *group* of eye diseases that causes damage to the **optic nerve**. It is usually caused by excessive pressure of fluid (the aqueous humor) in the eye. Glaucoma is referred to as the "sneak thief of sight" because it often occurs with no symptoms. However, glaucoma can be detected through an eye exam; because it occurs more frequently in older people (and in African Americans), professionals recommend increasingly frequent checkups, starting at age 35 (and even more frequently for African Americans).

Cataracts are caused by a clouding of the lens of the eye, which results in blurred vision. In children, the condition is called *congenital cataracts*, and distance and color vision are seriously affected. Surgery can usually correct the problems caused by cataracts.

Diabetes can cause **diabetic retinopathy**, a condition that results from interference with the blood supply to the retina.

Causes Primarily Affecting Children

The three most common causes of blindness in children are **cortical visual impairment (CVI)**, **retinopathy of prematurity (ROP)**, and **optic nerve hypoplasia (ONH)**. With respect to locus of causation, as a general rule, CVI occurs in the *brain*, ROP occurs in the *eye*, and ONH occurs in *nerve cells between the eye and the brain* (Zebehazy & Lawson, 2017).

For children, CVI is now the leading cause of visual impairment. CVI results from damage to parts of the *brain* responsible for vision. In other words, the eye itself is not always abnormal, but the mechanisms in the brain responsible for sight are dysfunctional. CVI often co-occurs with a wide range of other neurological disabilities, such as cerebral palsy, seizures, epilepsy, and so forth (Edmond & Foroozan, 2006; Weinstein et al., 2012).

We know from research that all children's brains are constantly changing and that different areas of the brain develop more rapidly at certain periods than at other times.

This plasticity of the developing brain in children with CVI can result in unexpected changes in visual functioning. For example, some individuals with CVI function better visually in low-light conditions (Good & Hou, 2006), and the eyesight of some can actually improve over time (Good, Hou, & Norcia, 2012). Such irregularities make studying blindness due to CVI particularly challenging for researchers and practitioners (Ely, 2016).

ROP results in abnormal growth of blood vessels in the eye, which then causes the retina to detach. The discovery of one of the causes of ROP involved a dramatic medical breakthrough. ROP began to appear more frequently in the 1940s in premature infants. In the 1950s, researchers determined that excessive concentrations of oxygen often administered to premature infants to prevent brain damage were causing blindness by affecting the growth of blood vessels in the eye. Since then, hospitals have been careful to monitor the amount of oxygen administered to premature infants. But this has not led to the elimination of ROP. Prematurity itself heightens the risk for ROP because blood vessels of the eye are not always fully developed until the baby is full term or close to full term. In 2013, the American Academy of Pediatrics (AAP) issued a policy statement asserting that low birthweight and/or premature babies should undergo a series of screening tests for ROP, and the AAP reaffirmed this policy in 2016 (Policy Statement: Screening Examination of Premature Infants for Retinopathy of Prematurity, 2013). Although not completely curable, scientists are making progress in retarding the progression of the condition through medical procedures (Chung, Kim, Ahn, & Koh, 2007; Mintz-Hittner & Kuffel, 2008).

ONH involves underdevelopment of the optic nerve. Although ONH can occur on its own (Borchert & Garcia-Filion, 2008), it is usually accompanied by myriad other neurological disorders (e.g., cerebral palsy, seizures, intellectual disabilities, autism), resulting in a variety of behavioral and cognitive problems (Borchert, 2012; Ek, Fernell, & Jacobson, 2005; Garcia et al., 2006). The exact cause or causes of ONH are still unknown although some researchers have pointed to health of the mother as a factor in some cases (Garcia-Filion, Fink, Geffner, & Borchert, 2010). Also, the prevalence of ONH is on the rise; however, it is not clear whether the increase is due to better diagnosis or some other, perhaps environmental, factors (Borchert & Garcia-Filion, 2008).

Retinitis pigmentosa (http://www.youtube.com/watch?v=fAf1_kbt5cw) is a hereditary condition that results in degeneration of the retina. It can start in infancy, early childhood, or the teenage years. Retinitis pigmentosa usually causes the field of vision to narrow (**tunnel vision**) and also affects one's ability to see in low light (**night blindness**).

Strabismus and nystagmus, two other conditions resulting in visual problems, are caused by improper muscle functioning. **Strabismus** is a condition in which one or both eyes are directed inward (crossed eyes) or outward. Left untreated, strabismus can result in permanent blindness because the brain will eventually reject signals from a deviating eye. Fortunately, most cases of strabismus can be corrected with eye exercises or surgery. Eye exercises sometimes involve the person's wearing a patch over the good eye for periods of time to force use of the eye that deviates. Surgery involves tightening or loosening the muscles that control eye movement. **Nystagmus** is a condition in which rapid involuntary movements of the eyes occur, usually resulting in dizziness and nausea. Nystagmus is sometimes a sign of brain malfunctioning and/or inner-ear problems.

MyLab Education Self-Check 12.2

MyLab Education Application Exercise 12.2:
Causes of Visual Impairments
Watch two videos that deal with identification and causes of visual impairments, and answer the questions that follow.

PSYCHOLOGICAL AND BEHAVIORAL CHARACTERISTICS

Language Development

Most authorities believe that lack of vision does not have a very significant effect on the ability to understand and use language (Wilton, 2011). Because auditory more than visual perception is the sensory modality through which we learn language, it's not surprising that studies have found that people who are blind are not impaired in language functioning. The child who is blind can still hear language and might even be more motivated than the sighted child to use language because it's the main channel through which she communicates with others.

Intellectual Ability

PERFORMANCE ON STANDARDIZED INTELLIGENCE TESTS At one time, it was popular for researchers to compare the intelligence of sighted people with that of persons with blindness. Most authorities now believe that such comparisons are virtually impossible because finding comparable tests is so difficult. From what is known, there is no reason to believe that blindness results in lower intelligence.

CONCEPTUAL ABILITIES It is also very difficult to assess the performance of children with visual impairment on laboratory-type tasks of conceptual ability. Many researchers, using conceptual tasks originally developed by noted psychologist Jean Piaget, have concluded that infants and very young children who are blind lag behind their sighted peers. This is usually attributed to the fact that they rely more on touch to arrive at conceptualizations of many objects, and touch is less efficient than sight. However, these early delays don't last long, especially once the children begin to use language to gather information about their environment (Perez-Pereira & Conti-Ramsden, 1999). Touch, however, remains a very critical sense throughout life for those who are blind.

An important difference between individuals with and without sight is that the latter need to take much more initiative to learn what they can from their environment. Sighted infants and children can pick up a lot of visual information incidentally. In a sense, the world comes to them; children who have visual impairment need to extend themselves out to the world to pick up some of the same information. Exploring the environment motorically, however, doesn't come easily for infants and young children with visual impairment, especially those who are blind. Some have serious delays in motor skills, such as sitting up, crawling, and walking (Zimmerman, 2011). Therefore, adults should do as much as possible to encourage infants and young children who are blind to explore their environment. It is critical that teachers and parents provide intensive and extensive instruction, including repetition, in order to help children with visual impairment develop their conceptual abilities.

Functional Skills

In many instances, what is just as important as intellectual and conceptual ability—if not more important—is the degree to which a person with visual impairment has functional skills such as using vision under non-clinical conditions in both familiar and unfamiliar settings. Carol Castellano, the mother of a child who is blind and the first vice president of the National Organization of Parents of Blind Children and president of New Jersey Parents of Blind Children, makes the point that the essence of having a visual impairment is needing to use a means other than simply eyesight to perform tasks (Castellano, 2005). This can range from using braille and magnifying devices to learning how to pour a glass of water (http://www.youtube.com/watch?v=xYsb2lVlxhE) without spilling it.

Orientation and Mobility

Orientation and mobility (O & M) skills refer to the ability to have a sense of where one is in relation to other people, objects, and landmarks (orientation) and to move through the environment (mobility). O & M skills are important for the successful adjustment of people with visual impairment. Research indicates that the ability to orient and move about the environment is associated with positive social adjustment (Zebehazy & Lawson, 2017) and positive employment outcomes (Cmar, 2015).

Mobility skills vary greatly among people with visual impairment. It is surprisingly difficult to predict which individuals will be the best travelers. For example, common sense tells us that mobility would be better among those who are not totally blind and those who lose their vision later in life, but this is not always the case. How much motivation and how much proper instruction one receives are critical to becoming a proficient traveler (Malik, 2015). In addition, research indicates that those who are totally blind actually develop better O & M skills than those who are partially sighted (Cameto & Nagle, 2007).

COGNITIVE MAPPING O & M skills depend to a great extent on spatial ability. Research has demonstrated that people who are blind can learn to make mental spatial representations of their environment, referred to as **cognitive mapping**, which can help them navigate through their environment (Iachini & Ruggiero, 2010). Cognitive mapping, sometimes referred to as mental mapping, involves the ability to integrate the relative position of various points in the spatial environment in order to navigate it more efficiently. Consider three sequential points—A, B, and C. A sequential mode of processing spatial information restricts a person's movement so that the person can move from A to C only by way of B. But a person with a cognitive map of points A, B, and C can go from A to C directly without going through B.

ECHOLOCATION Some persons who are blind, when walking along the street, seem able to sense objects in their path. This ability is sometimes referred to as having an **obstacle sense**—an unfortunate term in some ways, because many laypeople have taken it to mean that people who are blind somehow develop an extra sense. Research has determined that what is actually happening is that they are using **echolocation**, which is the ability to detect objects in the environment by auditory echoes (sound waves) created by footsteps, tapping a cane, or clicking one's tongue, for example. Up Close with Daniel Kish and Ben Underwood depicts two individuals with extremely well developed echolocation skills via tongue clicks.

Similar to sonar, echoes that bounce back can be used to interpret the location and size of objects. Bats, porpoises, dolphins, and whales also use echolocation to navigate their environment. And a number of experiments have shown that with experience, people who are blind can learn echolocation to a very high level of proficiency (Teng, Puri, & Whitney, 2012). It's through practice that they learn to do this. In fact, people who are sighted can also learn to use echolocation with enough practice (Teng & Whitney, 2011).

Although echolocation can be important for the mobility of someone without sight, by itself it doesn't make its user a highly proficient traveler. Extraneous noises (e.g., traffic, speech, rain, wind) can render obstacle sense unusable. Also, it requires walking at a fairly slow speed to be able to react in time. However, some researchers continue to study the phenomenon in the hope of developing mobility aids that can help sharpen echolocation ability in those who are blind (Miura, Muraoka, & Ifukube, 2010).

UP CLOSE with Daniel Kish and Ben Underwood Daniel Kish, blind since 13 months of age and arguably the most renowned echolocator in the world, taught himself to navigate his environment by using echoes from clicks of his tongue. Kish has become somewhat of a celebrity, founding World Access for the Blind, a nonprofit organization devoted to increasing public awareness of the potential of people with visual impairments. Among other things, he and his organization have focused on helping hundreds of children to learn echolocation skills.

Kish has volunteered himself to the research community as a subject of experiments with the hope of providing a better understanding of the scientific basis for echolocation.

For example, in one investigation, researchers took neuroimages of his brain while he engaged in echolocation. Significantly, the results suggested that when Kish was using echolocation, he was using the part of the brain people usually devote to *vision* and not *audition*.

Ben Underwood, another person with remarkable echolocation abilities, also received substantial media attention, both on television and the Internet (http://www.youtube.com/watch?v=XUXh-X1iveU). After losing his sight from cancer at age 3, Underwood gained notoriety as a teenager. Similar to Kish, his method of echolocation was tongue clicking. On January, 20, 2009, Ben Underwood died from cancer at the age of 16. •

Along with this pronounced ability to echolocate comes the common misconception that people who are blind automatically develop better acuity in their other senses. However, people who are blind don't have lowered thresholds of sensation in touch or hearing. What they can do is make better use of the sensations they obtain. Through concentration and attention, they learn to make very fine discriminations in touch and hearing (Cattaneo & Vecchi, 2011). In a similar vein, there is a myth that many of those who are born blind are also born with innate musical talent. There's no research to back up this claim; these individuals are more likely to focus on developing what musical talents they have because the sense of hearing is available to them.

Probably adding to the myth of inherent musical aptitude in people born blind is the special attention that the public gives to musical celebrities who are blind. In addition to Ray Charles, mentioned earlier in the chapter, there are several notable examples representing a variety of music genres, from winner of over 20 GRAMMYs, Stevie Wonder, to winner of the Van Cliburn Award, Nobuyuki Tsujii, to wildly popular Italian tenor, Andrea Bocelli, to winner of 9 GRAMMYs, Jose Feliciano.

Academic Achievement

Achievement tests are available in braille and large-print forms. Most professionals agree that direct comparisons of the academic achievement of students who are blind with that of sighted students must be interpreted cautiously because the two groups are tested under different conditions. The few studies that have been done suggest that both children with low vision and those who are blind are sometimes behind their sighted peers academically (Rapp & Rapp, 1992). Many authorities believe that when low achievement does occur, it is due not to the blindness itself, but to such things as low expectations or lack of exposure to braille.

Patrick, the student described in the accompanying Success Stories feature, began to learn braille as an older student. He enjoys reading braille instead of holding his book 2 inches from his right eye and struggling to use his remaining sight.

With respect to reading, we do know that learning to read braille is similar in some important ways to learning to read print. For example, **phonological awareness** (discussed in Chapter 6) is an important component of learning to read braille as well as print (Barlow-Brown & Connelly, 2002; Cattaneo & Vecchi, 2011; Gillon & Young, 2002; Veispak & Ghesquiere, 2010). So students who are blind and who have poor phonological awareness would be candidates for a type of "braille dyslexia." And some researchers have conjectured that there might be some for whom their poor braille reading skills are linked to difficulties in processing tactile information.

Social Adjustment

Most people with visual impairment are socially well adjusted. However, some do have a tendency to encounter problems with social competence (Zebehazy & Lawson, 2017; Zebehazy & Smith, 2011; Zimmerman, 2011). The road to social adjustment for people with visual impairment may be a bit more difficult for at least two reasons. First, social interactions among the sighted are often based on subtle cues, many of which are visual. Second, sighted society is often uncomfortable in its interactions with individuals who have visual impairment (Erin, 2006).

SUCCESS STORIES: Patrick Prepares for Transition from High School Through Functional Academics and Vocational Education

Patrick's mother, Audrey Pugh: "All I want anyone to do is give him a fair chance."

Nineteen-year-old Patrick Pugh is a high school junior with vision impairment and multiple disabilities.

Special educator Ricki Curry, an itinerant teacher of students with visual impairments, has worked closely with Patrick for 14 years. Patrick has no vision in his left eye and only partial sight in his right eye. His speech is slurred, and he does not have functional use of his left arm or leg. "Patrick is eager to learn new things," says Curry, who credits his success to intensive, relentless, and specific special education.

- **Intensive Instruction from Specialized Personnel.** Patrick started vision and physical therapy when he was 2 years old. Ricki Curry remembers the little boy whose eyes would lift aimlessly to the ceiling, not using what vision he had. "Our basic goal was for Patrick to learn to use his sight by tracking objects and looking at pictures, but as a 5-year-old, he was stubborn, difficult, and noncompliant," she recalls. Despite his reluctance, Patrick successfully learned literal information and concrete routines. He was highly distractible, and progress was very slow. His parents hoped that all he needed was extra time, so he stayed in a preschool for children with special needs until he was 7 years old.

  Patrick spent first grade in a self-contained class for children with learning disabilities in the nearest physically accessible elementary school. Curry continued to provide weekly sessions and to supervise his vision services. He was also given a personal aide to assist with mobility and visual modifications. "In some ways, kids with personal aides never encounter problems, so they don't learn any problem-solving skills!" says Curry. "On the other hand, there are some effective strategies that can be used by paraeducators." Patrick's hand use was limited, so his aide assisted him with writing. His teachers broke math down into small steps, individualized his reading, and taught him to use a large-print word processor.

- **Relentless Persistence Over Time.** Patrick finished elementary school 2 years older than most of his classmates yet able to do only rote math. His reading skills were concrete; he could decode text but had limited comprehension. "He could answer factual questions, but he couldn't make that leap to the abstract," recalls Curry. "Patrick was in a middle school science class learning about mitochondria. That's when it really hit me. Sure, he could learn the definition of mitochondria, but was this functional for him? He'd never use this word again!"

  Patrick was 13 years old when his mother and the individualized education program (IEP) team decided that he needed a class that emphasized functional academics, such as money skills. "At that point, we all knew this was what he needed," says Curry. "Patrick has multiple learning needs, and it takes him a long time to learn; it takes intensive care and a lot of specific teaching. This class gave him the right information at the right pace. We forgot about the mitochondria and we're now reading for comprehension."

- **Specific Goals for Transition and Vocational Education.** Patrick started high school at the age of 17, and a creative program was crafted for him blending functional academics, work experience, and independent living skills. He spent his mornings in two periods of functional English and math. He then boarded a van for the vocational center three afternoons a week, where he ate lunch with co-workers. He spent two afternoons at an independent living center learning to clean, shop, and travel around the community.

  Patrick Pugh and Ricki Curry worked 60 minutes daily on braille skills geared toward his vocational goals. "I think there's a job out there for Patrick," says Curry. "We've got 2 years to get those skills really sharp." According to Curry, he's exceeding everybody's expectations. "Every time we've taught him something, he's had some success in learning it." This description of Patrick does not surprise Audrey Pugh. "Opportunity is the main thing," she says. "All I want anyone to do is give him a fair chance."

  By Jean B. Crockett

SUBTLE VISUAL CUES Most of us who are sighted take for granted how often we use visual cues to help us in our social interactions. In growing up, we learn most of these cues incidentally by observing others. Thus, children with visual impairment often need to be taught directly how to use these cues (Jindal-Snape, 2005; Sacks, 2006). Facial expressions, such as smiling, are a good example of visual cues that don't come spontaneously for persons who have visual impairment. Social smiling is a reciprocal event—we respond to how others react to our smiles and vice versa. John M. Hull (1997), whose eyesight deteriorated gradually over several years, kept a diary of his experiences and likened smiling to sending dead letters, not knowing how and even if his smiles were being acknowledged.

SOCIETY'S DISCOMFORT WITH BLINDNESS Authorities point out that sighted people feel ill at ease when interacting with people with visual impairments, which then interferes with smooth social interaction. Unfortunately, some people who are blind feel that they need to go to great lengths to appear "normal." The following account, written by the National Federation of the Blind's president (himself blind), of one man's attempt to not appear different is humorous but poignant:

> Dr. Schroeder became a teacher and an administrator of public programs of education, but he was still affected by his beliefs about blindness. With the acquisition of the new job, Dr. Schroeder had the money to buy a house. He faced the problem of how to get the lawn mowed. He thought he might hire somebody to do it, but (he reasoned) if he asked a sighted person to mow his lawn, the neighbors would believe he was not able to do it himself because he was blind. This would reinforce their assessment of him as inferior. However, he was also afraid to mow the lawn himself because the neighbors might watch him do it, and if he missed a patch of grass, they would conclude that he was incompetent. He could, of course, cover the lawn in such a way that he would not miss any grass—going over it repeatedly in narrow strips—but this would look unusual and peculiar to the neighbors.
>
> Dr. Schroeder did not want to look peculiar. He decided that the best solution was for him to mow his lawn when the neighbors were not likely to observe. He decided to cut the grass at night. I cannot say how the neighbors reacted to this plan. However, if the objective is to seem normal, I doubt that mowing the lawn at night is the best way to accomplish this purpose.
>
> The efforts of Dr. Fred Schroeder to avoid looking conspicuous and to appear normal remind me of my own embarrassing experiences. How great a premium there is on seeming normal! (Maurer, 2000, p. 294)*

But even though some people who are blind, like Dr. Schroeder, might be uncomfortable about their blindness, in most cases the sighted person is the one who is more likely to feel awkward. This video provides more tips on social etiquette with people who are blind: (http://www.youtube.com/watch?v=P368_AsiMkA).

STEREOTYPIC BEHAVIORS An impediment to good social adjustment for some students with visual impairment is **stereotypic behaviors**: repetitive, stereotyped movements such as body rocking, poking or rubbing the eyes, repetitive hand or finger movements, and grimacing. These can begin as early as a few months of age. They are by no means exclusively found in children with more severe visual impairment although they tend to be more prevalent in those who are blind compared to those with low vision (Gal & Dyck, 2009). For many years, the term *blindisms* was used to refer to these behaviors because it was thought that they were manifested only in people who are blind; however, they are also sometimes characteristic of children with normal sight who have severe intellectual disabilities or autism.

Several competing theories concern the causes of stereotypic behaviors (Zimmerman, 2011). Some researchers believe that the behaviors are an individual's attempt to provide himself or herself with more stimulation to make up for a relative lack of sensory or social stimulation. Others believe them to be an individual's attempt to self-regulate stimulation in the face of overstimulation. In either case, most authorities believe that these behaviors serve to stabilize the person's arousal level (Warren, 1994).

Some professionals even disagree about how much one should intervene to reduce or eliminate stereotypic behaviors. On the one hand, in the extreme, these behaviors can interfere with learning and socialization and can even be physically injurious. On the other hand, in moderation, such behaviors might help maintain an appropriate level of arousal (Warren, 1994). In addition, some have argued for society's need to be more tolerant of stereotypic behaviors: "As researchers and advocates, . . . let us consider the idea that rocking is simply an idiosyncrasy or individual difference that should be ignored or for which we should demand greater awareness, tolerance, and understanding" (McHugh & Lieberman, 2003, p. 472).

---

*This material is reprinted with permission from the Braille Monitor, the leading publication of the National Federation of the Blind.

MyLab Education Self-Check 12.3

MyLab Education Application Exercise 12.3:
Psychological and Behavioral Characteristics
Watch videos about Sarah, Hannah, and Kyle, and then answer
questions about some of the psychological and behavioral
characteristics of people with visual impairments.

EDUCATIONAL CONSIDERATIONS

Lack of sight can severely limit a person's experiences because a primary means of obtaining information from the environment is not available. Making the situation even more difficult, educational experiences in the typical classroom are frequently visual. Nevertheless, most experts agree that, in many ways, students who have visual impairment should be educated in the same general way as sighted children. However, teachers need to make some important modifications. The most significant difference is that students with visual impairment have to rely on other sensory modalities to acquire information. If the teacher keeps in mind this difference, some of the most important teaching adjustments are based on common sense. A few examples (Bishop, 2004) are to call the student's name when addressing him or her; read aloud what you write on the board; allow extra time to complete tasks when necessary; and, perhaps most important, give *explicit directions*.

The student with little or no sight will possibly require special modifications in four major areas: (1) braille, (2) use of remaining sight, (3) listening skills, and (4) O & M training. The first three pertain directly to academic education, particularly reading; the last refers to skills needed for everyday living.

Braille

In 19th-century France, Louis Braille introduced a system of reading and writing for people who, like him, were blind. Although it was not the first method that was developed, Braille's was the one that became widely used.

Traditionally, there have been several braille codes, with each one associated with a different use, such as for math, or music, or computers. However, over the past several years, a movement arose to create just one code that would serve many purposes, thus resulting in more efficiency in writing and reading braille. **Unified English Braille (UEB)**, therefore, was developed as a way of combining these codes. Today, UEB is the preferred braille code for all English-speaking countries.

The basic unit of braille is a quadrangular cell, containing from one to six dots. Different patterns of dots represent letters, numbers, and even punctuation marks. Although there is one braille symbol for each letter of the alphabet, braille also consists

FOCUS ON

Louis Braille and the Development of Braille

Behind any major invention, there lies a fascinating story. Braille is no different. Most people credit Louis Braille with the first system those who are blind could use to read and write. However, that recognition actually goes to the French aristocrat and soldier, Captain Charles Barbier de la Serre. When his night-writing code, which was based on raised dots representing phonetic units, was rejected by the military, de la Serre presented it to the National Institute for the Young Blind. It didn't receive a very favorable review there, either, but it did serve as motivation for one of the institute's students, Louis Braille, to go on to perfect his own system (Kleege, 1999).

of a number of contractions whereby one symbol can stand for a word or a part of a word. Using contractions leads to faster reading and reduces the space and time required to transcribe braille. Research suggests that introducing contractions to young students in the earliest stages of reading instruction leads to better literacy skills (Emerson, Holbrook, & D'Andrea, 2009).

Generally, the best method of reading braille involves using both hands (Wright, Wormsley, & Kamei-Hannan, 2009; Zimmerman, 2011). There are variations on the two-handed method. One common way is for both hands to read together until near the end of the line, at which time the right hand continues to read along while the left hand slips down to the start of the next line, with the right hand then joining the left hand to start that next line.

Two basic means of writing in braille are the Perkins Brailler and the slate and stylus. The **Perkins Brailler** has six keys, one for each of the six dots of the cell. When depressed simultaneously, the keys leave an embossed print on the paper. More portable than the Perkins Brailler is the **slate and stylus**. This pen-shaped instrument is pressed through the opening of the slate, which holds the paper between its two halves.

Perhaps the most hotly debated topic in the field of visual impairment concerns whether students who are blind should be taught to use braille or another method of communication, such as a tape recorder or voice-activated computer. At one time, it was fairly common for students with blindness to use braille, but the percentage of students who are blind who use braille has steadily declined since the mid-1960s, when nearly half used braille. Today, it is estimated that only 8.6% of children use Braille as their primary mode of reading and writing (American Printing House for the Blind, 2015). Many within the community of people who are blind are alarmed at the reduced availability of braille and assert that it has led to a distressing rate of illiteracy (Castellano, 2005; Dixon, 2011). For the sighted, literacy involves the ability to read and write printed words. For those who are blind, literacy equates with the ability to read and write braille. They charge that too few sighted teachers are proficient in braille and that these teachers do little to discourage the notion held by some that using braille indicates inferiority. Whether a person is comfortable in identifying herself as blind is critical to whether she will be motivated to learn braille.

Ironically, advances in technology have also contributed to reduction in the use of braille. (We present some of these technologies later in the chapter.) Without doubt, technology has brought about many positive changes for people who are blind. Today, vast amounts of material can be accessed digitally and electronically. For example, books on tape, speech-recognition software, digital assistants, and computerized magnification devices have made it even easier to obtain and produce information. However, the question arises of whether such devices have made it *too* easy to acquire and generate such information. In other words, has easier access served as a disincentive to learning braille? It's also important to consider that relying on technology sometimes has drawbacks that may not be readily apparent. Consider computerized magnification. Straining to read enlarged print on a computer screen can be fatiguing to the eyes and body, thus reducing one's desire to read for pleasure: "Would you be tempted to read *War and Peace* on a computer screen with letters four inches high?" (Castellano, 2005, p. 25). Many authorities are concerned that, even when students do receive braille instruction, it is often not intense enough. In a survey of experts on braille usage, the respondents stated that in the early stages of braille acquisition, in particular, students need daily instruction for several years (Koenig & Holbrook, 2000). (See the accompanying Responsive Instruction on braille literacy instruction.) The need for intensive braille instruction presents a dilemma for school systems because of the lack of qualified braille instructors.

Advocates of braille also point out that it's essential for most students who are legally blind to learn braille to lead independent lives. Bolstering their argument is research indicating that adults who had learned braille in childhood as their primary medium for reading were employed at almost twice the rate of those who had used print as their primary medium (Ryles, 2000). A way of ensuring that braille becomes more readily available is through **braille bills**, now on the books in most states. Although the

RESPONSIVE INSTRUCTION

Meeting the Needs of Students With Visual Impairments

BRAILLE LITERACY INSTRUCTION

What the Research Says

For many years, access to high-quality braille literacy programs was hit-or-miss in this country. Barriers such as large caseloads, emphasis on core academic instruction over instruction in braille, lack of adequate assessment materials, and lack of administrative support for this specialized instruction all contributed to the challenge of delivering quality braille instruction (Hatlen, 1998). The 1997 amendments to the Individuals with Disabilities Education Act (IDEA) sought to change that by requiring all individualized education programs (IEPs) for students with visual impairments to provide for instruction in braille unless an evaluation clearly demonstrates that this is not appropriate for the child's needs both now and in the future.

Empirical research (Ryles, 1997) and professional recommendations (Rex, Koenig, Wormsley, & Baker, 1994) support the need for 1.5 to 2 hours of daily braille literacy instruction to foster high literacy levels for students with visual impairments. Braille literacy instruction includes the use of braille as a primary reading medium, particularly during the early elementary years similar to the period of print-literacy development for students without visual impairments, and as a secondary reading medium to supplement or support the use of print.

Research Study

Koenig and Holbrook (2000) designed a study to garner professional consensus related to braille literacy program delivery. A specific research technique, the Delphi method, provided them with a unique tool for determining consensus. The Delphi method requires surveying the same pool of respondents. In each round of surveys, respondents answer the questions but also provide comments or recommendations on how to change or improve the questions. Each time respondents receive the survey (after the initial round), they are provided with the compiled data and comments from the previous round. Final analysis reflects a minimum of three rounds of survey review and input.

Koenig and Holbrook selected 40 professionals for the study based on experience and expertise in teaching braille. The respondents represented various service delivery options (i.e., resource room, itinerant, and residential schools) and teaching capacities (i.e., those actively teaching and those who are no longer providing direct service but are professionals in the field). Round 1 of the survey included questions related to 11 areas of braille literacy and a "proposed level of service." Respondents indicated agreement or disagreement with the proposed level of service and/or offered alternative recommendations and comments. This process continued for three rounds of surveys.

Research Findings

Overall, the respondents reached consensus on the factors associated with high-quality braille literacy programs. Specific recommendations included:

1. Overwhelming and universal support for daily braille instruction for a period of 1.5 to 2 hours during the early elementary grades (kindergarten through third grade)
2. The need for early intervention, provided in moderate to short sessions, for concept development
3. Pre-braille instruction (e.g., exposure to names in braille, tactile labels, writing experiences) for preschool and kindergarten-age students for periods of 30 minutes to 1 hour
4. Daily contact for a period of 1 to 2 hours for students with print literacy skills who are just learning braille
5. Teaching listening skills such as aural-reading and live-reader skills on a moderate to periodic basis
6. Teaching keyboarding and word processing skills beginning in grades 1, 2, or 3
7. Braille slate and stylus instruction several days a week for moderate to short time periods beginning in third or fourth grade
8. Teaching students who are blind to write their signatures, spending 1 to 3 days per week for short sessions on this task beginning in middle school.

One point of contention was over how much time should be devoted to the development of dual media—that is, teaching both print and braille. Some respondents called for teaching both daily and long sessions; others expressed concern regarding overloading students or the importance of establishing one primary mode. Clearly, this issue requires more research and attention.

Applying the Research to Teaching

The authors of the study, as well as the Council for Exceptional Children's Division on Visual Impairments (DVI), stress that all literacy planning for students with visual impairments should be made on an individual basis (Koenig, Sanspree, & Holbrook, n.d.). The type(s) of reading mediums (print, braille, or both) selected for instruction should be determined after an assessment of the unique needs of the particular student. Thus, no medium is inherently superior; rather, different students will require different supports in order for them to become literate individuals. Therefore, teachers of students with visual impairments should use the preceding recommendations as a guideline for making individual determinations of services.

BY KRISTIN L. SAYESKI

specific provisions of these bills vary from state to state, the National Federation of the Blind (NFB), a major proponent of braille bills, has drafted a model bill that specifies two important components:

1. Braille must be available for students if any members of the individualized education program (IEP) team, including parents, indicate that it is needed.
2. Teachers of students with visual impairment need to be proficient in braille.

Federal law now reinforces the first component. The Individuals with Disabilities Education Act (IDEA) specifies that braille services and instruction are to be a part of the IEP unless all members of the team, including parents, agree that braille should not be used. Authorities now recommend that some students with low vision who can read large print or print with magnification should also be taught braille. Many students with low vision will experience deteriorating vision over the years. Learning braille at an early age prepares them for the time when their eyesight no longer allows them to read print.

Use of Remaining Sight

For many years, educators and parents expressed a great deal of resistance to having children with visual impairment use their sight in reading and other activities. Many myths contributed to this reluctance, including beliefs that holding books close to the eyes is harmful, strong lenses hurt the eyes, and using the eyes too much injures them. It's now recognized that this is true only in very rare conditions. In fact, most agree on the importance of encouraging people with visual impairment to use what sight they do have but not to the exclusion of braille for those who need it.

Two visual methods of aiding children with visual impairment to read print are large-print books and magnifying devices. **Large-print books** are simply books printed in larger-size type. The text in this book, printed primarily for sighted readers, is printed in 10-point type. Figure 12.3 shows print in 18-point and 24-point type, two of the most popular sizes for large-print materials. Type sizes for readers with visual impairment may range up to 30-point type.

The major difficulty with large-print books is that they are bigger than usual and therefore require a great deal of storage space. In addition, they are of limited availability, although, along with the American Printing House for the Blind, a number of commercial publishers are now publishing and marketing large-print books. Another potential disadvantage is that students who become dependent on large-print books may have difficulties when they encounter situations, such as many jobs, in which large-print materials are unavailable.

FIGURE 12.3

TYPEFACES COME IN VARIOUS SIZES. LARGE-PRINT BOOKS OFTEN USE 18-POINT TYPE AND 24-POINT TYPE

This is an example of 10-pt. type.

This is an example of 18-pt. type.

This is an example of 24-pt. type.

With advances in technology, more and more authorities are recommending **magnifying devices** instead of, or in addition to, large-print books (Zimmerman, Zebehazy, & Moon, 2010). With respect to reading speed and comprehension, using magnifying devices is at least as effective as using large-print books for many students (Lussenhop & Corn, 2003). Magnifying devices can be for close vision or distance vision. They can be portable, such as handheld magnifiers, monocular telescopes, or binocular telescopes that sit on eyeglass-type frames. Or they can be tabletop closed-circuit television scanners that present enlarged images on a television screen. Authorities highly recommend that students with low vision receive intensive instruction in the use of magnifying devices rather than being left on their own to use them (Corn & Koenig, 2002).

Listening Skills

The importance of listening skills for children who are blind cannot be overemphasized. Society tends to assume that listening skills will develop automatically in children who are blind. However, authorities agree that in most cases these children must be taught how to listen. In addition, teachers should provide a classroom environment as free from auditory distractions as possible.

Listening skills are becoming more important than ever because of the increasing accessibility of recorded material. The American Printing House for the Blind and the Library of Congress are major sources for these materials. Listeners can play the material at normal speed, or they can use a compressed-speech device that allows them to listen at about 250 to 275 words per minute. This method works by discarding very small segments of the speech. Some of the more sophisticated compressed-speech devices use a computer to eliminate those speech sounds that are least necessary for comprehension.

Orientation and Mobility Training

O & M training is crucial. The ability of people with a visual disability to navigate their environment determines significantly their level of independence and social integration. Societal changes have made being a pedestrian—with or without blindness—even more challenging (Barlow, Bentzen, & Bond, 2005; Huebner & Wiener, 2005; Sauerburger, 2005). Intersections are wider, often with multiple traffic signals for through, left-, and right-turn lanes that are set to change based on traffic flow. In addition, cars, especially hybrids, are now quieter and thus more difficult to detect. The National Highway Traffic Safety Administration (NHSTA) has instituted a "Quiet Car" rule mandating, that, as of 2019, electric vehicles make enough noise at low speeds to alert pedestrians that they are approaching.

Four general methods aid the O & M of people with visual impairment: the long cane, guide dogs, tactile maps, and human guides.

MyLab Education
Video Example 12.2

This video shows two students being taught how to use the long cane.

THE LONG CANE Professionals most often recommend the long cane for those individuals with visual impairments who need a mobility aid. It is called a **long cane** because it's much longer than the canes typically used for support or balance. Long canes can be straight, folded, or telescopic; the last two types are more compact but not as sturdy as the straight cane. The user receives auditory and tactual information about the environment by moving the cane along the ground. It can alert the user to drop-offs such as potholes or stairs, and can help to protect the lower part of the body from collision with objects.

Although watching a skilled user of the long cane can give the impression that it's easy to manipulate, intensive training in using the long cane is usually required (Sauerburger & Bourquin, 2010). Proper touch technique requires considerable coordination between the sweeping of the cane and the movement of the feet.

MyLab Education
Video Example 12.3

This video shows a student using a monocular, which functions similarly to a telescope, and helps with long distance vision.

GUIDE DOGS Guide dogs aren't as popular an option as most people tend to think. First, they must undergo extensive training. For example, the dogs not only need to "guide" their owners around obstacles, but among other things, they are expected to maintain a steady pace, stop at curbs on both sides of the street and at the bottom and top of stairs before being told to proceed, and recognize openings too small in height or width for their owner to fit. They need to have a temperament whereby they are not distracted by environmental

FOCUS ON

Guide Dogs

The use of dogs to help guide those who are blind dates at least as far back as the mid-16th century ("Guide Dog," n.d.). We can trace the formal training of guide dogs, however, to the early 1900s, when after World War I, Germany, the United States, and Great Britain established guide-dog schools to accommodate blinded veterans.

---

sights, sounds, and smells, including other dogs. In addition, the guide dog's disposition must be conducive to sitting quietly at its owner's feet for long periods of time.

Second, users of guide dogs require extensive training to learn how to use their dogs properly. The intensive training—as well as the facts that guide dogs are large, walk relatively fast, and need to be cared for—make them particularly questionable for children. Also, contrary to what most people think, the guide dog does not "take" the person who is blind anywhere. The person usually needs to know where he or she is going. The dog can be a safeguard against walking into dangerous areas.

Popular breeds for training are Labradors, Golden Retrievers, and German Shepherds. Because of humankind's natural affinity for dogs, it's important that the public keep in mind that the guide dog is a "worker" and not the same as a "pet."

TACTILE MAPS **Tactile maps** are embossed representations of the environment. People who are blind can orient themselves to their surroundings by touching raised symbols representing streets, sidewalks, buildings, and so forth. These maps can be displayed in public places, or more portable versions can be made from a type of paper.

Embossment, or raised symbols, has also been used to help people who are blind to appreciate environments that are considerably more vast than what are found locally. (See Up Close with Noreen Grice.)

MyLab Education
Video Example 12.4
Guide dog training is intensive and involves behavioral principles of praise and rewards.
http://www.youtube.com/watch?v=D-05qEC4qzEguide

UP CLOSE with Noreen Grice When Noreen Grice was an undergraduate working as an intern at the Boston Museum of Science in the 1980s, she happened to ask some students visiting from the Perkins School for the Blind what they had thought of the show. One youngster piped up, "That stunk!"

The experience with the Perkins students served as a catalyst for Grice's search for a method of presenting tactile representations of astronomical objects. Grice over the years has experimented with various methods of producing tactile images of heavenly bodies. In 2002, her quest culminated in the publication of *Touch the Universe* (http://www.youtube .com/watch?v=N3CLC2PtkcY). Consisting of photographs, embossed shapes, and a combination of braille and large-print captions, the book presents 14 photos taken with the Hubble Space Telescope. Planets, stars, and galaxies come to life for readers who have visual impairment as well as those with sight.

Now, about 30 years after her encounter with the Perkins students, Grice is president and founder of "You Can Do Astronomy LLC," and she continues to create astronomy books for people who are blind. •

HUMAN GUIDES Human guides undoubtedly enable people with visual impairment to move about accurately and safely. However, most O & M specialists don't recommend use of human guides as the primary means of navigation because it fosters too much dependence on other people. At times, however, the use of a human guide is warranted. Most who travel unaccompanied don't need help from others. However, if a person with visual impairment looks as though he or she needs assistance, you should first ask if help is wanted. If physical guidance is required, allow the person to hold on to your arm above the elbow and to walk a half-step behind you. Sighted people tend to grasp the arms of people with visual impairments and to sort of push them in the direction they are heading, which can be disorienting for the individual who is blind.

Technological Aids

Visual impairment is perhaps the disability area in which the most technological advances have been made. Consistent with the more mainstream world of technology, startup companies focused on the population of individuals with visual impairments are proliferating; and many of the major companies, such as Apple, are also now tapping into this market. The infusion of technology has occurred primarily in two general areas: communication and information access, and O & M. In addition, some highly experimental research has been conducted on artificial vision.

TECHNOLOGICAL AIDS FOR COMMUNICATION AND INFORMATION ACCESS Computers and software are available that convert printed material into synthesized speech or braille. Portable **braille notetakers** (http://www.youtube.com/watch?v=4qreEcYctI8) can serve the same function as the Perkins Brailler or slate and stylus, but they offer additional speech-synthesizer and word-processing capabilities. The user enters information with a braille keyboard and can transfer the information into a larger computer, review it using a speech synthesizer or braille display, or print it in braille or text.

Two services available for those who have visual impairments are Newsline® and Descriptive Video Service. **NFB-Newsline®** is a free service available through the NFB that allows individuals to access magazines and newspapers 24 hours a day from any touchtone telephone. Over 300 newspapers, including most of the major ones (e.g., *USA Today, The New York Times, The Wall Street Journal, The Washington Post, The Los Angeles Times*, and *The Toronto Globe and Mail*) are now available. Newsline is also available for iPhone. **Descriptive Video Service®** inserts a narrated description of key visual features of programs on television. It is also available in some movie theaters as well as some movies on videotape or DVD.

Great strides have been made in recent years to make computers and the World Wide Web more accessible for people with disabilities, including those who have visual impairments. With respect to computer software, **screen readers** (such as JAWS® for Windows®) can magnify information on the screen, convert on-screen text to speech, or do both.

TECHNOLOGICAL AIDS FOR ORIENTATION AND MOBILITY There are now a number of products available or under development designed to aid those who are blind with navigating the environment. Many of them take advantage of global positioning system (GPS) technology. Quite a few can be found on YouTube.

In general, technology-based travel aids are of two types: computer-based and experience-based (Karimi, Dias, Pearlman, & Zimmerman, 2014). The former rely on devices that depend on input based on *pre-existing* maps or routes developed using step-by-step algorithms. For example, one computer-based navigation aid first gathers data from a small robot that creates an initial map of an environment, such as a school building or an outdoor school campus. Then, as a blind traveler traverses the environment, he or she is provided cues on when to turn left, right, etc.

Some authorities are advocating that the computer-based approach be combined with an experience-based approach (Karimi et al., 2014). The experience-based approach allows for users to provide information about a route while traversing it. A user can make annotations along the way that may be useful to others when they travel the same route at a later time. For example, they could alert future travelers to places along the path that are more challenging due to construction or steepness of slopes (for wheelchair users).

Taking a cue from the popularity of video games in the sighted population, researchers are developing audio games, with the goal of helping those who are blind to improve their O & M skills. For example, one game used an audio-based virtual

MyLab Education
Video Example 12.5

This video shows a class of students using Perkins Braillers and the more technologically advanced braille lite notetakers.

MyLab Education
Video Example 12.6

For students with low vision, there are computerized magnification devices. This video shows two computerized magnifiers: Zoomtext for writing and a Closed Circuit Television (CCTV) magnification device for reading.

reality format, which included the playing of spatially localized sounds, such as doors closing, that identified the presence and location of objects as the player moved though the virtual environment (Connors, Chrastil, Sanchez, & Merabet, 2014). The goal of the game was for the player to move through the environment capturing as many "jewels" as possible while avoiding "monsters," which attempted to steal the jewels. Afterwards, those with higher performance on the game were better at moving through a "real" environment. Although the study would have been stronger had the researchers included a "control" group who did not play the game, the findings suggest that audio games hold promise for improving O & M skills.

ARTIFICIAL VISION Researchers have also made considerable progress in developing an artificial vision system for people who are blind. Several techniques are in the experimental stages, with different parts of the eye or brain the focus of the prosthesis—for example, the retina, the cornea, or the visual cortex of the brain (Reich, Maidenbaum, & Amedi, 2012). These surgeries are extremely complicated, and the results are highly variable. Even when the surgery is successful, those who have been blind since birth or from a very young age can find it overwhelming to adjust to the flood of visual sensations. See the accompanying Up Close with Mike May: Renaissance Man, describing the experiences of Mike May, who underwent such a surgery.

UP CLOSE with Mike May: Renaissance Man Mike May is the perfect example of a present-day Renaissance Man, an individual with an extensive range of interests and talents. Founder, president, and CEO of a major international business, clocked at 65 miles per hour as the world's fastest blind skier, and hired as the first blind political risk analyst for the CIA, Mike May, blind since age 3, has never shied away from challenges. But perhaps his biggest challenge was his decision in 1999 to undergo stem cell transplant surgery to restore sight in his one operable eye. And it wasn't just the pain from the surgery or the fact that he might lose the miniscule amount of light perception he had in that eye; it was facing the prospect of leaving the world of blindness to which he had adapted so comfortably and successfully. Even more daunting was the fact that virtually every other known case of individuals who had been blind and then been given sight had resulted in harmful psychological consequences (Kurson, 2005, 2007).

Fortunately, even though his vision remains very limited, Mike May has been up to the challenge and has not been driven into the depths of despair experienced by so many before him. He has taken the disappointment in stride and, in fact, has volunteered himself as a subject for researchers. One of their major findings is that the problems he now faces are based in the brain, not the eyes. After so many years of not having any visual input, May's brain has adapted in such a way that the cells responsible for sight have lost their function or changed functions.

When he is not having his brain scanned by neuroscientists, meeting presidents Carter, Reagan, Clinton, and Obama, breaking the world record in downhill skiing at the Paralympics of the Winter Olympics, traveling the world as an ambassador for promoting positive attitudes and accessibility for those who are blind since 1999, May applies his entrepreneurial skills as founder, president, and CEO of Sendero Group, a leading manufacturer of cutting-edge technologies for people who are blind. •

Video Example from YouTube

MyLab Education
Video Example 12.7

This interview with Mike May highlights his remarkable achievements. http://www.youtube.com/watch?v=bnefTJx2sCo&playnext=1&list=PL727AC0FEA51EDDB6&feature=results_video

---

CAUTIONS ABOUT TECHNOLOGY Words of caution are in order in considering the use of computerized and electronic devices. Supporters of braille argue that although technological devices can contribute much to reading and acquiring information, these devices cannot replace braille. Braille proponents are especially concerned that the slate and stylus be preserved as a viable method of taking notes. They point out that just as computers have not replaced paper and pen or pencil for people who are sighted, neither can computers take the place of the slate and stylus for people who are blind. And using a long cane is still considered essential.

Although technology might not be the answer to all the difficulties faced by people who are blind, there is no doubt that technology can make their lives easier and more productive. And as technologies develop for society in general, it is important that those who have visual impairments be able to take advantage of them.

Service Delivery Models

The four major educational placements for students with visual impairment, from most to least separate, are residential school, special class, resource room, and general education class with itinerant teacher help. In the early 1900s virtually all children who were blind were educated in residential institutions. Today, **itinerant teacher service**, wherein a vision teacher visits several different schools to work with students in their general education classrooms, is the most popular placement for students with visual impairment. The fact is, the number of students with visual impairment is so small that most schools find it difficult to provide services through special classes or resource rooms. The accompanying How Can I Help? feature illustrates how an itinerant teacher supports a fourth-grade student with a severe visual impairment.

Residential placement, however, is still a relatively popular placement model compared to other areas of disability. For example, approximately 4% of students with visual impairment between the ages of 6 and 21 are in a residential institution, whereas less than 0.5% of students with intellectual disabilities are so placed. The advantage of residential placement or special schools is that services can be concentrated to this relatively low-incidence population. For example, students in residential or special schools are more likely to receive O & M skills than those who are in regular schools (Cameto & Nagle, 2007). In the past, most children who were blind attended such institutions for several years; today some may attend on a short-term basis (e.g., 1 to 4 years). The prevailing philosophy of integrating children with visual impairments into classes with sighted children is also reflected in the fact that many residential facilities have established cooperative arrangements with local public schools wherein the staff of the residential facility usually concentrate on training for independent living skills such as mobility, personal grooming, and home management, whereas local school personnel emphasize academics.

ASSESSMENT OF PROGRESS

Teachers of students with visual impairments are required to assess both academic and functional skills. Academic assessments include braille skills for reading decoding and comprehension and Nemeth Code mathematics skills. Orientation and mobility skills are critical as part of a functional skills assessment.

Assessment of Academic Skills

The use of braille is a significant aspect of academic success for students with blindness or low vision, and IDEA requires inclusion of braille instruction in the IEP; thus, it's important for teachers to monitor the progress of these students in braille skills. **Curriculum-based measurement (CBM)** is an effective method for measuring the academic progress of students with visual impairments in the particular curriculum to which they are exposed. Braille versions of CBM reading passages have similar technical adequacy to CBM passages used with readers who are sighted (Morgan & Bradley-Johnson, 1995). Printed versions of passages can be translated into braille for use in monitoring students' braille reading rate and accuracy. However, teachers should modify standard CBM procedures for students with visual impairments because reading braille typically takes longer than reading print.

Teachers can also use CBM techniques in mathematics. Commercial CBM measures are available to monitor students' progress in computational fluency, and these measures can be translated into Nemeth Code for use with students with visual impairment. Standard CBM mathematics probes take approximately 2 to 4 minutes for sighted students (Thurber, Shinn, & Smolkowski, 2002), and the probe is scored by calculating the number of correct digits per minute.

Collaborating and Co-Teaching with Teachers of Students with Blindness or Low Vision

"I don't have time to learn braille!"

What Does It Mean to Be a Teacher of Students with Visual Impairments?

Collaboration for students with visual impairments often takes the form of working with itinerant special education teachers. This can be frustrating for general educators in that they are left "on their own" when the special educator is at another building. Therefore, in planning for collaboration, it's important that the general educator and itinerant teacher have time to plan for student needs that may arise at any time. Working with the general educator to plan for instruction, the teacher of students with visual impairments can offer expertise in:

1. Strategies for teaching listening and compensatory auditory skills
2. Techniques for modifying instructional methods and materials
3. Design of multisensory learning environments that encourage active participation by individuals with visual impairments in group and individual activities
4. Strategies for teaching basic concepts
5. Strategies for teaching organization and study skills
6. Strategies for teaching individuals with visual impairments to use thinking, problem-solving, and other cognitive strategies (Council for Exceptional Children, 2003)

Successful Strategies for Co-Teaching

Ricki Curry (an itinerant teacher) and Jenny Garrett (a fourth-grade teacher) talk about how they collaborated to fully include Dennis, a student with a severe visual impairment.

Jenny: My fourth-grade class consisted of 23 nine- and ten-year-old students, including two children with learning disabilities, one with severe behavior disorders, and Dennis. They began the year reading on anywhere from a first- to a sixth-grade level.

Ricki: Although he has some usable vision, Dennis can see no details from a distance of more than about 2 feet and uses large-print texts for reading.

Jenny: Dennis has some difficulty making friends because of his immaturity, his compulsive talking, and his inability to listen. On the other hand, he's got a good sense of humor and is quick with language. Dennis was in my class all day long for every academic subject. Ricki worked with him during language arts block, teaching braille. She came to school during the last half of my planning period, which gave us a daily opportunity to discuss assignments, homework, curricular adaptations, equipment, and the like. Homework was an enormous issue. Ricki helped him set up a notebook with a homework contract enclosed and a special highlighter, which he used to mark off completed assignments. He had to write down the assignments himself, remember to take the notebook home, complete the assignments, get a parent's signature, and get it back to school.

The hardest part of working with Dennis was the startup period. I had to get to know him, his visual capabilities, his strengths and weaknesses, his coping strategies. I began adapting my teaching style, using an easel rather than the blackboard so that he could scoot up to it. I had to decide how hard to push, what to expect from his parents, and what to demand from Dennis.

Ricki: I often found myself overwhelmed by the number of things that Jenny and/or Dennis needed help with in the short time that I was in the building. And so many things seemed to go wrong in the time between when I left one day and arrived again the next day! Although I was frustrated by the limitations imposed by time constraints, the beauty of the inclusion model was that I was very aware of the true gestalt of Dennis's program and knew exactly what he was involved in all the time. Had I not had an almost daily view of his classroom performance, I might not have believed how hard it was to integrate this very bright, verbal, personable child into Jenny's class.

Jenny: Collaboration works best when there is a match of personalities as well as energy, enthusiasm for teaching, and professionalism.

BY MARGARET P. WEISS

Assessment of Functional Skills

Orientation and mobility skills are critical to the successful adjustment of people with visual impairment, and thus should be the focus of assessment procedures. Traditional procedures for assessing O & M skills have comprised subjective checklists and self-report data. However, emerging technologies currently used for O & M training also offer promise for advancing progress-monitoring procedures. O & M instructors can use GPS as a systematic way to monitor their clients' travel proficiency. With some systems, they can gather data such as travel times, travel modes, routes, and trip duration. Evaluating these data frequently can help O & M instructors improve their clients' travel proficiency through data-based planning.

Testing Accommodations

IDEA requires appropriate accommodations or alternate assessments for students with disabilities who need them. Among the most common accommodations for students with blindness and low vision are presentation accommodations (e.g., test in braille, test in regular print with magnification, large-print test) and response accommodations (e.g., use of brailler). Scheduling accommodations are also important to students with visual impairments, given that students' reading rate in braille is usually slower than that of a sighted student. And with the burgeoning array of assistive technologies, states are having a difficult time keeping up with determining which accommodations should be allowed (Smith & Amato, 2012). Because of the low prevalence of visual impairments, these decisions are usually best made on an individual basis.

MyLab Education Self-Check 12.4

MyLab Education Application Exercise 12:4:
Accommodations in the Physical Environment
View and answer questions about the learning module Perspectives and Resources: Accommodations to the Physical Environment.

THE IRIS CENTER™

EARLY INTERVENTION

Researchers have documented that immediately after birth infants begin processing a wealth of visual information in their environment (Berk, 2005). This fact makes it easy to understand why intensive intervention should begin as early as possible to help the infant with visual impairment begin to explore the environment. As we noted earlier, many infants who are blind lag behind their peers in motor development. Consequently, O & M training is a critical component of preschool programming. At one time, O & M teachers thought that young children were not old enough to be taught mobility skills. Some parents, especially sighted parents, saw the use of a cane as too stigmatizing. Today, however, more and more preschoolers are learning cane techniques (http://www.youtube.com/watch?NR=1&feature=endscreen&v=YntKTaa3ciw).

As with all children, but all the more so because of restricted access to visual information, early literacy, numeracy, and cognitive skills should be addressed as soon as possible for those with visual impairments. Also, finger strength should be a focus in order to become a proficient user of braille (Zebehazy & Lawson, 2017).

Given that the classmates of a student with visual impairment are almost always sighted, there is a potential for social isolation. Research has shown that preschoolers with visual impairments are much less likely to initiate social interactions with their sighted peers, often preferring to be left alone (Zebehazy & Lawson, 2017). If not addressed early on, such passivity may continue on into adolescence and beyond.

Although many people believe that preschoolers with visual impairments should be educated in inclusive settings with sighted children, it's critical that teachers facilitate interactions between the children. We know from research that merely placing preschoolers who have visual impairments with preschoolers who are sighted doesn't lead to their interacting with one another (Celeste, 2006; D'Allura, 2002). Teachers must provide instruction in appropriate interactions using active engagement and repeated opportunities for learning.

Most authorities agree that it's extremely important to involve parents of infants with visual impairment in early intervention efforts. Parents can become actively involved in working at home with their young children, helping them with fundamental skills such as mobility and feeding, as well as being responsive to their infants' vocalizations. Parents, too, sometimes need support in coping with their reactions to having a baby with visual impairment.

TRANSITION TO ADULTHOOD

Two closely related areas are difficult for some adolescents and adults with visual impairment: independence and employment. The level of success attained by students with visual impairments in achieving independence and appropriate employment depends greatly on the kind of preparation and support they receive from their teachers and families.

Independent Living

With proper training, preferably starting no later than middle school, most people who are blind can lead very independent lives. However, evidence shows that many students who are blind aren't receiving the training necessary in daily living skills (Lewis & Iselin, 2002; Wolffe et al., 2002). Ironically, some professionals have asserted that the movement toward including students with visual impairment in general education and providing them access to the general education curriculum has led to a diminished emphasis on teaching skills necessary for independence (Spungin, 2003). They say that itinerant teachers often do not have enough time to do much direct teaching of daily living skills.

Many authorities also point out that a major reason why adolescents and adults with visual impairment might have problems becoming independent is because of the way society treats people without sight. A common mistake is to assume that they are helpless. Many people think of blindness as a condition to be pitied. People with visual impairment have a long history of arguing against paternalistic treatment by sighted society, often resisting governmental actions that were presumably designed to help them. For example, the NFB has passed resolutions opposing the *universal* installation of accessible pedestrian signals and underfoot raised dome detectable warnings. **Accessible pedestrian signals (APSs)** alert people who are blind to when it is safe to walk across an intersection. The most common types provide auditory or tactile cues or a combination of the two. The National Cooperative Highway Research Program (n.d.) has published a guide to best practices in implementing APSs. **Raised dome detectable warnings** alert people who are blind to unsafe areas, such as ledges next to tracks in subway stations.

The NFB has stated that APSs might be needed at some complex intersections, but that they are not needed universally (Maurer, 2003). They claim that APSs can be distracting and that continuously operating APSs add to noise pollution, which can interfere with the person's hearing traffic flow. The NFB asserts that the raised dome detectable warnings are also not needed in many instances and that they can lead to unstable walking conditions.

Underlying the NFB's objection to both of these travel aids is its concern that sighted society will view people who are blind as needing more accommodations than necessary, thus reinforcing the notion that they're helpless. Whether one agrees with the NFB or believes that it is being overly sensitive, there's no doubt that sighted society is inclined to take a paternalistic view toward people who are blind. The following account of a trip taken by students from the O & M Program of Louisiana Tech University to the World Trade Center in New York City points out—with considerable irony, given the tragedy of September 11, 2001—how misguided special treatment toward those who are blind can be. Presumably because of their blindness, the group experienced lax security in their trip up to the top of the building. Afterward, in the words of one of the students,

> we made jokes about lax security. If you want to bomb the trade center, just walk in with a white cane, and they will welcome you with open arms. There was a bit of irony in this. In 1993 the World Trade Center had been bombed, but at the moment I had forgotten one important detail about that event. . . .
>
> The thing which I had forgotten about that event was brought back to my attention. I don't remember if it was a graduate student, a center student, or a staff mem-

ber who said it, but as soon as the words were out, a little piece of irony clicked into place. In a federal penitentiary outside my home town of Springfield, Missouri, sits a blind man. His crime? He masterminded the (1993) bombing of the World Trade Center. When will they ever learn?

Society too loses something when it offers undeserved privileges to people it believes inferior. The general public loses the chance to experience the distinctiveness that we can add to society. . . . (T)hese people expect us all to be the same. They cannot tell the good guys from the bad guys in the blind minority. (Lansaw, 2000, pp. 964–965)*

Even though people who are blind can achieve virtually the same degree of independence as people who are sighted, it would be a mistake to assume that this comes naturally or easily. Many independent living skills that people who are sighted learn incidentally need to be taught explicitly to those who have visual impairments. The sighted often take for granted daily living skills because they seem so easy to do. Actually, many of these skills need to be taught directly. A simple example is handling money (http://www.youtube.com/watch?v=JuBaUtqqR50). People who are blind often learn to fold their bills in certain ways to keep track of $1 from $5, $10, etc.

Employment

Many working-age adults with visual impairment are unemployed, overqualified for the jobs they hold, and receive lower wages than are warranted (Kirchner & Smith, 2005; McDonnall, 2011). However, research shows that employers often don't understand that with appropriate accommodations blindness can be eliminated or reduced as a barrier to successful job performance (McDonnall, Cruden, & O'Mally, 2015).

Although the phrase, "you can be anything you want to be," is undoubtedly an overstatement, people like Tommy Edison, a blind film critic (http://www.youtube.com/watch?v=tEvHvZOyFcw&list=PL56F7928F8F332871) can give us pause. Research does indicate, however, that with proper transition programming, students with visual impairment, even those who are totally blind, can go on to hold jobs at every level of preparation—teachers, laborers, physicians, engineers. However, the transition programming should be intensive and extensive and include numerous well-supervised work experiences or internships (Cavenaugh & Giesen, 2012; Zebehazy & Lawson, 2017).

High on the list of ways to improve employment possibilities for those who are blind are job accommodations. Employees who are blind report that relatively minor adjustments can go a long way toward making it easier for them to function in the workplace. Suggested adaptations include improved transportation (e.g., car pools), better lighting, tinted office windows to filter light, prompt snow removal, regularly scheduled fire drills to ensure spatial orientation, hallways that are free of obstacles, and computer software (e.g., screen magnification programs) and reading machines that convert print into braille (Rumrill, Roessler, Battersby-Longden, & Schuyler, 1998; Rumrill, Schuyler, & Longden, 1997).

Visual impairment no doubt poses a real challenge for adjustment to everyday living. However, people with visual impairment are similar in many ways to people in the rest of society. Special and general educators need to achieve the delicate balance between providing special programming for students with visual impairment and treating them in the same manner as they do the rest of their students.

MyLab Education Self-Check 12.5

MyLab Education Application Exercise 12.5:
Transitioning to Adult Life: Kitchen Skills

Watch a video about adaptations and modifications for independent living skills. Then answer the questions that follow.

---

*This material is reprinted with permission from the Braille Monitor, the leading publication of the National Federation of the Blind.

▼ chapter twelve SUMMARY

wavebreakmedia/Shutterstock

How do professionals define and classify learners with blindness and low vision?

- Those using a legal definition use visual acuity and field of vision:
  - Blindness is visual acuity of 20/200 or less in the better eye with correction; low vision is 20/70 to 20/200.
  - Blindness is a field of vision no greater than 20 degrees.
- Those using an educational definition use method of reading:
  - Blindness is needing to use braille or aural methods.
  - Low vision is being able to read print (enlarged or magnified).

What is the prevalence of visual impairment?

- Blindness is primarily an adult disability.
- Fewer than 0.04% of students from age 6 to 21 are identified as having visual impairment.

What are some basic anatomical and physiological characteristics of the eye?

- Objects are seen when an electrical impulse travels from the optic nerve at the back of the eye to the occipital lobes of the brain.
- Light rays pass through the cornea, aqueous humor, pupil, lens, vitreous humor, and retina before reaching the optic nerve at the back of the brain.

How is visual ability measured?

- Visual acuity for far distances is most often measured by using the Snellen chart.
- Measures are also available for measuring visual acuity for near distances.
- Vision teachers can perform functional assessments to determine how students use their vision in everyday situations.

What causes visual impairments?

- The most common visual problems result from errors of refraction:
  - Myopia (nearsightedness)
  - Hyperopia (farsightedness)
  - Astigmatism (blurred vision)
- Some conditions affect both adults and children:
  - Glaucoma is a group of diseases causing damage to the optic nerve.
  - Cataracts cause clouding of the lens of the eye.
  - Diabetic retinopathy results from interference of the blood supply to the retina.
- Some conditions affect primarily children:
  - The three most common causes in children are cortical visual impairment, retinopathy of prematurity, and optic nerve hypoplasia.

- Cortical visual impairment results from brain damage or dysfunction.
- Retinopathy of prematurity can be caused by excessive concentrations of oxygen or other factors.
- Optic nerve hypoplasia involves underdevelopment of the optic nerve
- Retinitis pigmentosa, another cause primarily in children, usually causes tunnel vision and night blindness.

- Improper muscle functioning can cause visual problems:
  - *Strabismus* refers to the eyes being turned inward (crossed eyes) or outward.
  - *Nystagmus* refers to rapid involuntary movements of the eyes.

What are some of the psychological and behavioral characteristics of learners with visual impairments?

- Language development is largely unaffected, although subtle developmental delays can occur, especially in infancy.
- Individuals may experience early delays in conceptual development, which do not last long.
- Motor delays in infancy are common; it is important that adults encourage infants to explore their environment to help overcome these delays.
- Orientation and mobility (O & M) skills depend on spatial abilities:
  - People with visual impairment can process spatial information either sequentially or as a cognitive map; the latter is more efficient.
  - Some people with visual impairment use echolocation, the ability to detect objects by noting subtle changes in echoes as they move toward or away from the objects.
  - Two myths are that people who are blind have an extra sense and that they automatically develop better acuity in their other senses.
- Studies suggest that some students who are blind experience low academic achievement, which is most likely due to low expectations or lack of exposure to braille.
- Phonological awareness is important for learning to read print or braille.
- Any social adjustment problems that people with visual impairment have are largely due to sighted society's reactions to blindness.
- Some people with visual impairment engage in stereotypic (repetitive) behaviors:
  - Most authorities attribute stereotypic behaviors to an attempt to stabilize arousal levels.
  - Professionals disagree about whether to intervene with these behaviors.

What are some educational considerations for learners with visual impairments?

- The ability to read braille is a crucial skill:
  - Many authorities believe that the use of braille has slipped to dangerously low levels.
  - Braille bills have helped to ensure that students receive instruction in braille.
  - Federal law requires that braille be available if any member of the IEP team, including parents, thinks it necessary.
  - Authorities point out that many people with low vision can benefit from braille instruction.
- The use of remaining sight is an important skill:
  - Large-print books are useful, although the need for storage space is a drawback.
  - Magnifying devices can be used for close or distance vision.
- Listening skills are important.
- O & M skills are of critical importance.
  - Learning to use a long cane is very important.
  - Unfortunately, some individuals with blindness or low vision resist using a long cane because they think it stigmatizing.
  - Preschoolers and young children can learn cane techniques.
  - There is debate about whether those who are blind can be good mobility instructors.
- Some find using a guide dog very helpful.
  - Guide dogs are much more practical for adults than for children, and they and their owner need extensive training in order to be useful.
  - Guide dogs do not take people anywhere; people usually need to know where they are going.
  - Guide dogs can alert their owners to dangerous areas.
- Tactile maps can be very helpful.
- Human guides, although not recommended as a primary means of mobility, can be helpful at times.
- Technological aids are becoming increasingly important.
  - Technological aids are available for communication and information access. These include braille notetakers, personal data assistants, Newsline®, Descriptive Video Service®, and screen readers for computers.
  - Technological aids are available for O & M. These include obstacle-detection devices and the global positioning system (GPS).

- Learners with visual impairments should not become so dependent on technology that they neglect basic techniques, such as braille, the slate and stylus, and the long cane.
- Itinerant teacher service is the most common service delivery model, and compared to other areas of disability, residential placement is relatively popular.

How do professionals assess the progress of students with visual impairments in academic and functional skills and make testing accommodations for them?

- Teachers can monitor progress in braille skills involved in reading and mathematics using curriculum-based measurement (CBM).
- O & M instructors can monitor travel skills using GPS devices.
- Professionals can assess academic outcomes using braille versions of standardized academic tests.
- Testing accommodations often include testing in braille, large-print materials, or extended time.

What are some important considerations with respect to early intervention for learners with visual impairments?

- Intensive intervention should begin as early as possible.
- Inclusive settings can be beneficial, but it is important that the teacher facilitate interactions between students with visual impairments and sighted students.
- It is important to try to involve parents.
- Many authorities now recommend that preschoolers be taught cane techniques.

What are some important considerations with respect to transition to adulthood for learners with visual impairments?

- Most people who are blind can lead very independent lives.
- The current emphasis on inclusion needs to be viewed with caution to make sure it does not come at the expense of learning independent living skills.
- Sighted society needs to be careful not to treat those with visual impairments as helpless.
- Explicit teaching of independent living skills is essential.
- Many working-age adults with visual impairments are unemployed or are overqualified for the jobs they hold.
- Previous work experience is important for obtaining employment.
- Transition programming should be intensive and extensive.
- Job accommodations are essential.

▼ INTERNET RESOURCES

Pertinent Organizations

- Prevent Blindness America (www.preventblindness.org), founded in 1908, is a voluntary organization devoted to eye health and safety.

- World Access for the Blind (http://www.worldaccessfortheblind .org) provides advocacy for people with all forms of blindness.

- The National Federation of the Blind (www.nfb.org) is probably the leading organization devoted to advocacy for people who are blind.

- The National Braille Press's Center for Innovation (www .nbp.org/ic/nbp/technology/index.html) is devoted to making portable braille notetakers and other technologies affordable.

- The American Foundation for the Blind (http://www.afb .org/) is a major professional organization focused on blindness.

chapter thirteen

LEARNERS WITH LOW-INCIDENCE, MULTIPLE, AND SEVERE DISABILITIES

martin bowra/Shutterstock

▶ LEARNING OUTCOMES

Learning Outcome 13.1: Understand the most current definitions for and the prevalence of low-incidence, multiple, and severe disabilities.

Learning Outcome 13.2: Understand the definition, characteristics, prevalence, causes, and educational considerations associated with traumatic brain injury.

Learning Outcome 13.3: Understand the definition, prevalence, causes, psychological and behavioral characteristics, and educational considerations associated with deaf-blindness.

Learning Outcome 13.4: Learn about educational considerations for many students with low-incidence, multiple, and severe disabilities (e.g., augmentative or alternative communication, dealing with behavior problems, early intervention, and transition to adulthood).

MISCONCEPTIONS ABOUT Learners with Low-Incidence, Multiple, and Severe Disabilities

MYTH People with severe and multiple disabilities have problems so debilitating that the best they can hope for is employment in a sheltered workshop.

FACT With intensive and extensive instruction, many people with severe and multiple disabilities can now be employed in more integrated work settings.

MYTH People with severe and multiple disabilities have problems so debilitating that the best they can hope for is to live under close supervision in a large residential facility.

FACT With intensive and extensive instruction, many people with severe and multiple disabilities can now live independently or semi-independently by themselves or in a small community residential facility (CRF).

MYTH A person with traumatic brain injury (TBI) can be expected, with time, to recover completely and function without disabilities.

FACT Some people with TBI do recover completely, but many do not. Usually, a person with TBI has long-term disabilities that may be compensated for in many ways, but these disabilities don't ordinarily disappear completely, even with the best treatment and rehabilitation.

MYTH For students with Usher syndrome whose vision will deteriorate over time, it's best not to introduce braille and training with the long cane while their vision is still relatively good because to do so stigmatizes them.

FACT Braille and orientation and mobility training should not wait until the later stages of vision loss. Getting a head start on learning these complex skills almost always outweighs any stigmatization that might occur.

MYTH People who can't speak have extreme difficulty making themselves understood to others.

FACT With an appropriate augmentative or alternative communication (AAC) system, people who can't speak can carry on a normal conversation, sometimes very near the rate of speakers without disabilities. The flexibility, speed, and usefulness of communication with AAC systems are increasing rapidly with new technologies, and they now often allow a user to approximate typical verbal exchanges between speakers.

MYTH The only really effective way of controlling the undesirable behavior of people with severe and multiple disabilities is to use punishment.

FACT Functional behavioral assessment and positive behavioral supports are being used more frequently to replace undesirable behavior with desirable behavior—without the use of punishment. Often, the key is finding out what the person with severe and multiple disabilities is trying to communicate and helping him or her find a more effective, efficient way of communicating that to others.

MYTH Braille is only for people who are blind.

FACT It is helpful to teach braille to two groups of individuals who are not blind: (1) those who have visual impairments so severe that they can't read print reliably and (2) those whose condition will worsen with time to the point at which braille will be their only option.

GUIDING QUESTIONS

- What is the definition of low-incidence, multiple, and severe disabilities, and what is the prevalence?

- What is traumatic brain injury, and how might it affect education?

- How is deaf-blindness defined, and what are the special educational problems it entails?

- What educational considerations apply to many students with low-incidence, multiple, and severe disabilities?

T he definition of low-incidence, severe, and multiple disabilities, like the definition of all other categories of disabilities, is controversial. Disabilities are particularly mystifying when they are seldom seen, multiple, or severe. The causes and meanings of such disabilities, and the life course of the people who have them, may be particularly difficult to understand.

DEFINITION AND PREVALENCE

TASH (originally the Association for Persons with Severe Handicaps, then The Association for the Severely Handicapped, but now simply called TASH to avoid use of "handicapped" because some believe that the term is pejorative) is a major professional organization focused on individuals with severe disabilities. TASH defines a disability as "severe" if it results in the person needing ongoing support in more than one major life activity necessary to reside in the community and to enjoy a quality of life similar to that of members of the population without disabilities. Examples of life activities are such things as being able to communicate, engage in self-care, and learn skills to be employed and live in the community.

People with a severe disability in any area typically have more than one disability (Kauffman, Hallahan, Pullen, & Badar, 2018). Furthermore, a combination of mild disabilities may present severe educational problems (Kauffman, 2008). As noted in the Individuals with Disabilities Education Improvement Act of 2004 (IDEA): "Multiple disabilities means concomitant impairments . . . the combination of which causes such severe educational problems that they cannot be accommodated in special education programs solely for one of the impairments" (34 CFR, Sec. 300 (b)(6)). IDEA also states:

> The term "children with severe disabilities" refers to children with disabilities who, because of the intensity of their physical, mental, or emotional problems, need highly specialized education, social, psychological, and medical services in order to maximize their full potential for useful and meaningful participation in society and for self-fulfillment. The term includes those children with severe emotional disturbance (including schizophrenia), autism, severe and profound mental retardation, and those who have two or more serious disabilities, such as deaf-blindness, mental retardation and blindness, and cerebral palsy and deafness.
>
> Children with severe disabilities may experience severe speech, language, and/ or perceptual-cognitive deprivations, and evidence abnormal behaviors, such as failure to respond to pronounced social stimuli, self-mutilation, self-stimulation, manifestation of intense and prolonged temper tantrums, and the absence of rudimentary forms of verbal control, and may also have intensely fragile physiological conditions. (34 CFR, Sec. 315.4(d))

Low-incidence, severe, and multiple disabilities are often linked conceptually. They occur in only a relatively small percentage of cases of disability (Bruce & Ivy, 2017). Furthermore, nearly any low-incidence, severe disability will involve extensive and ongoing support in more than one major life activity. That is, low-incidence, severe, and multiple disabilities tend to go together. All of the low-incidence, severe, and multiple disabilities that we discuss in the chapter probably affect fewer than 1% of the population.

With these considerations in mind, in this chapter, we first discuss the categories and problems of traumatic brain injury and deaf-blindness. Then we discuss issues that apply to all categories of low-incidence, multiple, and severe disabilities: augmentative and alternative communication, behavior problems, early intervention, and transition to adulthood.

We mentioned severe and profound intellectual disability in Chapter 5 and discussed autism spectrum disorders in Chapter 9. However, much of what we present in this chapter applies to some individuals with autism and to those with severe or profound intellectual disability as well. Remember, though, that autism spectrum disorders can range from mild to severe, as is the case in all other categories of disability.

MyLab Education **Self-Check 13.1**

MyLab Education **Application Exercise 13.1:**
Multiple Disabilities and Severe Disabilities

Review the definitions of *severe and profound intellectual disabilities* and *multiple disabilities* in your text, and then answer the questions in this exercise.

TRAUMATIC BRAIN INJURY

Since 1990, when IDEA recognized the category of **traumatic brain injury (TBI)**, students with TBI have been eligible to be considered for special education and related services (Kauffman et al., 2018). Today, there is much greater understanding of the nature of TBI and the educational needs of students with TBI (e.g., http://www.ninds.nih.gov/ disorders/tbi/tbi.htm). Unlike cerebral palsy, TBI is brain damage that is acquired by trauma after a period of normal neurological development. TBI is a life-altering experience that results in neurological, cognitive, and psychosocial consequences (Trenchard, Rust, & Bunton, 2013).

Historically, recognition and treatment of disabilities are often triggered by the return of injured soldiers to civilian life. Because TBI is one of the most common injuries of the wars in Iraq and Afghanistan, perhaps the public will become more aware of and demand better treatment of those with TBI. Additionally, the national media has highlighted the significance of TBI as it relates to athletes. The celebrity status of many NFL players who have developed TBI as a result of sports injuries is also increasing awareness of and demand for better efforts at prevention, as well as early diagnosis and treatment.

MyLab Education
Video Example 13.1
Meet Rebekah and listen to her story about her life after experiencing a traumatic brain injury.

Definition and Characteristics

Commonly accepted definitions of TBI specify the following:

1. There is injury to the brain caused by an external force.
2. The injury is not caused by a degenerative or congenital condition.
3. There is a diminished or altered state of consciousness.
4. Neurological or neurobehavioral dysfunction results from the injury.

Most definitions also specify that the injury be followed by impairments in abilities required for learning in school and everyday functioning.

TBI can result from two categories of injury: open or closed. **Open head injuries** involve a penetrating head wound from such causes as a fall, gunshot, assault, vehicular accident, or surgery. Individuals with **closed head injuries** have no open head wound but may have brain damage caused by internal compression, stretching, or other shearing motion of neural tissues within the head. A common cause of closed head injuries is sporting and recreational accidents. For example, concussions in youth sports have received significant attention in recent years. For more information on such injuries read the Focus On Brain Injury in Athletics feature.

Soldiers have often acquired TBI as a result of improvised explosive devices (IEDs). They may experience either open head injuries, in which something penetrates the head or removes part of the brain, or closed head injuries, in which the concussive force of the explosion or the soldier's being thrown against an object damages the brain without creating an open wound. The effects of damage to the brain and the resulting symptoms can be severe with either type of injury.

The educational definition of TBI focuses on impairments in one or more areas important for learning. The federal (IDEA) definition of TBI states that it is

> an acquired injury to the brain caused by an external physical force, resulting in total or partial functional disability or psychosocial impairment, or both, that adversely affects a child's educational performance. The term applies to open or closed head injuries resulting in impairments in one or more areas, such as cognition; language; memory; attention; reasoning; abstract thinking; judgment; problem-solving; sensory, perceptual, and motor abilities; psychosocial behavior; physical functions; information processing; and speech. The term does not apply to injuries that are congenital or degenerative, or brain injuries induced by birth trauma. (34 CFR, Sec. 300.7(6)(12))

The effects of TBI range from very mild to profound, and TBI is often a part of or accompanied by other medical issues (Best, Heller, & Bigge, 2010). Often, the effects are immediate, and these immediate effects set TBI apart from most other disabilities—the child or youth is literally changed overnight. The sudden change presents particular difficulties to families and teachers, not to mention the individual sustaining the injury (Ashley, 2004; McDonald, 2013). However, sometimes the effects of TBI are not seen immediately after the injury but appear months or even years afterward. The possible effects of TBI include a long list of learning and psychosocial problems, such as:

- Problems remembering things
- Problems learning new information
- Speech and/or language problems
- Difficulty sequencing things
- Difficulty in processing information (making sense of things)
- Extremely uneven abilities or performance (able to do some things but not others)
- Extremely uneven progress (quick gains sometimes, no gains other times)
- Inappropriate manners or mannerisms
- Failure to understand humor or social situations
- Becoming easily tired, frustrated, or angered
- Unreasonable fear or anxiety
- Irritability
- Sudden, exaggerated swings of mood
- Depression
- Aggression
- Perseveration (persistent repetition of one thought or behavior)

From the length and variety of this list, it's not begging the question to state that narrowing down the definition of TBI is virtually impossible. In fact, perhaps the distinguishing feature of TBI is that it defies a narrow definition, reinforcing the basic principle of special education individualization and the importance of individualized education programs (IEPs). Just a few examples from research document problems in working memory (Raghubar, Barnes, Prasad, Johnson, Ewing-Cobbs, 2013), social skills (Anderson et al., 2013; Yeates et al., 2013), and depression (Ewing-Cobbs, Prasad, Mendez, Barnes, & Swank, 2013).

FOCUS ON

Brain Injury in Athletics

Sports-related concussions have occurred in all levels of athletics, including youth sports, since their inception. So why are we hearing about it in the media now? Is it simply a sense of greater awareness, or are concussions happening with greater frequency? The fact is, both are true. Sports-related concussions occur frequently in contact sports such as football, wrestling, boxing, and hockey, but they are also common in bicycling, playground accidents, and less combative sports like basketball and soccer (Centers for Disease Control and Prevention, 2011; McCrea et al., 2012). The incidence of concussions in organized sports resulting in emergency room visits has doubled in recent years for children ages 8 to 13, and more than doubled for children ages 14 to 19 (Bakhos, Lockhart, Myers, & Linakis, 2010).

Fortunately, new rules in organized athletics designed to help prevent serious TBI are a result of medical advances in the diagnosis and treatment of concussion, along with media attention and organized awareness efforts (e.g., *Heads Up—Concussion in Youth Sports*, Centers for Disease Control, https://www.cdc.gov/headsup/youthsports/index.html). The National Federation of State High School Associations has instituted new regulations for football that focus on concussion. Most states have passed laws that prevent players who have sustained a concussion in a sporting event from returning to play in the same game. (Visit the website for Law Atlas, click on Interactive Law Maps, and select Youth Sports TBI Laws to find out if your state has laws about youth sports and head injuries.)

Despite new awareness and medical advances in the prevention and treatment of concussion, problems still exist in athletics. An article in the *Chronicle of Higher Education* (Wolverton, 2013) cites concerns that athletic trainers in the National Collegiate Athletic Association (NCAA) answer directly to football coaches. Therefore, if players are injured (e.g., suffer a concussion), the trainers' job is to keep the player safe, but coaches want them back on the field.

Another challenge is that if a player is exhibiting symptoms, he or she may not disclose this to the coach for fear of losing playing time. However, the NCAA now provides guidelines for the evaluation of concussive symptoms on the sideline of sporting events and states that a player may not return to play until concussive symptoms have subsided completely. Enforcing these guidelines remains a critical issue in college athletics.

Repeated concussions put a person at risk for chronic traumatic encephalopathy (CTE). **Chronic traumatic encephalopathy (CTE)** is a degenerative brain disease caused by repetitive trauma to the brain. This trauma may include unsymptomatic subconcussive blows that are never even diagnosed, as well as more severe concussions and brain injuries (Lakhan & Kirchgessner, 2012). The first signs of CTE to appear are behavioral (e.g., impulsivity and physical and verbal abuse) and mood changes (e.g., depression and anxiety), followed by neurocognitive decline (e.g., problems with memory, executive functioning, and attention) (Stern et al., 2013).

Although the concept of a "punch-drunk syndrome" in boxers has been around since the early part of the 20th century (Martland, 1928), the recognition of concussions in many other sports causing long-term neurological symptoms did not come about until the early 2000s. The emergence of CTE as a medical condition in the scientific community originated with the case study of an autopsy performed on a deceased NFL football player reported by Dr. Bennet Omalu and his research team. Public awareness of CTE was sparked by the 2015 movie, *Concussion* (http://www.imdb.com/title/tt3322364/), which focused on Omalu (portrayed by Will Smith) and his struggles to convince the National Football League of the existence of CTE (Asken et al., 2016).

The tragic suicides of NFL players Junior Seau and Dave Duerson further publicized the debilitating effects of CTE. Both athletes' brains were donated to the National Institutes of Health to help researchers learn more about how to prevent and/or treat CTE. As they suspected, CTE in both athletes was confirmed. Research at Boston University's CTE center has found that 99 percent of the former NFL players studied had some level of CTE (Moran, 2017).

Unfortunately, as mentioned earlier, symptoms of CTE often do not appear at the time of the injury; instead, the repetition of this brain trauma shows up years later. Many athletes begin in youth sports and continue through high school and college. A selected few go on to play in professional leagues. The media has brought attention to the celebrities, but how many of our own children may one day feel the effects of the trauma their brains have experienced over years of participating in contact sports? Just as we need to attend more to the seriousness of diagnosed concussions, we must consider the danger of participating in contact sports and learn how to better protect the most important organ in the body, the brain.

One of the great difficulties with TBI is that it's often "invisible." True, in some cases, a person with TBI has paralysis, slurred speech, or some other indicator of brain damage that is quickly apparent. But in many cases, the person with TBI looks just like everyone else. The casual observer doesn't see anything obvious, as is true in some cases of physical disability. Recurrent concussions, for example, can affect a person's life in dramatic ways, but the individual may not manifest any visible evidence that a brain injury has taken place.

Prevalence

The exact prevalence of TBI is difficult to determine, but we do know that it occurs at an alarming rate among children and youths. We also know that 0.04% of the 6- to 21-year-old population are identified as needing special education services (U.S. Department of Education, 2016). Estimates suggest that 16% of those with TBI are considered to have moderate to severe impairment, with some cases leading to death (Trenchard et al., 2013). Males are more prone to TBI than females are, and the age range in which TBI is most likely to occur for both males and females is late adolescence and early adulthood. The Council for Exceptional Children (2001) refers to TBI as a "silent epidemic." TBI is considered an epidemic because of its increasing prevalence (Grandinette & Best, 2009; Stichter, Conroy, & Kauffman, 2008); and it's "silent" because many serious head injuries are unreported, and many cases of TBI go undetected or are mistaken for other disabilities. Some of the upsurge in TBI prevalence is due to increased survival rates because of medical advances. The prevalence of TBI is disconcerting because so many of the causes of TBI are entirely preventable or avoidable by following ordinary safety precautions.

MyLab Education
Video Example 13.2

Car accidents are a leading cause of TBI. Rebekah discusses the importance of wearing seatbelts. She was not wearing a seatbelt when she had an accident that led to a life-altering TBI.

Causes

Among children younger than 5 years old, accidental falls are the dominant cause of TBI, with vehicular accidents and child abuse causing substantial injuries as well. After age 5, and increasingly through adolescence, vehicular accidents (including accidents involving pedestrians, bicycles, motorcycles, and cars) account for the majority of TBI; assaults and gunshot wounds are increasingly prevalent among youths at older ages. Closed head injuries may be caused by a variety of events besides vehicular accidents, including a fall or abuse such as violent shaking of a child by an adult (see Lajiness-O'Neill & Erdodi, 2017).

Educational Considerations

The educational implications of TBI are varied and depend on the nature and severity of the injury and the age and abilities of the individual at the time of injury. A significant issue in educating someone who has experienced TBI is helping family members, teachers, and peers to respond appropriately to the sudden and sometimes dramatic changes that may occur in the student's academic abilities, appearance, behavior, and emotional state (Lajiness-O'Neill & Erdodi, 2017). Both general and special education teachers need training about TBI and its ramifications if students are to be reintegrated successfully into the schools and classrooms they attended before the injury (DePompei & Tyler, 2004; Grandinette & Best, 2009; Kauffman et al., 2018; Stichter et al., 2008). The following characteristics are essential features of appropriate education for students with TBI:

1. Well planned transition from a hospital or rehabilitation center to the school
2. A team approach involving regular and special educators, other specialized teachers, a guidance counselor, administrators, and the student's family
3. An individualized education program (IEP) concerned with cognitive, social/behavioral, and sensorimotor domains
4. Educational procedures to help students solve problems in focusing and sustaining attention for long periods, remembering previously learned facts and skills, learning new things, dealing with fatigue, and engaging in appropriate social behavior
5. Emphasis on the cognitive processes through which academic skills are learned, not just curriculum content
6. Plans for addressing long-term needs in addition to immediate and annual IEP goals

MyLab Education
Video Example 13.3

The Clubhouse is a program for individuals with Traumatic Brain Injury. Consider the benefits of such a program, including the individualization of the services for the participants.

It's critical that educators understand the implications of the brain injury for structuring the student's psychological and social environments in school (Best et al., 2010).

The teacher must focus on helping the student with TBI to recover cognitive abilities because these are most critical to academic and social progress. The abilities to remember and to make sense of academic information and social circumstances are key to the student's long-term success. The teacher must help the student learn to use coping mechanisms and alternative strategies, such as using a tape recorder, smartphone, planner, or other organizational devices and memory aids for whatever abilities cannot be recovered.

A major problem in reentry to school after TBI—at least if the consequences are serious—is that students with TBI tend to see themselves as not having changed, whereas peers and teachers are likely to notice that they are not the same. Dell Orto and Power (2000) note that our societal emphasis on productiveness, organization, independence, and achievement can contribute to negative attitudes toward a student with TBI. "Academic deficits displayed by survivors of TBI conflict with achievement values, not only causing discomfort in teachers, but frustration and perhaps a sense of rejection in the young person" (p. 22). Many teachers apparently don't want students with TBI in their classrooms, probably because these students exhibit characteristics that teachers find troublesome (just consider the bulleted list of learning and psychosocial problems presented earlier). Thus, a student's returning to school after TBI is a major issue that typically requires a team approach involving a variety of professionals, as we mentioned in our list of essential features of appropriate educational programs. Collaboration and problem solving by this team are essential to the success of the student's reentry.

The assessment of a student's academic and social skills following TBI is tricky because it's often difficult or impossible to separate physiological causes or reasons for difficulty with a task from other causes. More important than knowing precisely what difficulties have a physiological cause is pinpointing just what the student's academic and social learning difficulties are. Here again, a team approach is essential. Neurologists can often provide information about the consequences of TBI that helps teachers to set reasonable expectations and teach coping skills that help the student to compensate for abilities that will not return.

MyLab Education
Video Example 13.4

This video shows an example of the importance of interdisciplinary teamwork in implementing a successful educational program for a child with TBI.

LANGUAGE DISORDERS A student with TBI might acquire a language disorder after a period of normal development, or acquire a more severe language disorder than existed before the injury (see Chapter 10). Individuals with TBI comprise a very diverse population, although a disproportionate number of students with TBI have a pre-trauma history of learning problems or delayed speech and language.

Language or speech disorders are the greatest complicating factor in most students' return to school following TBI. A loss of ability to understand and formulate language due to brain injury is sometimes referred to as a **motor-speech disorder**, which we discussed in Chapter 10. The student may have trouble finding or saying words or constructing sentences that are appropriate for the topic of conversation or social context. Problems like these can be a source of frustration, anger, and confusion for students with TBI.

The language problems associated with TBI are primarily related to the cognitive and social demands of communication. The student might have problems with tasks that demand responding quickly, organizing, dealing with abstractions, sustaining attention (especially if there are distractions), learning new skills, responding appropriately in social situations, and showing appropriate affect. In fact, TBI can potentially disrupt all aspects of the give-and-take of social interaction that are required for effective communication.

The effects of TBI on language are extremely variable, and careful assessment of the given individual's abilities and disabilities is critically important. Interventions may range from making special accommodations, such as allowing more response time or keeping distractions to a minimum, to focusing on instruction in the social uses of language.

Depending on the site and degree of brain damage, a person with TBI may have motor control problems that interfere with communication, including the cognitive and social aspects of communication. Some students with TBI cannot communicate orally using the muscles of speech and must rely on alternative or augmentative communication systems, which we describe later in the chapter.

MyLab Education
Video Example 13.5

Chris sustained a head injury from a car accident. He discusses his difficulty with language, as well as the importance of art to allow him to have fulfillment in life.

SOCIAL AND EMOTIONAL PROBLEMS Brain injury may be accompanied by a variety of serious social and emotional effects. We know that TBI can cause violent aggression, hyperactivity, impulsivity, inattention, and a wide range of other emotional or behavioral problems, depending on just what parts of the brain are damaged. The possible effects of TBI include a long list of other psychosocial problems, some of which we listed previously as general characteristics.

The emotional and behavioral effects of TBI are determined by more than the physical damage; they also depend on the student's age at the time of injury and the social environment before and after the injury. Home, community, or school environments that foster misbehavior of any child or youth are known to be associated with increased risk for acquiring TBI. Such environments are extremely likely to worsen any emotional or behavioral problem resulting from TBI. Creating an environment that is conducive to and supportive of appropriate behavior is one of the great challenges of dealing effectively with the results of brain injury.

Many of the typical **behavior modification** or **behavior management** strategies that are used with other students who have emotional or behavioral difficulties are appropriate for use with students who have TBI. Consistency, predictability, and reinforcement (praise, encouragement, and other rewards) are particularly important (Persel & Persel, 2004), as is developing rapport with the student. Developing a good personal relationship with a student with TBI can be particularly challenging, as such students can be unpredictable, irritable, and angry with those who are trying to help (see ; Kauffman & Badar, 2018; Kauffman, Pullen, Mostert, & Trent, 2011).

TBI often shatters an individual's sense of self. Recovering one's identity can require a long period of rehabilitation and can be a painstaking process requiring multidisciplinary efforts (Best et al., 2010; Grandinette & Best, 2009). Effective education and treatment often require not only classroom behavior management but also family therapy, medication, cognitive training, and communication training.

MyLab Education **Self-Check 13.2**

MyLab Education **Application Exercise 13.2:**
Traumatic Brain Injury

Watch a video of Matt and his two teachers discussing his behaviors in the classroom. Then, answer a follow-up question.

DEAF-BLINDNESS

In Chapters 11 and 12, we noted that, depending on the level of severity, blindness or deafness can have a substantial impact on a person's ability to function independently. For those who are both deaf and blind, the impact can be even more profound than simply adding the effects of each disability. Because the primary avenues for receiving information—sight and sound—are limited, those who are deaf-blind are at risk for having extensive problems in communicating and in navigating their environments.

Although being cut off from the sights and sounds of daily life makes deaf-blindness one of the most challenging of all multiple disabilities, this doesn't mean that a person with deaf-blindness is doomed to a poor-quality life. In general, outcomes for individuals with deaf-blindness depend on at least three factors:

1. *The quality and intensity of instruction the person receives are critical.* Teachers of students with deaf-blindness "must make the most of every opportunity for learning. All interactions with adults and all aspects of the environment will be harnessed to help the child overcome the restrictions imposed by sensory impairments" (Hodges, 2000, p. 167).

2. *The degree and type of auditory impairment and visual impairment can vary dramatically in individuals with deaf-blindness.* The term *deaf-blindness* covers those with hearing impairments ranging from mild to profound. Likewise, the term covers those with visual impairments ranging from low vision (20/70 to 20/200 in the better eye with correction) to those who are totally blind. Despite some very notable exceptions, in general, the more severe the impairments, the greater is the impact on a person's ability to adapt.

3. *The vast majority of students who are deaf-blind have other disabilities and medical conditions.* For example, they may have intellectual disabilities, autism, and/or physical disabilities.

Definition

As we discussed in Chapters 11 and 12, considerable controversy exists over the definitions of deafness and blindness. As one might expect, this means that defining deaf-blindness is even more controversial than defining deafness or blindness separately. The Individuals with Disabilities Education Improvement Act (2004) describes deaf-blindness as an individual

> (1)(i) Who has a central visual acuity of 20/200 or less in the better eye with corrective lenses, or a field defect such that the peripheral diameter of visual field subtends an angular distance no greater than 20 degrees, or a progressive visual loss having a prognosis leading to one or both of these conditions:
>
> (ii) Who has a chronic hearing impairment so severe that most speech cannot be understood with optimum amplification, or a progressive hearing loss having a prognosis leading to this condition; and
>
> (iii) For whom the combination of impairments described in paragraphs (1)(i) and (ii) of this definition causes extreme difficulty in attaining independence in daily life activities, achieving psychosocial adjustment, or obtaining a vocation;
>
> (2) Who, despite the inability to be measured accurately for hearing and vision loss due to cognitive or behavioral constraints, or both, can be determined through functional and performance assessment to have severe hearing and visual disabilities that cause extreme difficulty in attaining independence in daily life activities, or obtaining vocational objectives; or
>
> (3) Who meets any other requirements that the Secretary may prescribe. (34 CFR, Sec. 396.4 (c)(2))

Prevalence

Deaf-blindness is very rare—much more rare, for example, than either deafness or blindness alone. The best estimate available is that only about 1 in 1,000 persons from birth to 21 years has deaf-blindness (National Center on Deaf-Blindness, 2015).

Causes

Causes of deaf-blindness can be grouped into three broad categories: (1) genetic/chromosomal syndromes, (2) prenatal conditions, and (3) postnatal conditions.

GENETIC/CHROMOSOMAL SYNDROMES Researchers are making enormous strides in discovering genetic/chromosomal syndromes involved in deaf-blindness. Some of these syndromes are inherited, and some result from damaged genetic and/or chromosomal material. Dozens of genetic/chromosomal syndromes are now known to be associated with deaf-blindness. The most common are CHARGE syndrome, Usher syndrome, and Down syndrome.

CHARGE Syndrome Caused by a gene mutation (Zentner, Layman, Martin, & Scacheri, 2010), **CHARGE syndrome** is characterized by a number of physical anomalies present at birth. These anomalies include such things as structural defects resulting in difficulties swallowing and breathing. Of the features of CHARGE syndrome, the most important for vision is coloboma. **Coloboma** refers to a condition in which the child is born with an abnormally shaped pupil and/or abnormalities of the retina or optic nerve. Coloboma can result in a variety of visual problems, including deficits in visual acuity and extreme sensitivity to light.

USHER Syndrome An inherited condition, **Usher syndrome** is characterized by hearing impairment and **retinitis pigmentosa**. As mentioned in Chapter 12, retinitis pigmentosa can result in vision problems starting in infancy, early childhood, or the teenage years, with the condition becoming progressively worse. It results in problems with seeing in low light, referred to as **night blindness**, and as it progresses, it results in a narrowing of the field of vision, referred to as **tunnel vision**.

Thus far, researchers have found that a mutation in any one of about 11 genes can result in Usher syndrome (National Institute on Deafness and Other Communication Disorders, 2010). Although Usher syndrome is one of the most common hereditary conditions causing deaf-blindness, its overall prevalence is very low. Estimates suggest that about 16,000 people in the United States have Usher syndrome (Wrong Diagnosis, 2010). The genetics of Usher syndrome show an interesting demographic pattern.

DOWN Syndrome Most often noted as a cause of intellectual disability (see Chapter 5), **Down syndrome** is also sometimes associated with deaf-blindness. Unlike Usher syndrome, which is inherited, Down syndrome results from damaged chromosomal material.

PRENATAL CONDITIONS Like Down syndrome, two of the most common types of **prenatal** conditions—**rubella**, sometimes referred to as **German measles**, and **congenital cytomegalovirus (CMV)**—can cause intellectual disability and/or deaf-blindness. When rubella occurs in a pregnant woman, especially in the first trimester, it can lead to a variety of disabilities, including deaf-blindness. Children born with CMV, a herpes virus, are also at risk for a variety of disabilities, including deaf-blindness.

POSTNATAL CONDITIONS Among the most common **postnatal** conditions that can cause deaf-blindness are **meningitis and TBI**. As we learned in Chapter 5, meningitis, which is an infection of the covering of the brain, can also cause intellectual disability. TBI, as we discussed earlier in this chapter, can result in a variety of other disabilities, as well as deaf-blindness.

FOCUS ON

The Genetics of Usher Syndrome and Its Geographic Distribution

About 1 in 75 people carries an Usher gene, but most don't realize they have it. Usher syndrome is an *autosomal-recessive disorder*, meaning that for a child to have the condition, both parents must be carriers of the gene. And with each such pregnancy, there is a one-in-four chance of the child having Usher syndrome. Thus, the chance of having a child with Usher syndrome is relatively rare even among those who carry the gene, and that is why the prevalence of Usher syndrome is so low. However, the odds of producing an offspring with Usher syndrome rise dramatically among people who are related.

Unfortunately, social forces have operated historically to make the likelihood of intermarriage higher among a certain cultural group: the Acadian French of south Louisiana. This has resulted in a relatively higher number of people with Usher syndrome in this area of the country. The high prevalence of Usher syndrome in south Louisiana is also the subject of a video narrated by the well-known neurologist Oliver Sacks, *The Ragin' Cajun Usher Syndrome*, produced by the British Broadcasting Company.

Ironically, events of the early 21st century may serve to reverse some of the social forces that led to a high incidence of Usher syndrome among Acadians. It's too early to tell, but Hurricane Katrina in 2005 and the British Petroleum oil spill in 2006 have resulted in a population displacement along the Louisiana Gulf Coast. It's possible that such dispersion will result in a decrease in intermarriage, which in turn would result in fewer offspring with Usher syndrome.

Psychological and Behavioral Characteristics

People who are deaf-blind can have significant problems in at least four areas: (1) accessing information, (2) communicating, (3) navigating the environment, and (4) achieving successful social emotional development (Hartshorne & Schmittel, 2016).

PROBLEMS ACCESSING INFORMATION For people who are deaf-blind, access to the usual sources of information (e.g., Internet, television, newspapers) is more difficult than for those who are sighted. And because communication depends largely on the availability of information, restricted access to information can have a negative impact on the ability to communicate. For one thing, without this store of world knowledge, there's much less to communicate about (Aitken, 2000).

MyLab Education
Video Example 13.6
This video shows a group lesson with deaf-blind students focused on increasing communication skills—oral and sign language.

PROBLEMS COMMUNICATING Most authorities agree that the biggest obstacle faced by people with deaf-blindness is communication. Without a strong commitment by teachers and other professionals and parents to providing a variety of opportunities for communication, the child who is deaf-blind can easily become socially isolated. The pattern for this isolation can begin at birth. The baby who is deaf and blind has limited ability to interact with his or her parents and the environment, presenting the context for an unpredictable world. For example, consider how the simple act of being picked up by an adult might be startling and be perceived as threatening (Pease, 2000). In the face of such experiences in infancy and early childhood, the child who is deaf-blind is a candidate for social isolation.

Once this pattern of isolation has been established, it's difficult to reverse. Therefore, it's not surprising that individuals who are deaf-blind are at risk for developing behavior disorders such as anxiety, depression, and even psychosis (Bodsworth, Clare, & Simblett, 2011; Dammeyer, 2011). It's critical that professionals and parents work together to provide an environment that's as supportive and rich in communication opportunities as possible.

No better example of the importance of providing a language-rich environment exists than the classic case of Helen Keller (1880–1968) and her teacher Anne Sullivan (1866–1936). Popularized by the classic movie *The Miracle Worker* (Green & Penn, 1962), Helen Keller's accomplishments are now familiar to most of us. Having lost her sight and hearing at the age of 19 months, Keller went on to extraordinary achievements, including graduating cum laude from Radcliffe College in 1904; publishing essays and books (including the much acclaimed *The Story of My Life*, 1905, written while she was in college and available in over 50 languages); touring the country lecturing on blindness; being a spokesperson for women's right to vote; and receiving the Presidential Medal of Freedom, the nation's highest civilian award. To see rare video footage of Helen Keller when she was younger and older, go to: http://www.youtube.com/watch?v=GzlriQv16gg and http://www.youtube.com/watch?v=8ch_H8pt9M8.

Helen Keller is testimony to the power of the human spirit to overcome overwhelming odds. However, just as important, she is testimony to the power of intensive and extensive special education instruction. As remarkable as she was, it's doubtful that Keller would have conquered her condition without the prolonged instruction from Annie Sullivan, herself born blind, who devoted nearly 50 years to being Keller's teacher and constant companion. Through persistence and intensive instruction, Sullivan was able to set Helen's mind free to learn language and higher concepts.

PROBLEMS NAVIGATING THE ENVIRONMENT As we discussed in Chapter 12, people who are blind or who have low vision can have significant difficulties with orientation and mobility (O & M). For people who are deaf-blind, these problems are often even more pronounced. Individuals who are blind and hearing can pick up auditory cues that help them in navigation. For example, being able to hear approaching traffic can be very helpful when crossing an intersection, and being able to hear such things as buses, trains, and construction noises can help a person who is blind to identify her location. However, people who are both deaf and blind are restricted in their ability to make use of auditory signals for navigating the environment.

FOCUS ON

Laura Bridgman (1829–1889), The First Documented Case of a Deaf-Blind Person to Learn Language

Sullivan and Keller are not the only famous teacher–student team to demonstrate the importance of intensive instruction for persons who are deaf-blind. Actually, predating the Keller-Sullivan relationship was the one of Laura Bridgman and Samuel Gridley Howe. Although most people are familiar with the story of Helen Keller, Laura Bridgman (1829–1889) was actually the first documented case of a deaf-blind person to learn language. Laura became ill with scarlet fever at the age of 2, and it left her deaf and blind.

Samuel Gridley Howe (1801–1876) was one of the 19th century's most daring social activists, reforming schools, prisons, and mental institutions as well as being a member of the "Secret Six," who lent financial support to John Brown's campaign to end slavery in the United States with his ill-fated launching of the raid at Harper's Ferry in 1859. Howe received his medical degree from Harvard University in 1824. After serving a 7-year stint as a surgeon in the Greek civil conflict, he returned to Boston. In 1832, he was named head of the Perkins Institution and Massachusetts School for the Blind (now named the Perkins School for the Blind).

After reading a newspaper account of Laura, Howe visited her parents and convinced them to send the 8-year-old to Perkins in 1837. There, he and his teachers worked painstakingly with Laura for several years. Although her achievements were not as spectacular as Keller's, Bridgman's accomplishments were extraordinary for the time, because many authorities believed that to be deaf-blind was to be mentally retarded. Furthermore, had it not been for Bridgman, Keller might never have received the instruction that unlocked her intellect. Helen's parents were alerted to the potential of teaching their own daughter after reading about Bridgman's accomplishments. Furthermore, Helen's teacher, Annie Sullivan, herself a former student at Perkins, consulted Howe's reports on Laura before embarking on her journey to tutor Helen.

The most important "lesson" of the Howe-Bridgman story might have been its sparking public interest in not only people who are deaf-blind but also those with other disabilities (Freeberg, 2001). Pioneers such as Samuel Gridley Howe began to open the eyes of society to the fact that people with disabilities were teachable.

SOCIAL-EMOTIONAL DEVELOPMENT Given the likelihood of being relatively isolated from interactions with their peers, it shouldn't be surprising that students who are deaf-blind are at risk for social-emotional difficulties (Hartshorne & Schmittel, 2016; Laugen, Jacobsen, Rieffe, & Wichstrøm, 2016). Typical developmental milestones such as attachment, the development of empathy, and friendships are more difficult due to these children's dual sensory impairments (Hartshorne & Schmittel, 2016).

> **MyLab Education Self-Check 13.3**
> **MyLab Education Application Exercise 13.3: Teaching Students with Deaf-Blindness**
> Watch a video in which the teacher is previewing the day's activities with the students, and then answer the question that follows.
>
>

Educational Considerations

The importance of early identification of deaf-blindness can't be overstated. As we have stressed in other chapters, early identification of any disability is important. But the fact that two senses—hearing and sight—are involved in deaf-blindness makes the need to intervene as early as possible of paramount importance (Anthony, 2016). In addition to educational intervention, early medical intervention, such as cochlear implants, is best provided as early as possible (Anthony, 2016).

From an educational perspective, the major needs of infants and preschoolers as well as of older students who are deaf-blind fall generally under the categories of communication and orientation and mobility. Both abilities, but especially communication, are required for social interaction. If these skills are taught effectively, then the social interaction of deaf-blind individuals is enhanced considerably (Janssen, Riksen-Walraven, & van Dijk, 2004).

In addressing needs for communication, orientation, and mobility, practitioners and parents should keep in mind at least two important principles: direct teaching and structured and predictable routines.

THE IMPORTANCE OF DIRECT TEACHING Many students with disabilities (e.g., intellectual disability, learning disabilities, blindness, deafness) are more reliant than those without disabilities on having teachers instruct them directly. Whereas students without disabilities can learn a great deal incidentally (e.g., from seeing or hearing things that happen around them), students with disabilities are often in greater need of having material taught to them directly (see Kauffman et al., 2018; Pullen & Hallahan, 2015). Because of their restricted sensory input, this need for direct teaching of information is even more pronounced for students who are deaf-blind than it is for children with other disabilities.

THE IMPORTANCE OF STRUCTURED AND PREDICTABLE ROUTINES To create a successful environment for learning, it's also critical that teachers and other professionals and parents provide a sense of security for students who are deaf-blind. One of the best ways to create this sense of security is through the use of predictable, structured routines (Chen, Alsop, & Minor, 2000; Miles, 1998; Smith, Smith, & Blake, 2010), discussed in detail in the Responsive Instruction feature.

COMMUNICATION The hands play a critical role in communication for most students who are deaf-blind. In effect, the hands become the "voice, or the primary means of expression" (Miles, 1999, p. 1). Professionals use a number of modes of communication that involve touch with people who are deaf-blind. Braille is the most obvious one along with touch cues, which often entails the special educator providing information by touching the hands or face of the student (Chen, Downing, & Rodriguez-Gil, 2000/2001). Also, adapted signs are often invaluable. Signs used by the Deaf community, such as American Sign Language and signed English, are visually based, which makes them difficult or impossible for people who are deaf-blind to use, depending on the severity of their visual impairment. A variety of tactual versions of signing (adapted signs) therefore have been created (Chen et al., 2000/2001). For example, for the reception of signs, the person who is deaf-blind can place his or her hands on the hands of the signer. For a demonstration, using rap, of deaf-blind tactile signing, go to: http://www.youtube.com/watch?v=LarnqAGeH6c&feature=relmfu. For the expression of signs, the teacher or parent can hold the hands of the person who is deaf-blind and guide him or her to produce signs.

ORIENTATION AND MOBILITY For people who have both visual impairment and hearing impairment, the need for **orientation and mobility (O & M)** training is even more important than for those who are only blind because they are at even greater risk of being unable to navigate their environment.

O & M training for people who have both visual and hearing impairments differs in at least two ways from O & M training for those with only visual impairment. First, adaptations are needed to communicate with people with deaf-blindness (Gense & Gense, 2004). The O & M instructor might need to use adaptations such as an interpreter, adapted signs, and/or touch cues to communicate with the student who is deaf-blind.

Second, it's sometimes necessary to alert the public that a traveler is deaf-blind. Even the best travelers with deaf-blindness occasionally become temporarily disoriented and need assistance. People with visual impairment who can hear can ask for assistance relatively easily. However, people who have both hearing and visual impairments may have a more difficult time communicating their needs to the public, and it won't always be obvious to the public that the person has both a visual and a hearing impairment. A

RESPONSIVE INSTRUCTION

Meeting the Needs of Students with Low-Incidence, Multiple, and Severe Disabilities

THE IMPORTANCE OF ESTABLISHING PREDICTABLE, STRUCTURED ROUTINES

What the Research Says

Researchers and practitioners from Project PLAI (Promoting Learning Through Active Interaction) have developed several modules for working with infants who have multiple disabilities and their families (Chen et al., 2000; Klein, Chen, & Haney, 2000). One of the modules focuses on establishing predictable routines. Specifically, for infants who are deaf-blind, they have recommended the following objectives:

- Create a predictable routine by identifying at least five daily activities that can be scheduled in the same sequence each day.
- Identify predictable sequences within specific activities (i.e., "subroutines").
- Identify and use specific auditory, visual, tactile, olfactory, and kinesthetic cues to help the infant anticipate familiar activities (Chen et al., 2000, p. 6).

The following describes how they implemented these objectives with 14-month-old Michael, his mother, Cecelia, and older sister, Kate. Michael was born prematurely and only weighed 1 pound, 8 ounces at birth. He was diagnosed with severe ROP (retinopathy of prematurity), cerebral palsy, and a hearing loss of undetermined severity.

An early interventionist helped Cecelia realize that Michael could better understand what was going on around him if his daily events were more predictable. In addition to the early morning and evening routines, Cecelia decided to try to increase the predictability of Michael's routines in several ways. After he finished his morning bottle, he would always get a bath. After the bath, Cecelia would put lotion on him and give him a shoulder and back massage. At bedtime, she would give him his bottle and then Kate would rock him while watching TV. Cecelia also realized that she and Michael had developed "subroutines." For example, after removing Michael's diaper and cleaning him, she would blow on his tummy and say, "Okay, all dry. All dry." Then she would sprinkle powder and put a new

diaper on him, say "All done," and give him a kiss while picking him up.

Other predictable routines and subroutines followed. Before going into Michael's room, Cecelia would always announce loudly, "Here comes Mommy." She would touch his shoulders before picking him up. Before putting him in the bath, she would put his foot in the water a couple of times, which helped him to stop screaming when he was placed in the tub. Before Cecelia gave Michael his back massage, she would rub some lotion on her fingers and let him smell it. (Chen et al., 2000, pp. 6–7)

Applying the Research to Teaching

Although the preceding example pertains to infants, predictable, structured routines are no less important for school-age children who have multiple disabilities, including deaf-blindness. School routines are particularly important for students who are deaf-blind because the only way for these children to learn is by doing. The students will be unable to learn through visually observing or hearing stimuli that will assist them in making sense of the world. Therefore, they will depend on the creation of a safe learning environment and trust with the primary instructor (Moss & Hagood, 1995). School routines that would benefit students who are deaf-blind follow:

1. *Turn-taking routines.* By keeping interactions balanced ("me, then you"), students will consistently know when to respond and be more active in their learning.
2. *Travel or movement routines.* If students do not feel comfortable moving around the classroom or school, they may choose to not move. Lack of mobility decreases opportunities for exploration, social interaction, and independence.
3. *Communication routines.* Students who are deaf-blind will rely on tactile communication. Students will be unable to make connections among input without direct interaction with others. Therefore, it is important to establish routines for communication as these students move from objects to gestures for communication.

BY KRISTIN L. SAYESKI

long cane can signal vision loss, but it does not indicate hearing impairment. Therefore, some professionals advocate the use of assistance cards. **Assistance cards** are usually relatively small (e.g., 3 × 6 inches) and can be held up by the person who is deaf-blind at a busy or unfamiliar intersection. The words on the card indicate that the person is asking for assistance—for example, "Please help me to CROSS STREET. I am both DEAF and VISUALLY IMPAIRED, so TAP ME if you can help. Thank you" (Franklin & Bourquin, 2000, p. 175).

SPECIAL CONSIDERATIONS FOR STUDENTS WITH USHER SYNDROME Students with Usher syndrome present some special educational challenges because most have progressive visual impairment. They might start out having relatively good vision, but their vision inevitably declines to the point at which they are legally, if not totally, blind. The effects of retinitis pigmentosa, which accompanies Usher syndrome, can sometimes be erratic and change rapidly, thus catching these students and their family off guard (Miner & Cioffi, 1999). Even when the deterioration occurs slowly over the course of several years, parents and teachers of children with Usher syndrome might neglect the importance of preparing them for the fact that they will one day have substantial visual impairment. Sometimes, they fear that the early introduction of braille and O & M training will stigmatize the children and damage their self-concept. However, most authorities now agree that braille instruction and O & M training should not be delayed until these students can no longer function as seeing individuals.

EDUCATIONAL CONSIDERATIONS FOR MANY STUDENTS WITH LOW-INCIDENCE, MULTIPLE, AND SEVERE DISABILITIES

Some of the devices and methods that we describe here might apply to any of the disabilities we discuss in this chapter. Communication, behavior management, early intervention, transition, employment, family involvement, and normalization are all frequent concerns with any of these disabilities.

Augmentative or Alternative Communication

For some individuals with severe and multiple disabilities, oral language is out of the question; they have physical or cognitive disabilities, usually as a result of neurological damage, that preclude their learning to communicate through normal speech. Educators and professionals must design a system of **augmentative and alternative communication (AAC)** for them. AAC includes any manual or electronic means by which such a person expresses wants and needs, shares information, engages in social closeness, or manages social etiquette (Beukelman, Yorkston, & Reichle, 2000; Gerenser & Forman, 2007; Heller & Bigge, 2010). Students for whom AAC must be designed range in intelligence from highly gifted to having profoundly intellectual disabilities, but they all have one characteristic in common: the inability to communicate effectively through speech because of a physical impairment. Some of these individuals cannot make any speech sounds at all; others need a system to augment their speech when they cannot make themselves understood because of environmental noise, difficulty in producing certain words or sounds, or unfamiliarity with the person with whom they want to communicate.

Manual signs or gestures are useful for some individuals. But many individuals with severe physical limitations cannot use their hands to communicate through the usual sign language; they must use another means of communication, usually involving special equipment. Dr. Nikki Kissane, now a surgeon, developed a simplified sign language system while a University of Virginia undergraduate student. (Search Nikki Kissane UVA to learn more.) Children and adults with limited speech capabilities can learn and use her simplified signs more easily than traditional signs.

The problems to be solved in helping individuals communicate in ways other than signing include selecting a vocabulary and giving them an effective, efficient means of indicating elements in their vocabularies. Although the basic ideas behind AAC are quite simple, selecting the best vocabulary and devising an efficient means of communication for many individuals with severe disabilities are extraordinarily challenging. As one AAC user put it, "The AAC evaluation should be done with the AAC user involved in the process from step one. It is the augmented speaker who will be using the device every day, both personally and professionally, not the AAC specialist" (Cardona, 2000, p. 237).

A variety of approaches to AAC have been developed, some involving relatively simple or so-called low-technology solutions and some requiring complex or high-technology solutions. Many different direct-selection and scanning methods have been devised for AAC, depending on individual capabilities. The system that is used may involve pointing with the hand or a head-stick, eye movements, or operation of a microswitch by foot, tongue, or head movement or breath control. Sometimes, the individual can use a typewriter or computer terminal that is fitted with a key guard so that keys are not likely to be pressed accidentally or use an alternative means for selecting keystrokes. Other students use communication boards, which offer an array of pictures, words, or other symbols and can be operated with either a direct-selection or scanning strategy. The content and arrangement of the board will vary, depending on the person's capabilities, preferences, and communication needs.

Today, researchers are finding increasingly innovative and creative technological solutions to the problem of nonvocal communication. At the same time, they are recognizing the importance of making decisions that are highly individualized and evidence-based. No one is well served by AAC that is not highly reliable from a scientific point of view. Researchers are attempting to make it possible for young AAC users to talk about the same kinds of things that other youngsters do. Other efforts are directed at training AAC users to tell those with whom they communicate how to interact with them more effectively—that is, to train AAC users in pragmatics. The important thing is that some people have physical limitations that preclude their efficient use of oral language and need an augmented or alternative means of communicating.

Users of AAC encounter three particular challenges that are not faced by natural communicators:

1. AAC is often much slower than natural communication—perhaps 1/20th the typical rate of speech. This can result in great frustration for both AAC users and natural communicators.
2. Users of AAC who are not literate must rely on a vocabulary and symbols that are selected by others. If the vocabulary and symbols, as well as other features of the system, are not well chosen, AAC will be quite limited in the learning and personal relationships it allows.
3. AAC must be constructed to be useful in a variety of social contexts, allow accurate and efficient communication without undue fatigue, and support the individual's learning of language and academic skills.

Progress in the field of AAC requires that all of these challenges be addressed simultaneously. AAC is increasingly focused on literacy and the right to use print, including writing, for communication. In many ways the emphasis on basic literacy skills parallels the emphasis on literacy for all students, regardless of disabilities (Yoder, 2001).

The remarkable increase in the power and availability of microcomputers (including small devices such as tablets and smartphones) is radically changing the ability to provide AAC and make sure that the user's words are communicated. New ways of using computer-based devices and new apps for such devices may lead to breakthroughs that will allow people with severe disabilities to communicate more effectively, even if they have extremely limited muscle control. Furthermore, existing software suggests ways of encouraging children to use their existing language skills.

Much information about AAC is now available on various websites. The International Society for Augmentative and Alternative Communication (ISAAC) publishes the professional journal *Augmentative and Alternative Communication* and maintains a website. Parents need to be aware of the availability of AAC and demand equipment and training that are effective for their child.

Behavior Problems

Some individuals who have certain severe or multiple disabilities engage in problematic behaviors such as self-stimulation, self-injury, tantrums, aggression toward others, or some combination of these. We caution that not all people with low-incidence, severe, or multiple disabilities exhibit the behavior problems we discuss here. Many people who are deaf-blind and many who have TBI, autism, or other severe or multiple disabilities do not engage in these behaviors. Nevertheless, most of the people who do exhibit these problems to a significant extent have severe and multiple disabilities. Moreover, behaviors of the type that we discuss here add a level of complexity and seriousness to any disability. Thus, finding solutions to these behavior problems is critical to treating the individual with respect and helping the person to participate in typical school and community activities (see Best et al., 2010; Heller, Forney, Alberto, Best, & Schwartzman, 2009).

Much controversy exists regarding the behavior problems of people with severe disabilities. Some educators and professionals assume that such problems simply will not occur if appropriate programs of instruction are provided. Others suggest that **functional behavioral assessment (FBA)**, **positive behavioral support (PBS)**, and nonaversive treatments (i.e., treatments in which punishment has no place) will be sufficient in all cases. However, others claim that positive behavioral supports and nonaversive treatments are insufficient in some cases to overcome behavior problems (e.g., Foxx, 2016; Mudford & Cullen, C., 2016; Mulick & Butter, 2016; Newsom & Kroeger, 2016).

SELF-STIMULATION **Self-stimulation** can be defined as any repetitive, stereotyped behavior that seems to have no immediately apparent purpose other than providing sensory stimulation. Self-stimulation (a form of stereotyped movement) may take a wide variety of forms, such as swishing saliva, twirling objects, hand-flapping, fixed staring, and the like. Repetitive, stereotyped behavior (sometimes called *stereotypy*) may have multiple causes, including social consequences, in addition to sensory stimulation (Bodfish, 2007).

Nearly everyone sometimes engages in some form of self-stimulation, such as lip-biting, hair-stroking, and nail-biting, but not at the high rate that characterizes a disability. Infants without disabilities engage in self-stimulation, and so do adults without disabilities, particularly when they are tired or bored. Only the high rate, lack of subtlety, and social inappropriateness of such self-stimulation differentiate it from the norm. Self-stimulation becomes problematic when it occurs at such a high rate that it interferes with learning or social acceptability or when it occurs with such intensity that it does injury. Some individuals with autism or other pervasive developmental disabilities engage in self-stimulation to the exclusion of academic and social learning. In most of these cases, it appears that only intrusive, directive intervention will be successful in helping the individual learn academic and social skills (Kauffman & Landrum, 2018).

SELF-INJURY **Self-injurious behavior (SIB)** is repeated physical self-abuse, such as biting, scratching, or poking oneself, head-banging, and so on (see Foxx, 2016). Unchecked, SIB often results in self-mutilation. Self-stimulation can be so frequent and intense that it becomes SIB. Hand-mouthing is self-stimulation of the kind that all infants do; even some adults without disabilities can be seen occasionally mouthing their hands. However, hand-mouthing becomes self-injurious for some people with severe developmental disabilities, resulting in serious skin lesions.

TANTRUMS Severe tantrums can include a variety of behaviors, including self-injury, screaming, crying, throwing or destroying objects, and aggression toward others. Sometimes, the event that sets off a tantrum is unknown, at least to the casual observer. Often, however, a tantrum is precipitated by a request or demand that the individual do something (perhaps a self-care task or some academic work), and the consequence of the tantrum is that the demand is withdrawn, thus reinforcing the tantrum behavior.

Tantrums impose a handicap on the individual who uses them to avoid learning or doing important things. They stymie socialization, as most people want to avoid interacting with someone who is likely to have a tantrum. Teachers and others who work most successfully with individuals who have tantrums do not withdraw reasonable demands for performance. They modify their demand or circumstances in some way or alternate their demands for performance in ways that are less likely to set off a tantrum.

AGGRESSION TOWARD OTHERS Not all aggression toward others is associated with tantrums. Some individuals with severe or multiple disabilities engage in calculated physical attacks that threaten or injure others (Gardner, 2007). Sometimes these attacks come without warning or only after subtle indications of imminent assault that only someone who knows the individual well is likely to perceive.

LACK OF DAILY LIVING SKILLS Lack of daily living skills refers to the absence or significant impairment of the ability to take care of one's basic needs, such as dressing, feeding, or toileting. Many people with severe and multiple disabilities must be taught the adaptive behavior that is expected of older children and adults. These adaptive behaviors include a wide variety of tasks involving clothing selection and dressing, food preparation and eating, grooming, socializing, using money, using public transportation, playing games or other recreation, and so on (Snell & Brown, 2006).

FUNCTIONAL BEHAVIORAL ASSESSMENT AND POSITIVE BEHAVIORAL INTERVENTION AND SUPPORT Problem behaviors are often related to a brain disorder or brain injury, even if the disorder is not understood. An example is severe autism, which often includes self-stimulation, self-injury, tantrums, or all of these. However, professionals and educators are increasing their emphasis on analyzing and changing the environments in which problem behavior is exhibited; that is, focusing on the immediate and alterable influences on behavior rather than on immutable or historical reasons for behavior (Best et al., 2010; Bodfish, 2007; Foxx, 2016).

In earlier chapters, we introduced the ideas of **functional behavioral assessment (FBA)** and **positive behavioral intervention and support (PBIS)**, primarily as they apply to students with less severe disabilities (see Chapters 7 to 9). However, these procedures may be particularly important for students with severe and multiple disabilities. FBA entails finding out why or under what circumstances problem behavior is exhibited, and PBIS involves creating an environment that supports appropriate behavior.

FBA often reveals how a student uses self-stimulation, SIB, tantrums, or aggression against others. A student might behave inappropriately to escape or avoid unpleasant or nonpreferred activities or tasks (see Kauffman & Landrum, 2018). In many instances, researchers and practitioners find that the student has no other effective and efficient means of communication. The task, therefore, is to figure out how the student is using unacceptable communication and teach the student a more effective, efficient, and acceptable means of letting others know what he or she wants or is feeling. FBA has led to the discovery that sometimes people with severe and multiple disabilities use inappropriate behavior to communicate a variety of their wants or needs (e.g., "Pay attention to me," "Let me out of here," "There's nothing to do," "There's too much to do," or "I don't want to do that now").

PBIS is the vehicle for teaching students how to behave more appropriately, making appropriate behavior "work" for their communication. In the case of students with severe and multiple disabilities, making PBIS a part of managing behavior across school, home, neighborhood, and community is particularly important. The accompanying Responsive Instruction box provides a more detailed discussion of PBIS for students with multiple or severe disabilities.

Early Intervention

Most children with multiple and severe disabilities are identified at birth or soon thereafter because their disabilities are very noticeable to parents, physicians, and/or nurses. Some newborns with severe and multiple disabilities require extensive medical treatment and therefore are immediately placed in **neonatal intensive care units (NICUs)**. NICUs are the equivalent of intensive care units (ICUs) for older children and adults, providing around-the-clock monitoring of bodily functions. The NICU staff consists of several specialists, often including specially trained nurses, physicians, respiratory care practitioners, occupational therapists, and social workers. Because NICUs are expensive to staff and administer, not all hospitals have them; therefore, newborns are sometimes transported from one hospital to another that has an NICU. Even though the infant is under constant medical supervision, most authorities agree that parents should be allowed to spend as much time as possible with their newborns to promote parent–infant bonding. Some NICUs allow parents to "room in" with their babies.

Other children with severe and multiple disabilities might seem typical at birth but are recognized as having pervasive developmental disabilities within the first couple years. In the case of very serious TBI, an individual might actually be developing normally until the event that causes severe brain damage. Early intervention therefore should be seen as having two meanings: (1) early in the child's life and (2) as soon as possible after the disability is detected.

The Division for Early Childhood (DEC) of the Council for Exceptional Children (CEC) recommends practices based on six criteria that are considered essential to early intervention programs in special education: (1) research- or value-based practices, (2) family-centered practices, (3) a multicultural perspective, (4) cross-disciplinary collaboration, (5) developmentally and chronologically age-appropriate practices, and (6) adherence to the principle of normalization (see Dunst & Espe-Sherwindt, 2017; Noonan & McCormick, 2006; see also discussion of normalization in Chapter 1).

RESEARCH- OR VALUE-BASED PRACTICES Early intervention programs should be based as much as possible on techniques that research has shown to be effective (Dunst & Espe-Sherwindt, 2017; Morris & Mather, 2008). Unfortunately, it is not always possible to conduct all the necessary research before an approach or technique is adopted. The CEC task force recommends that when research has not provided definitive evidence of an approach's effectiveness, the approach should be based on values held by the early childhood special education community. Some of these value-based practices are providing individualized practices for each child and family, communicating with family members in a nonpaternalistic manner and with mutual respect and caring, making center environments safe and clean, and providing opportunities for families to have access to medical decision making.

FAMILY-CENTERED PRACTICES At one time, the prevailing philosophy in early childhood special education programming ignored parents and families at best or viewed them primarily as potential negative influences on the child with disabilities. When early intervention programs did involve parents, the assumption often was that the parents had little to offer and were in need of training to improve their parenting skills. Although it's true that some parents do need to be educated about how to be better parents, to assume that this is always the case is paternalistic and off-putting to the majority of parents, who are very capable. For this reason, authorities now recommend that one not assume that parents have little or nothing to offer with respect to how to work with their children. Instead, they emphasize that parents, siblings, and extended family can be a valuable and integral part of the educational process for young children with disabilities.

As we discussed in Chapters 1, 2, and 4, IDEA also recognizes that parents and families should be central to the educational process for infants and toddlers. The requirement for individualized family service plans (IFSPs), in fact, dictates that the family be central in the decision-making process for the child. A family-centered philosophy means taking into account the particular priorities and needs of the family when developing an educational intervention plan for the child (see Section XI of Kauffman, Hallahan, & Pullen, 2017).

MULTICULTURAL PERSPECTIVE Given the changing ethnic demographics in the United States, it is critical that all special education programming be culturally sensitive. It's particularly important that early intervention professionals adopt a multicultural perspective because parents are often still coping with the stress of having had their child diagnosed with a disability (Dunst & Espe-Sherwindt, 2017; Noonan & McCormick, 2006). Having at least someone in the program who can speak the family's language is important. So is communicating respect, caring, and sensitivity. And it's important to provide services that are unbiased and nondiscriminatory with regard to disability, gender, race, religion, and ethnic and cultural orientation. Perhaps the most important multicultural factor, however, is providing services that are effective (Kauffman, Conroy, Gardner, & Oswald, 2008).

RESPONSIVE INSTRUCTION

Meeting the Needs of Students with Low-Incidence, Multiple, and Severe Disabilities

POSITIVE BEHAVIORAL INTERVENTION AND SUPPORT

What Is Positive Behavioral Intervention and Support?

Reauthorizations of the Individuals with Disabilities Education Act require teachers, school systems, and those involved with students who exhibit challenging behaviors to approach problematic behavior through a mechanism called positive behavioral intervention and support (PBIS). PBIS refers to the process of identifying alternative, acceptable ways to communicate through teaching more appropriate behaviors and/or changing the environment to reduce the likelihood of prompting the undesirable behavior (Kauffman, Nelson, Simpson, & Ward, 2017; Kogel, Kogel, & Dunlap, 1996). This approach to behavior management differs fundamentally from traditional behavior modification plans that focus on the elimination of target behaviors, yet do not take into account possible environmental or personal triggers when doing so. For example, a student's undesirable behavior of banging his head on his desk might be eliminated by placing a baseball cap on his head. Although this might appear to be an acceptable solution, if the student's banging was a sign of boredom or an anxiety-producing peer in the vicinity, the baseball cap solution does not address the function of the behavior, and it is likely that another behavior will manifest in response to the original source of the behavior.

PBIS, by contrast, is guided by two fundamental assumptions: (1) Each behavior carries a communicative intent, and (2) typically, multiple factors influence the presence of specific behavior. Interventions based on these assumptions, therefore, include a functional behavioral assessment (FBA) (Horner, Vaughn, Day, & Ard, 1996; Kauffman et al., 2017).

FBA seeks to identify the purpose of the behavior and supporting environmental conditions. The results of such assessment lead to the development of multifaceted plans that can include changing situational events, altering events that immediately precede the behavior, teaching alternative responses to the situation, and providing meaningful reinforcers to promote acceptable responses.

Applying the Research to Teaching

The following support strategies are all involved in implementing PBIS:

- Remove high-frustration activities (e.g., difficult assignments, undesirable directives).
- Select functional and meaningful (from the student's perspective) curricula.
- Reduce fear or anxiety about a situation through precorrection (e.g., a teacher might suggest what to do when feeling frustrated).
- Teach more appropriate ways to make requests or express oneself.
- Use behavior modification to reinforce desired behaviors and communicate nonacceptability.
- Create activities that build on student interest and strength.

One important component of implementing PBIS is to select functional and meaningful curricula for students. Typically, as students with multiple or severe disabilities progress through school, their curriculum becomes increasingly functional.

BY KRISTIN L. SAYESKI

CROSS-DISCIPLINARY COLLABORATION Because infants and young children with multiple and severe disabilities by definition have needs in multiple areas, best practice dictates the involvement of professionals from several disciplines. It's critical that these professionals collaborate in a coordinated way to provide high-quality services. Cross-disciplinary models vary, but the most essential feature for success is that the professionals in each of the disciplines work collaboratively, not independently. Some authorities also recommend that professionals should be willing to share roles.

DEVELOPMENTALLY AND CHRONOLOGICALLY AGE-APPROPRIATE PRACTICES The term **developmentally appropriate practice (DAP)** was first used by the National Association for the Education of Young Children, an organization that focuses on early childhood education for children without disabilities. DAP refers to the practice of using educational methods that are at the developmental levels of the child and that meet the child's individual needs. Many early childhood special educators agree with the notion of DAP, but they believe that it should be balanced with the need for using educational methods that are also chronologically age appropriate. They believe that young children with disabilities should be educated as much as possible alongside their same-age peers without disabilities rather than with much younger peers who do not have disabilities.

Transition to Adulthood

Transition to adulthood is a critical time for most people with severe and multiple disabilities. Special education has made great strides in developing transition services for people with disabilities. Much of this progress has been made because of a change in philosophy about how people with disabilities are treated, and this change is nowhere more evident than in the treatment of people with severe and multiple disabilities. For example, not long ago, the best employment that individuals with severe and multiple disabilities could hope for was in a **sheltered workshop**. Now, however, a much wider range of options is available, including, for some people, **competitive employment** alongside workers who do not have disabilities.

CHANGING PHILOSOPHY We can point to at least two principles of transition programming that reflect the change in philosophy toward treating people with severe disabilities with more dignity (Avellone & Taylor, 2017; Inge, 2017; Inge, Wehman, & Seward, 2017). First, as we noted in Chapter 5, is the emphasis on **self-determination**. As part of this emphasis on self-determination, professionals have developed a number of **person-centered plans**, which focus on the student's preferences and those of the family in planning for the future (Snell & Brown, 2006). Although person-centered planning is now part of most programs for people with severe disabilities, some have suggested that such plans are not a panacea (e.g., Osborne, 2005).

Second, authorities now recommend that natural supports be an integral part of transition planning. Rather than always creating new services for a person's particular needs, using **natural supports**, professionals first try to find the available resources already existing in the workplace or the community. With respect to work, the use of natural supports might mean training co-workers to provide assistance rather than immediately assuming that a **job coach** is required. With respect to community living, the use of natural supports might mean the person with a disability could live in an apartment, with assistance in **daily living skills** from a neighbor, family member, or paid attendant, rather than living in a residential facility with attendants.

VOCATIONAL PROGRAMMING A student's IEP must contain a transition plan, beginning no later than age 16 (and by age 14 when appropriate). The transition plan should contain recommendations for how to ready the student for the world of work and/or for postsecondary education or training.

For many students with severe and multiple disabilities, vocational training should begin in elementary school, because it might take several years for them to acquire all the skills needed to hold down a job successfully. In elementary school, the training might consist of learning to keep on schedule, building social skills, performing work-like tasks (e.g., helping to take attendance, collecting lunch money), and beginning to learn about different types of jobs.

In secondary school, the focus shifts to involving students in actual work situations in the community with the help of a job coach. The students should be involved in selecting these placements, which should vary sufficiently so that the students experience a good sample of the kinds of jobs available and can discover what they are good at and enjoy. In the early stages, this might involve the students' volunteering in several different types of placements. Later, it's preferable for students to engage in paid work placements. Being paid adds to the reality of the experience and provides an opportunity for students to learn how to handle finances.

COMMUNITY AND DOMESTIC LIVING SKILLS As we noted in Chapter 5, community living skills involve using transportation, shopping, using telephones, managing money, and using the Internet. Domestic living skills include preparing meals, doing laundry, doing housekeeping, performing yard maintenance, and so forth. Because students aren't that far away from the time when they will move out of their parents' home and because teaching domestic skills is often done in small groups, there are some advantages to using a setting other than their own home. Thus, domestic living skills are often taught in a school setting, such as the school cafeteria.

Another reason for using the school as the instructional setting some of the time is to ensure that the student with disabilities has a chance to interact with peers who do not have disabilities. Inclusion in regular school programs provides social opportunities for students, and social skills are critical for successful integration into the community and workplace (see Avellone & Taylor, 2017; Inge et al., 2017).

The last 30 to 40 years have brought enormous strides in preparing people with multiple and severe disabilities to lead productive lives as adults. It wasn't that long ago that people with multiple and severe disabilities were housed in large residential institutions and had minimal contact with the public. Today, with intensive and extensive instruction and the support of professionals and the community, many people with multiple and severe disabilities can aspire to work alongside persons without disabilities and live independently or semi-independently by themselves or in a small community residential facility (CRF).

MyLab Education **Self-Check 13.4**

MyLab Education **Application Exercise 13.4: Small Group Instruction for Students with Deaf-Blindness**

Watch a video in which a teacher is working on a language lesson with the students. Answer the questions that follow.

▼ chapter thirteen SUMMARY

martin bowra/Shutterstock

What is the definition of low-incidence, multiple, and severe disabilities, and what is the prevalence?

- Low-incidence, multiple, and severe disabilities are those that occur relatively infrequently and require extensive support in more than one major life activity, such as mobility, communication, self-care, independent living, employment, and self-sufficiency. Probably 1% or fewer of all learners have such low-incidence, multiple, or severe disabilities.

What is traumatic brain injury, and how might it affect education?

- Traumatic brain injury (TBI) is injury to the brain resulting in total or partial disability or psychosocial maladjustment that affects educational performance.
  - It may be the result of closed head injuries or open head injuries.
  - It may affect cognition, language, memory, attention, reasoning, abstract thinking, judgment, problem solving, sensory or perceptual and motor disabilities, psychosocial behavior, physical functions, information processing, or speech—all of which are important in school.

How is deaf-blindness defined, and what are the special educational problems it entails?

- Deaf-blindness is defined by significant impairments in both hearing and seeing, although the individual may have some residual hearing or sight.
  - Deaf-blindness may be caused by a variety of genetic and chromosomal syndromes, prenatal conditions, and postnatal conditions.
  - The person who is deaf-blind has difficulty accessing information, communicating, and navigating the environment.
  - Deaf-blindness requires direct teaching; predictable, structured routines; and emphasis on communication and mobility.

What educational considerations apply to many students with low-incidence, multiple, and severe disabilities?

- Communication, behavior management, early intervention, and transition to adulthood are concerns that apply to many learners with these disabilities.

  - Augmentative and alternative communication (AAC) is important for those who can't communicate effectively through speech.

  - Common behavior problems requiring special management include self-stimulation, self-injury, tantrums, aggression toward others, and lack of daily living skills, all of which may require functional behavioral assessment and positive behavioral support.

- Early intervention should be based on both research and values and be family centered, multicultural, cross disciplinary, and age appropriate, and feature normalization.

- Transition to adulthood should honor the concepts of person-centered planning and natural supports, feature vocational programming, and include community and domestic living skills.

▼ INTERNET RESOURCES

Pertinent Organizations

- The United Cerebral Palsy Association (www.ucp.org) provides information and resources for people with CP and their families.

- Two websites (www.deafblind.com and http://nationaldb.org) provide a variety of information about learners with low-incidence, multiple, and severe disabilities.

- More information about traumatic brain injury may be found at the Brain Injury Association of America (www .biausa.org).

chapter fourteen

LEARNERS WITH PHYSICAL DISABILITIES AND OTHER HEALTH IMPAIRMENTS

Blend Images-Kidstock/Brand X Pictures/Getty Images

► LEARNING OUTCOMES

Learning Outcome 14.1: Learn the definitions, classifications, and prevalence for physical disabilities and other health impairments.

Learning Outcome 14.2: Identify the issues associated with neuromotor impairments, orthopedic and musculoskeletal disorders, and other conditions affecting health and physical ability, and learn how physical disabilities can be prevented.

Learning Outcome 14.3: Understand some psychological and behavioral characteristics of people with physical disabilities and other

health impairments; and learn about prosthetics, orthoses, and other adaptive devices used by people with these conditions.

Learning Outcome 14.4: Learn about some educational considerations for people with physical disabilities and other health impairments.

Learning Outcome 14.5: Learn about issues that should be considered with respect to early intervention and transition to adulthood for individuals with physical disabilities and other health impairments.

MISCONCEPTIONS ABOUT Learners with Physical Disabilities and Other Health Impairments

MYTH Cerebral palsy is a contagious disease.

FACT Cerebral palsy is not a disease. It's a nonprogressive neurological injury. It's a disorder of muscle control and coordination caused by injury to the brain before or during birth or in early childhood.

MYTH Physical disabilities of all kinds are decreasing because of medical advances.

FACT Because of advances in medical technology, the number of children with physical disabilities is increasing. The number of survivors of serious medical conditions who develop normally or have mild impairments, such as hyperactivity and learning disabilities, is also increasing.

MYTH The greatest educational problem involving children with physical disabilities is providing highly specialized instruction.

FACT The greatest educational problem is teaching people without disabilities about what it's like to have a disability and how disabilities can be accommodated.

MYTH The more severe a person's physical disability is, the lower the person's intelligence is.

FACT A person can be severely physically disabled by cerebral palsy or another condition but have a brilliant mind.

MYTH People with epilepsy are mentally ill.

FACT People with epilepsy (seizure disorder) aren't any more or less disposed to mental illness than are those who don't have epilepsy.

MYTH Arthritis is found only in adults, particularly those who are elderly.

FACT Arthritic conditions are found in people of any age, including young children.

MYTH People with physical disabilities have no need for sexual expression.

FACT People with physical disabilities have normal sexual urges and need outlets for sexual expression.

MYTH Physical disabilities shape people's personalities.

FACT People with physical disabilities have the full range of personality characteristics found among those who don't have physical disabilities. No particular personality characteristics are associated with physical disability.

MYTH If a child with a physical disability such as cerebral palsy or spina bifida learns to walk as a young child, then he or she will maintain that ability throughout life.

FACT Continuing intervention through adolescence and adulthood—the entire life span—is required in many cases. Unless they have continued support for ambulation, adolescents or adults might find walking much more difficult or might give up walking, even if they learned to walk as children.

GUIDING QUESTIONS

- How are physical disabilities defined and classified?

- What is the prevalence of physical disabilities, and what is the need for special education?

- What are some major neuromotor impairments?

- What are some major orthopedic and musculo-skeletal disorders?

- What other conditions affect health or physical ability?

- How can physical disabilities be prevented?

- What are the psychological and behavioral characteristics of individuals with physical disabilities?

- What are prosthetics, orthoses, and adaptive devices?

- What are the major educational considerations for students with physical disabilities?

- Why is early intervention important, and on what should it focus?

- What are the major issues in transition for students with physical disabilities?

I n Western culture, many people are almost obsessed with their bodies. They don't just want to be healthy and strong; they want to be beautiful—well formed and attractive to others. In fact, some people seem to be more concerned about the impression their bodies make than they are about their own well-being. They might even endanger their health in an effort to become more physically alluring. It isn't really surprising, then, that people with physical disabilities must fight two battles: the battle to overcome the limitations imposed by their physical conditions and the battle to be accepted by others.

Individuals with physical disabilities or differences are often stared at, feared, teased, socially rejected, or treated cruelly. This has been the case throughout history, and it remains true today (for historical perspectives see Holmes, 2004; Metzler, 2006). Sometimes people feel embarrassed about someone else's disability and don't seem to understand the feelings of the person who has the disability. Or people might feel that an acquired physical disability must change someone's personality dramatically. In some cases involving traumatic brain injury, this is indeed the case (Kauffman & Badar, 2018). However, in most cases it is not.

In a story by Toney Earley (2000), *Jim the Boy*, Jim and his friend Penn, who had polio, are coming of age in a small rural town in North Carolina. Jim has mixed feelings of anger and fear when seeing his pal for the first time after Penn was paralyzed. We probably expect Jim's mixture of anger, fear, and inquisitiveness from a 10-year-old—wondering about death, the permanence of disability, how it feels to have the disability, and so on. But most of us have such feelings and questions, regardless of our age. And most people with physical disabilities share Penn's matter-of-factness and eagerness to be accepted and get on with life. (For more information about *Jim the Boy*, search the Internet for book reviews and book club reading guides.)

Although polio has been virtually eradicated by vaccination, many other causes of partial paralysis and other physical disabilities haven't been eliminated. As you read in Chapter 13, traumatic brain injury (TBI) is an example of a cause of physical disability that is actually increasing. Attitudes toward physical disabilities have not changed much in many ways, nor have the problems of having physical disabilities. Children with physical disabilities often face more than the problem of acceptance. For many, accomplishing the simple tasks of everyday living seems a minor—or major—miracle.

MyLab Education
Video Example 14.1

Sekai, a young man who has used a wheelchair since being in a car accident, explains how being in a wheelchair is nothing to feel sorry about. He says, "I am as normal as they are."

DEFINITION AND CLASSIFICATION

In this chapter, we consider children whose primary distinguishing characteristics are health or physical problems. *Children with physical disabilities or other health impairments* are those whose physical limitations or health problems interfere with school attendance or learning to such an extent that they require special services, training, equipment, materials, or facilities.

Children with physical disabilities might also have other disabilities of any type or special gifts or talents. Thus, the characteristics of children with physical disabilities are extremely varied. The child's physical condition is the proper concern of the medical profession, but when physical problems have obvious implications for education, teaching specialists are needed. The fact that the primary distinguishing characteristics of children with physical disabilities are medical conditions, health problems, or physical limitations highlights the necessity of interdisciplinary cooperation (Best, Heller, & Bigge, 2010).

Children may have **congenital anomalies** (defects with which they are born), or they may acquire disabilities through accident or disease after birth. Some physical disabilities are comparatively mild and transitory; others are profound and progressive, ending in total incapacitation and early death. Some are increasingly common chronic diseases. Discussing physical disabilities in general is difficult because the variety of these disabilities is so great. We've organized this chapter around specific conditions that fall into one of three categories: neuromotor impairments, orthopedic and musculoskeletal disorders, and other conditions that affect health or physical ability.

It's important to make distinctions between acute and chronic conditions. It's also important to understand the difference between episodic and progressive problems.

An **acute** illness or condition may be very serious or severe, but it either resolves on its own or with treatment (which may include hospitalization or medication), and the person recovers. Someone with a serious infection or who has a serious accident may, for example, become acutely ill or be in critical condition for a time but recover. However, a **chronic** condition is ongoing. It occurs or re-occurs over a long period of time; it usually does not resolve, even with the best treatment. A few examples of chronic conditions are cerebral palsy, muscular dystrophy, and arthritis.

An **episodic** condition occurs repeatedly, although most of the time the individual can function quite normally. Its occurrence is limited primarily to successive episodes. The episodes don't necessarily become more serious or severe over time. Asthma and seizure disorders (epilepsy), for example, tend to be episodic. However, a **progressive** condition is one that becomes more and more serious or severe over time, usually involving more and more complications or deterioration. Muscular dystrophy is an example of a physical problem that is usually progressive.

PREVALENCE AND NEED

Roughly 1% of the school-age population (about 500,000 children and youths) are classified as having physical disabilities. About 75,000 of these have orthopedic disabilities, but the vast majority has other health problems. This doesn't include students with traumatic brain injury or multiple disabilities or young children with developmental delays. Statistics show a dramatic increase in the percentage of the school population served by special education due to health problems (see, e.g., annual reports to Congress on implementation of federal special education laws). However, the needs of many students with physical disabilities are unmet because the number of children and youths with such disabilities is growing, and health and social service programs aren't keeping up.

Increases in prevalence might be due in part to improvements in the identification of and medical services provided to children with certain conditions. Ironically, medical advances have not only improved the chances of preventing or curing certain diseases and disorders but also increased the rate of survival of more children with severe medical problems—just as improved medical care means that more combat soldiers are surviving grievous wounds. Many children with severe and multiple disabilities and those with severe, chronic illnesses or severe injuries, who in the past wouldn't have survived long, today can have a normal life span. Therefore, declining mortality rates don't necessarily mean that there will be fewer individuals with disabilities. Moreover, improvements in medical care might not lower the number of individuals with disabilities unless there is also a lowering of risk factors in the environment—factors such as accidents, toxic substances, poverty, malnutrition, disease, and interpersonal violence.

MyLab Education Self-Check 14.1

MyLab Education Application Exercise 14.1:
Introducing Dr. Maxine Harper

Watch an interview with Dr. Harper, a former professor of Curriculum and Instruction at the University of Mississippi; then respond to a few questions.

NEUROMOTOR IMPAIRMENTS

Neuromotor impairment is caused by injury to the brain or spinal cord (neurological damage) that also affects the ability to move parts of one's body (motor impairment). It may be associated with injury to the brain before, during, or after birth. **Traumatic brain injury (TBI)**, which we discussed in Chapter 13, involves brain damage with an identifiable external cause (trauma) after birth (see Lajiness-O'Neill, Erdodi, & Lichtenstein, 2017). However, brain injury can be acquired from a variety of nontraumatic causes as well: hypoxia (reduced oxygen to the brain, as might occur in near drowning), infection of the brain or its linings, stroke, tumor, metabolic disorder (such as may occur with diabetes, liver disease, or kidney disease), or toxic chemicals or drugs.

In many cases of brain damage, it's impossible to identify the exact cause of the neuromotor impairment. The important point is that when a child's nervous system is damaged, no matter what the cause, muscular weakness or paralysis is often one of the symptoms. Because these children usually can't move about like most others, their education typically requires special equipment, special procedures, or other accommodations for their disabilities.

Cerebral Palsy

Cerebral palsy (CP) is not a disease. It's not contagious, it's not progressive (although improper treatment can lead to complications), and there are no remissions. Martin (2006) offers a succinct definition:

> Cerebral palsy is a disorder of movement and posture. It is caused by a brain injury that occurred before birth, during birth, or during the first few years after birth. The injury hinders the brain's ability to control the muscles of the body properly. The brain tells our muscles how to move and controls the tension of the muscles. Without the proper messages coming from the brain, infants with cerebral palsy have difficulty learning basic motor skills such as crawling, sitting up, or walking. (p. 2)

Cerebral palsy is more complicated than just an impairment of movement and posture, as Martin (2006) and others recognize. For practical purposes, CP can be considered part of a syndrome that includes motor dysfunction, psychological dysfunction, seizures, and emotional or behavioral disorders due to brain damage (see also Best & Bigge, 2010).

Some individuals with CP show only one indication of brain damage, such as motor impairment; others show combinations of symptoms. The usual definition of CP refers to paralysis, weakness, lack of coordination, and/or other motor dysfunction because of damage to the child's brain before it has matured. Symptoms can be so mild that they are detected only with difficulty or so profound that the individual is almost completely incapacitated.

Although no cure for CP is available, advances in medical and rehabilitation technology offer increasing hope of overcoming the disabilities resulting from neurological damage. For example, intensive long-term physical and occupational therapy in combination with a surgical procedure in which the surgeon cuts selected nerve roots below the spinal cord that cause spasticity in the leg muscles allows some children with spastic CP to better control certain muscles. Such treatment allows some nonambulatory children to walk and helps others to walk more normally.

CAUSES AND TYPES Anything that can damage the brain during its development can cause CP. Before birth, maternal infections, chronic diseases, physical trauma, or maternal exposure to toxic substances or X-rays, for example, can damage the brain of the fetus. During the birth process, the brain can be injured, especially if labor or birth is difficult or complicated. Premature birth, hypoxia, high fever, infections, poisoning, hemorrhaging, and related factors can cause harm after birth. In short, anything that results in oxygen deprivation, poisoning, cerebral bleeding, or direct trauma to the brain can be a possible cause of CP.

Although CP occurs at every social level, it is more often seen in children born to mothers in poor socioeconomic circumstances. Children who live in such circumstances have a greater risk of incurring brain damage because of factors such as malnutrition of the mother, poor prenatal and postnatal care, environmental hazards during infancy, and low birthweight. However, the prevalence of CP in children with very low birthweight has declined in recent years due to better neonatal treatment available for infants born prematurely (Robertson, Watt, & Yasui, 2007).

The two most widely accepted means of classification of CP specify the limbs that are involved and the type of motor disability. Some individuals have a mixture of various types of CP. Classification according to the extremities involved applies not just to CP but to all types of motor disability or paralysis. The most common classifications are **quadriplegia** (all four limbs are involved) and **paraplegia** (only the legs are involved).

Likewise, classification by type of movement applies not only to CP, but also to other types of neuromotor disabilities. **Spasticity** refers to stiffness or tenseness of muscles and inaccurate voluntary movement. **Choreoathetoid** is the term applied to abrupt, involuntary movements and difficulty maintaining balance. **Atonic** refers to floppiness or lack of muscle tone.

The important point about CP is that the brain damage affects strength and the ability to move parts of the body normally. The difficulty of movement may involve the limbs as well as the muscles involving facial expressions and speech. As a result, someone with CP might have difficulty moving or speaking or might exhibit facial contortions or drooling. But these results of brain damage don't necessarily mean that the person's intelligence or emotional sensitivity has been affected by the damage affecting muscle control.

ASSOCIATED DISABILITIES AND EDUCATIONAL IMPLICATIONS CP is a developmental disability—a multidisabling condition that is far more complex than a motor disability alone. When the brain is damaged, sensory abilities, cognitive functions, and emotional responsiveness as well as motor performance are usually affected. A high proportion of children with CP are found to have hearing impairments, visual impairments, perceptual disorders, speech problems, emotional or behavioral disorders, intellectual disability, or some combination of several of these disabling conditions in addition to motor disability. In a recent study, children with CP had a high prevalence of mental health problems and ADHD; however, specific disorders were difficult to detect because of their complexity (Bjorgaas, Elgen, Boe, & Hysing, 2013). They might also exhibit such characteristics as drooling or facial contortions.

Some individuals with CP have normal or above-average intellectual capacity, and a few test within the gifted range. Nevertheless, the average tested intelligence of children with CP is lower than the average for the general population. We must be very cautious in interpreting the test results of children with CP, however, because many standardized tests of intelligence and achievement might be inappropriate for individuals with special difficulties in perception, movement, or response speed. Furthermore, the movement

MyLab Education
Video Example 14.2

In this video, Kavana, who has cerebral palsy, receives physical therapy to improve her low muscle tone.

problems of a child with CP might become more apparent when the child is in a state of emotional arousal or stress; this can complicate using typical testing procedures, which tend to be demanding and stressful.

The educational problems of children who have CP are as multifaceted as their disabilities. Not only do these children need special equipment and procedures because of their physical disabilities but also they often require the same special educational procedures and equipment as children with vision, hearing, or communication disorders, learning disabilities, emotional or behavioral disorders, or intellectual disability. Careful and continuous educational assessment of the individual child's capabilities is particularly important. Teaching the child who has CP demands competence in many aspects of special education and experience in working with a variety of disabling conditions in a multidisciplinary setting (Best et al., 2010; Heller, Alberto, Forney, & Schwartzman, 2009).

Seizure Disorder (Epilepsy)

A person has a **seizure** when an abnormal discharge of electrical energy occurs in certain brain cells. The discharge spreads to nearby cells, and the effect may be loss of consciousness, involuntary movements, or abnormal sensory phenomena. The effects of the seizure depend on the location of the cells in which the discharge starts and how far the discharge spreads.

About 1 in 10 children has a seizure at some time, usually associated with a high fever or serious illness (Weinstein, 2002). However, this doesn't mean that 1 in 10 children has epilepsy. A person with **epilepsy** has a chronic neurological condition and has *recurrent* seizures (Arzimanoglou, Guerrini, & Aicardi, 2004; Weinstein, 2002). Because seizures reflect abnormal brain activity, it's not surprising that they occur more often in children with developmental disabilities (e.g., intellectual disability or cerebral palsy) than in children without disabilities (Best et al., 2010).

CAUSES AND TYPES Seizures are caused by damage to the brain. As brain imaging and molecular biology advance, scientists are arriving at a better understanding of risk for epilepsy (Barkovich, 2005). The most common immediate causes include lack of sufficient oxygen (hypoxia), low blood sugar (hypoglycemia), infections, and physical trauma. Certain conditions, such as those just listed, tend to increase the chances that neurochemical reactions will be set off in brain cells. In many cases, the causes are unknown. Some types of seizures may be progressive; that is, they may damage the brain or disrupt its functioning in such a way that having a seizure increases the probability of having another. Even though the cause of seizures isn't well understood, it's important to note that with proper medication, most people's seizures can be controlled.

Seizures can take many forms; neurologists still debate about the best way to classify them. However, educators should note that seizures may differ along at least the following dimensions:

- *Duration:* Seizures may last only a few seconds or for several minutes.
- *Frequency:* Seizures may occur as frequently as every few minutes or only about once a year.
- *Onset:* Seizures may be set off by certain identifiable stimuli or may be unrelated to the environment, and they may be totally unexpected or be preceded by certain internal sensations.
- *Movements:* Seizures may cause major convulsive movements or only minor motor symptoms (e.g., eye blinks).
- *Causes:* Seizures may be caused by a variety of conditions, including high fever, poisoning, trauma, and other conditions mentioned previously; but in many cases, the causes are unknown.
- *Associated disabilities:* Seizures may be associated with other disabling conditions or may be unrelated to any other medical problem or disability.
- *Control:* Seizures may be controlled completely by drugs, so that the individual has no more seizures, or they may be only partially controlled.

FOCUS ON

What to Do When Someone Has a Seizure

This is what medical authorities (WebMd) recommend when someone has a seizure.

If you witness a seizure, your account of the seizure will help a doctor diagnose and treat the person. Try to stay calm. Pay close attention to what happens during and after the seizure.

- **During a seizure:**
  - Protect the person from injury.
    - Keep him or her from falling if you can, or try to guide the person gently to the floor.
    - Try to move furniture or other objects that might injure the person during the seizure.
    - If the person is having a seizure and is on the ground when you arrive, try to position the person on his or her side so that fluid can leak out of the mouth. But be careful not to apply too much pressure to the body.
  - Do not force anything, including your fingers, into the person's mouth. Putting something in the person's mouth may cause injuries to him or her, such as chipped teeth or a fractured jaw. You could also get bitten.
  - Do not try to hold down or move the person. This can cause injury, such as a dislocated shoulder.
  - Pay close attention to what the person is doing so that you can describe the seizure to rescue personnel or doctors.

- How the person's body moved
- How long the seizure lasted
- How the person acted before the seizure
- How the person acted immediately after the seizure
- Whether the person suffered any injuries from the seizure

- **After a seizure:**
  - Check the person for injuries.
  - If you could not turn the person onto his or her side during the seizure, do so when the seizure ends and the person is more relaxed.
  - If the person is having trouble breathing, use your finger to gently clear his or her mouth of any vomit or saliva.
  - Loosen tight clothing around the person's neck and waist.
  - Provide a safe area where the person can rest.
  - Do not give anything to eat or drink until the person is fully awake and alert.
  - Stay with the person until he or she is awake and familiar with the surroundings. Most people will be sleepy or confused after a seizure.

http://www.webmd.com/epilepsy/tc/seizures-home-treatment

EDUCATIONAL IMPLICATIONS About half of all children with seizure disorders have average or higher intelligence—just as is true for the general population. Among children with seizure disorders who do not also have intellectual disability, however, the incidence of learning disabilities seems to be higher than among children who do not have seizure disorders (Arzimanoglou et al., 2004). Although many children with seizure disorders have other disabilities, some don't. Consequently, both general and special education teachers can expect to encounter children who have seizures.

With respect to the general public, see the Focus On: What to Do When Someone Has a Seizure feature.

General and special education teachers should also bear in mind the following (Arzimanoglou et al., 2004; Best et al., 2010):

1. General and special education teachers need to help dispel ignorance, superstition, and prejudice toward people who have seizures and provide calm management for the occasional seizure the child may have at school.
2. Special education teachers who work with students with severe intellectual disability or teach children with other severe developmental disabilities need to be prepared to manage more frequent seizures as well as to handle learning problems. The teacher should record the length of a child's seizure and the type of activity the child was engaged in before it occurred. This information will help physicians in diagnosis and treatment. If a student is being treated for a seizure disorder, the teacher should know the type of medication and its possible side effects. (Best et al., 2010)

Some children who don't have intellectual disability but have seizures exhibit learning and behavior problems. These problems might result from damage to the brain that causes other disabilities as well, or they might be the side effects of anticonvulsant medication or the result of mismanagement by parents and teachers. Teachers must be aware that seizures of any type can interfere with the child's attention or the continuity of education. Brief seizures might require the teacher to repeat instructions or allow the child extra time to respond. Frequent major convulsions might prevent even a bright child from achieving at the usual rate.

Many students with epilepsy have no learning problems at all. However, some do have learning disabilities, and children with epilepsy have emotional or behavioral disorders more often than those without epilepsy. If children with epilepsy do have problems in school, their school adjustment can be improved dramatically if they are properly assessed, placed, counseled, taught about seizures, and given appropriate work assignments. The quality of life of children with epilepsy is related to the same risk factors that affect quality of life for others with disabilities, including problems with **executive function** (see Chapter 7), problems with **adaptive behavior** (see Chapter 5), low IQ, psychosocial difficulties, low family income, and early age of onset (Sherman, Slick, & Eyrl, 2006).

Spina Bifida and Other Spinal Cord Injuries

Neurological damage can involve only the spinal cord, leaving the brain unaffected. Spinal cord injury can occur before or after birth, affecting the individual's ability to move or control bodily functions below the site of the injury (Best et al., 2010).

During early fetal development, the two halves of the embryo grow together or fuse at the midline. Incomplete closure results in congenital midline defects such as cleft lip and cleft palate. **Spina bifida** is a congenital midline defect that results from failure of the bony spinal column to close completely during fetal development. It is one type of **neural tube defect** (a malformation of the spine, spinal cord, or brain; see Barkovich, 2005; Liptak, 2002). The defect may occur anywhere from the head to the lower end of the spine. Because the spinal column is not closed, the spinal cord (nerve fibers) can protrude, resulting in damage to the nerves and paralysis and/or lack of function or sensation below the site of the defect.

Spina bifida is often accompanied by paralysis of the legs and of the anal and bladder sphincters because nerve impulses cannot travel past the defect. Surgery to close the spinal opening is performed in early infancy, but this doesn't repair the nerve damage.

Although spina bifida is one of the most common birth defects resulting in physical disability, its causes are not known entirely. We do know that many cases of spina bifida may be prevented by the addition of folic acid in the diets of women of childbearing age (U.S. Preventive Services Task Force, 2009; Youngblood et al., 2012). Additionally, recent scientific research has determined a possible genetic link in spina bifida (Copp, Stanier, & Green, 2013; Marini et al., 2011).

Spinal cord injuries resulting from accidents after birth are also a major cause of paralysis. The basic difference between spina bifida and other spinal cord injuries is that the individual who is injured after birth has gone through a period of normal development and must adjust to an acquired disability.

EDUCATIONAL AND SOCIAL IMPLICATIONS The extent of the paralysis resulting from a spinal cord injury depends on how high or low on the spinal column the injury is. Some children with spinal cord injuries can walk independently, some need braces, and others have to use wheelchairs. Lack of sensation and ability to control bodily functions also depend on the nature of the injury. Therefore, the implications for education are extremely varied. However, factors other than muscle weakness or paralysis alone affect a child's ability to walk. Careful analysis of motivation and other environmental inducements to walk are critically important.

Some children will have acute medical problems that might lead to repeated hospitalizations for surgery or treatment of infections. Lack of sensation in certain areas of the skin can increase the risk of burns, abrasions, and pressure sores. The child might need to be repositioned periodically during the school day and monitored carefully during some activities that involve risk of injury.

Spina Bifida and Learning Disabilities

Children with spina bifida (SB) often have intelligence in the average range—that is, they are not typically identified as having intellectual disabilities. However, children with SB are at an increased risk of learning disabilities (Coughlin & Montague, 2011; Hampton et al., 2013). In particular, learning disabilities affect mathematics abilities (Barnes et al., 2006; English, Barnes, Taylor, & Landry, 2009), reading comprehension (Hampton et al., 2013), and executive function (Stubberud, Langenbahn, Levine, Stanghelle, & Schanke, 2013). Identifying the academic strengths and weaknesses of children with spina bifida is critical—including IEP goals that focus on academic needs in addition to physical needs—and should be a focus of team meetings. Children with spina bifida are now living into adulthood. Their academic needs as well as their physical needs should be a part of their comprehensive plan to lead a fulfilling life.

Because the student with spina bifida has deficiencies in sensation below the defect, he or she may have particular problems in spatial orientation, spatial judgment, sense of direction and distance, organization of motor skills, and body image or body awareness. Lack of bowel and bladder control in some children will require periodic **catheterization**. Many children can be taught to do the procedure known as clean intermittent catheterization themselves, but teachers should know what to do or obtain help from the school nurse.

Enormous progress has been made in treating spina bifida and in including those who have paralysis as a result of the condition in schools and the larger society. Nevertheless, controversies sometimes arise regarding just what appropriate inclusion in school activities might entail. For example, a high school athlete with spina bifida took legal action to be included with runners without disabilities, even though she had to use a wheelchair on the track because her legs were paralyzed (Saslow, 2007). Furthermore, children with spina bifida may also have academic needs in addition to their physical needs.

ORTHOPEDIC AND MUSCULOSKELETAL DISORDERS

Some children are physically disabled because of defects or diseases of the muscles or bones. Even though they don't have neurological impairments, their ability to move is affected. Most of the time, muscular and skeletal problems involve the legs, arms, joints, or spine, making it difficult or impossible for the child to walk, stand, sit, or have use of their hands. The problems may be congenital or acquired after birth, and the causes can include genetic defects, infectious diseases, accidents, or developmental disorders.

Two of the most common musculoskeletal conditions affecting children and youths are **muscular dystrophy** and **juvenile rheumatoid arthritis**. Muscular dystrophy is a hereditary disease that is characterized by progressive weakness caused by degeneration of muscle fibers. No cure exists yet for muscular dystrophy, but advances in pharmacology are promising (Ruegg, 2013). Juvenile rheumatoid arthritis is a potentially debilitating disease in which the muscles and joints are affected; the cause and cure are unknown (Best et al., 2010). It can be a very painful condition and is sometimes accompanied by complications such as fever, respiratory problems, heart problems, and eye infections. Among children with other physical disabilities, such as cerebral palsy, arthritis may be a complicating factor that affects the joints and limits movement. These and other conditions can significantly affect a student's social and academic progress at school.

A wide variety of other congenital conditions, acquired defects, and diseases also can affect the musculoskeletal system. These include the spinal curvature known as **scoliosis** or missing or malformed limbs (see Best et al., 2010; Heller et al., 2009). In all these conditions, as well as in cases of muscular dystrophy and arthritis, the student's intelligence is unaffected unless additional disabilities are present. Regarding the musculoskeletal problem itself, special education is necessary only to improve the student's mobility, to ensure that the student maintains proper posture and positioning, to provide for education during periods of confinement to hospital or home, and to make the educational experience as normal as possible.

OTHER CONDITIONS AFFECTING HEALTH OR PHYSICAL ABILITY

In addition to the conditions we've discussed, an extremely wide array of diseases, physiological disorders, congenital malformations, and injuries can affect students' health and physical abilities and create a need for special education and related services. Chronic diseases and health conditions of children have increased dramatically during recent decades. These diseases and health-related conditions include childhood obesity (Powell, Harris, & Fox, 2013), diabetes (Tieh & Dreimane, 2013), and asthma (Mueller et al., 2013), for example.

Special educators need to be familiar with the range of physical disabilities and the types of accommodations that might be necessary to provide an appropriate education and related services (see Best et al., 2010; Heller et al., 2009; Lajiness-O'Neill et al., 2017). Moreover, teachers should understand that chronic diseases make many children's lives complicated and difficult because of possible hospitalizations, restrictions of activity, medications, teasing, and other consequences that, essentially, rob children of the experiences most of us associate with being kids (Zylke & DeAngelis, 2007).

Asthma is an increasingly common lung disease characterized by episodic inflammation or obstruction of the air passages such that the person has difficulty in breathing. Usually, the difficulty in breathing is reversible (i.e., is responsive to treatment). Severe asthma can be life threatening, and in some cases it severely restricts a person's activities. The disease can also get better or worse for poorly understood reasons, and the unpredictability of the condition can make finding satisfactory treatment difficult.

Cystic fibrosis (CF) is the most common autosomal recessive disease that leads to death (Gisler, von Kanel, Kraemer, Schaller, & Gallati, 2012). CF affects the lungs and the pancreas when the exocrine system produces a thick mucus that blocks the pancreatic ducts, the bronchi, and the intestines. Chronic illness in children with CF often means absences from school, which can be challenging to academic achievement. In recent years medical advances have led to longer life expectancies of individuals with CF. Although children born with CF in the 1970s and 1980s were expected to live into their teens, today their life expectancy has increased to the late 30s. An inspirational story about two young women with CF is shared in Up Close with Christina and Ali.

UP CLOSE with Christina and Ali In 2010, two sisters with CF decided to audition for *America's Got Talent (AGT)*. Although the girls, who had lost their older sister to CF in 2009, were told that they would never sing, they made it to the finals of AGT in Las Vegas. Since that time, they have released music that is meant to inspire those with CF or other life struggles. To learn more about Ali and Christina visit their website and follow them on Twitter, or go to a search engine and type in "cystic fibrosis christina and ali." •

Congenital malformations and disorders can occur in any organ system, and they may range from minor to fatal flaws in structure or function. In many cases, the cause of the malformation or disorder is not known; other conditions are known to be hereditary or caused by maternal infection or substance use, including alcohol, by the mother during pregnancy.

More children die in accidents each year than are killed by all childhood diseases combined. Millions of children and youths in the United States are seriously injured and disabled temporarily or permanently in accidents each year. Many of those who don't acquire TBI receive spinal cord injuries that result in partial or total paralysis below the site of the injury. Others undergo amputations or are incapacitated temporarily by broken limbs or internal injuries.

Children with **acquired immune deficiency syndrome (AIDS)** often acquire neurological problems, including intellectual disability, cerebral palsy, seizures, and emotional or behavioral disorders. Infants may contract the disease during the birth process. Although HIV does often result in neurological damage and cognitive impairment, it appears that at least in some cases the damage may be reversible with state-of-the-art drug therapies (Willen, 2006).

As children and youths with AIDS and other viral and bacterial infections live longer, owing to improved medical treatments, the need for special education and related services will increase. Teachers should be aware that if reasonable procedures are followed for preventing infections, no serious concern exists regarding transmission of HIV in the classroom (Best et al., 2010).

Fetal alcohol spectrum disorders result in disabilities acquired by children of mothers who abuse alcohol during pregnancy. The abuse of other substances by mothers also has negative implications for their children. If the mother is a substance abuser, then the probability of neglect and abuse by the mother after her baby is born is also high. Many women who are intravenous drug users not only risk chemical damage to their babies, but also might give them venereal diseases such as syphilis, which can result in disabilities. Children of mothers who are intravenous drug users are also at risk for being born with AIDS. If the number of substance-abusing mothers increases, then the number of infants and young children with severe and multiple disabilities will increase as well. In spite of the multiple causal factors involved, the prospects of effective early intervention with children who are exposed prenatally to drugs are much better than previously thought.

Some students have conditions that require particularly careful treatment because seemingly minor mistakes or oversights can have very serious consequences for them. Programs for students who are medically fragile must be particularly flexible and open to revision. Daily health care plans and emergency plans are essential, as are effective lines of communication among all who are involved with the student's treatment, care, and schooling. Decisions regarding placement of these students must be made by a team that includes health care providers and school personnel as well as the students and their parents.

More frequently, children are returning home from hospitalization able to breathe only with the help of a ventilator (a mechanical device that forces oxygen into the lungs through a tube inserted into the trachea). Whether it's appropriate for children who are dependent on ventilators or other medical technology to attend general education is debatable. Educators and parents together must make decisions in each individual case, weighing medical judgment about danger to the child as well as the interest of the child in being integrated with peers into as many typical school activities as possible.

PREVENTION OF PHYSICAL DISABILITIES

Although some physical disabilities aren't preventable by any available means, many or most are. For instance, failure to wear seat belts, helmets, and other safety devices accounts for many disabling injuries. Likewise, driving under the influence of alcohol or other drugs, careless storage of drugs and other toxic substances, careless storage of firearms, use of alcohol and other drugs during pregnancy, and a host of unsafe and unhealthful practices that could be avoided cause many disabilities. For example, lowering the incidence of obesity and increasing healthful diet and healthful physical activity could do much to prevent health complications of children, particularly diabetes (see Torpy, 2010).

Teenage mothers are more likely than older women to be physically battered. Teens are also more likely than older women to give birth to premature or low-birthweight babies, and these babies are at high risk for a variety of psychological and physical problems when they reach school age. Thus, preventing adolescent pregnancies would keep many babies from being born with disabilities. Inadequate prenatal care, including maternal infections and inadequate maternal nutrition during pregnancy, also contributes to the number of babies born with disabilities. And for young children, immunization against preventable childhood diseases could lower the number of those who acquire disabilities (see Heller et al., 2009). Although science is clear on the lack of any relationship between vaccinations and autism, vaccination against common childhood illnesses continues to be declined by some parents (see Boom & Healy, 2013; Eggert, 2013).

Child abuse is a significant contributing factor in creating physical disabilities in the United States, and its prevention is a critical problem. Many thousands of children, ranging from newborns to adolescents, are battered or abused each year. Teachers can play an extremely important role in detecting, reporting, and preventing child abuse and neglect because, next to parents, they are the people who spend the most time with children.

Children who are already disabled physically, intellectually, or emotionally are more at risk for abuse than are children without disabilities (Vig & Kaminer, 2002). Because children with disabilities are more vulnerable and dependent, they are easy targets for abuse by adults. Moreover, some of the characteristics of children with disabilities are sources of additional stress for their caretakers and may be contributing factors in physical abuse. These children often require more time, energy, money, and patience than children without disabilities. Parenting any child is stressful; parenting a child with a disability can demand more than some parents are prepared to give. It isn't surprising that children with disabilities are disproportionately represented among abused children and that the need for training is particularly great for parents of children with disabilities.

We mentioned in Chapters 1 and 5 that **phenylketonuria (PKU)** is now understood to be an inborn metabolic disorder that, untreated with a special diet, causes intellectual disability. PKU is generally thought of as a problem associated with intellectual disability, but it is also an issue involving other disabilities as well. Inborn metabolic disorders can result not only in intellectual disability but also in other disabilities associated with brain damage. Metabolic disorders may result in the buildup of **neurotoxins**, which can cause any of the disabilities associated with brain damage, including intellectual disability.

PKU isn't the only genetically determined metabolic disorder, and it is not simply a metabolic disorder that results in intellectual disability if it is untreated in early childhood. To prevent the negative effects of PKU (newborns are now routinely screened), it must be detected soon after birth so the infant can immediately be put on a special diet free of or very low in phenylalanine for the infant. At one time, individuals were taken off the diet by adolescence. But doctors now recommend that they stay on the diet for general health reasons. Furthermore, women must continue the diet during pregnancy to avoid damaging the fetus.

MyLab Education **Self-Check 14.2**

MyLab Education **Application Exercise 14.2: School Nurse**

Read the IRIS Center Module, *Perspectives and Resources: Provides Health Services for Students with Disabilities,* and answer a follow-up question.

PSYCHOLOGICAL AND BEHAVIORAL CHARACTERISTICS

Academic Achievement

It's impossible to make many valid generalizations about the academic achievement of children with physical disabilities because they vary so widely in the nature and severity of their conditions. The environmental and psychological factors that determine what a child will achieve academically also are extremely varied, and generalizations about academic outcomes aren't possible (see Best et al., 2010; Heller et al., 2009; Lajiness-O'Neill et al., 2017).

Many students with physical disabilities have erratic school attendance because of hospitalization, visits to physicians, bed-rest requirements, and so on. Some learn well with ordinary teaching methods; others require special methods because they have intellectual disability or sensory impairments in addition to physical disabilities. Because of the frequent interruptions in their schooling, some fall considerably behind their age peers in academic achievement, even though they have normal intelligence and motivation. The two major effects of a physical disability, especially if it is severe or prolonged, are that a child might be deprived of educationally relevant experiences and that he or she might not be able to learn to manipulate educational materials and respond to educational tasks the way most children do.

Some children with mild or transitory physical problems have no academic deficiencies at all; others have severe difficulties. Some students who have serious and chronic health problems still manage to achieve at a high level. Usually, these high-achieving children have high intellectual capacity, strong motivation, and teachers and parents who make every possible special provision for their education. Children with neurological impairments are, as a group, most likely to have intellectual and perceptual deficits and therefore to be behind their age peers in academic achievement.

Personality Characteristics

Research does not support the notion a certain personality type or self-concept is associated with any physical disability. Children and youths with physical disabilities are as varied in their psychological characteristics as children without disabilities, and they are apparently responsive to the same factors that influence the psychological development of other children. How children adapt to their physical limitations and how they respond to social-interpersonal situations greatly depend on how parents, siblings, teachers, peers, and the public react to them (Best et al., 2010; Heller et al., 2009; Lajiness-O'Neill et al., 2017).

PUBLIC REACTIONS Public attitudes can have a profound influence on how children with physical disabilities see themselves and on their opportunities for psychological adjustment, education, and employment. If the reaction is one of fear, rejection, or discrimination, these children might spend a great deal of energy trying to hide their stigmatizing differences. If the reaction is one of pity and an expectation of helplessness, people with disabilities will tend to behave in a dependent manner. To the extent that other people can see children with physical disabilities as people who have certain limitations but are otherwise just like everyone else, children and youths with disabilities will be encouraged to become independent, productive members of society.

Several factors seem to be causing greater public acceptance of people with physical disabilities. Professional and civic groups encourage support and decrease fear of people with disabilities through information and public education. People with physical disabilities are increasingly visible in the media, and they are often portrayed in a more realistic and positive light. Government insistence on the elimination of architectural barriers that prevent citizens with disabilities from using public facilities serves to decrease discrimination. Programs to encourage hiring workers with disabilities help the public to see those with physical disabilities as constructive, capable people. Laws that protect every child's right to public education bring more individuals into contact with people who have severe or profound disabilities. But many children with physical disabilities are still rejected, feared, pitied, or discriminated against. The more obvious the physical flaw, the more likely it is that the person will be perceived in negative terms by the public.

Public policy regarding children's physical disabilities has not met the needs of most of these children and their families. In particular, as successful medical treatment prolongs the lives of more and more children with severe, chronic illnesses and other disabilities, issues of who should pay the costs of treatment and maintenance (which are often enormous) and which children and families should receive the limited available resources are becoming critical.

CHILDREN'S AND FAMILIES' REACTIONS As we have suggested, children's reactions to their own physical disabilities are largely a reflection of how others respond to them (see Olrick, Pianta, & Marvin, 2002; Singh, 2003). Shame and guilt are learned responses; children will have such negative feelings only if others respond to them by shaming or blaming them (and those who are like them) for their physical differences. Children will be independent and self-sufficient (within the limits of their physical disabilities) rather than dependent and demanding only to the extent that they learn how to take care of their own needs. And they will have realistic self-perceptions and set realistic goals for themselves only to the extent that others are honest and clear in appraising their conditions.

However, certain psychological reactions are inevitable for children with physical disabilities, no matter how they are treated. The desire to participate in the same activities as most children and the fantasy that the disability will disappear are to be expected. With proper management and help, children can be expected eventually to accept their disability and live a happy life, even though they know the true nature of their condition. Fear and anxiety, too, can be expected. It's natural for children to be afraid when they are separated from their parents, hospitalized, and subjected to medical examinations and procedures that might be painful. In these situations, too, proper management can minimize emotional stress. Psychological trauma is not a necessary effect of hospitalization. The hospital environment may, in fact, be better than the child's home in the case of abused and neglected children.

Other important considerations regarding the psychological effects of a physical disability include the age of the child and the nature of the limitation (e.g., whether it is congenital or acquired, progressive or not). But even these factors are not uniform in their effects. A child with a relatively minor and short-term physical disability might become more maladjusted, anxious, debilitated, and disruptive than another child with a terminal illness because of the way the child's behavior and feelings are managed. Certainly, understanding the child's and the family's feelings about the disability is important. But it's also true that managing the consequences of the child's behavior is a crucial aspect of education and rehabilitation. Adolescence is a difficult time for most parents, and the fact that a child has a physical disability does not necessarily mean that the family will find a youngster's adolescence more difficult or less difficult.

Family support, school experiences, medical treatment, and attitudes have a very significant effect on the life of a child with a chronic health problem. Besides the school and society at large, the family and its cultural roots are important determinants of how and what children with physical disabilities will learn; therefore, it's important to take cultural values into account in teaching children not only about the academic curriculum but about their disability as well.

PROSTHETICS, ORTHOSES, AND ADAPTIVE DEVICES FOR DAILY LIVING

Many individuals with physical disabilities use prosthetics, orthoses, and other adaptive devices to help them function better on a daily basis. A **prosthesis** is an artificial replacement for a missing body part (e.g., an artificial hand or leg); an **orthosis** is a device that enhances the partial functioning of a part of a person's body (a brace or a device that allows a person to do something). **Adaptive devices** for daily living include a variety of adaptations of ordinary items found in the home, office, or school—such as a device to aid bathing or hand washing or walking—that make performing the tasks required for self-care and employment easier for the person who has a physical disability.

The most important principles to keep in mind are use of residual function, simplicity, and reliability. For example, the muscles of the arm, shoulder, or back operate an artificial hand. This might be too complicated or demanding for an infant or young child with a missing or deformed upper limb. Depending on the child's age, the length and function of the amputated limb, and the child's other abilities, a passive "mitt" or

MyLab Education
Video Example 14.3

In this video, a physical therapist helps a girl learn to use her prosthetic leg.

a variety of other prosthetic devices might be more helpful. Choice of the most useful prosthesis will depend on careful evaluation of each individual's needs. A person without legs may be taught to use her arms to move about in a wheelchair or to use her torso and arms to get about on artificial legs (perhaps also using crutches or a cane). Again, each individual's abilities and preferences must be evaluated in designing the prosthesis (see Best et al., 2010; Heller et al., 2009).

Two points regarding prosthetics, orthoses, and residual function must be kept in mind:

1. *Residual function is often important even when a prosthesis, orthosis, or adaptive device is not used.* For example, it may be crucial for the child with cerebral palsy or muscular dystrophy to learn to use the affected limbs as well as possible without the aid of any special equipment because using residual function alone will make the child more independent and can help to prevent or delay physical deterioration. Moreover, it's often more efficient for a person to learn not to rely completely on a prosthesis or orthosis, as long as he or she can accomplish a task without it.

2. *Spectacular technological developments often have very limited meaning for the immediate needs of the majority of individuals with physical disabilities.* It might be years before expensive experimental equipment is tested adequately and marketed at a cost that most people can afford, and a given device might be applicable only to a small group of individuals with an extremely rare condition. Even though a device may provide greater ability to participate in ordinary childhood activities, the current cost of some technological devices is clearly a barrier to their widespread use. Common standby prostheses, orthoses, and other equipment adapted to the needs of individuals will continue to be the most practical devices for a long time to come.

We don't mean to downplay the importance of technological advances for people with physical disabilities. Advances in technology and applications have provided extraordinary help for many students with disabilities (Best et al., 2010; Levy & O'Rourke, 2002; Lindsey, 2000). Our point here is that the greatest significance of a technological advance often lies in how it changes seemingly ordinary items or problems. For example, technological advances in metallurgy and plastics have led to the design of much more functional braces and wheelchairs. The heavy metal-and-leather leg braces that were formerly used by many children with cerebral palsy or other neurological disorders were cumbersome, difficult to apply, and not very helpful in preventing deformity or improving function. Those braces have been largely supplanted by braces constructed of thermoform plastic. Wheelchairs are being built of lightweight metals and plastics and redesigned to allow users to go places that are inaccessible to the typical wheelchair. And an increasing number of computerized devices are improving the movement and communication abilities of people with disabilities.

The greatest problem today isn't in devising new or more sophisticated assistive technology but rather in accurately evaluating children and youths to determine what would be most useful for them and then making that technology available. Most schools do not now make maximum use of available technology. Many children and youths who need prostheses or other assistive devices, such as computers, special vehicles, and self-help aids, are not carefully evaluated and provided with the most appropriate equipment.

Two social issues involving prosthetics are social acceptance and participation in sports. Returning war veterans who have lost limbs are sure to expose more people than ever to prosthetics (see Wood, 2011, 2012). In sports, a growing controversy over prosthetic limbs and surgical enhancements has become a matter of general public concern (see Goodman, 2007). Some are questioning whether prosthetic limbs and surgical enhancement (e.g., Lasik surgery and, inevitably, we predict, other prosthetic devices, including artificial computer-operated gadgets of all kinds) give competitors an unfair advantage (Longman, 2007; see also Howe, n.d.). In a sense, the controversy may parallel that of performance-enhancing drugs: What is fair and what is not, in athletic competitions?

MyLab Education
Video Example 14.4

This video highlights some of the advances in technology for individuals with physical disabilities, including Dorothy, who uses a hydraulic wheelchair.

EDUCATIONAL CONSIDERATIONS

Too often, we think of people who have physical disabilities as being helpless or unable to learn. It's easy to lower our expectations for them because we know that they are indeed unable to do some things. We forget, though, that many people with physical disabilities can learn to do many or all of the things that most people without disabilities do, although sometimes they must perform these tasks in different ways (e.g., a person who does not have the use of the hands might have to use the feet or mouth). Accepting the limitations imposed by physical disabilities without trying to see how much people can learn or how the environment can be changed to allow them to respond more effectively is an insulting and dehumanizing way of responding to physical differences. This is true in academics, but it is also the case in physical education. Adapted physical education is now a special educational feature of all school programs that make appropriate adaptations for students with disabilities (Kelly, Block, & Colombo-Dougovito, 2017). In addition to adaptive physical education in schools, individuals with disabilities can participate in many recreational activities with accommodations and modifications to equipment.

Adaptive Sports Iowa is a good example of an organization devoted to making several sports available to people with physical disabilities. To find out more information about Adaptive Sports Iowa, you can visit their website: http://www.adaptivesportsiowa .org/.

Educating students with physical disabilities isn't so much a matter of special instruction for children with disabilities as it is of educating the rest of the population (Best et al., 2010). People with physical disabilities solve many of their own problems, but their lives are often needlessly complicated because people without disabilities give no thought to what life is like for someone with specific physical limitations. Design adaptations in buildings, furniture, household appliances, and clothing can make it possible for someone with a physical disability to function as efficiently as a person without disabilities in a home, school, or community.

The objectives of educators and other professionals who work with children and youths with physical disabilities should include autonomy and self-advocacy (Best et al., 2010; Heller et al., 2009; Lajiness-O'Neill et al., 2017). Children with physical disabilities typically want to be self-sufficient, and they should be encouraged and taught the skills they need to take care of themselves to the maximum extent possible. This requires knowledge of the physical limitations created by the disability and sensitivity to the child's social and academic needs and perceptions—understanding the environmental and psychological factors that affect classroom performance and behavior.

Individualized Planning

Students with complex physical disabilities typically require a wide array of related services as well as special education. The individualized education programs (IEPs) for these students tend to be particularly specific and detailed. The instructional goals and objectives often include seemingly minute steps, especially for young children with severe disabilities (see Best et al., 2010; Heller et al., 2009; Lajiness-O'Neill et al., 2017). Many of the children under age 3 who need special education and related services are children with physical disabilities. These children, under federal law, have an **individualized family service plan (IFSP)** rather than an IEP (see Chapter 4 and Dunst & Espe-Sherwindt, 2017).

Educational Placement

Children with physical disabilities may be educated in any one of several settings, depending on the type and severity of the condition, the services available in the community, and the medical prognosis for the condition, but most are able to be in general education settings (Best et al., 2010; Nabors & Lehmkuhl, 2004; Lajiness-O'Neillet al., 2017). If children with physical disabilities ordinarily attend general education classes but must be hospitalized for more than a few days, they may be included in a class in the hospital itself. If they must be confined to their homes for a time, a visiting or homebound teacher can provide tutoring until they can return to general education. In these cases, which usually involve children who have been in accidents or who have conditions that are not permanently and severely disabling, relatively minor, commonsense adjustments are required to continue the children's education and keep them from falling behind their classmates. At the other extreme, usually involving serious or chronic disabilities, the child might be taught for a time in a hospital school or a special public school class designed specifically for children with physical disabilities.

MyLab Education
Video Example 14.5
This video is an example of a student with severe physical disabilities being integrated into a general education classroom.

Today, most children with disabilities are being integrated into the public schools because of advances in medical treatment; new developments in bioengineering, allowing them greater mobility and functional movement; decreases in or removal of architectural barriers and transportation problems; and the movement toward public education for all children. Any placement has positive and negative features, and the best decision for a particular child requires weighing the pros and cons. Working with a special educator to better understand a student's needs and how to meet those needs is imperative. For an example of how teachers can work together, read the accompanying How Can I Help? feature. Sometimes the benefits of a particular type of placement are either greatly exaggerated or almost completely dismissed.

Educational Goals and Curricula

Educational goals and curricula cannot be prescribed for children with physical disabilities as a group because their individual limitations vary so greatly. Even among children with the same condition, goals and curricula must be determined after assessment of each child's intellectual, physical, sensory, and emotional characteristics. A physical disability, especially a severe and chronic one that limits mobility, may have two implications for education: (1) The child might be deprived of experiences that children without disabilities have, and (2) the child might find it impossible to manipulate educational materials and respond to educational tasks the way most children do. For example, a child with severe CP can't take part in most outdoor play activities and travel experiences and might not be able to hold and turn pages in books, write, explore objects manually, or use a computer without special equipment. This student might require adapted physical education. Read the accompanying Responsive Instruction box for more on this topic (see also Kelly et al., 2017).

For children with an impairment that is only physical, curriculum and educational goals should ordinarily be the same as those for children without disabilities: reading, writing, arithmetic, and experiences designed to familiarize them with the world around them. In addition, special instruction might be needed in mobility skills, daily living skills, and occupational skills. Because of their physical impairments, these children might need special, individualized instruction in the use of mechanical devices that will help them to perform tasks that are much simpler for people without disabilities. Children with other disabilities in addition to physical limitations will require further adaptation of curricula (Best et al., 2010; Heller et al., 2009; Lajiness-O'Neillet al., 2017).

Educational goals for students with severe or profound disabilities must be related to their functioning in everyday community environments. Special educators and other professionals need to analyze community tasks (e.g., crossing streets, using money, riding public transportation, greeting neighbors) and plan efficient instruction for individuals with severe disabilities. Efficient instruction in such skills requires that teaching occur in the community environment.

Students with Physical Disabilities in the General Education Classroom

"But I'm not a nurse!"

Collaboration and Co-Teaching for Students with Physical Disabilities and Other Health Impairments

Students with physical disabilities often require complex systems of care, including services from health care professionals, related service personnel, and special educators. It is easy for everyone to forget about the students' cognitive and social needs because of the day-to-day physical needs. Even though a student with physical disabilities may have a wide range of services, the least restrictive environment for them may be the general education classroom. It is in this situation that collaboration with a special educator is important for the general education teacher to understand and meet the needs of these students.

What Does It Mean to Be a Teacher of Students with Physical Disabilities?

Special educators who work with students with physical disabilities must have skills related to learning and instruction, as well as skills in determining appropriate assistive technology devices, positioning, and socialization. According to the Council for Exceptional Children, special educators should be adept at the following:

1. Use adaptations and assistive technology to provide individuals with physical and health disabilities full participation and access to the general curriculum.
2. Identify instructional practices, strategies, and adaptations necessary to accommodate the physical and communication characteristics of individuals with physical and health disabilities.
3. Communicate adaptations of educational environments necessary to accommodate individuals with physical and health disabilities.
4. Implement specialized health care interventions.

These skills require a broad range of training for special educators, including medical management and extensive collaboration with health care providers and families. With this knowledge, special educators can collaborate with general education teachers to adjust instruction, change the physical environment of the classroom, and communicate successfully with students.

Successful Strategies for Co-Teaching

Jo is a special education teacher of 5- and 6-year-olds with CP and spina bifida. Charlotte is a general education teacher with a group of 28 kindergarten-aged students, some of whom have never had any school experiences. They describe their collaboration experiences.

Jo: We combined the children into two groups. Each group was made up of half my children and half of Charlotte's children. We'd occasionally put the two groups together. I became an expert in a certain content area. I taught it to two groups, and Charlotte did the same.

Charlotte: Our classes are scheduled for music together because of our collaboration. We had a music teacher come in who taught music to both classes as a large group; however, Jo and I did stay in the classroom to facilitate management needs because it was such a large group for one teacher to handle. In fact, we had to teach the music teacher some management ideas.

Charlotte: It was a good experience for her [the music teacher]; she was able to see how you can work with a range and variety of children. It's important to find someone who has a similar philosophy and treats children the way you do, but it also must be someone you can get along with, who has the same tolerance that you do. Had we not been friendly, liked each other, and respected the way each other did things, we would not have been successful. We have seen collaborations that were not as successful as ours because they did not develop out of commonalities.

Jo: One of the most demanding things about our collaboration was keeping up with the kids, keeping them on pace, and trying to make it valuable for them educationally. As much as I want this very worthwhile social experience for my special-needs kids, am I giving them the multisensory nuts-and-bolts special education that they need? I constantly have to try to strike a balance between the social needs of the children and the intense requirements of their special needs.

Charlotte: The most demanding thing about our collaboration was not working together ourselves, but effectively meeting the needs of the children. That's really the most demanding thing: living up to them.

Some students will have much more significant challenges than others, which can seem overwhelming for general education classroom teachers. Paraprofessional support is one tool for enabling more students with significant disabilities to be included in less restrictive settings.

BY MARGARET P. WEISS

The range of educational objectives and curricula for children with physical disabilities is often extended beyond the objectives and curricula typically provided for other students in school. For example, very young children and those with severe neuromuscular problems might need objectives and curricula focusing on the most basic self-care skills (e.g., swallowing, chewing, self-feeding). Older students might need not only to explore

RESPONSIVE INSTRUCTION

Meeting the Needs of Students with Physical Disabilities and Other Health Impairments

ADAPTED PHYSICAL EDUCATION

What the Research Says

Adapted physical education (APE) is an instructional service, not a setting or placement. Students receive APE when their disability necessitates a physical education program different from that of their peers. The difference can be in the form of an alternative activity, an instructional modification or adaptation, or different criteria for success. APE can be part of an integrated program for students with and without physical disabilities or can be a stand-alone program for students with disabilities only.

Who Qualifies for Adapted Physical Education?

Any student with an IEP may be eligible for APE. The Individuals with Disabilities Education Act (IDEA) requires that "physical education services, specially designed if necessary, must be made available to every child with a disability receiving a free appropriate public education." Necessary adaptations are determined by IEP team members. Any student with gross motor skill deficits or limitations in strength, flexibility, or physical fitness should be considered for APE services.

Strategies for Making Accommodations

Strategies for making accommodations to general physical education classes include (Auxter, Pyfer, & Huettig, 2005):

- Reduce the size of the playing field through reducing the size of the soccer field, goal area, basketball court, or length of a race.
- Change the size of equipment by using larger or more colorful balls, increasing the size of the bat but decreasing weight, using larger rackets, lighter bows, or scoops for catching.
- Reduce the playing area by adding more players to the field or court.
- Modify basic rules such as everyone plays seated, less mobile players get two or three bounces to get to the ball in tennis, rest periods or frequent substitutions are allowed, shorten the game, or partner activities.
- Use specialized equipment such as a ramp or bumpers for bowling, a batting tee, or a sit-ski for skiing.

The overarching aim for APE is for students to have access to activities that will support physical, recreational, and/or leisure goals. APE should take place in the least restrictive environment (LRE). Determining the LRE involves considerations of safety as well as opportunities for meaningful participation. For many students, the LRE will be the general education physical education class (Kelly et al., 2017).

BY KRISTIN L. SAYESKI

possible careers in the way all students should but also to consider the special accommodations their physical limitations demand for successful performance (see Best et al., 2010).

Although all students can profit from a discussion of death and dying, education about these topics might be particularly important in classrooms in which a student has a terminal illness. Teachers should be direct and open in their discussion of death and dying. Death shouldn't be a taboo subject; nor should teachers deny their own feelings or squelch the feelings of others. Confronted with the task of educating a child or youth with a terminal illness, teachers should seek available resources and turn to professionals in other disciplines for help (Heller et al., 2009).

Links with Other Disciplines

Children seldom have a single disability, and many children with physical disabilities have other disabilities as well. Therefore, multiple disciplines are often required, and special education is only one of many services needed.

Many children with physical disabilities will need the services of a physical therapist and/or occupational therapist. (For a description of classroom implications, see the Responsive Instruction feature, "Integrating Physical and Occupational Therapy in General Education Settings.") Both professionals can give valuable suggestions about helping children use their physical abilities to the greatest extent possible, continuing therapeutic management in the classroom, and encouraging independence and good work habits. The teacher should be particularly concerned with handling and positioning the child to

RESPONSIVE INSTRUCTION

Meeting the Needs of Students with Physical Disabilities and Other Health Impairments

INTEGRATING PHYSICAL AND OCCUPATIONAL THERAPY IN GENERAL EDUCATION SETTINGS

What the Research Says

The majority of students with physical disabilities receive related services as a part of their educational program. Related services can include anything from speech-language pathology to counseling to transportation. Two common related services for students with physical disabilities are occupational therapy and physical therapy. Researchers have found that the more integrated these types of services are into education settings, the more effective the outcomes are (see Heller et al., 2009).

Physical and Occupational Therapy

Understanding the differences between physical and occupational therapy can be confusing. Yet a clear understanding of the skills that are supported through these therapies is fundamental for creating the necessary bridge between out-of-class therapy and integrated therapy that supports student learning.

Physical therapy addresses sensory and gross motor functions. Physical therapists can assist students by identifying optimal positions for various tasks; teach students how to move within the classroom and school environment; and develop students' movement, strength, and coordination. Occupational therapists provide support for daily living skills such as dressing, bathing, and toileting as well as fine motor skills (handling small objects, handwriting, oral-motor skills).

Classroom Implications

As a classroom teacher, interdisciplinary collaboration among all service providers is a must. When planning for the integration of physical or occupational services in the classroom, the classroom teacher should consider the following questions:

- What are educationally relevant services versus medically relevant services? For example, an educationally relevant

service would be to work on transfer and handling techniques with the teacher and paraprofessional to position a student for instruction. A medically relevant therapy would be strength building.

- What are the educationally relevant IEP goals, and how can therapy support progress toward those goals? For example, mobility independence, ability to operate assistive technology, improved posture, and improved upper extremity coordination are all therapy goals that directly relate to improved educational outcomes.

- What type of service is necessary: direct, indirect, or both? Direct services involve hands-on treatment provided directly by the therapist. Preferably, these treatments occur within the natural environment (classroom, playground, gym) where the skill is expected. Indirect services, on the other hand, involve consultation or monitoring support. Under a consultation model, the therapist makes recommendations for instructional modifications, activity enhancement, environmental modifications, adaptation of materials, or schedule alterations. The therapist may even train the classroom teacher in ways to provide direct services. Monitoring involves periodic evaluations of student progress and related training for team members. A combination of direct and indirect services provides both direct services for certain goals or skills and consultation support for others.

- Is peer support appropriate? As students become more skilled, peer support can be solicited. This reduces the dependence a student has on any one individual and encourages interdependence—an important skill as students mature.

By working with therapists to identify ways to support therapy within the classroom, teachers learn ways to reduce the physical challenges students can encounter within general education settings, while fostering the development of necessary physical and occupational skills.

BY KRISTIN L. SAYESKI

minimize risk of further physical disability and to maximize efficient independent movement and manipulation of educational materials to enhance learning.

Specialists in prosthetics and orthoses design and build artificial limbs, braces, and other devices that help individuals who have physical disabilities to function more conventionally. Developing prosthetics and orthoses involves collaboration among several disciplines, such as medicine, biomechanics, and engineering. You can see the interaction of these disciplines if you go to https://www.youtube.com/watch?v=GFloqkkYmUM. By conferring with specialists, the teacher will better understand the function and operation of a child's prosthesis or orthosis and know what the child can and cannot be expected to do.

Cooperation with psychologists and social workers can be particularly important in the case of a child with a physical disability. Working with the child's family and community agencies is often necessary to prevent lapses in treatment. The child may also be particularly susceptible to psychological stress, so the teacher might need to consult the school psychologist to obtain an accurate assessment of intellectual potential.

Speech-language therapists are often called on to work with children with physical disabilities, especially those with cerebral palsy. The teacher will want advice from the speech-language therapist on how to maximize the child's learning of speech and language. Individuals of all ages need access to play and recreation, regardless of their physical abilities. Any adequate program for children or youths with physical disabilities will provide toys, games, and physical exercise to stimulate, amuse, and teach recreation skills and provide the youngster with options for productive leisure (Kelly et al., 2017). Physical education that is adapted to the abilities and disabilities of students is an important part of every sound school program.

MyLab Education Self-Check 14.4

MyLab Education Application Exercise 14.4:
Progress in General Education

Watch a video to see how Oscar, a student with serious physical and health impairments, is included in a general education classroom. Then answer the questions that follow.

MyLab Education Application Exercise 14.5:
Adaptive Devices

Use the textbook, the Internet, or another source to define *prosthetics, orthoses,* and *adaptive devices.* Then, watch a video about Kavana, and answer the questions that follow.

EARLY INTERVENTION

Early identification and intervention are critical for children with physical disabilities. Identifying signs of developmental delay so that intervention can begin as early as possible is important in preventing further disabilities that can result from lack of teaching and proper care. Early intervention also maximizes the outcome of therapy (see Dunst & Espe-Sherwindt, 2017). Communication skills are difficult for some children with physical disabilities, and they are a critical objective of any preschool program (see Chapter 9).

Besides communication, the first concern of teachers of young children with physical disabilities should be handling and positioning. *Handling* refers to how the child is picked up, carried, held, and assisted; *positioning* refers to providing support for the child's body and arranging instructional or play materials in certain ways. Proper handling makes the child more comfortable and receptive to education. Proper positioning maximizes physical efficiency and ability to manipulate materials; it also inhibits undesirable motor responses while promoting desired growth and motor patterns (Best et al., 2010). Proper positioning for one child might not be appropriate for another.

The teacher of young children with physical disabilities must know how to teach gross motor responses (e.g., head control, rolling over, sitting, standing, and walking) and must understand how abnormal reflexes that may be a part of developmental disabilities can interfere with learning basic motor skills. If the child has severe neurological and motor impairments, the teacher might need to begin by focusing on teaching the child to eat (e.g., how to chew and swallow) and to make the oral movements that are required for speech (Best et al., 2010; Lajiness-O'Neillet al., 2017). Fine motor skills, such as pointing, reaching, grasping, and releasing, can be critically important. These motor skills are best taught in the context of daily lessons that involve self-help and communication.

Motor skills shouldn't be taught in isolation, but as part of daily living and learning activities that will increase the child's communication, independence, creativity, motivation, and future learning. Learning social responsiveness, appropriate social initiation, how to play with others, and problem solving are other important goals for which the teacher must develop instructional strategies.

TRANSITION

Transition involves a turning point, a change from one situation or environment to another. When special educators speak of transition, they typically refer to change from school to work or from adolescence to adulthood. For children with physical disabilities, however, transition is perhaps a more pervasive concern than it is for children with other disabilities. It may involve discharge from intensive care or transition from hospital to home at any age. In fact, transition begins for some newborns immediately after they have been treated with sophisticated medical procedures. Nevertheless, we focus here on the transition concerns of adolescents and young adults with physical disabilities. Clearly, transition planning for many students with physical disabilities, including those who are supported by medical technology, is inadequate (see Inge, 2017; Scanlon, 2017).

Two areas of concern for transition stand out clearly for adolescents and young adults with physical disabilities: careers and sociosexuality. Adolescents begin contemplating and experimenting with jobs, social relations, and sexuality in direct and serious ways. For the adolescent with a physical disability, these questions and trial behaviors are often especially perplexing, not just to themselves but also to their families: Can I get and hold a satisfying job? Can I become independent? Will I have close and lasting friendships? Will anyone find me physically attractive? How can I gratify my sexual needs? Ordinary adolescents have a hard time coming to grips with these questions and the developmental tasks they imply; adolescents with physical disabilities often have an even more difficult time (see White, Schuyler, Edelman, Hayes, & Batshaw, 2002).

As we pointed out in discussing psychological characteristics, no formula predicts the emotional or behavioral problems a person with a given physical disability might have. The fact that children are enabled to walk doesn't mean that they will be able to walk all their lives. They might require continued services if they are to continue walking as adults (Bottos, Feliciangeli, Sciuto, Gericke, & Vianello, 2001). Much depends on the management and training the person has received and continues to receive as an adolescent and as an adult. Bottos and colleagues provide the following caution about interventions for CP: "Services for individuals with CP should be planned keeping in mind an entire life perspective rather than just the child-focused approach. Reduced contact when children grow up often results in a general deterioration of the quality of life of adults with disabilities and their careers" (2001, p. 526).

Choosing a Career

In working out an occupational goal for the adolescent or young adult with physical disabilities, it's important to carefully assess the individual's specific abilities, disabilities, and motivation. Postsecondary education must be considered in light of the individual's interests, strengths, demands, and accessibility. Some disabilities clearly rule out certain occupational choices. With other disabilities, high motivation and full use of residual function can make it possible to achieve unusual professional status.

One of the greatest problems in dealing with adolescents who have physical disabilities is helping them to attain a realistic employment outlook. Intelligence, emotional characteristics, motivation, and work habits must be assessed at least as carefully as physical limitations. Furthermore, the availability of jobs and the demands of certain occupations must be taken into account. The child who has moderate intellectual disability and severe spastic quadriplegia, for instance, is highly unlikely to have a career as

PEER CONNECTIONS | Tyler Rich

TYLER RICH was born with cerebral palsy, which affects the use of his legs. After using a walker for most of his life, he discovered the Segway Personal Transporter as a high school sophomore, joining a growing community of persons with disabilities who use Segways (http://www.segway.com/) to enhance their mobility. Tyler's interest in engineering prompted him to approach SegVator (http://www.segvator.com/), a company that made aftermarket products designed to enhance the functionality of the Segway Personal Transporter. He now tests many of their products, including car lifts and customized seating.

What do you do for fun? I love fly fishing, sailing, anything on the water. My grandfather lived on a sailboat, and I think love of the water is in my blood. I also work out several days a week. I used to use a walker, but now I put that energy towards going to the gym and working out to target specific muscles in my legs. It makes me feel good, and developing core strength also helps me to better control my Segway—although even before I had core strength I could still use it.

What is your favorite way to relax? I enjoy playing video games. And I read a lot; my favorite genre is satire.

What is your pet peeve? Ignorance. I try to educate people who are ignorant. If it doesn't work, I just go on about my business.

You mention that your pet peeve is ignorance. Is this ignorance about anything in particular? Ignorance in general? Could you tell us a bit more about this? By ignorance I'm referring to general closed-mindedness. When I approach someone I don't make judgments based on outward appearances. I get to know them and discover who they are as a person. If people were more accepting I think the world would be a lot better off.

Can you recall one teacher in particular who has been a positive influence in your life? Mr. Coughlin, my shop teacher in high school. Engineering is a real area of interest for me. Mr. Coughlin noticed that I was more experienced than most of the class and allowed me to work on my own projects instead of having to follow the curriculum. As a senior, I got to be a teaching assistant in his class.

Is there anyone else (celebrity, family member) whom you regard as a role model? Why are they a role model for you? Both of my grandfathers were role models for me. My mother's father was a woodworker, and I think that's where some of my interest in design and engineering came from. He lived on a sailboat, and my passion for sailing and other water activities probably comes from him. My dad's father designed machines and was always tinkering with something. I definitely take after him, too!

What is the most difficult thing for you about having a disability? Honestly, it's just not that big a deal for me. I was born with cerebral palsy, so I've never known life any other way. I can do anything in the world, but I might just do it differently from other people.

What are some of the misperceptions others have about your disability? Cerebral palsy is such a broad term. I'm very active and high functioning, but people sometimes think that I am paralyzed. Some people also assume that I have cognitive impairment, but in my case cerebral palsy only affects my mobility.

Has your disability affected your social relationships? If so, how? In order to be friends with me, someone has to be an accepting person—accepting of people's differences. Since this is the type of person I'd want to be friends with anyway, it works out well. I've made a lot of good friends through a program I participate in at a nearby ski resort. I am very active and don't want to be handled with kid gloves because of my cerebral palsy, and my friends in Wintergreen Adaptive Skiing Program understand that.

Are there any advantages to having a disability that others might be surprised to know? I really appreciate the value of hard work, and I don't feel entitled to things that I haven't earned. I've gotten to do a lot of very cool things in my life because I have been willing to work hard to reach my goals.

How do you think others perceive you? I think there can be a stigma of the Segway as a lazy person's device. People see me riding it, and think that I just don't want to walk. It's ironic, because I work so hard every day.

Please fill in the blank: I couldn't live without _____. My wits. I like thinking, of being cognizant of where I am.

What do you see your life looking like 10 years from now? In 10 years, I see myself working in Engineering. As an undergrad I plan to focus on studying mechanical engineering, and in graduate school I would like to explore biomedical engineering. Before I'm 35 years old I'd like to own a company that makes medical engineering products that make life easier for people with disabilities. Oh, and I'd also love fractional ownership of a jet plane.

a lawyer, a laboratory technician, or a clerk-typist. But what of a child who has physical disabilities because of CP but who has a bright mind and is highly motivated? Such a person might well overcome both the physical limitation and the associated social stigma and succeed in a wide variety of fields in which the work is more mental than physical. For instance, consider Tyler Rich, the young man introduced in the accompanying Peer Connections feature, who's on the path to a very bright career.

The occupational outlook for students with physical disabilities is as varied as the students themselves. Students with mild or transitory disabling conditions might not be affected at all in their occupational choices. Yet some with relatively mild physical disabilities might be unemployed or even unemployable because of inappropriate social and emotional behavior or poor work habits; they might need vocational rehabilitation training to function even in a vocation with limited demands. Some people with severe physical disabilities can use their intelligence, social skills, and residual physical abilities to the fullest and become competitive employees (or employers) in demanding occupations.

The outlook for employment of students with physical or multiple and severe disabilities has been improved dramatically by legislation and research and demonstration projects. More accessible transportation and buildings, increased skill in using technology to allow people to accomplish tasks at work, and greater commitment to preparing people with disabilities for work are resulting in more personal independence, economic self-sufficiency, and social acceptance, which benefit not only people with disabilities but the economy and society as well.

We now recognize that preparing for work begins in childhood. Long before adolescence, children, including those with physical disabilities, need to be taught about and to explore various careers. They need to be thinking about what they like to do as well as what they are particularly good at and about the demands and rewards of various kinds of jobs. The objective should be to help students select appropriate training and enter a career that makes maximum use of their abilities in ways that they find personally gratifying.

Supported employment for people with severe disabilities is a relatively new concept that is being widely adopted. In this approach, a person with a severe disability works in a regular work setting. She becomes a regular employee, performs a valued function in the same workplace as employees without disabilities, and receives fair remuneration. Training and continued support are necessary—hence the term *supported employment*. For example, a person with disabilities might be hired as a greeter at a store but might need training and continued support in such skills as making eye contact, smiling, welcoming shoppers to the store, and offering a shopping cart or information to customers. Training and continued support might also be required to help the person with disabilities know when to leave people alone and not insist on providing information or assistance that the customer does not want.

New technologies, especially in computing and other electronic devices, offer great promise for enabling students with physical disabilities to achieve personal independence, to acquire education and training that will make them employable, and to find employment. In some cases, the technology is readily available, and educators only need to become aware of available software and apps (e.g., software may allow functions of keys to be altered, save keystrokes, or provide substitutions for physical manipulation of materials).

Sometimes an individual's ability to use standard equipment is greatly enhanced by a simple modification such as orientation or location. Simply placing a keyboard in a vertical position over a monitor can enhance the ability of someone who uses a headstick to use a computer. (A headstick is an adaptive device that allows people who can't use their hands or feet, but who have control of neck muscles, to use a computer or accomplish other tasks.) Teachers must always look for simple, inexpensive, or cost-free ways to facilitate the performance of students with disabilities—to prevent an environment designed for people without disabilities from handicapping those who must do things a different way. Overlooking the seemingly obvious is perhaps the way in which we most frequently handicap people with disabilities.

Sociosexuality

Until fairly recently, physical disabilities were assumed to cancel human sexuality. People who were not typical physically, especially if they had limited mobility, were thought of as having no sex appeal for anyone and as having little or no ability or right to function sexually.

Fortunately, attitudes and experiences are changing. It's now recognized that people with disabilities have a right to family life education, including sex education, and to a full range of human relationships, including appropriate sexual expression. Sociosexual education for students with physical disabilities, as for all other children and youths, should begin early, continue through adulthood, and include information about the structures and functions of the body, human relationships and responsibilities, and alternative modes of sexual gratification. Youths with physical disabilities need to experience close friendships and warm physical contact that is not sexually intimate. But it is neither realistic nor fair to expect people with physical disabilities to keep all their relationships platonic or to limit themselves to fantasy. Most physical disabilities, even if severe, don't in themselves kill sexual desire or prevent sexual gratification, nor do they preclude marriage and children. The purpose of special education and rehabilitation is to make exceptional individuals' lives as full and complete as possible. In the case of youths with physical disabilities, this might involve teaching or providing alternative means of sexual stimulation and accepting sexual practices and relationships that are different from the norm. With sensitive education and rehabilitation, satisfying sociosexual expression can be achieved by all but a small minority of people with disabilities.

MyLab Education Self-Check 14.5

▼ chapter fourteen SUMMARY

How are physical disabilities defined and classified?

- Physical disabilities are physical limitations or health problems that interfere with school attendance or learning to such an extent that special services, training, equipment, materials, or facilities are required.

  - May be congenital or acquired

  - May be acute or chronic, episodic, or progressive

  - May be accompanied by other disabilities, such as intellectual disability and emotional or behavioral disorders, or special gifts or talents

- Major categories are neuromotor impairments, orthopedic or musculoskeletal disorders, and other conditions that affect health or physical abilities.

What is the prevalence of physical disabilities, and what is the need for special education?

- About 1% of the child population has a physical disability or health impairment.

  - About one-fifth of these children have multiple disabilities.

  - About one-tenth of these children have orthopedic problems.

  - Most (80%) of these children have chronic health problems.

What are some major neuromotor impairments?

- All involve damage to the brain before, during, or soon after birth or damage to the spinal cord.

  - Cerebral palsy, characterized by paralysis, weakness, uncoordination, and/or other motor dysfunction, sometimes by intellectual disability or other disabilities

  - Seizure disorder, an abnormal electrical discharge in the brain

  - Spina bifida, the failure of the spinal column to close during fetal development

Blend Images-KidStock/
Brand X Pictures/Getty
Images

What are some major orthopedic and musculoskeletal disorders?

- Muscular dystrophy, a degenerative disease causing a progressive weakening and wasting away of muscle

- Juvenile rheumatoid arthritis, acute inflammation around the joints that may cause chronic pain and other complications

What other conditions affect health or physical ability?

- Fetal alcohol syndrome (FAS), now one of the most common causes of malformation and intellectual disability, caused by the mother's abuse of alcohol during pregnancy

- AIDS, a life-threatening viral infection that often involves neurological complications such as intellectual disability, seizures, cerebral palsy, and emotional or behavioral disorders

- Accidents

How can physical disabilities be prevented?

- Safety precautions, better health care, prevention of pregnancy in early teens, prevention of child abuse, prevention of conditions that cause brain or spinal injury

What are the psychological and behavioral characteristics of individuals with physical disabilities?

- No generalizations are possible.
- Much depends on the reactions of family and the public.

What are prosthetics, orthoses, and adaptive devices?

- Prosthetics are artificial body parts.
- Orthoses enhance the function of a body part.
- Adaptive devices aid daily activity.

What are the major educational considerations for students with physical disabilities?

- Education must make the most of the student's assets.
- Education should be as normal as possible and equip the student for daily living as well as employment or further education.

Why is early intervention important, and on what should it focus?

- Early intervention is important in preventing further disability and maximizing the child's development.
- Early intervention should focus on communication, handling, positioning, and social skills.

What are the major issues in transition for students with physical disabilities?

- Transition may involve movement from one setting to another as well as preparation for adulthood.
  - Choice of and preparation for a career are important issues.
  - Sociosexuality is another critical issue.

▼ INTERNET RESOURCES

Pertinent Organizations

- The United Cerebral Palsy Association provides information and resources for people with cerebral palsy and their families (http://www.ucp.org).
- The Epilepsy Foundation of America provides invaluable information about epilepsy (http://www.efa.org).
- Information about spina bifida can be obtained from the Spina Bifida Association (http://www.spinabifidaassociation.org) or from the National Spinal Cord Injury Association (http://www.spinalcord.org).
- For more information about specific diseases and conditions, consider the following organizations and resources:

  The Asthma and Allergy Foundation of America (http://www.aafa.org)
  The National Cystic Fibrosis Foundation (http://www.cff.org)
  The National Multiple Sclerosis Society (http://www.nmss.org)

- The National Organization for Rare Diseases (http://www.rarediseases.org)
- For more information on fetal alcohol spectrum disorders, visit the site of the National Organization on Fetal Alcohol Syndrome (http://www.nofas.org).

chapter fifteen

LEARNERS WITH SPECIAL GIFTS AND TALENTS

▶ LEARNING OUTCOMES

Learning Outcome 15.1: Learn about the definition and prevalence of giftedness.

Learning Outcome 15.2: Understand the origins of giftedness, how students with special gifts and talents are identified, and some psychological and behavioral characteristics of people with special gifts and talents.

Learning Outcome 15.3: Learn about the effect of cultural values on students with special gifts and talents and groups of

students with special gifts and talents who are neglected.

Learning Outcome 15.4: Learn about some educational considerations for people with special gifts and talents.

Learning Outcome 15.5: Learn about issues that should be considered with respect to early intervention and transition to adulthood for individuals with special gifts and talents.

MISCONCEPTIONS ABOUT Learners with Special Gifts and Talents

MYTH People with special intellectual gifts are physically weak, socially inept, have narrow interests, and are prone to emotional instability and early decline.

FACT Wide individual variations exist among individuals with special intellectual gifts, and most are healthy, well adjusted, socially attractive, and morally responsible.

MYTH People who have special gifts or talents are in a sense superhuman.

FACT People with special gifts or talents are not superhuman; rather, they are human beings with extraordinary gifts in particular areas. And like everyone else, they may have particular faults.

MYTH People with special gifts or talents tend to be mentally unstable.

FACT Those with special gifts or talents are about as likely to be well adjusted and emotionally healthy as those who do not have such gifts.

MYTH We know that 3% to 5% of the population has special gifts or talents.

FACT The percentage of the population that is found to have special gifts or talents depends on the definition of *giftedness* used. Some definitions include only 1% or 2% of the population; others, over 20%.

MYTH Giftedness is a stable trait, always consistently evident in all periods of a person's life.

FACT Some of the remarkable talents and outstanding productivity of people with special gifts develop early and continue throughout life; in other cases, a person's gifts or talents are not noticed until adulthood. Occasionally, a child who shows outstanding ability becomes a nondescript adult.

MYTH People who have special gifts do everything well.

FACT Some people who are characterized as having a special gift have superior abilities of many kinds; others have clearly superior talents in only one area.

MYTH People have special intellectual gifts if they score above a certain level on intelligence tests.

FACT IQ is only one indication of one kind of giftedness. Creativity and high motivation are as important as general intelligence. Gifts or talents in some areas, such as the visual and performing arts, are not assessed by tests that measure IQ.

MYTH Students who have a true gift or talent for something will excel without special education. They need only the incentives and instruction that are appropriate for all students.

FACT Some children with special gifts or talents will perform at a remarkably high level without special education of any kind, and some will make outstanding contributions even in the face of great obstacles to their achievement. But most will not come close to achieving at a level commensurate with their potential unless their talents are deliberately fostered by instruction that is appropriate for their advanced abilities.

GUIDING QUESTIONS

- How is giftedness defined?
- What is the prevalence of giftedness?
- What are the origins of giftedness?
- How is giftedness identified?
- What are the psychological and behavioral characteristics of students with special gifts and talents?
- How do cultural values affect the education of students with special gifts and talents?

- What groups of students with special gifts and talents are neglected?
- What are the major educational considerations for students with special gifts and talents?
- What are the major problems of early intervention for children with special gifts and talents?
- What provisions are made for transition of students with special gifts and talents?

People who have special gifts or the potential for gifted performance can go through life unrecognized. They might seem unremarkable to the people who are closest to them. Sometimes their special talents or gifts aren't discovered because their families and friends don't think their special abilities are very important. And sometimes they aren't recognized because they aren't given opportunities or training. Especially in the case of those who are poor or members of minority groups, students with extraordinary gifts or talents may be deprived of chances to demonstrate and develop their potential. How many more outstanding artists and scientists would we have if all talented students had the opportunity and the training necessary to develop their talents to the fullest possible extent? We know that we'd have more, but we don't know how many more (see Callahan & Hertberg-Davis, 2013a).

Unlike disabilities, gifts and talents are abilities that nearly everyone believes should be fostered deliberately and celebrated. Yet giftedness is not without risk of stigma and rejection. Many people have a low level of tolerance for others who eclipse ordinary people in some way, especially in academic knowledge or achievement. Children who achieve far beyond the level of their average peers may be criticized, socially isolated, or pressured by their parents, other children, or school personnel to be like everyone else (Freeman, 2005; Plucker & Callahan, 2017). In fact, they may be teased, bullied, rejected, or hated (you may want to explore http://highability.org/ and evaluate what you see there in the light of our comments on social status, self-perception, mental illness, and stigma).

Some of the problems of giftedness parallel those of disabling conditions. For instance, defining and identifying children with special gifts or talents involve the same difficulties as defining and identifying children with intellectual disability or emotional or behavioral disorders (see Kauffman, Hallahan, Pullen, & Badar, 2018; Kauffman & Landrum, 2018; see also Landrum, Wiley, Tankersley, & Kauffman, 2014). All of the theoretical and philosophical issues involving disability and special education apply also to giftedness and special education (see Anastasiou & Kauffman, 2011, 2012, 2013; Kauffman & Anastasiou, in press). Nevertheless, an underlying philosophical issue regarding giftedness makes us think differently about this exceptionality: Most of us feel a moral obligation to help people who are at some disadvantage compared to the average person, who have differences that prevent them from achieving ordinary levels of competence unless they're given special help. But we may not feel the same moral obligation to help people who have special gifts, who are already ahead of most of us, to become even better and to distinguish themselves further by fulfilling their highest promise (see Gallagher, 2013; Plucker & Callahan, 2017).

MyLab Education
Video Example 15.1
Early elementary school teachers can play a crucial role in spotting giftedness in students early, which helps ensure that these students reach their potential.

The desirability or necessity of helping the highest-achieving students to reach their full potential is often questioned. Today, the emphasis is on programs to develop the talents of *all* students, with less special attention given to those who might be identified as gifted or talented. Some researchers have noted this trend toward downplaying or neglecting giftedness (Gallagher, 2000b, 2013; Kauffman et al., 2018; Plucker & Callahan, 2014, 2017; Plucker & Peters, 2016). The neglect of our most talented students is an ugly secret of contemporary American public education policy (http://www.brainy-child.com/) (DiGennaro, 2007).

DEFINITION

Students with special gifts excel in some way compared to other students of the same age. Beyond this almost meaningless statement, however, little agreement exists among educators about how giftedness should be defined (see Plucker & Callahan, 2017). School systems have widely differing practices regarding the education of students with special gifts or talents, because the term *gifted* has no clear-cut definition. Disagreements about definition are due primarily to differences of opinion regarding the following questions:

1. *In what ways do students with a special gift or talent excel?* Do they excel in general intelligence, insight, creativity, special talents, and achievements in academic subjects or in a valued line of work, moral judgment, or some combination of factors? Perhaps nearly everyone is gifted in some way or other. Which kind of giftedness is most important? Which kind of giftedness should be encouraged?

2. *How is giftedness measured?* Is it measured by standardized tests of aptitude and achievement, teacher judgments, past performance in school or everyday life, or some other means? If it's measured in any one particular way, some individuals will be overlooked. If past performance is the test, giftedness is being defined after the fact. Which measurement techniques are valid and reliable? Which measurements will identify students who have the potential to develop special gifts or talents?

3. *To what degree must a student excel to be considered to have a special gift or talent?* Must the student do better than 50%, 80%, 90%, or 99% of the comparison group? The number of individuals with special gifts will vary depending on the criterion (or criteria) for giftedness. What percentage of the population should be considered to have special gifts?

4. *Who should be in the comparison group?* Should the comparison group comprise every student of the same chronological age, the other students in the same school, all students of the same ethnic or racial origin, or some other grouping? Almost everyone is the brightest or most capable in some group. Which group should set the standard?

5. *Why should students with special gifts be identified?* What social or cultural good is expected to come from their identification? Is it important to meet individual students' educational needs? Are national economic or security issues at stake? Does identifying these individuals maintain an elite group or social power? By providing special educational opportunities for these students, will others reap personal or social benefits? What criteria will be used to judge whether identifying students with special gifts or talents pays off?

Giftedness, or *talent*, like *intellectual disability*, is whatever we choose to make it. Someone can be considered gifted (or to have intellectual disabilities) one day and not the next, or in one place but not another, simply because an arbitrary definition has been changed. The definitions that professionals use have no inherent rightness or wrongness. Some definitions might be more logical, more precise, or more useful than others, but we are still unable to say that they are more correct in some absolute sense. We have to struggle with the concepts of gift and talent and the reasons for identifying individuals with gifts or talents before we can make any decisions about definition. Any definition of giftedness is shaped to a large extent by what the surrounding culture believes is most useful or necessary for its survival. Giftedness is defined, not discovered (see Callahan & Hertberg-Davis, 2013b; Lohman, 2006; Plucker & Callahan, 2014, 2017).

Even the terminology of *giftedness* can be rather confusing. Besides the word *gifted*, a variety of other terms have been used to describe individuals who are superior in some way: talented, creative, insightful, genius, and precocious, for example.

- *Precocity* refers to remarkable early development. Precocious children develop gifts in such areas as language, music, or mathematics at a very young age.
- *Insight* may be defined as separating relevant from irrelevant information, finding novel and useful ways of combining relevant bits of information, or relating new and old information in a novel and productive way.
- *Genius* has sometimes been used to indicate a particular aptitude or capacity in any area. More often, it has been used to indicate extremely rare intellectual powers (often assumed to be indicated by IQ) or creativity.
- *Creativity* refers to the ability to express novel and useful ideas, to sense and elucidate novel and important relationships, and to ask previously unthought of, but crucial, questions.
- *Talent* ordinarily has been used to indicate a special ability, aptitude, or accomplishment.
- *Giftedness*, as we use the term in this chapter, refers to cognitive (intellectual) superiority (not necessarily of genius caliber), creativity, and motivation in combination and of sufficient magnitude to set children apart from the vast majority of their age peers and make it possible for them to contribute something of particular value to society.

The lack of consensus about what giftedness means poses problems for government definitions. No federal law requires special education for students with special gifts or talents, although federal legislation encourages states to develop programs and support research. The federal mandate for special education applies only if the student has a disability in addition to giftedness (see Huefner, 2006; Yell, 2016). However, most states mandate programs, and the most common elements of state definitions are (1) general intellectual ability, (2) specific academic aptitude, (3) creative thinking ability, (4) advanced ability in the fine arts and performing arts, and (5) leadership ability.

The field of special education is beginning to appreciate the different ways in which giftedness can be expressed in various areas of human endeavor. Likewise, educators are starting to acknowledge the extent to which the meaning of giftedness is rooted in cultural values (Lohman, 2006; see also Plucker & Callahan, 2017). There are many different abilities and many different ways of measuring them. What's considered giftedness and how it's measured depend to a large extent on what a culture values and believes. Most experts now acknowledge that intelligence isn't all there is to giftedness.

Recognizing the many facets of human intelligence has led to dissatisfaction with previous conceptualizations of general intelligence that reduced it to a single number (IQ) that was assumed to be unchangeable. Sternberg (1997, 2017; also, search the Web for "triarchic theory of intelligence") described a theory of intelligence that suggests three main kinds of giftedness: analytic, synthetic, and practical:

- *Analytic giftedness* involves being able to take a problem apart—to understand the parts of a problem and how they are interrelated, which is a skill typically measured by conventional intelligence tests.
- *Synthetic giftedness* involves insight, intuition, creativity, or adeptness at coping with novel situations, skills that are typically associated with high achievement in the arts and sciences.
- *Practical giftedness* involves applying analytic and synthetic abilities to the solution of everyday problems, the kinds of skills that characterize people who have successful careers.

A popular idea today is that individuals have "multiple intelligences" (Gardner & Hatch, 1989; see Chan, 2006 and Sternberg, 2017; also, search the Web for "multiple intelligences"). However, the concept of multiple intelligences is seen by many as scientifically untenable because it is not supported by research (Lloyd & Hallahan, 2007; Willingham, 2009). The theory of multiple intelligences is widely held to be legitimate, but few, if any, reliable applications of the theory to teaching exist (see Callahan & Hertberg-Davis, 2013b; Plucker & Callahan, 2017).

Today, most experts in educating students with special gifts and talents suggest that giftedness refers to superior abilities in specific areas of performance, which may be exhibited under some circumstances but not others. Even though giftedness is believed to be a remarkable ability to do something that society values, it's not an inherent, immutable trait that a person necessarily carries for life (Reis & Renzulli, 2009; Renzulli & Delcourt, 2013; Renzulli & D'Souza, 2014). Moreover, having a special gift in one area doesn't mean that a person is good at everything—or even that someone who is a good thinker about one thing is a good thinker about all things (http://www.nagc.org/). People become extraordinarily good at something only by developing their ability to do that particular thing. Ability is not a mental ability that can be used in any way one wants. All measures of intellectual ability, with no exceptions, tap into what has already been developed (Lohman, 2006).

PREVALENCE

Federal reports and legislation have assumed that 3% to 5% of the U.S. school population could be considered to have special gifts or talents. The prevalence of giftedness is a function of the definition that is used; if giftedness is defined as the top x percent on a given criterion, the question of prevalence has been answered. Of course, if x percent refers to a percentage of a national sample, the prevalence of gifted pupils in a given school or cultural group may vary from that of the comparison group, regardless of the criteria that are used to measure performance (see Callahan, 2011).

MyLab Education Self-Check 15.1

MyLab Education Application Exercise 15.1: Where Does Your State Stand?

This exercise asks you to consider IDEA-related services for students who are gifted and/or talented, and the variation across states with respect to how they are identified and served.

ORIGINS OF GIFTEDNESS

As defined today, giftedness isn't something that sets people apart in every way from people who are average. Instead, it refers to specific, valued, and unusual talents that people may exhibit during some periods of their life. The main factors that contribute to giftedness therefore are really much the same as those that foster any type of behavior, whether typical or exceptional:

1. Genetic and other biological factors, such as neurological functioning and nutrition
2. Social factors, such as family, school, the peer group, and community

We are all combinations of the influences of our genetic inheritances and social and physical environments. What environments foster gifted performance? We can often change students' environments; we cannot yet change their genetic makeup.

Although giftedness may be determined in part by one's genetic inheritance, whatever genetic combinations are involved are exceedingly complex and not distributed according to race or social class. The idea that giftedness is entirely inherited is one of the worst ideas associated with gifted education (Gallagher, 2006). However, children are not born with equal capabilities. Some learn much faster than others, and in a multicultural society it's particularly difficult to define ideas, concepts, or abilities that should be most highly valued and then identify students who should be included among those who are gifted or talented.

Families, schools, peer groups, and communities have a profound influence on the development of giftedness. Stimulation, opportunities, expectations, demands, and rewards for performance all affect children's learning.

How can families, schools, and the larger culture nurture children's giftedness? Research has shown that parents differ greatly in their attitudes toward and management of the giftedness of their children. Home and family are critically important, especially in the child's younger years (see Muratori et al., 2006; Robinson, 2013). In the families of highly successful persons:

- Someone in the family (usually one or both parents) had a personal interest in the child's talent and provided great support and encouragement for its development.
- The parents were role models (at least at the start of their child's development of talent), especially in terms of lifestyle.
- There was specific parental encouragement of the child to explore, to participate in home activities related to the area of developing talent, and to join the family in related activities. Small signs of interest and capability by the child were rewarded.
- Parents took it for granted that their children would learn in the area of talent, just as they would learn language.
- The family exhibited expected behaviors and values related to the talent, holding to clear schedules and standards for performance appropriate for the child's stage of development.
- Teaching was informal and occurred in a variety of settings. Early learning was exploratory and much like play.
- The family interacted with a tutor/mentor and received information to guide the child's practice—including specific tasks to be accomplished, information or specific points to be emphasized or problems to be solved, a set time by which the child could be expected to achieve specific goals and objectives, and the amount of time to be devoted to practice.
- Parents observed practice, insisted that the child put in the required amount of practice time, provided instruction where necessary, and rewarded the child for doing something especially well or meeting a standard.
- Parents sought special instruction and special teachers for the child.
- Parents encouraged participation in events (recitals, concerts, contests, etc.) in which the child's capabilities were displayed in public.

The ways in which schools can nurture children's giftedness have received too little attention (Brighton & Jarvis, 2017); Robinson, Shore, & Enersen, 2007). Yet the ways in which schools identify giftedness, group children for instruction, design curricula, and reward performance have profound effects on what the most able students achieve. When schools facilitate the performance of all students who can achieve at a superior level in specific areas, giftedness is found among children of all cultural and socioeconomic groups.

IDENTIFICATION OF GIFTEDNESS

Measuring giftedness is a complicated matter (Borland, 2014; Lohman, 2006; Plucker & Callahan, 2017). Appropriate methods of early identification will help children with special talents achieve self-fulfillment and aid them in developing their special potential to make a unique and valuable contribution to society.

The most common methods of identifying giftedness include IQ (based on group or individual tests), standardized achievement test scores, teacher nominations, parent nominations, peer nominations, self-nominations, and evaluations of student work or performance. In fact, strong arguments can be made not to disregard the traditional psychometric test-score approach altogether (Robinson, 2005). Typically, some combination of several of these methods is used (http://www.youtube.com/watch?v=WjjVTPpimDk).

In devising identification procedures that are fair to individuals from all cultural and ethnic groups and all social classes, educators must take into account the varied definitions of giftedness and recognize the effects of cultural variation on children's behavior (Borland, 2014; Plucker & Callahan, 2017). In addressing multicultural differences, it's important to recognize the variations of socioeconomic status, language, and values that occur within various ethnic and cultural groups, not just between them. Hunsaker and Callahan (1995) proposed eight general identification principles to help ensure fairness:

1. Assessments exceed a narrow conception of talent.
2. Separate and appropriate identification strategies are used to identify different aspects of giftedness.
3. Reliable and valid instruments and strategies are used to assess talent.
4. Appropriate instruments are employed for underserved populations.
5. Each child is viewed as an individual, recognizing the limits of a single score on any measure.
6. A multiple-measure/multiple-criteria approach is followed.
7. Appreciation is shown for the value of the individual case study and the limitations of combinations of scores.
8. Identification and placement are based on individual students' needs and abilities rather than on the numbers who can be served.

Identification methods should focus on balancing concern for identifying only those students whose capabilities are markedly above average with concern for including all who show promise for gifted performance (see Callahan & Hertberg-Davis, 2013b; Plucker & Callahan, 2017; Robinson, 2005).

PSYCHOLOGICAL AND BEHAVIORAL CHARACTERISTICS

Giftedness has been recognized in some form in every society throughout recorded history. In many societies, individuals with special gifts have been stereotyped in one of two ways: (1) as physically weak, socially inept, narrow in interests, and prone to emotional instability and early decline; or, in the opposite direction, (2) as superior in intelligence, physique, social attractiveness, achievement, emotional stability, and moral character and immune to ordinary human frailties and defects. Although it might be possible to find a few individuals who seem to fit one stereotype or the other, the vast majority of people with special gifts or talents fit neither.

Nevertheless, stereotypes persist (see Plucker & Peters, 2016). A still-common misperception is that genius predisposes people to mental illness. The idea that giftedness and insanity are linked is one of the worst misconceptions of the field (Gallagher, 2006). Some people with special gifts and talents accomplish remarkable things in spite of, not because of, mental illness or physical disability (see Goldsmith, 2005; Martin, Burns, & Schonlau, 2010; Mueller, 2009).

Perhaps it shouldn't be surprising that the majority of students who show giftedness enter occupations that demand greater-than-average intellectual ability, creativity, and motivation. Most find their way into the ranks of professionals and managers, and many distinguish themselves among their peers in adulthood (Renzulli & D'Souza, 2014). But not all such students enjoy occupational success in demanding jobs; some choose career paths that do not make use of their talents, or they otherwise fail to distinguish themselves.

The self-concepts, social relationships, and other psychological characteristics of students with special gifts or talents have been matters of considerable interest (Assouline & Colangelo, 2006; Robinson et al., 2007). Many of these students are happy, well liked by their peers, emotionally stable, and self-sufficient. They may have wide and varied interests and perceive themselves in positive terms. Nevertheless, some gifted students experience bullying and are traumatized by it (Peterson & Ray, 2006). Giftedness can be stigmatizing. But, regardless of the reason for bullying—the bullied student has a disability or is gifted or is different in some other way—it's important to address it in effective ways (see Leff, Waanders, Waasdorp, & Paskewich, 2014).

Students with intellectual gifts are often acutely sensitive to their own feelings and those of others and they are highly concerned about interpersonal relationships, intrapersonal states, and moral issues. Using their advanced cognitive abilities appears to help many of these children develop at a young age the social and emotional adjustment strategies used by most adults. In short, many (but not all) students with high intellectual gifts are self-aware, self-assured, socially skilled, and morally responsible.

However, assuming that gifted students never need education in morality is a terrible mistake. Students identified as gifted sometimes bully others (Peterson & Ray, 2006). Moreover, individuals can and have used their special gifts for nightmarish purposes. Therefore, it's important to recognize the enormous potential for both good and evil purposes to which special gifts and talents can be put and to help individuals who have such gifts and talents see the value of using them in the service of what is morally right.

Giftedness includes a wide variety of abilities and degrees of difference from average (Plucker & Callahan, 2017). Moreover, the nature and degree of an individual's giftedness may affect his or her social and emotional adjustment and educational and psychological needs. Consider, for example, that categorizing only people with IQs of 180 or higher as "gifted" is roughly like categorizing only those individuals with IQs of 20 or less as having "intellectual disabilities." In fact, children who are exceptionally precocious—those whose talents are extremely rare—may constitute a group for which extraordinary adaptations of schooling are required (just as extraordinary adaptations are required for children with very severe intellectual disabilities) (see Gross, 2000, 2002; von Karolyi & Winner, 2005). Child prodigies are children whose development and accomplishments meet or exceed those of adults with extraordinary talent. They often astonish others by their talent at an early age, and they often need opportunities that more typical students don't require and would find intimidating. For an example of a musical prodigy, see the accompanying feature, Up Close with Geoff Gallante, "A Child Prodigy on Trumpet."

UP CLOSE with Goeff Gallante *Geoff Gallante: A Child Prodigy on Trumpet* Geoff Gallante has already had a remarkable career, although he is quite young. He started playing the trumpet at age 4. As a 6-year-old, he had already played with Wynton Marsalis and Maynard Ferguson. He's also appeared on national television and played with many well-known performers and groups, both jazz and orchestral (http://www.youtube.com/watch?v=Bh2Fk5T0Xmo). •

MyLab Education Self-Check 15.2

MyLab Education Application Exercise 15.2: "What Is Giftednes?"

Listen to the comments of a student teacher and a professor talking about gifted students; then respond to the questions that follow.

CULTURAL VALUES REGARDING STUDENTS WITH SPECIAL GIFTS AND TALENTS AND THEIR EDUCATION

In American culture, it's difficult to elicit sympathy and next to impossible to arrange sustained public support for education that meets the needs of children with special gifts, especially intellectual gifts (Gallagher, 2000a, 2004; Murray, 2005). This is not a peculiarly American problem, but there's something self-limiting, if not self-destructive, about a society that refuses to acknowledge and nourish the special talents of its children who have the greatest gifts (see De Hahn, 2000; DiGennaro, 2007; Gallagher, 2013; Murray, 2005; Renzulli & D'Souza, 2014).

Video Example from

YouTube

MyLab Education
Video Example 15.2

In this video, Gabriel uses his gifts and talents to affect change for children with disabilities in Gaborone, Botswana in sub-Saharan Africa. Gabriel, like many other students with intellectual gifts, is acutely sensitive to his own feelings and those of others and highly concerned about interpersonal relationships, intrapersonal states, and moral issues.

Gallagher (2000a) described American society's ambivalence toward students with special gifts or talents. Our society loves the good things that people with extraordinary gifts produce, but it hates to acknowledge superior intellectual performance. Opponents of special education for students with special gifts argue that it's inhumane and un-American to segregate such students for instruction and to allocate special resources for educating those who are already advantaged. There is the danger of leaving some children out when only the ablest are selected for special programs. However, it seems impossible to argue against special education for students with special gifts and talents without arguing against special education in general, because all special education involves recognizing and accommodating unusual individual differences (Kauffman et al., 2018). Drawing a line is necessary if you are going to have any special service or special program of any kind (see Kauffman, 2013; Kauffman & Lloyd, 2017).

NEGLECTED GROUPS OF STUDENTS WITH SPECIAL GIFTS AND TALENTS

Students who are disadvantaged by economic needs, racial discrimination, disabilities, or gender bias are often overlooked in programs for gifted and talented students. In fact, many groups of gifted learners are neglected in a diverse, multicultural society (Callahan, 2011; Callahan & Hertberg-Davis, 2013a, 2013c). Two facts cannot be ignored:

1. Children from higher socioeconomic levels already have many of the advantages, such as more appropriate education, opportunities to pursue their interests in depth, and intellectual stimulation, that special educators recommend for those with special gifts or talents.
2. Far too many individuals with special gifts or talents are disadvantaged by life circumstances or disabilities and have been overlooked and discriminated against, resulting in a tremendous waste of human potential.

Underachievers

Identifying underachieving gifted students is very difficult, in part because no universally accepted definition exists (Siegle & McCoach, 2013). Students can fail to achieve at a level consistent with their abilities for a variety of reasons, including low expectations, lack of motivation, the influence of peers, family trauma, and other causes (Robinson et al., 2007; Siegle & McCoach, 2013). Many females achieve far less than they have the ability to achieve because of social or cultural barriers to their selection or progress in certain careers, even though males are most often identified by teachers as underachieving gifted students. Students who are members of racial or ethnic minorities also are often underachievers because of bias in identifying or programming for their abilities. Likewise, students with obvious disabilities are frequently overlooked or denied opportunities to achieve.

Underachievement of children with special gifts or talents can result from any of the factors that lead to underachievement in any group, such as emotional conflicts or a chaotic, neglectful, or abusive home environment. A frequent cause is inappropriate school programs—schoolwork that is unchallenging and boring because these students have already mastered most of the material or because teachers have low expectations or mark students down for their misbehavior. A related problem is that underachievers with special gifts or talents often develop negative self-images and negative attitudes toward school. When students show negative attitudes toward school and self, any special abilities they might have will likely be overlooked.

One way of preventing or responding to underachievement is allowing students to skip grades or subjects so that school becomes more nurturing and provides greater interest and challenge. However, acceleration is not always appropriate, nor is it typically sufficient by itself to address the problems of the underachieving student with exceptional abilities. Counseling, individual and family therapy, and a variety of supportive or remedial strategies are possible alternatives or additions to acceleration.

Underachievement must not be confused with nonproductivity. A lapse in productivity doesn't necessarily indicate that the student is underachieving. Students with extraordinary ability should not be expected to be constantly producing something remarkable. But this highlights the difficulty in defining giftedness: How much time must elapse between episodes of creative productivity before we say that someone no longer exhibits giftedness or has become an underachiever? We noted earlier that giftedness is in the performance, not the person. Yet we know that the unrelenting demand for gifted performance is unrealistic and can be inhumane.

Students from Low Socioeconomic Status Families or Who Live in Remote Areas

MyLab Education
Video Example 15.3
Teachers should be careful not to allow their own biases to influence their judgment as to the potential of minority students.

Children who are reared in poverty might not have toys, reading materials, opportunities for travel and exploration, good nutrition and medical care, and many other advantages that more affluent families typically provide. Lack of basic necessities and opportunities for learning can mask intelligence and creativity. Families of children in inner-city areas don't have the financial resources to provide the opportunities and early experiences to foster talent. Yet support for gifted students from low-income families often appears to be an easy target for elimination in tight state or local budgets (see Chandler, 2015; Murray, 2005).

Children who live in rural or remote areas might not have access to many of the educational resources typically found in more populated regions. Many of those who live in remote areas also experience economic deprivation and lack the advantages that children from affluent families have (Davis & Rimm, 2004; Plucker, 2013).

Cultural- and Ethnic-Minority Groups

Some ethnic groups, such as many ethnic minorities from Asian countries, are included in programs for gifted students more often than would be suggested by their percentage of the general population (see Oh & Callahan, 2013). However, other ethnic groups, especially African Americans and Spanish-speaking students, are underrepresented in programs for gifted students (Grisson & Redding, 2016; Hebert, 2013; Worrell, 2013; Yoon & Gentry, 2009).

Some of the greatest challenges in the field today are identifying culturally diverse and disadvantaged students with special abilities and then including and retaining these students in special programs (Callahan & Hertberg-Davis, 2013a; Ford, 2015; Moore, Ford, & Milner, 2005; Robinson et al., 2007). Some cultural and ethnic groups have been sorely neglected in programs for students with special gifts or talents (you may want to go to http://blogs.scientificamerican.com/ and search for "gifted minorities"). Many ethnic minority students with special gifts or talents remain underachievers, even if they recognize the importance of achievement in American society (Borland, 2004; Lohman, 2005; Tomlinson, Ford, Reis, Briggs, & Strickland, 2004).

Appropriate identification and programming for students with special gifts or talents can be assumed to result in approximately equal proportions among all ethnic groups. However, this proportionality will likely occur only if educators renew efforts to achieve the following:

- Devise and adopt culturally sensitive identification criteria.
- Provide counseling to raise the educational and career aspirations of students in underrepresented groups.
- Make high-achieving models from all ethnic groups available.
- Retain underrepresented ethnic students in programs for gifted students.
- Adopt a workable system to ensure the inclusion of underrepresented groups.
- Build relationships with the families of minority children.

MyLab Education
Video Example 15.4

For some cultures, giftedness in traditional academics is not valued as much as success in work and contributing to the family and community.

MyLab Education
Video Example 15.5

Some students with Asperger syndrome can benefit from gifted programming. Allowing them to put their special skills to use for the benefit of the entire class is a nice way to help their social assimilation into the general education classroom.

Ultimately, the larger social-environmental issue of making families and communities safe, as well as intellectually stimulating, for children and youths of all cultural and ethnic backgrounds must be addressed (Borland, 2004; Gallagher, 2000a; Plucker & Callahan, 2017). Equal opportunity for development outside the school environment would help address the underrepresentation of minority students in programs for students with extraordinary abilities (see Davis & Rimm, 2004; Ford & Moore, 2006).

Students with Disabilities

The education of students with both disabilities and special gifts or talents is a newly emerging field (see Coleman & Roberts, 2015). The idea that students can be **twice exceptional** (meaning that they have both a disability and a special gift or talent) (see Kalbfleisch, 2013; Missett, 2013) is, as Gallagher (2006) noted, one of the best ideas in gifted education.

The major goals of special education for twice-exceptional students are identifying gifted and talented students with specific disabilities, performing research and development, preparing teachers and other professionals to work with such children and youths, improving interdisciplinary cooperation for the benefit of such children and youths, and preparing students for adult living. Educators should consider the full range of programs for gifted and talented students for those who are twice exceptional, including acceleration. The accompanying Responsive Instruction, "Twice Exceptional Students in Advanced Placement Classes," provides a summary of the early stages of the research on instructional strategies for these students.

Our stereotypic expectations of people with disabilities frequently keep us from recognizing their abilities. For example, if a child lacks the ability to speak or to be physically active or presents a demeanor associated with intellectual dullness (e.g., drooling, slumping, dull eyes staring), we tend to assume that the child has intellectual disability. The fact is, students with physical characteristics typically associated with severe intellectual disabilities might be intellectually brilliant; unless this is acknowledged, however, the talents of students with cerebral palsy and other physical disabilities can be easily overlooked. Students with special gifts or talents and hearing impairment also can be overlooked if their communication skills are poorly developed, if their teachers are not looking for signs of talent, or if they are taught by teachers who have limited competence in communicating with people who are deaf. Students with learning disabilities involving written language may be overlooked (Assouline, Nicpon, & Whiteman, 2010). In fact, students with disabilities associated with communication problems, such as autism spectrum disorder or mental disorders, may be found to be gifted (Assouline, Nicpon, & Doobay, 2009; Coleman & Roberts, 2015; Martin et al., 2010). And people with physical disabilities may be found to have an extraordinary talent that we might not expect, as illustrated by the example of Doug Landis, an artist whose work we featured in Chapter 1 earlier.

Giftedness occurs in combination with disabilities of nearly every description. Marie Curie, twice the winner of the Nobel Prize (physics and chemistry), suffered from profound depression (Goldsmith, 2005). Consider also Evelyn Glennie, a deaf percussionist (http://www.youtube.com/watch?v=IlOemXqTOW8), and Timothy Cordes, a blind physician. They don't fit the stereotypes we hold. True, they are not typical of people with their disabilities—or of people who do not have their disabilities, for that matter. Fortunately, their disabilities did not preclude their pursuit of their areas of special talent.

We don't want to foster the myth that giftedness is found as often among students with disabilities as among those who do not have disabilities. But clearly, students with special gifts or talents as well as disabilities have been a neglected population. A key factor in meeting these students' needs is the collaboration of a variety of disciplines and institutions to provide appropriate technology and training.

RESPONSIVE INSTRUCTION

Meeting the Needs of Students with Special Gifts and Talents

TWICE EXCEPTIONAL STUDENTS IN ADVANCED PLACEMENT CLASSES

What the Research Says

For students who are twice-exceptional (that is, they have a diagnosed disability but also demonstrate areas of high ability or talent), their high school experience tends to be focused on addressing their disability rather than their talents (Schultz, 2012). For example, when developing a student's individualized education program, educators tend to identify objectives that target deficit areas—not areas of strength. Yet, success in college can be fostered through a rigorous and robust high school curriculum. Therefore, twice-exceptional students can benefit from participation in advanced placement courses provided that appropriate accommodations or supports are in place.

Research Study

Schultz (2012) conducted a study to identify barriers and supports that exist for students with disabilities participating in advanced placement (AP) courses. For the study, Schultz interviewed parents, teachers, guidance counselors, and college students who had identified disabilities and who had participated in AP courses while in high school. Participants answered interview questions that included information about school culture, accommodations, and academic experiences.

Research Findings

Several themes emerged from Schultz's research. First, school culture played an important role in determining access to AP classes. Some schools operated under the assumption that AP classes were exclusively for honors students, while other schools had more open philosophies in terms of accessibility to these classes. A second, similar theme was equity. While the College Board's *Equity Policy Statement* encourages *any* student willing to challenge himself or herself to participate in more rigorous coursework, some guidance counselors viewed "equity" as treating all students the same, particularly in regard to selection criteria for AP classes. In some cases,

these criteria served as a barrier to entry for students with disabilities. Another theme was lack of AP enrollment as part of transition planning. Even though the students who participate in AP classes were college bound, they did not enroll in AP courses as part of their transition planning. Incorporating such coursework into a plan could strengthen students' preparation for the transition to college. In general, Schultz also found that students either did not receive their required IEP accommodations or were discouraged from requesting them. Again, the notion that fairness means that everyone gets the same treatment was a common sentiment.

Finally, both advocacy and mentoring provided significant support for students. It was clear from the interviews that parents had advocated early for their children to have access to advanced or challenging work throughout their educational careers. Similarly, adult mentors such as special education teachers or guidance counselors were frequently instrumental in providing guidance and encouragement for students to enroll in AP courses.

Applying the Research to Teaching

Many schools and school districts may be unaware of how their culture or policies create barriers to access to AP courses for students who are twice exceptional. Schools should embrace the *Equity Policy Statement of the College Board* and encourage a wider range of students who are interested in challenging themselves to participate in advanced coursework. Similarly, special education teachers can give guidance to general educators on how to provide accommodations and supports that do not sacrifice quality or lower standards of expectations. Finally, all school personnel from special educators to guidance counselors to advanced placement teachers should recognize the important role they can play in terms of mentoring and supporting students who are twice exceptional. Indeed, positive mentoring can boost confidence and facilitate risk taking—essential components of success.

BY KRISTIN L. SAYESKI

Females

Females comprise the largest group of neglected students with special gifts or talents. Females with extraordinary capabilities today have many opportunities for education and choice of careers that were denied to females a generation ago, but there are many opportunities that still elude them (see Goldsmith, 2005; Plucker & Callahan, 2017; Reis, 2013).

Cultural factors work against the development and recognition of females with special gifts or talents. Females simply have not had equal opportunity and motivation to enter many academic disciplines or careers that have by tradition been dominated by males, such as chemistry, physics, medicine, and dentistry. When females have entered these fields, they have often been rewarded inappropriately (according to irrelevant criteria) for their performance. English literature has tended to portray females as wives, mothers, or "weaker" sisters, who are either dependent on males or sacrifice themselves for the sake of males. Such barriers to giftedness in females have been brought forcefully to public attention (see Davis & Rimm, 2004; Plucker & Callahan, 2014, 2017).

Females with special gifts or talents lag behind males in many measures of achievement and aptitude (e.g., professional and career achievement, standardized test scores, grades) and tend not to pursue courses of study or careers involving science, engineering, and math. In short, they are underrepresented in many fields of advanced study and in professions and careers that carry high status, power, and pay. We can only presume to know the reasons for their underrepresentation. Factors that have contributed to the situation might include lower parental expectations for females, overemphasis on and glamorization of gender differences, school and societal stereotypes of gender roles, and educational practices that are detrimental to achievement (e.g., less attention to high-achieving girls, expectations of less independence of girls).

Research suggests that the problems of neglect and underrepresentation of females with exceptional abilities are much more complex than previously believed. Like underrepresentation of ethnic and cultural minorities, the problems involving females are closely tied to cultural, social, and political issues, and they do not have simple or easy solutions. Nevertheless, the education of females with special gifts or talents might be improved by encouraging females to take risks by enrolling in challenging courses, to make career choices appropriate for their abilities, and to explore avenues that break stereotypical female roles.

MyLab Education **Self-Check 15.3**

MyLab Education **Application Exercise 15.3:**
The Home Environment

Watch a video in which Dr. Irma Olmedo discusses how the home environment affects students' behavior in school, and answer the question that follows.

Gender Identity

Neglect of females is quite clear, but gender identity is also an issue in identification of individuals with special gifts and talents. Outstanding achievement may be stereotypically male or female, carrying suspicion that an individual who excels in an activity that has been dominated by the opposite sex is gay, bisexual, or transgendered. Zephyrus Todd, for example, transgendered to male after gaining fame as a highly gifted little girl called "Super Awesome Sylvia," an amazing robot-maker (Selk, 2017). He first was a role model for girls in science, a male-dominated field. Our society still struggles in many ways with gender identity, and one aspect of that struggle is decoupling gender identity and the identification of gifted and talented individuals.

EDUCATIONAL CONSIDERATIONS

The focus of education is now on talent development across the full spectrum of abilities in particular areas of functioning (see Plucker & Callahan, 2017; Robinson et al., 2007; Tomlinson et al., 2002). However, this point of view includes the recognition that equity for many students with special gifts and talents may require special education (Kauffman et al., 2018). No federal requirement exists for special education for gifted students. State and local policies are uneven and often inadequate (Van Tassel-Baska, 2006).

All students at all ages have relative talent strengths, and schools should help students to identify and understand their own best abilities. Students whose talents are at exceptionally higher levels than those of their peers should have access to instructional resources and activities commensurate with their talents (Davis & Rimm, 2004). The one-size-fits-all mentality that is at least partly an outgrowth of the inclusion movement reflects a mistaken view of human development. Highly talented young people suffer boredom and negative peer pressure in heterogeneous classrooms. Students at all ages and grade levels are entitled to challenging and appropriate instruction if they are to develop their talents fully (see Callahan, 2013; Plucker & Callahan, 2017). For some, this instruction might be available only in a setting apart from their age mates. Effective instruction should be a greater concern than keeping a student in a classroom with age peers.

The belief that students with special gifts or talents don't need special education designed for their needs is among the most awful ideas anyone can hold and works against talent development, for it justifies doing nothing in schools to meet the needs of gifted students. It fosters the idea that all students, no matter what their needs, should be included in general education and it lowers expectations for the performance of gifted students (Gallagher, 2006). As we noted earlier, family support plays a crucial role in the development of talent, but many students also need special school supports if they are to achieve to their full potential. The consensus of leaders in the field is that special education for students with special gifts or talents should have three characteristics:

1. A curriculum designed to accommodate the students' advanced cognitive skills (see Van Tassel-Baska & Stambaugh, 2006)
2. Instructional strategies consistent with the learning of students with extraordinary abilities in the particular content areas of the curriculum (see Davis & Rimm, 2004; Dixon & Moon, 2006)
3. Administrative arrangements facilitating appropriate grouping of students for instruction (see Callahan, 2000, 2001, 2011, 2013; Plucker & Callahan, 2017; Robinson et al., 2007)

States and localities have devised a wide variety of plans for educating students with special gifts or talents. Generally, the plans can be described as providing **enrichment** (additional experiences provided to students without placing them in a higher grade) or **acceleration** (placing the students ahead of their age peers).

Many variations of enrichment and acceleration have been invented, ranging from general education placement with little or no assistance for the teacher to special schools offering advanced curricula in special areas such as science and mathematics or the arts. STEM high schools—special high schools emphasizing science, technology, engineering, and mathematics—are appropriate for some gifted students (see Ambrose, 2010). Between the extremes of regular classrooms in which the teacher tries to go it alone and special schools for gifted students are consulting teacher programs, resource rooms, community mentor programs (in which highly talented students work individually with professionals), independent study programs, special classes, and rapid advancement of students through the usual grades, including early admission to high school or college.

Not every community offers all possible options. The types of services offered vary greatly within the school systems of given states and from state to state. As one might expect, large metropolitan areas typically offer more program options than small towns or rural areas.

Some of the educational options for students with high ability, such as acceleration and inclusion, are extremely controversial. Acceleration and advanced placement seem to be particularly effective (Gavin & Adelson, 2014). However, no single type of program option meets the needs of all students who have special gifts or talents (see Callahan, 2013). Ideally, assessment, identification, and instruction are closely linked, whether students have disabilities or special gifts and talents—or both. When including students with disabilities and special gifts and talents, it is important to use strategies that meet the needs of both types of students.

Advances in telecommunications, the presence of computers in the home and classroom, and the call for excellence in U.S. education are three developments with implications for educating the most able students. The possible uses of computers for enhancing the education of extraordinarily high-performing students are enormous. Using software tutorials, accessing data banks, playing or inventing intellectually demanding computer games, writing and editing in English and foreign languages, learning computer languages, and solving advanced problems in mathematics are only a few of the possibilities (see Plucker & Callahan, 2017; Robinson et al., 2007).

EARLY INTERVENTION

The giftedness of young children presents special problems of definition, identification, programming, and evaluation (Brighton & Jarvis, 2017; Porter, 2005; Robinson et al., 2007; Ruf, 2005). Although educators have made progress in building model programs and providing better services for young children with special gifts, negative attitudes toward such efforts persist. Barriers inhibiting the development of better education for these children include lack of parental advocacy, lack of appropriate teacher training, an emphasis on older students of extraordinary ability, financial constraints, and legal roadblocks such as laws preventing early admission to school. The barriers to early identification and programming for students with special gifts or talents include school policies and ideologies that refuse to advance students to grades beyond their chronological age peers.

Many questions remain unanswered about the education of young children who have special gifts. Relatively little is known about how advantageous it is to identify and provide programs for such children before they are in third or fourth grade or how best to train parents and teachers to work with preschoolers with special abilities. Young children with disabilities need the best possible early intervention to make sure that all of their abilities, including any special gifts they might have, are not overlooked (see Odom & Wolery, 2006; Porter, 2005).

Although not a panacea, early admission to school and acceleration through grades and subjects offer significant advantages for some young students with special gifts or talents. What many young children with special abilities need most is the freedom to make full and appropriate use of school systems as they now exist. They need the freedom to study with older children in specific areas in which their abilities are challenged. Such children need to be able to get around the usual eligibility rules so that they can go through the ordinary curriculum at an accelerated rate. Unfortunately, relatively few preschoolers with special gifts receive the kind of educational programming appropriate for their abilities. See the accompanying Responsive Instruction feature, "Acceleration: A Nation Deceived Report."

MyLab Education
Video Example 15.6
No matter the model, for example acceleration or enrichment, a key component should be parent involvement.

MyLab Education
Video Example 15.7
Acceleration, when individualized, can be an effective way to meet the needs of gifted students.

MyLab Education Self-Check 15.4

MyLab Education Application Exercise 15.4: Characteristics of Students Who Are Gifted

Consider the characteristics of gifted students suggested by the comments of teachers and family members in two videos, and respond to the accompanying questions.

TRANSITION TO ADULTHOOD

For students with special gifts or talents who are achieving near their potential and who have been given opportunities to take on adult roles, the transitions from childhood to adolescence to adulthood and from high school to higher education or employment are

HOW CAN I HELP? Working with Gifted Students in the General Education Classroom

"How can I challenge him when half of my students have difficulty reading?"

Working with students with gifts and talents can be especially challenging for classroom teachers, considering the wide range of achievement levels in today's classrooms. Collaboration with a teacher of students with special gifts and talents can help general education teachers challenge all students. Collaboration to meet the needs of gifted students is often difficult. Instruction in a differentiated classroom is based on student readiness and includes constant assessment of student skill and knowledge, varying of activities or assignments for individuals, and the active exploration of topics at varying levels by individuals or groups of students. This can be quite difficult to manage with 20 or 30 students who have a wide range of skills. Teachers of gifted students can help manage the classroom when groups and individuals are working, assess student progress, and collect resources.

Consider a differentiated activity designed to help all students learn the water cycle.

Students choose one of six possible activities to complete in class (time permitting) or as homework.

A. Design a cartoon that illustrates your journey as a water droplet. Include an appropriate caption.

B. Draw an accurate version of the water cycle that includes all steps. Be sure to show the processes that get a water droplet from one step to another.

C. Create a fictional story about the journey of a water droplet. Base it on your water droplet's journey.

D. Design a similar game using another cycle we have studied (e.g., the carbon cycle or the nitrogen cycle). Write out or sketch one possible journey. How does this journey differ from your journey as a water droplet?

E. Create a bar graph of your journey and the journey of two other droplets, based on the amount of time spent at each station. For data, refer to your paper clip chain and the chains of two classmates.

F. Create a local version of the water cycle. Be sure to include the names of local rivers, bays, oceans, mountains, and so on.

This lesson can be used with students of all achievement levels; however, the instructional support necessary for all students to understand the lesson varies. Collaborating with a teacher of students with special gifts and talents would allow both teachers to provide instructional support, observe student work, and develop subsequent lessons. Differentiation to this extent may not be possible without this collaboration.

BY MARGARET P. WEISS

---

typically not very problematic. Particularly by adolescence, these students tend to be aware of their relative strengths and weaknesses. This means that they might not see themselves as gifted in their areas of relative weakness even though they perform as well as or better than the majority of their age peers in those areas (Plucker & Stocking, 2001; Robinson et al., 2007).

In many ways, transitions for these youths tend to mirror the problems in transitions faced by adolescents and young adults with disabilities (see Kohler & Field, 2006). Not all adolescents and young adults with special gifts or talents take transitions in stride. Many need personal and career counseling and a networking system that links students to school and community resources (Herbert & Kelly, 2006; Neihart, Reis, Robinson, & Moon, 2002).

If there is a central issue in the education of adolescents with special gifts or talents, it is that of acceleration versus enrichment (see Callahan & Hertberg-Davis, 2013a; Colangelo, Assouline, & Marron, 2013; Plucker & Callahan, 2017). Proponents of enrichment believe that these students need continued social contact with their age peers. They argue that such students should follow the curriculum of their age peers and study topics in greater depth. Proponents of acceleration believe that the only way to provide challenging and appropriate education for students with special gifts and talents is to let them compete with older students. These educators argue that because the cognitive abilities of these students are advanced beyond their years, these students should proceed through the curriculum at an accelerated pace.

RESPONSIVE INSTRUCTION

Meeting the Needs of Students with Special Gifts and Talents

ACCELERATION: A NATION DECEIVED REPORT

What the Research Says

In *A Nation Deceived: How Schools Hold Back Its Brightest Students*, Colangelo, Assouline, and Gross (2004a) summarized 50 years of research on the various forms of acceleration and came to the singular conclusion that acceleration, in many of its forms and under many different circumstances, benefits gifted students both academically and socially. Unfortunately, concern over ability tracking (an extreme form of ability grouping that sorts students based on global measures such as IQ or GPA) has spilled over into concern about acceleration programs. Acceleration, not a form of tracking, is any educational program that moves students through at a faster rate or younger than typical age. Effective acceleration programs match the level and complexity of the curriculum to the readiness and motivation of the student.

A Nation Deceived dispels many myths associated with acceleration including the belief that the majority of students are not socially mature enough to advance grades, holding students to their grade level is the "safer" educational route, and acceleration results in gaps in students' knowledge. The report touches upon the 18 types of acceleration found in schools today and reviews the relevant research associated with each practice. The types of acceleration are early admission to kindergarten, early admission to first grade, grade skipping, continuous progress, self-paced instruction, subject-matter acceleration/partial acceleration, combined classes, curriculum compacting, telescoping curriculum, mentoring, extracurricular programs, correspondence courses, early graduation, concurrent/dual enrollment, advanced placement, credit by examination, acceleration in college, and early entrance into middle school, high school, or college.

BY KRISTIN L. SAYESKI

Acceleration for adolescents with special gifts or talents can mean enrollment in advanced placement courses, early entrance to college, or enrollment in college courses while they are attending high school (see Callahan, 2003; Colangelo et al., 2004b; Muratori et al., 2006). Some of the most highly gifted students might even be admitted early to graduate study. Other students with special gifts or talents who are nonetheless less dramatically different from their age peers may not benefit from radical acceleration.

Acceleration programs, particularly in mathematics, have been evaluated very favorably (see Assouline & Lupkowski-Shoplik, 2003; Brody & Stanley, 2005; Muratori et al., 2006; Plucker & Callahan, 2017). In fact, early entrance to college on a full-time or part-time basis appears to work very well for adolescents, as long as it is done with care and sensitivity to the needs of individual students. It's important to provide counseling and support services for students who enter college early to ensure that they have appropriate, rewarding social experiences that enhance their self-esteem, as well as academic challenges and successes.

Beyond acceleration and enrichment, adolescents with special gifts or talents often need attention to social and personal development if they are to make successful and gratifying transitions to adulthood and careers (Assouline & Colangelo, 2006; see also Callahan, 2013). Like other groups of students with special characteristics and needs, they may benefit from opportunities to socialize with and learn from other students who have similar characteristics and face similar challenges. They may be able to obtain particular benefit from reflecting on the nature and meaning of life and the directions they choose for themselves. Given proper supports, they can often make use of self-determination and survival skills (see Neihart et al., 2002).

MyLab Education Self-Check 15.5

▼ chapter fifteen SUMMARY

How is giftedness defined?

- Students with special gifts excel in some way compared to others of the same age. However, little agreement exists about how giftedness should be defined. Disagreements about definition include:
    - What is to be measured
    - How it is to be measured
    - The degree to which one must excel
    - The comparison group
    - Reasons for identifying giftedness
- Giftedness is actually whatever we wish to make it.
- There may be different kinds of giftedness, such as analytic, synthetic, and practical intelligence.

What is the prevalence of giftedness?

- Prevalence depends on definition; school systems across the nation typically identify about 3% to 5% of students as gifted.

What are the origins of giftedness?

- Both biological (primarily genetic) and social factors (e.g., family, school, peer group, community) are involved.
    - No one knows precisely how much each of these two factors contributes to giftedness, especially in the individual case.
    - We can alter many social factors but not genetic factors, and more attention needs to be given to how schools foster giftedness.

How is giftedness identified?

- Individual intelligence tests have been the traditional means of identifying giftedness.
- More attention is being given now to additional, culturally sensitive identification procedures, including nomination by peers, parents, teachers, and self as well as to interests and accomplishments.

What are the psychological and behavioral characteristics of students with special gifts and talents?

- Gifted students typically learn to read at an early age and achieve other developmental milestones earlier than most children.

Fuse/Corbis/Getty Images

- Gifted students are typically good at many things.
- Gifted students typically like school and like learning.
- Gifted students are subject to the same psychological and physical problems as other students.

How do cultural values affect the education of students with special gifts and talents?

- American culture is ambivalent about giftedness, liking the good things that giftedness brings but disliking intellectual superiority and identifying individuals with intellectual gifts.

What groups of students with special gifts and talents are neglected?

- Underachievers are often overlooked.
- Students who are from low socioeconomic status families and those living in remote areas are often unrecognized.
- Students from cultural- and ethnic-minority groups are often neglected.
- Students who also have disabilities are often not identified.
- Females are underrepresented.

What are the major educational considerations for students with special gifts and talents?

- Acceleration and enrichment are the two most common ways of accommodating gifted students; and both have advantages and disadvantages, proponents and opponents.

What are the major problems of early intervention for children with special gifts and talents?

- Lack of research to indicate effective ways of identifying giftedness in young children (i.e., before third or fourth grade) is a major problem.

What provisions are made for transition of students with special gifts and talents?

- The problems of gifted adolescents tend to mirror those of students with disabilities of the same age, and many will need personal counseling about further education and career paths.
- Acceleration (including early admission to college) and enrichment (including advanced placement courses) are the two primary accommodations.

▼ PERTINENT ORGANIZATIONS

- The National Association for Gifted Children (http://www.nagc.org/) offers much useful information for teachers, school administrators, and parents.
- The Association for the Gifted, a division of CEC (the Council for Exceptional Children) known as CEC-TAG, maintains useful information for teachers and teachers in training (http://www.cectag.org/).

- The National Society for the Gifted and Talented (http://www.nsgt.org/) has the mission of advancing the development of gifted, talented, and high potential youth by providing opportunities, advocacy, and exemplary programs and practices.
- The World Council for Gifted and Talented Children (http://www.world-gifted.org/) is a nonprofit organization that provides advocacy and support for gifted children throughout the world.

GLOSSARY

A

Acceleration: An approach in which students with special gifts or talents are placed in grade levels ahead of their age peers in one or more academic subjects.

Accessible pedestrian signal (APSs):   Devices for people who are blind to let them know when the "walk" signal is on at intersections; can be auditory, tactile, or both.

Accommodations: Changes in the delivery of instruction, type of student performance, or method of assessment that do not significantly change the content or conceptual difficulty of the curriculum.

Acquired apraxia: As in developmental apraxia, there are problems in motor planning such that the child has difficulty in producing speech sounds and organizing words and word sounds for effective communication. However, the problem is known to be caused by neurological damage.

Acquired immune deficiency syndrome (AIDS):   A virus-caused illness resulting in a breakdown of the immune system; currently, no known cure exists.

Acute: A serious state of illness or injury from which someone often recovers with treatment.

Adaptations: Changes in curricular content or conceptual difficulty or changes in instructional objectives and methods.

Adapted signs: Using sign language in such a way as to help those who also have visual impairment communicate, such as holding the hands of the individual while guiding them to sign.

Adaptive behavior: The social and practical intelligence used in people's everyday lives; along with IQ, is considered in making a determination of intellectual disability.

Adaptive behavior skills: Skills needed to adapt to one's living environment (e.g., communication, self-care, home living, social skills, community use, self-direction, health and safety, functional academics, leisure, and work); usually estimated by an adaptive behavior survey; one of two major components (the other is intellectual functioning) of the AAMR definition.

Adaptive devices: Special tools that are adaptations of common items to make accomplishing self-care, work, or recreation activities easier for people with physical disabilities.

Adderall: A psychostimulant for ADHD; its effects are longer acting than those of Ritalin.

Adventitiously deaf: Deafness that occurs through illness or accident in an individual who was born with normal hearing.

Affective disorder: A disorder of mood or emotional tone characterized by depression or elation.

Aggression: Behavior that intentionally causes others harm or that elicits escape or avoidance responses from others.

Aim line: Used in CBM; based on expected growth norms, a line drawn from the baseline data point to the anticipated end of instruction.

Americans with Disabilities Act (ADA):   Civil rights legislation for persons with disabilities ensuring nondiscrimination in a broad range of activities.

Amniocentesis: A medical procedure that allows examination of the amniotic fluid around the fetus; sometimes recommended to determine the presence of abnormality.

Androgen: A hormone that is responsible for controlling the development of male characteristics.

Anoxia: Deprivation of oxygen; can cause brain injury.

Anxiety disorder: A disorder characterized by anxiety, fearfulness, and avoidance of ordinary activities because of anxiety or fear.

Aphonia: Loss of voice.

Applied behavior analysis (ABA):   Highly structured approach that focuses on teaching functional skills and continuous assessment of progress; grounded in behavioral learning theory.

Apraxia: The inability to plan and coordinate speech.

Aqueous humor: A watery substance between the cornea and lens of the eye.

Asperger syndrome: One of five autism spectrum disorders; a milder form of autism without significant impairments in language and cognition; characterized by primary problems in social interaction.

Assistance card: A relatively small card containing a message that alerts the public that the user is deaf-blind and needs assistance in crossing the street.

Asthma: A lung disease characterized by episodic difficulty in breathing, particularly exhaling, due to inflammation obstruction of the air passages.

Astigmatism: Blurred vision caused by an irregular cornea or lens.

Atonic: Lack of muscle tone; floppiness.

Atresia: Absence or closure of a part of the body that is normally open.

Attention deficit hyperactivity disorder (ADHD):   A condition characterized by severe problems of inattention, hyperactivity, and/or impulsivity; often found in people with learning disabilities.

Audiologist: An individual trained in audiology, the science dealing with hearing impairments, their detection, and remediation.

Audiometric zero: The lowest level at which people with normal hearing can hear.

Auditory-oral approach: A method of teaching communication to people who are deaf that stresses the use of visual cues, such as speechreading and cued speech.

Auditory-verbal approach: Part of the oral approach to teaching students who have hearing impairment; stresses teaching the person to use his or her remaining hearing as much as possible; heavy emphasis on use of amplification; heavy emphasis on teaching speech.

Augmentative and alternative communication (AAC): Alternative forms of communication that do not use the oral sounds of speech or that augment the use of speech.

Auricle: The visible part of the ear, composed of cartilage; collects the sounds and funnels them via the external auditory canal to the eardrum.

Autism savant syndrome: A condition in which the individual displays behaviors characteristic of autism spectrum disorder but also has remarkable skills or talents (e.g., musical, artistic talents), which often involve preoccupation with memorization of facts.

Autism spectrum disorders (ASD): A disability wherein symptoms fall on a continuum from relatively mild to severe; DSM-5 divides them into two general domains: "social communication impairment" and "repetitive/restricted behaviors."

Autistic regression: Circumstances whereby a child develops normally but then loses some speech and social skills; usually occurs between 1 and 3 years old; cause unknown.

B

Basal ganglia: A set of structures within the brain that include the caudate, globus pallidus, and putamen, the first two being abnormal in people with ADHD; generally responsible for the coordination and control of movement.

Baseline data point: Used in CBM; the beginning score gathered before an intervention begins, e.g., the number of correct words per minute that a student reads before receiving a fluency intervention.

Behavior management: Strategies and techniques used to increase desirable behavior and decrease undesirable behavior. May be applied in the classroom, home, or other environment.

Behavior modification: Systematic control of environmental events, especially of consequences, to produce specific changes in observable responses. May include reinforcement, punishment, modeling, self-instruction, desensitization, guided practice, or any other technique for strengthening or eliminating a particular response.

Behavioral inhibition: The ability to stop an intended response, to stop an ongoing response, to guard an ongoing response from interruption, and to refrain from responding immediately; allows executive functions to occur; delayed or impaired in those with ADHD.

Behavioral parent training (BPT): Parent interventions that concentrate on training parents to use behavioral principles to modify their child's difficult behavior.

Behavioral phenotype: A collection of behaviors, including cognitive, language, and social behaviors as well as psychopathological symptoms, that tend to occur together in people with a specific genetic syndrome.

Bicultural-bilingual approach: An approach for teaching students with hearing impairment that stresses teaching American Sign Language as a first language and English as a second language and promotes the teaching of Deaf culture.

Braille: A system in which raised dots allow people who are blind to read with their fingertips; each quadrangular cell contains from one to six dots, the arrangement of which denotes different letters and symbols.

Braille bills: Legislation passed in several states to make braille more available to students with visual impairment; specific provisions vary from state to state, but major advocates have lobbied for (1) making braille available if parents want it, and (2) ensuring that teachers of students with visual impairment are proficient in braille.

Braille notetakers: Portable devices that can be used to take notes in braille, which are then converted to speech, braille, or text.

C

Cataracts: A condition caused by clouding of the lens of the eye; affects color vision and distance vision.

Catheterization: Insertion of a tube into an organ of the body to inject a fluid or to withdraw a fluid, such as urine from the bladder.

Center-based program: A program implemented primarily in a school or center, not in the student's home.

Central coherence: The inclination to bring meaning to stimuli by conceptualizing it as a whole; thought to be weak in people with ASD.

Cerebellum: An organ at the base of the brain responsible for coordination and movement; site of abnormal development in persons with ADHD.

Cerebral palsy (CP): A condition characterized by paralysis, weakness, lack of coordination, and/or other motor dysfunction; caused by damage to the brain before it has matured.

CHARGE syndrome: A genetic syndrome resulting in deaf-blindness; characterized by physical anomalies, often including coloboma (abnormalities of the pupil, retina, and/or optic nerve), cranial nerves, heart defects, atresia (absence or closure) of the chonae (air passages from nose to throat), retardation in growth and mental development, genital abnormalities, ear malformation and/or hearing loss.

Choanae: Air passages from the nose to the throat.

Choreoathetoid: Characterized by involuntary movements and difficulty with balance; associated with choreoathetoid cerebral palsy.

Chorionic villus sampling (CVS): A method of testing the unborn fetus for a variety of chromosomal abnormalities, such as Down syndrome; a small amount of tissue from the chorion (a membrane that eventually helps form the placenta) is extracted and tested; can be done earlier than amniocentesis but the risk of miscarriage is slightly higher.

Chromosomal disorder: Any of several syndromes resulting from abnormal or damaged chromosome(s); can result in intellectual disabilities.

Chromosome: A rod-shaped entity in the nucleus of the cell; contains genes, which convey hereditary characteristics; each cell in the human body contains 23 pairs of chromosomes.

Chronic: A long-lasting condition; not temporary.

Chronic traumatic encephalopathy (CTE): A degenerative brain disease caused by repeated brain trauma, some of which might not been severe enough symptomatically to diagnose; symptoms can include early dementia, depression, risk of suicide, deficits in working memory.

Chronological age: Refers to how old a person is; used in comparison to mental age to determine IQ. IQ = (mental age ÷ chronological age) × 100.

Classwide peer tutoring (CWPT): An instructional procedure in which all students in the class are involved in tutoring and being tutored by classmates on specific skills as directed by their teacher.

Cleft palate: A condition in which there is a rift or split in the upper part of the oral cavity; may include the upper lip (cleft lip).

Clinical history: A history both from the patient and from a close contact such as parents, spouse, or significant other.

Closed head injury: Damage to the brain that occurs without penetration of the skull; might be caused by a blow to the head or violent shaking by an adult.

Coaching: A technique whereby a friend or therapist offers encouragement and support for a person with ADHD.

Cochlea: A snail-shaped organ that lies below the vestibular mechanism in the inner ear; its parts convert the sounds coming from the middle ear into electrical signals that are transmitted to the brain.

Cochlear implantation: A surgical procedure that allows people who are deaf to hear some environmental sounds; an external coil fitted on the skin by the ear picks up sound from a microphone worn by the person and transmits it to an internal coil implanted in the bone behind the ear, which carries it to an electrode implanted in the cochlea of the inner ear.

Cognition: The ability to solve problems and use strategies; an area of difficulty for many persons with learning disabilities.

Cognitive mapping: A nonsequential way of conceptualizing the spatial environment that allows a person who has visual impairment to know where several points in the environment are simultaneously; allows for better mobility than does a strictly sequential conceptualization of the environment.

Cognitive training: A group of training procedures designed to change thoughts or thought patterns.

Collaborative consultation: An approach in which a special educator and a general educator collaborate to come up with teaching strategies for a student with disabilities. The relationship between the two professionals is based on the premises of shared responsibility and equal authority.

Coloboma: A condition of the eye in which the pupil is abnormally shaped and/or there are abnormalities of the retina or optic nerve; can result in loss of visual acuity and extreme sensitivity to light.

Common Core State Standards (CCSS): A common set of standards in English language arts and Math for K–12.

Common Core State Standards Initiative: A movement aimed at having all states accept a common set of standards for states for K–12; led by The National Governors Association (NGA) and the Council of Chief State School Officers (CCSSO).

Communication: The process of sharing information.

Communication disorders: Impairments in the ability to use speech or language to communicate.

Communicative function: Acts of communication, such as requesting, rejecting, commenting, arguing, and reasoning.

Communicative intent: The need to communicate for social reasons; thought to be lacking in most children with autism.

Community residential facility (CRF): A place, usually a group home, in an urban or residential neighborhood where about 3 to 10 adults with intellectual disabilities live under supervision.

Comorbidity: Co-occurrence of two or more conditions in the same individual.

Competitive employment: A workplace that provides employment that pays at least minimum wage and in which most workers do not have disabilities.

Comprehension monitoring: The ability to keep track of one's own comprehension of reading material and to make adjustments to comprehend better while reading; often deficient in students with learning disabilities.

Conduct disorder: A disorder characterized by overt, aggressive, disruptive behavior or covert antisocial acts such as stealing, lying, and fire setting; may include both overt and covert acts.

Conductive hearing impairment: A hearing impairment, usually mild, resulting from malfunctioning along the conductive pathway of the ear (i.e., the outer or middle ear).

Congenital: A characteristic or condition that is present at birth; might or might not be due to genetic factors.

Congenital anomaly: An irregularity (anomaly) that is present at birth; might or might not be due to genetic factors.

Congenital cytomegalovirus (CMV): The most frequently occurring viral infection in newborns; can result in a variety of disabilities, especially hearing impairment.

Congenitally deaf: Deafness that is present at birth; can be caused by genetic factors, by injuries during fetal development, or by injuries occurring at birth.

Connexin-26 gene: A gene, the mutation of which causes deafness; the leading cause of congenital deafness in children.

Constant time delay: An instructional procedure whereby the teacher makes a request while simultaneously prompting the student and then over several occasions makes the same request and waits a constant period of time before prompting; often used with students with intellectual disabilities.

Content enhancement: The modification of curriculum materials to make them more salient or prominent, e.g., graphic organizers and mnemonics.

Contingency-based self-management: Rewards based on use of self-management techniques.

Continuous performance test (CPT): A test measuring a person's ability to sustain attention to rapidly presented stimuli; can help in the diagnosis of ADHD.

Cooperative learning: A teaching approach in which the teacher places students with heterogeneous abilities (for example, some might have disabilities) together to work on assignments.

Cooperative teaching: An approach in which general educators and special educators teach together in the general classroom; it helps the special educator know the context of the general education classroom better.

Coping skills interventions (CSI): Parent interventions that concentrate on training parents to use strategies to cope with their responses to their child's difficult behavior.

Cornea: A transparent cover in front of the iris and pupil in the eye; responsible for most of the refraction of light rays in focusing on an object.

Cortical visual impairment (CVI): A poorly understood childhood condition that apparently involves dysfunction in the visual cortex; characterized by large day-to-day variations in visual ability.

Co-teaching: A special educator working side-by-side with a general educator in a classroom, both teachers providing instruction to the group.

Cranial nerves: Twelve pairs of nerves that connect the brain with various muscles and glands in the body.

Creativity: The ability to express novel and useful ideas, to sense and elucidate new and important relationships, and to ask previously unthought of, but crucial, questions.

Cued speech: A method to aid speechreading in people with hearing impairment; the speaker uses hand shapes to represent sounds.

Curriculum-based language and communication assessment (CBLA): Curriculum-based assessment that focuses on speech, language, and communication skills needed to learn the school curriculum.

Curriculum-based measurement (CBM): A formative evaluation method designed to evaluate performance in the curriculum to which students are exposed; usually involves giving students a small sample of items from the curriculum in use in their schools; proponents argue that CBM is preferable to comparing students with national norms or using tests that do not reflect the curriculum content learned by the students.

Customized employment: Based on an assessment of the individual's strengths, weaknesses, and interests, the job matches the person's profile of interests and skills.

Cystic fibrosis (CF): An inherited disease affecting primarily the gastrointestinal (GI) tract and respiratory organs; characterized by thick, sticky mucous that often interferes with breathing or digestion.

D

Daily living skills: Skills required for living independently, such as dressing, toileting, bathing, cooking, and other typical daily activities of adults without disabilities.

Decibels: Units of relative loudness of sounds; zero decibels (0 dB) designates the point at which people with normal hearing can just detect sound.

Decoding: The ability to convert print to spoken language; dependent on phonemic awareness and understanding of the alphabetic principles; a significant problem for many people with reading disabilities.

Deinstitutionalization: A social movement starting in the 1960s whereby large numbers of persons with intellectual disabilities and/or mental illness are moved from large mental institutions into smaller community homes or into the homes of their families; recognized as a major catalyst for integrating persons with disabilities into society.

Deinstitutionalization movement: Advocates crusade for closing of large residential institutions for people with intellectual and mental disabilities; begun in 1950s and up through the 1970s.

Descriptive Video Service®: A service for use of people with visual impairment that provides audio narrative of key visual elements; available for several public television programs and some videos of movies.

Developmental apraxia: A disorder of speech or language involving problems in motor planning such that the child has difficulty in producing speech sounds and organizing words and word sounds for effective communication. The cause may be unknown.

Developmentally appropriate practice (DAP): Educational methods for young children that are compatible with their developmental levels and that meet their individual needs; coined by the National Association for the Education of Young Children.

Diabetic retinopathy: A condition resulting from interference with the blood supply to the retina; the fastest-growing cause of blindness.

Dialects: A variation of a language that differs from that standard language based on phonology, vocabulary, or grammar. Dialects may be distinct to members of a particular group (e.g., ethnic group, regional group).

Direct Instruction (DI): A method of teaching academics, especially reading and math; emphasizes drill and practice and immediate feedback; lessons are precisely sequenced, fast-paced, and well-rehearsed by the teacher.

Disability: A disability is an inability to do something as a result of a specific impairment.

Dopamine: A neurotransmitter, the levels of which may be abnormal in people with ADHD.

Down syndrome: A condition resulting from an abnormality with the 21st pair of chromosomes; the most common abnormality is a triplet rather than a pair (the condition sometimes referred to as trisomy 21); characterized by intellectual disability and such physical signs as slanted-appearing eyes, hypotonia, a single palmar crease, shortness, and a tendency toward obesity.

Due process hearing: A non-court proceeding held before an impartial hearing officer.

Dynamic assessments: An interactive assessment process that involves ongoing analysis of student learning in response to an intervention.

Dysarthria: A condition in which brain damage causes impaired control of the muscles used in articulation.

Dyscalculia: Specific learning disabilities in mathematics. Not all mathematics disabilities are alike; individuals with dyscalculia may have difficulty with number sense, math computation, problem solving, etc.

Dysfluencies: Hesitations, repetitions, and other disruptions of normal speech flow.

Dyslexia: A term for reading disabilities; used more often by those in the medical profession than those who are educators.

E

Early expressive language delay (EELD): A significant lag in the development of expressive language that is apparent by age 2.

Early intensive behavioral intervention (EIBI): A program anchored in the applied behavioral analysis tradition that emphasizes the role of parents as interventionists, and requires considerable time commitments from therapists and parents in implementing very structured training on discrete skills. Some researchers have found it to be effective in improving language and functional skills in many, although not all, young children with autism.

Early intervening services: IDEA allows for academic or behavioral supports or related services for students in grades K-12—with an emphasis on K-3—to be provided for students who have not yet been identified as having a disability but need these supports to be successful in the general education curriculum. No more than 15% of IDEA funds may be used for these efforts.

Echolalia: The parroting repetition of words or phrases either immediately after they are heard or later; often observed in individuals with autism spectrum disorders.

Echolocation: Ability to detect objects in the environment by auditory echoes (sound waves) created by footsteps, tapping a cane, clicking one's tongue. Similar to sonar, the echoes can be used to interpret the location and size of objects. This ability is used by bats and porpoises, and can be developed in humans.

Education for All Handicapped Children Act: Also known as Public Law 94-142, which became law in 1975 and is now known as the Individuals with Disabilities Education Act (IDEA). Retitled in 1990 and reauthorized in 1997 and 2004.

Electroencephalography (EEG): A method of measuring the electrical activity of the brain.

Emotional disturbance: The term used in federal special education laws and regulations for problematic behavior that interferes with education; the federal term used to indicate the problems of emotionally disturbed students.

Emotional or behavioral disorders: The terminology proposed by the National Mental Health and Special Education Coalition to replace the federal terminology "emotional disturbance."

Encephalitis: An inflammation of the brain; can affect the child's mental development adversely.

Encopresis: Bowel incontinence; soiling oneself.

Enrichment: An approach in which additional learning experiences are provided for students with special gifts or talents while the students remain in the grade levels appropriate for their chronological ages.

Enuresis: Urinary incontinence; wetting oneself.

Epilepsy: A pattern of repeated seizures.

Episodic: Occurring in episodes; a temporary condition that will pass but may recur.

Event-related potentials: The brain's response resulting from a specific sensory, cognitive, or motor event.

Exceptionality group: People who share a collection of specific abilities or disabilities.

Executive functioning: The ability to regulate one's behavior through working memory, inner speech, control of emotions and arousal levels, and analysis of problems and communication of problem solutions to others; delayed or impaired in people with ADHD.

Expected growth norms: Used with CBM; the rate at which the average student is expected to learn given typical instruction.

Expressive language: Encoding or sending messages in communication.

External otitis: An infection of the skin of the external auditory canal; also called swimmer's ear.

Externalizing behavior: Acting-out behavior; aggressive or disruptive behavior that is observable as behavior directed toward others.

Extreme male brain: A description sometimes applied to persons with autism based on some researchers' claims that high levels of androgen (a hormone that is responsible for controlling the development of male characteristics) in amniotic fluid are more likely to result in autistic traits in children.

F

Familiality studies: A method of determining the degree to which a given condition is inherited; looks at the prevalence of the condition in relatives of the person with the condition.

Family activity settings: Activities that families routinely engage in, such as mealtimes and seasonal celebrations; can be focal points for the implementation of PBSs.

Family-centered model: A consumer-driven model that encourages the family to make its own decisions with respect to services while mobilizing resources and supports for the family's goals.

Family characteristics: A component of the Turnbulls' family systems model; includes type and severity of the disability as well as such things as size, cultural background, and socioeconomic background of the family.

Family functions: A component of the Turnbulls' family systems model; includes such things as economic, daily care, social, medical, and educational needs.

Family interaction: A component of the Turnbulls' family systems model; refers to how cohesive and adaptable the family is.

Family life cycle: A component of the Turnbulls' family systems model; consists of birth and early childhood, childhood, adolescence, and adulthood.

Family systems theory: Stresses that the individual's behavior is best understood in the context of the family and the family's behavior is best understood in the context of other social systems.

Fetal alcohol spectrum disorders (FASD): A range of disorders in children whose mothers consumed large quantities of alcohol during pregnancy.

Fetal alcohol spectrum (FAS): Abnormalities associated with the mother's drinking alcohol during pregnancy; defects range from mild to severe, including growth retardation, brain damage, intellectual disability, hyperactivity, anomalies of the face, and heart failure; also called *alcohol embryopathy*.

Fingerspelling: Spelling the English alphabet by various finger positions on one hand.

Fragile X syndrome: A condition in which the bottom of the X chromosome in the twenty-third pair of chromosomes is pinched off; can result in a number of physical anomalies as well as intellectual disabilities; occurs more often in males than females; thought to be the most common hereditary cause of intellectual disabilities.

Free appropriate public education (FAPE): The primary intent of federal special education law, that the education of all children with disabilities will in all cases be free of cost to parents (i.e., at public expense) and appropriate for the particular student.

Frontal lobes: Two lobes located in the front of the brain; responsible for executive functions; site of abnormal development in people with ADHD.

Functional academics: Teaching academics, such as reading and math, in the context of daily living skills; goal is for student to learn skills to function independently, such as reading labels on goods at stores, using a computer to fill out job applications; used most often with students who have intellectual disabilities.

Functional behavioral assessment (FBA): Evaluation that consists of finding out the consequences (what purpose the behavior serves), antecedents (what triggers the behavior), and setting events (contextual factors) that maintain inappropriate behaviors.

Functional magnetic resonance imaging (fMRI): An adaptation of the MRI used to detect changes in the brain while it is in an active state; unlike a PET scan, it does not involve using radioactive materials.

Functional magnetic resonance spectroscopy (fMRS): An adaptation of the MRI used to detect changes in the brain while it is in an active state; unlike a PET scan, it does not involve using radioactive materials.

Functional vision assessment: An appraisal of an individual's use of vision in everyday situations.

G

Genius: A word sometimes used to indicate a particular aptitude or capacity in any area; rare intellectual powers.

Giftedness: Refers to cognitive (intellectual) superiority, creativity, and motivation of sufficient magnitude to set the child apart from the vast majority of age peers and make it possible for the child to contribute something of particular value to society.

Glaucoma: A condition often, but not always, due to excessive pressure in the eyeball; the cause is unknown; if untreated, blindness results.

Graphic organizers: A way of enhancing content visual displays using lines, circles, and boxes to organize information.

Guardianship: A legal term that gives a person the authority to make decisions for another person; can be full, limited, or temporary; applies in cases of parents who have children who have severe cognitive disabilities.

Gullibility: An inclination to believe highly questionable statements or claims, despite scanty evidence; considered by some to be a key characteristic of persons with intellectual disabilities, especially those who have mild intellectual disabilities.

H

Handicap: A handicap is a disadvantage imposed on an individual.

Hand-over-hand guidance: A tactile learning strategy for persons who are deaf-blind; the teacher places his or her hands over those of the person who is deaf-blind and guides them to explore objects.

Hand-under-hand guidance: A tactile learning strategy for persons who are deaf-blind; the teacher places his or her hands underneath part of the student's hand or hands while the child is exploring objects.

Heat maps: A graphic map using different colors to represent a distribution of variables (e.g., people from different ethnic groups, religious affiliations; species of birds, mammals, etc.).

Heritability studies: A method of determining the degree to which a condition is inherited; a comparison of the prevalence of a condition in identical (i.e., monozygotic, from the same egg) twins versus fraternal (i.e., dizygotic, from two eggs) twins.

Herpes simplex: A viral disease that can cause cold sores or fever blisters; if it affects the genitals and is contracted by the mother-to-be in the later stages of fetal development, it can cause mental subnormality in the child.

Hertz (Hz): A unit of measurement of the frequency of sound; refers to the highness or lowness of a sound.

Hidden curriculum: The dos and don'ts of social interactions that most people learn incidentally or with little instruction but that remain hidden for those with Asperger syndrome.

History: A patient's "story" of his or her functioning in life with respect to strengths and weaknesses; considered crucial by many physicians in the diagnosis of ADHD.

Homophenes: Sounds that are different but that look the same with regard to movements of the face and lips (i.e., visible articulatory patterns).

Human immunodeficiency virus (HIV): The virus that leads to AIDS; a type of retrovirus that gradually disables the body's immune system, eventually leading to AIDS. The virus has been detected in the bloodstream of a person who is said to be "HIV positive."

Hydrocephalus: A condition characterized by enlargement of the head because of excessive pressure of the cerebrospinal fluid.

Hyperactive child syndrome: A term used to refer to children who exhibit inattention, impulsivity, and/or hyperactivity; popular in the 1960s and 1970s.

Hyperopia: Farsightedness; vision for near objects is affected; usually results when the eyeball is too short.

I

In vitro fertilization: The procedure of removing eggs from the mother, fertilizing them with the father's sperm in a laboratory, then returning them to the mother's uterus; used to help infertile couples conceive.

Inborn errors of metabolism: Deficiencies in enzymes used to metabolize basic substances in the body, such as amino acids, carbohydrates, vitamins, or trace elements; can sometimes result in intellectual disabilities; PKU is an example.

Inclusion: Mainstreaming; the idea of placing students with disabilities in general education classes and other school activities.

Incus: The anvil-shaped bone in the ossicular chain of the middle ear.

Individualized education program (IEP): IDEA requires an IEP to be drawn up by the educational team for each exceptional child; the IEP must include a statement of present educational performance, instructional goals, educational services to be provided, and criteria and procedures for determining that the instructional objectives are being met.

Individualized family service plan (IFSP): A plan mandated by PL 99-457 to provide services for young children with disabilities (under three years of age) and their families; drawn up by professionals and parents; similar to an IEP for older children.

Individuals with Disabilities Education Act (IDEA): The Individuals with Disabilities Education Act was enacted in 1990 and reauthorized in 1997 and 2004; it replaced PL 94-142, enacted in 1975. This federal law requires that to receive funds under the act, every school system in the nation must provide a free, appropriate public education for every child between the ages of three and twenty-one, regardless of how or how seriously he or she may be disabled.

Individuals with Disabilities Education Improvement Act (IDEIA): The Individuals with Disabilities Education Act is a federal law that guarantees services to individuals with disabilities. That law was reauthorized in 2004 and titled at that time the Individuals with Disabilities Education Improvement Act.

Informal reading inventory (IRI): A method of assessing reading in which the teacher has the student read progressively more difficult series of word lists and passages; the teacher notes the difficulty level of the material read and the types of errors the student makes.

Insight: The ability to separate and/or combine various pieces of information in new, creative, and useful ways.

Intellectual disabilities: The newer term for "mental retardation"; a disability in intelligence and adaptive behavior.

Interim alternative educational setting (IAES): A temporary placement outside general education for students whose behavior is extremely problematic, but in which their education is continued.

Internalizing behavior: Acting-in behavior; anxiety, fearfulness, withdrawal, and other indications of an individual's mood or internal state.

In vitro fertilization: A method of promoting pregnancy; a procedure whereby a woman's egg or eggs are taken from her ovaries, and male sperm are placed with the egg(s) in the laboratory.

IQ–achievement discrepancy: Academic performance markedly lower than would be expected on the basis of a student's intellectual ability.

Iris: The colored portion of the eye; contracts or expands, depending on the amount of light striking it.

Itinerant teacher services: Services for students who have visual impairment in which the special education teacher visits several different schools to work with students and their general education teachers; the students attend their local schools and remain in general education classrooms.

J

Job coach: A person who assists adult workers with disabilities (especially those with intellectual disabilities), providing vocational assessment, instruction, overall planning, and interaction assistance with employers, family, and related government and service agencies.

Joint attention: The process by which one person alerts another to a stimulus via nonverbal means, such as gazing or pointing.

Juvenile rheumatoid arthritis: A systemic disease with major symptoms involving the muscles and joints.

K

Kurzweil 1000: A computerized device that converts print into speech for persons with visual impairment; the user places the printed material over a scanner that then reads the material aloud by means of an electronic voice.

L

Language: An arbitrary code or system of symbols to communicate meaning.

Language disorders: Oral communication that involves a lag in the ability to understand and express ideas, putting linguistic skill behind an individual's development in other areas, such as motor, cognitive, or social development.

Language-based reading impairment: A reading problem that is based on a language problem.

Large-print books: Books having a font-size that is larger than the usual 10-point type; a popular size for large print books is 18-point type.

Larynx: The structure in the throat containing the vocal apparatus (vocal cords); laryngitis is a temporary loss of voice caused by inflammation of the larynx.

Learned helplessness: A motivational term referring to a condition in which a person believes that no matter how hard he or she tries, failure will result.

Least restrictive environment (LRE): A legal term referring to the fact that exceptional children must be educated in as normal an environment as possible.

Left temporal lobe: An area on the left side of the brain; neuroimaging studies indicate it is responsible for speech, language, and reading abilities and is dysfunctional in persons with reading disabilities.

Legally blind: A person who has visual acuity of 20/200 or less in the better eye even with correction (e.g., eyeglasses) or has a field of vision so narrow that its widest diameter subtends an angular distance no greater than 20 degrees.

Lens: A structure that refines and changes the focus of the light rays passing through the eye.

Literary braille: Braille symbols used for most writing situations.

Locus of control: A motivational term referring to how people explain their successes or failures; people with an internal locus of control believe that they are the reason for success or failure, whereas people with an external locus of control believe that outside forces influence how they perform.

Long cane: A mobility aid used by individuals with visual impairment, who sweep it in a wide arc in front of them; proper use requires considerable training; the mobility aid of choice for most travelers who are blind.

Low birth weight (LBW): Babies who are born weighing less than 5.5 pounds; usually premature; at risk for behavioral and medical conditions, such as intellectual disabilities.

Low vision: A term used by educators to refer to individuals whose visual impairment is not so severe that they are unable to read print of any kind; they may read large or regular print, and they may need some kind of magnification.

M

Magnetic resonance imaging (MRI): A neuroimaging technique whereby radio waves are used to produce cross-sectional images of the brain; used to pinpoint areas of the brain that are dysfunctional.

Magnifying devices: Often recommended for people with low vision; can be for close vision (e.g., handheld magnifier) or distance vision (e.g., monocular telescope or binocular telescope mounted on eyeglass frames).

Malleus: The hammer-shaped bone in the ossicular chain of the middle ear.

Manifestation determination: Determination that a student's misbehavior is or is not a manifestation of a disability.

Manual alphabet: Letters of the alphabet, each of which is represented by a different hand shape.

Maternal serum screening (MSS): A method of screening the fetus for developmental disabilities such as Down syndrome or spina bifida; a blood sample is taken from the mother and analyzed; if it is positive, a more accurate test such as amniocentesis or CVS is usually recommended.

Meningitis: A bacterial or viral infection of the linings of the brain or spinal cord; can cause a number of disabilities.

Mental age: Age level at which a person performs on an IQ test; used in comparison to chronological age to determine IQ. IQ = (mental age ÷ chronological age) × 100.

Metacognition: One's understanding of the strategies available for learning a task and the regulatory mechanisms needed to complete the task.

Microcephalus: A condition causing development of a small, conical-shaped head; proper development of the brain is prevented, resulting in intellectual disabilities.

Mild mental retardation or intellectual disability: A classification used to specify an individual whose IQ is approximately 50–70.

Milieu teaching: A naturalistic approach to language intervention in which the goal is to teach functional language skills in a natural environment.

Mind-wandering: Difficulty in keeping a train of thought because of thinking about something other than what one is doing; sometimes accompanied by one's inability to recall what topic(s) he or she was thinking about.

Minimal brain injury: A term used to describe a child who shows behavioral but not neurological signs of brain injury; the term is not as popular as it once was, primarily because of its lack of diagnostic utility (i.e., some children who learn normally show signs indicative of minimal brain injury); a term used to refer to children who exhibit inattention, impulsivity, and/or hyperactivity; popular in the 1950s and 1960s.

Mixed hearing impairment: A hearing impairment resulting from a combination of conductive and sensorineural hearing impairments.

Mnemonics: The use of memory-enhancing cues to help one remember something; techniques that aid memory, such as using rhymes, songs, or visual images to remember information.

Moderate mental retardation or intellectual disabilities: A classification used to specify an individual whose IQ is approximately 35–50.

Modifications: Changes made in instruction or assessment to make it possible for a student with a disability to respond more normally.

Molecular genetics: Study of the structure and function of genes at the molecular level.

Momentary time sampling: An interval recording procedure used to capture a representative sample of a target behavior over a specified period of time.

Morphology: The study within psycholinguistics of word formation; how adding or deleting parts of words changes their meaning.

Motor-speech disorder: Loss or impairment of the ability to understand or formulate language because of accident or illness.

Multicultural education: Aims to change educational institutions and curricula so they will provide equal educational opportunities to students regardless of their gender, social class, ethnicity, race, disability, or other cultural identity.

Multidisciplinary team: A team of individuals from different disciplines, e.g., general education, special education, school psychology, speech/language pathology, that typically decides whether a struggling student should be referred for special education evaluation or whether and what interventions should be tried to see if the student improves.

Muscular dystrophy: A hereditary disease characterized by progressive weakness caused by degeneration of muscle fibers.

Mute: Possessing no, or almost no, language; characteristic of many with autism.

Myopia: Nearsightedness; vision for distant objects is affected; usually results when eyeball is too long.

N

Native-language emphasis: An approach to teaching language-minority pupils in which the student's native language is used for most of the day and English is taught as a separate subject.

Natural supports: Resources in person's environment that can be used for support, such as friends, family, co-workers.

Nemeth Code: Braille symbols used for mathematics and science.

Neonatal intensive care unit (NICU): A special unit in a hospital designed to provide around-the-clock monitoring and care of newborns who have severe physical problems; staffed by professionals from several disciplines, such as nursing, social work, occupational therapy, respiratory therapy, and medicine; similar to an intensive care unit for older children and adults.

Neural tube defect: Any defect involving the spinal cord.

Neuronal underconnectivity: Deficiency in communication among neurons (cells) in the brain; considered a major problem in persons with autism spectrum disorders.

Neurotoxin: A substance known to damage nerve cells.

Neurotransmitters: Chemicals involved in sending messages between neurons in the brain.

Neurotypicals: A term coined by people with Asperger syndrome to describe people who do not have neurological disabilities.

NFB-Newsline®: A free service available through the National Federation of the Blind, allows individuals to access magazines and newspapers 24 hours a day from any touchtone telephone.

Night blindness: A condition characterized by problems in seeing at low levels of illumination; often caused by retinitis pigmentosa.

Nonverbal learning disabilities: A term used to refer to individuals who have a cluster of disabilities in social interaction, math, visual-spatial tasks, and tactual tasks.

Norepinephrine: A neurotransmitter, the levels of which may be abnormal in people with ADHD.

Nuchal translucency ultrasound: A method of screening for Down syndrome; fluid from behind the fetus's neck and protein from the mother's blood are analyzed.

Nystagmus: A condition in which there are rapid involuntary movements of the eyes; sometimes indicates a brain malfunction and/or inner-ear problems.

O

Obstacle sense: A skill possessed by some people who are blind, whereby they can detect the presence of obstacles in their environments; research has shown that it is not an indication of an extra sense, as popularly thought; it is the result of learning to detect subtle changes in the pitches of high-frequency echoes.

Occipital lobes: An area in the posterior portion of the brain, largely devoted to visual perceptual processing; deficiencies in communication with the frontal lobes are implicated in autism spectrum disorder.

Open head injury: A brain injury in which there is an open wound in the head, such as a gunshot wound or penetration of the head by an object, resulting in damage to brain tissue.

Optic nerve: The nerve at the back of the eye, which sends visual information back to the brain.

Optic nerve hypoplasia (ONH): A condition resulting in underdevelopment of the optic nerve; often accompanied by brain abnormalities, which can result in other problems (e.g., speech and/or cognitive disabilities); one of the most common causes of childhood blindness.

Oralism–manualism debate: The controversy over whether the goal of instruction for students who are deaf should be to teach them to speak or to teach them to use sign language.

Orientation and mobility (O & M) skills: The ability to have a sense of where one is in relation to other people, objects, and landmarks and to move through the environment.

Orthosis: A device designed to restore, partially or completely, a lost function of the body (e.g., a brace or crutch).

Ossicles: Three tiny bones (malleus, incus, and stapes) that together make possible an efficient transfer of sound waves from the eardrum to the oval window, which connects the middle ear to the inner ear.

Otitis media: Inflammation of the middle ear.

Otoacoustic emissions: Low-intensity sounds produced by the cochlea in response to auditory stimulation; used to screen hearing problems in infants and very young children.

Oval window: The link between the middle and inner ears.

P

Paradoxical effect of Ritalin: The now discredited belief that Ritalin, even though a stimulant, acts to subdue a person's behavior and that this effect of Ritalin is evident in people with ADHD but not in those without ADHD.

Paraplegia: A condition in which both legs are paralyzed.

Partial participation: An approach in which students with disabilities, while in the general education classroom, engage in the same activities as students without disabilities but on a reduced basis; the teacher adapts the activity to allow each student to participate as much as possible.

Peer-assisted learning strategies (PALS): Based on research-proven, best practices in reading, such as phonological awareness, decoding, and comprehension strategies. PALS involves the pairing of a higher performing student with a lower performing student, with the pairs then participating in highly structured tutoring sessions. The students take turns being the "coach" (tutor) and the "reader" (tutee).

Peer confederates: Peers who assist the teacher.

Peer tutoring: A method that can be used to integrate students with disabilities in general education classrooms, based on the notion that students can effectively tutor one another. The role of learner or teacher may be assigned to either the student with a disability or the student who does not have a disability.

Peer-mediated instruction: The deliberate use of a student's classroom peer(s) to assist in teaching an academic or social skill.

Perinatal: The time of birth.

Perkins Brailler: A system that makes it possible to write in braille; has six keys, one for each of the six dots of the cell, which leave an embossed print on the paper.

Perseveration: A tendency to repeatedly engage in the same behaviors; often found in people with brain injury, as well as those with ADHD.

Person-centered planning: A method of planning for people with disabilities that places the person and his family at the center of the planning process.

Pervasive Developmental Disorder not Otherwise Specified (PDD-NOS): One of five autism spectrum disorders; pervasive delay in development that does not fit into any of the other diagnostic categories.

Phenylketonuria (PKU): A metabolic genetic disorder caused by the inability of the body to convert phenylalanine to tyrosine; an accumulation of phenylalanine results in abnormal brain development.

Phonemes: Distinct sound elements that make up words.

Phonemic awareness: One's ability to understand that words are made up of sounds or phonemes.

Phonological awareness: The ability to understand that speech flow can be broken into smaller sound units such as words, syllables, and phonemes; lack of such awareness is generally thought to be the reason for the reading problems of many students with learning disabilities.

Phonological disorders: A disorder that occurs in children who are younger than 9 years old that results in the impaired ability to produce sounds in the child's own language.

Phonological recoding: Unraveling the individual sounds of a word and then blending them together to say the word.

Phonology: The study of how individual sounds make up words.

Pivotal response teaching (PRT): Based on the assumption that some skills are critical, or pivotal, in order for the individual to be able to function in other areas.

Positive behavior intervention plan (BIP): A plan for changing behavior with an emphasis on positive reinforcement (rewarding) procedures.

Positive behavioral intervention and support (PBIS): Systematic use of the science of behavior to find ways of supporting desirable behavior rather than punishing the undesirable behavior; positive reinforcement (rewarding) procedures that are intended to support a student's appropriate or desirable behavior.

Positive behavioral support (PBS): Positive reinforcement (rewarding) procedures intended to support a student's appropriate or desirable behavior.

Positron emission tomography (PET) scans: A computerized method for measuring bloodflow in the brain; during a cognitive task, a low amount of radioactive dye is injected in the brain; the dye collects in active neurons, indicating which areas of the brain are active.

Postlingual deafness: Deafness occurring after the development of speech and language.

Postnatal: The time after birth.

Practical intelligence: Ability to solve everyday problems.

Prader-Willi syndrome: Caused by inheriting from one's father a lack of genetic material on the fifteenth pair of chromosomes; leading genetic cause of obesity; degree of intellectual disabilities varies, but the majority fall within the mild intellectual disability range.

Pragmatics: The study within psycholinguistics of how people use language in social situations; emphasizes the functional use of language rather than the mechanics.

Precocity: Remarkable early development.

Prefrontal lobes: Two lobes located in the very front of the frontal lobes; responsible for executive functions; site of abnormal development in people with ADHD.

Prelingual deafness: Deafness that occurs before the development of spoken language, usually at birth.

Prelinguistic communication: Communication through gestures and noises before the child has learned oral language.

Prenatal: The time before birth.

Prereferral: The process of referring a child suspected of having a disability to a multidisciplinary team that decides whether the student should be referred for special education evaluation or whether adjustments in teaching should be tried first to see if the student improves.

Prereferral teams (PRTs): Teams made up of a variety of professionals, especially general and special educators, who work with general education teachers to come up with strategies for teaching difficult-to-teach children. Designed to influence general educators to take ownership of difficult-to-teach students and to minimize inappropriate referrals to special education.

Prevalence: The percentage of a population or number of individuals having a particular exceptionality.

Primary language disorder: A language disorder that has no known cause.

Profound mental retardation or intellectual disabilities: A classification used to specify an individual whose IQ is below approximately 20.

Progressive: A disease or condition that worsens over time and from which one seldom or never recovers with treatment.

Progressive time delay: An instructional procedure whereby the teacher makes a request while simultaneously prompting the student and then over several occasions gradually increases the latency between the request and the prompt; often used with students with intellectual disabilities.

Progress monitoring: Assessments are frequent, measures that teachers administer at regular intervals and that provide information on whether a student is learning as expected. These assessments may be given to a large number of students in a short period of time.

Prosody: Reading while using intonation and expression or emphasis to make the reading sound like spoken language.

Prosthesis: A device designed to replace, partially or completely, a part of the body (e.g., artificial teeth or limbs).

Psychoanalytic: Related to psychoanalysis, including the assumptions that emotional or behavior disorders result primarily from unconscious conflicts and that the most effective preventive actions and therapeutic interventions involve uncovering and understanding unconscious motivations.

Psychostimulants: Medications that activate dopamine levels in the frontal and prefrontal areas of the brain that control behavioral inhibition and executive functions; used to treat persons with ADHD.

Pupil: The contractile opening in the middle of the iris of the eye.

Pure-tone audiometry: A test whereby tones of various intensities and frequencies are presented to determine a person's hearing loss.

Q

Quadriplegia: A condition in which all four limbs are paralyzed.

R

Raised dome detectable warnings: Bumps in the pavement that are designed to alert people who are blind to unsafe areas.

Reading comprehension: The ability to understand what one has read.

Reading fluency: The ability to read effortlessly and smoothly; consists of the ability to read at a normal rate and with appropriate expression; influences one's reading comprehension.

Receptive language: Decoding or understanding messages in communication.

Reciprocal teaching: A cognitive teaching strategy whereby the student gradually assumes the role of co-instructor for brief periods; the teacher models four strategies for the students to use: (1) predicting, (2) questioning, (3) summarizing, and (4) clarifying; a method in which students and teachers are involved in a dialogue to facilitate learning.

Refraction: The bending of light rays as they pass through the structures (cornea, aqueous humor, pupil, lens, vitreous humor) of the eye.

Repeated readings: Students repeatedly (several times a week) read the same short passages aloud until they read at an appropriate pace with few or no errors.

Resonance: The quality of the sound imparted by the size, shape, and texture of the organs in the vocal tract.

Response-to-intervention (RTI) or response-to-treatment approach: A way of determining whether a student has a learning disability; increasingly intensive levels of instructional intervention are delivered, and if the student does not achieve, at some point, he or she is determined to have a learning disability or is referred for special education evaluation.

Retina: The back portion of the eye, containing nerve fibers connected to the optic nerve.

Retinitis pigmentosa: A hereditary condition resulting in degeneration of the retina; causes a narrowing of the field of vision and affects night vision.

Retinopathy of prematurity (ROP): A condition resulting from administration of an excessive concentration of oxygen at birth; causes scar tissue to form behind the lens of the eye.

Retrieval of information from long-term memory (RLTM): In contrast to short-term memory, which involves remembering something occurring just a few seconds ago, long-term memory involves remembering something longer ago; the length varies from one study to the next, from only about a minute to several decades.

Ritalin: The most commonly prescribed psychostimulant for ADHD; its generic name is methylphenidate.

Rubella (German measles): A serious viral disease, which, if it occurs during the first trimester of pregnancy, is likely to cause a deformity in the fetus.

S

Scaffolded instruction: Teachers provide assistance to students when they are first learning tasks and then gradually reduce it so that eventually students do the tasks independently.

Schizophrenia: According to the National Institute of Mental Health, a chronic and severe mental disorder that affects how a person thinks, feels, and behaves; people with schizophrenia may seem like they have lost touch with reality; symptoms usually start between the ages of 16 and 30.

Scoliosis: An abnormal curvature of the spine.

Screening instruments: Quick measures administered to determine who may need further assessment.

Screen reader: Software for computers that magnifies images on the screen and/or converts text on the screen to speech.

Secondary language disorder: A language disorder that is caused by another disorder or disability, such as intellectual disabilities, hearing impairment, or brain injury.

Seizure (convulsion): A sudden alteration of consciousness, usually accompanied by motor activity and/or sensory phenomena; caused by an abnormal discharge of electrical energy in the brain.

Self-determination: Having control over one's life, not having to rely on others for making choices about one's quality of life; develops over one's life span.

Self-injurious behavior (SIB): Behavior causing injury or mutilation of oneself, such as self-biting or head-banging; usually seen in individuals with severe and multiple disabilities.

Self-instruction: A type of cognitive training technique that requires individuals to talk aloud and then to themselves as they solve problems.

Self-monitoring: A type of cognitive training technique that requires individuals to keep track of their own behavior.

Self-regulation: Refers generally to a person's ability to regulate his or her own behavior (e.g., to employ strategies to help in a problem-solving situation); an area of difficulty for persons who have intellectual disabilities.

Self-stimulation: Any repetitive, stereotyped activity that seems only to provide sensory feedback.

Semantics: The study of the meanings attached to words and sentences.

Sensorineural hearing impairment: A hearing impairment, usually severe, resulting from malfunctioning of the inner ear.

Severe mental retardation or intellectual disabilities: A classification used to specify an individual whose IQ is approximately 20–35.

Sheltered workshop: A facility that provides a structured environment for people with disabilities in which they can learn skills; can be either a transitional placement or a permanent arrangement.

Sheltered-English approach: A method in which language-minority students are taught all their subjects in English at a level that is modified constantly according to individuals' needs.

Short-term memory (STM): The ability to recall information after a short period of time.

Sign language: A manual language used by people who are deaf to communicate; a true language with its own grammar.

Signing English systems: Used simultaneously with oral methods in the total communication approach to teaching students who are deaf; different from American Sign Language because the signs maintain the same word order as spoken English.

Simultaneous communication: The use of both manual and oral communication by people who are deaf.

Slate and stylus: A method of writing in braille in which the paper is held in a slate while a stylus is pressed through openings to make indentations in the paper.

Sleep apnea: Cessation of breathing while sleeping.

Smarter Balanced Assessment Consortium (SBAC): A collection of states that are developing a common assessment to accompany the Common Core State Standards.

Snellen chart: Used in determining visual acuity; consists of rows of letters or Es arranged in different positions; each row corresponds to the distance at which a normally sighted person can discriminate the letters; does not predict how accurately a child will be able to read print.

Social intelligence: One's ability to understand and interpret social interactions between people, such as whether someone is angry or happy; a component of adaptive behavior, which, in addition to IQ, is used to determine whether someone has intellectual disabilities.

Social support: Emotional, informational, or material aid provided to a person or a family; this informal means of aid can be very valuable in helping families of children with disabilities.

Spasticity: Characterized by muscle stiffness and problems in voluntary movement; associated with spastic cerebral palsy.

Special education: Special, individualized instruction provided according to federal, state, and local laws and designed to meet individual educational needs of a student with disabilities or giftedness or both; the profession of special education.

Specific language impairment (SLI): A language disorder with no identifiable cause; language disorder not attributable to hearing impairment, intellectual disabilities, brain dysfunction, or other plausible cause; also called specific language disability.

Speech: The formation and sequencing of oral language sounds during communication.

Speech audiometry: A technique that tests a person's detection and understanding of speech, rather than using pure tones to detect hearing loss.

Speech disorders: Oral communication that involves abnormal use of the vocal apparatus, is unintelligible, or is so inferior that it draws attention to itself and causes anxiety, feelings of inadequacy, or inappropriate behavior in the speaker.

Speech-language pathologist (SLP): Speech-language pathologists work with individuals who have disorders related to speech, language, communication, swallowing, voice, or fluency. SLPs may work in the heath care profession or in schools. SLPs assess, diagnose, and treat individuals with speech and language disorders.

Speech-reception threshold (SRT): The decibel level at which a person can understand speech.

Speechreading: A method that involves teaching children to use visual information from a number of sources to understand what is being said to them; more than just lipreading, which uses only visual clues arising from the movement of the mouth in speaking.

Spina bifida: A congenital midline defect resulting from failure of the bony spinal column to close completely during fetal development.

Stapes: The stirrup-shaped bone in the ossicular chain of the middle ear.

Stereotyped motor or verbal behaviors: Repetitive, ritualistic motor behaviors such as twirling, spinning objects, flapping the hands, and rocking, similar to those that are evident in some people who are blind.

Strabismus: A condition in which the eyes are directed inward (crossed eyes) or outward.

Strattera: A nonstimulant medication for ADHD; affects the neurotransmitter norepinephrine.

Strauss syndrome: Behaviors of distractibility, forced responsiveness to stimuli, and hyperactivity; based on the work of Alfred Strauss and Heinz Werner with children with intellectual disabilities.

Stuttering: Speech characterized by abnormal hesitations, prolongations, and repetitions; may be accompanied by grimaces, gestures, or other bodily movements indicative of a struggle to speak, anxiety, blocking of speech, or avoidance of speech.

Subculture: A culture that is associated with or part of a larger culture; a culture that is not the entire culture of a nation or other entity. Sometimes called "microculture," but a subculture is not necessarily small or a minority of a larger culture.

Summary of performance (SOP): Now required by federal law, schools must develop an SOP for each student with a disability as the student exits secondary school whether by graduating or exceeding the age of eligibility. SOPs are designed to provide a summary of relevant information, such as assessment reports; accommodations that have been provided; and recommendations for future accommodations, assistive technology, and support services for use in employment, training, or postsecondary schooling.

Supported competitive employment: A workplace where adults who have disabilities earn at least minimum wage and receive ongoing assistance from a specialist or job coach; the majority of workers in the workplace do not have disabilities.

Supported employment: A method of integrating people with disabilities who cannot work independently into competitive employment; includes use of an employment specialist, or job coach, who helps the person with a disability function on the job.

Supported living: An approach to living arrangements for those with disabilities and/or intellectual disabilities that stresses living in natural settings rather than institutions, big or small.

Supports: Resources and strategies that promote a person's development, education, interests, and personal well-being; critical to the AAIDD's conceptualization of intellectual disabilities.

Synaesthesia: Occurs when the stimulation of one sensory or cognitive system results in the stimulation of another sensory or cognitive system.

Syntax: The way words are joined together to structure meaningful sentences; grammar.

Syphilis: A venereal disease that can cause mental subnormality in a child, especially if it is contracted by the mother-to-be during the latter stages of fetal development.

Systematic instruction: Teaching that involves instructional prompts, consequences for performance, and transfer of stimulus control; often used with students with intellectual disabilities.

T

Tactile map: An embossed representation of the environment that people who are blind can use to orient themselves to their surroundings.

Talent: Ordinarily has been used to indicate a special ability, aptitude, or accomplishment.

Task analysis: The procedure of breaking down an academic task into its component parts for the purpose of instruction; a major feature of Direct Instruction.

Tetra-amelia: A birth anomaly in which all four limbs of the fetus or baby are missing.

Text telephone (TT): A device connected to a telephone by a special adapter; allows communication over the telephone between people who have hearing impairment and those with hearing; sometimes referred to as a TTY (teletype) or TTD (telecommunication device for the deaf).

Theory of mind (ToM): The ability to take another's perspective in a social exchange; the ability to infer another person's feelings, intentions, desires, etc.; impaired in those with ASD.

Tiered assignment: Assignments varying in difficulty but on a single topic.

Total communication approach: An approach for teaching students with hearing impairment that blends oral and manual techniques.

Touch cues: Tactual signals used to communicate with persons who are deaf-blind; can be used to signify a variety of messages.

Toxins: Poisons in the environment that can cause fetal malformations; can result in cognitive impairments.

Transition plan: A plan defined in a student's IEP that specifies the student's goals and services related to transitioning from high school to post-high school experiences. The Individuals with Disabilities Education Act requires that the IEP include the transition plan before the age of 16.

Transliteration: A method used by most sign language interpreters in which the signs maintain the same word order as that of spoken English; American Sign Language (ASL) is also used by some interpreters.

Traumatic brain injury (TBI): Injury to the brain (not including conditions present at birth, birth trauma, or degenerative diseases or conditions) resulting in total or partial disability or psychosocial maladjustment that affects educational performance; may affect cognition, language, memory, attention, reasoning, abstract thinking, judgment, problem solving, sensory or perceptual and motor disabilities, psychosocial behavior, physical functions, information processing, or speech.

Traveling notebook: A system of communication in which parents and professionals write messages to each other by way of a notebook or log that accompanies the child to and from school.

Trisomy 21: A type of Down syndrome in which the twenty-first chromosome is a triplet, making forty-seven, rather than the normal forty-six, chromosomes in all.

Tunnel vision: A condition characterized by problems in peripheral vision, or a narrowing of the field of vision.

Twice exceptional: Possession of both a disability and a special gift or talent.

Tympanic membrane (eardrum): The anatomical boundary between the outer and middle ears; the sound gathered in the outer ear vibrates here.

U

Unified English Braille: A combination of literary braille and braille codes for technical fields, such as the Nemeth Code for science and mathematics; not yet widely adopted.

Universal design: The design of new buildings, tools, and instructional programs to make them usable by the widest possible population of potential users.

Universal design for learning (UDL): Designing lessons that are appropriate for all learners.

Usher syndrome: An inherited syndrome resulting in hearing loss and retinitis pigmentosa, a progressive condition characterized by problems in seeing in low light and tunnel vision; there are three different types of Usher syndrome, differing with respect to when it occurs developmentally and the range of the major symptoms of hearing impairment, vision impairment, and balance problems.

V

Vestibular mechanism: Located in the upper portion of the inner ear; consists of three soft, semicircular canals filled with a fluid; sensitive to head movement, acceleration, and other movements related to balance.

Video relay service (VRS): A service, using a sign language interpreter, a video camera or computer, and an Internet connection, that allows persons who are deaf to communicate with those who are hearing.

Visual acuity: The ability to see fine details; usually measured with the Snellen chart.

Vitreous humor: A transparent, gelatinous substance that fills the eyeball between the retina and the lens of the eye.

Vocabulary base: The words that a person knows the definition of such that he or she can use each word appropriately in communicating.

Vyvanse: A stimulant that is sometimes prescribed to treat symptoms of attention deficit hyperactivity disorder in children.

W

Williams syndrome: A condition resulting from deletion of material in the seventh pair of chromosomes; often results in mild to moderate intellectual disabilities, heart defects, and elfin facial features; people affected often display surprising strengths in spoken language and sociability while having severe deficits in spatial organization, reading, writing, and math.

Working memory (WM): The ability to remember information while also performing other cognitive operations.

Wraparound service systems: Involve using not only educational services but also available community services (e.g., mental health, social welfare, juvenile justice, and so forth) in order to meet the individualized needs of children and their families.

Z

Zero tolerance: A school policy, supported by federal and state laws, that having possession of any weapon or drug on school property will automatically result in a given penalty (usually suspension or expulsion) regardless of the nature of the weapon or drug or any extenuating circumstances.

Zika virus: A virus caused mostly by the bite of an infected *Aedes* species mosquito; pregnant women, if infected, can pass the virus to their unborn fetus, which can result in various birth defects.

REFERENCES

CHAPTER 1

Bateman, B. D. (2007). Law and the conceptual foundations of special education practice. In J. B. Crockett, M. M. Gerber, & T. J. Landrum (Eds.), *Achieving the radical reform of special education: Essays in honor of James M. Kauffman* (pp. 95–114). Mahwah, NJ: Erlbaum.

Bateman, B. D. (2017). Individual education programs for children with disabilities. In J. M. Kauffman, D. P. Hallahan, & P. C. Pullen (Eds.), *Handbook of special education* (2nd ed., pp. 87–104). New York: Routledge.

Bateman, B. D., & Linden, M. A. (2006). *Better IEPs: How to develop legally correct and educationally useful programs* (4th ed.). Verona, WI: Attainment.

Board of Education of Hendrick Hudson v. Rowley, 484 US 176 (1982).

Crockett, J. B., & Kauffman, J. M. (1999). *The least restrictive environment: Its origins and interpretations in special education*. Mahwah, NJ: Erlbaum.

Crockett, J. B., & Kauffman, J. M. (2001). The concept of the least restrictive environment and learning disabilities: Least restrictive of what? Reflections on Cruickshank's 1977 guest editorial for the *Journal of Learning Disabilities*. In D. P. Hallahan & B. K. Keogh (Eds.), *Research and global perspectives in learning disabilities: Essays in honor of William M. Cruickshank* (pp. 147–166). Mahwah, NJ: Erlbaum.

Data Accountability Center. (2013). *Individuals with Disabilities Education Act (IDEA) Data Tables*. Retrieved from https://www.ideadata.org/TABLES35TH/B1-17.pdf.

Earley, P. (2006). *Crazy: A Father's search through America's mental health madness*. New York: Penguin.

Edens, E. L., Kasprow, W., Tsai, J., & Rosenheck, R. A. (2011). Association of substance use and VA service-connected disability benefits with risk of homelessness among veterans. *American Journal of Addiction, 20*, 412–419. doi:10.1111/j.1521-0391.2011.00166.x.

Endrew F. v. Douglas County School District, 580 1-16 (March 22, 2017).

Gelman, J. A., Pullen, P. L., & Kauffman, J. M. (2004). The meaning of highly qualified and a clear roadmap to accomplishment. *Exceptionality, 12*, 195–207. dio:10.1207/s15327035ex1204_2

Gerber, M. M. (2017). History. In J. M. Kauffman, D. P. Hallahan, & P. C. Pullen (Eds.), *Handbook of special education* (2nd ed., pp. 3–15). New York: Routledge.

Gladwell, M. (2008). *Outliers: The story of success*. New York: Little, Brown.

Goin, M. K. (2007, July 8). The wrong place to treat mental illness. *The Washington Post*, p. B7.

Holmes, M. S. (2004). *Fictions of affliction: Physical disability in Victorian culture*. Ann Arbor, MI: University of Michigan Press.

Huefner, D. S. (2006). *Getting comfortable with special education law: A framework for working with children with disabilities* (2nd ed.). Norwood, MA: Christopher Gordon.

Itard, J. M. G. (1962). *The wild boy of Aveyron*. (G. Humphrey & M. Humphrey, Trans.). Upper Saddle River, NJ: Pearson.

Kanner, L. (1964). *A history of the care and study of the mentally retarded*. Springfield, IL: Charles C. Thomas.

Kauffman, J. M. (2005). Waving to Ray Charles: Missing the meaning of disability. *Phi Delta Kappan, 86*(6), 520–521, 524.

Kauffman, J. M. (2008). 44: Special education. In T. L. Good (Ed.), *21st Century education: A reference handbook* (pp. 405–413). Thousand Oaks, CA: Sage.

Kauffman, J. M. (2010). *The tragicomedy of public education: Laughing, crying, thinking, fixing*. Verona, WI: Attainment.

Kauffman, J. M. (2014). How we prevent the prevention of emotional and behavioral difficulties in education. In P. Garner, J. M. Kauffman, & J. G. Elliott (Eds.), *The Sage handbook of emotional and behavioral difficulties* (2nd ed., pp. 505–516). London: Sage.

Kauffman, J. M., Anastasiou, D., Badar, J., Travers, T. C., & Wiley, A. L. (2016). Inclusive education moving forward. In J. P. Bakken & F. E. Obiakor (Eds.), *Advances in special education, Vol. 32—General and special education in an age of change: Roles of professionals involved* (pp. 153–177). Bingley, UK: Emerald.

Kauffman, J. M., & Brigham, F. J. (2009). *Working with troubled children*. Verona, WI: Attainment.

Kauffman, J. M., & Hallahan, D. P. (2005). *Special education: What it is and why we need it*. Boston: Allyn & Bacon.

Kauffman, J. M., & Hallahan, D. P. (2009). Parental choices and ethical dilemmas involving disabilities: Special education and the problem of deliberately chosen disabilities. *Exceptionality, 17*, 45–62. doi:10.1080/09362830802667835

Kauffman, J. M., Hallahan, D. P., & Pullen, P. C. (Eds.). (2017). *Handbook of special education* (2nd ed.). New York: Routledge.

Kauffman, J. M., & Hung, L. Y. (2009). Special education for intellectual disability: Current trends and perspectives. *Current Opinion in Psychiatry, 22*, 452–456. doi:10.1097/YCO.0b013e32832eb5c3

Kauffman, J. M., & Konold, T. R. (2007). Making sense in education: Pretense (including NCLB) and realities in rhetoric and policy about schools and schooling. *Exceptionality, 15*, 75–96. doi:10.1080/09362830701294151

Kauffman, J. M., & Landrum, T. J. (2006). *Children and youth with emotional and behavioral disorders: A history of their education*. Austin, TX: Pro-Ed.

Kauffman, J. M., & Landrum, T. J. (2009). Politics, civil rights, and disproportional identification of students with emotional and behavioral disorders. *Exceptionality*. doi:10.1080/09362830903231903

Kauffman, J. M., Mock, D. R., Tankersley, M., & Landrum, T. J. (2008). Effective service delivery models. In R. J. Morris & N. Mather (Eds.), *Evidence-based interventions for students with learning and behavioral challenges* (pp. 359–378). Mahwah, NJ: Erlbaum.

Landrigan, P. J., Lambertini, L., & Birnbaum, L. S. (2012). A research strategy to discover the environmental causes of autism and neurodevelopmental disabilities. *Environmental Health Perspectives, 120*, 258–260. doi:10.1289/ehp.1104285

Losure, Mary (2013). *Wild boy: The real life of the savage of Aveyron*. Somerville, MA: Candlewick Press.

MacMillan, D. L., & Forness, S. R. (1998). The role of IQ in special education placement decisions: Primary and determinative or peripheral and inconsequential? *Remedial and Special Education, 19*, 239–253.

Martin, E. W., Jr. (2013). *Breakthrough: Federal special education legislation 1965–1981*. Sarasota, FL: Bardolf.

Mercier, C., & Picard, S. (2011). Intellectual disability and homelessness. *Journal of Intellectual Disability Research, 55*, 441–449. doi:10.1111/j.1365-2788.2010.01366.x

Metzler, I. (2006). *Disability in medieval Europe: Thinking about physical impairment during the Middle Ages, c. 1100–1400*. New York: Routledge.

National Research Council. (2001). *Educating children with autism*. Washington, DC: National Academy Press.

Nomani, A. Q. (2007, April 29). My brother's battle—and mine. *The Washington Post*, p. B2.

Pinker, S. (2002). *The blank slate: The modern denial of human nature*. New York: Viking.

Powers, R. (2017). *No one cares about crazy people; The chaos and heartbreak of mental health in America*. New York: Hachette.

Pullen, P. C., & Hallahan, D. P. (2015). What is special education? In B. D. Bateman, J. W. Lloyd, & M. Tankersley, *Understanding special education issues: Who, where, what, when, how & why* (pp. 36–50). New York: Routledge.

Rauch, S. A., & Lanphear, B. P. (2012). Prevention of disability in children. *Future of Children, 22*, 193–217. doi:10.1353/foc.2012.0006

Rothstein, R., Jacobsen, R., & Wilder, T. (2006, November). *"Proficiency for all"—An oxymoron*. Paper presented at symposium on "Examining America's commitment to closing achievement gaps: NCLB and its alternatives." Teachers College, Columbia University, New York.

Sapp, W., & Hatlen, P. (2010). The expanded core curriculum: Where we have been, where we are going, and how we can get there? *Journal of Visual Impairment & Blindness, 104*, 338–348.

Stichter, J. P., Conroy, M. A., & Kauffman, J. M. (2008). *An introduction to students with high-incidence disabilities.* Upper Saddle River, NJ: Merrill/Pearson.

Turnbull, H. R. (2007). A response to Professor Vitello. *Remedial and Special Education, 28,* 69–71. doi:10.1177/07419325070280020501

U.S. Department of Education. (2016). *38th Annual Report to Congress on the Implementation of the Individuals with Disabilities Education Act, 2016.* Washington, DC: Author.

Vitello, S. J. (2007). Shared responsibility reconsidered: A response to Professor Turnbull on IDEIA 2004 accountability and personal responsibility. *Remedial and Special Education, 28,* 66–68. doi:10.1177/07419325 070280020401

Winzer, M. A. (1993). *The history of special education: From isolation to integration.* Washington, DC: Gallaudet University Press.

Wolfensberger, W. (1972). *The principle of normalization in human services.* Toronto: National Institute on Mental Retardation.

Yell, M. L. (2006). *The law and special education* (2nd ed.). Upper Saddle River, NJ: Pearson.

Yell, M. L., Crockett, J. B., Shriner, J. G., & Rozalski, M. (2017). Free appropriate education and the least restrictive environment. In J. M. Kauffman, D. P. Hallahan, & P. C. Pullen (Eds.), *Handbook of special education* (2nd ed., pp. 55–70). New York: Routledge.

Yell, M. L., & Drasgow, E. (2005). *No child left behind: A guide for professionals.* Upper Saddle River, NJ: Merrill/Pearson.

Yell, M. L., Katsiyannis, A., & Bradley, M. R. (2017). The Individuals with Disabilities Education Act: The evolution of special education law. In J. M. Kauffman, D. P. Hallahan, & P. C. Pullen (Eds.), *Handbook of special education* (2nd ed., pp. 55–70). New York: Routledge.

Yell, M. L., Rogers, D., & Rogers, E. L. (1998). The legal history of special education: What a long, strange trip it's been! *Remedial and Special Education, 19,* 219–228.

Zelder, E. Y. (1953). Public opinion and public education for the exceptional child—court decisions 1873–1950. *Exceptional Children, 19,* 187–198.

Zigmond, N. (2007). Delivering special education is a two-person job: A call for unconventional thinking. In J. B. Crockett, M. M. Gerber, & T. J. Landrum (Eds.), *Achieving the radical reform of special education: Essays in honor of James M. Kauffman* (pp. 115–137). Mahwah, NJ: Erlbaum.

Zigmond, N., & Kloo, A. (2017). General and special education are (and should be) different. In J. M. Kauffman, D. P. Hallahan, & P. C. Pullen (Eds.), *Handbook of special education* (2nd ed., pp. 249–262). New York: Routledge.

Zigmond, N., Kloo, A., & Volonino, V. (2009). What, where, and how? Special education in the climate of full inclusion. *Exceptionality, 17,* 189–204. doi:10.1080/09362830903231986

Zordan, P., Sciorati, C., Campana, L., Cottone, L., Clementi, E., Querini, P., & Brunelli, S. (2013). The nitric oxide-donor molsidomine modulates the innate inflammatory response in a mouse model of muscular dystrophy. *European Journal of Pharmacology.* doi:10.1016/j.ejphar.2013.05.007

CHAPTER 2

Anastasiou, D., & Keller, C. (2017). Cross-national differences in special education: A typological approach. In J. M. Kauffman, D. P. Hallahan, & P. C. Pullen (Eds.), *Handbook of special education* (2nd ed., pp. 911–923). New York: Routledge.

Avellone, L. E., & Taylor, J. (2017). Preparing students with low-incidence disabilities for community living opportunities. In J. M. Kauffman, D. P. Hallahan, & P. C. Pullen (Eds.), *Handbook of special education* (2nd ed., pp. 758–770). New York: Routledge.

Bateman, B. D. (2007). Law and the conceptual foundations of special education practice. In J. B. Crockett, M. M. Gerber, & T. J. Landrum (Eds.), *Achieving the radical reform of special education: Essays in honor of James M. Kauffman* (pp. 95–114). Mahwah, NJ: Erlbaum.

Bateman, B. D. (2017). Individual education programs for children with disabilities. In J. M. Kauffman, D. P. Hallahan, & P. C, Pullen (Eds.), *Handbook of special education* (2nd ed.. pp. 87–104). New York: Routledge.

Bateman, B. D., & Linden, M. A. (2006). *Better IEPs: How to develop legally correct and educationally useful programs* (4th ed.). Verona, WI: Attainment.

Boardman, A. G., & Vaughn, S. (2007). Response to intervention as a framework for prevention and identification of learning disabilities: Which comes first, identification or intervention? In J. B. Crockett, M. M. Gerber, & T. J. Landrum (Eds.), *Achieving the radical reform of special education: Essays in honor of James M. Kauffman* (pp. 15–35). Mahwah, NJ: Erlbaum.

Burns, M. K., Silberglitt, B., Christ, T. J., Gibbons, K. A., & Coolong-Chaffin, M. (2016). Using oral reading fluency to evaluate response to intervention and to identify students not making sufficient progress. P. Yaacov & K. D. Cummings (Eds.), *The Fluency Construct* (pp. 123–140). New York: NY: Springer.

Cheney, D., Flower, A., & Templeton, T. (2008). Applying Response to Intervention metrics in the social domain for students at-risk of developing emotional or behavioral disorders. *Journal of Special Education, 42*(2), 108–126.

Common Core State Standards Initiative. (2012). Frequently asked questions. Retrieved from http://www.corestandards.org/resources/frequently-asked-questions.

Cook, B. G., & Friend, M. (1998). Co-teaching: Guidelines for creating effective practices. In E. L. Meyen, G. A. Vergason, & R. J. Whelan (Eds.), *Educating students with mild disabilities: Strategies and methods* (2nd ed., pp. 453–479).

Cook, S. C., McDuffie-Landrum, K. A., Oshita, L., & Cook, B. G. (2017). Co-teaching for students with disabilities: A critical and updated analysis of the empirical literature. In J. M. Kauffman, D. P. Hallahan, & P. C. Pullen (Eds.), *Handbook of special education* (2nd ed, pp. 233–248). New York: Routledge.

Council for Exceptional Children. (1998). *What every special educator must know* (3rd ed.). Reston, VA: Author.

Crockett, J. B., & Kauffman, J. M. (1999). *The least restrictive environment: Its origins and interpretations in special education.* Mahwah, NJ: Erlbaum.

Crockett, J. B., & Kauffman, J. M. (2001). The concept of the least restrictive environment and learning disabilities: Least restrictive of what? Reflections on Cruickshank's 1977 guest editorial for the *Journal of Learning Disabilities.* In D. P. Hallahan & B. K. Keogh (Eds.), *Research and global perspectives in learning disabilities: Essays in honor of William M. Cruickshank* (pp. 147–166). Mahwah, NJ: Erlbaum.

Cruickshank, W. M. (1977). Guest editorial. *Journal of Learning Disabilities, 10,* 193–194. doi:10.1177/00222194770100040 1

Duhon, G. J., Mesmer, E. M., Atkins, M. E., Greguson, L. A., & Olinger, E. S. (2009). Quantifying intervention intensity: A systematic approach to evaluating student response to increasing intervention frequency. *Journal of Behavioral Education, 18,* 101–118.

Endrew F. v. Douglas County School District, 580 1-16 (March 22, 2017).

Fairbanks, S., Sugai, G., Guardino, D., & Lathrop, M. (2007). Response to intervention: Examining classroom behavior support in second grade. *Exceptional Children, 73,* 288–310.

Falk, K. B., & Wehby, J. H. (2001). The effects of peer-assisted learning strategies on the beginning reading skills of young children with emotional or behavioral disorders. *Behavioral Disorders, 26,* 344–359.

Finn, C. E., Jr., Rotherham, A. J., & Hokanson, C. R., Jr. (Eds.). (2001). *Rethinking special education for a new century.* New York: Thomas B. Fordham Foundation.

Fuchs, D., & Fuchs, L. S. (1994). Inclusive schools movement and the radicalization of special education reform. *Exceptional Children, 60,* 294–309.

Fuchs, D., Fuchs, L. S., & Compton, D. L. (2012). Smart RTI: A next-generation approach to multilevel prevention. *Exceptional Children, 78,* 263–279.

Fuchs, D., Fuchs, L. S., & Stecker, P. M. (2010). The "blurring" of special education in a new continuum of general education placements and services. *Exceptional Children, 76,* 301–323.

Fuchs, D., Fuchs, L. S., Thompson, A., Svenson, E., Yanb, L., Otaiba, S. A., et al. (2001). Peer-assisted learning strategies in reading: Extensions for kindergarten, first grade, and high school. *Remedial and Special Education, 22,* 15–21. doi:10.1177/074193250102200103

Fuchs, D., Mock, D., Morgan, P. L., & Young, C. L. (2003). Responsiveness-to-intervention: Definitions, evidence, and implications for the learning disabilities construct. *Learning Disabilities Research and Practice, 18,* 157–171. doi:10.1111/1540-5826.00072

Fuchs, L. S., Fuchs, D., Compton, D. L., Bryant, J. D., Hamlett, C. L., & Seethaler, P. M. (2007). Mathematics screening and progress monitoring at first grade: Implications for responsiveness-to-intervention. *Exceptional Children, 73,* 311–330.

Fulk, B. M., & King, K. (2001). Classwide peer tutoring at work. *Teaching Exceptional Children, 34*(2), 49–53.

Gardner, R., Cartledge, G., Seidl, B., Woolsey, M. L., Schley, G. S., & Utley, C. A. (2001). Mt. Olivet after-school program: Peer-mediated interventions for at-risk students. *Remedial and Special Education, 22,* 22–33. doi:10.1177/074193250102200104

Gliona, M. F., Gonzales, A. K., & Jacobson, E. S. (2005). Dedicated, not segregated: Suggested changes in thinking about instructional environments and the language of special education. In J. M. Kauffman & D. P. Hallahan (Eds.), *The illusion of full inclusion: A comprehensive critique of a current special education bandwagon* (2nd ed., pp. 135–146). Austin, TX: Pro-Ed.

Greenwood, C. R., Arrega-Mayer, C., Utley, C. A., Gavin, K. M., & Terry, B. (2001). Class-wide peer tutoring learning management system: Applications with elementary-level English language learners. *Remedial and Special Education, 22,* 34–47. doi:10.1177/074193250102200105

Hallahan, D. P. (2007). Learning disabilities: Whatever happened to intensive instruction? *LDA Newsbriefs, 42*(1), 1, 3–4, 24.

Hockenbury, J. C., Kauffman, J. M., & Hallahan, D. P. (1999–2000). What's right about special education? *Exceptionality, 8*(1), 3–11.

Hoover, J. J., & Patton, J. R. (2004). Differentiating standards-based education for students with diverse needs. *Remedial and Special Education, 25,* 74–78. doi:10.1177/07419325 5040250020101 https://www.ideadata.org/TABLES35TH/B3-2.pdf

Hudson, T. M., & McKenzie, R. G. (2016). Evaluating the Use of RTI to Identify SLD: A Survey of State Policy, Procedures, Data Collection, and Administrator Perceptions. *Contemporary School Psychology, 20*(1), 31–45.

Huefner, D. S. (2006). *Getting comfortable with special education law: A framework for working with children with disabilities* (2nd ed.). Norwood, MA: Christopher Gordon.

Hughes, C.A., & Dexter, D.D. (2011). Response to intervention: A research-based summary. *Theory Into Practice, 50,* 4–11.

Imray, P., & Colley, A. (2017). *Inclusion is dead: Long live inclusion.* New York: Routledge.

Inge, K. J. (2017). Section X editor: Transition of adults with low incidence disabilities. In J. M. Kauffman, D. P. Hallahan, & P. C. Pullen (Eds.), *Handbook of special education* (2nd ed., p. 739). New York: Routledge.

Johns, B. H. (2003). NCLB and IDEA: Never the twain should meet. *Learning Disabilities: A Multidisciplinary Journal, 12*(3), 89–91.

Kauffman, J. M. (1995). Why we must celebrate a diversity of restrictive environments. *Learning Disabilities Research and Practice, 10,* 225–232.

Kauffman, J. M. (1999–2000). The special education story: Obituary, accident report, conversion experience, reincarnation, or none of the above? *Exceptionality, 8*(1), 61–71.

Kauffman, J. M. (2002). *Education deform: Bright people sometimes say stupid things about education.* Landham, MD: Scarecrow Education.

Kauffman, J. M. (2004). The president's commission and the devaluation of special education. *Education and Treatment of Children, 27,* 307–324.

Kauffman, J. M. (2014). Past, present, and future in EBD and special education. In B. Cook, M. Tankersley, & T. Landrum (Eds.), *Advances in learning and behavioral disabilities, Vol. 27: Classroom behavior, contexts, and interventions* (pp. 63–87). Bingley, UK: Emerald.

Kauffman, J. M., Bantz, J., & McCullough, J. (2002). Separate and better: A special public school class for students with emotional and behavioral disorders. *Exceptionality, 10,* 149–170.

Kauffman, J. M., & Hallahan, D. P. (1997). A diversity of restrictive environments: Placement as a problem of social ecology. In J. W. Lloyd, E. J. Kame'enui, & D. Chard (Eds.), *Issues in educating students with disabilities* (pp. 325–342). Mahwah, NJ: Erlbaum.

Kauffman, J. M., & Hallahan, D. P. (2005a). *Special education: What it is and why we need it.* Boston: Allyn & Bacon/Pearson.

Kauffman, J. M., & Hallahan, D. P. (Eds.) (2005b). *The illusion of full inclusion: A comprehensive critique of a current special education bandwagon* (2nd ed.). Austin, TX: Pro-Ed.

Kauffman, J. M., & Hallahan, D. P. (2009). Parental choices and ethical dilemmas involving disabilities: Special education and the problem of deliberately chosen disabilities. *Exceptionality, 17,* 45–62. doi:10.1080/09362830802667835

Kauffman, J. M., Hallahan, D. P., Pullen, P. C., & Badar, J. (2018). *Special education: What it is and why we need it.* New York: Routledge.

Kauffman, J. M., & Konold, T. R. (2007). Making sense in education: Pretense (including NCLB) and realities in rhetoric and policy about schools and schooling. *Exceptionality, 15,* 75–96.

Kauffman, J. M., & Landrum, T. J. (2007). Educational service interventions and reforms. In J. W. Jacobson, J. A. Mulick, & J. Rojahn (Eds.), *Handbook of intellectual and developmental disabilities* (pp. 173–188). New York: Springer.

Kauffman, J. M., McGee, K., & Brigham, M. (2004). Enabling or disabling? Observations on changes in the purposes and outcomes of special education. *Phi Delta Kappan, 85,* 613–620.

Kauffman, J. M., Mock, D. R., Tankersley, M., & Landrum, T. J. (2008). Effective service delivery models. In R. J. Morris & N. Mather (Eds.), *Evidence-based interventions for students with learning and behavioral challenges* (pp. 359–378). Mahwah, NJ: Erlbaum.

Kauffman, J. M., Pullen, P. L., Mostert, M. P., & Trent, S. C. (2011). *Managing classroom behavior: A reflective case-based approach* (5th ed.). Upper Saddle River, NJ: Pearson.

Kauffman, J. M., & Sasso, G. M. (2006a). Certainty, doubt, and the reduction of uncertainty: A rejoinder. *Exceptionality, 14,* 109–120.

Kauffman, J. M., & Sasso, G. M. (2006b). Toward ending cultural and cognitive relativism in special education. *Exceptionality, 14,* 65–90.

Kauffman, J. M., & Wiley, A. L. (2004). How the President's Commission on Excellence in Special Education (PCESE) devalues special education. *Learning Disabilities: A Multidisciplinary Journal, 13,* 3–6.

Kavale, K. A., Kauffman, J. M., Bachmeier, R. J., & LeFever, G. G. (2008). Response-to-intervention: Separating the rhetoric of self-congratulation from the reality of specific learning disability identification. *Learning Disability Quarterly, 31,* 135–150.

Kourea, L., Cartledge, G., & Musti-Rao, S. (2007). Improving reading skills of urban elementary students through total class peer tutoring. *Remedial and Special Education, 28,* 95–107. doi:10.1177/07419325070280020801

Landrum, T. J., & Kauffman, J. M. (2006). Behavioral approaches to classroom management. In C. M. Evertson & C. S. Weinstein (Eds.), *Handbook of classroom management: Research, practice, and contemporary issues* (pp. 47–71). Mahwah, NJ: Erlbaum.

Lazarus, S. S., Thurlow, M. L., Lail, K. E., & Christensen, L. (2009). A longitudinal analysis of state accommodations policies: Twelve years of change 1993–2005. *Journal of Special Education, 43*(2), 67–80.

Lloyd, J. W., & Hallahan, D. P. (2007). Advocacy and reform of special education. In J. B. Crockett, M. M., Gerber, & T. J. Landrum (Eds.), *Achieving the radical reform of special education: Essays in honor of James M. Kauffman* (pp. 245–263). Mahwah, NJ: Erlbaum.

Maheady, L., Harper, G. F., & Mallette, B. (2001). Peer-mediated instruction and interventions with students with mild disabilities. *Remedial and Special Education, 22,* 4–14. doi:10.1177/074193250102200102

Martin, E. W. (1995). Case studies on inclusion: Worst fears realized. *The Journal of Special Education, 29,* 192–199.

Mellard, D. F. & Johnson, E. S. (2008). *RTI: A practitioner's guide to implementing response to intervention.* Thousand Oaks, CA: Corwin Press.

Mercer, C. D., Mercer, A. R., & Pullen, P. C. (2011). *Teaching students with learning problems* (8th ed.). Upper Saddle River, NJ: Pearson.

Miller, S. P. (2002). *Validated practices for teaching students with diverse needs and abilities.* Boston: Allyn & Bacon/Pearson.

Mock, D. R., & Kauffman, J. M. (2002). Preparing teachers for full inclusion: Is it possible? *The Teacher Educator, 37,* 202–215. doi:10.1080/08878730209555294

Mock, D. R., & Kauffman, J. M. (2005). The delusion of full inclusion. In J. W. Jacobson, J. A. Mulick, & R. M. Fuchs (Eds.), *Fads: Dubious and improbably treatments for developmental disabilities* (pp. 113–128). Mahwah, NJ: Erlbaum.

Moore, T. (2007, January 19). Classroom distinctions. *The New York Times,* p. A27.

Mostert, M. P., Kavale, K. A., & Kauffman, J. M. (Eds.). (2008). *Challenging the refusal of reasoning in special education.* Denver, CO: Love.

National Governors Association Center for Best Practices, Council of Chief State School Officers. (2010). *Common Core State Standards.* Washington, DC: National Governors Association Center for Best Practices, Council of Chief State School Officers.

Noonan, M. J., & McCormick, L. (2006). *Young children with disabilities in natural environments: Methods and procedures.* Baltimore: Brookes.

O'Connor, R. E., Sanchez, V., & Kim, J. J. (2017). Responsiveness to intervention and multi-tiered systems of support for reducing reading difficulties and identifying learning disability. In J. M. Kauffman, D. P. Hallahan, & P. C. Pullen (Eds.), *Handbook of special education* (2nd ed., pp. 189–202). New York: Routledge.

Pierangelo, R., & Giuliani, G. A. (2006). *Assessment in special education: A practical approach* (2nd ed.). Boston: Allyn & Bacon/Pearson.

Pisha, B., & Coyne, P. (2001). Smart from the start: The promise of universal design for learning. *Remedial and Special Education, 22,* 197–203. doi:10.1177/074193250102200402

Pugach, M. C., & Warger, C. L. (2001). Curriculum matters: Raising expectations for students with disabilities. *Remedial and Special Education, 22,* 194–196. doi:10.1177/074193250102200401.

Pullen, P. C., & Hallahan, D. P. (2015). What is special education? In B. D. Bateman, J. W. Lloyd, & M. Tankersley, *Understanding special education issues: Who, where, what, when, how & why* (pp. 36–50). New York: Routledge.

Quenemoen, R. F., & Thurlow, M. (2017). Standards-based reforms and students with disabilities. In J. M. Kauffman, D. P. Hallahan, & P. C. Pullen (Eds.), *Handbook of special education* (2nd ed., pp. 203–217). New York: Routledge.

Sasso, G. M. (2001). The retreat from inquiry and knowledge in special education. *The Journal of Special Education, 34,* 178–193.

Sasso, G. M. (2007). Science and reason in special education: The legacy of Derrida and Foucault. In J. B. Crockett, M. M. Gerber, & T. J. Landrum (Eds.), *Achieving the radical reform of special education: Essays in honor of James M. Kauffman* (pp. 143–167). Mahwah, NJ: Erlbaum.

Scanlon, D. J. (2017). Section IX editor: Transition of adults with high incidence disabilities. In J. M. Kauffman, D. P. Hallahan, & P. C. Pullen (Eds.), *Handbook of special education* (2nd ed., pp. 687–689). New York: Routledge.

Scruggs, T. E., Mastropieri, M. A., & McDuffie, K. A. (2007). Co-teaching in inclusive classrooms: A metasynthesis of qualitative research. *Exceptional Children, 73,* 392–416.

Silberglitt, B., Parker, D., & Muyskens, P. (2016). Assessment: Periodic assessment to monitor progress. In Jimerson, S. R., Burns, M. K., & A. M. VanDerHeyden (Eds.) *Handbook of response to intervention: The science and practice of multi-tiered systems of support* (pp. 271–291). New York, NY: Springer.

Simpson, R. L., & Kauffman, J. M. (2007). Inclusão de alunos deficientes em salas de aula regulares (Inclusion of students with disabilities in general education). In J. M. Kauffman & J. A. Lopes (Eds.), *Pode a educação especial deixar de ser especial?* (pp. 167–190). Braga, Portugal: Psiquilíbrios Edições.

Spooner, F., Baker, J. N., Harris, A. A., Ahlgrim-Delzell, L., & Browder, D. M. (2007). Effects of training in universal design for learning on lesson plan development. *Remedial and Special Education, 28,* 108–116. doi:10.1177/0741932507028002010

Thurlow, M. L. (2000). Standards-based reform and students with disabilities: Reflections on a decade of change. *Focus on Exceptional Children, 33*(3), 1–16.

Thurlow, M. L. (2010). Special issue: Testing students with disabilities. *Applied Measurement in Education, 23,* 121–131.

Thurlow, M. L. (Summer 2012). Common core standards: The promise and the peril for students with disabilities. *The Special Edge, 25*(3), 1, 6.

Thurlow, M. L., Nelson, J. R., Teelucksingh, W., & Draper, I. L. (2001). Multiculturalism and disability in a results-based educational system: Hazards and hopes for today's schools. In C. A. Utley & F. E. Obiakor (Eds.), *Special education, multicultural education, and school reform: Components of quality education for learners with mild disabilities* (pp. 155–172). Springfield, IL: Charles C. Thomas.

Tomlinson, C. A. (2001). *How to differentiate instruction in mixed-ability classrooms* (2nd ed.). Alexandria, VA: Association for Supervision and Curriculum Development.

U.S. Department of Education. (1995). *Seventeenth annual report to Congress on the implementation of the Individuals with Disabilities Education Act.* Washington, DC: Author. Retrieved from http://www.ed.gov/about/reports/annual/osep/2002/index.html

U.S. Department of Education. (2005). *Twenty-seventh annual report to Congress on implementation of the Individuals with Disabilities Education Act.* Washington, DC: Author.

U.S. Department of Education. (2009). *Twenty-eighth annual report to Congress on implementation of the Individuals with Disabilities Education Act.* Washington, DC: Author.

U.S. Department of Education. (2016). *Thirty-eighth annual report to Congress on implementation of the Individuals with Disabilities Education Act.* Washington, DC: Author.

Walsh, J. M., & Jones, B. (2004). New models of cooperative teaching. *Teaching Exceptional Children, 36*(5), 14–20.

Warnock, M. (2005). *Special educational needs: A new look. Impact No. 11.* London: Philosophy of Education Society of Great Britain.

Yell, M. L. (2006). *The law and special education* (2nd ed.). Upper Saddle River, NJ: Pearson.

Yell, M. L., Crockett, J. B., Shriner, J. G., & Rozalski, M. (2017). Free appropriate education and the least restrictive environment. In J. M. Kauffman, D. P. Hallahan, & P. C. Pullen (Eds.), *Handbook of special education* (2nd ed., pp. 71–86). New York: Routledge.

Zigmond, N. (2003). Where should students with disabilities receive special education services? Is one place better than another? *The Journal of Special Education, 37,* 193–199. doi:10.1177/00224669030370030901

Zigmond, N. (2007). Delivering special education is a two-person job: A call for unconventional thinking. In J. B. Crockett, M. M. Gerber, & T. J. Landrum (Eds.), *Achieving the radical reform of special education: Essays in honor of James M. Kauffman* (pp. 115–137). Mahwah, NJ: Erlbaum.

Zigmond, N., & Kloo, A. (2017). General and special education are (and should be) different. In J. M. Kauffman, D. P. Hallahan, P. C. Pullen (Eds.), *Handbook of special education* (2nd ed., pp. 249–261). New York: Routledge.

Zirkel, P. A. (2011). State laws and guidelines for RTI: Additional implementation features. *Communique, 39.* Retrieved from http://www.nasponline.org/publications/cq/39/7/professional-practice-state-laws.aspx

CHAPTER 3

Abedi, J., Hofstetter, C., & Lord, C. (2004). Assessment accommodations for English language learners: Implications for policy-based empirical research. *Review of Educational Research, 74,* 1–28. doi:10.3102/00346543074001001

Albus, D., Thurlow, M., Liu, K., & Bielinski, J. (2005). Reading test performance of English-language learners using an English Dictionary. *The Journal of Educational Research, 98,* 245–254. doi:10.3200/JOER.98.4.245-256

Artiles, A. J., Rueda, R., Salazar, J. J., & Higareda, I. (2005). Within-group diversity in minority disproportionate representation: English language learners in urban school districts. *Exceptional Children, 71,* 283–301.

Associated Press. (2004, April 18). Gay teens harassed at school: Persecution leads to law. *Charlottesville Daily Progress,* p. A11.

Banks, J. A., & Banks, C. A. (2016). *Multicultural education: Issues and perspectives* (9th ed.). Hoboken, NJ: Wiley.

Bateman, B. D. (1994). Who, how, and where: Special education's issues in perpetuity. *The Journal of Special Education, 27,* 509–520. doi:10.1177/002246699402700410

Bell, K. (2004). GLSEN in tough times: Training educators about LGBT issues in a challenging political, economic, and educational climate. *Beyond Behavior, 13*(3), 29–30.

Bennett, L. (2000). Equality by design: Three charter schools try new approaches to integration. *Teaching Tolerance, 17,* 43–49.

Calhoon, M. B., Al Otaiba, S., Cihak, D., King A., & Avalos, A. (2007). Effects of a peer-mediated program on reading skill acquisition for two-way bilingual first-grade classroom. *Learning Disability Quarterly, 30,* 169–184.

Calhoon, M. B., Al Otaiba, S., Greenberg, D., King, A., & Avalos, A. (2006). Improving reading skills in predominantly Hispanic Title 1 first-grade classrooms: The promise of peer-assisted learning strategies. *Learning Disabilities Research & Practice, 21,* 261–272. doi:10.1111/j.1540-5826.2006.00222.x

Collins, K. (2000). No place for bigotry: An anti-bias club changes the atmosphere at a suburban high school. *Teaching Tolerance, 17,* 26–27.

Council for Exceptional Children. (2000). Improving results for culturally and linguistically diverse students. *Research Connections in Special Education, 7.*

Denton, C. A., Anthony, J. L., Parker, R., & Hasbrouck, J. E. (2004). The effects of two tutoring programs on the English reading development of Spanish-English bilingual students. *Elementary School Journal, 104,* 289–305.

Dunn, L. M. (1968). Special education for the mildly retarded? Is much of it justifiable? *Exceptional Children, 35*, 5–21.

Evertson, C. M., & Weinstein, C. S. (Eds.). (2006). *Handbook of classroom management: Research, practice, and contemporary issues.* Mahwah, NJ: Erlbaum.

Fulk, B. M., & King, K. (2001). Classwide peer tutoring at work. *Teaching Exceptional Children, 34*(2), 49–53.

Gallucci, J. P. (2000). Signs of remembrance: A school for the deaf celebrates Dia de los Muertos. *Teaching Tolerance, 18*, 30–31.

Gerstein, J. (2017, April 10, 07:03 PM EDT). Full bench of 4th Circuit to hear Trump travel ban case in May. *Politico*, Retrieved from http://www.politico.com/story/2017/04/donald-trump-travel-ban-federal-appeals-court-case-237084.

Gersten, R., & Baker, S. (2000). What we know about effective instructional practices for English-language learners. *Exceptional Children, 66*, 454–470.

Gerstein, J. (2017, June 1). Trump administration asks Supreme Court to reinstate travel ban. *Politico*. Retrieved from: http://www.politico.com/story/2017/06/01/trump-travel-ban-supreme-court-239050

Good, R. H., & Kaminski, R. A. (Eds.). (2002). *Dynamic Indicators of Basic Early Literacy Skills* (6th ed.). Eugene, OR: Institute for the Development of Educational Achievement. Available: http://dibels.uoregon.edu

Greenwood, C. R., Arrega-Mayer, C., Utley, C. A., Gavin, K. M, & Terry, B. J. (2001). Classwide peer tutoring learning management system: Applications with elementary-level English language learners. *Remedial and Special Education, 22*, 34–47. doi:10.1177/074193250102200105

Hammill, D. D. (2004). What we know about correlates of reading. *Exceptional Children, 70*, 453–468.

Kauffman, J. M., Conroy, M., Gardner, R., & Oswald, D. (2008). Cultural sensitivity in the application of behavior principles to education. *Education and Treatment of Children, 31*, 239–262.

Kauffman, J. M., & Hallahan, D. P. (2005). *Special education: What it is and why we need it.* Boston: Allyn & Bacon/Pearson.

Kauffman, J. M., & Landrum, T. (2009). Politics, civil rights, and disproportional identification of students with emotional and behavioral disorders. *Exceptionality, 17*, 177–188. doi:10.1080/09362830903231903

Kauffman, J. M., Mostert, M. P., Trent, S. C., & Pullen, P. L. (2011). *Managing classroom behavior: A reflective case-based approach* (5th ed.). Upper Saddle River, NJ: Pearson.

Kissinger, K. (2017). *Anti-bias education in the early childhood classroom.* New York, NY: Routledge.

Klingner, J. K., & Edwards, P. A. (2006). Cultural considerations with response to intervention models. *Reading Research Quarterly, 41*, 108–117. doi:10.1598/RRQ.41.1.6

Linan-Thompson, S., Vaughn, S., Prater, K., & Cirino, P. T. (2006). The response to intervention of English language learners at risk for reading problems. *Journal of Learning Disabilities, 39*, 390–398. doi:10.1177/00222194060390050201

MacSwan, J., & Rolstad, K. (2006). How language proficiency tests mislead us about ability: Implications for English language learner placement in special education. *Teachers College Record, 108*, 2304–2328. doi:10.1111/j.1467-9620.2006.00783.x

McAfee, M. (2000). Welcome to Park Day School: A Bay Area teacher shares her independent school's commitment to community. *Teaching Tolerance, 18*, 24–29.

McCardle, P., & Leung, C. Y. Y. (2006). English language learners: Development and intervention. *Topics in Language Disorders, 26*, 302–304.

McCardle, P., McCarthy, J. M., & Leos, K. (2005). English language learners and learning disabilities: Research agenda and implications for practice. *Learning Disabilities Research & Practice, 20*, 68–78. doi:10.1111/j.1540-5826.2005.00122.x

McDonnell, L. M., McLaughlin, M. J., & Morison, P. (Eds.). (1997). *Educating one and all: Students with disabilities and standards-based reform.* Washington, DC: National Academy Press.

McIntyre, T. (2007). *Are behaviorist interventions inappropriate for culturally different youngsters with learning and behavior disorders?* Retrieved from http://maxweber.hunter.cuny.edu/pub/eres/EDSPC715_MCINTYRE/CBehModR.html

Morgan, P. L., Farkas, G., Hillemeier, M. M., Mattison, R., Maczuga, S., & Cook, M. (2015). Minorities are disproportionately underrepresented in special education: Longitudinal evidence across five disability conditions. *Educational Researcher, 44*(5).

Mundy, L. (2002, March 31). A world of their own. *The Washington Post Magazine*, pp. 22–29, 38–43.

Oswald, D. P., Coutinho, M. J., Best, A. M., & Singh, N. (1999). Ethnic representation in special education, the influence of school related economic and demographic variables. *Journal of Special Education, 32*, 194–206. doi:10.1177/002246699903200401

Pavri, S. (2001). Loneliness in children with disabilities: How teachers can help. *Teaching Exceptional Children, 33*(6), 52–58.

Peck, A., & Scarpati, S. (2004). Literacy instruction and research. *Teaching Exceptional Children, 36*(6), 71.

Pierce, R. L., Adams, C. M., Speirs Neumeister, K. L., Cassady, J. C., Dixon, F. A., & Cross, T. L. (2007). Development of an identification procedure for a large urban school corporation: Identifying culturally diverse and academically gifted elementary students. *Roeper Review, 29*, 113–118. doi:10.1080/02783190709554394

Pollard-Durodola, S. D., Mathes, P. G., Vaughn, S., Cardenas-Hagan, E., & Linan-Thompson, S. (2006). The role of oracy in developing comprehension in Spanish-speaking English language learners. *Topics in Language Disorders, 26*, 365–384.

Pullen, P. C., & Hallahan, D. P. (2015). What is special education? In B. D. Bateman, J. W. Lloyd, & M. Tankersley, *Understanding special education issues: Who, where, what, when, how & why* (pp. 36–50). New York: Routledge.

Ravitch, D. (2003). *The language police: How pressure groups restrict what students learn.* New York: Knopf.

Reyna, V. F. (2004). Why scientific research? The importance of evidence in changing educational practice. In P. McCardle, & V. Chhabra (Eds.), *The voice of evidence in reading research* (pp. 47–58). Baltimore: Paul H. Brookes.

Shealey, M. W., & Callins, T. (2007). Creating culturally responsive literacy programs in inclusive classrooms. *Intervention in School and Clinic, 42*, 195–197. doi:10.1177/10534512070420040101

Singh, N. N., Baker, J., Winton, A. S. W., & Lewis, D. K. (2000). Semantic equivalence of assessment instruments across cultures. *Journal of Child and Family Studies, 9*, 123–134. doi:10.1023/A:1009424003319.

Skiba, R. J., Poloni-Staudinger, L., Simmons, A. B., Feggins-Azziz, L.R., & Chung, C. (2005). Unproven links: Can poverty explain ethnic disproportionality in special education? *Journal of Special Education, 39*, 130–144. doi:10.1177/00224669050390030101

Takaki, R. (1994). Interview: Reflections from a different mirror. *Teaching Tolerance, 3*(1), 11–15.

Thurlow, M. L., Nelson, J. R., Teelucksingh, W., & Draper, I. L. (2001). Multiculturalism and disability in a results-based educational system: Hazards and hopes for today's schools. In C. A. Utley & F. E. Obiakor (Eds.), *Special education, multicultural education, and school reform: Components of quality education for learners with mild disabilities* (pp. 155–172). Springfield, IL: Charles C. Thomas.

Tyler, N. C., Yzquierdo, Z., Lopez-Reyna, N., & Flippin, S. S. (2004). Cultural and linguistic diversity and the special education workforce: A critical overview. *The Journal of Special Education, 38*, 22–38. doi:10.1177/00224669040380010301

U.S. Department of Education. (2016). *38th Annual Report to Congress on the Implementation of the Individuals with Disabilities Education Act, 2016.* Washington, DC: Author.

Utley, C. A., & Obiakor, F. E. (2001a). Learning problems or learning disabilities of multicultural learners: Contemporary perspectives. In C. A. Utley & F. E. Obiakor (Eds.), *Special education, multicultural education, and school reform: Components of quality education for learners with mild disabilities* (pp. 90–117). Springfield, IL: Charles C. Thomas.

Utley, C. A., & Obiakor, F. E. (2001b). Multicultural education and special education: Infusion for better schooling. In C. A. Utley & F. E. Obiakor (Eds.), *Special education, multicultural education, and school reform: Components of quality education for learners with mild disabilities* (pp. 3–29). Springfield, IL: Charles C. Thomas.

Utley, C. A., & Obiakor, F. E. (Eds.). (2001c). *Special education, multicultural education, and school reform: Components of quality education for learners with mild disabilities.* Springfield, IL: Charles C. Thomas.

Vaughn, S., Cirino, P. T., Linan-Thompson, S., Mathes, P. G., Carlson, C. D., Cardenas-Hagan, E., Pollard-Durodola, S. D., Fletcher, J. M., & Francis, D. J. (2006). Effectiveness of a Spanish intervention and an English intervention for English language learners at risk for reading problems. *American Educational Research Journal, 43*, 449–487. doi:10.3102/0002831204300344

Vaughn, S., Linan-Thompson, S., Mathes, P. G., Cirino, P. T., Carlson, C. D., Pollard-Durodola, S. D., et al. (2006). Effectiveness of a Spanish intervention for first-grade English language learners at risk for reading difficulties. *Journal of Learning Disabilities, 39*, 56–73. doi:10.1177/00222194060390010601

Vaughn, S., Mathes, P., Linan-Thompson, S., Cirino, P., Carlson, C. Pollard-Durodola, S., et al. (2006). Effectiveness of an English intervention for first-grade English language learners at risk for reading problems. *The Elementary School Journal, 107*, 153–180. doi:10.1086/510653

Vaughn, S., Mathes, P., Linan-Thompson, S., & Francis, D. (2005). Teaching English language learners at risk for reading difficulties to read in Spanish or English. *Learning Disabilities Research & Practice, 20*(1), 58–67. doi:10.1111/ j.1540-5826.2005.00121.x

Villegas, A. M., & Lucas, T. (2007). The culturally responsive teacher. *Educational Leadership, 64*(6), 28–33.

Wiesel, E. (2004, July 4). The America I love. *Parade*, pp. 4–5.

Xu, Y., Gelfer, J. I., Sileo, N., Filler, J., & Perkins, P. (2008). Effects of peer tutoring on young children's social interactions. *Early Child Development and Care, 178*, 617–635. doi:10.1080/03004430600857485

CHAPTER 4

Anderson, L., Larson, S., Lakin, C., & Kwak, N. (2002). Children with disabilities: Social roles and family impacts in the NHIS-D. *DD Data Brief, 4*(1), 1–11.

Bailey, D. B., Raspa, M., Humphreys, B. P., & Sam, A. M. (2011). Promoting family outcomes in early intervention. In J. M. Kauffman & D. P. Hallahan (Eds.), *The handbook of special education* (pp. 668–684). New York: Routledge.

Bell, R. Q., & Harper, L. V. (1977). *Child effects on adults*. Hillsdale, NJ: Erlbaum.

Bellefontaine, S., Hastings, P., Parker, R., & Forman, D. (2006, June 19). Child compliance to mothers and fathers: Sequential analysis of a clean-up task. Paper presented at the annual meeting of the XVth Biennial International Conference on Infant Studies, Westin Miyako, Kyoto, Japan. Retrieved from http://www.allacademic.com/meta/p94058_index.html

Berry, J. O., & Hardman, M. L. (1998). *Lifespan perspectives on the family and disability*. Boston: Allyn & Bacon.

Blacher, J., & Baker, B. L. (2007). Positive impact of intellectual disability on families. *American Journal on Mental Retardation, 112*, 330–348. doi:10.1352/0895-8017(2007)112[0330:PIOIDO]2.0.CO;2

Brooks-Gunn, J., & Lewis, M. (1984). Maternal responsivity in interactions with handicapped infants. *Child Development, 55*, 858–868.

Cantwell, J., Muldoon, O., & Gallagher, S. (2015). The influence of self-esteem and social support on the relationship between stigma and depressive symptomology in parents caring for children with intellectual disabilities. *Journal of Intellectual Disability Research, 59*, 948–957. doi:10.1111/jir.12205

Drotar, D., Baskiewicz, A., Irvin, N., Kennell, J., & Klaus, M. (1975). The adaptation of parents to the birth of an infant with a congenital malformation: A hypothetical model. *Pediatrics, 56*, 710–717.

Esquivel, S. L., Ryan, C. S., & Bonner, M. (2008). Involved parents' perceptions of their experiences in school-based team meetings. *Journal of Educational and Psychological Consultation, 18*, 234–258. doi:10.1080/ 10474410802022589

Ferguson, P. M. (2002). A place in the family: An historical interpretation of research on parental reactions to having a child with a disability. *The Journal of Special Education, 36*, 124–130. doi:10.1177/00224669020360030201

Fiedler, C. R., Simpson, R. L., & Clark, D. M. (2007). *Parents and families of children with disabilities: Effective school-based support services*. Upper Saddle River, NJ: Merrill/ Pearson.

Floyd, F. J., Purcell, S. E., Richardson, S. S., & Kupersmidt, J. B. (2009). Sibling relationship quality and social functioning of children and adolescents with intellectual disability. *American Journal of Intellectual and Developmental Disabilities, 114*, 110–127. doi:10.1352/2009.114.110-127

Fox, L., Vaughn, B. J., Wyatte, M. L., & Dunlap, G. (2002). "We can't expect other people to understand": Family perspectives on problem behavior. *Exceptional Children, 68*, 437–450.

Gallagher, P. A., Powell, T. H., & Rhodes, C. A. (2006). *Brothers & sisters: A special part of exceptional families* (3rd ed.). Baltimore: Brookes.

Glidden, L. M., & Jobe, B. M. (2006). Brief research report: The longitudinal course of depression in adoptive and birth mothers of children with intellectual disabilities. *Journal of Policy and Practice in Intellectual Disabilities, 2*, 139–142. doi:10.1111/j.1741-1130.2006.00067.x

Gouin, J. P., da Estrela, C., Desmarais, K., & Barker, E. T. (2016). The impact of formal and informal support on health in the context of caregiving stress. *Family Relations: Interdisciplinary Journal of Applied Family Studies, 65*, 191–206.

Grasso, F. (2014). Parenting children with disabilities: Some theoretical reflections and experimental data, coded by the ICF, about the effect of child disability on parental perception of their own offspring. *Life Span and Disability, 28*, 207–231.

Groneberg, J. G. (2008). *Road map to Holland: How I found my way through my son's first two years with Down syndrome*. New York: New American Library.

Guralnick, M. J., Neville, B., Hammond, M. A., & Connor, R. T. (2008). Mothers' social communicative adjustments to young children with mild developmental delays. *American Journal on Mental Retardation, 113*, 1–18.

Harry, B. (2002). Trends and issues in serving culturally diverse families of children with disabilities. *The Journal of Special Education, 36*, 131–138. doi:10.1177/00224669020360030301

Hastings, R. P., Daley, D., Burns, C., & Beck, A. (2006). Maternal distress and expressed emotion: Cross-sectional and longitudinal relationships with behavior problems of children with intellectual disabilities. *American Journal on Mental Retardation, 111*, 48–61. doi:10.1352/ 0895-8017(2006)111[48:MDAEEC]2.0.CO;2

Howell, A., Hauser-Cram, P., & Kersh, J. E. (2007). Setting the stage: Early child and family characteristics as predictors of later loneliness in children with developmental disabilities. *American Journal on Mental Retardation, 112*, 18–30. doi:10.1352/0895-8017(2007)112 [18:STSECA]2.0.CO;2

Jurbergs, N., Palcic, J., & Kelley, M. L. (2007). School–home notes with and without response cost: Increasing attention and academic performance in low-income children with attention-deficit/hyperactivity disorder. *School Psychology Quarterly, 22*, 358–379. doi:10.1037/1045-3830.22.3.358

Kauffman, J. M., Mostert, M. P., Trent, S. C., & Pullen, P. L. (2011). *Managing classroom behavior: A reflective case-based approach*. Upper Saddle River, NJ: Pearson.

Kelley, M. L. (1990). *School–home notes: Promoting children's classroom success*. New York: Guilford Press.

Keogh, B. K., Garnier, H. E., Bernheimer, L. P., & Gallimore, R. (2000). Models of child–family interactions for children with developmental delays: Child-driven or transactional? *American Journal on Mental Retardation, 105*, 32–46.

Lambie, R. (2000). *Family systems within educational contexts: Understanding at-risk and special-needs students*. Denver, CO: Love.

Laxman, D. J., McBride, B. A., Jeans, L. M., Dyer, W. J., Santos, R. M., Kern, J. L., Sugimura, N., Curtiss, S. L., & Weglarz-Ward, J. M. (2015). Father involvement and maternal depressive symptoms in families of children with disabilities or delays. *Maternal and Child Health Journal, 19*, 1078–1086.

Lenhard, W., Breitenbach, E., Ebert, H., Schindelhauer-Deutscher, H. J., Zang, K. D., & Henn, W. (2007). *Intellectual and Developmental Disabilities, 45*, 98–102. doi:10.1352/ 1934-9556(2007)45[98:AOMTTC]2.0.CO;2

Lewin, A., Mitchell, S. J., Waters, D., Hodgkinson, S., & Southammakosane, C. (2015). The protective effects of father involvement for infants of teen mothers with depressive symptoms. *Maternal and Child Health Journal, 19*, 1016–1023.

Lindo, E. J., Kliemann, K. R., Combes, B. H., & Frank, J. A. (2016). Managing stress levels of parents of children with developmental disabilities: A meta-analytic review of interventions. *Family Relations: Interdisciplinary Journal of Applied Family Studies, 65*, 207–224.

Livingston, M. (2013, July 2). The rise of single fathers: A ninefold increase since 1960. *Pew Research Social & Demographic Trends*, Retrieved from http://www.pewsocialtrends.org/2013/07/02/the-rise-of-single-fathers/.

Lucyshyn, J. M., Horner, R. H., Dunlap, G., Albin, R. W., & Ben, K. R. (2002). Positive behavior support with families. In J. M. Lucyshyn, G. Dunlap, & R. W. Albin (Eds.), *Families and positive behavior support: Addressing problem behavior in family contexts* (pp. 3–43). Baltimore: Brookes.

Magana, S., Schwartz, S. J., Rubert, M. P., & Szapocznik, J. (2006). Hispanic caregivers of adults with mental retardation: Importance of family functioning. *American Journal* on *Mental Retardation, 111*, 250–262. doi:10.1352/0895-8017(2006)111[250:H-COAWM]2.0.CO;2

Mahoney, G., & Robenalt, K. (1986). A comparison of conversational patterns between mothers and their Down syndrome and normal infants. *Journal of the Division for Early Childhood, 10*, 172–180.

Mangelsdorf, S. C., & Schoppe-Sullivan, S. J. (2007). Introduction: Emergent family systems. *Infant Behavior & Development, 30*, 60–62. doi:10.1016/j.infbeh.2006.11.006

Meadow-Orlans, K. P., Mertens, D. M., & Sass-Lehrer, M. A. (2003). *Parents and their deaf children: The early years.* Washington, DC: Gallaudet University Press.

Meyer, D. J., & Vadasy, P. F. (2008). *Sibshops: Workshops for siblings of children with special needs.* Baltimore: Brookes.

Mueller, T. G. (2017). Promoting collaborative partnerships with families. In J. M. Kauffman, D. P. Hallahan, & P. C. Pullen (Eds.), *Handbook of special education* (2nd ed., pp. 773–792). New York: Routledge.

Mueller, T. G., Singer, G. H., & Draper, L. M. (2008). Reducing parental dissatisfaction with special education in two school districts: Implementing conflict prevention and alternative dispute resolution. *Journal of Educational and Psychological Consultation, 18*, 191–233. doi:10.1080/10474410701864339

Orsmond, G. I., & Seltzer, M. M. (2000). Brothers and sisters of adults with mental retardation: Gendered nature of the sibling relationship. *American Journal on Mental Retardation, 105*, 486–508.

Orsmond, G. I., Seltzer, M. M., Greenberg, J. S., & Krauss, M. W. (2006). Mother–child relationship quality among adolescents and adults with autism. *American Journal on Mental Retardation, 111*, 121–137. doi:10.1352/0895-8017(2006)111[121:MRQAAA]2.0.CO;2

O'Shea, D. J., & O'Shea, L. J. (2001). Why learn about students' families? In D. J. O'Shea, L. J. O'Shea, R. Algozzine, & D. J. Hammitte (Eds.), *Families and teachers of individuals with disabilities: Collaborative orientations and responsive practices* (pp. 5–24). Boston: Allyn & Bacon.

O'Shea, D. J., O'Shea, L. J., Algozzine, R., & Hammitte, D. J. (Eds.). (2001). *Families and teachers of individuals with disabilities: Collaborative orientations and responsive practices.* Boston: Allyn & Bacon.

Parette, H. P., & Petch-Hogan, B. (2000). Approaching families: Facilitating culturally/linguistically diverse family involvement. *Teaching Exceptional Children, 33*(2), 4–10.

Plant, K. M., & Sanders, M. R. (2007). Predictors of care-giver stress in families of preschool-aged children with developmental disabilities. *Journal of Intellectual Disability Research, 51*, 109-124. doi: 10.1111/j.1365-2788.2006.00829.x

Rossiter, L., & Sharpe, D. (2001). The siblings of individuals with mental retardation: A quantitative integration of the literature. *Journal of Child and Family Studies, 10*, 65–84. doi:10.1023/A:1016629500708

Scorgie, K., & Sobsey, D. (2000). Transformational outcomes associated with parenting children who have disabilities. *Mental*

Retardation, 38, 195–206. doi:10.1352/0047-6765(2000)038 <0195:TOAWPC>2.0.CO;2

Shattuck, R. M., & Kreider, R. M. (2013). Social and economic characteristics of currently unmarried women with a recent birth: 2011. *American Community Survey Reports.* Retrieved from http://www.census.gov/prod/2013pubs/acs-21.pdf.

Shivers, C. M., & Dykens, E. M. (2017). Adolescent siblings of individuals with and without intellectual and developmental disabilities: Self-reported empathy and feelings about their brothers and sisters. *American Journal on Intellectual and Developmental Disabilities, 122*, 62–77. doi:10.1352/1944-7558-122.1.62

Sileo, N. M., & Prater, M. A. (2012). *Working with families of children with special needs: Family and professional partnerships and roles.* Upper Saddle River, NJ: Pearson.

Silverman, A. (2005). *No overalls for Sophie!* KJZZ, The National Public Radio Affiliate in Phoenix, AZ.

Singer, G. H. S. (2006). Meta-analysis of comparative studies of depression in mothers of children with and without developmental disabilities. *American Journal on Mental Retardation, 111*, 155–169. doi:10.1352/0895-8017(2006)111 [155:MOCSOD]2.0.CO;2

Singer, G. H. S. (2017). Introduction to Section XI: Parent and family issues in special education. In J. M. Kauffman, D. P. Hallahan, & P. C. Pullen (Eds.), *Handbook of special education* (2nd ed., pp. 771–772). New York: Routledge.

Singer, G. H. S., Goldberg-Hamblin, S. E., Peckham-Hardin, K. D., Barry, L., & Santarelli, G. E. (2002). Toward a synthesis of family support practices and positive behavior support. In J. M. Lucyshyn, G. Dunlap, & R. W. Albin (Eds.), *Families and positive behavior support: Addressing problem behavior in family contexts* (pp. 155–183). Baltimore: Brookes.

Singer, G. H. S., Maul, C., Wang, M., & Ethridge, B. L. (2017). Resilience in families of children with disabilities: Risk and protective factors. In J. M. Kauffman, D. P. Hallahan, & P. C. Pullen (Eds.), *Handbook of special education* (2nd ed., pp. 793–810). New York: Routledge.

Skinner, D., Bailey, D. B., Correa, V., & Rodriguez, P. (1999). Narrating self and disability: Latino mothers' construction of identities vis-à-vis their child with special needs. *Exceptional Children, 65*, 481–495.

Skotarczak, L., & Lee, G. K. (2015). Effects of parent management training programs on disruptive behavior for children with a developmental disability: A meta-analysis. *Research in Developmental Disabilities, 38*, 272–287. doi:10.1016/j.ridd.2014.12.004

Slonims, V., & McConachie, H. (2006). Analysis of mother–infant interaction in infants with Down syndrome and typically developing infants. *American Journal on Mental Retardation, 111*, 273–289. doi:10.1352/0895-8017

Smith, L. E., Greenberg, J. S., Seltzer, M. M., & Hong, J. (2008). Symptoms and behavior problems of adolescents and adults with autism: Effects of mother–child relationship quality, warmth, and praise. *American Journal on Mental Retardation, 113*, 387–402. doi:10.1352/ 2008.113:387-402

Stoneman, Z., & Gavidia-Payne, S. (2006). Marital adjustment in families of young children with disabilities: Associations with daily hassles and problem-focused coping. *American Journal on Mental Retardation, 111*, 1–14. doi:10.1352/ 0895-8017(2006)111 [1:MAI-FOY]2.0.CO;2

Taylor, N. E., Wall, S. M., Liebow, H., Sabatino, C. A., Timberlake, E. M., & Farber, M. Z. (2005). Mother and soldier: Raising a child with a disability in a low-income military family. *Exceptional Children, 72*, 83–99.

Technical Assistance Alliance for Parent Centers. (2009). *About the Alliance.* Retrieved from http://www.taalliance.org/about/index.asp

Turnbull, H. R., Shogren, K. A., & Turnbull, A. P. (2011). Evolution of the parent movement. In J. M. Kauffman & D. P. Hallahan (Eds.), *Handbook of special education* (pp. 639–653). New York: Routledge.

Turnbull, A., & Turnbull, R. (2006). Fostering family–professional partnerships. In M. E. Snell & F. Brown (Eds.), *Instruction of students with severe disabilities* (6th ed.). Upper Saddle River, NJ: Merrill/Pearson.

Turnbull, A., Turnbull, R., Erwin, E., & Soodak, L. (2006). *Families, professionals, and exceptionality: Positive outcomes through partnerships and trust.* Upper Saddle River, NJ: Merrill/Pearson.

UNICEF Office of Research. (2013). Child well-being in rich countries: A comparative review. *Innocenti Report Card 11.* http://www.unicef-irc.org/Report-Card-11/.

Warger, C. (2003–2004). *Five homework strategies for teaching students with disabilities.* ERIC Clearinghouse on Disabilities and Gifted Education. Retrieved from http://www.ericdigests.org/2002-1/homework.html

Werner, E. E. (2004). Journeys from childhood to midlife: Risk, resilience, and recovery. *Pediatrics, 114*, 492.

Zuckerman, K. E., Lindly, O. J., & Sinche, B. (2016) Parent beliefs about the causes of learning and developmental problems among children with autism spectrum disorder: Results from a national survey. *American Journal on Intellectual and Developmental Disabilities, 121*, 432–447. doi:10.1352/1944-7558-121.5.432

Zuniga, M. E. (1992). Families with no roots. In E. W. Lynch & M. J. Hanson (Eds.), *Developing cross-cultural competence* (2nd ed., pp. 151–179). Baltimore: Brookes.

CHAPTER 5

AAMR Ad Hoc Committee on Terminology and Classification. (2010). *Mental retardation: Definition, classification, and systems of supports* (11th ed.). Washington, DC: American Association on Mental Retardation.

Abbeduto, L., Brady, N., & Kover, S. T. (2007). Language development and Fragile X syndrome: Profiles, syndrome-specificity, and within-syndrome differences. *Mental Retardation and Development Disabilities Research Reviews, 13*, 36–46. doi:10.1002/mrdd.20142

Abbeduto, L., Keller-Bell, Y., Richmond, E. K., & Murphy, M. M. (2006). Research on language development and mental retardation: History, theories, findings, and future directions. *International Review of Research in Mental Retardation, 32*, 1–39. doi:10.1016/S0074-7750(06)32001-0

Abbeduto, L., Murphy, M. M., Cawthon, S. W., Richmond, E. K., Weissman, M. D., Karadottir, S., et al. (2003). Receptive language skills of adolescents and young adults with Down or Fragile X syndrome. *American Journal on Mental Retardation, 108,* 149–160.

Abbeduto, L., Murphy, M. M., Richmond, E. K., Amman, A., Beth, P., Weissman, M. D., et al. (2006). Collaboration in referential communication: Comparison of youth with Down syndrome or Fragile X syndrome. *American Journal on Mental Retardation, 111,* 170–183. doi:10.1352/0895-8017(2006)111 [170:CIRCCO]2.0.CO:2

Ager, A. (2003). *The BILD Life Experiences Checklist Manual.* Birmingham, England: British Institute of Learning Disabilities.

Agran, M., Fodor-Davis, J., Moore, S., & Deer, M. (1989). The application of a self-management program on instruction-following skills. *Journal of the Association for the Severely Handicapped, 14,* 147–154.

Alvarez, H. (2008, January 10). Alzheimer's disease in individuals with Down syndrome. *eMedicine,* Retrieved from http://emedicine. medscape.com/article/1136117-overview

Atkins v. State of Virginia, 536 U.S. 304 (2002).

Bailey, D. B., Raspa, M., Holiday, D., Bishop, E., & Olmsted, M. (2009). Functional skills of individuals with Fragile X syndrome: A lifespan cross-sectional analysis. *American Journal of Intellectual and Developmental Disabilities, 114,* 289–303. doi:10.1352/1944-7558-114.4.289-303

Baumeister, A. A. (2006). Mental retardation: Confusing sentiment with science. In H. N. Switsky & S. Greenspan (Eds.), *What is mental retardation? Ideas for an evolving disability in the 21st Century* (rev. ed., pp. 95–126). Washington, DC: American Association on Mental Retardation.

Bebko, J. M., & Luhaorg, H. (1998). The development of strategy use and metacognitive processing in mental retardation: Some sources of difficulty. In J. A. Burack, R. M. Hodapp, & E. Zigler (Eds.), *Handbook of mental retardation and development* (pp. 382–407). New York: Cambridge University Press.

Beck, S., Wojdyla, D., Say, L., Betran, A. P., Merialdi, M., Requejo, J. H. & Van Look, P. F. A. (2010). The worldwide incidence of preterm birth: A systematic review of maternal mortality and morbidity. *Bulletin of the World Health Organization, 88,* 31–38. doi:10.2471/BLT.08.062554

Belser, R. C., & Sudhalter, V. (2001). Conversational characteristics of children with fragile X syndrome: Repetitive speech. *American Journal on Mental Retardation, 106,* 28–38.

Blatt, B., & Kaplan, F. M. (1966). *Christmas in purgatory.* Boston, MA: Allyn & Bacon.

Brown, R. I., & Brown, I. (2005). The application of quality of life. *Journal of Intellectual Disability Research, 49,* 718–727. doi:10.1111/i.1365-2788.2005.00740.x

Caballo, C., Crespo, M., Jenaro, C., Verdugo, M. A., & Martinez, J. L. (2005). Factor structure of the Schalock and Keith Quality of Life Questionnaire (QOL-Q): Validation on Mexican and Spanish samples. *Journal of Intellectual Disability Research, 49,* 773–776. doi:10.1111/j.1365-2788.2005.00750.x

Carr, J. (1994). Annotation: Long term outcome for people with Down's syndrome. *Journal*

of Child Psychology and Psychiatry, 35, 425–439. doi:10.1111/j.1469-7610.1994.tb01732.x

Carter, E. W., Hughes, C., Guth, C. B., & Copeland, S. R. (2005). Factors influencing social interaction among high school students with intellectual disabilities and their general education peers. *American Journal on Mental Retardation, 110,* 366–377. doi:10.1352/0 895-8017(2005)110[366:FISIAH]2.0.CO;2

Chapman, D. A., Scott, K. G., & Mason, C. A. (2002). Early risk factors for mental retardation: Role of maternal age and maternal education. *American Journal on Mental Retardation, 107,* 46–59.

Cummins, R. A. (2005a). Instruments for assessing quality of life. In J. Hogg & A. Langa (Eds.), *Assessing adults with intellectual disabilities: A service provider's guide* (pp. 119–137). Malden, MA: Blackwell.

Cummins, R. A. (2005b). Issues in the systematic assessment of quality of life. In J. Hogg & A. Langa (Eds.), *Assessing adults with intellectual disabilities: A service provider's guide* (pp. 9–22). Malden, MA: Blackwell.

Davis, S. (1997). *The Human Genome Project: Examining the Arc's concerns regarding the Human Genome Project's ethical, legal, and social implications.* Presentation at the DOE Human Genome Program Contractor-Grantee Workshop VI. Retrieved from www.ornl.gov/hgmis/resource/arc.html

Delquadri, J. C., Greenwood, C. R., Stretton, K., & Hall, R. V. (1983). The peer tutoring spelling game: A classroom procedure for increasing opportunity to respond and spelling performance. *Education and Treatment of Children, 6,* 225–239.

Devlin, P. Enhancing job performance. *Intellectual and Developmental Disabilities, 49,* 221–232.

Dimitropoulos, A., Feurer, I. D., Butler, M. G., & Thompson, T. (2001). Emergence of compulsive behavior and tantrums in children with Prader-Willi syndrome. *American Journal on Mental Retardation, 106,* 39–51.

Drasgow, E., Wolery, M., Chezan, L. C., Halle, J., & Hajiaghamohseni, Z. (2017). Systematic instruction of students with significant cognitive disabilities. In J. M. Kauffman, D. P. Hallahan, & P. C. Pullen (Eds.), *Handbook of special education* (2nd ed., pp. 632–648). New York: Routledge.

Drew, C. J., & Hardman, M. L. (2007). *Intellectual disabilities across the life span* (9th ed.). Upper Saddle River, NJ: Pearson.

Dykens, E. (2001). Introduction to special issue. *American Journal on Mental Retardation, 106,* 1–3.

Dykens, E. M., Hodapp, R. M., & Finucane, B. M. (2000). *Genetics and mental retardation syndromes: A new look at behavior and interventions.* Baltimore: Brookes.

Dymond, S. K. (2017). Functional curriculum for students with significant cognitive disabilities. In In J. M. Kauffman, D. P. Hallahan, & P. C. Pullen (Eds.). *The handbook of special education* (2nd ed, pp. 675–686). New York: Routledge.

Evenhuis, H. M. (1990). The natural history of dementia in Down's syndrome. *Archives of Neurology, 47,* 263–267.

Everson, J. M., & Trowbridge, M. H. (2011). Preparing students with low-incidence disabilities for community living opportunities.

In J. M. Kauffman & D. P. Hallahan (Eds.). *The handbook of special education.* New York: Routledge.

Fidler, D. J., Hepburn, S. L., Most, D. E., Philofsky, A., & Rogers, S. J. (2007). Emotional responsivity in young children with Williams syndrome. *American Journal on Mental Retardation, 112,* 194–206. doi:10.1352/0895-8017(2007)112 [194:ERIY-CW]2.0.CO;2

Fidler, D. J., Hodapp, R. M., & Dykens, E. M. (2002). Behavioral phenotypes and special education: Parent report of educational issues for children with Down syndrome, Prader-Willi syndrome, and Williams syndrome. *The Journal of Special Education, 36,* 80–88. doi:10.1177/ 00224669020360020301

Fraser, J., & Mitchell, A. (1876). Kalmuc idiocy: Report of a case with autopsy, with notes on sixty-two cases. *Journal of Mental Science, 22,* 161–179.

Glidden, L. M. (2006). An update on the label and definitional asynchrony: The missing *mental* and *retardation* in mental retardation. In H. N. Switsky & S. Greenspan (Eds.), *What is mental retardation? Ideas for an evolving disability in the 21st century* (rev. ed., pp. 39–49). Washington, DC: American Association on Mental Retardation.

Greenspan, S. (2004). Why Pinocchio was victimized: Factors contributing to social failure in people with mental retardation. *International Review of Research in Mental Retardation, 28,* 121–144. doi:10:10.1016/ S0074-7750(04)28004-1

Greenspan, S. (2006a). Functional concepts in mental retardation: Finding the natural essence of an artificial category. *Exceptionality, 14,* 205–224. doi:10.1207/ s1532703ex1404_3

Greenspan, S. (2006b). Mental retardation in the real world: Why the AAMR definition is not there yet. In H. N. Switsky & S. Greenspan (Eds.), *What is mental retardation? Ideas for an evolving disability in the 21st century* (rev. ed., pp. 165–183). Washington, DC: American Association on Mental Retardation.

Greenspan, S. (2009). Foolish action in adults with intellectual disabilities: The forgotten problem of risk-unawareness. In L. Glidden (Ed.), *International review of research in mental retardation* (Vol. 36, pp. 147–194). New York: Elsevier. doi:10.1016/s0074-7750(08)00005-0

Greenspan, S., Loughlin, G., & Black, R. S. (2001). Credulity and gullibility in people with developmental disorders: A framework for future research. *International Review of Research in Mental Retardation, 24,* 101–135. doi:10.1016/S0074-7750(01)80007-0

Greenspan, S., & Olley, J. G. (2015). Variability of IQ test scores. In Polloway, E. A. (Ed.), *The death penalty and intellectual disability* (p. 41–153).Washington, DC: American Association on Intellectual and Developmental Disabilities.

Greenspan, S., & Switsky, H. N. (2006). Lessons from the *Atkins* decision for the next AAMR manual. In H. N. Switsky & S. Greenspan (Eds.), *What is mental retardation? Ideas for an evolving disability in the 21st century* (rev. ed., pp. 283–302). Washington, DC: American Association on Mental Retardation.

Greenwood, C. R. (1991). Classwide peer tutoring: Longitudinal effects on the reading, language, and mathematics achievement of at-risk students. *Reading & Writing Quarterly, 7,* 105–123.

Hagerman, R. J. (2001). Fragile X syndrome. In S. B. Cassidy & J. E. Allanson (Eds.), *Management of genetic syndromes* (pp. 165–183). New York: Wiley-Liss.

Haldeman-Englert, C. (2008, February). Williams syndrome. *Medline Plus,* Retrieved from http://www.nlm.nih.gov/medlineplus/ency/article/001116.htm

Hatton, D. D., Wheeler, A. C., Skinner, M. L., Bailey, D. B., Sullivan, K. M., Roberts, J. E., et al. (2003). Adaptive behavior in children with Fragile X syndrome. *American Journal on Mental Retardation, 108,* 373–390.

Hodapp, R. M., & Dykens, E. M. (2007). Behavioral effects of genetic mental retardation disorders. In J. W. Jacobson, J. A. Mullick, & J. Rojahn (Eds.), *Handbook of intellectual and developmental disabilities* (pp. 115–131). New York: Springer.

Hodapp, R. M., & Fidler, D. J. (1999). Special education and genetics: Connections for the 21st century. *Journal of Special Education, 33,* 130–137. doi:10.1177/002246699903300301

Hof, P. R., Bouras, C., Perl, D. P., Sparks, L., Mehta, N., & Morrison, J. H. (1995). Age-related distribution of neuropathologic changes in the cerebral cortex of patients with Down's syndrome. *Archives of Neurology, 52,* 379–391.

Inge, K. J., & Moon, M. S. (2011). Preparing students with low incidence disabilities to work in the community. In J. M. Kauffman & D. P. Hallahan (Eds.). *The handbook of special education.* New York, Routledge.

Institute of Education Sciences, National Center for Special Education Research. (2009, July). *Facts from NLTS2: Secondary Experiences and Academic Performance of students with mental retardation.* Retrieved from http://nces.ed.gov/pubSearch/pubsinfo.asp?pubid=NCSER20093020

John, A. E., Rowe, M. L., & Mervis, C. B. (2009). Referential communication skills of children with Williams syndrome: Understanding when messages are not adequate. *American Journal of Intellectual and Developmental Disabilities, 114,* 85–99. doi:10.1352/2009.114.85-99

Kasari, C., Freeman, S. F. N., & Hughes, M. A. (2001). Emotion recognition by children with Down syndrome. *American Journal on Mental Retardation, 106,* 59–72.

Kaufman, S. Z. (1999). *Retarded isn't stupid, mom!* (rev. ed.). Baltimore: Brookes.

Kazdin, A. E. (n.d.). Helping parents with intellectual disabilities raise their children: A review of *The health and wellness program: A parenting curriculum for families at risk.* Retrieved from http://psycnet.apa.org/critiques/52/14/16.html

Kemp, C., & Carter, M. (2006). Active and passive task related behavior, direction following and the inclusion of children with disabilities. *Education and Training in Developmental Disabilities, 41,* 14–27.

Lakin, K. C., Prouty, R., Coucouvanis, K. (2006). Changing patterns in the size settings for persons with intellectual and developmental disabilities, 1977-2005. *Mental Retardation, 44,* 306–309.

Lancioni, G. E., O'Reilly, M. F., Seedhouse, P., Furniss, F., & Cunha, B. (2000). Promoting independent task performance by persons with severe developmental disabilities through a new computer-aided system. *Behavior Modification, 24,* 700–718. doi:10.1177/0145445500245005

Levorato, M. C., Roch, M. Florit, E. (2011). Role of verbal memory in reading text comprehension of individuals with Down syndrome. *American Journal of Developmental Disabilities, 116,* 99–110. doi:10.1352/1944-7558-116.2.99.

MacMillan, D. L., Gresham, F. M., Bocian, K. M., & Lambros, K. M. (1998). Current plight of borderline students: Where do they belong? *Education and Training in Mental Retardation and Developmental Disabilities, 33,* 83–94.

Mank, D., Cioffi, A., & Yovanoff, P. (2003). Supported employment outcomes across a decade: Is there evidence of improvement in the quality of implementation? *Mental Retardation, 41,* 188–197.

Margallo-Lana M. L., Moore, P. B., Kay, D. W., Perry, R. H., Reid, B. E., Berney, T. P., & Tyrer, S. P. (2007). Fifteen-year follow-up of 92 hospitalized adults with Down's syndrome: incidence of cognitive decline, its relationship to age and neuropathology. *Journal of Intellectual Disabilities, 51,* 463–477.

Martin, J. E., Rusch, F. R., James, V. L., Decker, P. J., & Trtol, K. A. (1982). The use of picture cues to establish self-control in the preparation of complex meals by mentally retarded adults. *Applied Research in Mental Retardation, 3,* 105–119. doi:10.1016/0270-3092(82)90001-7

McDonnell, J. J. (2017). Instructional contexts for students with significant cognitive disabilities. In J. M. Kauffman, D. P. Hallahan, & P. C. Pullen (Eds.), *Handbook of special education* (2nd ed.). New York: Routledge.

McDonnell, J. J., Hardman, M. L., & McDonnell, A. P. (2003). *An introduction to persons with moderate and severe disabilities* (2nd ed.). Boston: Allyn & Bacon.

McNeil, D. G., Romero, S., & Tavernise, S. (2016, February 7). Search to explain birth defects in Brazil led to Zika virus. *New York Times,* CLXV, #57135.

Mechling, L. C., Gast, D. L., & Fields, E. A. (2008). Evaluation of a portable DVD player and system of least prompts to self-prompt cooking task completion by young adults with moderate intellectual disabilities. *The Journal of Special Education, 42,* 179–190. doi:10.1177/ 0022466907313348

Medline Plus. (2007, October 19). Inborn errors of metabolism. Retrieved from http://www.nlm.nih.gov/medlineplus/ency/article/002438.htm

Mervis, C. B., & Becerra, A. M. (2007). Language and communicative development in Williams syndrome. *Mental Retardation and Developmental Disabilities Research Reviews, 13,* 3–15. doi:10.1002/mrdd.20140

Mervis, C. B., Klein-Tasman, B. P., & Mastin, M. E. (2001). Adaptive behavior of 4- through 8-year-old children with Williams syndrome. *American Journal on Mental Retardation, 106,* 82–93.

Meyer, G. A., & Batshaw, M. L. (2002). Fragile X syndrome. In M. L. Batshaw (Ed.), *Children with disabilities* (5th ed.). Baltimore: Brookes.

Moldavsky, M., Lev, D., & Lerman-Sagie, T. (2001). Behavioral phenotypes of genetic syndromes: A reference guide for psychiatrists. *Journal of the American Academy of Child and Adolescent Psychiatry, 40,* 749–761. doi:10.1097/00004583-200107000-00009

Morgan, P. L., Farkas, G., Hillemeier, M. M., Mattison, R., Maczuga, S., Li, H., & Cook, M. (2015). Minorities are disproportionately underrepresented in special education: longitudinal evidence across 5 disabilities conditions. *Educational Researcher, 44* (5), 278–292. doi:10.3102/0013189X15591157.

Mortweet, S. L., Utley, C. A., Walker D., Dowson, H. L., Delquadri, J. C., Reddy, S. S., & Ledford, D. (1999). Classwide peer tutoring: Teaching students with mild mental retardation in inclusive classrooms. *Exceptional Children, 65,* 524–536.

National Institute of Neurological Disorders and Stroke. (2008, October 29). *NINDS Microcephaly Information Page.* Retrieved from http://www.ninds.nih.gov/disorders/microcephaly/microcephaly.htm

Newman, L., Wagner, M., Cameto, R., & Knokey, A. (2009). *The post-high school outcomes of youth with disabilities up to 4 years after high school. A report from the National Longitudinal Transition Study-2 (NLTS2)* (NCSER 2009-3017). Washington, DC: U. S. Government Printing Office.

Patton, J. P., & Keyes, D. W. (2006). Death penalty issues following *Atkins. Exceptionality, 14,* 237–255. doi:10.1207/s15327035ex1404_5

Percy, M., Lewkis, S. Z., & Brown, I. (2007). Introduction to genetics and development. In I. Brown & M. Percy. (Eds.), *A comprehensive guide to intellectual disabilities* (pp. 87–108). Baltimore: Brookes.

Polloway, E. A., Bouck, E., Patton, J. R., & Lubin, J. (2017). Intellectual and developmental disabilities. In J. M. Kauffman, D. P. Hallahan, & P. C. Pullen (Eds.), *Handbook of special education* (2nd ed., pp. 265–285). New York: Routledge.

Polloway, E. A., Smith, J. D., & Antoine, K. (2010). Biological causes. In M. Beirne-Smith, J. R. Patton, & S. H. Kim (Eds.), *Intellectual disabilities* (8th ed.). Upper Saddle River, NJ: Pearson.

Prouty, R., Coucouvanis, K., & Lakin, K. C. (2007). HCBS recipients are increasingly likely to live with parents or other relatives. *Intellectual and Developmental Disabilities, 45,* 359–361.

Roberts, J. E., Price, J., & Malkin, C. (2007). Language and communication development in Down syndrome. *Mental Retardation and Developmental Disabilities Research Reviews, 13,* 26–35. doi:10.1002/mrdd.20136

Rueda, R., Monzo, L., Shapiro, J., Gomez, J., & Blacher, J. (2005). Cultural models of transition: Latina mothers of young adults with developmental disabilities. *Exceptional Children, 71,* 401–414.

Sands, D., & Wehmeyer, M. (2005). Teaching goal setting and decision making to students with developmental disabilities. In M. L. Wehmeyer, M. Agran, M. L. Wehmeyer,

& M. Agran (Eds.), *Mental retardation and intellectual disabilities: Teaching students using innovative and research-based strategies* (pp. 273–296). Auckland, New Zealand: Pearson.

Schalock, R. L., Brown, I., Brown, R. I., Cummins, R., Felce, D., Matikka, L., et al. (2002). Quality of life: Its conceptualization, measurement, and application. A consensus document. *Mental Retardation, 40,* 457–470. doi:10.1352/0047-6765(2002)040<0457:C-MAAOQ>2.0.CO;2

Schalock, R. L., & Keith, K. D. (1993). *Quality of life questionnaire.* Worthington, OH: IDA Publishing.

Skiba, R., Artiles, A. J., Kozleski, E. B., Losen, D. J., & Harry, E. G. (2015). Risks and consequences of oversimplifying educational inequities: A response to Morgan et al. (2015). *Educational Researcher, 45,* 221-225. doi:10.3102/0013189X1664606.

Snell, M. E., Luckasson, R., et al. (2009). Characteristics and needs of people with intellectual disability who have higher IQs. *Intellectual and Developmental Disabilities, 47,* 220–233. doi:10.1352/1934-9556-47.3.220

Sparrow, S. S., Chicchetti, D. V., & Saulnier, C. A. (2016). *Vineland Adaptive Behavior scales* (3rd ed.). Circle Pines, MN: American Guidance Service.

Spinath, F. M., Harlaar, N., Ronald, A., & Plomin, R. (2004). Substantial genetic influence on mild mental impairment in early childhood. *American Journal on Mental Retardation, 109,* 34–43.

Spinelli, C. G. (2006). *Classroom assessment for students in special and general education* (2nd ed.). Upper Saddle River, NJ: Merrill/Pearson.

Stancliffe, R. J., Lakin, K. C., Larson, S. A., Engler, J., Taub, S., Fortune, J., & Bershadsky, J. (2012). Demographic characteristics, health conditions, and residential service use in adults with Down syndrome in 25 US states. *Intellectual and Developmental Disabilities, 50* (2), 92–108. doi:10.1352/1934-9556-50.2.92.

Switsky, H. N. (2006). The importance of cognitive-motivational variables in understanding the outcome performance of persons with mental retardation: A personal view from the early twenty-first century. *International Review of Research in Mental Retardation, 31,* 1–29. doi:10.1016/S0074-7750(05)31001-9

Tarleton, B., & Ward, L. (2007). "Parenting with support": The views and experiences of parents with intellectual disabilities. *Journal of Policy and Practice in Intellectual Disabilities, 4,* 194–202. doi:10.1111/j.1741-1130.2007.00118.x

Tasse, M. J., Schalock, R. L., Balboni, G., Bersani Jr., H., Borthwick-Duffy, S. A., Spreat, S., Thissen, D., Widaman, K. F., & Zhang, D. (2012). The construct of adaptive behavior: It's conceptualization, measurement, and use in the field of intellectual disability. *American Journal of Developmental Disabilities, 117,* 291–303. doi:10.1352/1944-7558-117.4.291.

Taylor, H. G., Klein, N., Minich, N. M., & Hack, M. (2000). Middle-school-age outcomes in children with very low birthweight. *Child Development, 71,* 1495–1511. doi:10.1111/1467-8624.00242

Taylor, R. L., Richards, S. B., & Brady, M. P. (2005). *Mental retardation: Historical perspectives, current practices, and future directions.* Boston: Allyn & Bacon.

Thompson, J. R., Bradley, V. J., Buntinx, W. H. E., Schalock, R. L., Shogren, K. A., Snell, M. E., et al. (2009). Conceptualizing supports and the support needs of people with intellectual disability. *Intellectual and Developmental Disabilities, 47,* 135–146. doi:10.1352/1934-9556-47.2.135

Tichá, R., Lakin, K. C., Larson, S.A., Stancliffe, R. J., Taub, S., Engler, J., Moseley, C. (2012). Correlates of everyday choice and support related choice for 8,892 randomly sampled adults with intellectual and developmental disabilities in 19 states. *Intellectual and Developmental Disabilities, 50,* 486–504.

Tymchuk, A. J. (2006). *The health and wellness program: A parenting curriculum for families at risk.* Baltimore: Brookes.

U.S. Department of Education. (2016). *Thirty-eighth annual report to Congress on implementation of the Individuals with Disabilities Education Act.* Washington, DC: Author.

Urv, T. K., Zigman, W. B., & Silverman, W. (2008). Maladaptive behaviors related to dementia status in adults with Down syndrome. *American Journal of Mental Retardation, 113,* 73–86. doi:10.1352/0895-8017(2008)113[73:MBRTDS]2.0.CO;2

Wade, C., Llewellyn, G., & Matthews, J. (2008). Review of parent training interventions for parents with intellectual disability. *Journal of Applied Research in Intellectual Disabilities, 21,* 351–366. doi:10.1111/j.1468-3148.2008.00449.x

Wallace, R. A., & Dalton, A. J. (2011). What we can learn from study of Alzheimer's disease in patients with Down syndrome for early-onset Alzheimer's disease in the general population? *Alzheimers Research & Therapy, 3,* doi:10.1186/alzrt72

Wechsler, D. (2003). *Wechsler intelligence scale for children* (4th ed.). San Antonio, TX: Psychological Corporation.

Wehmeyer, M. L., Garner, N., Yeager, D., Lawrence, M., & Davis, A. K. (2006). Infusing self-determination into 18–21 services for students with intellectual or developmental disabilities: A multi-stage, multiple component model. *Education and Training in Developmental Disabilities, 41,* 1–13.

Wehymeyer, M. L., & Mithaug, D. E. (2006). Self-determination, causal agency, and mental retardation. *International Review of Research in Mental Retardation, 31,* 31–71. doi:10.1016/S0074-7750(05)31002-0

Wehmeyer, M. L., & Shogren, K. A. (2017, in press). Access to the general education curriculum for students with significant cognitive disabilities. In J. M. Kauffman, D. P. Hallahan, & P. C. Pullen (Eds.), *Handbook of special education* (2nd ed.). New York: Routledge.

Weijerman, M. E., van Furth, A. M., Vonk Noordegraaf, T., Van Wouwe, J. P., Broers, C. J. M., & Gemeke, R. J. B. J. (2008). Prevalence, neonatal characteristics, and first year mortality of Down syndrome: A national study, *Journal of Pediatrics, 152,* 15–19. doi:10.1016/j.jpeds.2007.09.045.

Whitaker, S. (2008). The stability of IQ in people with low intellectual ability: An analysis of the literature. *Intellectual and Developmental Disabilities, 46,* 120–128. doi:10.1352/0047-6765(2008)46[120:TSOII-P]2.0.CO;2

Winsor, J., & Butterworth, J. (2008). Participation in integrated employment and community-based nonwork services for individuals supported by state disability agencies. *Intellectual and Developmental Disabilities, 46,* 166–168. doi:10.1352/0047-6765(2008)46[166:PIIEAC]2.0.CO;2

Woods, G. W., Freedman, D. D., & Derning, T. J. (2015). Intellectual disability and comorbid disorders. In Polloway, E. A. (Ed.), *The death penalty and intellectual disability* (p. 279–292). Washington, DC: American Association on Intellectual and Developmental Disabilities.

Ysseldyke, J., & Olsen, K. (1999). Putting alternate assessments into practice: What to measure and possible sources of data. *Exceptional Children, 65,* 175–185.

CHAPTER 6

Aarnoudse-Moens, C. S. H., Weisglas-Kuperus, N., van Goudoever, J. B., & Oosterlaan, J. (2009). Meta-analysis of neurobehavioral outcomes in very preterm and/or very low birth weight children. *Pediatrics, 124,* 717–728. doi:10.1542/peds.2008-2816

Adams, G. L., & Engelmann, S. (1996). *Research on direct instruction: 25 years beyond DISTAR.* Seattle: Educational Achievement Systems.

Al-Yagon, M. (2007). Socioemotional and behavioral adjustment among school-age children with learning disabilities: The moderating role of maternal personal resources. *The Journal of Special Education, 40,* 205–217. doi:10.1177/ 00224669070400040201

Allsopp, D. H., Kyger, M. M., & Lovin, L. (2008). Mathematics dynamic assessment: Informal assessment that responds to the needs of struggling learners in mathematics. *Teaching Exceptional Children, 40,* 6–16.

American Psychiatric Association. (2013). "Specific Learning Disorder." American Psychiatric Publishing. Retrieved from http://www.dsm5.org/Documents/Specific%20Learning%20Disorder%20Fact%20Sheet.pdf.

Bear, G. G., Kortering, L. J., & Braziel, P. (2006). School completers and noncompleters with learning disabilities: Similarities in academic achievement and perceptions of self and teachers. *Remedial and Special Education, 27,* 293–300. doi:10.1177/07419325060700050401

Beichtman, J. H., Hood, J., & Inglis, A. (1992). Familial transmission of speech and language impairment: A preliminary investigation. *Canadian Journal of Psychiatry, 37,* 151–156.

Bender, W. N., Rosenkrans, C. B., & Crane, M. K. (1999). Stress, depression, and suicide among students with learning disabilities: Assessing the risk. *Learning Disability Quarterly, 22,* 143–156. doi:10.2307/1511272

Berkeley, S., Bender, W. N., Peaster, L. G., & Saunders, L. (2009). Implementation of response to intervention: A snapshot of progress. *Journal of Learning Disabilities, 42,* 85–95. doi:10.1177/ 0022219408326214

Bryan, T., Burstein, K., & Ergul, C. (2004). The social-emotional side of learning disabilities: A science-based presentation of the state of the art. *Learning Disability Quarterly, 40,* 27, 45–51. doi:10.2307/1593631

Bryan, T. H., Donahue, M., Pearl, R., & Sturm, C. (1981). Learning disabled children's conversational skills—The "TV Talk Show." *Learning Disability Quarterly, 4,* 250–260. doi:10.2307/1510946

Bryan, T. H., & Sullivan-Burstein, K. (1998). Teacher-selected strategies for improving homework completion. *Remedial and Special Education, 19,* 263–275. doi:10.1177/074193259801900502

Case, L. P., Harris, K. R., & Graham, S. (1992). Improving the mathematical problem-solving skills of students with learning disabilities. *The Journal of Special Education, 26,* 1–19.

Chevalier, T. M., Parrila, R., Ritchie, K. C., & Deacon, S. H. (2017). The role of metacognitive reading strategies, metacognitive study and learning strategies, and behavioral study and learning strategies in predicting academic success in students with and without a history of reading difficulties. *Journal of Learning Disabilities, 50,* 34–48. doi: 10.1177/0022219415588850.

Clarizio, H. F., & Phillips, S. E. (1986). Sex bias in the diagnosis of learning disabled students. *Psychology in the Schools, 23,* 44–52. doi:10.1002/1520-6807(198601)23:1<44::AID-PITS2310230108>3.0.CO;2-L.

Cobb, R. B., & Alwell, M. (2009). Transition planning/coordinating interventions for youth with disabilities: A systematic review. *Career Development for Exceptional Individuals, 32,* 70–81. doi:10.1177/0885728809336655

Cohen, S., & Janicki-Deverts, D. (2012). Who's stressed? Distributions of psychological stress in the United Stattes in probability samples from 1983, 2006, and 2009. *Journal of Applied Social Psychology, 42,* 1320–1334.

Cook, S. C., McDuffie-Landrum, K. A., Oshita, L., & Cook, B. G. (2017). Co-teaching for students with disabilities: A critical and updated analysis of the empirical literature. In J. M. Kauffman, D. P. Hallahan, & P. C. Pullen (Eds.), *Handbook of special education.* (2nd ed., pp. 233–248). New York: NY: Routledge.

Cortiella, C. (2009). *The state of learning disabilities.* New York: National Center for Learning Disabilities. Retrieved from www.ld.org/stateofld

Cortiella, C., & Horowitz, S. H. (2014). *The state of learning disabilities: Facts, trends and emerging issues.* New York: National Center for Learning Disabilities. Retrieved from https://www.ncld.org/wp-content/uploads/2014/11/2014-State-of-LD.pdf

Council for Exceptional Children. (2003). *What every special educator must know: Ethics, standards, and guidelines for special educators* (5th ed.). Arlington, VA: Author.

Culbertson, W. C., & Zillmer, E. A. (2017). "Tower of London (TOL-DX)" (2nd ed.). Multi-Health-Systems. Retrieved from http://www.mhs.com/product.aspx-?gr=edu&prod=toldx&id=overview.

Daniel, S. S., Walsh, A. K., Goldston, D. B., Arnold, E. M., Reboussin, B. A., & Wood, F. B. (2006). Suicidality, school dropout, and reading problems among adolescents. *Journal of Learning Disabilities, 39,* 507–514. doi:10.1177/ 00222194060390060301

DeFries, J. C., Gillis, J. J., & Wadsworth, S. J. (1993). Genes and genders: A twin study of reading disability. In A. M. Galaburda (Ed.), *Dyslexia and development: Neurobiological aspects of extra-ordinary brains* (pp. 187–294). Cambridge, MA: Harvard University Press.

Deno, S. L. (1985). Curriculum-based measurement: The emerging alternative. *Exceptional Children, 52,* 219–232.

Deshler, D. D., & Hock, M. F. (2007). Adolescent literacy: Where we are, where we need to go. In M. Pressley, A. K. Billman, K. H. Perry, K. E, Reffitt, & J. M. Reynolds (Eds.), *Shaping literacy achievement: Research we have, research we need* (pp. 98–128). New York: Guilford Press.

DeThorne, L. S., Hart, S. A., Petrill, S. A., Deater-Deckard, K., Thompson, L. A., Schatschneider, C., et al. (2006). Children's history of speech-language difficulties: Genetic influences and associations with reading-related measures. *Journal of Speech, Language, and Hearing Research, 49,* 1280–1293. doi:10.1044/1092-4388(2006/092).

Duckworth, A. L., & Kern, M. L. (2011). A meta-analysis of the convergent validity of self-control measures. *Journal of Research in Personality, 45,* 259–268. doi.org/10.1016/j.jrp.2011.02.004.

Eicher, J. D., Montgomery, A. M., Akshoomoff, N., Amaral, D. G., Bloss, C. S., Libiger, O., . . . Gruen, J. R. (2016). Dyslexia and language impairment associated genetic markers influence cortical thickness and white matter in typically developing children. *Brain Imaging and Behavior, 10,* 272–282. doi:10.1007/s11682-015-9392-6.

Ellis, A. (2001). *Research on educational innovations* (3rd ed.). Larchmont, NY: Eye On Education.

Ellis, A. K., & Fouts, J. T. (1997). *Research on educational interventions.* Larchmont, NY: Eye on Education.

Ellis, E. S., & Howard, P. W. (2007, Spring). Graphic organizers: Power tools for teaching students with learning disabilities. *Current Practice Alerts, 13.* Retrieved from http://www.teachingld.org/pdf/alert13.pdf

Engelmann, S., & Bruner, E. C. (1969). DISTAR reading I: An instructional system. Chicago: SRA.

Epstein, M. H., Munk, D. D., Bursuck, W. D., Polloway, E. A., & Jayanthi, M. (1998). Strategies for improving home–school communication about homework for students with disabilities. *Journal of Special Education, 33,* 166–176. doi:10.1177/002246699903300304.

Evens, A., Hryhorczuk, D., Lanphear, B. P., Rankin, K. M., Lewis, D. A., Forst, L., & Rosenberg, D. (2015). *Environmental Health, 14*(21), 1–9. doi:10.1186/s12940-015-0008-9.

Foegen, A., Jiban, C., & Deno, S. (2007). Progress monitoring measures in mathematics: A review of the literature. *The Journal of Special Education, 41,* 121–139. doi:10.1177/0022466907041002010

Frostig, M., & Horne, D. (1964). *The Frostig program for the development of visual perception: Teacher's guide.* Chicago: Follett.

Fuchs, D., & Fuchs, L. S. (2005). Peer-assisted learning strategies: Promoting word recognition, fluency, and reading comprehension in young children. *The Journal of Special Education, 39,* 34–44. doi:10.1177/00 224669050390010401

Fuchs, D., Fuchs, L., & Burish, P. (2000). Peer-assisted learning strategies: An evidence-based practice to promote reading achievement. *Learning Disabilities Research & Practice, 15*(2), 85–91. doi:10.1207/SLDRP1502_4

Fuchs, D., Fuchs, L. S., McMaster, K. L., Yen, L., & Svenson, E. (2004). Nonresponders: How to find them? How to help them? What do they mean for special education? *Teaching Exceptional Children, 37,* 72–77.

Fuchs, D., Mock, D., Morgan, P. L., & Young, C. L. (2003). Responsiveness-to-intervention: Definitions, evidence, and implications for the learning disabilities construct. *Learning Disabilities Research & Practice, 18,* 157–171. doi:10.1111/1540-5826.00072

Fuchs, L. S. (2003). Assessing intervention responsiveness: Conceptual and technical issues. *Learning Disabilities Research & Practice, 18,* 172–186. doi:10.1111/1540-5826.00073

Fuchs, L. S., Deno, S. L., & Mirkin, P. K. (1984). The effects of frequent curriculum-based measurement and evaluation of pedagogy, student achievement and student awareness of learning. *American Educational Research Journal, 24,* 449–460.

Fuchs, L. S., Fuchs, D., Hamlett, C. L., Walz, L., & Germann, G. (1993). Formative evaluation of academic progress: How much growth can we expect? School Psychology Review, 22, 27–48.

Fuchs, L. S., Powell, S. R., Seethaler, P. M., Cirino, P. T., Fletcher, J. M., Fuchs, D., & Hamlett, C. L. (2011). The development of arithmetic and word-problem skill among students with mathematics disability. In J. M. Kauffman & D. P. Hallahan (Eds.), *Handbook of special education.* New York: Routledge.

Gabrieli, J. D. E. (2009). Dyslexia: A new synergy between education and neuroscience. *Science, 325,* 280–283. doi:10.1126/science.1171999

Gajria, M., Jitendra, S., Sood, S., & Sacks, G. (2007). Improving comprehension of expository text in students with LD: A research synthesis. *Journal of Learning Disabilities, 40,* 210–225. doi:10.1177/00222194070400 030301.

Geary, D. C., Hoard, M. K., Nugent, L. & Bailey, D. H. (2011). Mathematical cognition deficits in children with learning disabilities and persistent low achievement: A five-year prospective study. *Journal of Educational Psychology, 104,* 206-223. doi:10.1037/a0025398. 10.1037/a0025398

Gersten, R., Chard, D. J., Jayanthi, M., Baker, S. K., Morphy, P., & Flojo, J. (2009). Mathematics instruction for students with learning disabilities: A meta-analysis of instructional components. *Review of Educational Research, 79,* 1202–1242. doi:10.3102/0034654309334431

Good, R. H., Simmons, D. C., & Kame'enui, E. J. (2001). The importance and decision-making utility of a continuum of fluency-based indicators of foundational reading skills for third-grade high-stakes outcomes. *Scientific Studies of Reading, 5,* 257–288. doi:10.1207/S1532799XSSR0503_4

Graham, S., & Harris, K. R. (2003). Students with learning disabilities and the process of writing: A meta-analysis of SRSD studies. In H. L. Swanson, K. R. Harris, & S. Graham (Eds.), *Handbook of learning disabilities* (pp. 323–344). New York: Guilford.

Graham, S., & Harris, K. R. (2011). Writing and students with disabilities. In J. M. Kauffman & D. P. Hallahan (Eds.), *Handbook of special education*. New York: Routledge.

Guttorm, T. K., Leppanen, P. H. T., Poikkeus, A.-M., Eklund, K. M., Lyytinen, P., & Lyytinen, H. (2005). Brain event-related potentials (ERPs) measured at birth predict later language development in children with and without risk for dyslexia. *Cortex, 41*, 291–303. doi:10.1016/S0010-9452(08)70267-3

Hallahan, D. P. (1975). Comparative research studies on the psychological characteristics of learning disabled children. In W. M. Cruickshank & D. P. Hallahan (Eds.), *Perceptual and learning disabilities in children. Vol. 1: Psychoeducational practices* (pp. 29–60). Syracuse, NY: Syracuse University Press.

Hallahan, D. P. (1992). Some thoughts on why the prevalence of learning disabilities has increased. *Journal of Learning Disabilities, 25*, 523–528. doi:10.1177/002221949202500806

Hallahan, D. P., & Cruickshank, W. M. (1973). *Psychoeducational foundations of learning disabilities.* Upper Saddle River, NJ: Pearson.

Hallahan, D. P., Kneedler, R. D., & Lloyd, J. W. (1983). Cognitive behavior modification techniques for learning disabled children: Self-instruction and self-monitoring. In J. D. McKinney & L. Feagans (Eds.), *Current topics in learning disabilities* (Vol. 1, pp. 207–244). New York: Ablex.

Hallahan, D. P., Lloyd, J. W., Kauffman, J. M., Weiss, M. P., & Martinez, E. A. (2005). *Learning disabilities: Foundations, characteristics, and effective teaching.* Boston: Allyn & Bacon.

Hallahan, D. P., & Mercer, C. D. (2002). Learning disabilities: Historical perspectives. In R. Bradley, L. Danielson, & D. P. Hallahan (Eds.), *Identification of learning disabilities: Research to practice* (pp. 1–67). Mahwah, NJ: Erlbaum.

Hallgren, B. (1950). Specific dyslexia (congenital word blindness: A clinical and genetic study). *Acta Psychiatrica et Neurologica, 65*, 1–279.

Hammill, D. D., Leigh, J. E., McNutt, G., & Larsen, S. C. (1981). A new definition of learning disabilities. *Learning Disability Quarterly, 4*, 336–342.

Harris, K. R., Graham, S., & Mason, L. H. (2003). Self-regulated strategy development in the classroom: Part of a balanced approach to writing instruction for students with disabilities. *Focus on Exceptional Children, 35*(7), 1–16.

Hayworth, C. M. A., Kovas, Y., Harlaar, N., Hayiou-Thomas, M. E., Petrill, S. A., Dale, P. S., & Plomin, R. (2009). Generalist genes and learning disabilities: A multivariate genetic analysis of low performance in reading, mathematics, language and general cognitive ability in a sample of 8000 12-year-old twins. *The Journal of Child Psychology and Psychiatry, 50*, 1318–1325. doi:10.1111/j.1469-7610.2009.02114.x.

Hoeft, F., Ueno, T., Reiss, A. L., Meyler, A., Whitfield-Gabrieli, S., Glover, S., & Gabrieli, J. D. E. (2007). Prediction of children's reading skills using behavioral, functional, and structural neuroimaging measures. *Behavioral Neuroscience, 121*, 602–613. doi:10.1037/0735-7044.121.3.602

Hosp, M. K., Hosp, J. L., & Howell, K. W. (2007). *The abcs of CBM: A practical guide to curriculum-based measurement.* New York: Guilford.

Hudson, R., Lane, H., & Pullen, P. (2005). Reading fluency assessment and instruction: What, why, and how? *The Reading Teacher, 58*, 702–714.

Kauffman, J. M., & Hallahan, D. P. (2005). *Special education: What it is and why we need it.* Boston: Allyn & Bacon.

Kephart, N. C. (1971). *The slow learner in the classroom* (2nd ed.). Columbus, OH: Merrill/Pearson.

Kirk, S. A. (1963). Behavioral diagnosis and remediation of learning disabilities. In *Proceedings of the Conference on Exploration into the Problems of the Perceptually Handicapped Child, First Annual Meeting, Vol. 1.* Chicago: April 6, 1963.

Kirk, S. A., & Kirk, W. D. (1971). *Psycholinguistic learning disabilities: Diagnosis and remediation.* Urbana: University of Illinois Press.

Kourea, L., Cartledge, G., & Musti-Rao, S. (2007). Improving the reading skills of urban elementary students through total class peer tutoring. *Remedial and Special Education, 28*, 95–107. doi:10.1177/07419325070280020801.

Kuder, S. J. (2017). Vocabulary instruction for secondary students with reading disabilities: An updated research review. *Learning Disability Quarterly*, 1–10. doi:10.1177/0731948717690113.

Kunsch, C. A., Jitendra, A. K., & Sood, S. (2007). The effects of peer-mediated instruction in mathematics for students with learning problems: A research synthesis. *Learning Disabilities Research & Practice, 22*, 1–12. doi:10.1111/j.1540-5826.2007.00226.x.

Lanphear B, Dietrich K., Auinger P., & Cox C. (2000). Cognitive deficits associated with blood l.ead concentrations < 10 μg/dL in US children and adolescents. *Public Health Reports, 115*, 521–529.

Lasley II, T. J., Matczynski, T. J., & Rowley, J. B. (2002). *Instructional models: Strategies for teaching in a diverse society.* Belmont, CA: Wadsworth/Thomas Learning.

Leinhardt, G., Seewald, A., & Zigmond, N. (1982). Sex and race differences in learning disabilities classrooms. *Journal of Educational Psychology, 74*, 835–845. doi:10.1037/0022-0663.74.6.835

Levin, J. R. (1993). Mnemonic strategies and classroom learning: A twenty year report card. *Elementary School Journal, 27*, 301–321.

Lewis, B. A. (1992). Pedigree analysis of children with phonology disorders. *Journal of Learning Disabilities, 25*, 586–597. doi:10.1177/002221949202500908

Lewis, B. A., & Thompson, L. A. (1992). A study of development of speech and language disorders in twins. *Journal of Speech and Hearing Research, 35*, 1086–1094.

Lindstrom, L. E., & Benz, M. R. (2002). Phases of career development: Case studies of young women with learning disabilities. *Exceptional Children, 69*, 67–83.

Lubin, J., & Polloway, E. A. (2016). Mnemonic instruction in science and social studies for students with learning problems: A review. *Learning Disabilities: A Contemporary Journal, 14*, 207–224.

Maag, J. W., & Reid, R. (2006). Depression among students with learning disabilities: Assessing the risk. *Journal of Learning Disabilities, 39*, 3–10. doi:10.1177/00222194060390010201

MacMillan, D. L., Gresham, F. M., & Bocian, K. M. (1998). Discrepancy between definitions of learning disabilities and school practices: An empirical investigation. *Journal of Learning Disabilities, 31*, 314–326. doi:10.1177/002221949803100401

MacMillan, D. L., & Siperstein, G. N. (2002). Learning disabilities as operationally defined by schools. In R. Bradley, L. Danielson, & D. P. Hallahan (Eds.), *Identification of learning disabilities: Research to practice* (pp. 287–333). Mahwah, NJ: Erlbaum.

Madaus, J. W., & Banerjee, M. (2011). Transition to postsecondary education. In J. M. Kauffman & D. P. Hallahan (Eds.), *Handbook of special education.* New York: NY: Routledge.

Maheady, L., Harper, G. F., & Mallette, B. (2003, Spring). Classwide peer tutoring. *Current Practice Alerts.* Retrieved from http://www.teachingld.org/pdf/PeerTutoring_rev1.pdf.

Mammarella, I. C., Ghisi, M., Bomba, M., Bottesi, G., Caviola, S., Broggi, F., & Nacinovich, R. (2016). Anxiety and depression in children with nonverbal learning disabilities, reading disabilities, or typical development. *Journal of Learning Disabilities, 49*, 130-139. doi:10.1177/0022219414529336.

Margalit, M. (2006). Loneliness, the salutogenic paradigm and learning disabilities: Current research, future directions, and interventional implications. *Thalamus, 24*, 38–48.

Mastropieri, M. A., & Scruggs, T. E. (1998). Constructing more meaningful relationships in the classroom: Mnemonic research into practice. *Learning Disabilities Research & Practice, 13*, 138–145.

Mastropieri, M. A., Scruggs, T. E., & Whedon, T. B. (1997). Using mnemonic strategies to teach information about U.S. Presidents: A classroom-based investigation. *Learning Disability Quarterly, 20*, 13–21. doi:10.2307/1511089.

Mattison, R. E., & Mayes, S. D. (2012). Relationships between learning disability, executive function, and psychopathology in children with ADHD. *Journal of Attention Disorders, 16*, 138–146. doi:10.1177/1087054710380188

McGrady, H. J., Lerner, J. W., & Boscardin, M. L. (2001). The educational lives of students with learning disabilities. In P. Rodis, A. Garrod, & M. L. Boscardin (Eds.), *Learning disabilities and life stories* (pp. 177–193). Boston: Allyn & Bacon.

McMaster, K., & Espin, C. (2007). Technical features of curriculum-based measurement in writing: A review of the literature. *The Journal of Special Education, 41*, 68–84. doi:10.1177/ 0022466907041020301

Mercer, C. D., Mercer, A. R., & Pullen, P. C. (2011). *Teaching students with learning problems*. Boston: Pearson.

Molfese, D. M. (2000). Predicting dyslexia at 8 years of age using neonatal brain responses. *Brain and Language, 72*, 238–245. doi:10.1006/ brln.2000.2287

Morgan, P. L., & Fuchs, D. (2007). Is there a bidirectional relationship between children's reading skills and reading motivation? *Exceptional Children, 73*, 165–183.

Murawski, W. W., & Swanson, H. L. (2001). A meta-analysis of co-teaching research: Where are the data? *Remedial and Special Education, 22*, 258–267. doi:10.1177/074193250102200501

National Institute of Child Health and Human Development. (2000). *Report of the National Reading Panel: Teaching children to read: An evidence-based assessment of the scientific research literature on reading and its implications for instruction*. Washington, DC: National Institute of Child Health and Human Development. Retrieved from http://www.nichd.nih.gov/publications/nrp/upload/smallbook_pdf.pdf

National Joint Committee on Learning Disabilities. (1989, September 18). *Modifications to the NJCLD definition of learning disabilities*. Letter from NJCLD to member organizations. Washington, DC: Author.

National Joint Committee on Learning Disabilities. (2006). *Learning disabilities and young children: Identification and intervention*. Retrieved from http://www.ldonline.org/article/11511

O'Connor, Sanchez, & Kim (2017). Multi-tiered systems of support and responsiveness to intervention models for reducing reading difficulties and identifying learning disability. In J. M. Kauffman, D. P. Hallahan, & P. C. Pullen (Eds.), *Handbook of special education* (2nd ed., pp. 189–202). New York: Routledge.

Olson, R., Wise, B., Conners, F., Rack, J., & Fulker, D. (1989). Specific deficits in component reading and language skills: Genetic and environmental influences. *Journal of Learning Disabilities, 22*, 339–348. doi:10.1177/002221948902200604

Pastor, P. N., & Reuben, C. A. (2008). Diagnosed attention deficit hyperactivity disorder and learning disability: United States: 2004-2006. *Vital Health Statistics, Series 10*(237): 1–14.

Peng, P., & Fuchs, D. (2017). A randomized control trial of working memory training with and without strategy instruction: Effects on young children's working memory and comprehension. *Journal of Learning Disabilities, 50*, 62–80. doi:10.1177/0022219415594609

Pennington, B. F. (1990). Annotation: The genetics of dyslexia. *Journal of Child Psychology and Child Psychiatry, 31*, 193–201. doi:10.1111/j.1469-7610.1990.tb01561.x.

Peterson, R. L., & Pennington, B. F. (2015). Developmental dyslexia. *Annual Review of Clinical Psychology, 11*, 283–307. doi:10.1146/annurev-clinpsy-032814-112842.

Petrill, S. A., Deater-Deckard, K., Thompson, L. A., DeThorne, L. S., & Schatschneider, C. (2006). Reading skills in early readers: Genetic and shared environmental influences. *Journal of Learning Disabilities, 39*, 48–55. doi:10.1177/00222194060390010501

Plomin, R., & Kovas, Y. (2005). Generalist genes and learning disabilities. *Psychological Bulletin, 131*, 592–617. doi:10.1037/0033-2909.131.4.592

Prevatt, F., Welles, T. L., Li, H., & Proctor, B. (2010). The contribution of memory and anxiety to math performance of college students with learning disabilities. *Learning Disabilities Research & Practice, 25*, 39–47. doi:10.1111/j.1540-5826.2009.00299.x

Pullen, P. C. (2002, October 1). Expert connection: Phonological awareness. *TeachingLD.org*. Retrieved from http://TeachingLD.org/expert_connection/phonological.html

Pullen, P. C., & Hallahan, D. P. (2015). What is special education? In B. D. Bateman, J. W. Lloyd, & M. Tankersley, M. *Understanding special education Issues: Who, where, what, when, how & why* (pp. 36–50). New York: Routledge.

Pullen, P. C., Lane H. B., Ashworth, K. E., & Lovelace, S. (2017). Learning disabilities. In J. M. Kauffman, D. P. Hallahan, & P. C. Pullen (Eds.), *Handbook of special education* (2nd ed.). New York: Routledge.

Queen, O. (2001). Blake Academy and the Green Arrow. In P. Rodis, A. Garrod, & M. L. Boscardin (Eds.), *Learning disabilities and life stories* (pp. 3–16). Boston: Allyn & Bacon.

Raskind, W. H. (2001). Current understanding of the genetic basis of reading and spelling disability. *Learning Disability Quarterly, 24*, 141–157. doi:10.2307/1511240.

Raskind, W. H., Beate, P., Richards, T., Eckert, M. M., & Berninger, V. W. (2013). The genetics of reading disabilities: From phenotypes to candidate genes. *Frontiers in Psychology, 3*, 1–20. doi:org/10.3389/fpsyg.2012.00601.

Reiff, H. B., Gerber, P. J., & Ginsberg, R. (1997). *Exceeding expectations: Successful adults with learning disabilities*. Austin, TX: Pro-Ed.

Reyna, S. E., Grineski, S. E., & Collins, T. W. (2017). Residential exposure to air toxics is linked to lower grade point averages among school children in El Paso, Texas, USA. *Population and Environment. 37*, 319–340. doi:10.1007/s11111-015-0241-8.

Reynolds, C. A., Hewitt, J. K., Erickson, M. T., Silberg, J. L., Rutter, M., Simonoff, E., et al. (1996). The genetics of children's oral reading performance. *Journal of Child Psychology and Psychiatry, 37*, 425–434. doi:10.1111/j.1469-7610.1996.tb01423.x

Rojewski, J. W., & Gregg, N. (2011). Career decision-making and postsecondary attainment of work-bound youth with high incidence disabilities. In J. M. Kauffman, D. P. Hallahan, & P. C. Pullen (Eds.), *Handbook of special education* (2nd ed., pp. 705–717). New York: Routledge.

Rooney, K. J. (1998). *Independent strategies for efficient study*. Richmond, VA: Educational Enterprises.

Rourke, B. P. (1995). *Syndrome of nonverbal learning disabilities: Neurodevelopmental manifestations*. New York: Guilford Press.

Rubenstein, K., Matsushita, M., Berninger, V. W., Raskind, W. H., & Wijsman, E. M. (2011). Genome scan for spelling deficits: Effects of verbal IQ on models of transmission and trait localization. *Behavior Genetics, 41*, 31–42.

Saygin, Z. M., Norton, E. S., Osher, D. E., Beach, D. E., Cyr, A. B., Ozernov-Palchik, O., Yendiki, A., . . . Gabrielli, J. D. E. (2013). *The Journal of Neuroscience, 33*, 13251–13258. doi:10.1523/jneurosci.4383-12.2013.

Scanlon, D., Patton, J. R., & Raskind, M. (2017). Transition to daily living for persons with high incidence disabilities. In J. M. Kauffman, D. P. Hallahan, & P. C. Pullen (Eds.), *Handbook of special education* (2nd ed., pp. 718–733). New York: Routledge.

Schiff, R., Ben-Shushan, Y. N., & Ben-Artzi, E. (2017). Metacognitive strategies: A foundation for early word spelling and reading in kindergartners with SLI. *Journal of Learning Disabilities 50*, 143–157. doi:10.1177/0022219415589847.

Schulte-Korne, G., Deimel, W., Muller, K., Gutenbrunner, C., & Remschmidt, H. (1996). Familial aggregation of spelling disability. *Journal of Child Psychology and Psychiatry, 37*, 817–822. doi:10.1111/j.1469-7610.1996.tb01477.x

Schulte-Korne, G., Ziegler, A., Deimel, W., Schumaker, J., Plume, E., Bachmann, C., et al. (2006). Interrelationship and familiality of dyslexia related quantitative measures. *Annals of Human Genetics, 71*, 160–175. doi:10.1111/j.1469-1809.2006.00312.x

Scruggs, T., Mastropieri, M., Brigham, F. J. & Milman, L. M. (2017). Science and social studies. In J. M. Kauffman, D. P. Hallahan, & P. C. Pullen (Eds.), *Handbook of special education* (2nd ed., pp. 571–585). New York: Routledge.

Semrud-Clikeman, M., Walkowiak, J., Wilkinson, A., & Minne, E. P. (2010). Direct and indirect measures of social perception, behavior, and emotional functioning in children with Asperger's disorder, nonverbal learning disability, or ADHD. *Journal of Abnormal Child Psychology, 38*, 509–519. doi:10.1007/s10802-009-9380-7

Sexton, M., Harris, K. R., & Graham, S. (1998). Self-regulated strategy development and the writing process: Effects on essay writing and attributions. *Exceptional Children, 64*, 295–311.

Shalev, R. S. (2004). Developmental dyscalculia. *Journal of Child Neurology, 19*, 765–771.

Shaywitz, S. E., Shaywitz, B. A., Fletcher, J. M., & Escobar, M. D. (1990). Prevalence of reading disability in boys and girls: Results of the Connecticut Longitudinal Study. *Journal of the American Medical Association, 264*, 998–1002.

Spekman, N. J., Goldberg, R. J., & Herman, K. L. (1992). Learning disabled children grow up: A search for factors related to success in the young adult years. *Learning Disabilities Research & Practice, 7*, 161–170. doi:10.1080/00220671.2010.514690

Sperling, R. A., Richmond, A. S., Ramsay, C. M., & Klapp, M. (2012). The measurement and predictive ability of metacognition in middle school learners. *The Journal of Educational Research, 105*, 1–7.

Sreckovic, M. E., Common, E. A., Knowles, M. M., & Lane, K. L. (2014). A review of self-regulated strategy development for writing for students with EBD. *Behavioral Disorders, 39*, 56–77.

Swanson, H. L., & Jerman, O. (2006). Math disabilities: A selective meta-analysis of the literature. *Review of Educational Research, 76*, 249–274. doi:10.3102/00346543076002249

Swanson, H. L., Kehler, P, & Jerman, O. (2010). Working memory, strategy knowledge, and strategy instruction in children with reading disabilities. *Journal of Learning Disabilities*, *43*, 24–47. doi:10.1177/0022219409338743

Swanson, H. L., Zheng, X., & Jerman, O. (2009). Working memory, short-term memory, and reading disabilities: A selective meta-analysis of the literature. *Journal of Learning Disabilities*, *42*, 260–287. doi:10.1177/0022219409331958

Tarver, S. G. (1999, Summer). Direct instruction. *Current Practice Alerts*, *2*. Retrieved from http://www.teachingld.org/pdf/Alert2.pdf.

Teglasi, H., Schussler, L., Gifford, K., Annotti, L. A., Sanders, C., & Liu, H. (2015). Child behavior questionnaire–short form for teachers: Informant correspondences and divergences. *Assessment*, *22*, 730-748. doi.org.proxy.its.virginia.edu/10.1177/1073191114562828.

U.S. Department of Education. (2016). 38th Annual Report to Congress on the Implementation of the *Individuals with Disabilities Education Act*. Washington, DC: Author.

Vaughn, S., & Fuchs, L. S. (2003). Redefining learning disabilities as inadequate response to instruction: The promise and potential problems. *Learning Disabilities Research & Practice*, *18*, 137–146. doi:10.1111/1540-5826.00070

Willows, D. M. (1998). Visual processes in learning disabilities. In H. L. Swanson (Ed.), *Handbook of assessment of learning disabilities: Theory, research, and practice* (pp. 147–175). Austin, TX: Pro-Ed.

Worling, D. E., Humphries, T., & Tannock, R. (1999). Spatial and emotional aspects of language inferencing in nonverbal learning disabilities. *Brain and Language*, *70*, 220–239. doi:10.1006/brln.1999.2156

Wright, V. R., Chau, M., & Aratani, Y. (2010). *Who are America's poor children: The official story*. The National Center for Children in Poverty. Retrieved from http://www.nccp.org/publications/pdf/text_912.pdf.

Zhang, N., Baker, H. W., Tufts, M., Raymond, R. E., Salihu, H., & Elliott, M. R. (2013). Early childhood lead exposure and academic achievement: Evidence from Detroit Public Schools, 2008–2010. *American Journal of Public Health*, *103*, 72–77.

Zigmond, N., & Kloo, A. (2017). General and special education are (and should be) different. In J. M. Kauffman, D. P. Hallahan, & P. C. Pullen (Eds.), *Handbook of special education* (2nd ed., pp. 249–261). New York: Routledge.

CHAPTER 7

American Psychiatric Association. (2013). *Diagnostic and statistical manual of mental disorders* (5th ed.). Washington, DC: Author.

Alderson, R. M., Kasper, L. J., Hudec, K. L., & Patros, C. H. G. (2013). Attention-deficit/hyperactivity disorder (ADHD) and working memory in adults: A meta-analytic review. *Neuropsychology*, *27*, 287–302. doi:10.1037/a0032371.

Arnsten, A. F. T., Berridge, C. W., & McCracken, J. T. (2009). The neurological basis Attention-Deficit/Hyperactivity Disorder. *Primary Psychiatry*, *16*, 47–54.

Ayduk, O., Mendoza-Denton, R., Mischel, W., Downey, G., Peake, P. K., & Rodriguez, M. (2000). Regulating the interpersonal self: Strategic self-regulation for coping with rejection sensitivity. *Journal of Personality and Social Psychology*, *79*, 776–792. doi:10.1037/0022-3514.79.5.776.

Barbaresi, W. J., Katusic, S. K., Colligan, R. C., Weaver, A. L., Leibson, C. L., & Jacobsen, S. J. (2006). Long-term stimulant medication treatment of ADHD: Results from a population based study. *Journal of Developmental and Behavioral Pediatrics*, *27*, 1–10. doi:10.1079/ 00004703-200602000-00001

Barkley, R. A. (1997). Behavioral inhibition, sustained attention, and executive functions: Constructing a unifying theory of ADHD. *Psychological Bulletin*, *121*, 65–94. doi:10.1037/0033-2909.121.1.65

Barkley, R. A. (2000a). *A new look at ADHD: Inhibition, time, and self-control* [video manual]. Baltimore: Guilford Press.

Barkley, R. A. (2000b). *Taking charge of ADHD: The complete, authoritative guide for parents* (rev. ed.). New York: Guilford Press.

Barkley, R. A. (2006a). Associated cognitive, developmental, and health problems. In R. A. Barkley (Ed.), *Attention-deficit hyperactivity disorder: A handbook for diagnosis and treatment* (3rd ed., pp. 122–183). New York: Guilford Press.

Barkley, R. A. (2006b). Etiologies. In R. A. Barkley (Ed.), *Attention-deficit hyperactivity disorder: A handbook for diagnosis and treatment* (3rd ed., pp. 219–247). New York: Guilford Press.

Barkley, R. A. (2006c). History. In R. A. Barkley (Ed.), *Attention-deficit hyperactivity disorder: A handbook for diagnosis and treatment* (3rd ed., pp. 3–75). New York: Guilford Press.

Barkley, R. A. (2006e). A theory of ADHD. In R. A. Barkley (Ed.), *Attention-deficit hyperactivity disorder: A handbook for diagnosis and treatment* (3rd ed., pp. 297–334). New York: Guilford Press.

Barkley, R. A., & Edwards, G. (2006). Diagnostic interview, behavior rating scales, and medical examination. In R. A. Barkley (Ed.), *Attention-deficit hyperactivity disorder: A handbook for diagnosis and treatment* (3rd ed., pp. 337–368). New York: Guilford Press.

Barkley, R. A., & Murphy, K. R. (2007). Comorbid psychiatric disorders in adults with ADHD. *The ADHD Report*, *15*(2), 1–7. doi:10.1521/adhd.2007.15.2.1

Barkley, R. A. Murphy, K., & Kwanik, D. (1996). Psychological adjustment and adaptive impairments in young adults with ADHD. *Journal of Attention Disorders*, *1*, 41–54. doi:10.1177/108705479600100104.

Barkley, R. A., & Peters, H. (2012). Earliest reference to ADHD in the medical literature? Melchior Adam Weikard's description in 1775 of "Attention Deficit" (Mangel der Aufmerksamkeit, Attentio Volubilis). *Journal of Attention Disorders*, *16*, 623–630. doi:10.1177/1087054711432309.

Bateman, B., Warner, J. O., Hutchinson, E., Dean, T., Rowlandson, P., Gant, C., et al. (2004). The effects of a double blind, placebo controlled, artificial food colourings and benzoate preservative challenge on hyperactivity in a general population sample

of preschool children. *Archives of Disease in Childhood*, *89*, 506–511. doi: 10.1136/adc.2003.031435

Bauermeister, J. J., Canino, G., Polanczyk, G., & Rohde, L. A. (2010). ADHD across cultures: Is there evidence for a bidimensional organization of symptoms? *Journal of Clinical & Adolescent Psychology*, *39*, 362–372. doi:10.1080/ 15374411003691743

Biederman, J., Petty, C. R., Monuteaux, M. C., Fried, R., Byrne, D., Mirto, T., & Faraone, S. V. (2010). Adult psychiatric outcomes of girls with attention deficit hyperactivity disorder: 11-year follow-up in a longitudinal case-control study. *American Journal of Psychiatry*, *167*, 409–417. doi:10.1176/appi.ajp.2009.09050736

Birch, H. G. (1964). *Brain damage in children: The biological and social aspects*. Baltimore: Williams & Wilkins.

Bradshaw, L. G., & Kamal, M. (2017). Prevalence of ADHD in Qatari school-age children, *Journal of Attention Disorders*, *21*, 442–449.

Campbell, S. B., & von Stauffenberg, C. (2009). Delay and inhibition as early predictors of ADHD symptoms in third grade. *Journal of Abnormal Child Psychology*, *37*, 1–15. doi:10.1007/s10802-008-9270-4.

Casey, B. J., Somerville, L. H., Gotlib, I. H., Ayduk, O., Franklin, N. T., Askren, M. K. . . . Shoda, Y. (2011). Behavioral and neural correlates of delay of gratification 40 years later. *Proceedings of the National Academy of Sciences*, *108*, 14998–15003. doi: 10.1073/pnas.1108561108.

Castle, L., Aubert, R. E., Verbrugge, R. R., Khalid, M., & Epstein, R. S. (2007). Trends in medication treatment for ADHD. *Journal of Attention Disorders*, *10*, 335–342. doi:10.1177/ 1087054707299597

Centers for Disease Control and Prevention. (2010, November). Increasing prevalence of parent-reported attention-deficit/hyperactivity Disorder Among Children––United States, 2003 and 2007. *Morbidity and Mortality Weekly Report*, *59*, 1439–1443. Retrieved from http://www.cdc.gov/mmwr/preview/mmwrhtml/mm5944a3.htm.

Cepeda, N. J., Cepeda, M. L., & Kramer, A. F. (2000). Task switching and attention deficit hyperactivity disorder, *Journal of Abnormal Child Psychology*, *28*, 213–226. doi:10.1023/A:1005143419092

Cheung, K., & Theule, J. (2016). Parental psychopathology in families of children with ADHD: A meta-analysis. *Journal of Child and Family Studies*, *25*, 3451–3461.

Childress, A. C. (2016). A critical appraisal of atomoxetine in the management of ADHD. *Therapeutics and Clinical Risk Management*, *12*, 27-39. doi:10.2147/TCRM.S59270

Crichton, A. (1798). *An inquiry into the nature and origins of mental derangement* (Vols. I and II). London: Strand Publishers.

Christakis, D. A., Zimmerman, F. J., DiGiuseppe, D. L., & McCarty, C. A. (2004). Early television exposure and subsequent attentional problems in children. *Pediatrics*, *113*, 708–713. doi:10.1542/peds.113.4.708

Cobb, B., Sample, P. L., Alwell, M., & Johns, N. R. (2006). Cognitive-behavioral interventions, dropout, and youth with disabilities. *Remedial and Special Education*, *27*, 259–275. doi: 10.1177/07419325060270050201

Conners, C. K. (2007). *Conners-3*. Boston: Pearson.

Conners, C. K., Erhardt, D., & Sparrow, E. (2000). *Conners' Adult ADHD Rating Scales*. North Tonawanda, NY: Multi-Health Systems.

Connor, D. F. (2006). Simulants. In R. A. Barkley (Ed.), *Attention-deficit hyperactivity disorder: A handbook for diagnosis and treatment* (3rd ed., pp. 608–647). New York: Guilford Press.

Corkum, P., Andreou, P., Schachar, R., Tannock, R., & Cunningham, C. (2007). The telephone interview probe: A novel measure of treatment response in children with attention deficit hyperactivity disorder. *Educational and Psychological Measurement, 67*, 169–185. doi:10.1177/0013164406292038

Cox, D. J., Merkel, R. L., Kovatchev, B., & Seward, R. (2000). Effect of stimulant medication on driving performance of young adults with attention-deficit hyperactivity disorder. *Journal of Nervous and Mental Disease, 188*, 230–234. doi:10.1097/00005053-200004000-00006

Cruickshank, W. M., Bentzen, F. A., Ratzeburg, F. H., & Tannhauser, M. T. (1961). *A teaching method of brain-injured and hyperactive children*. Syracuse, NY: Syracuse University Press.

Cruickshank, W. M., Bice, H. V., & Wallen, N. E. (1957). *Perception and cerebral palsy*. Syracuse, NY: Syracuse University Press.

Danckaerts, M., Sonuga-Barke, E. J. S., Banaschewski, T., Buitelaar, J., Dopfner, M., Hollis, C., & Coghill, D. (2010). The quality of life of children with attention deficit/hyperactivity disorder: A systematic review. *European Child and Adolescent Psychiatry, 19*, 83–105. doi:10.1007/s00787-009-0046-3

Davies, S., & Witte, R. (2000). Self-management and peer-monitoring within a group contingency to decrease uncontrolled verbalizations of children with attention-deficit/hyperactivity disorder. *Psychology in the Schools, 37*, 135–147. doi:10.1002/(SICI)1520-6807(200003)37:2[lt]135::AID-PITS5[gt]3.0.C0;2-U

Dittman, C. K. (2016). The impact of early classroom inattention on phonological processing and wordreading development. *Journal of Attention Disorders, 20*, 653–664.

DuPaul, G. J., Arbolino, L. A., & Booster, G. D. (2009). Cognitive-behavioral interventions for attention-deficit/hyperactivity disorder. In M. J. Mayer, J. E. Lochman, & F. M. Gresham (Eds.), *Cognitive-behavioral interventions for emotional and behavioral disorders: School-based practices* (pp. 295–327). New York: Guilford Press.

DuPaul, G. J., Barkley, R. A., & Connor, D. F. (1998). Stimulants. In R. A. Barkley (Ed.), *Attention-deficit hyperactivity disorder: A handbook for diagnosis and treatment* (pp. 510–551). New York: Guilford Press.

DuPaul, G. J., & Eckert, T. L. (1997). The effects of school-based interventions for attention deficit hyperactivity disorder: A meta-analysis, *School Psychology Review, 26*, 5–27.

DuPaul, G. J., Eckert, T. L., & McGoey, K. E. (1997). Interventions for students with attention-deficit/hyperactivity disorder: One size does not fit all. *School Psychology Review, 26*, 369–381.

DuPaul, G. J., & Ervin, R. A. (1996). Functional assessment of behaviors related to attention-deficit hyperactivity disorder: Linking assessment to intervention design. *Behavior Therapy, 27*, 601–622. doi:10.1016/S0005-7894(96)80046-3

Ebejer, J. L., Medland, S. E., van der Werf, J., Gondro, C., Henders, A. K., Lynskey, M., . . .Duffy, D. L. (2012). Attention deficit hyperactivity disorder in Australian adults: Prevalence, persistence, conduct problems and disadvantage. PLoS ONE, 7, e47404. doi:10.1371/journal.pone.0047404.t005

Ervin, R. A., DuPaul, G. J., Kern, L., & Friman, P. C. (1998). Classroom-based functional and adjunctive assessments: Proactive approaches to intervention selection for adolescents with attention deficit hyperactivity disorder. *Journal of Applied Behavior Analysis, 31*, 65–78. doi:10.1901/jaba.1998.31–65.

Evans, S. W., Pelham, W. E., Smith, B. H., Bukstein, O., Gnagy, E. M., Greiner, A. R., et al. (2001). Dose-response effects of methylphenidate on ecologically valid measures of academic performance and classroom behavior in adolescents with ADHD. *Experimental and Clinical Pharmacology, 9*, 163–175.

Feingold, B. (1975). *Why your child is hyperactive*. New York: Random House.

Fischer, M., Barkley, R. A., Smallish, L., & Fletcher, K. (2007). Hyperactive children as young adults: Driving abilities, safe driving behavior, and adverse driving outcomes. *Accident Analysis and Prevention, 39*, 94–105. doi:10.1016/j.aap.2006.06.008

Floet, A. M. W., Scheiner, C., & Grossman, L. (2010). Attention-deficit/hyperactivity disorder. *Pediatrics in Review, 31*, 56–69. doi:10.1542/pir.31-2-56

Forness, S. R., & Kavale, K. A. (2002). Impact of ADHD on school systems. In P. Jensen & J. R. Cooper (Eds.), *Attention deficit hyperactivity disorder: State of the science; Best practices* (pp. 1–20). Kingston, NJ: Civic Research Institute.

Frazier, T. W., Youngstrom, E. A., Glutting, J. J., & Watkins, M. W. (2007). ADHD and achievement: Meta-analysis of the child, adolescent, and adult literatures and a concomitant study with college students. *Journal of Learning Disabilities, 40*, 49–65. doi:10.1177/0022219407040001040.

Franklin, M. S., Mrazek, M. D., Anderson, C. L., Johnston, C., Smallwood, J., Kingstone, A., & Schooler, J. W. (2014). The relationship between mind-wandering, meta-awareness, and ADHD symptomatology, *Journal of Attention Disorders, 21*, 475–486.

Fredriksen, M., Dahl, A. A., Martinsen, E. W., Klungsoyr, O., Faraone, S. V., Dawn, E. P. (2014). Childhood and persistent ADHD symptoms associated with educational failure and long-term occupational disability in adult ADHD. ADHD: Attention Deficit Hyperactivity Disorder, 6, 87–99. doi:10.1007/s12402-014-0126-1.

Frodl, T., & Skokauskas, N. (2012). Meta-analysis of structural MRI studies in children and adults with attention deficit hyperactivity disorder indicates treatment effects. *Acta Psychiatrica Scandinavica, 125*, 114–126. doi:10.1111/j.1600-0447.2011.01786x.

Goldstein, K. (1936). The modification of behavior consequent to cerebral lesions. *Psychiatric Quarterly, 10*, 586–610.

Goldstein, K. (1939). *The organism*. New York: American Book Co.

Goldstein, S., & Kennemer, K. (2009). Neuropsychological aspects of attention-deficit hyperactivity disorder. In C. R. Reynolds & E. Fletcher-Janzen (Eds.). *Handbook of clinical child neuropsychology* (3rd ed., pp. 617–633). New York: Springer.

Graham, S., Fishman, E. J., Reid, R., & Hebert, M. (2016). Writing characteristics of students with attention deficit hyperactive disorder: A meta-analysis. *Learning Disabilities Research & Practice, 31*, 75–89. doi:http://dx.doi.org.proxy.its.virginia.edu/10.1111/ldrp.12099

Graves, S. L., & Serpell, Z. (2013). Racial differences in medication use in a national sample of children with ADHD enrolled in special education. *School Mental Health, 5*, doi:10.1007/s12310-0139105-5.

Hallahan, D. P., & Cottone, E. A. (1997). Attention deficit hyperactivity disorder. In T. E. Scruggs & M. A. Mastropieri (Eds.), *Advances in learning and behavioral disabilities, Vol. 11* (pp. 27–67). Greenwich, CT: JAI Press.

Hallahan, D. P., Lloyd, J. W., Kneedler, R. D., & Marshall, K. J. (1982). A comparison of the effects of self-versus teacher-assessment on on-task behavior. *Behavior Therapy, 13*, 715–723.

Hallahan, D. P., Lloyd, J. W., Kosiewicz, M. M., Kauffman, J. M., & Graves, A. W. (1979). Self-monitoring of attention as a treatment for a learning disabled boy's off-task behavior. *Learning Disability Quarterly, 2*(3), 24–32.

Hallahan, D. P., Marshall, K. J., & Lloyd, J. W. (1981). Self-recording during group instruction: Effects on attention to task. *Learning Disability Quarterly, 4*, 407–413.

Hallowell, E. M., & Ratey, J. J. (2006). *Delivered from distraction: Getting the most out of life with attention deficit disorder*. New York: Ballentine Books.

Harris, K. R., Friedlander, B. D., Saddler, B., Frizzelle, R., & Graham, S. (2005). Self-monitoring of attention versus self-monitoring of academic performance: Effects among students with ADHD in the general education classroom. *The Journal of Special Education, 39*, 145–156. doi:10.1177/002246699703100108

Hart, H., Radua, J., Nakao, T. Mataix-Cols, D., & Rubia, K. (2013). Meta-analysis of functional magnetic imaging studies of inhibition and attention in attention-deficit/hyperactivity disorder. *JAMA Psychiatry, 70*, 185–198. doi:10.1001/jamapsychiatry.2013.277.

Hechtman, L., Swanson, J. M. Sibley, M. H. Stehli, A. Owens, E. B., Mitchell, J. T . . . , & Nichols, J. Q. (2016). Functional adult outcomes 16 years after childhood diagnosis of Attention-Deficit/Hyperactivity Disorder: MTA results. *Journal of the American Academy of Child and Adolescent Psychiatry, 55*, 945–952.

Hoffmann, H. (1865). Die Geschichte vom Zappel-Philipp [The Story of Fidgety Philip]. In *Der Struwwelpeter* [Shaggy Peter]. Germany: Pestalozzi-Verlag.

Horner, R. H., & Carr, E. G. (1997). Behavioral support for students with severe disabilities: Functional assessment and comprehensive intervention. *The Journal of Special Education, 31*, 1–11.

Hvolby, A. (2015). Associations of sleep disturbance with ADHD: Implications for treatment. *Attention Deficit Hyperactivity Disorders*, 7, 1–18.

IDEA Data Tables. (2013). Percent of students ages 6–21 served under IDEA. Retrieved from https://www.ideadata.org/TABLES35TH/B1-17.pdf.

Kang, J.-H., Lin, H.-C., & Chung, S.-D. (2012). Attention-deficit/hyperactivity disorder increased the risk of injury: A population-based follow-up study. *Acta Paediatrica*, 102, 640–643. doi:10.1111/apa.12213.

Katusic, S. K., Barbaresi, W. J., Colligan, R. C., Weaver, A. L., Leibson, C. L., & Jacobsen, S. J. (2005). Psychostimulant treatment and risk for substance abuse among young adults with a history of attention-deficit/hyperactivity disorder: A population-based, birth cohort study. *Journal of Child and Adolescent Psychopharmacology*, 15, 764–776. doi:10.1089/cap.2005.15.764

Kohn, A. (1993). *Punished by rewards: The trouble with gold stars, incentive plans, A's, praise, and other bribes.* Boston: Houghton Mifflin.

Lakhan, S. E., & Kirchgessner, A. (2012). Prescription stimulants in individuals with and without attention deficit hyperactivity disorder: misuse, cognitive impact, and adverse effects. *Brain and Behavior*, 2, 661–677. doi:10.1002/brb3.78.

Landau, S., Milich, R., & Diener, M. B. (1998). Peer relations of children with attention-deficit hyperactivity disorder. *Reading and Writing Quarterly: Overcoming Learning Difficulties*, 14, 83–105.

Lawrence, V., Houghton, S., Tannock, R., Douglas, G., Durkin, K., & Whiting, K. (2002). ADHD outside the laboratory: Boys' executive function performance on tasks in videogame play and on a visit to the zoo. *Journal of Abnormal Child Psychology*, 30, 447–462. doi:10.1023/ A:1019812829706

Levy, F., Barr, C., & Sunohara, G. (1998). Directions of aetiologic research on attention deficit hyperactivity disorder. *Australian and New Zealand Journal of Psychiatry*, 32, 97–103. doi:10.3109/00048679809062715

Li, D., Sham, P. C., Owen, M. J., & He, L. (2006). Meta-analysis shows significant association between dopamine system genes and attention deficit hyperactivity disorder (ADHD). *Human Molecular Genetics*, 15, 2276–2284. doi:10.1093/ hmg/ddl152

Lloyd, J. W., Hallahan, D. P., Kauffman, J. M., & Keller, C. E. (1998). Academic problems. In R. J. Morris & T. R. Kratochwill (Eds.), *The practice of child therapy* (pp. 167–198). Boston: Allyn & Bacon.

Marshall, R. M., Hynd, G. W., Handwerk, M. J., & Hall, J. (1997). Academic underachievement in ADHD subtypes. *Journal of Learning Disabilities*, 30, 635–642. doi:10.1177/002221949703000607

Meszaros, A., Czobor, P., Balint, S., Komlosi, S., Simon, V., & Bitter, I. (2009). Pharmacotherapy of adult attention deficit hyperactivity disorder (ADHD) a meta-analysis. *International Journal of Neuropsychopharmacology*, 12, 1137–1147.

Michielsen, M., Semeijn, E., Comijs, H. C., van de Ven, P., Beekman, A. T. F., Deeg, D. J. H., & Kooij, J. J. S. (2012). Prevalence of attention-deficit hyperactivity disorder in older adults in the Netherlands. *The British Journal of Psychiatry*, 201, 298–305. doi:10.1192/bjp.bp.111.101196

Mikami, A., Jack, A., & Lerner, M. D. (2009). Attention-deficit/hyperactivity disorder. In J. L. Matson (Ed.), *Social behavior and skills in children* (pp. 159–185). New York: Springer.

Milberger, S., Biederman, J., Faraone, S. V., Guite, J., & Tsuang, M. T. (1997). Pregnancy, delivery and infancy complications and attention deficit hyperactivity disorder: Issues of gene– environment interaction. *Biological Psychiatry*, 41, 65–75. doi:10.1016/0006-3223(95)00653-2

Miller, F. G., & Lee, D. L. (2013). Do functional behavioral assessments improve intervention effectiveness for students diagnosed with ADHD? A single-subject meta-analysis. *Journal of Behavioral Education*, 22, 253–282. doi:10.1007/s10864-013-9174-4.

Millichap, J. G., & Yee, M. M. (2012). The diet factor in attention-deficit/hyperactivity disorder. *Pediatrics*, 129, 330–337. doi:10.1542/peds.2011-2199.

Mischel, W., & Ebbesen, E. B. (1970). Attention in delay of gratification. *Journal of Personality and Social Psychiatry*, 16, 329–337. doi:10.1037/h0029815.

Mohr-Jensen, C., & Steinhausen, H.-C. (2016). A meta-analysis and systematic review of the risks associated with childhood attention-deficit hyperactivity disorder on long-term outcome of arrests, convictions, and incarcerations. *Clinical Psychology Review*, 48, 32–42.

Mowinckel, Pedersen, M. L., Eilertsen, E., & Biele, G. (2015). A meta-analysis of decision-making and attention in adults with ADHD. *Journal of Attention Disorders*, 19, 355–367. doi:10.1177/1087054714558872.

MTA Cooperative Group. (1999). A 14-month randomized clinical trial of treatment strategies for attention-deficit/hyperactivity disorder. *Archives of General Psychiatry*, 56, 1073–1086.

National Institutes of Health. (1998). Diagnosis and Treatment of Attention Deficit Hyperactivity Disorder. NIH Consensus Statement Online 1998 Nov 16–18; 16(2), 1–37. Retrieved September from http://consensus.nih.gov/1998/1998AttentionDeficitHyperactivityDisorder110html.htm

National Institute of Mental Health. (2012). "Attention Deficit Hyperactivity Disorder." National Institutes of Health: NIH Publication No. 12-3572. Retrieved from http://www.nimh.nih.gov/health/publications/attention-deficit-hyperactivity-disorder/index.shtml.

Neuman, R. J., Lobos, E., Reich, W., Henderson, C. A., Sun, L.-W., & Todd, R. D. (2007). Prenatal smoking exposure and dopaminergic genotypes interact to cause a severe ADHD subtype. *Biological Psychiatry*, 61, 1320–1328. doi:10.1016/j.biopsych.2006.08.049

Nigg, J. T., Nikolas, M., Knottnerus, G. M., Cavanagh, K., & Friderici, K. (2010). Confirmation and extension of association of blood lead with attention-deficit/hyperactivity disorder (ADHD) and ADHD symptom domains at population-typical exposure levels. *The Journal of Child Psychology and Psychiatry*, 51, 58–65. doi:10.1111/j.1469-7610.2009.02135.x

Palmer, E. D., & Finger, S. (2001). An early description of ADHD (Inattentive Subtype): Dr. Alexander Crichton and 'mental restlessness' (1798). *Child Psychology and Psychiatry Review*, 6, 66–73. doi:10.1017/S1360641701002507

Pasamanick, B., Lilienfeld, A. M., & Rogers, M. E. (1956). Pregnancy experience and the development of behavior disorders in children. *American Journal of Psychiatry*, 112, 613–617.

Pfiffner, L. J., Barkley, R. A., & DuPaul, G. J. (2006). Treatment of ADHD in school settings. In R. A. Barkley (Ed.), *Attention-deficit hyperactivity disorder: A handbook for diagnosis and treatment* (3rd ed., pp. 122–183). New York: Guilford Press.

Pinel, J. P. J. (2006). *Biopsychology* (5th ed.). Boston: Allyn & Bacon.

Pingault JB, Côté SM, Galéra C, Genolini C, Falissard B, Vitaro F, Tremblay RE. (2013) Childhood trajectories of inattention, hyperactivity and oppositional behaviors and prediction of substance abuse/dependence: A 15-year longitudinal population-based study. *Molecular Psychiatry*, 18, 806–812.

Polanczyk, G. A., Salum, L. S., Sugaya, A. C., & Rohde, L. A. (2015). Annual Research Review: A meta-analysis of the worldwide prevalence of mental disorders in children and adolescents. *Journal of Child Psychology and Psychiatry*, Online at: https://www.researchgate.net/publication/271842422

Polanczyk, G., Silva de Lima, M., Horta, B. L., Biederman, J., & Rhode, L. A. (2007). The worldwide prevalence of ADHD: A systematic review and metaregression analysis. *American Journal of Psychiatry,* 164, 942–948. doi:10.1176/ appi.ajp.164.6.942

Posner, K., Pressman, A. W., & Greenhill, L. L. (2009). ADHD in preschool children. In T. E. Brown (Ed.), *ADHD comorbidities: Handbook for ADHD complications in children and adults* (pp. 37–53). Washington, DC: American Psychiatric Publishing.

Ramsay, J. R. (2010). *Nonmedication treatments for adult ADHD: Evaluating impact on daily functioning and well-being.* Washington, DC: American Psychological Association.

Reid, R., & Lienemann, R. O. (2006). Self-regulated strategy development for written expression with students with attention deficit/hyperactivity disorder. *Exceptional Children*, 73, 53–68.

Reid, R., Trout, A. L., & Schartz, M. (2005). Self-regulation interventions for children with attention deficit/hyperactivity disorder. *Exceptional Children*, 71, 361–377.

Richards, T. L., Deffenbacher, J. L., Rosen, L. A., Barkley, R. A., & Rodricks, T. (2007). Driving anger and driving behavior in adults with ADHD. *Journal of Attention Disorders*, 10, 54–64. doi:10.1177/1087054705284244

Rowland, A. S., Umbach, D. M., Catoe, K. E., Stallone, L., Long, S., Rabiner, D., et al. (2001). Studying the epidemiology of attention-deficit hyperactivity disorder: Screening method and pilot results. *Canadian Journal of Psychiatry*, 46, 931–940.

Rucklidge, J., Brown, D., Crawford, S., & Kaplan, B. (2007). Attributional styles and psychosocial functioning of adults with ADHD: Practice issues and gender differences. *Journal of Attention Disorders, 10,* 288–298. doi:10.1177/1087054706289942

Sanchez-Mora, C., Cormand, B., Ramos-Quiroga, J. A., Hervas, A., Bosch, R., Palomar, G., Nogueira, M., . . . Ribases, M. (2013). Evaluation of common variants in 16 genes involved in the regulation of neurotransmitter release in ADHD. *European Neuropsychopharmacology, 23,* 426–435. doi:10.1016/j.euroneuro.2012.07.014

Schachar, R., Mota, V. L., Logan, G. D., Tannock, R., & Klim, P. (2000). Confirmation of an inhibitory control deficit in attention-deficit/hyperactivity disorder. *Journal of Abnormal Child Psychology, 28,* 227–235. doi:10.1023/A:1005140103162

Schatz, D. B., & Rostain, A. L. (2007). ADHD with comorbid anxiety: A review of the current literature. *Journal of Attention Disorders, 10,* 141–149. doi:10.1177/1087054706286698

Scheffler, R. M., Brown, T. T., Fulton, B. D., Hinshaw, S. P., Levine, P., & Stone, S. (2009). Positive association between attention-deficit/hyperactivity disorder medication use and academic achievement during elementary school. *Pediatrics, 123,* 1273–1279. doi:10.1542/peds.2008-1597

Schlam, T. R., Wilson, N. L., Shoda, Y., Mischel, W., & Ayduk, O. (2012). Preschoolers' delay of gratification predicts their body mass 30 years later. *The Journal of Pediatrics, 162,* 90–93. doi:10.1016/j.jpeds.2012.06.049

Semrud-Clikeman, M., Steingard, R. J., Filipek, P., Biederman, J., Bekken, K., & Renshaw, P. F. (2000). Using MRI to examine brain–behavior relationships in males with attention deficit disorder with hyperactivity. *Journal of the American Academy of Child and Adolescent Psychiatry, 39,* 477–484. doi:10.1097/00004583-200004000-00017

Shapiro, E. S., DuPaul, G. J., & Bradley-Klug, K. L. (1998). Self-management as a strategy to improve the classroom behavior of adolescents with ADHD. *Journal of Learning Disabilities, 31,* 545–555. doi:10.1177/002221949803100604

Shilon, Y., Pollak, Y., Aran, A., Shaked, S., & Gross-Tsur, V. (2011). Accidental injuries are more common in children with attention deficit hyperactivity disorder compared with their non-affected siblings. *Care, Health, and Development, 38,* 366–370. doi:10.1111/j.1365-2214.2011.01278.x

Shoda, Y., Mischel, W., & Peake, P. K. (1990). Predicting adolescent cognitive and self-regulatory competencies from preschool delay of gratification: Identifying diagnostic conditions. *Developmental Psychology, 26,* 978–986. doi:10.1037/0012-1649.26.6.978

Silvestri, R., Gagliano, A., Aricò, I., Calarese, T., Cedro, C., Bruni, O., & Bramanti, P. (2009). Sleep disorders in children with attention-deficit/hyperactivity disorder (ADHD) recorded overnight by video-polysomnography. *Sleep Medicine, 10,* 1132–1138. doi:10.1016/j.sleep.2009.04.003

Sjowall, D., Roth, L., Lindqvist, S., & Thorell, L. B. (2012). Multiple deficits in ADHD: Executive dysfunction, delay aversion, and emotional deficits. *Journal of Child Psychology and Psychiatry, 54,* 619–627. doi:10.1111/jcpp.12006

Spencer, T. J., Biederman, J., & Wilens, T. E. (2010). Medications used for attention-deficit/ hyperactivity disorder. In M. K. Dulcan (Ed.), *Dulcan's textbook of child and adolescent psychiatry* (published online). American Psychiatric Publishing. Retrieved from http://www.psychiatryonline.com/content.aspx?aid=468068

Still, G. F. (1902). Some abnormal psychical conditions in children. *The Lancet, 1,* 1008–1012, 1077–1082, 1153–1168.

Strauss, A. A., & Werner, H. (1942). Disorders of conceptual thinking in the brain-injured child. *Journal of Nervous and Mental Disease, 96,* 153–172.

Substance Abuse and Mental Health Services Administration. (2015). Center for Behavioral Health Statistics and Quality. Treatment Episode Data Set (TEDS): 2003-2013. National Admissions to Substance Abuse Treatment Services. BHSIS Series S-75, HHS Publication No. (SMA) 15-4934. Rockville, MD: Substance Abuse and Mental Health Services Administration.

Tankersley, M. (1995). A group-oriented contingency management program: A review of research on the good behavior game and implications for teachers. *Preventing School Failure, 40,* 59–72.

Tripp, G., & Alsop, B. (2001). Sensitivity to reward delay in children with attention deficit hyperactivity disorder (ADHD). *Journal of Child Psychology and Psychiatry, 42,* 691–698. doi:10.1111/1469-7610.00764

Tripp, G., & Wickens, J. R. (2009). Neurobiology of ADHD. *Neuropharmacology, 57,* 579–589. doi:10.1016/j.neuropharm.2009.07.026

Vaughn, S., Schumm, J. S., & Arguelles, M. E. (1997). The ABCDEs of Co-teaching. *Teaching Exceptional Children, 30*(2), 4–10.

Volkow, N. D., Wang, G.-J., Newcorn, J., Telang, F., Solanto, M. V., Fowler, J. S., et al. (2007). Depressed dopamine activity in caudate and preliminary evidence of limbic involvement in adults with attention-deficit/hyperactivity disorder. *Archives of General Psychiatry, 64,* 932–940. doi:10.1001/archpsyc.64.8.932

Vorstman, J. A. S., & Ophoff, R. A. (2013). Genetic causes of developmental disorders. *Current Opinion Neurology, 26,* 128–136. doi:10.1097/WCO.0b013e32835f1a30

Walcott, C. M., Scheemaker, A., & Bielski, K. (2009). A longitudinal investigation of inattention and preliteracy development. *Journal of Attention Disorders, 14,* 79–85. doi:10.1177/ 1087054709333330

Wang, T., Liu, K., Li, Z., Yang, X., Liu, Y., Shi, W., & Chen, L. (2017). Prevalence of attention deficit/hyperactivity disorder among children and adolescents in China: A systematic review and meta-analysis. *BMC Psychiatry.* Available online: https://bmcpsychiatry.biomedcentral.com/articles/10.1186/s12888-016-1187-9

Weiss, L. (1992). *Attention deficit disorder in adults.* Lanham, MD: Taylor Publishing.

Weiss, M., Hechtman, L., & Weiss, G. (2000). ADHD in parents. *Journal of the American Academy of Child and Adolescent Psychiatry, 39,* 1059–1061. doi:10.1097/00004583-200008000-00023

Werner, H., & Strauss, A. A. (1939). Types of visuo-motor activity in their relation to low and high performance ages. *Proceedings of the American Association on Mental Deficiency, 44,* 163–168.

Werner, H., & Strauss, A. A. (1941). Pathology of figure-background relation in the child. *Journal of Abnormal and Social Psychology, 36,* 236–248. doi:10.1037/h0058060

Weyandt, L. L. (2009a). Attention-deficit/hyperactivity disorder in adults. In M. C. Smith & N. DeFrates-Densch, N. (Eds.), *Handbook of research on adult learning and development* (pp. 670–692). New York: Routledge.

Weyandt, L. L. (2009b). Executive functions and attention deficit hyperactivity disorder. *The ADHD Report, 17*(6), 1–7. doi:10.1521/adhd.2009.17.6.1

Weyandt, L. L., & DuPaul, G. (2006). ADHD in college students. *Journal of Attention Disorders, 10,* 9–19. doi:10.1177/1087054705286061

Weyandt, L. L., & DuPaul, G. J. (2013). Academic, social, and psychological functioning, *College students with ADHD: Current issues and future directions.* New York, NY: Springer.

Whalen, C. K., Henker, B., Ishikawa, S. S., Jamner, L. D., Floro, J. N., Johnston, J. A., et al. (2006). An electronic diary study of contextual triggers and ADHD: Get ready, get set, get mad. *Journal of the American Academy of Child and Adolescent Psychiatry, 45,* 166–174. doi:10.1097/01.chi.0000189057.67902.10

Wilens, T. E., & Biederman, J. (1992). Pediatric psychopharmacology: The stimulants. *Pediatric Clinics of North America, 15*(1), 191–222.

Willcutt, E. G., Chhabildas, N., & Pennington, B. F. (2001). Validity of the DSM-IV subtypes of ADHD. *ADHD Report, 9*(1), 2–5. doi:10.1521/adhd.9.1.2.16970

Willcutt, E. G., Pennington, B. F., Boada, R., Ogline, J. S., Tunick, R. A., Chhabildas, N. A., et al. (2001). A comparison of the cognitive deficits in reading disability and attention-deficit/hyperactivity disorder. *Journal of Abnormal Psychology, 110,* 157–172. doi:10.1037/0021-843X.110.1.157

Willcutt, E. G., Pennington, B. F., Duncan, L., Smith, S. D., Keenan, J. M., Wadsworth S., DeFries, J. C. . . . Olson, R. K. (2010). Understanding the complex etiologies of developmental disorders: Behavioral and molecular genetic approaches. *Journal of Developmental and Behavioral Pediatrics, 31,* 533–544. doi:10.1097/DBP.0b013e3181ef42a1

Wolraich, M. L., Wilson, D. B., & White, J. W. (1995). The effect of sugar on behavior or cognition in children: A meta-analysis. *Journal of the American Medical Association, 274,* 1617–1621.

Woodward, L. J., Fergusson, D. M., & Horwood, L. J. (2000). Driving outcomes for young people with attentional difficulties in adolescence. *Journal of the American Academy of Child and Adolescent Psychiatry, 39,* 627–634. doi:10.1097/00004583-200005000-00017

Zheng, C., Lichtenstein, P., Asherson, P. J., & Larsson, H. (2013). Developmental twin study of attention problems: High heritabilities throughout development. *Journal of American Medical Association Psychiatry, 70,* 311–318. doi:10.1001/jamapsychiatry.2013.287

CHAPTER 8

Anastasiou, D., Gardner, R., & Michail, D. (2011). Ethnicity and exceptionality. In J. M. Kauffman & D. P. Hallahan (Eds.), *Handbook of special education*. New York: Routledge.

Anastasiou, D., Kauffman, J. M., & Michail, D. (2016). Disability in multicultural theory: Conceptual and social justice issues. *Journal of Disability Policy Studies, 27*(1), 3–12. doi:10.1177/1044207314558595.

Anastasiou, D., Morgan, P. L., Farkas, G., & Wiley, A. (2017). Minority disproportionate representation in special education: Politics and evidence, issues and implications. In J. M. Kauffman, D. P. Hallahan, & P. C. Pullen (Eds.), *Handbook of special education* (2nd ed., pp. 897–910). New York: Routledge.

Blake, C., & Behan, D. (2014). Do teacher training courses prepare new teachers to meet the challenges of EBD students? In P. Garner, J. M. Kauffman, & J. G. E. Elliott (Eds.), *Sage handbook of emotional and behavioral difficulties* (2nd ed., pp. 401–413). London: Sage Publications.

Bower, E. M. (1982). Defining emotional disturbance: Public policy and research. *Psychology in the Schools, 19*, 55–60. doi:10.1002/1520-6807 (19820108)19: 1<55::AID-PITS2310190112>3.0.CO;2-2

Brigham, F. J., Ahn, S. Y., Stride, A. N., & McKenna, J. W. (2016). FAPE accompli: Misapplication of the principles of inclusion and students with EBD. In J. P. Bakken, F. E. Obiakor, & A. Rotatori (Eds.), *Advances in special education, Vol. 31a—General and special education in an age of change* (pp. 31–47). Bingley, UK: Emerald.

Brigham, F. J., & Kauffman, J. M. (1998). Creating supportive environments for students with emotional or behavioral disorders. *Effective School Practices, 17*(2), 25–35.

Cheney, D. A., Cumming, T., & Slemrod, T. (2014). Secondary education and promising practices for students with EBD. In H. M. Walker & F. M. Gresham (Eds.), *Handbook of evidence-based practices for students having emotional and behavioral disorders* (pp. 344–360). New York: Guilford.

Chesapeake Institute. (1994, September). *National agenda for achieving better results for children and youth with serious emotional disturbance.* Washington, DC: Author.

Colvin, G. (2004). *Managing the cycle of acting-out behavior in the classroom.* Eugene, OR: Behavior Associates.

Cook, B. G. & Ruhaak, A. E. (2014). Causality and emotional or behavioral disorders: An introduction. In P. Garner, J. M. Kauffman, & J. G. E. Elliott (Eds.), *Sage handbook of emotional and behavioral difficulties* (2nd ed., pp. 97–108). London: Sage Publications.

Cooper, P. (2014). Biology, emotion and behavior: The importance of a biopsychosocial perspective in understanding EBD. In P. Garner, J. M. Kauffman, & J. G. E. Elliott (Eds.), *Sage handbook of emotional and behavioral difficulties* (2nd ed., pp. 109–130). London: Sage Publications.

Costello, E. J., Egger, H., & Angold, A. (2005). 1-year research update review: The epidemiology of child and adolescent psychiatric disorders: I. Methods and public health burden. *Journal of the American Academy of Child and Adolescent Psychiatry, 44*, 972–986.

Costello, E. J., Foley, D., & Angold, A. (2006). 10-year research update review: The epidemiology of child and adolescent psychiatric disorders: II. Developmental epidemiology. *Journal of the American Academy of Child and Adolescent Psychiatry, 45*, 8–25.

Coutinho, M. J., & Oswald, D. P. (2011). Gender and exceptionality. In J. M. Kauffman & D. P. Hallahan (Eds.), *Handbook of special education* (pp. 759–772). New York: Routledge.

Cullinan, D. (2004). Classification and definition of emotional and behavioral disorders. In R. B. Rutherford, M. M. Quinn, & S. R. Mathur (Eds.), *Handbook of research in emotional and behavioral disorders* (pp. 32–53). New York: Guilford.

Cullinan, D. (2007). *Students with emotional and behavior disorders: An introduction for teachers and other helping professionals* (2nd ed.). Upper Saddle River, NJ: Merrill/Pearson.

Davies, J. D., & Ryan, J. (2014). Voices from the Margins: The perceptions of pupils with emotional and behavioral difficulties about their educational experiences. In P. Garner, J. M. Kauffman, & J. G. E. Elliott (Eds.), *Sage handbook of emotional and behavioral difficulties* (2nd ed., pp. 349–362). London: Sage Publications.

Dunlap, G., & Fox, L. (2014). Supportive interventions for young children with social, emotional, and behavioral delays and disorders. In H. M. Walker & F. M. Gresham (Eds.), *Handbook of evidence-based practices for students having emotional and behavioral disorders* (pp. 503–517). New York: Guilford.

Dunlap, G., Strain, P. S., Fox, L., Carta, J. J., Conroy, M., Smith, B. J., et al. (2006). Prevention and intervention with young children's challenging behavior: Perspectives regarding current knowledge. *Behavioral Disorders, 32*, 29–45.

Eber, L., Malloy, J. M., Rose, J., & Flamini, A. (2014). School-based wraparound for adolescents: The RENEW model for transition-aged youth with or at-risk of EBD. In H. M. Walker & F. M. Gresham (Eds.), *Handbook of evidence-based practices for students having emotional and behavioral disorders* (pp. 378–393). New York: Guilford.

Evans, S. W., Rybak, T., Strickland, H., & Owens, J. S. (2014). The role of school mental health models in preventing and addressing children's emotional and behavior problems. In H. M. Walker & F. M. Gresham (Eds.), *Handbook of evidence-based practices for students having emotional and behavioral disorders* (pp. 394–409). New York: Guilford.

Evertson, C., & Weinstein, C. (Eds.). (2006). *Handbook of classroom management: Research, practice and contemporary issues.* Mahwah, NJ: Erlbaum.

Forness, S. R., & Beard, K. Y. (2007). Strengthening the research base in special education: Evidence-based practice and interdisciplinary collaboration. In J. Crockett, M. Gerber, & T. Landrum (Eds.), *Achieving the radical reform of special education* (pp. 169–188). Mahwah, NJ: Erlbaum.

Forness, S. R., Freeman, S. F. N., Paparella, T., Kauffman, J. M., & Walker, H. M. (2012). Special education implications of point and cumulative prevalence for children with emotional or behavioral disorders. *Journal of Emotional and Behavioral Disorders, 20*, 1–14.

Forness, S. R., & Knitzer, J. (1992). A new proposed definition and terminology to replace "serious emotional disturbance" in Individuals with Disabilities Act. *School Psychology Review, 21*, 12–20.

Forness, S. R., Walker, H. M., & Serna, L. A. (2014). Establishing an evidence base: Lessons learned from implementing randomized controlled trials for behavioral and pharmacological interventions. In H. M. Walker & F. M. Gresham (Eds.), *Handbook of evidence-based practices for students having emotional and behavioral disorders* (pp. 567–582). New York: Guilford.

Fox, J. J., & Gable, R. A. (2004). Functional behavioral assessment. In R. B. Rutherford, M. M. Quinn, & S. R. Mathur (Eds.), *Handbook of research in emotional and behavioral disorders* (pp. 143–162). New York: Guilford.

Furlong, M. J., Morrison, G. M., & Fisher, E. S. (2005). The influences of the school contexts and processes on violence and disruption in American schools. In P. Clough, P. Garner, J. T. Pardeck, & F. K. O. Yuen (Eds.), *Handbook of emotional and behavioural difficulties in education* (pp. 106–120). London: Sage.

Furlong, M. J., Morrison, G. M., & Jimerson, S. (2004). Externalizing behaviors of aggression and violence and the school context. In R. B. Rutherford, M. M. Quinn, & S. R. Mathur (Eds.), *Handbook of research in emotional and behavioral disorders* (pp. 243–261). New York: Guilford.

Garner, P. (2014). Curriculum interventions: Linking behaviour to student learning. In P. Garner, J. M. Kauffman, & J. G. E. Elliott (Eds.), *Sage handbook of emotional and behavioral difficulties* (2nd ed., pp. 291–302). London: Sage Publications.

Garner, P., Kauffman, J. M., & Elliott, J. G. E. (Eds.) (2014). *Sage handbook of emotional and behavioral difficulties* (2nd ed.). London: Sage Publications.

Goldstein, R. N. (2014). *Plato at the Googleplex: Why philosophy won't go away.* New York: Random House.

Gresham, F. M., & Elliott, S. N. (2014). Social skills assessment and training in EBD: Evidence-based practices. In H. M. Walker & F. M. Gresham (Eds.), *Handbook of evidence-based practices for students having emotional and behavioral disorders* (pp. 152–172). New York: Guilford.

Gresham, F. M., & Kern, L. (2004). Internalizing behavior problems in children and adolescents. In R. B. Rutherford, M. M. Quinn, & S. R. Mathur (Eds.), *Handbook of research in emotional and behavioral disorders* (pp. 262–281). New York: Guilford.

Gresham, F. M., & Walker, H. M. (2014). The evidence basis for emotional and behavioral disorders in school settings and contexts. In H. M. Walker & F. M. Gresham (Eds.), *Handbook of evidence-based practices for students having emotional and behavioral disorders* (pp. 9–14). New York: Guilford.

Grigorenko, E. (2014). Genetics and EBD. In P. Garner, J. M. Kauffman, & J. G. E. Elliott (Eds.), *Sage handbook of emotional and behavioral difficulties* (2nd ed., pp. 131–144). London: Sage Publications.

Hallenbeck, B. A., & Kauffman, J. M. (1995). How does observational learning affect the behavior of students with emotional or behavioral disorders? A review of research. *Journal of Special Education, 29,* 45–71. doi:10.1177/002246699502900103

Heubeck, B. G., & Lauth, G. (2014). Parent training for behavioral difficulties during the transition to school: Promises and challenges for prevention and early intervention. In P. Garner, J. M. Kauffman, & J. G. E. Elliott (Eds.), *Sage handbook of emotional and behavioral difficulties* (2nd ed., pp. 317–333). London: Sage Publications.

Hornby, G., & Evans, B. (2014). Including students with significant EBDs in mainstream settings. In P. Garner, J. M. Kauffman, & J. G. E. Elliott (Eds.), *Sage handbook of emotional and behavioral difficulties* (2nd ed., pp. 335–348). London: Sage Publications.

Jimenez-Barbero, J. A., Rukiz-Hernandez, J. A., Llor-Zaragoza, L., Periz-Garcia, M., & Llor-Esteban, B. (2016). Effectiveness of anti-bullying school programs: A meta-analysis. *Children and Youth Services Review, 61,* 165–175.

Jones, V., Dohrn, E., & Dunn, C. (2004). *Creating effective programs for students with emotional and behavioral disorders.* Boston: Allyn & Bacon.

Kauffman, J. M. (1997). Conclusion: A little of everything, a lot of nothing is an agenda for failure. *Journal of Emotional and Behavioral Disorders, 5,* 76–81.

Kauffman, J. M. (1999). How we prevent the prevention of emotional and behavioral disorders. *Exceptional Children, 65,* 448–468.

Kauffman, J. M. (2010). The problem of early identification. In H. Ricking & G. C. Schulze (Eds.), *Förderbedarf in der emotionalen und sozialen Entwiklung: Prävention, Interdisziplinarität, und Professionalisierung* (pp. 171–177). Bad Heilbrunn, Germany: Klinkhardt Verlag.

Kauffman, J. M. (2011). *Toward a science of education: The battle between rogue and real science.* Verona, WI: Attainment.

Kauffman, J. M. (2013). Labeling and categorizing children and youth with emotional and behavioral disorders in the USA: Current practices and conceptual problems. In T. Cole, H. Daniels, & J. Visser (Eds.), *The Routledge international handbook of emotional and behavioural difficulties* (2nd ed., pp. 15–21). London: Routledge.

Kauffman, J. M. (2014a). Epilogue: Science is a hard mistress. In H. M. Walker & F. M. Gresham (Eds.), *Handbook of evidence-based practices for students having emotional and behavioral disorders* (pp. 583–585). New York: Guilford.

Kauffman, J. M. (2014b). Prologue. On following the scientific evidence. In H. M. Walker & F. M. Gresham (Eds.), *Handbook of evidence-based practices for students having emotional and behavioral disorders* (pp. 1–5). New York: Guilford.

Kauffman, J. M. (2014c). How we prevent the prevention of emotional and behavioural difficulties in education. In P. Garner, J. M. Kauffman, & J. G. Elliott (Eds.), *Handbook of emotional and behavioural difficulties* (2nd ed., pp. 505–516). London: Sage.

Kauffman, J. M., & Anastasiou, D. (in press). On cultural politics in special education: Is much of it justifiable? *Journal of Disability Policy Studies.*

Kauffman, J. M., & Badar, J. (2014). Instruction, not inclusion, should be the central issue in special education: An alternative view from the USA. *Journal of International Special Needs Education, 17,* 13–20.

Kauffman, J. M., & Badar, J. (2016). It's instruction over place—not the other way around! *Phi Delta Kappan, 98*(4), 55–59. doi:10.1177/0031721716681778

Kauffman, J. M., Bantz, J., & McCullough, J. (2002). Separate and better: A special public school class for students with emotional and behavioral disorders. *Exceptionality, 10,* 149–170.

Kauffman, J. M., & Brigham, F. J. (2009). *Working with troubled children.* Verona, WI: Attainment.

Kauffman, J. M., Conroy, M., Gardner, R., & Oswald, D. (2008). Cultural sensitivity in the application of behavior principles to education. *Education and Treatment of Children, 31,* 239–262. doi:10.1353/etc.0.0019

Kauffman, J. M., & Landrum, T. J. (2006). *Children and youth with emotional and behavioral disorders: A brief history of their education.* Austin, TX: Pro-Ed.

Kauffman, J. M., & Landrum, T. J. (2009). Politics, civil rights, and disproportional identification of students with emotional and behavioral disorders. *Exceptionality, 17,* 177–188. doi:10.1080/09362830903231903

Kauffman, J. M., & Landrum, T. J. (2013). *Cases in emotional and behavioral disorders of children and youth* (2nd ed.). Upper Saddle River, NJ: Merrill/Pearson.

Kauffman, J. M., & Landrum, T. J. (2018). *Characteristics of emotional and behavioral disorders of children and youth* (11th ed.). Upper Saddle River, NJ: Merrill/Pearson.

Kauffman, J. M., Mock, D. R., & Simpson, R. L. (2007). Problems related to underservice of students with emotional or behavioral disorders. *Behavioral Disorders, 33,* 43–57.

Kauffman, J. M., Mock, D. R., Tankersley, M., & Landrum, T. J. (2008). Effective service delivery models. In R. J. Morris & N. Mather (Eds.), *Evidence-based interventions for students with learning and behavioral challenges* (pp. 359–378). Mahwah, NJ: Erlbaum.

Kauffman, J. M., Nelson, C. M., Simpson, R. L., & Mock, D. R. (2017). Contemporary issues. In J. M. Kauffman, D. P. Hallahan, & P. C. Pullen (Eds.), *Handbook of special education* (2nd ed., pp. 16–28). New York: Routledge.

Kauffman, J. M., Pullen, P. L., Mostert, M. P., & Trent, S. C. (2011). *Managing classroom behavior: A reflective case-based approach* (5th ed.). Upper Saddle River, NJ: Merrill/Pearson.

Kauffman, J. M., Simpson, R. L., & Mock, D. R. (2009). Problems related to underservice: A rejoinder. *Behavioral Disorders, 34,* 172–180.

Kauffman, J. M., Ward, D. M., & Badar, J. (2016). The delusion of full inclusion. In R. M. Foxx & J. A. Mulick (Eds.), *Controversial therapies for autism and intellectual disabilities* (2nd ed., pp. 71–86). New York: Taylor & Francis.

Kazdin, A. E. (2008). *The Kazdin method for parenting the defiant child.* Boston: Houghton Mifflin.

Keogh, B. K. (2003). *Temperament in the classroom: Understanding individual differences.* Baltimore: Brookes.

Kerr, M. M., & Nelson, C. M. (2010). *Strategies for addressing behavior problems in the classroom* (6th ed.). Upper Saddle River, NJ: Merrill/Pearson.

Konopasek, D., & Forness, S. R. (2004). Psychopharmacology in the treatment of emotional and behavioral disorders. In R. B. Rutherford, M. M. Quinn, & S. R. Mathur (Eds.), *Handbook of research in emotional and behavioral disorders* (pp. 352–368). New York: Guilford.

Konopasek, D. E., & Forness, S. R. (2014). Issues and criteria for the effective use of psychopharmacological interventions in schooling. In H. M. Walker & F. M. Gresham (Eds.), *Handbook of evidence-based practices for students having emotional and behavioral disorders* (pp. 457–472). New York: Guilford.

Landrum, T. J. (2017). Emotional and behavioral disorders. In J. M. Kauffman, D. P. Hallahan, & P. C. Pullen (Eds.), *Handbook of special education* (2nd ed., pp. 312–324). New York: Routledge.

Landrum, T. J., Wiley, A. L., Tankersley, M., & Kauffman, J. M. (2014). Is EBD "special," and is "special education" an appropriate response? In P. Garner, J. M. Kauffman, & J. G. E. Elliott (Eds.), *Sage handbook of emotional and behavioral difficulties* (2nd ed., pp. 69–81). London: Sage Publications.

Lane, K. L., & Menzies, H. M. (Eds.). (2010). Academic problems. *Behavioral Disorders* [special issue].

Lane, K, L., Menzies, H. M., Oakes, W. P., & Germer, K. A. (2014). Screening and identification approaches for detecting students at-risk. In H. M. Walker & F. M. Gresham (Eds.), *Handbook of evidence-based practices for students having emotional and behavioral disorders* (2nd ed., pp. 129–151). New York: Guilford.

Learoyd-Smith S., & Daniels, H. (2014). Social context, cultures and environments. In P. Garner, J. M. Kauffman, & J. G. E. Elliott (Eds.), *Sage handbook of emotional and behavioral difficulties* (2nd ed., pp. 145–164). London: Sage Publications.

Leff, S. S., Waanders, C., Waasdorp, T. E., & Paskewich, B. S. (2014). Bullying, harassment and relational aggression in school settings. In H. M. Walker & F. M. Gresham (Eds.), *Handbook of evidence-based practices for students having emotional and behavioral disorders* (pp. 277–291). New York: Guilford.

Locher, C., Koechlin, H., Zion, S. R., Werner, C., Pine, D. S., Kirsch, I., Kessler, R. C., & Kossowsky, J. (2017, August 30). Efficacy and safety of selective serotonin reuptake inhibitors, serotonin-norepinephrine reuptake inhibitors, and placebo for common psychiatric disorders among children and adolescents: A systematic review and meta-analysis. *JAMA Psychiatry.* doi:

10.1001/jamapsychiatry.2017.2432. Retrieved September 2, 2017 from http://jamanetwork.com.proxy.its.virginia.edu/journals/jamapsychiatry/fullarticle/2652447.

Marshall, K., Brown, W. H., Conroy, M. A., & Knopf, H. (2017). Early intervention and prevention of disability: Preschoolers. In J. M. Kauffman, D. P. Hallahan, & P. C. Pullen (Eds.), *Handbook of special education* (2nd ed., pp. 850–864). New York: Routledge.

Martens, B. K., & Lambert, T. (2014). Conducting functional behavioral assessments for students with emotional/behavioral disorders. In H. M. Walker & F. M. Gresham (Eds.), *Handbook of evidence-based practices for students having emotional and behavioral disorders* (pp. 243–257). New York: Guilford.

Mash, E. J., & Barkley, R. A. (Eds.). (2014). *Child psychopathology* (3rd ed.). New York: Guilford.

Masia, C. L., Klein, R. G., Storch, E. A., & Corda, B. (2001). School-based behavioral treatment for social anxiety disorder in adolescents: Results of a pilot study. *Journal of the American Academy of Child and Adolescent Psychiatry, 40,* 780–786.

Mattison, R. E. (2004). Psychiatric and psychological assessment of emotional and behavioral disorders during school mental health consultation. In R. B. Rutherford, M. M. Quinn, & S. R. Mathur (Eds.), *Handbook of research in emotional and behavioral disorders* (pp. 163–180). New York: Guilford.

Mattison, R. E. (2014). The interface between child psychiatry and special education in the treatment of EBD students in school settings. In H. M. Walker & F. M. Gresham (Eds.), *Handbook of evidence-based practices for students having emotional and behavioral disorders* (pp. 104–128). New York: Guilford.

Mayer, M. J., & Cornell, D. G. (Eds.). (2010). New perspectives on school safety and violence prevention. *Educational Researcher* [special issue], *39*(5). doi:10.3102/0013189X09356778

McGrath, H. (2014). Directions in teaching social skills to students with EBD. In P. Garner, J. M. Kauffman, & J. G. E. Elliott (Eds.), *Sage handbook of emotional and behavioral difficulties* (2nd ed.). London: Sage Publications.

Mundschenk, N. A., & Simpson, R. L. (2014). Defining emotional/behavioral disorders: The quest for affirmation. In P. Garner, J. M. Kauffman, & J. G. E. Elliott (Eds.), *Sage handbook of emotional and behavioral difficulties* (2nd ed., pp. 43–53). London: Sage Publications.

Nelson, C. M., & Kauffman, J. M. (1977). Educational programming for secondary school age delinquent and maladjusted pupils. *Behavioral Disorders, 2,* 102–113.

Nelson, C. M., Leone, P. E., & Rutherford, R. B. (2004). Youth delinquency: Prevention and intervention. In R. B. Rutherford, M. M. Quinn, & S. R. Mathur (Eds.), *Handbook of research in emotional and behavioral disorders* (pp. 282–301). New York: Guilford.

Nelson, J. R., Benner, G. J., & Bohaty, J. (2014). Addressing the academic performance problems and challenges of EBD students. In H. M. Walker & F. M. Gresham (Eds.), *Handbook of evidence-based practices for students having emotional and behavioral disorders* (pp. 363–377). New York: Guilford.

Nicholson, T. (2014). Academic achievement and behavior. In P. Garner, J. M. Kauffman, & J. G. E. Elliott (Eds.), *Sage handbook of emotional and behavioral difficulties* (2nd ed., pp. 303–316). London: Sage Publications.

O'Brennan, L. M., Furlong, M. J., O'Malley, M. D., & Jones, C. N. (2014). The influence of school contexts and processes on violence and disruption. In P. Garner, J. M. Kauffman, & J. G. E. Elliott (Eds.), *Sage handbook of emotional and behavioral difficulties* (2nd ed., pp. 165–176). London: Sage Publications.

Oliver, R. M., Cress, C. J., Savolainen, H., & Epstein, M. H. (2014). Strength-based assessment issues, tools, and practices in school-related contexts in the U.S. and Finland. In H. M. Walker & F. M. Gresham (Eds.), *Handbook of evidence-based practices for students having emotional and behavioral disorders* (pp. 229–242). New York: Guilford.

O'Mahoney, P. (2014). Childhood emotional and behavioural problems and later criminality: Continuities and discontinuities. In P. Garner, J. M. Kauffman, & J. G. E. Elliott (Eds.), *Sage handbook of emotional and behavioral difficulties* (2nd ed., pp. 189–204). London: Sage Publications.

Otten, K., & Tuttle, J. (2010). *How to reach and teach children with challenging behavior.* San Francisco: Jossey-Bass.

Place, M., & Elliott, J. G. E. (2014). The importance of the 'E' in EBD. In P. Garner, J. M. Kauffman, & J. G. E. Elliott (Eds.), *Sage handbook of emotional and behavioral difficulties* (2nd ed., pp. 83–93). London: Sage Publications.

Polloway, E. A., Kauffman, J. M., Charles, A., Smith, T. E. C., & Patton, J. R. (2017). *Emotional and behavioral disorders: An analysis of demographic trends, state terminology, and definitions.* Unpublished manuscript, Lynchburg College.

Reinke, W. M., Frey, A. J., Herman, K., & Thompson, C. V. (2014). The management of collaborative school and home interventions to develop successful students (e.g., the family and school checkup models). In H. M. Walker & F. M. Gresham (Eds.), *Handbook of evidence-based practices for students having emotional and behavioral disorders* (pp. 432–445). New York: Guilford.

Rogers-Adkinson, D., & Griffith, P. (Eds.). (1999). *Communication disorders and children with psychiatric and behavioral disorders.* San Diego: Singular.

Schaffner, L. (2006). *Girls in trouble with the law.* New Brunswick, NJ: Rutgers University Press.

Scull, A. (2015). *Madness in civilization: A cultural history of insanity from the Bible to Freud, from the madhouse to modern medicine.* Princeton, NJ: Princeton University Press.

Seeley, J. R., Severson, H. H., & Fixsen, A. (2014). Empirically-based targeted prevention approaches for addressing externalizing and internalizing behavior disorders within school contexts. In H. M. Walker & F. M. Gresham (Eds.), *Handbook of evidence-based practices for students having emotional and behavioral disorders* (pp. 307–323). New York: Guilford.

Skiba, R., Middelberg, L. V., & McClain, M. B. (2014). Multicultural issues for schools and EBD students: Disproportionality in discipline and special education. In H. M. Walker & F. M. Gresham (Eds.), *Handbook of evidence-based practices for students having emotional and behavioral disorders* (pp. 54–70). New York: Guilford.

Skiba, R. J., & Rausch, M. K. (2006). Zero tolerance, suspension, and expulsion: Questions of equity and effectiveness. In C. Evertson & C. Weinstein (Eds.), *Handbook of classroom management: Research, practice, and contemporary issues* (pp. 1063–1089). Mahwah, NJ: Erlbaum.

Sprague, J., & Walker, H. (2000). Early identification and intervention for youth with antisocial and violent behavior. *Exceptional Children, 66,* 367–379.

Sprague, J. R., Jolivette, K., & Nelson, C. M. (2014). Applying positive behavior intervention and supports in alternative education programs and secure juvenile facilities. In H. M. Walker & F. M. Gresham (Eds.), *Handbook of evidence-based practices for students having emotional and behavioral disorders* (pp. 261–276). New York: Guilford.

Stichter, J. P., Conroy, M. A., & Kauffman, J. M. (2008). *An introduction to students with high-incidence disabilities.* Upper Saddle River, NJ: Merrill-Prentice Hall.

Swan, A. J., Cummings, C. M., Caporino, N. E., & Kendall, P. C. (2014). Anxiety disorders: Evidence-based intervention approaches. In H. M. Walker & F. M. Gresham (Eds.), *Handbook of evidence-based practices for students having emotional and behavioral disorders* (pp. 324–343). New York: Guilford.

Thomas, J. M., & Guskin, K. A. (2001). Disruptive behavior in young children: What does it mean? *Journal of the American Academy of Child and Adolescent Psychiatry, 40,* 44–51.

Unruh, D. K., & Murray, C. J. (2014). Improving transition outcomes for students with emotional and behavioral disorders. In H. M. Walker & F. M. Gresham (Eds.), *Handbook of evidence-based practices for students having emotional and behavioral disorders.* New York: Guilford.

Van Acker, R., Boreson, L., Gable, R. A., & Patterson, T. (2005). Are we on the right course? Lessons learned about current FBA/BIP practices in schools. *Journal of Behavioral Education, 14*(1), 35–56. doi:10.1007/s10864-005-0960-5

Vidair, H. B., Sauro, D., Blocher, J., Scudellari, L., & Hoagwood, K. E. (2014). Empirically supported school-based mental health programs targeting academic and mental health functioning: An update. In H. M. Walker & F. M. Gresham (Eds.), *Handbook of evidence-based practices for students having emotional and behavioral disorders* (pp. 15–53). New York: Guilford.

Wagner, M. (2014). The longitudinal outcomes and post high-school status of students with EBD. In H. M. Walker & F. M. Gresham (Eds.), *Handbook of evidence-based practices for students having emotional and behavioral disorders* (pp. 86–103). New York: Guilford.

Walker, H. M., & Gresham, F. M. (Eds.) (2014), *Handbook of evidence-based practices for students having emotional and behavioral disorders*. New York: Guilford.

Walker, H. M., Ramsey, E., & Gresham, F. M. (2003–2004a). Heading off disruption: How early intervention can reduce defiant behavior—and win back teaching time. *American Educator, 27*(4), 6–21.

Walker, H. M., Ramsey, E., & Gresham, F. M. (2003–2004b). How disruptive students escalate hostility and disorder—and how teachers can avoid it. *American Educator, 27*(4), 22–27, 47.

Walker, H. M., Ramsey, E., & Gresham, F. M. (2004). *Antisocial behavior in school: Strategies and best practices* (2nd ed.). Pacific Grove, CA: Brooks/Cole.

Walker, H. M., Severson, H. H., Seeley, J. R., Feil, E. G., Small, J., Golly, A. M., Frey, A. J., Lee, J., Sumi, W. C., Woodbridge, M., Wagner, M, & Forness, S. R. (2014). The evidence base of the First Step to Success early intervention for preventing emerging antisocial behavior patterns. In H. M. Walker & F. M. Gresham (Eds.), *Handbook of evidence-based practices for students having emotional and behavioral disorders* (pp. 518–536). New York: Guilford.

Walker, H. M., Small, J., Severson, H. H., Seeley, J. R., & Feil, E. G. (2014). Multiple-gating approaches in universal screening within school and community settings: Practice and methodological considerations. In R. J. Kettler, T. A. Glover, C. A. Albers, & K. Feeney-Kettler (Eds.), *Universal screening in educational settings: Identification, implementation, and interpretation* (pp. 303–316). Washington, DC: American Psychological Association.

Walker, H. M., & Sprague, J. R. (2007). Early, evidence-based intervention with school-based behavior disorders: Key issues, continuing challenges, and promising practices. In J. B. Crockett, M. M. Gerber, & T. J. Landrum (Eds.), *Achieving the radical reform of special education: Essays in honor of James M. Kauffman* (pp. 37–58). Mahwah, NJ: Erlbaum.

Walker, H. M., Yell, M. L., & Murray, C. (2014). Identifying EBD students in the context of schooling under the federal ED definition: Where we've been, where we are, and where we need to go. In P. Garner, J. M. Kauffman, & J. G. E. Elliott (Eds.), *Sage handbook of emotional and behavioral difficulties* (2nd ed., pp. 55–68). London: Sage Publications.

Wolf, M. M., Braukmann, C. J., & Ramp, K. A. (1987). Serious delinquent behavior as part of a significantly handicapping condition. *Journal of Applied Behavior Analysis, 20*, 347–359.

Yell, M. L., Gatti, S. N., & Allday, R. A. (2014). Legislation, regulation, and litigation and the delivery of support services to EBD students in school settings. In H. M. Walker & F. M. Gresham (Eds.), *Handbook of evidence-based practices for students having emotional and behavioral disorders* (pp. 71–85). New York: Guilford.

Yell, M. L., Katsiyannis, A., & Bradley, M. R. (2017). The Individuals with Disabilities Education Act: The evolution of special education law. In J. M. Kauffman, D. P. Hallahan, & P. C. Pullen (Eds.), *Handbook of special education* (2nd ed., pp. 55–70). New York: Routledge.

Zigmond, N., & Kloo (2017). General and special education are (and should be) different. In J. M. Kauffman, D. P. Hallahan, & P. C. Pullen (Eds.), *Handbook of special education* (2nd ed., pp. 249–261). New York: Taylor & Francis.

CHAPTER 9

Adams, J.B., Johansen, L.J., Powell, L.D., Quig, D., & Rubin, R.A. (2011). Gastrointestinal flora and gastrointestinal status in children with autism-comparisons to typical children and correlation with autism severity. *BMC Gastroenterology, 11*, No. 22. doi:doi.org/10.1186/1471-230X-11-22.

Adamson, L. B., Bakeman, R., Deckner, D. F., & Romiski, M. (2009). Joint engagement and the emergence of language in children with autism and Down syndrome. *Journal of Autism and Developmental Disorders, 39*, 84–96. doi:10.1007/s10803-008-0601-7

Adreon, D., & Stella, J. (2001). Transition to middle and high school: Increasing the success of students with Asperger syndrome. *Intervention in School and Clinic, 36*, 266–271. doi:10.1177/105345120103600502

American Psychiatric Association. (2013). *Diagnostic and statistical manual* (5th ed.), *DSM-5*. Arlington, VA: American Psychiatric Publishing.

Anderson, S., & Meints, K. (2016). Brief report: The effects of equine-assisted activities on the social functioning in children and adolescents with autism spectrum disorder. *Journal of Autism and Developmental Disorders, 46*, 3344–3352. doi:10.1007/s10803-016-2869-3

Asperger, H. (1991). The "Autistic Psychopathy" in childhood. In U. Frith (Ed. & Trans.), *Autism and Asperger syndrome* (pp. 37–92). Cambridge, UK: Cambridge University Press, 1991. (Original work published 1944)

Autism Genome Project Consortium. (2007). Mapping autism risk loci using genetic linkage and chromosomal rearrangements. *Nature Genetics, 39*, 319–328. doi:10.1038/ng1985

Auyeung, B., Baron-Cohen, S., Ashwin, E., Knickmeyer, R., Taylor, K., & Hackett, G. (2009). Fetal testosterone and autistic traits. *British Journal of Psychology, 100*, 1–22. doi:10.1348/ 00712608X311731

Barbeau, E. B., Mendrek, A., & Motton, L. (2009). Are autistic traits autistic? *British Journal of Psychology, 100*, 23–28. doi:10.1348/ 000712608X337788

Barger, B. D., Campbell, J. M., & McDonough, J. D. (2013). Prevalence and onset of regression within autism spectrum disorders. *Journal of Autism and Developmental Disorders, 43*, 817–828. doi: http://dx.doi.org/10.1007/s10803-012-1621-x.

Barnhill, G. P. (2016). Supporting students with Asperger syndrome on college campuses: Current practices. *Focus on Autism and Other Developmental Disabilities, 31*, 3–15. doi:10.1177/1088357614523121.

Baron-Cohen, S. (2002). The extreme male brain theory of autism. *Trends in Cognitive Sciences, 6*, 248–254. doi:10.1016/S1364-6613(02)01904-6

Baron-Cohen, S. (2003). *The essential difference: Men, women and the extreme male brain*. London: Penguin.

Baron-Cohen, S., Auyeung, B., Ashwin, E., & Knickmeyer, R. (2009). Fetal testosterone and autistic traits: A response to three fascinating commentaries. *British Journal of Psychology, 100*, 39–47. doi:10.1348/000712608X394271

Baron-Cohen, S., Leslie, A. M., & Frith, U. (1985). Does the autistic child have a "theory of mind"? *Cognition, 21*, 37–46. doi:10.1016/0010-0277(85)90022-8

Baron-Cohen, S., Wheelright, S., Skinner, R., Martin, J., & Clubley, E. (2001). The autism-spectrum quotient (AQ): Evidence from Asperger syndrome/high functioning autism, males and females, scientists, and mathematicians. *Journal of Autism and Developmental Disorders, 31*, 5–17. doi:http://dx.doi.org/10.1023/A:1005653411471

Bell, R. Q., & Harper, L. V. (1977). *Child effects on adults*. Hillsdale, NJ: Erlbaum.

Bellini, S., & Hopf, A. (2007). The development of the autism social skills profile: A preliminary analysis of psychometric properties. *Focus on Autism and Other Developmental Disabilities, 22*, 80–87. doi:10.1177/10883576070220020801

Ben-Sasson, A., Hen, L., Fluss, R., Cermak, S. A., Engel-Yeger, B., & Gal, E. (2009). A meta-analysis of sensory modulation symptoms in individuals with autism spectrum disorders. *Journal of Autism and Developmental Disorders, 39*, 1–11. doi:10.1007/s10803-0593-3

Bettelheim, B. (1967). *The empty fortress*. New York: Free Press.

Bishop, D. V. M., Whitehouse, A. J. O., Watt, H. J., & Line, E. A. (2008). *Developmental Medicine & Child Neurology, 50*, 1–5.

Bishop-Fitzpatrick L., Minshew, N. J., & Eack, S. M. (2013). A systematic review of psychosocial interventions for adults with autism spectrum disorders. *Journal of Autism and Developmental Disorders, 43*, 687–694. doi:10.1007/s10803-012-1615-8.

Bleuler, E. (1951). *Textbook of psychiatry* (A. A. Brill, Trans.). New York: Dover. (Original work published 1916)

Borgi, M., Loliva, D., Cerino, S., Chiarotti, F., Venerosi, A., Bramini, M. . . ., & Cirulli, F. (2016). Effectiveness of a standardized equine-assisted therapy program for children with autism spectrum disorder. *Journal of Autism and Developmental Disorders, 46*, 1–9. doi:10.1007/s10803-015-2530-6

Bozkus-Genc, G., & Yucesoy-Ozkan, S. (2016). Meta-analysis of pivotal response training for children with autism spectrum disorder. *Education and Training in Autism and Developmental Disabilities, 51*, 13–26.

Buie, T., Campbell, D.B., Fuchs, G.J., 3rd, Furuta, G.T., Levy, J., Vandewater, J., . . . Beaudet, A.L., et al. (2010). Evaluation, diagnosis, and treatment of gastrointestinal disorders in individuals with ASDs: A consensus report. Pediatrics 125 (Suppl 1), S1–S18.

Burton, C. E., Anderson, D. H., Prater, M. A., & Dyches, T. T. (2012). Video self-modeling on an iPad to teach math skills to adolescents with autism and intellectual disability. *Focus on Autism and Other Developmental Disabilities, 28*(2), 67–77. doi:10.1177/1088357613478829.

Causton-Theoharis, J., Ashby, C., & Cosier, M. (2009). Islands of loneliness: Exploring social interaction through the autobiographies of individuals with autism. *Intellectual and Developmental Disabilities, 47*, 84–96. doi:10.1352/1934-9556-47.2.84

Cederlund, M., Hagberg, B., Billstedt, E., Gillberg, I. C., & Gillberg, C. (2008). Asperger syndrome and autism: A comparative longitudinal follow-up study more than 5 years after original diagnosis. *Journal of Autism and Developmental Disorders, 38*, 72–85. doi:10.1007/s10803-007-0364-6

Centers for Disease Control and Prevention. (2008, October 20). *Update: Measles outbreaks continue in U.S.* Retrieved from http://cdc.gov/Features/MeaslesUpdate/

Centers for Disease Control and Prevention. (2013, June 27). "Autism Spectrum Disorders: Data and Statistics." Retrieved from http://www.cdc.gov/ncbddd/autism/data.html

Centers for Disease Control and Prevention. (2016, April 1). Prevalence and characteristics of autism spectrum disorder among children aged 8 years—autism and developmental disabilities monitoring network, 11 sites, United States, 2012, *Modality and Mortality Weekly Report, Surveillance Summaries, 65*(3), 1–23. Retrieved from https://www.cdc.gov/mmwr/volumes/65/ss/ss6503a1.htm

Clifford, S. M., & Dissanayake, C. (2008). The early development of joint attention in infants with autistic disorder using home video observations and parental interview. *Journal of Autism and Developmental Disorders, 38*, 791–805. doi:10.1007/s10803-007-0444-7

Cohen, I. L., Schmidt-Lackner, S., Romanczyk, R., & Sudhalter, V. (2003). The PDD behavior inventory: A rating scale for assessing response to intervention in children with pervasive developmental disorder. *Journal of Autism and Developmental Disabilities, 33*, 31–45. doi:10.1023/A:1022226403878

Cohen, I. L., & Sudhalter, V. (2005). *PDD Behavior Inventory (PDDBI).* Lutz, FL: Psychological Assessment Resources.

Colle, L., Baron-Cohen, S., Wheelwright, S., & van der Lely, H. K. J. (2008). Narrative discourse in adults with high-functioning autism or Asperger syndrome. *Journal of Autism and Developmental Disorders, 38*, 28–40. doi:10.1007/s10803-007-0357-5

Constantino, J. N., & Gruber, C. P. (2005). *The social responsiveness scale (SRS).* Los Angeles: Western Psychological Services.

Coo, H., Ouellette-Kuntz, H., Lloyd, J. E. V., Kasmara, L., Holden, J. J. A., & Lewis, M. E. S. (2008). Trends in autism prevalence: Diagnostic substitution revisited. *Journal of Autism and Developmental Disorders, 38*, 1036–1046. doi:10.1007/s10803-007-0478-x

Courchesne, E., Campbell, K., & Solso, S. (2011). Brain growth across the life span in autism: Age-specific changes in anatomical pathology. *Brain Research, 1380*, 138–145. doi: http://dx.doi.org/10.1016/j.brainres.2010.09.101.

Coury, D. L., Ashwood, P., Fasano, A., Fuchs, G., Geraghty, M., Kaul, . . . Jones, N. E. (2012). Gastrointestinal conditions in children with autism spectrum disorder: Developing a research agenda. *Pediatrics 130* (Suppl 2), S160–S168.

Doi, H., Takashi, X. F., Kanai, C., Ohta, H., Yoki, H., Iwanami, A. . . . Shinohara, K. (2013). Recognition of facial expressions and prosodic cues with graded emotional intensities in adults with Asperger syndrome. *Journal of Autism and Developmental Disorders, 43*, 2099–2113. doi: http://dx.doi.org/10.1007/s10803-013-1760-8

Down, J. L. (1887). *On some of the mental affections of childhood and youth.* London, England: Churchill.

Duifhuis, E. A., den Boer, J. C., Doornbos, A., Buitelaar, J. K., Oosterling, I. J., & Klip, H. (2017). The effect of Pivotal Response Treatment in children with autism spectrum disorders: A non-randomized study with a blinded outcome measure. *Journal of Autism and Developmental Disorders, 47*, 231–242.

Editors of *The Lancet.* (2010, February 2). Retraction—Ileal-lymphoid-nodular hyperplasia, non-specific colitis, and pervasive developmental disorder in children. *The Lancet.* Retrieved from http://www.thelancet.com/journals/lancet/article/PIIS0140-6736%2810%2960175-4/fulltextdoi:10.1016/S0140-6736(10)60175-4

Eisenberg, L., & Kanner, K. (1956). Early infantile autism, 1943–1955. *American Journal of Orthopsychiatry, 26*, 556–566.

Elder, L. M., Dawson, G., Toth, K., Fein, D., & Munson, J. (2008). Head circumference as an early predictor of autism symptoms in younger siblings of children with autism spectrum disorder. *Journal of Autism and Developmental Disorders, 38*, 1104–1111. doi:10.1007/s10803-007-04959

Eldevik, S., Hastings, R. P., Hughes, J. C., Jahr, E., Eikeseth, S., & Cross, S. (2009). Meta-analysis of Early Intensive Behavioral Intervention for children with autism. *Journal of Clinical Child & Adolescent Psychology, 38*, 439–450. doi:10.1080/15374410902851739

Elison, J. T., Paterson, S. J., Wolff, J. J., Reznick, J. S., Sasson, N. J., Gu, H., . . . Piven, J. (2013). White matter microstructure and atypical visual orienting in 7-month-olds at risk for autism. *American Journal of Psychiatry, 170*, 899–908. doi:http://dx.doi.org/10.1176/appi.ajp.2012.12091150

Falter, C. M., Plaisted, K. C., & Davis, G. (2008). Male brains, androgen, and the cognitive profile in autism: Convergent evidence from 2D:4D and congenital adrenal hyperplasia. *Journal of Autism and Developmental Disorders, 38*, 997–998. doi:10.1007/s10803-008-0552-z.

Fenson, L. (2007). *MacArthur-Bates Communicative Development Inventories (CDIs)* (3rd ed.). Baltimore: Brookes.

Fenson, L., Marchman, V. A., Thal, D. J., Dale, P. S., Reznick, J. S., & Bates, E. (2006). *MacArthur-Bates Communicative Development Inventories (CDIs)* (2nd ed.). Baltimore: Brookes.

Flaherty, D. K. (2011). The vaccine-autism connection: A public health crisis caused by unethical medical practices and fraudulent science. *Annals of Pharmacotherapy, 45*, 1302–1304. doi:10.1345/aph

Fombonne, E. (2001). Is there an autism epidemic? *Pediatrics, 107*, 411–412. doi:10.1542/peds.107.2.411

Freed, G. L., Clark, S. J., Butchart, A. T., Singer, D. C., & Davis, M. M. (2010). Parental vaccine safety concerns in 2009. *Pediatrics, 125*, 654–659. doi:http://dx.doi.org/10.1542/peds.2009-1962.

Freeman, S. F. N., Gulsrud, A., & Kasari, C. (2015). Brief report: Linking early joint attention and play abilities to later reports of friendships for children with ASD. *Journal of Autism and Developmental Disorders, 45*, 2259–2266. doi:http://dx.doi.org.proxy.its.virginia.edu/10.1007/s10803-015-2369-x

Frith, U. (2003). *Autism: Explaining the enigma* (2nd ed.). Malden, MA: Blackwell.

Fukomoto, A., Hashimoto, T., Ito, H., Nishimura, M., Tsuda, Y., Miyazaki, M., & Kagami, S. (2008). Growth of head circumference in autistic infants during the first year of life. *Journal of Autism and Developmental Disorders, 38*, 411–418.

Gabriels, R. L., Pan, Z., Dechant, B., Agnew, J. A., Brim, N., & Mesibov, G. (2015). Randomized controlled trial of therapeutic horseback riding in children and adolescents with autism spectrum disorder. *Journal of the American Academy of Child & Adolescent Psychiatry, 54*, 541–549. doi:10.1016/j.jaac.2015.04.007.

General Medical Council. (2010, May 24). Determination on serious professional misconduct (SPM) and sanction. Retrieved from http://www.gmc-uk.org/Wakefield_SPM_and_SANCTION.pdf_32595267.pdf

Gerhardt, P. F. (2003). Transition support for learners with Asperger syndrome: Toward a successful adulthood. In R. W. Du Charme & T. P. Gullotta (Eds.). *Asperger syndrome: A guide for professionals and families* (pp. 157–171). New York: Kluwer Academic/Plenum.

Glessner, J. T., Wang, K., Cai, G., Korvatska, O., Kim, C. E., Wood, S., & Hakonarson, H. (2009). Autism genome-wide copy number variation reveals ubiquitin and neuronal genes. *Nature, 459*, 569–573. doi:10.1038/nature07953

Grandin, T. (1995). *Thinking in pictures.* New York: Doubleday.

Grandin, T. (2002, May 6). First person: Myself. *Time*, 56.

Grindle, C. F., Hastings, R. P., Saville, M., Hughes, J.C., Huxley, K., Kovshoff, H. . . . Remington, B. (2012). Outcomes of a behavioral education model for children with autism in a mainstream school setting. *Behavior Modification, 36*, 298–319. doi:10.1177/0145445512441199

Guber, P. (Producer), & Levinson, B. (Director). (1988). *Rain Main* [Motion picture]. United States: United Artists.

Hart, J. E., & Whalon, K. J. (2012). Using video self-modeling via iPads to increase academic responding of an adolescent with autism spectrum disorder and intellectual disability. *Education and Training in Autism and Developmental Disabilities, 47*(4), 438–446.

Hendricks, D., & Wehman, P. (2009). Transition from school to adulthood for youth with autism spectrum disorders: Review and recommendations. *Focus on Autism and Other Developmental Disorders, 24*(2), 77–88. doi:10.1177/1088357608329827

Hertz-Picciotto, I., & Delwiche, L. (2009). The rise of autism and the role of age at diagnosis. *Epidemiology, 20*, 84–90. doi:10.1097/EDE.0b013e3181902d15

Hewetson, A. (2002). *The stolen child: Aspects of autism and Asperger syndrome.* Westport, CT: Bergin & Garvey.

Horner, R. H., Albin, R. W., Sprague, J. R., & Todd, A. W. (2000). Positive behavior support. In M. E. Snell & F. Brown (Eds.), *Instruction of students with severe retardation* (5th ed., pp. 207–243). Upper Saddle River, NJ: Merrill/Pearson.

Howlin, P., Magiati, I., & Charman, T. (2009). Systematic review of Early Intensive Behavioral Interventions for children with autism. *American Journal on Intellectual and Developmental Disabilities, 114*, 23–41. doi:10.1352/2009.114:23–41

Hurl, K., Wightman, J., Haynes, S. N., & Virues-Ortega, J. (2016). Does a pre-intervention functional assessment increase intervention effectiveness? A meta-analysis of within-subject interrupted time-series studies. *Clinical Psychology Review, 47*, 71–84. doi:10.1016/j.cpr.2016.05.003.

IDEA Data Accountability Center. (2013). "Data Tables for OSEP State Reported Data." Retrieved from https://www.ideadata.org/PartBData.asp

Individuals With Disabilities Education Improvement Act of 2004. (2004). 20 U.S.C. § 1400 *et seq.*

Institute of Medicine. (2004). *Immunization safety review: Vaccines and autism.* Washington, DC: National Academies Press.

Joint Attention. (n.d.). In *Wikipedia.* Retrieved from http://en.wikipedia.org/wiki/Joint_attention

Just, M. A., Keller, T. A., Malave, V. L., Kana, R. K., & Varma, S. (2012). Autism as a neural system disorder: A theory of frontal-posterior underconnectivity. *Neuroscience and Biobehavioral Reviews, 36*, 1292–1313. doi:http://dx.doi.org/10.1016/j.neubiorev.2012.02.007

Kaland, N., Callesen, K., Moller-Nielson, A., Mortensen, E. L., & Smith, L. (2008). Performance of children and adolescents with Asperger syndrome or high functioning autism on advanced theory of mind tasks. *Journal of Autism and Developmental Disorders, 38*, 1112–1123. doi:10.1007/s10803-007-0496-8.

Kang, D. W., Park, J. G., Ilhan, Z. E., Wallstrom, G., Labaer, J., Adams, J. B., & Krajmalnik-Brown, R. (2013). Reduced incidence of Prevotella and other fermenters in intestinal microflora of autistic children. *PLoS ONE 8*, e68322.

Kanner, L. (1973). *Childhood psychosis: Initial studies and new insights* (pp. 1–43). Washington, DC: V. H. Winston. (Reprinted from Autistic disturbances of affective contact. *Nervous Child, 2*, 217–250, by L. Kanner, 1943.)

Koegel, L. K., Koegel, R. L., Harrower, J. K., & Carter, C. M. (1999). Pivotal response intervention I: Overview of approach. *Journal of the Association for Persons with Severe Handicaps, 24*, 174–185. doi:10.2511/rpsd.24.3.174

Koegel, R. L., & Koegel, L. K. (Eds.). (2006). *Pivotal response treatments for autism: Communication, social, and academic development.* Baltimore, MD: Brookes.

Kohane, I. S., McMurry, A., Weber, G., MacFadden, D., Rappaport, L., Kunkel, L., . . . Churchill, S. (2012). The co-morbidity burden of children and young adults with autism spectrum disorders. *PLoS ONE 7*, e33224.

Kuusikko, S., Pollock-Wurman, R., Jussila, K., Carter, A. S., Mattila, M.-J., Ebeling, H., & Moilanen, I. (2008). Social anxiety in high-functioning children and adolescents with autism and Asperger syndrome. *Journal of Autism and Developmental Disorders, 38*, 1697–1709. doi:10.1007/s10803-008-0555-9.

Landa, R. J., Holman, K. C., & Garrett-Mayer, E. (2007). Social and communication development in toddlers with early and later diagnosis of autism spectrum disorders. *Archives of General Psychiatry, 64*, 853–864.

Lanning, B. A., Baier, M. E., Matyastik, I.-H., Krenck, N., & Tubbs, D. (2014). Effects of equine assisted activities on autism spectrum disorder. *Journal of Autism and Developmental Disorders, 44*, 1897–1907. doi:10.1007/s10803-014-2062-5

Le Couteur, A., Haden, G., Hammal, D., & McConachie, H. (2008). Diagnosing autism spectrum disorders in pre-school children using two standardised [sic] assessment instruments: The ADI-R and the ADOS. *Journal of Autism and Developmental Disorders, 38*, 362–372. doi:10.1007/s10803-007-0403-3

Lotter, V. (1966). Epidemiology of autistic conditions in young children: I. Prevalence. *Social Psychiatry, 1*, 124–137. doi:10.1007/BF00584048

Luna, B., Doll, S. K., Hegedus, S. J., Minshew, N. J., & Sweeney, J. A. (2007). Maturation of executive function in autism. *Biological Psychiatry, 61*, 474–481. doi:10.1016/j.biopsych.2006.02.030

Luyster, R., Lopez, K., & Lord, C. (2007). Characterizing communicative development in children referred for autism spectrum disorders using the MacArthur-Bates Communicative Development Inventory (CDI). *Journal of Child Language, 34*, 623–654. doi:10.1017/ S0305000907008094

Luyster, R., Qiu, S., Lopez, K., & Lord, C. (2007). Predicting outcomes of children referred for autism using the MacArthur-Bates Communicative Development Inventory. *Journal of Speech, Language, and Hearing Research, 50*, 667–681. doi:10.1044/1092-4388(2007/047).

MacDonald, R., Parry-Cruwys, D., Dupere, S., & Ahearn, W. (2014). Assessing progress and outcome of early intensive behavioral intervention for toddlers with autism. *Research in Developmental Disabilities, 35*, 3632–3644. doi:10.1016/j.ridd.2014.08.036.

Mason, R. A., Davis, H. S., Ayres, K. M., Davis, J. L., & Mason, B. A. (2016). Video self-modeling for individuals with disabilities: A best-evidence, single case meta-analysis. *Journal of Developmental and Physical Disabilities, 28*, 623–642. doi:10.1007/s10882-016-9484-2

Matson, J. L., Tureck, K., Turygin, N., Beighley, J., & Rieske, R. (2012). Trends and topics in Early Intensive Behavioral Interventions for toddlers with autism. *Research in Autism Spectrum Disorders, 6*, 1412–1417. doi:10.1016/j.rasd.2012.02.010

Mazza, M., Mariano, M., Peretti, S., Masedu, F., Pino, M. C., & Valenti, M. (2017, February 18). *Journal of Autism and Developmental Disorders.* First online: doi:10.1007/s10803-017-3069-5

Mazurek, M. O., & Wenstrup, C. (2013). Television, video game and social media use among children with ASD and typically developing siblings. *Journal of Autism and Developmental Disorders, 43*, 1258–1271. doi:http://dx.doi.org/10.1007/s10803-012-1659-9

Miller, J. S., Bilder, D., Farley, M., Coon, H., Pinborough-Zimmerman, J., Jenson, W., . . . McMahon, W. M. (2013). Autism spectrum disorder reclassified: A second look at the 1980s Utah/UCLA Autism Epidemiologic Study. *Journal of Autism and Developmental Disorders, 43*, 200-210. doi:10.1007/s10803-012-1566-0

Mills, J. L., Hediger, M. L., Molloy, C. A., Chrousos, G. P., Manning-Courtney, P., Yu, K. F., et al. (2007). Elevated levels of growth-related hormones in autism and autism spectrum disorder. *Clinical Endocrinology, 67*, 230–237.

Muller, R. A. (2007). The study of autism as a distributed disorder. *Mental Retardation and Developmental Disabilities Research Reviews, 13*, 85–95. doi:10.1002/mrdd.20141

Murch, S. H., Anthony, A., Casson, D. H., Malik, M., Berelowitz, M., Dhillon, A. P., et al. (2004). Retraction of an interpretation. *The Lancet, 363*, 750. doi:10.1016/S0140-6736(04)15715-2

Murray, D. S., Creaghead, N. A., Manning-Courtney, P., Shear, P. K., Bean, J., & Prendville, J. (2008). The relationship between joint attention and language in children with autism spectrum disorders. *Focus on Autism and Other Developmental Disabilities, 23*, 5–8. doi:10.1177/1088357607311443

Myles, B. S. (2003). Social skills instruction for children with Asperger syndrome. In R. W. Du Charme & T. P. Gullotta (Eds.). *Asperger syndrome: A guide for professionals and families* (pp. 21–42). New York: Kluwer Academic/Plenum.

Myles, B. S., & Simpson, R. L. (2001). Understanding the hidden curriculum: An essential social skill for children and youth with Asperger syndrome. *Intervention in School and Clinic, 36*, 279–286. doi:10.1177/105345120103600504

Myles, B. S., & Simpson, R. L. (2003). *Asperger syndrome: A guide for parents and teachers.* Austin, TX: Pro-Ed.

Naess, P. (Director), & Bass, R. (2005). *Mozart and the Whale* [Motion picture]. United States: Millennium Films.

National Institute of Health. (2013, August 21). National Institute of Neurological Diseases and Stroke: "Autism Fact Sheet." Retrieved from http://www.ninds.nih.gov/disorders/autism/detail_autism.htm

National Research Council. (2001). *Educating children with autism.* Washington, DC: National Academy Press.

O'Haire, M. E. (2013). Animal-assisted intervention for autism spectrum disorder: A systematic literature review. *Journal of Autism and Developmental Disorders, 43*, 1606–1622. doi: 10.1007/s10803-012-1707-5

Page, T. (2007, August 20). Parallel play: A lifetime of restless isolation explained. *The New Yorker*, pp. 36–41.

Parracho, H. M., Bingham, M.O., Gibson, G. R., and McCartney, A. L. (2005). Differences between the gut microflora of children with autistic spectrum disorders and that of healthy children. *Journal of Medical Microbiology, 54*, 987–991.

Piven, J., Arndt, S., Bailey, J., & Andreason, N. C. (1996). Regional brain enlargement in autism: A magnetic resonance imaging study. *Journal of the American Academy of Child and Adolescent Psychiatry, 35*, 530–536. doi:10.1097/00004583-199604000-00020

Ratto, B., Reznick, J. S., & Turner-Brown, L. (2016). Cultural effects on the diagnosis of autism spectrum disorder among Latinos. *Focus on Autism and Other Developmental Disabilities, 31*, 275–283.

Reichow, B., & Wolery, M. (2009). Comprehensive synthesis of Early Intensive Behavioral Interventions for young children with autism based on the UCLA Young Autism Project Model. *Journal of Autism and Developmental Disorders, 39*, 23–41. doi:10.1007/s10803-008-0596-0

Robertson, A. E., & Simmons, D. R. (2013). The relationship between sensory sensitivity and autistic traits in the general population. *Journal of Autism and Developmental Disorders, 43*, 775–784. doi: http://dx.doi.org/10.1007/s10803-012-1608-7

Sallows, G. O., & Graupner, T. D. (2005). Intensive behavioral treatment for children with autism: Four-year outcome and predictors. *American Journal on Mental Retardation, 110*, 417–438. doi:10.1352/0895-8017(2005)110[417:IBTFCW] 2.0.CO;2

Scheuermann, B., & Webber, J. (2002). *Autism: Teaching does make a difference*. Stamford, CT: Wadsworth Group.

Schieve, L. A., Gonzalez, V., Boulet, S. L., Visser, S. N., Rice, C. E., Braun, K. V. N., & Boyle, C. A. (2012). Concurrent medical conditions and health care use and needs among children with learning and behavioral developmental disabilities, National Health Interview Survey, 2006-2010. *Research in Developmental Disabilities: A Multidisciplinary Journal, 33*, 467–476.

Schopler, E., Van Bourgondien, M. E., Wellman, G. J., & Love, S. R. (2010). *Childhood Autism Rating Scale*, Second Edition, Pearson/Psych Corp.

Scott, J. (Producer), & Hicks, S. (Writer/Director). (1996). *Shine* [Motion picture]. Australia: New Line Cinema.

Sebat, J., Lakshmi, B., Malhotra, D., Troge, J., Lese-Martin, C., Walsh, T., et al. (2007). Strong association of de novo copy number mutations with autism. *Science, 316*, 445–449. doi:10.1126/ science.1138659

Semrud-Clikeman, M., Fine, J. G., & Bledsoe, J. (2013, June 9). Comparison among children with children autism spectrum disorder, nonverbal learning disorder and typically developing children on measures of executive functioning. *Journal of Autism and Developmental Disorders*, published online. doi:http://dx.doi.org/10.1007/s10803-013-1871-2

Shattuck, P. T. (2006). The contributions of diagnostic substitution to the growing administrative prevalence of autism in U.S. special education. *Pediatrics, 117*, 1028–1037. doi:10.1542/peds.2005-1516

Shattuck, P. T., Carter, S., Narendorf, S. C., Cooper, B., Sterzing, P. R., Wagner, M., & Taylor, J. L. Postsecondary education and employment among youth with an autism spectrum disorder. *Pediatrics, 129*, 1042–1049. doi:10.1542/peds.2011-2864

Shore, S. (2003). My life with Asperger syndrome. In R. W. Du Charme & T. P. Gullotta (Eds.), *Asperger syndrome: A guide for professionals and families* (pp. 189–209). New York: Kluwer Academic/Plenum.

Simpson, R. L., de Boer-Ott, S. R., Griswold, D. E., Myles, B. S., Byrd, S. E., Ganz, J. B., et al. (2005). *Autism spectrum disorders: Interventions and treatments for children and youth*. Thousand Oaks, CA: Corwin Press.

Simpson, R. L., de Boer-Ott, S. R., & Smith-Myles, B. (2003). Inclusion of learners with autism spectrum disorders in general education settings. *Topics in Language Disorders, 23*, 116–133. doi:10.1097/00011363-200304000-00005

Skuse, D. H. (2009). Commentary: Is autism really a coherent syndrome in boys, or girls? *British Journal of Psychology, 100*, 33–37. doi:10.1348/ 000712608X369459

Smithson, P. E., Kenworthy, L., Wills, M. C., Jarrett, M., Atmore, K., & Yerys, B. E. (2013). Real world executive control impairments in preschoolers with autism spectrum disorders. *Journal of Autism and Developmental Disorders, 43*, 1967–1975. doi:10.1007/s10803-012-1747-x.

Stichter, J., Conroy, M., O'Donnell, R., & Reichow, B. (2017). Current issues and trends in the education of children and youth with autism spectrum disorders. In J. M. Kauffman, D. P. Hallahan, & P. C. Pullen (Eds.). *Handbook of special education*. New York: Routledge.

Stone, W. L., McMahon, C. R., Yoder, P. J., & Walden, T. A. (2007). Early social-communicative and cognitive development of younger siblings of children with autism spectrum disorders. *Archives of Pediatric and Adolescent Medicine, 161*, 384–390. doi:10.1001/archpedi.161.4.384

Sulzer-Azaroff, B., Hoffman, A. O., Horton, C. B., Bondy, A., & Frost, L. (2009). The Picture Exchange Communication System (PECS): What do the data say? *Focus on Autism and Other Developmental Disabilities, 24*(2), 89–103. doi:10.1177/1088357609332743

Sutcliffe, J. S. (2008). Genetics: Insights into the pathogenesis of autism. *Science, 321*, 208–209. doi:10.1126/science.1160555

Tager-Flusberg, H., Rogers, S., Cooper, J., Landa, R., Lord, C., Paul, R.,..., & Yoder, P. (2009). Defining spoken language benchmarks and selecting measures of expressive language development for children with Autism Spectrum Disorders. *Journal of Speech, Language, and Hearing Research, 52*, 643–652. doi:10.1044/1092-4388(2009/08-0136)

Tammet, D. (2006). *Born on a blue day: A memoir of Asperger's and an extraordinary mind*. London: Hodder & Stoughton.

Tick, B., Bolton, P., Happé, F., Rutter, M., & Rijsdijk, F. (2016). Heritability of autism spectrum disorders: A meta-analysis of twin studies. *Journal of Child Psychology and Psychiatry, 57*, 585–595. http://dx.doi.org.proxy.its.virginia.edu/10.1111/jcpp.12499

Treffert, D. A. (2013, August 6). Savant syndrome: Realities, myths, and misconceptions. *Journal of Autism and Developmental Disorders*. doi:http://dx.doi.org/10.1007/s10803-013-1906-8

Uljarevic, M., & Hamilton, A. (2013). Recognition of emotions in autism: A formal meta-analysis. *Journal of Autism and Developmental Disabilities, 43*, 1517–1526. doi: http://dx.doi.org/10.1007/s10803-012-1695-5

van Rijn, S., de Sonneville, L., Lahuis, B., Pieterse, J., van Engeland, H., & Swaab, H. (2013). Executive function in MCDD and PDD-NOS: A study of inhibitory control, attention regulation, and behavioral adaptivity. *Journal of Autism and Developmental Disabilities, 43*, 1356–1366. doi: http://dx.doi.org/10.1007/s10803-012-1688-4

Venker, C. E., Ray-Subramanian, C. E., Bolt, D. M., & Weismer, S. E. (2013, August 2). Trajectories of autism severity in early childhood. *Journal of Autism and Developmental Disabilities*. Published online. doi:10.1007/s10803-013-1903-y

Volk, H. E., Lurmann, F., Penfold, B., Hertz-Picciotto, I., & McConnell, R. (2013). Traffic-related air pollution, particulate matter, and autism. *JAMA, Psychiatry, 70*, 71–77. doi:10.1001/jamapsychiatry.2013.266

Volkmar, F. R., & Pauls, D. (2003). Autism. *The Lancet, 362*, 1133–1141. doi:10.1016/S0140-6736(03)14471-6

Wakefield, A. J., Murch, S. H., Anthony, A., Linnell, J., Casson, D. M., Malik, M., et al. (1998). Illeal-lymphoid-nodular hyperplasia, non-specific colitis, and pervasive developmental disorder in children. *The Lancet, 351*, 637–641. doi:10.1016/S0140-6736(97)11096-0.

Wang, Y., Zhang, Y.-B., Liu, L.-L., Ji-Fang, C., Wang, J., Shum, D. H. K., van Amelsvoort, T., & Chan, R. C. K. (2017). A meta-analysis of working memory impairments in autism spectrum disorders. *Neuropsychology Review, 27*, 46–61. doi:10.1007/s11065-016-9336-y

Ward, S. C., Whalon, K., Rusnak, K., Wendell, K., & Paschall, N. (2013). The association between therapeutic horseback riding and the social communication and sensory reactions of children with autism. *Journal of Autism and Developmental Disorders, 43*, 2190–2198. doi:10.1007/s10803-013-1773-3

Wehman, P. H., Schall, C. M., McDonough, J., Kregel, J., Brooke, V., Molinelli, A. . . . Thiss, W. (2013, July 27). *Journal of Autism and Developmental Disorders*, Published online. doi:10.1007/s10803-013-1892-x

Werner, E., & Dawson, G. (2005). Validation of the phenomenon of autistic regression using home videotapes. *Archives of General Psychiatry, 62*, 889–895.

Wiig, E. H., Semel, E., & Secord, W. A. (2013). Clinical evaluation of language fundamentals (5th ed.). Upper Saddle River, NJ: Pearson.

Wing, L. (1981). Asperger syndrome: A clinical account. *Psychological Medicine, 11*, 115–129. doi:10.1017/S0033291700053332

Wing, L., & Potter, D. (2002). The epidemiology of autistic spectrum disorders: Is prevalence rising? *Mental Retardation & Developmental Disabilities Research Reviews, 8*(3), 151–161. doi:10.1002/mrdd.10029

Wolff, J. J., Gu, H., Gerig, G., Elison, J. T., Styner, M., Gouttard, S., . . . Piven, J. (2012). Differences in white matter fiber tract development present from 6 to 24 months in infants with autism. *American Journal of Psychiatry, 169,* 589–600. doi:http://dx.doi.org/10.1176/appi.ajp.2011.11091447

Wong, C., Odom, S. L., Hume, K. A., Cox, A. W., Fettig, A., Kucharczyk, S., ... & Schultz, T. R. (2015). Evidence-based practices for children, youth, and young adults with autism spectrum disorder: A comprehensive review. *Journal of Autism and Developmental Disorders, 45,* 1951–1966.

CHAPTER 10

Anderson, N. B., & Shames, G. H. (2011). *Human communication disorders* (8th ed.). Upper Saddle River, NJ: Pearson.

Audet, L. R., & Tankersley, M. (1999). Implications of communication and behavioral disorders for classroom management: Collaborative intervention techniques. In D. Rogers-Adkinson & P. Griffith (Eds.), *Communication disorders and children with psychiatric and behavioral disorders* (pp. 403–440). San Diego: Singular.

Bernthal, J. E., Bankson, N. W., & Flipsen Jr., P. (2017). *Articulation and phonological disorders: Speech sound disorders in children* (8th ed.). Upper Saddle River, NJ: Pearson.

Calandrella, A. M., & Wilcox, M. J. (2000). Predicting language outcomes for young prelinguistic children with developmental delay. *Journal of Speech, Language and Hearing Research, 43,* 1061–1071. PMid:11063230

Campbell, S. L., Reich, A. R., Klockars, A. J., & McHenry, M. A. (1988). Factors associated with dysphonia in high school cheerleaders. *Journal of Speech and Hearing Disorders, 53,* 175–185. PMid:3361859

Cannito, M. P., Yorkston, K. M., & Beukelman, D. R. (Eds.). (1998). *Neuromotor speech disorders: Nature, assessment, and management.* Baltimore: Brookes.

Catts, H., Adlof, S., Hogan, T., & Ellis Weismer, S. (2005). Are specific language impairment and dyslexia distinct disorders? *Journal of Speech, Language, and Hearing Research, 48,* 1378–1396. doi:10.1044/1092-4388(2005/096)

Catts, H. W., Fey, M. E., Zhang, X., & Tomblin, J. (2001). Estimating the risk of future reading difficulties in kindergarten children: A research-based model and its clinical implications. *Language, Speech, and Hearing Services in Schools, 32,* 38–50. doi:10.1044/0161-1461(2001/004)

Choudhury, N., & Benasich, A. A. (2003). A family aggregation study: The influence of family history and other risk factors on language development. *Journal of Speech, Language, and Hearing Research, 46,* 261–272. doi:10.1044/ 1092-4388(2003/021)

Conti-Ramsden, G., Durkin, J., & Simkin, Z. (2010). Language and social factors in the use of cell phone technology by adolescents with and without specific language impairment (SLI). *Journal of Speech, Language, and Hearing Research, 53,* 196–208. doi:10.1044/0192-4388(2009/08/0241)

Conture, E. G. (2001). *Stuttering: Its nature, diagnosis, and treatment.* Boston: Allyn & Bacon.

DeThorne, L. S., Petrill, S. A., Schatschneider, C., & Cutting, L. (2010). Conversational language use as a predictor of early reading development: Language history as a modeling variable. *Journal of Speech, Language, and Hearing Research, 53,* 209–223. doi:10.1044/0192-4388(2009/08/0060).

Ehren, B. J., & Nelson, N. W. (2005). The responsiveness to intervention approach and language impairment. *Topics in Language Disorders, 25,* 120–131.

Fey, M. E., Catts, H. W., & Larrivee, L. S. (1995). Preparing preschoolers for academic and social challenges of school. In M. E. Fey, J. Windsor, & S. F. Warren (Eds.), *Language intervention: Preschool through the elementary years* (pp. 3–37). Baltimore: Brookes.

Foundas, A. L. (2001). The anatomical basis of language. *Topics in Language Disorders, 21*(3), 1–19.

Goldstein, B., & Iglesias, A. (2004). Language and dialectical variations. In J. E. Bernthal, N. W. Bankson, & P. Flipsen Jr. (2017), *Articulation and phonological disorders: Speech sound disorders in children* (8th ed., pp. 277–301). Upper Saddle River, NJ: Pearson.

Gustason, G., & Zawolkow, E. (1993). *Signing exact English dictionary.* Los Alamitos, CA: Modern Signs Press.

Hallahan, D. P., Lloyd, J. W., Kauffman, J. M., Weiss, M., & Martinez, E. (2005). *Introduction to learning disabilities* (3rd ed.). Boston: Allyn & Bacon.

Hammer, C. S., & Weiss, A. L. (2000). African American mothers' views of their infants' language development and language-learning environment. *American Journal of Speech-Language Pathology, 9,* 126–140.

Harris, Y. R., & Schroeder, V. M. (2013). Language deficits or differences: What we know about African American vernacular English in the 21st century. *International Education Studies, 6,* 194–204. doi:10.5539/ies.v6n4p194

Hart, B., & Risley, T. R. (1995). *Meaningful differences in the everyday experience of young American children.* Baltimore: Brookes.

Hulit, L. M., & Howard, M. R. (2010). *Born to talk: An introduction to speech and language development* (4th ed.). Boston: Allyn & Bacon.

Justice, L. M. (2006). *Communication sciences and disorders: An introduction.* Upper Saddle River, NJ: Pearson.

Klein, H. B., & Moses, N. (1999). *Intervention planning for adults with communication problems: A guide for clinical practicum and professional practice.* Boston: Allyn & Bacon.

Kohnert, K., Windsor, J., & Yim, D. (2006). Do language-based processing tasks separate children with language impairment from typical bilinguals? *Learning Disabilities Research and Practice, 21,* 19–29. doi:10.1111/j.1540-5826.2006.00204.x

Koury, L. N. (2007). Service delivery issues in early intervention. In R. Lubinski, L. A. C. Golper, & C. M. Frattali (Eds) *Professional issues in speech language pathology and audiology* (pp. 349–370). Clifton Park, NY: Thomson Delmar.

Lane, H. B., & Pullen, P. C. (2004). *Phonological awareness assessment and instruction: A sound beginning.* Boston: Allyn & Bacon.

MacArthur, C. A., Pilippakos, Z., Graham, S., & Harris, K. (2012). Writing instruction. In B. Wong & D. Butler (Eds.) *Learning about learning disabilities* (4th ed., pp. 240–270). San Diego, CA: Academic Press.

McCabe, P. C., & Marshall, D. J. (2006). Measuring the social competence of preschool children with specific language impairment: Correspondence among informant ratings and behavioral observations. *Topics in Early Childhood Special Education, 26,* 234–246. doi:10.1177/02711214060260040401

McGregor, K. K. (2000). The development and enhancement of narrative skills in a preschool classroom: Towards a solution to clinician–client mismatch. *American Journal of Speech-Language Pathology, 9,* 55–71.

McNeil, B. C., Justice, L. M., Gillon, G T., & Schuele, C. M. (2017). Phonological awareness: Description, assessment, and intervention. In J. E. Bernthal, N. W. Bankson, & P. Flipsen Jr., *Articulation and phonological disorders: Speech sound disorders in children* (8th ed., pp. 302–324). Upper Saddle River, NJ: Pearson.

Mercer, C. D., & Pullen, P. C. (2009). *Students with learning disabilities* (7th ed.). Upper Saddle River, NJ: Merrill/Pearson.

Mullen, R., & Schooling, T. (2010). The National Outcomes Measurement System for pediatric speech-language pathology. *Language, Speech, and Hearing Services in Schools, 41,* 44–60. doi:10.1044/0161-1461(2009/08-0051)

Muter, V., Hulme, C., Snowling, M. J., & Stevenson, J. (2004). Phonemes, rimes, vocabulary and grammatical skills as foundations of early reading development: Evidence from a longitudinal study. *Developmental Psychology, 40,* 665–681. doi:10.1037/0012-1649.40.5.665

Nelson, K. (1993). The psychological and social origins of autobiographical memories. *Psychological Science, 4,* 7–14. doi:10.1111/j.1467-9280.1993.tb00548.x

Nelson, K. (1998). *Language in cognitive development: The emergence of the mediated mind.* Cambridge University Press.

Onslow, M., Packman, A., & Payne P. A. (2007). Clinical identification of early stuttering: Methods, issues, and future directions. *Asia Pacific Journal of Speech Pathology and Audiology, 10,* 15–31.

Owens, R. E., Jr. (2014). *Language disorders: A functional approach to assessment and intervention* (6th ed.). Upper Saddle River, NJ: Pearson.

Owens, R. E., Jr., Evans, D. E., & Haas, B. A. (2000). *Introduction to communication disorders: A life span perspective.* Boston: Allyn & Bacon.

Owens, R. E., Metz, D. E., & Farinella, K. A. (2015). *Introduction to communication disorders: A lifespan evidence-based perspective* (5th ed.). Upper Saddle River, NJ: Pearson.

Peterson, R. L., Pennington, B. F., Shriberg, L. D., & Boada, R. (2009). What influences literacy outcome in children with speech sound disorder? *Journal of Speech, Language, and Hearing Research, 52,* 1175–1188. doi:10.1044/0192-4388(2009/08-0024)

Prizant, B. M. (1999). Early intervention: Young children with communication and emotional/behavioral problems. In

D. Rogers-Adkinson & P. Griffith (Eds.), *Communication disorders and children with psychiatric and behavioral disorders* (pp. 295–342). San Diego: Singular.

Raspberry, W. (2001, August 21). Bi-English education: Low-income children might benefit from early immersion in standards. *Charlottesville Daily Progress*, p. A6.

Robinson, R. L., & Crowe, T. A. (2001). Fluency and voice. In D. M. Ruscello (Ed.), *Tests and measurements in speech-language pathology* (pp. 163–183). Boston: Butterworth-Heinemann.

Rogers-Adkinson, D., & Griffith, P. (Eds.). (1999). *Communication disorders and children with psychiatric and behavioral disorders*. San Diego: Singular.

Sawyer, D. J. (2006). Dyslexia: A generation of inquiry. *Topics in Language Disorders, 26*, 95–109.

Silliman, E. R., & Scott, C. M. (2006). Language impairment and reading disability: Connections and complexities. *Learning Disabilities Research and Practice, 21*, 1–7. doi:10.1111/j.1540-5826.2006.00202.x

Snowling, M. J., & Hayiou-Thomas, M. E. (2006). The dyslexia spectrum: Continuities between reading, speech, and language impairments. *Topics in Language Disorders, 26*, 110–126.

Soto, G., Solomon-Rice, P., & Caputo, M. (2009). Enhancing the personal narrative skills of elementary school-aged students who use AAC: The effectiveness of personal narrative intervention. *Journal of Communication Disorders, 42*, 43–57. doi:10.1016/j.jcomdis.2008.08.001

Staskowski, M., & Nelson, N. W. (2007). Service delivery issues in educational settings. In R. Lubinski, L. A. C. Golper, & C. M. Frattali (Eds.), *Professional issues in speech language pathology and audiology* (pp. 329–348). Clifton Park, NY: Thomson Delmar.

Stockman, I. J. (2010). A review of developmental and applied language research on African American children: From a deficit to difference perspective on dialect differences. *Language, Speech, and Hearing Services in Schools, 41*, 23–38. doi:10.1044/0161-1461(2009/08-0086).

The Stuttering Foundation (2017). Prevalence. Retrieved from http://www.stutteringhelp.org/prevalence.

Throneburg, R. N., Calvert, L. K., Sturm, J. J., Paramboukas, A. A., & Paul, P. J. (2000). A comparison of service delivery models: Effects on curricular vocabulary skills in the school setting. *American Journal of Speech-Language Pathology, 9*, 10–20.

Tomblin, J. B. (2010). The EpiSLI database: A publically available data base on speech and language. *Language Speech Hearing Services in Schools*.

Vellutino, F. R., Fletcher, J. M., Snowling, M. J., & Scanlon, D. M. (2004). Specific reading disability (dyslexia): What have we learned in the past four decades? *Journal of Child Psychology and Psychiatry, 45*, 2–40. doi:10.1046/j.0021-9630.2003.00305.x

Vinson, B. (2011). *Language disorders across the lifespan* (3rd ed.). Boston, MA: Cengage Learning.

Warren, S. F., & Abbaduto, L. (1992). The relation of communication and language development to mental retardation. *American Journal on Mental Retardation, 97*, 125–130. PMid:1418929

Yoder, P. J., & Warren, S. F. (2001). Relative treatment effects of two prelinguistic communication interventions on language development of toddlers with developmental delays vary by maternal characteristics. *Journal of Speech and Hearing Research, 44*, 224–237. doi:10.1044/1092-4388(2001/019)

CHAPTER 11

Aldersley, S. (2002). Least restrictive environment and the courts. *Journal of Deaf Studies and Deaf Education, 7*, 189–199. doi:10.1093/deafed/7.3.189

Allinder, R. M., & Eccarius, M. A. (1999). Exploring the technical adequacy of curriculum-based measurement in reading for children who use manually coded English. *Exceptional Children, 65*, 271–288.

American Academy of Otolaryngology—Head and Neck Surgery. (2007). *Noise & Hearing Protection*. Retrieved from http://www.ent-net.org/healthinfo/hearing/noise_hearing.cfm

Andrews, J., Hamilton, B., Misener-Dunn, K., & Clark, M. D. (2016). Early reading for young deaf and hard of hearing children: Alternative frameworks. *Psychology, 7*(4), 510–522. Retrieved from http://www.scirp.org/journal/psyh

Andrews, J. F., Leigh, I. W., & Weiner, M. T. (2004). *Deaf people: Evolving perspectives from psychology, education, and sociology*. Boston: Allyn & Bacon.

Andrews, J. F., & Zmijewski, G. (1997). How parents support home literacy with deaf children. *Early Child Development and Care, 127*, 131–139. doi:10.1080/0300443971270111

Bornstein, M. H., Selmi, A. M., Haynes, O. M., Painter, K. M., & Marx, E. S. (1999). Representational abilities and the hearing status of child/mother dyads. *Child Development, 70*, 833–852. doi:10.1111/1467-8624.00060

Brashear, H., Henderson, V., Park, K-H., Hamilton, H., Lee, S., & Starner, T. (2006). American Sign Language recognition game development for deaf children. In *Proceedings of the 8th International ACM SIGACCESS Conference on Computers and Accessbility* (pp. 79–86). Portland, OR: ACM Press.

Brill, R. G., MacNeil, B., & Newman, L. R. (1986). Framework for appropriate programs for deaf children. *American Annals of the Deaf, 131*, 65–77.

Buchino, M. A. (1993). Perceptions of the oldest hearing child of deaf parents. *American Annals of the Deaf, 138*, 40–45.

Campbell, R., & MacSweeney, M. (2004). Neuroimaging studies of crossmodal plasticity and language processing in deaf people. In G. A. Calvert, C. Spence, & B. E. Stein (Eds.), *The handbook of multisensory processing* (pp. 773–784). Cambridge, MA: MIT Press.

Cawthon, S. (2009). Professional development for teachers of students who are deaf or hard of hearing: Facing the assessment challenge. *American Annals of the Deaf, 154*, 50–61. doi:10.1353/aad.0.0073

Cawthon, S. W. (2010). Science and evidence of success: Two emerging issues in assessment accommodations for students who are deaf or hard of hearing. *Journal of Deaf Studies and Deaf Education, 15*, 185–203. doi:10.1093/deafed/enq002

Centers for Disease Control and Prevention. (2016, June 17). Cytomegalovirus (CMV) and Congenital CMV Infection. Retrieved from https://www.cdc.gov/cmv/

Cheng, S., & Rose, S. (2009). Investigating the technical adequacy of curriculum-based measurement in written expression for students who are deaf or hard of hearing. *Journal of Deaf Studies and Deaf Education, 14*, 503–515. doi:10.1093/deafed/enp013

Christiansen, J. B. (2009). The 2006 protest at Gallaudet University: Reflections and explanations. *Sign Language Studies, 10*, 69–89. doi:10.1353/sls.0.0033

Clark, M. D., Galloza, A., Keith, C. L., Tibbitt, J. S., Wolsey, J. A., & Zimmerman, H. G. (2015, May 4). Eye gaze: Learning to look and looking to learn. *ADVANCE for Speech and Hearing*. Retrieved from http://speech-language-pathology-audiology.advanceweb.com/Features/Articles/Eye-Gaze-Development-in-Infants.aspx

Council for Exceptional Children. (2003). *What every special educator must know: Ethics, standards, and guidelines for special educators* (5th ed.). Arlington, VA: Author.

Emery, S. D., Middleton, A., & Turner, G. H. (2010). Whose deaf genes are they anyway? The Deaf community's challenge to legislation on embryo selection. *Sign Language Studies, 10*, 155–169. doi:10.1353/sls.0.0037

Emmorey, K. (2002). *Language, cognition, and the brain: Insights from sign language research*. Mahwah, NJ: Erlbaum.

Enns, C., Zimmer, K., Broszeit, C., & Rabu, S. (2013). Assessing ASL development: Receptive skills test. Winnipeg, Canada: Northern Signs Research.

Feldman, H. M., Dollaghan, C. A., Campbell, T. F., Colborn, D. K., Janosky, J., Kurs-Lasky, M., et al. (2003). Parent-reported language skills in relation to otitis media during the first 3 years of life. *Journal of Speech, Language, and Hearing Research, 46*, 273–287. doi:10.1044/1092-4388(2003/022)

Gallaudet Research Institute. (2011, April). *Regional and National Summary Report of Data from the 2009-10 Annual Survey of Deaf and Hard of Hearing Children and Youth*. Washington, DC: GRI, Gallaudet University. Retrieved from http://research.gallaudet.edu/Demographics/2010_National_Summary.pdf.

Geers, A. E., & Hayes, H. (2011). Reading, writing, and phonological processing skills of adolescents with 10 or more years of cochlear implant experience. *Ear and Hearing, 32*, 49S.

Geers, A. E., Moog, J. S., Biedenstein, J., Brenner, C., & Hayes, H. (2009). Spoken language scores of children using cochlear implants compared to hearing age-mates at school entry. *Journal of Deaf Studies and Deaf Education, 14*, 371–385. doi:10.1093/deafed/enn046

Gilliver, M., Cupples, L., Ching, T., Leigh, G., & Gunnourie, M. (2016). Developing sound skills for reading: Teaching phonological awareness to preschoolers with hearing loss. *Journal of Deaf Studies and Deaf Education, 21*, 268–279.

Goldin-Meadow, S. (2003). *The resilience of language: What gesture creation in deaf children can tell us about how all children learn language.* New York: Psychology Press.

Kegl J., Senghas A., & Coppola, M. (1999). Creation through contact: Sign language emergence and sign language change in Nicaragua. In M. DeGraff (Ed.), *Comparative grammatical change: The intersection of language acquisition, creole genesis, and diachronic syntax* (pp. 179–237). Cambridge, MA: MIT Press.

Kluwin, T. N., Stinson, M. S., & Colarossi, G. M. (2002). Social processes and outcomes of inschool contact between deaf and hearing peers. *Journal of Deaf Studies and Deaf Education, 7,* 200–213. doi:10.1093/deafed/7.3.200

Ladd, P. (2003). *Understanding Deaf culture: In search of Deafhood.* Clevedon, England: Multilingual Matters.

Lane, H. (1984). *When the mind hears: A history of the deaf.* New York: Random House.

Lane, H. (1992). *The mask of benevolence: Disabling the Deaf community.* New York: Knopf.

Lane, H. (2002). Do deaf people have a disability? *Sign Language Studies, 2,* 356-379.

Lane, H., Hoffmeister, R., & Bahan, B. (1996). *A journey into the Deaf world.* San Diego, CA: Dawn Sign Press.

Laugen, N., Jacobsen, K. H., Rieffe, C., Carolien, L. (2016). Predictors of psychosocial outcomes in hard-of-hearing preschool children, *Journal of Deaf Studies and Deaf Education, 21,* 259–267.

Lazarus, S. S., Thurlow, M. L., Lail, K. E., Eisenbraun, K. D., & Kato, K. (2006). *2005 state policies on assessment participation and accommodations for students with disabilities* (Synthesis Report 64). Minneapolis, MN: University of Minnesota, National Center on Educational Outcomes. Retrieved from http://education.umn.edu/NCEO/OnlinePubs/Synthesis64/

Lederberg, A. R., & Golbach, T. (2002). Parenting stress and social support in hearing mothers of deaf and hearing children: A longitudinal study. *Journal of Deaf Studies and Deaf Education, 7,* 330–345.

Lederberg, A. R., Miller, E. M., Easterbrooks, S. R., & Connor, C. M. (2014). Foundations for literacy: An early literacy intervention for deaf and hard-of-hearing children. *Journal of Deaf Studies and Deaf Education, 19,* 438-455.

Lee, S., Henderson, V., & Brashear, H. (2005, June). *CopyCat: An ASL game for deaf children.* Paper presented at the meeting of the Rehabilitation Engineering & Assistive Technology Society of North America Student Design Competition, Atlanta, GA.

Lomas, G., Andrews, J. F., & Shaw, P. C. (2017). Deaf and hard of hearing students. In J. M. Kauffman, D. P. Hallahan, & P. C. Pullen (Eds.). *Handbook of special education.* (2nd ed., pp. 338–357. New York: Routledge.

Lucas, C., Bayley, R., McCaskill, C., & Hill, J. (2015). The intersection of African American English and Black American Sign Language. *International Journal of Bilingualism, 19,* 156–168.

Lucas, C., & McCaskill, C. (2007). American Sign Language. In M. Montgomery & E. Johnson, *The new encyclopedia of southern culture Vol 5* (pp. 40–42). Chapel Hill, NC: University of North Carolina Press.

Marschark, M. (2002). *Language development in children who are deaf: A research synthesis.* Alexandria, VA: National Association of State Directors of Special Education (NASDE).

Marschark, M., Pelz, J. B., Convertino, C., Sapare, P., Arndt, M. E., & Seewagen, R. (2005). Classroom interpreting and visual information processing in mainstream education for deaf students: Live or Memorex®? *American Educational Research Journal, 42,* 727–761. doi:10.3102/000283120 42004727

Marschark, M., Sapare, P., Convertino, C., & Seewagen, R. (2005). Access to postsecondary education through sign language interpreting. *Journal of Deaf Studies and Deaf Education, 10,* 38–50. doi:10.1093/deafed/eni002

Marschark, M., Sapare, P., Convertino, C., Seewagen, R., & Maltzen, H. (2004). Comprehension of sign language interpreting: Deciphering a complex task situation. *Sign Language Studies, 4,* 345–368. doi:10.1353/sls.2004.0018

Martin, D., Bat-Chava, Y., Lalwani, A., & Waltzman, S. B. (2010). Peer relationships of deaf children with cochlear implants: Predictors of peer entry and peer interaction success. *Journal of Deaf Studies and Deaf Education, 16,* 108–120. doi:10.1093/deafed/enq037.

Mason, T. C. (2005). Cross-cultural instrument translation: Assessment, translation, and statistical applications. *American Annals of the Deaf, 150,* 67–72. doi:10.1353/aad.2005.0020

McCaskill, C., Lucas, C., Bayley, R., Hill, J., King, R., Baldwin, P., & Hogue, R. (2011). *The hidden treasure of Black ASL: It's history and structure.* Washington, DC: Gallaudet University Press.

Meadow-Orlans, K. P. (1987). An analysis of the effectiveness of early intervention programs for hearing-impaired children. In M. J. Guralnick & F. C. Bennett (Eds.), *The effectiveness of early intervention for at-risk and handicapped children* (pp. 325–362). New York: Academic Press.

Meadow-Orlans, K. P. (1990). Research on developmental aspects of deafness. In D. F. Moores & K. P. Meadow-Orlans (Eds.), *Educational and developmental aspects of deafness* (pp. 283–298). Washington, DC: Gallaudet University Press.

Mehra, S., Eavey, R. D., & Keamy, D. G. (2009). The epidemiology of hearing impairment in the United States: Newborns, children, and adolescents. *Otolaryngology—Head and Neck Surgery, 140,* 461–472. doi:10.1016/j.otohns.2008.12.022

Mekonnen, M., Hannu, S., Elina, L., & Matti, K. (2016). The self-concept of deaf/hard-of-hearing students. *Journal of Deaf Studies and Deaf Education, 21,* 345–351.

Menchel, R. S. (1988). Personal experience with speechreading. *Volta Review, 90*(5), 3–15.

Middleton, A., Emery, S. D., & Turner, S. D. (2010). Views, knowledge, and beliefs about genetics and genetic counseling among deaf people. *Sign Language Studies, 10,* 170–196. doi:10.1353/sls.0.0038

Miller, E. M., Lederberg, A. R., & Easterbrooks, S. R. (2013). Phonological awareness: Explicit instruction for young deaf and hard-of-hearing children. *Journal of Deaf Studies and Deaf Education, 18,* 206–227. doi:10.1093/deafed/ens067

Mitchell, R. E., & Karchmer, M. A. (2004). Chasing the mythical ten percent: Parental hearing status of deaf and hard of hearing students in the United States. *Sign Language Studies, 4,* 138–163. doi:10.1353/sls.2004.0005

Mitchell, R. E., & Karchmer, M. A. (2005). Parental hearing status and signing among deaf and hard of hearing children. *Sign Language Studies, 5,* 231–244. doi:10.1353/sls.2005.0004

Moeller, M. P., & Luetke-Stahlman, B. (1990). Parents' use of signing exact English: A descriptive analysis. *Journal of Speech and Hearing Disorders, 55,* 327–338.

Morere, D., & Allen, T. (Eds.). (2012). *Assessing literacy in deaf individuals: Neurocognitive measurement and predictors.* New York: Springer.

Mueller, V., & Hurtig, R. (2010). Technology-enhanced shared reading with deaf and hard-of-hearing children: The role of a fluent signing narrator. *Journal of Deaf Studies and Deaf Education, 15,* 72–101. doi:10.1093/deafed/enp023

Mundy, L. (2002, March 31). A world of their own. *The Washington Post Magazine,* pp. 22–31.

National Institute on Deafness and Other Communication Disorders. (2016, May 3). Cochlear Implants. Retrieved fromhttps://www.nidcd.nih.gov/health/cochlear-implants.

Nicaraguan sign language. (2010, March 15). Wikipedia. Retrieved from http://en.wikipedia.org/wiki/Nicaraguan_Sign_Language

National Institute on Deafness and Other Communication Disorders. (2011, March). Cochlear Implants. Retrieved from http://www.nidcd.nih.gov/health/hearing/pages/coch.aspx/

National Institute on Deafness and Other Communication Disorders. (2017, September). Quick Statistics About Hearing. Retrieved from https://www.nidcd.nih.gov/health/statistics/quick-statistics-hearing#2.

Northern, J., & Downs, M. (2014). *Hearing in children* (6th ed.). San Diego, CA: Plural Publishing.

Padden, C. (1996). Early bilingual lives of deaf children. In I. Parasnis (Ed.), *Cultural and Language Diversity: Reflections on the Deaf Experience* (pp. 99–116). Cambridge, MA: Cambridge University Press.

Padden, C., & Humphries, T. (1988). *Deaf in America: Voices from a culture.* Cambridge, MA: Harvard University Press.

Padden, C., & Humphries, T. (2005). *Inside deaf culture.* Cambridge, MA: Harvard University Press.

Park, J., & Lombardino, L. J. (2012). A comparison of phonological processing skills of children with mild to moderate sensorineural hearing loss and children with dyslexia. *American Annals of the Deaf, 157,* 289–306. doi:10.1353/aad.2012.1621.

Park, J., Lombardino, L. J., & Ritter, M. (2013). Phonology matters: A comprehensive investigation of reading and spelling skills of school-age children with mild to moderate hearing loss. *American Annals of the Deaf*, *158*, 20–40. doi:10.1353/aad.2013.0013.

Paul, P. (1998). *Literacy and deafness: The development of reading, writing, and literate thought*. Boston: Allyn & Bacon.

Powers, S. (2003). Influences of student and family factors on academic outcomes of mainstream secondary school deaf students. *Journal of Deaf Studies and Deaf Education*, *8*, 57–78. doi:10.1093/deafed/8.1.57

Punch, R. (2016). Employment and adults who are deaf or hard of hearing: Current status and experiences of barriers, accommodations, and stress in the workplace. *American Annals of the Deaf*, *161*, 384–397.

Punch, R., Creed, P. A., & Hyde, M. B. (2006). Career barriers perceived by hard-of-hearing adolescents: Implications for practice from a mixed-methods study. *Journal of Deaf Studies and Deaf Education*, *11*, 225–237.

Punch, R., Hyde, M., & Creed, P. A. (2004). Issues in the school-to-work transition of hard of hearing adolescents. *American Annals of the Deaf*, *149*, 28–38. doi:10.1353/aad.2004.0015

Quigley, S., Jenne, W., & Phillips, S. (1968). *Deaf students in colleges and universities*. Washington, DC: Alexander Graham Bell Association for the Deaf.

Reagan, T. (1990). Cultural considerations in the education of deaf children. In D. F. Moores & K. P. Meadow-Orlans (Eds.), *Educational and developmental aspects of deafness* (pp. 73–84). Washington, DC: Gallaudet University Press.

Renaissance Learning. (2006). *STAR early literacy assessment*. Wisconsin Rapids, WI: Author.

Sanghavi, D. M. (2006, December 5). Wanting babies like themselves, some parents choose genetic defects. *The New York Times*. Retrieved from www.nytimes.com/2006/12/05/health/05essa.html?ex=1322974800&en=9fbb1b0e738b-55d1&ei=5088partner=rssnyt&emc=rss

Sarant, J. Z., Harris, D. C., & Bennet, L.A. (2015). Academic outcomes for school-aged children with severe to profound hearing loss and early unilateral and bilateral cochlear implants. *Journal of Speech, Language, and Hearing Research (58)*3, 1017–1032. doi:10:1044/2015_JSLHR-H-14-0075

Schick, B., Williams, K., & Kupermintz, H. (2006). Look who's being left behind: Educational interpreters and access to education for deaf and hard-of-hearing students. *Journal of Deaf Studies and Deaf Education*, *11*, 3–20. doi:10.1093/deafed/enj007

Schirmer, B. R. (2001). *Psychological, social, and educational dimensions of deafness*. Boston: Allyn & Bacon.

Schroedel, J. G., & Geyer, P. D. (2000). Long-term career attainments of deaf and hard of hearing college graduates: Results from a 15-year follow-up survey. *American Annals of the Deaf*, *145*, 303–314.

Seal, B. C. (2004). *Best practices in educational interpreting* (2nd ed.). Boston: Allyn & Bacon.

Senghas, A. (2003). Intergenerational influence and ontogenetic development in the emergence of spatial grammar in Nicaraguan Sign Language. *Cognitive Development*, *18*, 511–531. doi:10.1016/j.cogdev.2003.09.006

Sheridan, M. (2001). *Inner lives of deaf children: Interviews and analysis*. Washington, DC: Gallaudet University Press.

Siegel, L. (2000). The educational and communication needs of deaf and hard of hearing children: A statement of principle on fundamental educational change. *American Annals of the Deaf*, *145*, 64–77.

Simms, L., Andrews, J., & Smith, A. (2005). A balanced approach to literacy instruction for deaf signing students, *Balanced Reading Instruction*, *12*, 39–54.

Simms, L., Baker, S., & Clark, M. D. (2013). The standardized visual communication and sign language checklist for signing children. *Sign Language Studies*, *14*, 101–124.

Snow, C., Burns, N., & Griffin, P. (1998). *Preventing reading difficulties in young children*. Washington, DC: National Academy of the Sciences.

Stokoe, W. C. (1960). *Sign language structure*. Silver Spring, MD: Linstok Press.

Stokoe, W. C., Casterline, D. C., & Croneberg, C. G. (1976). *A dictionary of American Sign Language on linguistic principles* (2nd ed.). Silver Spring, MD: Linstok Press.

Takruri, L. (2006, October 30). Gallaudet exposes debate over deafness. *The Washington Post*. Retrieved from http://www.washingtonpost.com/wp-dyn/content/article/2006/10/30/AR2006103000087.html

Tapper, J., & Sandell, C. (2006, May 10). *Is deaf university president not 'deaf enough'?* ABC News Internet Ventures. Retrieved from http://www.abcnews.go.com/WNT/story?id=1947073

Thrasher, R. D. (2009, October 26). Middle ear, otitis media with effusion. *eMedicine*, Retrieved from http://emedicine.medscape.com/article/858990-overview

Trezek, B., Wang, Y., & Paul, P. (2010). *Reading and deafness: theory, research, and practice*. Clifton Park, NY: Delmar.

U.S. Department of Education, National Center on Student Progress Monitoring. (2006). *Review of progress monitoring tools*. Retrieved from http://www.studentprogress.org/chart/chart.asp

U.S. Department of Education, Office of Special Education and Rehabilitative Services, Office of Special Education Programs. (2016). *38th Annual Report to Congress on the Implementation of the Individuals with Disabilities Education Act*. Washington, DC: Author. Retrieved from https://www2.ed.gov/about/reports/annual/osep/2016/parts-b-c/38th-arc-for-idea.pdf

Walker, L. A. (1986). *A loss for words: The story of deafness in a family*. New York: Harper & Row.

Wang, Y., Spychala, H., Harris, R. S., & Oettig, T. L. (2013). The effectiveness of a phonics-based early intervention for deaf and hard of hearing preschool children and its possible impact on reading skills in elementary school: A case study. *American Annals of the Deaf*, *158*, 107–120. doi:10.1353/aad.2013.0021.

Waters, D., Campbell, R., Capek, C. M., Woll, B., David, A. S., McGuire, P. K., et al. (2007). Fingerspelling, signed language, text and picture processing in deaf native signers: The role of the mid-fusiform gyrus. *NeuroImage*, *35*, 832–840. doi:10.1016/j.neuroimage.2007.01.025

Wauters, L. N., & Knoors, H. E. T. (2007). Social integration of deaf children in inclusive settings. *Journal of Deaf Studies and Deaf Education*, *13*, 21–36. doi:10.1093/deafed/enm028

CHAPTER 12

American Printing House for the Blind (2015). *Annual report 2015: The joy of independence*. Louisville, KY: American Printing House for the Blind.

Barlow, J. M., Bentzen, B. L., & Bond, T. (2005). Blind pedestrians and the changing technology and geometry of signalized intersections: Safety, orientation, and independence. *Journal of Visual Impairment and Blindness*, *99*, 587–598.

Barlow-Brown, F., & Connelly, V. (2002). The role of letter knowledge and phonological awareness in young Braille readers. *Journal of Research in Reading*, *25*, 259–270. doi:10.1111/1467-9817.00174

Berk, L. E. (2005). *Infants and children: Infants through middle childhood* (5th ed.). Boston: Allyn & Bacon.

Bishop, V. E. (2004). *Teaching visually impaired children* (3rd ed.). Springfield, IL: Charles C. Thomas.

Borchert, M. (2012). Reappraisal of the optic nerve hypoplasia syndrome. *Journal of Neuro-Ophthalmology*, *32*, 58–67. doi:10.1097/WNO.0b013e31824442b8.

Borchert, M., & Garcia-Filion, P. (2008). The syndrome of optic nerve hypoplasia. *Current Neurology and Neuroscience Reports*, *8*, 395–403. doi:10.1007/s11910-008-0061-7.

Cameto, R., & Nagle, K. (2007). Orientation and mobility skills of secondary school students with visual impairments. Facts from NLTS2. NCSER 2008-3007. Retrieved from http://ies.ed.gov/ncser/pdf/20083007.pdf

Castellano, C. (2005). *Making it work: Educating the Blind/VI student in the regular school*. Greenwich CT: Information Age Publishing.

Cattaneo, Z., & Vecchi, T. (2011). *Blind vision: The neuroscience of visual impairment*. Cambridge, MA: MIT Press.

Celeste, M. (2006). Play behaviors and social interactions of a child who is blind: In theory and practice. *Journal of Visual Impairment and Blindness*, *100*, 75–90.

Chung, E. J., Kim, J. H., Ahn, H. S., & Koh, H. J. (2007). Combination of laser photocoagulation and intravietreal bevacizumab (Avastin®) for aggressive zone I retinopathy of prematurity. *Graef's Archive of Clinical Experimental Ophthalmology*, *245*, 1727–1730. doi:10.1007/s00417-007-0661-y.

Cmar, J. L. (2015). Orientation and mobility skills and outcome expectations as predictors of employment for young adults with visual impairments. *Journal of Visual Impairment and Blindness*, *109*, 95–106.

Connors, E. C., Chrastil, E. R., Sanchez, J., & Merabet, L. B. (2014). Action video game play and transfer of navigation and spatial cognition skills in adolescents who are blind. *Frontiers in Human Neuroscience*, *8*, 133.

Corn, A. L., & Koenig, A. J. (2002). Literacy for students with low vision: A framework for delivering instruction. *Journal of Visual Impairment and Blindness, 96,* 305–321.

Council for Exceptional Children. (2003). *What every special educator must know: Ethics, standards, and guidelines for special educators* (5th ed.). Arlington, VA: Author.

D'Allura, T. (2002). Enhancing the social interaction skills of preschoolers with visual impairments. *Journal of Visual Impairment and Blindness, 96,* 576–584.

Edmond, J. C., & Foroozan, R. (2006). Cortical visual impairment in children. *Current Opinion in Ophthalmology, 17,* 509-512.

Ely, M. S. (2016). Cerebral/Cortical visual impairment (CVI): The responsibility of practitioners in the field of visual impairment in a changing landscape. *Journal of Visual Impairment and Blindness, 110,* 201–206.

Emerson, R. W., Holbrook, M. C., & D'Andrea, F. M. (2009). Acquisition of literacy skills by young children who are blind: Results from the ABC Braille Study. *Journal of Visual Impairment and Blindness, 103,* 610–624.

Erin, J. N. (2006). Teaching social skills to elementary and middle school students with visual impairments. In S. Z. Sacks & K. E. Wolffe (Eds.), *Teaching social skills to students with visual impairments: From theory to practice* (pp. 364–404). New York: American Foundation for the Blind.

Gal, E., & Dyck, M. J. (2009). Stereotyped movements among children who are visually impaired. *Journal of Visual Impairment and Blindness, 103,* 754–765.

Garcia-Filion, P., Fink, C., Geffner, M. E., & Borchert, M. (2010). Optic nerve hypoplasia in North America: A re-appraisal of perinatal risk factors. *Acta Ophthalmologica, 88,* 527–534. doi:10.1111/j.1775-3768.2008.0145.x.

Garcia, M. L., Ty, E. B., Taban, M., Rothner, A. D., Rogers, D., & Traboulsi, E. I. (2006). Systemic and ocular findings in 100 patients with optic nerve hypoplasia. *Journal of Child Neurology, 21,* 949–-956. doi:10.1177/0883073806021011701.

Gillon, G. T., & Young, A. A. (2002). The phonological-awareness skills of children who are blind. *Journal of Visual Impairment and Blindness, 96,* 38–49.

Good, W. V., & Hou, C. (2006). Sweep visual evoked potential grating acuity thresholds paradoxically improve in low-luminance conditions in children with cortical visual impairment. *Investigative Ophthalmology & Visual Science, 47,* 3220–3224.

Good, W. V., Hou, C., & Norcia, A. M. (2012). Spatial contrast sensitivity vision loss in children with vertical visual impairment. *Investigative Ophthalmology & Visual Science, 53,* 7730–7734.

Grice, N. (2002). *Touch the universe.* Washington DC: Joseph Henry Press, National Academies Press.

Guide dog. (n.d.). In *Wikipedia.* Retrieved January 2, 2013 from http://www.youtube.com/watch?v=TQCqbICydZo.

Hatlen, P. (1998). Goal 8: Educational and developmental goals, including instruction, will reflect the assessed needs of each student in all areas of academic and disability-specific core curricular. In A. L. Corn & K.

M. Huebner (Eds.), *A report to the nation: The national agenda for the education of children and youths with visual impairments, including those with multiple disabilities* (pp. 50–52). New York: AFP Press.

Huebner, K. M., & Wiener, W. (2005). Guest editorial. *Journal of Visual Impairment and Blindness, 99,* 579–583.

Hull, J. M. (1997). *On sight and insight: A journey into the world of blindness.* Oxford, England: Oneworld Publications.

Iachini, T., & Ruggiero, G. (2010). The role of visual experience in mental scanning of actual pathways: Evidence from blind and sighted people. *Perception, 39,* 953–969.

Jernigan, K. (1992, June). Equality, disability, and empowerment. *Braille Monitor, 35,* 292–298.

Jindal-Snape, D. (2005). Self-evaluation and recruitment of feedback for enhanced social interaction by a student with visual impairment. *Journal of Visual Impairment and Blindness, 99,* 486–498.

Karimi, H. A., Dias, M. B., Pearlman, J., & Zimmerman, G. J. (2014). Wayfinding and navigation for people using social navigation networks. *EAI Endorsed Transactions on Collaborative Computing, 1*(2), 1–13.

Kirchner, C., & Smith, B. (2005). Transition to what? Education and employment outcomes for visually impaired youths after high school. *Journal of Visual Impairment and Blindness, 99,* 499–504.

Kleege, G. (1999). *Sight unseen.* New Haven, CT: Yale University Press.

Koenig, A. J., & Holbrook, M. C. (2000). Ensuring high-quality instruction for students in braille literacy programs. *Journal of Visual Impairment and Blindness, 94,* 677–694.

Koenig, A. J., Sanspree, M. J., & Holbrook, M. C. (n.d.). Determining the reading medium for students with visual impairments. *D.V.I. Quarterly.* Retrieved from http://www.ed.arizona.edu/dvi/Postion%20Papers/determining_Read_med.htm

Kurson, R. (2005, June). Into the light. *Esquire.* Retrieved from http://www.esquire.com/print-this/ESQ0605BLIND_114.2

Kurson, R. (2007). *Crashing through: A true story of risk, adventure, and the man who dared to see.* New York: Random House.

Kuusisto, S. (2004, June). Elegy for Ray Charles.

Kuusisto, S. (2006). *Eavesdropping.* New York: W. W. Norton.

Lansaw, J. (2000, December). Citizenship and the irony at the top of the world. *Braille Monitor, 43,* 963–965.

Lewis, S., & Iselin, S. A. (2002). A comparison of the independent living skills of primary students with visual impairments and their sighted peers: A pilot study. *Journal of Visual Impairment and Blindness, 96,* 335–344.

Lussenhop, K., & Corn, A. L. (2003). Comparative studies of the reading performance of students with low vision. *RE:view, 34,* 57–69.

Malik, S. (2015). *Orientation and mobility training in special education curriculum on the social adjustment problems of visually impaired children in family.* Proceedings of The Multidisciplinary Academic Conference, 439–456.

Maurer, M. (2000, April). Blindness, quotas, and the disadvantages of civil rights. *Braille Monitor, 43,* 287–296.

Maurer, M. (2003). The Federation is attacked for seeking to enhance mobility and safety. *Braille Monitor, 46,* 1–5.

McDonnall, M. C. (2011). Predictors of employment for youths with visual impairments: Findings from the Second National Longitudinal Transition Study. *Journal of Visual Impairment & Blindness, 105,* 453–466.

McDonnall, M. C., & Crudden, A. (2009). Factors affecting the successful employment of transition-age youths with visual impairments. *Journal of Visual Impairment and Blindness, 103,* 329–341.

McDonnall, M. C., Cruden, A., & O'Mally, J. (2015). Predictors of employer attitudes toward people who are blind or visually impaired as employees. *Journal of Vocational Rehabilitation, 42,* 41–50.

McHugh, E., & Lieberman, L. (2003). The impact of developmental factors on stereotypic rocking of children with visual impairments. *Journal of Visual Impairment and Blindness, 97,* 453–473.

Mintz-Hittner, H. A., & Kuffel, R. R. (2008). Intravitreal injection of bevacizumab (avastin) for treatment of stage 3 retinopathy of prematurity in zone i or posterior zone II. *Retina, 28,* 831-838. doi:10.1097/IAE.0b013e318177f934

Miura, R., Muraoka, T., & Ifukube, T. (2010). Comparison of obstacle sense ability between the blind and the sighted: A basic psychophysical study of designs of acoustic assistive devices. *Acoustical Science and Technology, 31,* 137–147. doi:10.1250/ast.31.137

Morgan, S. K., & Bradley-Johnson, S. (1995). Technical adequacy of curriculum-based measurement for Braille readers. *School Psychology Review, 24,* 94–103.

National Cooperative Highway Research Program. (n.d.) Accessible pedestrian signals: A guide to best practices. Retrieved from http://www.apsguide.org/index.cfm

National Eye Institute. (2010, May). Facts about retinopathy of prematurity (ROP). Retrieved from http://www.nei.nih.gov/health/rop/rop.asp#5

National Federation of the Blind. (2006). NFB-NEWSLINE® Retrieved from http://www.nfb.org/nfb/Newspapers_by_Phone.asp?SnID=389319

Perez-Pereira, M., & Conti-Ramsden, G. (1999). *Language development and social interaction in blind children.* East Sussex, England: Psychology Press, Ltd.

Policy Statement: Screening Examination of Premature Infants for Retinopathy of Prematurity. (2013). *Pediatrics.* 131(1):189–195. http://pediatrics.aappublications.org/content/131/1/189. Reaffirmed February 2016.

Rapp, D. W., & Rapp, A. J. (1992). A survey of the current status of visually impaired students in secondary mathematics. *Journal of Visual Impairment and Blindness, 86,* 115–117.

Reich, L., Maidenbaum, S., & Amedi, A. (2012). The brain as flexible task machine: Implications for visual rehabilitation using non-invasive and invasive approaches. *Current Opinion in Neurology, 25,* 86–95. doi:http://dx.doi.org/10.1097/WCO.0b013e32834ed723

Rex, E. J., Koenig, A. J., Wormsley, D., & Baker, R. (1994). *Foundations of braille literacy.* New York: American Foundation for the Blind.

Rumrill, P. D., Schuyler, B. R., & Longden, J. C. (1997). Profiles of on-the-job accommodations needed by professional employees who are blind. *Journal of Visual Impairment and Blindness, 91*, 66–76.

Ryles, R. (2000). Braille as a predictor of success. In *Braille into the next millennium*. Washington, DC: National Library Service for the Blind and Physically Handicapped and Friends of Libraries for Blind and Physically Handicapped Individuals in North America.

Ryles, R. N. (1997). The relationship of reading skills on employment, income, education, and reading habits. *Journal of Visual Impairment & Blindness, 83*, 306–313.

Sacks, S. Z. (2006). The development of social skills: A personal perspective. In S. Z. Sacks & K. E. Wolffe (Eds.), *Teaching social skills to students with visual impairments: From theory to practice* (pp. 3–19). New York: American Foundation for the Blind.

Sauerburger, D. (2005). Street crossings: Analyzing risks, developing strategies, and making decisions. *Journal of Visual Impairment and Blindness, 99*, 659–663.

Sauerburger, D., & Bourquin, E. (2010). Teaching the use of a long cane step by step: Suggestions for progressive, methodical instruction. *Journal of Visual Impairment & Blindness, 104*, 299–304.

Schroeder, F. K. (2002). Research and future opportunities for the blind. *Braille Monitor, 45*, 581–586.

Smith, D. W., & Amato, S. (2012). Synthesis of available accommodations for students with visual impairments on standardized assessments. *Journal of Visual Impairment & Blindness, 106*, 203–214.

Spungin, S. J. (2003). Cannibalism is alive and well in the blindness field. *Journal of Visual Impairment and Blindness, 97*, 69–71.

Teng, S., Puri, A., & Whitney, D. (2012). Ultrafine spatial acuity of blind expert human echolocators. *Experimental Brain Research, 216*, 483–488. doi:10.1007/s00221-011-2951-1.

Teng, S., & Whitney, D. (2011). The acuity of echolocation: Spatial resolution in sighted persons compard to the performance of an expert who is blind. *Journal of Visual Impairment & Blindness, 105*, 20–31.

Thurber, R. S., Shinn, M. R., & Smolkowski, K. (2002). What is measured in mathematics tests? Construct validity of curriculum-based mathematics measures. *School Psychology Review, 31*, 498–513.

Veispak, A., & Ghesquiere, P. (2010). Could specific braille reading difficulties result from developmental dyslexia? *Journal of Visual Impairment & Blindness, 104*, 228-238.

Weinstein, J. M., Gilmore, R. O., Shaikh, S. M., Kunselman, A. R., Trescher, W. F., Tashima, L. M., . . . Fesi, J. D. (2012). Defective motion processing in children with cerebral visual impairment due to periventricular white matter damage. *Developmental Medicine and Neurology, 54*, e1–e8. doi:10.1111/j.1469-8749.2010.03874.x

Wilton, A. P. (2011). Implications of parent-child interaction for early language development of young children with visual impairments. *Insight: Research and Practice in Visual Impairment and Blindness, 4*, 139–147.

Wolffe, K. E., Sacks, S. Z., Corn, A. L., Erin, J. N., Huebner, K. M., & Lewis, S. (2002). Teachers of students with visual impairments: What are they teaching? *Journal of Visual Impairment and Blindness, 96*, 293–303.

Wright, T., Wormsley, D. P., & Kamei-Hannan, C. (2009). Hand movements and Braille reading efficiency: Data from the Alphabetic Braille and Contracted Braille Study. *Journal of Visual Impairment and Blindness, 103*, 649–661.

Zebehazy, K. T., & Lawson, L. (2017). Blindness and low vision. In J. M. Kauffman, D. P. Hallahan, & P. C. Pullen (Eds.) *Handbook of special education* (2nd ed., pp. 358–376). New York: Routledge.

Zebehazy, K. T., & Smith, T. J. (2011). An examination of characteristics related to social skills of youths with visual impairments. *Journal of Visual Impairment & Blindness, 105*, 84–95.

Zimmerman, G. J., Zebehazy, K. T., & Moon, M. L. (2010). Optics and low vision devices. In A. L. Corn & J. Erin (Eds.), *Foundations of low vision: Clinical and functional perspectives* (2nd ed., pp. 192–237). New York: AFB Press.

CHAPTER 13

Aitken, S. (2000). Understanding deafblindness. In S. Aitken, M. Buultjens, C. Clark, J. T. Eyre, & L. Pease (Eds.), *Teaching children who are deafblind: Contact, communication, and learning* (pp. 1–34). London: David Fulton.

Anderson, V., Beauchamp, M. H., Yeates, K. O., Crossley, L., Hearps, S. J. C., & Catroppa, C. (2013). Social competence at 6 months following childhood traumatic brain injury. *Journal of the International Neuropsychological Society, 19*, 539–550. doi:10.1017/S1355617712001543

Anthony, T. L. (2016). Early identification of infants and toddlers with deafblindness. *American Annals of the Deaf, 161*, 412–423.

Ashley, M. J. (Ed.). (2004). *Traumatic brain injury: Rehabilitative treatment and case management* (2nd ed.). Boca Raton, FL: CRC Press.

Asken, B. M., Sullan, M. J., Snyder, A. R., Houck, Z. M., Bryant, V. E., Hizel, L. P., . . . Bauer, R. M. (2016). Factors influencing clinical correlates of chronic traumatic encephalopathy (CTE): A review. *Neuropsychology Review, 26*, 340–363. doi:10.1007/s11065-016-9327-z.

Avellone, L. E., & Taylor, J. (2017). Preparing students with low-incidence disabilities for community living opportunities. In J. M. Kauffman, D. P. Hallahan, & P. C. Pullen (Eds.), *Handbook of special education* (2nd ed., pp. 758–770). New York: Routledge.

Bakhos, L. L., Lockhart, G. R., Myers, R., & Linakis, J. G. (2010). Emergency department visits for concussion in young child athletes. *Pediatrics, 126*, e550–e556. doi:10.1542/peds.2009-3101

Best, S. J., Heller, K. W., & Bigge, J. L. (2010). *Teaching individuals with physical or multiple disabilities* (6th ed.). Upper Saddle River, NJ: Pearson.

Beukelman, D. R., Yorkston, K. M., & Reichle, J. (Eds.). (2000). *Augmentative and alternative communication for adults with acquired neurologic disorders*. Baltimore: Brookes.

Bodfish, J. W. (2007). Stereotypy, self-injury, and related abnormal repetitive behaviors. In J. W. Jacobson, J. A. Mulick, & J. Rojahn (Eds.), *Handbook of intellectual and developmental disabilities* (pp. 481–505). New York: Springer.

Bodsworth, S. M., Clare, I.C.H., Simblett, S. K., & Deafblind UK. (2011). Deafblindness and mental health: Psychological distress and unmet need among adults with dual sensory impairment, *British Journal of Visual Impairment, 29*, 6–26.

Bruce, S. M., & Ivy, S. E. (2017). Severe and multiple disabilities. In J. M. Kauffman, D. P. Hallahan, & P. C. Pullen (Eds.), *Handbook of special education* (2nd ed., pp. 411–427). New York: Routledge.

Cardona, G. W. (2000). Spaghetti talk. In M. Oken-Fried & H. A. Bersani (Eds.), *Speaking up and spelling it out: Personal essays on augmentative and alternative communication* (pp. 237–244). Baltimore: Brookes.

Centers for Disease Control and Prevention. (2011, October 6). Press Release: CDC finds 60 percent increase in youth athletes treated for TBIs. Retrieved from http://www.cdc.gov/media/releases/2011/p1006_TBI_Youth.html.

Chen, D., Alsop, L., & Minor, L. (2000). Lessons from Project PLAI in California and Utah: Implications for early intervention services to infants who are deaf-blind and their families. *Deaf-Blind Perspectives, 7*(3), 1–8.

Chen, D., Downing, J., & Rodriguez-Gil, G. (2000/2001). Tactile learning strategies for children who are deaf-blind: Concerns and considerations from Project SALUTE. *Deaf-Blind Perspectives, 8*(2), 1–6.

Council for Exceptional Children. (2001). Traumatic brain injury: The silent epidemic. *CEC Today, 7*(7), 1, 5, 15.

Cullen, C., & Mudford, O. C. (2005). Gentle teaching. In J. W. Jacobson, R. M. Foxx, & J. A. Mulick (Eds.), *Controversial therapies for developmental disabilities: Fad, fashion, and science in professional practice* (pp. 423–432). Mahwah, NJ: Erlbaum.

Dammeyer, J. (2011). Mental and behavioral disabilities among people with congenital deafblindness. *Research in Developmental Disabilities, 32*, 571–575. doi:10.1016/j.ridd.2010.12.019

Dell Orto, A. E., & Power, P. W. (2000). *Brain injury and the family: A life and living perspective* (2nd ed.). Washington, DC: CRC Press.

DePompei, R., & Tyler, J. (2004). Children and adolescents: Practical strategies for school participation. In M. J. Ashley (Ed.), *Traumatic brain injury: Rehabilitative treatment and case management* (2nd ed., pp. 559–580). Boca Raton, FL: CRC Press.

Dunst, C. J., & Espe-Sherwindt, M. (2017). Contemporary early intervention models, research and practice for infants and toddlers with disabilities and delays. In J. M. Kauffman, D. P. Hallahan, & P. C. Pullen (Eds.), *Handbook of special education* (2nd ed., pp. 831–849) New York: Routledge.

Ewing-Cobbs, L., Prasad, M. R., Mendez, D., Barnes, M. A., & Swank, P. (2013). Social interaction in young children with inflicted and accidental traumatic brain injury: Relations with family and social outcomes. *Journal of International Neuropsychological Society, 19*, 497–507. doi:10.1017/S1355617713000210

Foxx, R. M. (2016). The perpetuation of the myth of nonaversive treatment of severe behavior. In R. M. Foxx & J. A. Mulick (Eds.), *Controversial therapies for autism and intellectual disabilities: Fad, fashion and science in professional practice* (2nd ed., pp. 223–244). New York: Routledge.

Foxx, R. M. (2016). Why ABA is not a fad, a pseudoscience, a duibious or controversial treatment, or politically correct. In R. M. Foxx & J. A. Mulick (eds.), *Controversial therapies for autism and intellectual disabilities* (2nd ed., pp. 422–432). New York: Taylor & Francis.

Franklin, P., & Bourquin, E. (2000). Picture this: A pilot study for improving street crossings for deaf-blind travelers. *RE:view, 31*, 173–179.

Freeberg, E. (2001). *The education of Laura Bridgman: First deaf and blind person to learn language.* Cambridge, MA: Harvard University Press.

Gardner, W. I. (2007). Aggression in persons with intellectual disabilities and mental disorders. In J. W. Jacobson, J. A. Mulick, & J. Rojahn (Eds.), *Handbook of intellectual and developmental disabilities* (pp. 541–562). New York: Springer.

Gense, D. J., & Gense, M. (2004). *The importance of orientation and mobility skills for students who are deaf-blind.* Retrieved from http://dblink.org/lib/o&m.htm

Gerenser, J., & Forman, B. (2007). Speech and language deficits in children with developmental disabilities. In J. W. Jacobson, J. A. Mulick, & J. Rojahn (Eds.), *Handbook of intellectual and physical disabilities* (pp. 563–579). NY: Springer.

Grandinette, S., & Best, D. J. (2009). Traumatic brain injury. In K. W. Heller, P. E. Forney, P. A. Alberto, S. J. Best, & M. N. Schwartzman, *Understanding physical, health, and multiple disabilities* (2nd ed., pp. 118–138). Upper Saddle River, NJ: Pearson.

Green, P. M. (Producer), & Penn, A. (Director). (1962). *The Miracle Worker.* United States: Paramount Pictures.

Hartshorne, T. S., & Schmittel, M. C. (2016). Social-emotional development in children and youth who are deafblind. *American Annals of the Deaf, 161*, 441–453.

Heller, K. W., & Bigge, J. L. (2010). Augmentative and alternative communication. In S. J. Best, K. W. Heller, & J. L. Bigge, *Teaching individuals with physical or multiple disabilities* (6th ed., pp. 221–254). Upper Saddle River, NJ: Pearson.

Heller, K. W., Forney, P. E., Alberto, P. A., Best, S. J., & Schwartzman, M. N. (2009). *Understanding physical, health, and multiple disabilities* (2nd ed.). Upper Saddle River, NJ: Pearson.

Hodges, L. (2000). Effective teaching and learning. In S. Aitken, M. Buultjens, C. Clark, J. T. Eyre, & L. Pease (Eds.), *Teaching children who are deafblind: Contact, communication, and learning* (pp. 167–199). London: David Fulton Publishers.

Horner, R. H., Vaughn, B., Day, H. M. & Ard, B. (1996) The relationship between setting events and problem behavior. In L. K. Koegel, R. L. Koegel, & G. Dunlab (Eds.), *Positive behavioral support: Including people with difficult behavior in the community* (pp. 381–402). Baltimore: Brookes.

Inge, K. J. (2017). Section X. Transition from school to adulthood for students with low-incidence disabilities. In J. M. Kauffman, D. P. Hallahan, & P. C. Pullen (Eds.), Handbook of special education (2nd ed., pp. 739–740). New York: Routledge.

Inge, K. J., Wehman, P., & Seward, H. (2017). Preparing students with low incidence disabilities to work in the community. In J. M. Kauffman, D. P. Hallahan, & P. C. Pullen (Eds.), *Handbook of special education* (2nd ed., pp. 741–757). New York: Routledge.

Janssen, M. J., Riksen-Walraven, J. M., & van Dijk, J. P. M. (2004). Enhancing the interactive competence of deafblind children: Do intervention effects endure? *Journal of Developmental and Physical Disabilities, 16*, 73–94. doi:10.1023/B:JODD.0000010040.54094.0f

Kauffman, J. M. (2008). Special education. In T. L. Good (Ed.), *21st century education: A reference handbook* (pp. 405–413). Thousand Oaks, CA: Sage.

Kauffman, J. M., & Badar, J. (2018). *The scandalous neglect of children's mental health: The role of schools.* New York: Routledge.

Kauffman, J. M., Conroy, M., Gardner, R., & Oswald, D. (2008). Cultural sensitivity in the application of behavior principles to education. *Education and Treatment of Children, 31*, 239–262. doi:10.1353/etc.0.0019

Kauffman, J. M., & Hallahan, D. P. (2005). *Special education: What it is and why we need it.* Boston: Allyn & Bacon.

Kauffman, J. M., Hallahan, D. P., & Pullen, P. C. (Eds.). (2017). *Handbook of special education* (2nd ed., Section XI, pp. 771–828). New York: Routledge.

Kauffman, J. M., Hallahan, D. P., Pullen, P. C., & Badar, J. (2019). *Special education: What it is and why we need it* (2nd. ed.). New York: Routledge.

Kauffman, J. M., & Landrum, T. J. (2018). *Characteristics of emotional and behavioral disorders of children and youth* (11th ed.). Upper Saddle River, NJ: Merrill/Pearson.

Kauffman, J. M., Nelson, C. M., Simpson, R. L., & Ward, D. R. (2017). Contemporary issues. In J. M. Kauffman, D. P. Hallahan, & P. C. Pullen (Eds.), *Handbook of special education* (2nd ed., pp. 16–28). New York: Taylor & Francis.

Kauffman, J. M., Pullen, P. L., Mostert, M. P., & Trent, S. C. (2011). *Managing classroom behavior: A reflective case-based approach* (5th ed.). Upper Saddle River, NJ: Pearson.

Keller, H. (1905). *The story of my life.* New York: Grosset & Dunlap.

Klein, M. D., Chen, D., & Haney, C. M. (2000). *Promoting learning through active interation: A guide to early communication with young children who have multiple disabilities.* Baltimore: Brookes.

Koegel, L. K., Koegel, R. L., & Dunlap, G. (Eds.). (1996). *Positive behavioral support: Including people with difficult behavior in the community.* Baltimore: Brookes.

Lajiness-O'Neill, R., & Erdodi, L. A., & Lichtenstein, J. D. (2017). Traumatic brain injury. In J. M. Kauffman, D. P. Hallahan, & P. C. Pullen (Eds.), *Handbook of special education* (2nd ed., pp. 377–393). New York: Routledge.

Lakhan, S. E., & Kirchgessner, A. (2012). Chronic traumatic encephalopathy: the dangers of getting "dinged." *SpringerPlus, 1.* doi:10.1186/2193-1801-1-2.

Laugen, N. J., Jacobsen, K. H., Rieffe, C., & Wichstrøm, L. (2016). Predictors of psychosocial outcomes in hard-of-hearing preschool children. *Journal of Deaf Studies & Deaf Education, 21*, 259–267.

Martland, H. (1928). Punch drunk. *Journal of the American Medical Association, 91*, 1103–1107.

McCrea, M., Guskiewicz, K., Randolph, C., Barr, W. B., Hammeke, T. A., Marshall, S. W., Powell, M. R., Ahn, K. W., Wang, Y., & Kelly, J. P. (2012). Incidence, clinical course, and predictors of prolonged recovery time following sport-related concussion in high school athletes. *Journal of International Neuropsychological Society, 19*, 497–507. doi:10.1017/S1355617712000872

McDonald, S. (2013). Impairments in social cognition following severe traumatic brain injury. *Journal of the International Neuropsychological Society, 19*, 231–246. doi:10.1017/S1355617712001506

Miles, B. (1998). *Overview of deaf-blindness.* Monmouth, OR: DB-LINK. Retrieved from www.tr.wou.edu/dblink/Overview2.htm

Miles, B. (1999, March 9). *Talking the language of the hands.* Retrieved from www.tr.wou.edu/dblink/hands2.htm

Miner, I., & Cioffi, J. (1999, October 25). *Usher syndrome in the school setting.* Retrieved from www.tr.wou.edu/dblink/usherfulltext.htm

Moran, B. (2017, July 24). *CTE Found in 99 percent of former NFL players studied: Data suggest disease may be more common in football players than previously thought.* Retrieved October 22 from https://www.bu.edu/research/articles/cte-former-nfl-players/

Morris, R. J., & Mather, N. (Eds.). (2008). *Evidence-based interventions for students with learning and behavioral challenges.* London: Taylor & Francis.

Moss, K., & Hagood, L. (1995). *Teaching strategies and content modifications for the child with deaf blindness.* Austin, TX: Texas School for the Blind and Visually Impaired.

Mudford, O. C., & Cullen, C. (2016). Auditory Integration Training: A critical review (1991-2014). In R. M. Foxx & J. A. Mulick (Eds.), *Controversial therapies for autism and intellectual disabilities: Fad, fashion and science in professional practice* (2nd ed., pp. 270–282). New York: Routledge.

Mulick, J. A., & Butter, E. M. (2016). Positive behavior support: A paternalistic, utopian delusion. In R. M. Foxx & J. A. Mulick (Eds.), *Controversial therapies for autism and intellectual disabilities: Fad, fashion and science in professional practice* (2nd ed., pp. 303–321). New York: Routledge.

National Center on Deaf-Blindness. (2015). 2015 *National Deaf-Blind Child Count: Overall Population Demographics.* Retrieved from https://nationaldb.org/pages/show/2015-national-deaf-blind-child-count/overall-population-demographics#summary

National Data Accountability Center. (2013, August). Individuals with Disabilities Education Act (IDEA) data. Retrieved from https://www.ideadata.org/default.asp

National Institute on Deafness and Other Communication Disorders. (2010, June 7). Usher syndrome. Retrieved from http://www.nidcd.nih.gov/health/hearing/usher.asp

Newsom, C. & Kroeger, K. A. (2016). Nonaversive treatment. In R. M. Foxx & J. A. Mulick (Eds.), *Controversial therapies for autism and intellectual disabilities: Fad, fashion and science in professional practice* (2nd ed., pp. 322–338). New York: Routledge.

Noonan, M. J., & McCormick, L. (2006). *Young children with disabilities in natural environments*. Baltimore: Brookes.

Osborne, J. G. (2005). Person-centered planning: A *faux fixe* in the service of humanism? In J. W. Jacobson, R. M. Foxx, & J. A. Mulick (Eds.), *Controversial therapies for developmental disabilities: Fad, fashion, and science in professional practice* (pp. 313–329). Mahwah, NJ: Erlbaum.

Pease, L. (2000). Creating a communicating environment. In S. Aitken, M. Buultjens, C. Clark, J. T. Eyre, & L. Pease (Eds.), *Teaching children who are deafblind: Contact, communication, and learning* (pp. 35–82). London: David Fulton Publishers.

Persel, C. S., & Persel, C. H. (2004). The use of applied behavior analysis: Traumatic brain injury rehabilitation. In M. J. Ashley (Ed.), *Traumatic brain injury: Rehabilitative treatment and case management* (2nd ed., pp. 403–453). Boca Raton, FL: CRC Press.

Pullen, P. C., & Hallahan, D. P. (2015). What is special education? In B. D. Bateman, J. W. Lloyd, & M. Tankersley, M. (Eds.). *Understanding special education Issues: Who, where, what, when, how & why* (pp. 36–50). New York: Routledge.

Raghubar, K. P., Barnes, M. A., Prasad, M., Johnson, C. P., & Ewing-Cobbs, L. (2013). Mathematical outcomes and working memory in children with TBI and orthopedic injury. *Journal of the International Neuropsychological Society, 19*, 254–263. doi:10.1017/S1355617712001543

Smith, K. G., Smith, I. M., & Blake, K. (2010). CHARGE syndrome: An educator's primer. *Education and Treatment of Children, 33*, 289–314.

Stichter, J. P., Conroy, M. A., & Kauffman, J. M. (2008). *An introduction to students with high-incidence disabilities*. Upper Saddle River, NJ: Merrill-Prentice Hall.

Stern, R. A., Daneshvar, D. H., Baugh, C. M., Seichepine, D. R., Montenigro, P. H., Riley, D. O., . . . McHale, L. (2013). Clinical presentation of chronic traumatic encephalopathy. *Neurology, 81*, 1122–1129.

The National Collegiate Athletic Association. (2012). *2012–2013 NCAA sports medicine handbook*. Indianapolis, IN: Author.

Trenchard, S. O., Rust, S., & Bunton, P. (2013). A systematic review of psychosocial outcomes within 2 years of paediatric traumatic brain injury in a school-aged population. *Brain Injury, 27*, 1217–1237. doi:10.3109/02699052.2013.812240.

U.S. Department of Education. (2016). *38th Annual Report to Congress on the Implementation of the Individuals with Disabilities Education Act*. Washington, DC: Author.

Westling, D. L., & Fox, L. (2000). *Teaching students with severe disabilities* (2nd ed.). Upper Saddle River, NJ: Merrill.

Wolverton, B. (2013, September 2). Coach makes the call. *The Chronicle of Higher Education*. http://www.chronicle.com/article/Trainers-Butt-Heads-With/141333.

Wrong Diagnosis. (2010, June 26). Prevalence and incidence of Usher syndrome. Retrieved from http://www.wrongdiagnosis.com/u/usher_syndrome/prevalence.htm

Yeates, K. O., Gerhardt, C. A., Bigler, E. D., Abildskov, T., Dennis, M., Rubin, K. H., Stancin, T., Taylor, H. G., & Vannatta, K. (2013). Peer relationships of children with traumatic brain injury. *Journal of International Neuropsychological Society, 19*, 518–527. doi:10.1017/S1355617712001531

Yoder, D. E. (2001). Having my say. *Augmentative and Alternative Communication, 17*, 2–10.

Zentner, G. E., Layman, W. S., Martin, D. M., & Scacheri, P. C. (2010). Molecular and phenotypic aspects of CHD7 mutation in CHARGE syndrome. *American Journal of Medical Genetics Part A, 152A*, 674–686.

CHAPTER 14

Arzimanoglou, A., Guerrini, R., & Aicardi, J. (2004). *Aicardi's epilepsy in children* (3rd ed.). Philadelphia: Lippincott Williams & Wilkins.

Auxter, D., Pyfer, J., & Huettig, C. (2005). *Principles and methods of adapted physical education and recreation* (10th ed.). New York: McGraw-Hill.

Barkovich, A. J. (2005). *Pediatric neuroimaging* (4th ed.). Philadelphia: Lippincott Williams & Wilkins.

Barnes, M. A., Wilkinson, M., Khemani, E., Boudesquie, A., Dennis, M., & Fletcher, J. M. (2006). Arithmetic processing in children with spina bifida: Calculation accuracy, strategy use, and fact retrieval fluency. *Journal of Learning Disabilities, 39*(2), 174–187.

Best, S. J., & Bigge, J. L. (2010). Cerebral palsy. In S. J. Best, K. W. Heller, & J. L. Bigge, *Teaching individuals with physical or multiple disabilities* (6th ed.). Upper Saddle River, NJ: Merrill/Pearson.

Best, S. J., Heller, K. W., & Bigge, J. L. (2010). *Teaching individuals with physical or multiple disabilities* (6th ed.). Upper Saddle River, NJ: Merrill/Pearson.

Bjorgaas, H. M., Elgen, I., Boe, T., & Hysing, M. (2013). Mental health in children with cerebral palsy: Does screening capture the complexity? *Scientific World Journal*. doi:10.1155/2013/468402

Boom, J. A., & Healy, C. M. (2013). Standard childhood vaccines: Parental hesitancy or refusal. Retrieved from http://www.uptodate.com/contents/standard-childhood-vaccines-parental-hesitancy-or-refusal

Bottos, M., Feliciangeli, A., Sciuto, L., Gericke, C., & Vianello, A. (2001). Functional status of adults with cerebral palsy and implications for treatment of children. *Developmental Medicine and Child Neurology, 43*, 516–528. doi:10.1017/ S0012162201000950

Copp, A. J., Stainier, N., & Greene, D. E. (2013). Neural tube deficits: Recent advances, unsolved questions, and controversies. *The Lancet, 12*, 799–809.

Coughlin, J., & Montague, M. (2011). The effects of strategy instruction on the mathematical problem solving of adolescents with spina bifida. *The Journal of Special Education, 45*, 171–183. doi:10.1177/0022466910363913

Dunst, C. J., & Espe-Sherwindt, M. (2017). Contemporary intervention models, research and practice for infants and toddlers with disabilities and delays. In J. M. Kauffman, D. P. Hallahan, & P. C. Pullen (Eds.), *Handbook of special education* (2nd ed., pp. 831–849). New York: Routledge.

Earley, T. (2000). *Jim the boy*. Boston: Little, Brown.

Eggert, D. (2013, August 11). Michigan has high rate of parents refusing vaccines. *Detroit Free Press*. Retrieved from http://www.freep.com/article/20130811/NEWS06/308110113/.

English, L. H., Barnes, M. A., Taylor, H. B., & Landry, S. H. (2009). Mathematical development in spina bifida. *Developmental Disabilities Research Reviews, 15*, 28–34. doi:10.1002/ddrr.48

Gisler, F. M., von Kanel, T., Kraemer, R., Schaller, A., & Gallati, S. (2013). Identification of SNPs in the cystic fibrosis interactome influencing pulmonary progression in cystic fibrosis. *European Journal of Human Genetics, 21*, 397–403. doi:10.1038/ejhg.2012.181.

Goodman, E. (2007, May 29). Wheels competing with feet. *Charlottesville Daily Progress*, A8.

Hampton, L. E., Fletcher, J. M., Cirino, P., Blaser, S., Kramer, L. A., & Dennis, M. (2013). Neuropsychological profiles of children with aqueductal stenosis and spina bifida myelomeningocele. *Journal of the International Neuropsychological Society, 19*, 127–136. doi:10.1017/S1355617712001117

Heller, K. W., Alberto, P. A., Forney, P. E., & Schwartzman, M. N. (2009). *Understanding physical, sensory, and health impairments: Characteristics and educational implications* (2nd ed.). Upper Saddle River, NJ: Pearson.

Holmes, M. S. (2004). *Fictions of affliction: Physical disability in Victorian culture*. Ann Arbor, MI: University of Michigan Press.

Howe, M. (n.d.). *Born to run*. Retrieved from http://www.spectrum.ieee.org/print/2189

Inge, K. J. (2017). Section X. Transition from school to adulthood for students with low-icidence disabilities. In J. M. Kauffman, D. P. Hallahan, & P. C. Pullen (Eds.), *Handbook of special education* (2nd ed., pp. 739–740). New York: Routledge.

Kauffman, J. M., & Badar, J. (2018). *The scandalous neglect of children's mental health needs: What schools can do*. New York: Routledge.

Kelly, L. E., Block, M. E., & Colombo-Dougovito, A. (2017). Physical education. In J. M. Kauffman, D. P. Hallahan, & P. C. Pullen (Eds.), *Handbook of special education* (2nd ed., pp. 586–605). New York: Routledge.

Lajiness-O'Neill, R., Erdodi, L. A., & Lichtenstein, J. D. (2017). Traumatic brain injury. In J. M. Kauffman, D. P. Hallahan, & P. C. Pullen (Eds.), *Handbook of special education* (2nd ed., pp. 377–393). New York: Routledge.

Levy, S. E., & O'Rourke, M. (2002). Technological assistance: Innovations for independence. In M. L. Batshaw (Ed.), *Children with disabilities* (5th ed., pp. 629–645). Baltimore: Brookes.

Lindsey, J. E. (Ed.). (2000). *Technology and exceptional individuals* (3rd ed.). Austin, TX: Pro-Ed.

Liptak, G. (2002). Neural tube defects. In M. L. Batshaw (Ed.), *Children with disabilities* (5th ed., pp. 467–492). Baltimore: Brookes.

Longman, J. (2007, May 15). An amputee sprinter: Is he disabled or too-abled? *The New York Times*. Retrieved from http://www.nytimes.com/2007/05/15/sports/othersports/15runner.html?ex=1183176000&en=1a1cac2e919125c0&ei=5070

Marini, N. J., Hoffmann, T. J., Lammer, E. J., Hardin, J., Lazaruk, K., Stein, J. B., Gilbert, D. A., . . . & Rine, J. (2011). A genetic signature of Spina Bifida risk from pathway-informed comprehensive gene-variant analysis. *Plos One, 6*, 1–11.

Martin, S. (2006). *Teaching motor skills to children with cerebral palsy and similar movement disorders: A guide for parents and professionals*. Bethesda, MD: Woodbine House.

Metzler, I. (2006). *Disability in medieval Europe: Thinking about physical impairment during the Middle Ages, c. 1100–1400*. New York: Routledge.

Mueller, G. A., Wolf, S., Bacon, E., Forbis, S., Langdon, L., & Lemming, C. (2013). Contemporary topics in pediatric pulmonology for the primary care clinician. *Current Problems in Pediatric and Adolescent Health Care, 43*, 130–156.

Nabors, L. A., & Lehmkuhl, H. D. (2004). Children with chronic medical conditions: Recommendations for school mental health clinicians. *Journal of Developmental and Physical Disabilities, 16*, 1–19. doi:10.1023/B:JODD.0000010036.72472.55

Olrick, J. T., Pianta, R. C., & Marvin, R. S. (2002). Mother's and father's responses to signals of children with cerebral palsy during feeding. *Journal of Developmental and Physical Disabilities, 14*, 1–17. doi:10.1023/A: 1013537528167

Powell, L. M., Harris, J. L., & Fox, T. (2013). Food marketing expenditures aimed at youth: Putting the numbers in context. *American Journal of Preventive Medicine, 45*, 453–461. Retrieved from http://dx.doi.org/10.1016/j.amepre.2013.06.003

Robertson, C. M. T., Watt, M., & Yasui, Y. (2007). Changes in the prevalence of cerebral palsy for children born very prematurely within a population-based program over 30 years. *Journal of the American Medical Association, 297*, 2733–2740.

Ruegg, U. T. (2013). Pharmacological prospects in the treatment of Duchenne muscular dystrophy. *Current Opinion in Neurology, 26*, 577–584.

Saslow, E. (2007, April 12). In Maryland, a fight to the finish line: Wheelchair racer's quest for inclusion spurs debate. *The Washington Post*, A1, A16.

Scanlon, D. J. (Ed.). (2017). Section IX. What it will mean to transition: Transition and high incidence disabilities. In J. M. Kauffman, D. P. Hallahan, & P. C. Pullen (Eds.), *Handbook of special education* (2nd ed., pp. 687–690). New York: Routledge.

Sherman, E. M. S., Slick, D. J., & Eyrl, K. L. (2006). Executive dysfunction is a significant predictor of poor quality of live in children with epilepsy. *Epilepsia, 47*, 1936–1942. doi:10.1111/j.1528-1167.2006.00816.x

Singh, D. K. (2003). Families of children with spina bifida: A review. *Journal of Developmental and Physical Disabilities, 15*, 37–55. doi:10.1023/A:1021452220291

Stubberud, J., Langenbahn, D., Levine, B., Stanghelle, J., & Schanke, A-K. (2013). Goal management training of executive functions in patients with spina bifida: A randomized controlled trial. *Journal of the International Neuropsychological Society, 19*(6), 672–685. doi:10.1017/S1355617713000209

Tieh, P. & Dreimane, D. (2013). Type 2 diabetes mellitus in children and adolescents. *Indian Journal of Pediatrics*. Retrieved from http://www.PubMed.gov

Torpy, J. M. (2010). Chronic diseases of children. *Journal of the American Medical Association, 303*(7), 682. doi:10.001/jama.303.7.682

U.S. Preventive Services Task Force. (2009). Folic Acid for the prevention of neural tube defects: U.S. preventive services task force recommendation statement. *Annals of Internal Medicine, 150*, 626–632.

Vig, S., & Kaminer, R. (2002). Maltreatment and developmental disabilities in children. *Journal of Developmental and Physical Disabilities, 14*, 371–386. doi:10.1023/A:1020334903216

Weinstein, S. (2002). Epilepsy. In M. L. Batshaw (Ed.), *Children with disabilities* (5th ed., pp. 493–523). Baltimore: Brookes.

White, P. H., Schuyler, V., Edelman, A., Hayes, A., & Batshaw, M. L. (2002). Future expectations: Transition from adolescence to adulthood. In M. L. Batshaw (Ed.), *Children with disabilities* (5th ed., pp. 693–705). Baltimore: Brookes.

Willen, E. J. (2006). Neurocognitive outcomes in pediatric HIV. *Mental Retardation and Developmental Disabilities Research Reviews, 12*, 223–228. doi:10.1002/mrdd.20112

Wood, D. (2011, October 10; updated 2012, April 16). Beyond the battlefield: From a decade of war, an endless struggle for the severely wounded. *Huffington Post*. Retrieved from http://www.huffingtonpost.com/2011/10/10/beyond-the-battlefield-part-1-tyler-southern_n_999329.html?ref=politics

Youngblood, M. E., Williamson, R., Bell, K. N., Johnson, Q., Kancherla, V., & Oakley, G. P. (2013). 2012 Update on global prevention of folic acid-preventable Spina Bifida and Anencephaly. *Birth Defects Research*, 1–6.

Zylke, J. W., & DeAngelis, C. D. (2007). Pediatric chronic diseases—stealing childhood. *Journal of the American Medical Association, 297*, 2765–2766.

CHAPTER 15

Ambrose, D. (Ed.). (2010). STEM high schools. *Roeper Review, 32*(1), special issue.

Anastasiou, D., & Kauffman, J. M. (2011). A social constructionist approach to disability: Implications for special education. *Exceptional Children, 77*, 367–384.

Anastasiou, D., & Kauffman, J. M. (2012). Disability as cultural difference: Implications for special education. *Remedial and Special Education, 33*, 139–149.

Anastasiou, D., & Kauffman, J. M. (2013). The social model of disability: Dichotomy between impairment and disability. *Journal of Medicine and Philosophy, 38*, 441–459.

Assouline, S. G., & Colangelo, N. (2006) Social-emotional development of gifted adolescents. In F. A. Dixon & S. M. Moon (Eds.), *The handbook of secondary gifted education* (pp. 65–86). Waco, TX: Prufrock Press.

Assouline, S. G., & Lupkowski-Shoplik, A. (2003). *Developing mathematical talent: A guide for challenging and educating gifted students*. Waco, TX: Prufrock Press.

Assouline, S. G., Nicpon, M. F., & Doobay, A. (2009). Profoundly gifted girls and autism spectrum disorder. *Gifted Child Quarterly, 53*, 89–105. doi:10.1177/0016986208330565

Assouline, S. G., Nicpon, M. F., & Whiteman, C. (2010). Cognitive and psychosocial characteristics of gifted students with written language disability. *Gifted Child Quarterly, 54*, 102–115. doi:10.1177/0016986209355974

Borland, J. H. (2004). *Issues and practices in the identification and education of gifted students from under-represented groups*. Storrs, CT: National Research Center on the Gifted and Talented.

Borland, J. H. (2014). Identification of gifted students. In J. A. Plucker & C. M. Callahan, *Critical issues and practices in gifted education: What the research says* (2nd ed., pp. 323–342). Waco, TX: Prufrock Press.

Brighton, C. M., & Jarvis, J. M. (2017). Early identification and intervention in gifted education: Developing talent in diverse learners. In J. M. Kauffman, D. P. Hallahan, & P. C. Pullen (Eds.), *Handbook of special education* (2nd ed., pp. 882–893). New York: Routledge.

Brody, L. E., & Stanley, J. C. (2005). Youths who reason exceptionally well mathematically and/or verbally. In R. J. Sternberg & J. E. Davidson (Eds.), *Conceptions of giftedness* (2nd ed., pp. 20–37). New York: Cambridge University Press.

Callahan, C. M. (2000). Evaluation as a critical component of program development and implementation. In K. A. Heller, F. J. Monks, R. J. Sternberg, & R. F. Subotnik (Eds.), *International handbook of giftedness and talent* (2nd ed., pp. 537–548). New York: Pergamon.

Callahan, C. M. (2001). Evaluating learner and program outcomes in gifted education. In F. A. Karnes & S. M. Bean (Eds.), *Methods and materials for teaching the gifted* (pp. 253–298). Waco, TX: Prufrock Press.

Callahan, C. M. (2003). *Advanced placement and international baccalaureate programs for talented students in American high schools: A focus on science and mathematics*. Storrs, CT: National Research Center on the Gifted and Talented.

Callahan, C. M. (2011). Special gifts and talents. In J. M. Kauffman & D. P. Hallahan (Eds.), *Handbook of special education* (pp. 304–317). New York: Routledge.

Callahan, C. M. (2013). Evaluating services offered to gifted and talented students: A planning guide. In C. M. Callahan & H. L. Hertberg-Davis (Eds.), *Fundamentals of gifted education: Considering multiple perspectives* (pp. 440–447). New York: Taylor & Francis.

Callahan, C. M., & Hertberg-Davis, H. L. (Eds.). (2013a). *Fundamentals of gifted education: Considering multiple perspectives.* New York: Taylor & Francis.

Callahan, C. M., & Hertberg-Davis, H. L. (2013b). Beliefs, philosophies, and definitions. In C. M. Callahan & H. L. Hertberg-Davis (Eds.), *Fundamentals of gifted education: Considering multiple perspectives* (pp. 13–20). New York: Taylor & Francis.

Callahan, C. M., & Hertberg-Davis, H. L. (2013c). Heterogeneity among the gifted: Not an oxymoron. In C. M. Callahan & H. L. Hertberg-Davis (Eds.), *Fundamentals of gifted education: Considering multiple perspectives* (pp. 329–330). New York: Taylor & Francis.

Chan, D. W. (2006). Perceived multiple intelligences among male and female Chinese gifted students in Hong Kong: The structure of the Student Multiple Intelligences Profile. *Gifted Child Quarterly, 50,* 325–338.

Chandler, M. A. (2015, June 7). District renews focus on gifted. *The Washington Post,* C1, C6.

Colangelo, N., Assouline, S. G., & Gross, M. U. M. (2004a). *A nation deceived: How schools hold back America's brightest students. Vol. I.* Iowa City, IA: Connie Belin & Jacqueline N. Blank International Center for Gifted Education and Talent Development.

Colangelo, N., Assouline, S. G., & Gross, M. U. M. (Eds.). (2004b). *A nation deceived: How schools hold back America's brightest students. Vol. II.* Iowa City, IA: Connie Belin & Jacqueline N. Blank International Center for Gifted Education and Talent Development.

Colangelo, N., Assouline, S. G., & Marron, M. A. (2013). Evidence trumps beliefs: Academic acceleration is an effective intervention for high-ability students. In C. M. Callahan & H. L. Hertberg-Davis (Eds.), *Fundamentals of gifted education: Considering multiple perspectives* (pp. 164–175). New York: Taylor & Francis.

Coleman, M. R., & Roberts, J. L. (2015, October). Special Issue: Twice Exceptional Learners. *Gifted Child Today, 38*(4), 204–256.

Council for Exceptional Children. (2001). *Performance-based standards.* Retrieved from www.cec.sped.org/ps/perf_based_stds/index.html

Davis, G. A., & Rimm S. B. (2004) *Education of the gifted and talented* (5th ed.). Boston: Allyn & Bacon.

De Hahn, E. L. H. (2000). Cross-cultural studies in gifted education. In K. A. Heller, F. J. Monks, R. J. Sternberg, & R. F. Subotnik (Eds.), *International handbook of giftedness and talent* (2nd ed., pp. 549–561). New York: Pergamon.

DiGennaro, J. (2007, February 10). Gifted minds we need to nurture. *The Washington Post,* A17.

Dixon, F. A., & Moon, S. M. (Eds.). (2006). *The handbook of secondary gifted education.* Waco. TX: Prufrock Press.

Ford, D. Y. (2015, January). Culturally responsive gifted classrooms for culturally different students: A focus in invitational learning. *Gifted Child Today, 38*(1), 67–69.

Ford, D. Y., & Moore, J. L. (2006). Being gifted and adolescent: Issues and needs of students of color. In F. A. Dixon & S. M. Moon (Eds.),

The handbook of secondary gifted education (pp. 113–136). Waco, TX: Prufrock Press.

Freeman, J. (2005). Permission to be gifted: How conceptions of giftedness can change lives. In R. J. Sternberg & J. E. Davidson (Eds.), *Conceptions of giftedness* (2nd ed., pp. 80–97). New York: Cambridge University Press.

Gallagher, J. J. (2000a). Changing paradigms for gifted education in the United States. In K. A. Heller, F. J. Monks, R. J. Sternberg, & R. F. Subotnik (Eds.), *International handbook of giftedness and talent* (2nd ed., pp. 681–693). New York: Pergamon.

Gallagher, J. J. (2000b). Unthinkable thoughts: Education of gifted students. *Gifted Child Quarterly, 44,* 5–12. doi:10.1177/001698620004400102

Gallagher, J. J. (2004). Public policy and acceleration of gifted students. In N. Colangelo, S. G. Assouline, & M. U. M. Gross (Eds.), *A nation deceived: How schools hold back America's brightest students. Vol. II* (pp. 39–45). Iowa City, IA: Connie Belin & Jacqueline N. Blank International Center for Gifted Education and Talent Development.

Gallagher, J. J. (2006). According to Jim: Best and worst of gifted education. *Roeper Review, 29,* 10.

Gallagher, J. J. (2013). Political issues in gifted education. In C. M. Callahan & H. L. Hertberg-Davis (Eds.), *Fundamentals of gifted education: Considering multiple perspectives* (pp. 358–368). New York: Taylor & Francis.

Gardner, H., & Hatch, T. (1989). Multiple intelligences go to school: Educational implications of the theory of multiple intelligences. *Educational Researcher, 18*(8), 4–9.

Gavin, M. K., & Adelson, J. L. (2014). Mathematics gifted education. In J. A. Plucker & C. M. Callahan, *Critical issues and practices in gifted education: What the research says* (2nd ed., pp. 387–412). Waco, TX: Prufrock Press.

Goldsmith, B. (2005). *Obsessive genius: The inner world of Marie Curie.* New York: Norton.

Grissom, J. A., & Redding, C. (2016). Discretion and disproportionality: Explaining the underrepresentation of high-achieving students of color in gifted programs. *AERA Open, 2*(1), 1–25.

Gross, M. U. M. (2000). Issues in the cognitive development of exceptionally and profoundly gifted individuals. In K. A. Heller, F. J. Monks, R. J. Sternberg, & R. F. Subotnik (Eds.), *International handbook of giftedness and talent* (2nd ed., pp. 179–192). New York: Pergamon.

Gross, M. U. M. (2002). Social and emotional issues for exceptionally intellectually gifted students. In M. Neihart, S. M. Reis, N. M. Robinson, & S. M. Moon (Eds.), *The social and emotional development of gifted children. What do we know?* (pp. 19–29). Waco, TX: Prufrock Press.

Hebert, T. P. (2013). Gifted Latino students: Overcoming barriers. In C. M. Callahan & H. L. Hertberg-Davis (Eds.), *Fundamentals of gifted education: Considering multiple perspectives* (pp. 412–423). New York: Taylor & Francis.

Herbert, T. P., & Kelly, K. R. (2006). Identity and career development in gifted students.

In F. A. Dixon & S. M. Moon (Eds.), *The handbook of secondary gifted education* (pp. 35–64). Waco, TX: Prufrock Press.

Huefner, D. S. (2006). *Getting comfortable with special education law: A framework for working with children with disabilities* (2nd ed.). Norwood, MA: Christopher-Gordon.

Hunsaker, S. L., & Callahan, C. M. (1995). Creativity and giftedness: Published instrument uses and abuses. *Gifted Child Quarterly, 39,* 110–114. doi:10.1177/001698629503900207

Kalbfleisch, M. L. (2013). Twice-exceptional students: Gifted students with learning disabilities. In C. M. Callahan & H. L. Hertberg-Davis (Eds.), *Fundamentals of gifted education: Considering multiple perspectives* (pp. 458–469). New York: Taylor & Francis.

Kauffman, J. M. (2013). Labeling and categorizing children and youth with emotional and behavioral disorders in the USA. In T. Cole, H. Daniels, & J. Visser (Eds.), *The Routledge international companion to emotional and behavioural difficulties* (pp. 15–21). London: Routledge.

Kauffman, J. M., & Anastasiou, D. (in press). On cultural politics in special education: Is much of it justifiable? *Journal of Disability Policy Studies.*

Kauffman, J. M., & Hallahan, D. P. (2005). *Special education: What it is and why we need it.* Boston: Allyn & Bacon.

Kauffman, J. M., Hallahan, D. P., Pullen, P. C., & Badar, J. (2018). *Special education: What it is and why we need it* (2nd. ed.). New York: Routledge.

Kauffman, J. M., & Konold, T. R. (2007). Making sense in education: Pretense (including NCLB) and realities in rhetoric and policy about schools and schooling. *Exceptionality, 15,* 75–96.

Kauffman, J. M., & Landrum, T. J. (2018). *Characteristics of emotional and behavioral disorders of children and youth* (11th ed.). Upper Saddle River, NJ: Pearson.

Kauffman, J. M., & Lloyd, J. W. (2017). Statistics, data, and special education decisions: Basic links to realities. In J. M. Kauffman, D. P. Hallahan, & P. C. Pullen (Eds.), *Handbook of special education* (2nd., pp. 29–39). New York: Taylor & Francis.

Kohler, P. D., & Field, S. (2006). Transition-focused education: Foundation for the future. In B. G. Cook & B. R. Schirmer (Eds.), *What is special about special education? Examining the role of evidence-based practices* (pp. 86–99). Austin, Tx: Pro-Ed.

Landrum, T. J., Wiley, A. L., Tankersley, M., & Kauffman, J. M. (2014). Is EBD "special," and is "special education" an appropriate response? In P. Garner, J. M. Kauffman, & J. G. E. Elliott (Eds.), *SAGE handbook of emotional & behavioral difficulties* (pp. 69–81). London: Sage Publications.

Leff, S. S., Waanders, C., Waasdorp, T. E., & Paskewich, B. S. (2014). Bullying, harassment and relational aggression in school settings. In H. M. Walker & F. M. Gresham (Eds.), *Handbook of evidence-based practices for students having emotional and behavioral disorders* (pp. 277–291). New York: Guilford.

Lloyd, J. W., & Hallahan, D. P. (2007). Advocacy and reform of special education. In J. B. Crockett, M. M. Gerber, & T. J. Landrum

(Eds.), *Achieving the radical reform of special education: Essays in honor of James M. Kauffman* (pp. 245–263). Mahwah, NJ: Lawrence Erlbaum Associates.

Lohman, D. F. (2005, September). *Identifying academically talented minority students* (RM05216). Storrs, CT: University of Connecticut, National Research Center on the Gifted and Talented.

Lohman, D. F. (2006). Exploring perceptions and awareness of high ability. *Roeper Review, 29,* 32–40.

Martin, L. T. Burns, R. M., & Schonlou, M. (2010). Mental disorders among gifted and nongifted youth: A selected review of the epidemiological literature. *Gifted Child Quarterly, 54,* 31–41. doi:10.1177/0016986209352684

Missett, T. C. (2013). Gifted students with emotional and behavioral disabilities. In C. M. Callahan & H. L. Hertberg-Davis (Eds.), *Fundamentals of gifted education: Considering multiple perspectives* (pp. 369–376). New York: Taylor & Francis.

Moore, J. L., Ford, D. Y., & Milner, H. R. (2005). Recruitment is not enough: Retaining African American students in gifted education. *Gifted Child Quarterly, 49,* 51–67.

Mueller, C. E. (2009). Protective factors as barriers to depression in gifted and nongifted adolescents. *Gifted Child Quarterly, 53,* 3–14. doi:10.1177/0016986208326552

Muratori, M. C., Stanley, J. C., Gross, M. U. M., Ng., L., Tao, T., Ng., J., et al. (2006). Insights from SMPY's greatest former child prodigies: Drs. Terence ("Terry") Tao and Lenhard ("Lenny") Ng reflect on their talent development. *Gifted Child Quarterly, 50,* 307–324.

Murray, S. (2005, July 19). Grants for gifted children face major threat from budget ax. *The Washington Post,* A19.

Neihart, M., Reis, S. M., Robinson, N. M., & Moon, S. M. (Eds.). (2002). *The social and emotional development of gifted children. What do we know?* Waco, TX: Prufrock Press.

Odom, S. L., & Wolery, M. (2006). A unified theory of practice in early intervention/early childhood special education. In B. G. Cook & B. R. Schirmer (Eds.), *What is special about special education? Examining the role of evidence-based practices* (pp. 72–85). Austin, TX: Pro-Ed.

Oh, S., & Callahan, C. M. (2013). Asian American gifted students: The model minority. In C. M. Callahan & H. L. Hertberg-Davis (Eds.), *Fundamentals of gifted education: Considering multiple perspectives* (pp. 401–411). New York: Routledge.

Peterson, J. S., & Ray, K. E. (2006). Bullying among the gifted: The subjective experience. *Gifted Child Quarterly, 50,* 252–269.

Plucker, J. A. (2013). Students from rural environments. In C. M. Callahan & H. L. Hertberg-Davis (Eds.), *Fundamentals of gifted education: Considering multiple perspectives* (pp. 424–434). New York: Taylor & Francis.

Plucker, J., & Callahan, C. M. (Eds.). (2014). Critical issues and practices in gifted education: What the research says (2nd ed.). Waco, TX: Prufrock Press.

Plucker, J. A., & Callahan, C. M. (2017). Special gifts and talents. In J. M. Kauffman, D. P. Hallahan, & P. C. Pullen (Eds.), *Handbook of special education* (2nd ed., pp. 428–444). New York: Routledge.

Plucker, J. A., & Peters, S. J. (2016). *Excellence gaps in education: Expanding opportunities for talented students.* Cambridge, MA: Harvard Education Press.

Plucker, J. A., & Stocking, V. B. (2001). Looking outside and inside: Self-concept development of gifted adolescents. *Exceptional Children, 67,* 535–548.

Porter, L. (2005). *Gifted young children: A guide for teachers and parents* (2nd ed.). Berkshire, England: Open University Press.

Reis, S. M. (2013). Is this really still a problem? The special needs of gifted girls and women. In C. M. Callahan & H. L. Hertberg-Davis (Eds.), *Fundamentals of gifted education: Considering multiple perspectives* (pp. 343–357). New York: Taylor & Francis.

Reis, S. M., & Renzulli, J. S. (2009). Myth 1: The gifted and talented constitute one single homogeneous group and giftedness is a way of being that stays in the person over time and experiences. *Gifted Child Quarterly, 53,* 233–235. doi:10.1177/ 0016986209346824

Renzulli, J. S., & Delcourt, M. A. B. (2013). Gifted behaviors versus gifted individuals. In C. M. Callahan & H. L. Hertberg-Davis (Eds.), *Fundamentals of gifted education: Considering multiple perspectives* (pp. 36–48). New York: Taylor & Francis.

Renzulli, J. S., & D'Souza, S. (2014). Intelligences outside the normal curve: Co-cognitive factors that contribute to the creation of social capital and leadership skills in young people. In J. A. Plucker & C. M. Callahan, *Critical issues and practices in gifted education: What the research says* (2nd ed., pp. 343–362). Waco, TX: Prufrock Press.

Robinson, A., Shore, B. M., & Enersen, D. L. (2007). *Best practices in gifted education: An evidence-based guide.* Waco, TX: Prufrock Press.

Robinson, N. M. (2005). In defense of a psychometric approach to the definition of academic giftedness: A conservative view from a die-hard liberal. In R. J. Sternberg & J. E. Davidson (Eds.), *Conceptions of giftedness* (2nd ed., pp. 280–294). New York: Cambridge University Press.

Robinson, N. M. (2013). Parents and the development and education of gifted students. In C. M. Callahan & H. L. Hertberg-Davis (Eds.), *Fundamentals of gifted education: Considering multiple perspectives* (pp. 236–247). New York: Taylor & Francis.

Ruf, D. L. (2005). *Losing our minds: Gifted children left behind.* Scottsdale, AZ: Great Potential Press.

Schuiltz, S. M. Twice-exceptional students enrolled in advanced placement classes. *Gifted Child Quarterly, 56,* 119–133.

Selk, A. (2017, October 5). Making his own path: Super Awesome Sylvia was a role model to girls in science, producing how-to videos and giving speeches across the world. Then he realized he was a boy. *Washington Post,* C1, C3

Siegle, D., & McCoach, D. B. (2013). Underachieving gifted students. In C. M. Callahan & H. L. Hertberg-Davis (Eds.), *Fundamentals of gifted education: Considering multiple perspectives* (pp. 377–387). New York: Taylor & Francis.

Sternberg, R. J. (1997). A triarchic view of giftedness: Theory and practice. In N. Colangelo & G. A. Davis (Eds.), *Handbook of gifted education* (2nd ed., pp. 43–53). Boston: Allyn & Bacon.

Sternberg, R. J. (2015). Multiple intelligences in the new age of thinking. In S. Goldstein, D. Princiotta, & J. Naglieri (Eds.), *Handbook of intelligence: Evolutionary theory, historical perspective, and current concepts* (pp. 229–242). New York, NY: Springer.

Sternberg, R. J. (2017). Theories of intelligence. In S. I. Pfeiffer (Ed.), *Handbook of giftedness and talent.* Washington, DC: American Psychological Association.

Tomlinson, C. A., Ford, D. Y., Reis, S. M., Briggs, C. J., & Strickland, C. A. (Eds.). (2004). *In search of the dream: Designing schools and classrooms that work for high potential students from diverse cultural backgrounds.* Washington, DC: National Association for Gifted Children.

Tomlinson, C. A., Kaplan, S. N., Renzulli, J. S., Purcell, J., Leppien, J., & Burns, D. (2002). *The parallel curriculum: A design to develop high potential and challenge high-ability learners.* Thousand Oaks, CA: Corwin.

Van Tassel-Baska, J. (2006). A content analysis of evaluation findings across 20 gifted programs: A clarion call for enhanced gifted program development. *Gifted Child Quarterly, 50,* 199–215.

Van Tassel-Baska, J., & Stambaugh, T. (2006). *Comprehensive curriculum for gifted learners* (3rd ed.). Boston: Allyn & Bacon.

Von Karolyi, C., & Winner, E. (2005). Extreme giftedness. In R. J. Sternberg & J. E. Davidson (Eds.). *Conceptions of giftedness* (2nd ed., pp. 377–394). New York: Cambridge University Press.

Willingham, D. T. (2009). *Why don't students like school? A cognitive scientist answers questions about how the mind works and what it means for your classroom.* San Francisco: Jossey-Bass.

Worrell, F. C. (2013). Gifted African Americans. In C. M. Callahan & H. L. Hertberg-Davis (Eds.), *Fundamentals of gifted education: Considering multiple perspectives* (pp. 388–400). New York: Taylor & Francis.

Yell, M. L. (2016). *Law and special education* (4th ed.). Upper Saddle River, NJ: Pearson.

Yoon, S. Y., & Gentry, M. (2009). Racial and ethnic representation in gifted programs. *Gifted Child Quarterly, 53,* 121–136. doi:10.1177/00169862 08330564

NAME INDEX

SUBJECT INDEX